STRAIN OF DISCOURSE

THE 30 GREATEST NBA PLAYERS OF ALL-TIME

© Danny Bennett, 2020.

@danjosephbennett

Table of Contents.

It's recommended that you read this book from beginning to end, but an index of each player profiled can be found on the last page

All statistics current through the conclusion of the 2019-20' NBA season

For Becca, forever ago—for the love, for the support, and for never losing sight of you and me stuff.

Foreword.

I used to attempt to keep up with all major sports—perhaps it was a self-appointed obligation to maintain my reputation as a 'sports guy', or maybe to inflate my 'masculinity'—but by 2020, other sports have been cast aside. I hate-follow the NFL for fantasy football purposes, I'm confident I couldn't name you one player in baseball's NL Central division, and while I grew up a huge hockey fan in Detroit, I'm now hopeless if I have to carry a hockey conversation. It's simply all about the NBA for me. I see it as the perfect blend of competition, athleticism, teamwork and *just* the right amount of shameful melodrama amongst grown men.

I think the most bizarre attachment I have to the league is how I use the NBA Finals' as a historical benchmark to remind me of what I was doing in my life around the time the NBA was crowning a champion. **2018 Finals'**—Due to a colossal scheduling error, I was on my way to Japan during game one. Only when I landed did I read about LeBron's virtuoso 51-point game, as well as J.R. Smith forgetting what the score was at the end of regulation. **2013 Finals'**—I was living in Chicago, and believing the game to be over, actually l*eft* my friend's house before the conclusion of game six. Only to check my phone and see that a Ray Allen three-point shot had somehow tied the game. **2008 Finals'**—I was in college and working at a crumby bar in Kalamazoo. I remember working the night of the game four Celtic comeback, and watching people go nuts in the bar. **2007 Finals'**—I actually have no recollection. I know who played, I know what the outcome was, and I know all of the legacy implications of the result. But the wound LeBron inflicted on me as a Detroit fan during the 2007 Eastern Conference Finals was too fresh to watch anymore basketball that season. **2004 Finals'**—Well, I have no recollection of many of those Finals' games, but for more celebratory reasons. On that topic, and before we go on this journey through the NBA's greatest players, it's only fair that I come clean on where my NBA allegiances lie. Per my 2019-20' NBA League Pass habits, there are three teams for which I don't miss any games. However, the origin and nature of those attachments vary greatly.

The Detroit Pistons are my primary allegiance, and it comes with the most conventional backstory. Growing up in metro-Detroit during the illustrious *Grant Hill* era—not a lot of winning, but a lot of maroon and turquoise merchandise—one was frequently reminded by one's elders of the heroic *Bad Boy* era. As much as I loved watching Don Reid, Theo Ratliff, Terry Mills, Stacey Augmon, Lindsey Hunter and Bison Dele sport those horrific uniforms in the mid-to-late 90s, Isiah Thomas, Joe Dumars, Dennis Rodman, Rick Mahorn, Bill Laimbeer and Vinnie Johnson continued to cast a shadow over Detroit basketball throughout the 90s. Ironically, the end of the *Grant Hill* era was precisely the beginning of the *Going to Work* era, as newly minted Piston executive, Joe Dumars, somehow pulled off this stunning sequence of events between 2000 and 2004:

a) Insisted that Ben Wallace be part of the Grant Hill deal to Orlando in 2000.
b) Maximized a bad 2002 draft with its third-best player at twenty-third overall [Tayshaun].
c) Lured Chauncey via free agency to point guard the team a few weeks later.
d) Swindled then Wizard player/team president (MJ) into taking Stackhouse for Rip.
e) Completed the process by landing Rasheed at the trade deadline in 2004.
f) Stomped out the Lakers in the 2004 Finals' and simultaneously..
g) Joined Jerry West as the only other player to win a Finals' MVP and a championship as Team President for the same franchise.

Detroit's four-year ascent aligned tightly with my high school years, where basketball became the only sport I played. Shit, my first job was working in the parking lot of the Palace of Auburn Hills, which was no more than eleven minutes away from the house I grew up in. The Pistons remained highly competitive as I went away to college, but the *Going to Work* run ended with LeBron's iconic *48-Special* in game five of the 2007 Eastern Conference Final, and then a six-game loss to the Celtics in the 2008 ECF. I graduated from college (somehow) in the spring of 2009, and Detroit Basketball has been deliciously sub-mediocre for the entirety of the prior decade. It didn't stop me from watching the games regardless of where I was living. My love for basketball is inexorably tied to the Pistons, regardless of their current un-follow-ability.

Secondly, I don't miss any Toronto Raptor games. While this is a newer attachment, the origin story probably makes sense with some context. My wife is from Toronto and the Raptors rapid ascent and subsequent (implausible) championship provided a connective cause within our family, that for me, yielded a genuine emotional investment in their success. Despite a small wedding in the fall of 2017, my wife insisted that we also throw a massive second wedding for all of our friends and family in the spring of 2019. Despite my resistance to the idea (and overall contentment with just one wedding), we ultimately threw another wedding on May 31st, 2019 in Siesta Key, Florida.

The evening of *May 30th,* 2019 happened to be game one of the 2019 NBA Finals'. Because we were hosting more than 50 people that made their way to Florida from Ontario, we obviously needed to arrange some kind of watch party for game one. I'll never forget the glorious collection of people who came together to watch the Raptors give the Warriors the business in game one of the 2019 Finals'. We got back home to Orlando a few days later and proceeded to watch the Raptors capture an NBA championship. My wife's father, someone who's loved basketball his whole life, was one of the first in line for tickets when the Raptors were announced as an expansion team in 1995. That fanbase endured some horrendous basketball, and it was pretty special to watch them win a championship, particularly when I felt uniquely connected to it.

It was really the way the Raptors defended their title in the marathon 2019-20' season that locked me into 'every night fan' status. I have my wife Becca to thank for this one. We moved to from Orlando to Salt Lake City just prior to the 2019-20' season. When the campaign got under way, my wife insisted that we devote primary League Pass priority to the Raptors.[1] I was resistant at first, but I quickly fell in love with an organization that was seemingly attempting to re-create the institutional stability and consistency of the 2000s and 2010s San Antonio Spurs. Ravaged by injury early in the season, the Raptors continued to win with lineups that might not have been favored against a handful of G-League teams. Despite an earlier than desired exit from the 2020 playoffs, I'm all in on this team going forward.[2]

The Los Angeles Lakers are the third team I follow very closely, and this represents the most complicated of my allegiances. Having a rooting interest in both the Lakers and Pistons is like a brunch banquet with the Montagues and the Capulets—I was raised to absolutely hate the Lakers. The stabilizing variable in this corrosive equation was the decision by my favorite player—Kentavious Caldwell-Pope—to become a Laker. I'm just kidding. While I was happy to see a divisive Detroit draft pick find his niche on a championship-winning team, I have other motivations for tuning into a basketball team that I was raised to despise

LeBron James is my connection to the Los Angeles Lakers. I've been an advocate for LeBron's success since around the time people started questioning whether or not he would have any. Joining team LeBron satisfied plenty of things that were probably missing from my life around that time. While I still actively cheer for LeBron's success, I'm a lot less vocal about it, and not *quite* as emotionally attached. To really appreciate this deeply rooted loyalty I have within the NBA, we need to isolate a moment where LeBron's legacy was in the balance, and my allegiance was truly tested. I'll need you to travel back in time with me to April 28th, 2012, right around 3:00pm.

Picture game one of the first-round matchup between the Chicago Bulls and Philadelphia 76ers. In the waning moments, Derrick Rose performed an especially aggressive euro-hop and his left anterior cruciate ligament (and the hearts of everyone in metro-Chicago) ripped in half. I was living in Chicago at the time and I remember the room I was in, the people that were around me, and what I did the night it happened—which is fairly profound, given I was still engaged in frequent mid-twenties knuckleheadery. Watching the air come out of that city was unlike anything I've ever seen. However, the visceral connection I have to that moment isn't based on the impact the injury had on the league as a whole, or noble unbiased feelings of empathy I had for the dark moment in Chicago sports that was unfolding.

Hell no. I grew up in metro-Detroit, and hating Chicago teams was in my blood. But more than that, I was a vindictive, self-conscious, argumentative and annoying LeBron James supporter. With the one-seeded Bulls no longer a threat, LeBron's Heat should have had a leisurely stroll to the Finals', and while I wasn't rooting for Derrick to tear his knee or celebrating when he did (in public), I was happy to swim in the river of Chicago fan tears that flowed through the Loop. At this point, and at the expense of my own sanity, I'd spent the past 3+ years as a vocal LeBron fan. Lest we forget for a moment what it meant to admit you were sympathetic to LeBron's cause *post-decision*—not dissimilar to revealing you were a Scientologist. In fact, I'm sure people were starting to integrate my LeBron support into their personal descriptions of me—Danny Bennett = nice dude .. decent hang .. big LeBron guy.

---

[1] Naturally, I pushed back, but what was I going to do? Watch the Sekou Doumbouya Pistons? Actually .. yes.

[2] Is it just me, or is Giannis going to look excellent in a Raptor uniform? See you soon, big fella ;)

Five weeks later, In the early morning of June 6th, 2012, I found myself at Nick's Beer Garden in Wicker Park. I was hate-watching a replay of the Celtics beating the Heat to take a 3-2 lead in the Eastern Conference Finals. This loss meant a trip back to Boston, and a loss in Boston meant the weight of the sports world crashing squarely on the back of LeBron. The opening that Derrick's injury created hadn't really mattered, and the Heat had their backs to the wall again. This pending collapse also meant a rush of feelings that were all too familiar.

Disappointment in 2009 when SVG's Magic out-strategized the 66-win Cavs. Embarrassment in 2010 when Boston capitalized on LeBron's classic game five no-show. Rock Bottom Depression in 2011 after the Finals' loss to Dallas. To this day, I'm unable to accurately articulate my emotions after that loss. For now, I will call it embarr-e-disgust-i-bullshit-dammit-fuck-ed. I shattered my phone after the Mavs won game six. It's true—part of my exploded Blackberry struck my friend Quinn. I still have Post-Traumatic-J.J. Barea-Syndrome from the 2011 NBA Finals'.[3]

I now had to slog my way through two more days of work before Thursday night's game six. The anticipation was sure to bring chain-smoking and anxiety for me reminiscent of Stringer Bell right before his demise. But it wasn't Omar Little or Brother Mouzone coming for me, nor was it Pierce, Rondo, Allen or KG. It was the fear that LeBron would continue to fall short of the lofty (and just) expectations that had been attached to his career. It was the pending humiliation for being so wrong about a player whose ability I'd perceived to be singular and generational. But really, it was the historic hazing I was about to receive from the many people who were ready to remind me of how annoying I'd been in support of LeBron. During the 2010 playoffs, I made a bet with my buddy Adam that LeBron would eventually become the greatest player of all-time. Adam's originally from Chicago and rightfully believed MJ's claim to the throne to be unassailable. The only stakes for the bet? Upon LeBron's retirement, the loser would have to write a concession essay with no fewer than three sources to back up the surrender. Let's just say that Adam liked to remind me in those first couple years, the moment LeBron was eliminated, just how far LeBron had to go. What a dick.

Despite struggling to contain Rondo[4] in the first two games, Miami took a 2-0 lead in this series. Rondo led the league in assists and was still in his prime, but with Pierce (age 34), Garnett (36) and Ray Allen (36), these Celtics were four years removed from their championship season and gutting out one final run. Those LeBron Heat teams, while great, were often guilty of playing down to their opponent, and this series was no different. Vintage KG (24 points, 10 rebounds) helped bring a game three Celtics victory. Rondo (15 points, 15 assists, go ahead game-winning bucket) led the Celtics to an overtime victory to even up the series. Miami then lost a game five rock fight at home, during which both teams shot 40% from the field. Just like that, the narrative of going back to the Finals' to avenge the embarr-e-disgust-i-bullshit-dammit-fuck-ed loss from the previous year was quickly going up in flames.

A game seven Miami loss meant NBA writers wouldn't have to reach too deep to write their series' recaps—the high-mileage narratives that'd followed the Heat around for two

---

[3] For real. When I hear J.J. Barea's name, or when any announcer says 'Nowitzki will go to the free throw line', I wince noticeably.

[4] Playoff Rondo put up a career-high 44 points in game two. For those unaware, Rajon Rondo categorizes his play through a 1-5 ranking system (a real thing). He says level 5 is reserved for the Finals', but that was level 5 Rondo for sure. I'm pretty sure game six of the 2020 Finals' was level 5 Rondo too.

seasons would effectively write themselves: *LeBron can't win a big game..The Bosh/Wade/James thing doesn't work..Will LeBron ever win a championship?* Since coming into the league, LeBron had been Nike's golden ticket. But if his brand was becoming one of unmet expectations, losing, and trademark collapses, how marketable would LeBron actually be going forward? The sharks were certainly circling June 7ᵗʰ, 2012. Boston fans were filing into TD Garden with their ugly girlfriends like a horde of hammerheads .. and their ugly hammerhead shark girlfriends.

I typically preferred to watch games at the apartment by myself, as to not subject the normal world to the madness and self-deprecation that came with exercising my LeBron mania during the months of April through June. My roommate definitely hated me at the time, and I believe the high volume of stressful Miami Heat watching was the primary reason. He wasn't into basketball at all, but he heard me yelling at Dwayne Wade so often that he would mock me by yelling 'God-Damn-Dwayne-Wade!' all the time. Truth be told, poor guy witnessed my peak LeBron insanity. I didn't notice it then, but the looks he gave me in response to both *LeBron-rejoicing* and *LeBron-wallowing* explicitly revealed a high level of confusion over why I cared so much. That confusion is shared across the non-sports-loving population, and I guess it's as good a time as any to address exactly how I had gotten that deep regarding LeBron.

From a basketball perspective, who doesn't love a phenom? Everyone could hear the LeBron buzz after the 2001 *Sports Illustrated* cover, but it became a steady roar for me in December 2002 when LeBron flexed Oak Hill on national television.[5] The next landmark LeBron moment happened in my Kalamazoo dorm room in the Fall of 2004. My roommate and best friend were hard at work drinking Busch Lights and building our NBA2K dynasties on Xbox .. *I mean*, studying and discussing our futures. Despite my *Going to Work* Pistons having just hung a championship banner, I felt compelled to trade every valuable asset to the Cavaliers, just to be able to virtually play out LeBron's very promising future as a Piston. Fast forward a few hazy college years to May 31ˢᵗ, 2007. LeBron was enjoying the high approval rating that tends to accompany promising young Unicorn players in the NBA, but a tied Eastern Conference Final with my Pistons afforded LeBron an opportunity to take the next step. I can't remember why, but I was watching the game at a friend's house who didn't like basketball, and there were no other sports fans there. Picture the sad guy watching a basketball game in a room by himself. We all know what happened that night—my red Tashaun Prince jersey wiped away a few tears after that double-OT loss, but how could you not marvel at what LeBron had just done?

After that series,[6] I went from appreciation to actively rooting for the guy. 08', 09' and 10' didn't bring a title for LeBron, but that didn't stop me from making sure everyone around

---

[5] This is a forever re-watchable broadcast. Top five best aspects—5) The mainlining of the LeBron Phenomenon to the masses through a since extinct medium called 'ESPN 2'. 4) A dominating 31, 13 and 6 from LeBron. 3) The crack broadcaster team of Bilas, Shulman, Walton and Vitale. No explanation necessary. 2) A first quarter LeBron tomahawk for the ages. 1) Securing the unrealistic expectations we would always have for LeBron—The opening montage showcased a dozen NBA hall-of-famers (or soon to be hall-of-famers). Which was then bookended with a LeBron high school highlight reel, insinuating that he would join them soon. Yikes.

[6] Make no mistake—the Pistons, then and forever, are my NBA priority. *But* did *you* watch them between 2009 and 2020?? Unfortunately for me, I did. They weren't bad enough to snare a Unicorn in the draft, and only made the playoffs three times (first-round sweeps in 09', 16' and 19'). It's all good though because Luke Kennard will end up being better than Donovan Mitchell. **smashes everything on desk**

me knew how great he was. Ultimately, Decision 1.0 marked the point of no return, and where the non-basketball factors come into play.

My decision to support LeBron was aided by the fact that I've always been a strict contrarian. Naturally, Raphael, the outsider, was always my favorite Ninja Turtle when I was a kid. As the anti-LeBron sentiment grew in the late 2000s and the approval rating began to plummet, it only emboldened me to drill down on my defense and support for LeBron's abilities. I was ready to root for LeBron regardless of where he decided to play in the summer of 2010. But when he chose Miami and became a full-on Bond villain, it presented a situation where I could be in the vast minority in my support for something that was undeniably great— PERFECT! I knew I was standing on a small corner of the NBA world, and it was exactly where I wanted to be.

Winning a game facing elimination on the road, in Boston no less, is a nightmare in a bottle. I've always hated the Celtics, but fully acknowledge that when they're a contender (splice out the post-Bird, pre-KG years) they have the best home court advantage in the league. On this night however, and for the remainder of LeBron's reign over the Eastern Conference, he would prove impervious to the Paul Pierce trash talking, the Heinsohn[7] cackling and the chaotic Boston environment at large. We've all heard the notion that a player or team needs to take 'the crowd out of it early', but never has that strategy been utilized more effectively than during this game. Howard Beck, then with the *New York Times*, wrote in his game recap— *James Takes Game Six Personally*:

> No Matter the outcome, James had the most at stake, his reputation
> seemingly riding on every shot. So, he took a lot of them.

LeBron missed his first shot, and a quick Ray Allen bucket gave Boston the first lead of the game. In the form of a warning shot dunk that gave Miami an 8-4 lead, LeBron's first bucket came at the 9:01 mark in the first quarter. This was the first of *12 made shots in a row for him*—a streak that wasn't broken until there were seven seconds left in the second quarter. Of the 12 consecutive makes, there were 2 dunks and a layup that also drew a foul, but the other 9 makes were the following number of feet from the basket—21, 12, 25, 8, 9, 12, 14, 16 & 19.

On top of hitting everything that came off his fingertips, LeBron also entered basketball computer mode. Boston tried a zone in the second quarter, which LeBron inoculated by getting to the middle and got a few easy look over Rondo. Boston started inching up on LeBron's jumper, so he got Pierce and Rondo in the air for a few easy trips to the free throw line. We were really seeing an exposition of the full LeBron arsenal during a significant pressure moment. With D-Wade having one of the worst playoff halves of his career, LeBron grabbed hold of the game, the series, the playoffs, and his legacy all at once. Despite the efforts of Breen, Jackson and Van Gundy, it was hard to describe how locked in he was.

As LeBron continued to smother Boston, it progressively felt more theatrical. On its face, we were all still watching a basketball game. But like Beck said, LeBron was fighting for his reputation with every shot, and you could feel that in real time. You could sense a star

---

[7] I hate the Celtics, but Tommy Heinsohn is a legend. He's the only person to be a part of the Celtics organization for all 17 of their championships! Amazing!

ascending to another level beyond the success they'd already experienced. Amid peak-*McConaissance*, it was like watching McConaughey navigate the projects in that classic *True Detective* tracking shot. It was like watching Al Pacino rise in the *Sollozzo and McCluskey* murder scene. It was like watching star-actor-Denzel become Hollywood-force-Denzel in *Training Day*.

King Kong definitely didn't have shit on LeBron in that first half, and he was asking Paul Pierce if Pierce *liked to get wet* every chance he got. On 12 of 14 from the field, LeBron put up 30 in the first two quarters. He had the Celtics on a string and had a dagger every time Boston tried to stay attached. Mickael Pietrus wasn't able to get into his airspace, and Paul Pierce was fully swept up in the LeBron supernova. Pierce shot a cool 22% from the floor and was 0-6 from three in this game. I have to go back and check the tape, but I'm pretty sure his PER in this game was equal to Michael Scott's in the legendary warehouse basketball game.

Meanwhile, after wiping myself off, I'd stepped outside for some cool-down-post-LeBron-euphoria cigarettes. My chosen nicotine vehicle was further illuminating the special part of my brain reserved for LeBron success.[8] As my brain is running a mile-a-minute picturing how heroic this win might look if they held on, it was also hard to ignore the fact that a thirteen-point lead far from ensured a victory. What if the faucet shut off at halftime and LeBron came out flat in the second half? How revved up would the sharks be after another LeBron collapse with all of the lights on? Boston was smart enough to know that LeBron shooting jump shots was where they preferred him to be—what if he went cold?

I had been tricked before. A year prior, Miami held a 15-point lead with 7:14 left in game two of the 2011 Finals'. LeBron and friends were looking at a chance to take a 2-0 series lead and hold the Mavs under 80 points in the process. But, in one of the league's more dramatic cosmic shifts, Dallas came back. The Heat led 88-73 at that point, and each team would get off 10 shots in the final 7:14. The trouble was, Dallas would go 9 of 10 from the field down the stretch, and Miami went 1 of 10.

With the frustration of watching Don Draper go after another trashy 6.5 in a smoky Midtown bar instead of staying faithful to either of his 9+ wives,[9] LeBron let that one slip out of his fingers. LeBron went 0-4 down this stretch including missing back-to-back potential dagger threes with around one minute left. Dirk badly outdueled him in those final six minutes—9 points on 4 of 5 from the field, 3 rebounds, 2 assists and the go-ahead last-second bucket. LeBron couldn't close it out, and I couldn't pour vodka into a glass quick enough. That historic and narrative-altering loss was to blame for what is still a Mt. Rushmore hangover for me the following day. Miami won the next one, but we all know what happened after that, and *many* experts could only describe it as an embarr-e-disgust-i-bullshit-dammit-fuck-ed collapse.

---

[8] I'm no neuroscientist, but I'm pretty sure this region is sandwiched between self-fulfillment and the deep love I have for my wife.

[9] Seriously dude? Rachel Menkel (Dept. Store Owner), Suzanne Farrell (Sally's teacher) & Dr. Faye Miller (Psychologist turned side-piece[technically Don wasn't married to Megan yet]) were all at least 8's in their own right. But Midge Daniels (artistic/forgettable), Bobby Barrett (annoying comic's wife) and Sylvia Rosen (lived in Don's building, Sally walked in on them) were all totally unforgivable. Betty was stunning early on, and Megan Draper was rather lovely throughout. Need I remind you of the *Zou Bisou Bisou* rendition she did for Don's birthday in the Season 5 premiere? C'mon man!!

Bron was so tentative after game two of that series, and it's likely that if he were able to hold on to that game two lead, the Heat get that 2011 banner. However, that collapse exposed to the world that LeBron wasn't ready for mountaintop-level adversity. That vulnerability[10] would have manifested somewhere else down the line, and he would have encountered his bottom eventually. Prior to that, he'd experienced scrutiny, maybe heavy scrutiny, but most would agree it was commensurate with the expectations that come along with his capabilities. But he had never gone to the very bottom. In my opinion, knowing what that bottom felt like was instrumental in the game six performance we're now centered on.

On October 12th, 2018, *HBO* and *Uninterrupted* premiered the second episode of *The Shop*. LeBron, without any unclear words, confirmed that the 2011 Finals' loss sparked the pivot which allowed him to get to the next step. The statement was preceded by a conversation between Drake, Mav Carter and LeBron on how greatness is really defined by staying power and overcoming challenge.

MC: *What was your greatest challenge, Bron, was it [20]11?*

LBJ: *It was eleven, yeah. I had seven great seasons, eight great seasons, went to Miami my first year, and thought it would be easy. I knew I still had to work hard, but I thought it would be easy because I was teaming up with some guys that were some real players. You go down there and that first year we lose that finals. It felt like the world had caved in. First of all, I was wearing a hat that I wasn't accustomed to, and I bought into it, because at that point in time in my life I was still caring about what other people thought. But that moment right there, that moment shaped me for who I am today. Without that moment, I wouldn't be here today.*

MC: *So, you're happy you lost that Finals' today?*

LBJ: *I'm not happy that I lost, but I left that finals like 'Yo Bron, what the fuck was you on?' You was overthinking everything, you didn't show up, you didn't do what you were supposed to do and now you can't sleep at night because you didn't give it all that you had, in the sense that you know you could have done better. After that finals I was like that's never happening again. I may lose again, I may not win everything, but I'm never going to fail like that.*

MC: *And you feel like that was the greatest failure of your career?*

LBJ: *Nah, that was my greatest achievement.*

MC: *If you're really good, your greatest failure is the beginning of the greatest thing in your life. Like, when you fail miserably, that's actually the beginning*

---

[10] This also confirms to me that if LeBron had met Kobe in either the 2009 or 2010 Finals', Kobe would have eaten him alive. Kobe was a hardened savage at that point, and LeBron was still vulnerable, as the 2011 Finals' exposed.

of something great. So, you felt like that was the beginning of something great?

LBJ: *That was my greatest achievement.*

MC: *To overcome it?*

LBJ: *Mm-hmm.*

Hearing LeBron candidly re-address this critical point in his career only confirmed what I already knew about the 2011 Finals' importance in shaping the player that we've come to know over the past eight or nine years. In the context of game six of the 2012 Eastern Conference Finals, it didn't put the ball through the basket for him in the first half, but it sure as hell reminded LeBron to be the one taking the shots, come hell or high water.

To my great relief, the second half picked up where the first one ended. During the second half, LeBron did regress from ballistic-*Super Saiyan*, temporarily encountering basketball divinity, to simply playing like a league MVP in his prime. Fortunately, that was enough to keep Boston outside of striking distance. LeBron sprinkled in buckets to sustain a comfortable Miami lead, but as the clock ticked under 3 minutes left in the third quarter, Boston did have some momentum as they'd cut the lead to 10 and Miami's offense was starting to sputter. Yet, as he had done the whole game, LeBron stepped into a three and squashed another surge as the shot clock nearly expired. Prior to that, LeBron had a steely, nearly Anton Chigurh-esque emotionless demeanor. But after that dagger, he expressed a little swagger in the form of a mean mug for all to see. As long as you're rooting for the road team, there's nothing quite like the silence/low groaning noise of a raucous crowd after a dagger shot in a big game. The Miami lead would never be fewer than 11 points after that, and even as the lead expanded into the fourth quarter, Spoelstra didn't bring LeBron out of the game until three minutes were left.

Maybe the Dirk comeback was on his mind and he didn't want to take his foot off the gas. Whatever the rationale, LeBron checked out of the game with 45 points, 15 rebounds and 5 assists. It was the first 45-15-5 since Wilt-freaking-Chamberlain in 1964. The Heat won 98-79, and like LeBron's legacy, survived to play another day.

LeBron was the easy choice for the post-game interview, and Doris Burke would be the one posing the questions. The first question was a relative softball, and earned a softball-ish response:

DB: *LeBron, no player has to play under the kind of scrutiny and pressure that you do—how do you stand and deliver the kind of performance that you did tonight?*

LBJ: (no smiles) *I just wanted to try and lead my team the best way I could, whatever I need to do out there on the floor, I tried to be there for them tonight. I'm glad we were able to get this win and force the game seven.*

Doris clearly wasn't going to ignore the gravity of the moment. She got right to the heart of the stakes, the pressure and the historical implications of this game which I've been trying to convey for the last couple thousand words. The second question was quick, but so direct that it caught LeBron off guard. It also provoked the response which confirmed a change in LeBron:

> DB: *What is it like knowing that regardless of what happens with the team, the failure rests on your shoulders?*
>
> LBJ (slightly taken aback): *I just go out and do what I've been taught—and that's to play at a high level and have fun with it. And at the end of the day I won't regret anything. If I know I played hard and I gave it my all, I won't regret anything no matter the outcome, and that's where I've been this whole season.*

Enter 'live with the results' LeBron—a professional at the top of his field who through experiencing his very bottom, had gained the maturity and focus required to mentally pivot toward solely concentrating on the things he could control. LeBron, with little emotion, had just expressed that he's happy to live with the results after providing us a dissertation on how to respond when your back is to the wall. This declaration that typically accompanies a losing effort—'well, I gave it my all and fell short'—followed one of the great all-time NBA performances, and to me, illustrated a vivid image of the healthier mindset that LeBron had deliberately cultivated and ultimately achieved.

It was widely publicized that LeBron had spent time training with Hakeem in the summer prior to that season. The intention was to play out of the post more often in the 2011-2012 campaign.[11] I say LeBron could have scrimmaged every day in the offseason with the *Monstars*. He could even have Mike Mancias[12] utilize their alien technology to create a serum that would net immediate muscle recovery. Even if LeBron closed out every workout by shooting 5,000 threes with Chip Engelland,[13] I still don't see a path to LeBron's current legacy standing that doesn't include him finding psychological peace with the things that were said about him. It wasn't just a matter of more time in the gym, although that too was a prerequisite. He knew that he had to broaden his comprehension of the intangibles that accompany the level of greatness he sought. He succeeded, and he's been on a warpath through the NBA ever since that game six in Boston.

So .. yeah .. between 2010-ish and 2016-ish, I was pretty lost in the weeds fighting for LeBron's legacy. I've continued to care about LeBron's legacy in real time, but now it's more of a hobby that I'm ashamed of, opposed to the tiresome crusade to annoy everyone I came across. When it appeared that defending LeBron was a less dire responsibility, I emerged from the fray with a hefty book of current and recent NBA knowledge. The data may have been accumulated because of its adjacent position from my myopic, LeBron-oriented perspective on the NBA, but it was there nonetheless, and I've since poured immeasurable energy into building

---

[11] Which he did. He was 7-7 for 15 points on post-ups against Boston in that game six.
[12] LeBron's personal trainer/nutritionist that has been working with him since his rookie season.
[13] Long-tenured shooting coach for the San Antonio Spurs.

on that knowledge. While the reasons for boarding the LeBron train are a little shaky, even in my own re-telling, the journey fast-tracked me to a destination where I care more about the NBA than I could have previously thought was possible. That's why I watch the Lakers every night.

I have private interests in the NBA, but they were noticeably ironed out in the process of writing this book. Over the past five years, I've flirted with different creative outlets for my obsession with the NBA—I've been a part of several NBA-oriented podcasts, and experimented with writing one-off pieces about certain NBA developments that I found were being underreported. But mostly, it's been a one-way flow of content traffic from NBA writers to my ears and eyes. This book isn't a means for me to get off a number of takes that I'm desperate for others to read—yes, shooters shoot, and I'm going to get some shots up—but mostly, completion of this project marks fulfillment of a challenge to myself to not just consume the work of others, but to create my own.

We're going to disagree on plenty of assertions I'll make throughout this book. There will be metaphors that won't make sense, there will be pop culture references that are understood by fewer than 5% of readers, and certain takes will be downright confrontational to your NBA sensibilities. However, I've only failed you if you don't think I've put the work in. I'll live with the results because I think I've put the work in. Before we start running down my list of the all-time greatest players in the history of the NBA, why don't we zoom in on my approach and the framework that we'll be navigating.

Introduction.

Maybe an actual writer like Malcolm Gladwell can write a book about this for me, but there is something undeniably compelling about the ranking of something that we care about. Click-bait poachers have certainly figured out that people fall for the allure of a desirable list all the damn time—*16 Best Dressed Actresses At The Oscars* (or) *11 Foods You Should Totally Be Eating Today, Ranked*—Blah, blah, blah. I miss the good ole' days of the internet (at 34, I *can* actually say that) when all you had were a few pop-up adds. Now, it seems like every web page I go to has 436 different things going on.[14] Sigh. Whatever the forces are, we just can't get enough of lists, especially when they're ordering things we care about.

One list that's resonated with me for a long time is *Rolling Stone's 500 Greatest Albums of All Time*. The list was put together by the editors of *Rolling Stone* in 2003, based on the results of two polls completed by 271 artists, producers, industry executives and journalists. My hazy mid-2000s college years saw me re-centering my musical obsession around classic rock, the booming indie scene and aftershocks of the NYC rock-resurgence. Needless to say, ever since the list came out, I've loved referencing/dissecting/hating/praising this list over the years. Reasonably speaking, providing a narrow definition for what constitutes greatness in the creation of popular music is a silly exercise, given the vast subjectivity every single person has in their valuation process. *But son of a bitch if it's not a good time.*

I could probably write a book about the gripes I have with the list—namely a Led Zeppelin record not appearing until #29, or Pink Floyd's *Dark Side of the Moon* not being higher than #43. A higher-profile gripe that many have is the apparent shade toward hip-hop (*Illmatic* #402, *The Low End Theory* #153, *Ready to Die* #134). Clearly the philosophy for Rolling Stone was to give shine to the artists whose music was tangibly, indelibly influential to future artists (or even unborn genres as a whole, like hip-hop).[15] Rolling Stone offered a revised list in 2012, so I was sure they would give some more shine to hip-hop (and they kind-of did). Kanye's 2005 triumph *Late Registration* debuted at #118, the highest of any of the 16 post-2003 additions to

---

[14] Remember the *Chappelle's Show* episode (S2:E6) where Dave imagined what the internet would look like if it were a real place? What does that look like now? I have to imagine there are 58 people bothering you instead of one, and all of them already know what you're looking for. Thanks Zuckerberg!

[15] But *Illmatic* at #402? C'mon man.

the ranking. They also added a few more hip-hop albums, including Lil' Wayne's *Carter III*, which if you were born between 1982 and 1990, is an album you've listened to between 1,982 and 1,990 times. All of this to say—even with 250+ expert contributors, the list will never be perfect. No one will ever be totally content with it.

My stepdad and I bonded over basketball from a pretty early age, and when he told me stories of all-time great NBA players, I could feel there was a certain mystique attached to them. The way he talked about Isiah Thomas or MJ or Bird bared a closer resemblance to the description someone would provide for a war hero, more so than one of an athlete. It always made all-time greats seem truly legendary, in an actual sense, not just a hyperbolic sense. In the right context, that could be said of great players from any sport. However, I believe basketball has the unique ability to illuminate individuality (more than baseball or football). Greatness within those more specialized sports, generally speaking, is defined more by the frequency of completing a position's more narrow role, versus the style with which you complete it.[16] I think hockey and soccer also allow for players to be effective through a wider variety of styles, which makes those sports, like basketball, more ripe for fruitful 'best-ever' debates. Great basketball players somehow have their own 'brand' of individual, almost proprietary greatness that I'm obsessed with.

As we know, in trying to appraise that greatness, there isn't one factor, stat, category (or any five of them) that make a player great, or greater than another player for that matter. And clearly, it's not just the stats either—greatness, in the all-time NBA power dynamic context, commonly includes the personal profile of a player. The player has to win, they have to rack up some hardware and stats, but they also have to uphold a certain reputation for them to be considered an all-time great. But how exactly do you rank certain players above others with so much subjectivity baked into how we appreciate or don't appreciate certain player's attributes within that profile?

I've spent much more time than I'd care to admit trying to solve this puzzle numerically. I was convinced that if I crunched the right numbers, I could create a model that would spit out definitive rankings, allowing us to skip the debates that will inevitably go on as long as the NBA exists. I mean, if I weighed out traditional and advanced stats, include regular season and playoff figures, and then consider them appropriately toward different players' careers, I could compute the greatest players of all-time .. right? The result was a basic metric for calculating greatness, that is far from perfect, but I liked it enough to include it in the profile of every player I selected for my ranking. Let's call it the Greatness Index.

In constructing the parameters of the model, I chose six different categories to weigh into a player's Greatness Index score—All-NBA First-Team selections, All-Defense selections, League MVPs, Playoff Win Shares, Championships and Finals' MVPs. It was challenging to pick the appropriate weights for each contributing achievement, especially making sure the metric

---

[16] I started drawing up a comparison to baseball, but after 3 minutes of researching baseball statistics I started nodding off. MLB and NFL greatness is more defined by surpassing certain statistical markers, and by doing so for extended periods of time. I think in basketball it matters more *how* you reach those thresholds. For example, we celebrate Tom Brady because of his systematic ability to not just hit certain markers throughout a game, but to also do so at the end of games—but the markers for success remain the same, and are celebrated by his ability to hit them, not exactly by the means through which he does so. Does that make sense? Okay, I'll quit while I'm behind.

was able to traverse different eras of the NBA. We'll disagree on some of the choices, but this was the methodology:

All-NBA First-Team **(8 points)**—All-NBA teams date back to the league's inaugural season in 1946-47', and I especially liked the idea of exclusively using First-Team selections because they're especially difficult to earn, and denote that a player was truly one of the best players in the league that season.

All-Defense **(6 points)**—All-Defensive teams only date back to the 1968-69' season, short-handing the great defenders of the Russell-era (none more so than Bill Russell himself).[17] However, making these teams is also very difficult, and I wanted to reward, if not over reward, a player's defensive reputation. I chose to do overall selections, instead of separating First-Team and Second-Team selections, largely to mitigate weirdness like the 2012-13' vote—Joakim Noah and Tyson Chandler tying for a first-team selection (?) while 2012-13' Defensive Player of the Year, Marc Gasol, was selected to the All-Defense *Second* team (the only All-Defense selection of his career).

MVPs **(10 points)**—League MVP awards are also incredibly hard to win, and date back to the 1955-56' season. I feel it is the most prestigious regular season accomplishment and is weighted as such versus the other two regular season achievements.

Playoff Win Shares **(Player's Total x 3)**—I put a lot of thought into the best way to reward playoff success that wasn't necessarily championship success. My first thought was to reward playoff success by the number of times a player's team won a playoff round, or maybe just by counting the number of playoff wins a player has. I couldn't really make those figures work, and I also couldn't seem to get any of today's advanced stats to work either. Basically, all of the really comprehensive advanced stats begin tracking during the 1973-74' season (the NBA began tracking many modern stats that season—steals, blocks, possessions per game). However, there is one fairly sturdy metric that works across every era of the NBA—*Basketball Reference's* Win Shares. Per the website—'Win Shares is a player statistic which attempts to divvy up credit for team success to the individuals on the team'. Taking a player's career *Playoff* Win Shares and multiplying them by three allows for every player's postseason contribution to count similarly. Win Shares reward players who may have been playing at a high level but were on teams that weren't destined for championship contention. It technically hurts the very greatest players because their Win Shares earned during the Finals' accumulate the same as first-round playoff competition, thus their high-profile moments are not justly amplified. However,

---

[17] The fact that steals and blocks were not counted until the early 70s drastically hurts the profiles of the players within the Russell-era. All of their advanced stats would be much higher, and based on available data, it's conceivable that Wilt Chamberlain or Bill Russell could have averaged in excess of 8 blocks per game. Reddit user 'dantheman9758' used tea leaves from newspapers and actual game film to determine that within a sample of 112 games, spanning Wilt's entire career (1960-1973), he averaged 8.8 blocks. He did the same for a 135-game sample spanning data across Russell's career (1956-1969), which had Russell averaging 8.1 blocks per game. It's not especially reliable data, but how inflated are the legends of those players if, conservatively, each of them claimed 6+ blocks per game?

multiplying their totals by three allows the very greatest, and specifically the most prolific, to amass points through rewarding their perpetual championship contention.

Championships (12 Points)—The sterling measure of team greatness, but one that can be unfairly weaponized to expand or discredit the legacies of individual players. I wanted championships to be important, but not reward so many points that it might exclude players that had fewer shots at winning championships.

Finals' MVPs (12 Points)—Often times a formality and not given to the most important player, but it remains the MVP award for excellence at the highest level and should be rewarded as such.

To demonstrate how I calculated the Greatness Index score for each player, let's use a player who I love but who will not make my ranking of the 30 greatest players ever—Chauncey Billups:

Chauncey Billups' Career Accomplishments		
All-NBA First-Team (0)	x 8	= 0
All-Defense (2)	x 6	= 12
League MVP (0)	x 10	= 0
Playoff Win Shares (20.6)	x 3	= 61.8
Championships (1)	x 12	= 12
Finals' MVP (1)	x 12	= 12
Greatness Index Score = 97.8		

Chauncey's score of 97.8 is good for the 53rd highest score in the Greatness Index database—not too bad for Mr. Big Shot! You can probably imagine how the scores go up for the players who stack up these accolades throughout their career. I will be referencing the results of the Greatness Index throughout the book, and each player I chose for my list will have their score in the heading of their profile. The choices I made for my ranking certainly don't run in lockstep with what is reflected in the Greatness Index results. A player's score in the metric is just one vantage point from which to view their historical profile. *But son of a bitch if it's not a good time.*

I also wanted to incorporate credible lists from brave souls who have undertaken this exercise in the past. Bill Simmons' 2010 *The Book of Basketball* is probably the most comprehensive basketball document in existence. Bill's player ranking within that book is also the deepest list ever done (96 players).[18] To honor Bill Simmons and his epic biography of professional basketball, I will include a ranking that is central to the criteria he used in selecting his list. Early in Bill's book, he tells a story of the first time he met Isiah Thomas. Having chided

---

[18] Simmons' book is insanely well-researched. Don't get me wrong, I did a preposterous amount of research for this book, but Bill's book is truly the holy document of professional basketball. My ranking will teach you a thing or two about NBA history, but in a much more random, jumping around type-of way. Simmons' book gives a rich chronological backlog of the NBA's genesis, and key events that shaped the league through the years.

Thomas for years in his columns, which resulted in Isiah publicly threatening Simmons, Bill was understandably terrified of the encounter. However, after an awkward introduction, they had a meaningful conversation during which Isiah Thomas exposed to Bill Simmons what he perceived to be *The Secret* of basketball. I'm paraphrasing, but the secret ultimately suggests that camaraderie, selflessness and a singular focus on team-oriented objectives were the hidden truths behind building winning situations that last. Those things inevitably come under fire when individual teammates desire more money, playing time and notoriety. So, for each player that I'll be profiling in my book, I'll be giving them a ranking between 1 and 100, for my perceived appreciation that player has or had for *The Secret*.

Someone whose actual ranking I'll be including with all of my players, is Ben Taylor's. No one has done a more thorough and nuanced list of NBA all-time players than Taylor. He defines his list (of 40 players) more as listing the players with the most value added to a team. In his words the list *ranks the players who have provided the largest increase in the odds of a team winning championships over the course of their careers*. His approach to evaluating players by this manner was instructive and perspective-altering for me. As a tribute to his incredible analytical work, I'll be including the ranking he gives to each of my players as well.[19]

As someone who loves appropriately ranking players, I really do love advanced stats. Basically, I love having as many clubs in my bag as possible. Furthermore, I'm very proud to be a fan of a sport that has arrived at a place where truly advanced mathematical methodology is being used by every franchise's front office. The problem is, I haven't been in direct contact with *real* mathematics since college,[20] and for someone who is easily confused by the everyday challenges of adulthood, you could probably imagine how incapable I am of explaining the methodology behind most NBA advanced stats. That being said, there will never be a replacement for watching the games to analyze a player's true impact. Advanced stats, to me, serve as a means to justify what we believe we're seeing, and furthermore, to provide fair comparisons to players we might not get to see play very often. To paraphrase the Basketball Analytics Godfather, Dean Oliver—*it's important to watch a lot of games, but the stats watch every game.*

In my quest to integrate cutting edge advanced stats into each player's profile—not just the caveman math behind the Greatness Index— I reached out to the creator of PIPM (Player Impact Plus-Minus), Jacob Goldstein. Jacob Goldstein (@JacobEGoldstein), of *bball-index.com*, published his Player Impact Plus-Minus model in early 2018. PIPM is the most complete metric that we have in establishing a player's true impact on both sides of the ball.[21] Creating an appropriately weighted plus-minus metric has been the holy grail for advanced metric nerds for many years now—RAPM/RPM, BPM, RAPTOR etc. Implementation of luck-adjusted net rating

---

[19] Taylor wrote an excellent book titled *Thinking Basketball*, and he has an equally excellent podcast by the same name.

[20] Looking through my undergrad transcript is like peering into the written records of a lost civilization—I barely remember half of these classes—*Ocean Systems, Peoples of the World, Basic Italian I*, etc. By far the best part of my transcript are the two classes I managed an 'A' in during the totality of my undergrad degree—*The Genesis and Development of Rock and Roll* (and) *Drug Use: Personal and Societal Impact* (!!!)

[21] *538's RAPTOR* model is really good too, perhaps better, but because it's dynamism is based on using player tracking data, it's only able to track player performance since 2013-14' (the first season of player tracking).

and luck-adjusted on/off data (methodology designed by Nathan Walker (@bbstats))[22] were real game-changers, and have created a widely-respected metric across the basketball analytics community. A big thanks to Mr. Goldstein for allowing a knucklehead like me to plug the metric into my ranking. Because I will butcher an attempt to translate the PIPM concept into words, I give you the explanation posted on Goldstein's site, *bball-index.com*:

> *Player Impact Plus-Minus is a metric that combines traditional box score value with luck-adjusted on/off player data to estimate how much value a player adds to their team.*
>
> *Luck-adjusted data, developed by Nathan Walker, is used to adjust for factors that are out of an individual team or player's control. For instance, free throw shooting and three-point shooting can cause wide variance in the specific ratings, but in studies it has been shown that teams and players have limited control over makes or misses. Another example is adjusting for rebounding and turnovers to attempt to limit the noise from the final values.*
>
> *The box score component is calculated off a regression from a 15-year RAPM sample. Especially on offense, there is real value to be found in the traditional box score. Combining that with more advanced play by play data, PIPM is able to see who is adding value that the box score is unable to capture.*

Let's use an example of a player's PIPM profile, and stick with my guy Chauncey Billups:

PIPM	O-PIPM	D-PIPM	Peak—2007-08'	Wins Added
+1.71 (132nd)	+2.42	-0.71	+4.26 (91st)	107.60 (57th)

PIPM suggests a player's overall impact by combining their offensive and defensive contributions for both regular season and playoff games.

- Chauncey's career PIPM is +1.71, the sum of his +2.42 O-PIPM and -0.71 Defensive-PIPM scores (with his all-time rank—132nd—in parenthesis).
- Chauncey's peak PIPM of +4.26 was achieved during the 2007-08' season (with his rank among all-time peaks—91st—in parenthesis).
- Wins Added is the PIPM estimation for the number of wins a given player is responsible for over the course of their career (with their all-time rank in parenthesis). Think of Wins Added as a more dynamic version of Win Shares.

---

[22] You may remember a kerfuffle a few years ago when Kawhi Leonard ranked conspicuously low in ESPN's proprietary defensive RPM breakout—87th to be exact. It was a glaring hole in the model that was stemming from the Spurs' opponents shooting 37% from three, most of those makes being out of the (preposterously large) hands of Kawhi Leonard. Nathan Walker's work on the PIPM model accounts for factors like this that a player is unable to control. Helping make it the best measurement we have for evaluating a player's overall impact.

This is a pretty good score. His defensive impact is lower than I'd have expected, but perhaps a reflection of the poor defenses he played within outside of his Detroit tenure. Whatever the case may be, his defensive figure illuminates a noteworthy aspect of PIPM—defense matters. For example, Rudy Gobert has a career +0.35 O-PIPM, which is pretty low, and suggests a fairly anemic offensive player. But because he has a bonkers +3.74 D-PIPM, he has the 19th best-ever career PIPM. Conversely, James Harden boasts the 20th best-ever career PIPM with a D-PIPM of -0.76 (but a stellar +4.77 O-PIPM). That is to say, in an era that tends to value offense more than ever, don't be surprised to see this model reward defensive-minded players for their efforts.

Unfortunately, PIPM is limited by the fact that many contemporary stats were not recorded until the 1973-74' NBA season. To avoid rating players on an uneven scale, I'll omit PIPM from players who primarily played in the Russell-era (pre-1969). As I will for every player, I will list Russell-era player rankings for Playoff PER[23] and Playoff Win Shares. The thinking here is that the majority of PIPM data is from regular season play, and because Russell-era all-time great players have such a large data set for postseason performance, it works well for them too. Here are Chauncey's figures for those metrics:

Playoff PER	Playoff Win Shares	Playoff O-Win Shares	Playoff D-Win Shares
19.11 (67th)	20.60(21st)	15.02 (13th)	5.58 (54th)

13th all-time for Playoff Offensive Win Shares is pretty fucking legit, Mr. Billups. While his PER reflects a player who wasn't super efficient, the accumulated Playoff Win Shares demonstrate all the winning that the Pistons did during their six consecutive trips to the Eastern Conference Finals!

If I'm getting way too math-ey for you, rest assured that this book will not be a Statistics 100 course. While I appreciate the genesis of a hyper-analytical approach to NBA coverage and player performance, I think there's a notion that if you haven't fully embraced analytics that you're somehow archaic in your basketball analysis. I think that we have many different ways to interpret the game and its players now, and that is absolutely a good thing. These interpretations are well-represented by the options we have for NBA-minded content in our podcast feed. Please use this very technical chart as a guide:

---

[23] Player Efficiency Rating (PER) was developed by John Hollinger as an all-in-one measure of a player's performance, and like Win Shares, it is pretty reliable pre-1973-74'. 20 is a very good score, 25 is a great score, and 30 is an all-time great score.

21

I listen to all of these habitually, but enjoy them for different reasons. Nate Duncan and Danny Leroux's *Dunc'ed On* Podcast is unquestionably the most frequent, deeply analytical and readily available coverage of the NBA.[24] I genuinely learn a lot from their work, but sometimes it sounds like I'm listening to a joy-less criminal deposition. Simmons will dedicate at least one segment a week to talking about hoops, and it's usually quite fun, but doesn't entail nearly the nitty-gritty analysis.[25] The sweet spot for me is Zach Lowe's podcast, *The Lowe Post*. Analytical, but doesn't put me to sleep or make me feel dumb. Entertaining and personal, but Zach is very conscious of not letting non-basketball conversations get off the rails. All of these different interpreters of the NBA exemplify all of the different approaches there are to absorb, acknowledge and ultimately rank player performance in the league. For me, that sweet spot will fall on the analytical side of the spectrum, but I enjoy all manner of NBA analysis. That, generally speaking, has been my approach to this ranking—striving for an analysis that is driven mainly by a score of statistics, but not ignoring the player narratives that so-often run alongside a player's statistical profile.

There's another distinction I've made many times when having this conversation, so I deemed it important to include. If you were to make a list of simply the best basketball players, it would skew heavily toward modern players, given the many advantages they enjoy—the advancement of exercise science, nutrition and sleep.[26] For instance, I can't value Bill Russell's rings exactly as heavily as I do modern players, because he played against tiny white dudes who had to work roofing jobs in the summer and were probably (definitely) smoking cigarettes at halftime. However, Russell was the common denominator for the most dominating sports dynasty in the history of North American professional sports, so where does that leave us? I'm not exactly sure, but I do know that I evaluate players more on how they performed against their actual competition, more than how they might fare, hypothetically, against players from a different era.

I poured myself into this project because I find discourse around the NBA's greatest players to be intolerable. I want to cut through real and imagined narratives to construct the best possible ranking, and I ultimately believe that this conversation is best served by designating tiers for the players involved:

Tier I	Tier II	Tier III
4 Players	**10 Players**	**16 Players**

---

[24] I'm a proud *Dunc'ed On Prime* subscriber.

[25] The Russillo-Simmons hoops-oriented podcasts are absolutely some of the best basketball content available. Russillo reels Simmons back in just enough to make for excellent NBA banter.

[26] Simply put, I think 'greatest-ever' conversations are either a) Greatest Player in a Vacuum—'I don't care how good Russell was, Shaq would have steamrolled him'. Or b) Greatest Player Within Proper Context—'Russell's teams were so completely dominant against their competition in the 1960's, that it doesn't matter if he'd stack up physically against modern day bigs'. I'm leaning toward (b), which is ultimately more challenging and subjective.

My ranking is of the 30 greatest players of all-time, but I won't be numbering them individually. My thinking is that there will inevitably be arbitrary rank among players if you list them one-after-another.

To demonstrate how I plan to utilize tiers, let's use the top 30 television shows, according to Alan Sepinwall & Matthew Zoller Steitz' 2016 book—*TV (The Book)*—in the same manner that I'll be carrying out my ranking. Their top 30 shows are as follows:

1) *The Simpsons* 2) *The Sopranos* 3) *The Wire* 4) *Cheers* 5) *Breaking Bad* 6) *Mad Men* 7) *Seinfeld* 8) *I Love Lucy* 9) *Deadwood* 10) *All in the Family* 11) *M*A*S*H** 12) *Hill Street Blues* 13) *The Shield* 14) *The Twilight Zone* 15) *Arrested Development* 16) *The Larry Sanders Show* 17) *The Honeymooners* 18) *Louie* 19) *The Mary Tyler Moore Show* 20) *The X-Files* 21) *Curb Your Enthusiasm* 22) *SpongeBob SquarePants* 23) *Twin Peaks* 24) *Lost* 25) *Buffy the Vampire Slayer* 26) *Freaks & Geeks* 27) *My So-Called Life* 28) *Oz* 29) *The Dick Van Dyke Show* 30) *Friday Night Lights*

Converted into my format, they would look like this:

Tier I	**Tier II**	**Tier III**
The Simpsons	*Breaking Bad*	*Arrested Development*
The Sopranos	*Mad Men*	*The Larry Sanders Show*
The Wire	*Seinfeld*	*The Honeymooners*
Cheers	*I Love Lucy*	*Louie*
	Deadwood	*The Mary Tyler Moore Show*
	All in the Family	*The X-Files*
	M*A*S*H*	*Curb Your Enthusiasm*
	Hill Street Blues	*SpongeBob SquarePants*
	The Shield	*Twin Peaks*
	The Twilight Zone	*Lost*
		Buffy the Vampire Slayer
		Freaks & Geeks
		My So-Called Life
		Oz
		The Dick Van Dyke Show
		Friday Night Lights

Let's go back to *Rolling Stone's* list, and place the top 30 albums of that ranking within my tiered system:

Tier III

Blue – Joni Mitchell
Led Zeppelin – Led Zeppelin[27]
Who's Next – The Who
The Joshua Tree – U2
Rumours – Fleetwood Mac
James Brown Live at The Apollo – James Brown
Innervisions – Stevie Wonder
Plastic Ono Band – John Lennon
The Complete Recordings – Robert Johnson
The Great Twenty-Eight – Chuck Berry
Thriller – Michael Jackson
Astral Weeks – Van Morrison
Born to Run – Bruce Springsteen
Nevermind – Nirvana
Blood on the Tracks – Bob Dylan
Are You Experienced? – The Jimi Hendrix Experience

Tier II

Abbey Road – The Beatles
The Velvet Underground – The Velvet Underground & Nico
Kind of Blue – Miles Davis
The Sun Sessions – Elvis Presley
The White Album – The Beatles
Blonde on Blonde – Bob Dylan
London Calling – The Clash
Exile on Main Street – The Rolling Stones
What's Going On? – Marvin Gaye
Rubber Soul – The Beatles

Tier I

Highway 61 Revisited – Bob Dylan
Revolver – The Beatles
Pet Sounds – The Beach Boys
Sgt. Pepper's Lonely Hearts Club Band – The Beatles

Subjectivity is unavoidable in any conversation about the greatest NBA players because each and every one of us that cares about this stuff comes to the table with bias. What I'm aiming to accomplish with the wide mobility a player can have, especially across Tier III, is a representative range of where I could conceivably see that player ranked, dependent on the approach being utilized to appraise their greatness.

I decided on the number 30 because beyond that threshold the player pool gets way too deep and I would inevitably be encouraged to make increasingly subjective choices. For example, If I did a Tier IV to constitute the 31st through 50th greatest players of all-time, I could have conceivably selected from 60 to 80 players that might be deserving of a selection for those 20 spots. Intrinsically, there is a narrowing of subjectivity that occurs as you march toward the

---

[27] WTF, man.

mountaintop of NBA all-time greatness—thus, why the tiers get smaller, as do the margins for placement, as we get closer to the very greatest players of all-time.

Enough with the pre-amble. We're going to start with Tier III—the 15th through 30th greatest players in NBA history—their profiles presented in random order. From there we'll work our way to the mountaintop together.

Julius Erving

	The Secret	Greatness Index	Ben Taylor Rank
	90 / 100	117.32 (40th)	16th

PIPM	O-PIPM	D-PIPM	Peak—1979-80'	Wins Added
+2.85 (41st)	+2.01	+0.84	+4.36 (85th)	111.66 (47th)

Playoff PER	Playoff Win Shares	Playoff O-Win Shares	Playoff D-Win Shares
19.96 (47th)	16.44 (34th)	9.29 (42nd)	7.16 (32nd)

The **A**merican **B**asketball **A**ssociation, if you need a refresher, was a professional basketball league that aimed to compete with, or earn a lucrative merger with, the NBA. The league somehow operated for nine seasons between 1967 and 1976, while perpetually mitigating financial issues, disputes with the NBA over rights to young players, and general systematic discord at nearly every level.[28] There is no truer testament to the dysfunction within the ABA than the fact that there were seven different commissioners in the league's nine seasons (the NBA has had five commissioners in 70+ seasons). It was a mess.[29] Even as the league dwindled to just six franchises after the 1975-76' season—losing Memphis, Utah, San Diego and Virginia franchises along the way—it would finally earn the merger it so coveted at the campaign's conclusion. The two leagues had been barreling toward an agreement for years, and the settlement of the Oscar Robertson Suit in 1976 paved the way for an agreement to happen. In recent years, the ABA had enticed a lot of quality talent with big-money contracts (that were sneakily stretched across 10, 15, even 20 years). By 1976, the NBA needed an influx of exciting players to revive the long-term viability of the league, and were willing to absorb The Pacers, Nets, Spurs and Nuggets to do so. The real reason the NBA made a deal though? The NBA needed Julius Erving.

---

[28] Everything I've read about the ABA makes it seem like _Semi-Pro_ may actually serve as a fairly realistic historical document to what the ABA was like. Well, minus all the cocaine in the real ABA.

[29] Honestly, it wasn't all bad though. I don't plan to touch on the ABA beyond this segment so I'm going to just get it all out of my system. The NBA would eventually adopt the Three-Point Shot, the drafting of underclassmen and the slam-dunk competition as tangible additions to the league—all of which originated in the ABA.

After becoming one of just six players to average 20 points and 20 rebounds during their college career,[30] Erving jumped from UMass Amherst to the ABA after two seasons. He dominated his rookie season for the Virginia Squires, and was now draft-eligible for the 1972 NBA draft. Which initiated a trifecta of hardly imaginable 'what-ifs?'

1. He was drafted twelfth-overall by the Milwaukee Bucks, but because of a tangled web of legal nonsense, The Squires retained his rights and his jump to the NBA was halted. Imagine if he'd gone to Milwaukee! Oscar Robertson was approaching the end of his career, but the prospect of Dr. J and Kareem riding out their primes together is terrifying! How many more titles would the Bucks have won? Does Kareem go to L.A.?[31] Does Boston then win 6 titles in the 80's?

2. Erving dominated again for Virginia in 1972-73', but the Squires had to sell him at the end of the season because they were so broke. That came two years after Virginia moved all-time great Rick Barry, and in another year they would have to move George Gervin to San Antonio. So, had they kept their shit together and been one of the teams included in the merger, we could have all collectively laughed that the 'Virginia Squires' was a passable name for a professional franchise.

3. As a New York Net, Doc would dominate for the ABA's remaining three seasons, ascending beyond the league's best player, and establishing himself as the league's best chance for a merger. When the NBA absorbed The Nuggets, Pacers, Spurs and Erving's Nets in 1976, each team was required to pay $3.2M as each team was treated as a pseudo-expansion team. The Nets, however, were required to pay an additional $4.8M indemnity to the Knicks (for cutting in on their market). Unable to pay this, the Nets offered Julius Erving to the Knicks if they would waive the indemnity—*to which the Knicks declined!* From there, the Bucks, Lakers and 76ers started inquiring about Erving's availability, and eventually Philly won the sweepstakes for a $3M fee and a fresh $3M contract for Doc (the combination of the two was why Doc wore number 6 for Philly). The Nets effectively traded Dr. J for an opportunity to be in the NBA, and imploded after the deal. The Knicks were mediocre for awhile, but it's hard not to think about what Doc's legend would have been, had his NBA prime been spent electrifying the Garden. Or what if he'd gotten swooped up by the Lakers?

---

[30] Amazing bar trivia ask—Bill Russell, Paul Silas, Artis Gilmore, Spencer Haywood, Kermit Washington and Julius Erving. If someone gets that right, you haaaaave to pick up their tab.

[31] Yeah. He wanted out of Milwaukee bad. He told the team at a private dinner instead of going to the press. A novel concept by 2020 standards.

The Lakers probably miss out on Magic a few years later, and maybe Magic keeps his initial plan of playing for his hometown Detroit Pistons[32]—Dammit!

'Dr. J' earned ABA MVP all three of the final seasons leading up to the merger, including two ABA championship campaigns with his New York Nets. Apart from the valuable commodity he was as a basketball player on the court, Julius Erving was a legitimate draw as an entertainer. Other ABA players acknowledged Erving's undeniable greatness as giving legitimacy to an otherwise floundering league. In an archived UPI article from March 7th, 1987, former ABA player M.L. Carr said of Dr. J:

> *What happened was, every guy in the league was very proud to say that Julius Erving was a part of us .. Julius was our masterpiece -- our showcase. We used to say, 'Hey, we got a guy over here that can play with anyone'.*[33]

The greatness of Julius Erving extended to serve as a measure of confidence for his fellow ABA players that would soon be competing against NBA players in 1976-77'. They did pretty damn well too—former ABA players filled 10 of 24 available all-star slots in the first merged season. Plus, 5 of the 10 starters in the 1977 NBA Finals' were guys who'd been playing in the ABA the previous season. An organic kinship developed among former ABA players, as they were able to recall the crumby conditions and chaos that defined much of their time in the league.   Kind of like when the *Michael Scott Paper Company* was bought out by *Dunder Mifflin*—upon re-integrating with their *Dunder Mifflin* colleagues, Michael, Ryan and Pam reveled in the bond that was cemented during their tumultuous, fast-paced and ultimately, short-lived tenure with the *Michael Scott Paper Company*. Yeah, exactly like that.

Dr. J was immediately a very good NBA player. He led the Sixers to those 1977 Finals', and captained a Philadelphia squad that reached two more NBA Finals' before finally breaking through to win Doc's only NBA championship in 1982-83'. He would retire a few seasons later having been selected an all-star in every single season of his basketball career (5 ABA, 11 NBA).

Julius Erving was an undeniably dynamic scorer with a multitude of unique physical gifts. This is one of many players I didn't get a chance to see play, but the video is very telling about what Erving did well. In the open court, he is *the* most terrifying player I've ever watched. The lazy comp here would be 2006-2014 LeBron, and maybe his open court stuff wasn't that

---

[32] Jeannie Buss was on Zach Lowe's podcast January 22nd 2019, and told a story about the first time Magic met the Buss family. The Buss family are the long-time owners of the Los Angeles Lakers. Jeannie tells the story of how Magic was flown to L.A. shortly after being drafted by the Lakers, and promptly brought to the Buss family estate. The old man (Dr. Jerry Buss) instructed Jeannie to keep Magic company before the meeting. Apparently, during the first exchange between Magic and Jeannie, Magic indicated his desire to play his three years for the Lakers, then to return home and play for his hometown Detroit Pistons. Jeannie, in a panic, ran to tell this to her father who calmly responded—'the moment he puts on the uniform and plays in the Forum, he'll never look back'. Dammit!

[33] Hubie Brown quote in the *Basketball: A Love Story – People Say Dr. J was great in the NBA, Listen, in the ABA, that's where he did his stuff. On the Break, he did things that were amazing. But the big thing was the love of Doc. No player would blindside Doc into the stanchion. If you did, your own players would whup your ass. That's how much respect Doc had.*

nuclear, but his ability was still unbelievable in that regard. To the point that it made me anxious watching how fast he would run in space and mercilessly spike the ball. Then, instead of tearing off into the 12th row, he lands and trots back to his end of the court, effortlessly, casually. Additionally, he was exceptional at getting to the basket in the half-court, even when the defense saturated the paint in expectation of his rapid arrival. I kind of knew the above traits to some degree, but was very surprised at how good Dr. J was at establishing position down low, and while using a variety of moves, getting himself easy buckets. Defensively, all signs point toward him being a plus player on this end. He was guilty of leaking out to try and get quick points in transition. Yet, he always had very high block and steal rates, and he was part of extremely good defensive teams in Philadelphia in the late 70s/early 80s. Doc's career D-PIPM of +0.84 is very respectable, and in line with the type of defending he demonstrates on film.

Every once in a while, right when we thought we had it all pretty well figured out, something comes along in the stream of something we love that serves to re-calibrate what we thought we knew. For instance, during the course of rock music, certain moments demonstrated a pivot or a yarn-wrapped thumbtack in determining the landscape of influence that allowed the genre to progress. Take your pick, but I'd say—Buddy Holly and The Crickets touring the UK in 58', The Beatles playing the Ed Sullivan show in 64', The Beatles releasing *Sgt. Pepper's Lonely Hearts Club Band* in 67', The Ramones playing their first gig at CBGBs in 74', David Bowie completing the 'Berlin Trilogy' in 79', Nirvana's *Nevermind* released in September 91', The Strokes residency at The Mercury Lounge[34] in December 2000.

Similarly, in basketball, certain players come along to flip the script on how the game is supposed to be played. Like the list of moments in rock, they don't have to be the greatest or most dynamic performers, it's the fact that in their moment they altered how we perceived the game to be played. Dr. J's explosive, fast-paced play and power-dunking represent one of those pivot moments in the NBA, and basketball at-large. Take your pick, but I'd say—George Mikan forcing the league to widen the foul lane and implement goaltending, Elgin Baylor and Bill Russell playing above the rim, Wilt Chamberlain forcing the league to, again, expand the foul lane and goaltending rules, [Dr. J flying through the air], Larry Bird's contract negotiation in 1983 that yielded 'Bird Rights' and a 'soft' salary cap, Michael Jordan influencing the league to begin marketing its players individually, Allen Iverson making whites uncomfortable while speaking to the interiority of black American culture, Steph Curry punctuating the three-point era by being able to make shots from anywhere on the court. An imperfect list by any measure,

---

[34] If you like rock music and haven't read Lizzy Goodman's *Meet Me In the Bathroom*, you are definitely fucking up. In Oral History format, it details the rare moment in music and creativity that New York City incubated early in the late 90s and early 00s. Joe Levy, Rock writer/editor, has a quote about the Strokes' role in that moment that gave me goosebumps when I first read it – *This all happened in a place where other things happened a long time ago. This was a block away from the St. Mark's church where Patti Smith and Lenny Kaye started what would [be] the Patti Smith Group. They started it there because that's where Jack Kerouac read and because at the time Patti lived down the street. And it wasn't by accident that she lived down the street on Tenth Street, because the whole Andy Warhol crowd used to live in the East Village and the Velvet Underground used to play on St. Mark's Place. All of this stuff doesn't happen by accident, it's not a coincidence. It's not a straight line either—you don't go, 'Oh, Velvet Underground, Patti Smith, Karen O.' It doesn't go Velvet Underground, Strokes. It's a long distance to travel from one to the other but there is a continuum, there is a vibe, there is a place where those bands have roots. It does matter, it matters to the sound. .. Whoa. I'd like to write like that when I grow up.*

but you see where I'm going here. This quote from the great New York Post columnist, Mike Vaccaro, in *Basketball: A Love Story*, sums it up for me:

> *I grew up about 10 minutes away from Nassau Coliseum. Obviously, Julius Erving was amazing to behold. One of my earliest recollections is a commercial of him dunking a basketball backwards, and it was the first time I had ever seen that. It seemed otherworldly, like something a Martian would do. Then I remember watching him a couple weeks later in person, doing the same thing and thinking to myself, 'I Don't know if I could ever do that, but I could watch that all day'.*

I asked my stepdad about what made Dr. J great, and I think he also nails it:

> *In my opinion, it was the introduction of the best athlete on the team playing the three and attacking the rim on the break. As a young man in the ABA, his athleticism seemed implausible—he could touch the top of the back board, but wasn't just a jumper, he could score, rebound and block shots. At that time and before, the four and five dominated the offense. That's why Wilt, Kareem and Moses Malone all averaged 25 a game. Even the Big O [Oscar Robertson] couldn't change that paradigm. Championships came through the front court. The Pistons and Mr. Jordan changed all of that. To me, he was like Jordan—Air before Air.*

Why he belongs in this tier? I don't acknowledge ABA statistics, because it feels like grading on an uneven scale, but he's probably higher for a lot of people that do. If you're talking about a guy who won 4 MVPs and 3 Championships in the NBA, he's probably a Tier II player. Alas, his profile is a little blurry because of the five high-level seasons that were spent in the ABA. Aside from hardware, his efficiency figures fall short of what I'd prefer to see for a Tier II player. It's difficult to compare across eras, but Dr. J had a vulnerability that would just be eaten up by the modern NBA—he was observably way better at dribbling with one hand than the other. For a guy without a really steady jumper, I'm convinced that there are ways to strategize him out of a playoff series in 2020. The skill requirements are different as we traverse the different eras of the NBA, but I just can't get too far past that chink in his armor. However, he's a true legend of the game whose impact and influence cannot be overstated.

Scottie Pippen

The Secret	Greatness Index	Ben Taylor Rank
100 /100	226.74 (12th)	25th

PIPM	O-PIPM	D-PIPM	Peak—1993-94'	Wins Added
+2.93 (36th)	+1.41	+1.53	+4.99 (53rd)	174.98 (19th)

Playoff PER	Playoff Win Shares	Playoff O-Win Shares	Playoff D-Win Shares
18.35 (83rd)	23.58 (12th)	9.46 (41st)	14.12 (5th)

A pillar of every lasting dynasty in the NBA has been success on draft day:

- ✓ 60s Celtics—In the 1956 draft, Red Auerbach swindles no fewer than ten people in acquiring Bill Russell, Tommy Heinsohn and K.C. Jones in the same draft.[35]
- ✓ 80s Lakers—In the 1979 draft, the Lakers won a coin toss to earn the first-overall pick (Magic Johnson). In the 1982 draft, the Lakers again had the first-overall pick (James Worthy).[36]
- ✓ 80s Celtics—In the 1977 draft, the Celtics draft Cedric Maxwell, future Finals' MVP, twelfth-overall. In the 1978 draft, Red Auerbach drafts Larry Bird sixth-overall, even though he would be ineligible for another year. In the 1980 draft, the Celtics trade their first-overall pick to Golden State

---

[35] Auerbach was the primary architect of the Celtics roster from 1950 to 2006, and one of the most forward-thinking executives in the history of professional sports. Russell, Heinson and K.C. Jones are all Hall-of-Famers.
[36] Both picks were the compensation for trades that then Laker GM, Bill Sharman, had previously made with teams that utterly bottomed out the year that the pick conveyed.

for Robert Parish and the third-overall pick (then select Kevin McHale with that pick).[37]

- ✓ *90s Bulls—In the 1984 draft, Michael Jordan falls to the Bulls at the third-overall pick. In the 1987 draft, the Bulls trade the eighth-overall pick, Olden Polynice, and future draft considerations to the Sonics for their fifth-overall choice, Scottie Pippen. Also in the 1987 draft, the Bulls selected Horace Grant tenth-overall. In the 1989 draft, The Bulls selected B.J. Armstrong eighteenth-overall. In the 1990 draft, The Bulls selected Toni Kukoč twenty-ninth-overall.*
- ✓ 2000s Spurs—In the 1997 draft, the Spurs took Tim Duncan with the first-overall pick, after bottoming-out the previous season in the wake of David Robinson's injuries. In the 1999 draft, the Spurs took Manu Ginobili fifty-seventh-overall. In the 2001 draft, the Spurs selected Tony Parker twenty-eighth-overall. A few days after the 2011 draft, the Spurs would trade George Hill for the Pacers fifteenth-overall pick, Kawhi Leonard.
- ✓ 2000s Lakers—In the 1996 draft, Jerry West swindled freaking everyone by deliberately down-playing his draft target's value (while secretly coveting him), and trading Vlade Divac for his target, Charlotte's thirteenth-overall pick—Kobe Bryant. In the 1996 draft, the Lakers also took Derek Fisher with the twenty-fourth-overall pick.
- ✓ 2010s Warriors—In the 2009 draft, the Warriors took Steph Curry seventh-overall. In the 2011 draft, the Warriors took Klay Thompson eleventh-overall. In the 2012 draft, the Warriors selected Draymond Green thirty-fifth-overall.

Chicago jumped from 27 to 38 wins in MJ's 1984-85' rookie season. A few years later, in the 1987-88' rookie campaign of Scottie Pippen and Horace Grant, the Bulls would jump again from 40 to 50 wins. It wasn't crystal clear then, but Jordan had his running mate for what is probably the most impressive dynasty in modern sports. Pippen flashed ridiculous physical ability, and dynamic two-way versatility early on, but little did anyone know that it was his temperament, accountability and commitment to winning that would coalesce perfectly in Chicago and allow them to achieve dynastic success.

---

[37] Also, Red would trade beloved Gerald Henderson after the 1984 championship for Seattle's 1986 first-round pick, which would convey as the second-overall pick used to draft Lenny Bias. If you didn't watch the *30 for 30* and are unaware, Bias—a generational talent that would have extended the Celtics 80s dynasty, died from a drug overdose a few days after the 1986 draft. The tape of his collegiate play at the University of Maryland made it clear to me that he was going to be a force in the NBA, and a completely insane 'what-if' had he lived to play.

The Bulls continued to grow together, especially after consecutive Eastern Conference Final losses in 89' & 90' to the *Bad Boy* Pistons. Chicago pushed Detroit to six games in 1989, and seven games in 1990. Just before tipoff in game seven of the 1990 series, Pippen came down with a migraine. Scottie was terrible in that game with just 2 points on 1 for 10 shooting from the field. Coupled with a controversial exit from the 89' series after a Laimbeer elbow, Pippen quickly became a scapegoat for why the Bulls hadn't earned a championship yet. On May 25th, 1991, with the Bulls up 2-0 against the Pistons and poised to finally slay that dragon, *Chicago Tribune* writer Sam Smith wrote an article with a title that addressed the narrative— *Pippen Still Battling A Curse That Has Haunted Him.* In the article, a year after the game seven migraine, Scottie details his memory of the headache coming on:

> *I realized it was a big game, but I felt good about it. I ate dinner out the night before and went to a movie, nothing real exciting. I was relaxed and looking forward to the game, but I wasn`t nervous. Breakfast went fine and then came the warmups . . .*

> *I started asking my teammates about the lights,* Pippen said. He speaks about the time without emotion. His eyes are hard and his voice firm. He has long since come to grips with his frustration and faces its residue with more determination than despair.

> *I was asking if the lights were dim or something. Then I ran to Mark (Pfeil, then Bulls trainer) and asked him to give me a couple of aspirin. I thought maybe that would calm me down. But that seemed to energize it. It got worse, and when the game started I couldn`t focus. And 25,000 people screaming didn`t make it any better.*

This was really a brilliant article[38], and I highly recommend Sam Smith's *The Jordan Rules* book that was written during that 1990-91' Bulls season. Pippen would close out the article with his outlook on the future:

> *I feel like people are always going to be looking at my play, especially in big games. There will be no letting down because of my past. But I`m just approaching the game that I`m playing to win it, and whatever I`ve done doesn`t really matter.*

> *The thing is, I`d just like to get back to that last game again,* says Scottie Pippen. *It`s what I`ve thought about for a long time. Then I can say I*

---

[38] Smith would say this of Pippen's game in the article—*He fills numerous roles for the Bulls. He`s a playmaker and a rebounder, a scorer and defender. He is one of the few players in the game who can take the ball off the backboard on one end, travel the length of the court and finish with a score on the other end. Usually, only MVPs like Michael Jordan and Magic Johnson can do that.*

was there and I played. Just to get the opportunity and to perform. It's something I think about. Now I've got the chance.

Every great player's pursuit of finding their best version typically requires them to come face-to-face with their bottom. Whispers about his poise in big game situations was enough to propel Pippen to his best season in 1990-91', and the Bulls would get their vengeance in a sweep of the Pistons. You can see Pippen's progression through his stat lines from those 89' through 91' Eastern Conference Finals against Detroit:

	PTS	MP	REBS	ASTS	STLS	BLKS
1989 ECF vs. Detroit (L)	9.7	33.3	7.3	3.0	1.5	1.3
1990 ECF vs. Detroit (L)	16.6	40.0	6.3	3.7	2.0	0.9
1991 ECF vs. Detroit (W)	22.0	38.0	7.8	5.3	3.0	2.0

As great players tend to do, Scottie Pippen responded to the criticism and helped the Bulls breakthrough for their first ever championship in the 1991 Finals'. The Bulls beat up the Magic-led Lakers in a five-game route, thanks to Pippen going 32 points, 13 rebounds, 7 assists and 5 steals in the title-clinching game five. With the 90s under way, Scottie and MJ grabbed the torch from Magic, Isiah and Bird, and were poised for global domination.

In 1991-92', Pippen upped his play again to average 21 points, 7 rebounds and 7 assists. After not being selected to the All-Star game the year prior, Pippen would appear in the game for the first of six consecutive seasons in 1992. The Bulls won 67 games, earned the number one spot in Offensive Rating and number four in Defensive Rating on their way to a second-consecutive championship. 1992-93' would be a similar story with an identical conclusion for the Chicago Bulls—capping off the rare NBA three-peat of championships.

When MJ walked away to play baseball before the 1993-94' season, NBA spectators had the opportunity to see a Jordan-less Bulls team compete against the rest of the league. Without question, everyone was curious how far Scottie could take the Bulls on his own, allowing everyone to test out their takes on exactly how important Pippen was to Chicago's success. Pippen willingly stepped into the leading-man role, and the Bulls won 55 games that year, just two fewer than the previous season with Michael Jordan at the helm.[39] Pippen finished third in MVP voting, but the Bulls were far less efficient offensively, and weren't considered championship contenders heading into the 1994 postseason, where they were bounced in the second round by the Knicks. The 1994-95' season began pretty rough, in part because Horace Grant had left for Orlando, leaving a gaping hole at power forward. That season received an overwhelming jolt back to life when MJ returned toward the end of the regular season.

Unable to re-integrate on-the-fly after Jordan's return, the Bulls would fall short in the 1995 playoffs.[40] Chicago exploded in 1995-96' for 72 wins, on their way to the first of three more championships. Pippen assumed the role he was born to play—a nuclear three-and-d

---

[39] It's no surprise, given the opportunity, that 1993-94' was Pippen's peak PIPM season.

[40] Worth mentioning that Pippen led Chicago in points, rebounds, assists, steals and blocks in 1994-95'. Only Dave Cowens (78'), KG (03'), LeBron (09') and Giannis (17') have completed that major feat.

wingman, who had upped his three-point shooting to 37% on five attempts per game. Pippen was also anchoring a defense that didn't have a traditional rim-protector, all while shouldering the 20 points per game requirement that comes along with being the team's second offensive option. The Bulls nearly matched their dominance in the following season, winning 69 regular season games, and capturing the 1996-97' championship. 1997-98' would prove to be a steep challenge for the now-aging Bulls.[41] Nevertheless, MJ and Pippen edged the Jazz in the Finals', with MJ's unforgettable jumper over Bryon Russell punctuating the end of the Chicago run, which amassed six championships in eight seasons. Pippen played six more seasons[42] after that final championship, but his career is obviously defined by his tenure with the Bulls.

Looking at tape of Scottie Pippen was genuinely thrilling for me. He was an absolutely ridiculous defender—putting perimeter players in the torture chamber on the wing, and demonstrating the ability to front much bigger players on the block with his humanoid-bird-creature-7'3" wingspan. You can take your pick, but I'm confident in saying either MJ or Pippen was the greatest perimeter defender of all-time. I would lean toward Pippen because of the length and switch-ability.[43] Offensively, he was at his best when he was playing in transition, which naturally accentuated his array of physical gifts. He lacked the half-court ability to score when compared to more polished iso-scorers, but more than made up for it with a profound ability to pass and create opportunities for his teammates. One of the league's truly overlooked all-time passers, Pippen's most dynamic offensive skillset was definitely the variety of precision passes he was capable of, playing within Phil Jackson's Triangle Offense.

In the limited opportunity we had to see Scottie Pippen playing without Michael Jordan, there was evidence to suggest his potential as a perennial All-NBA caliber player with MVP upside. But we don't need to extrapolate the data we have from when he played without MJ to determine what a truly great player he was on his own. Pippen holds many distinctions to me—best perimeter defender of all-time, second-best player on six championship teams, top-five most-versatile players in the history of the game. Yet, his doctorate-level understanding of Bill Simmons' and Isiah Thomas' *Secret of Basketball*, might be his most distinguishing characteristic. He continually sacrificed the advancement of his own personal brand and financial compensation commensurate with his value, to be part of a winning team. On top of that, this dude put up with Jordan's heavily-abrasive style for a decade. We know that Jordan punched at least two of his teammates, and at some point, tested every single guy he played with, one way or another. Pippen lived with the figurative punches (maybe literal ones?), and there is reason to believe that Pippen's similar nastiness as a player even helped yield the very

---

[41] They should totally make a documentary about that season.

[42] Easy to forget his prominent role on the 1999-00' *Jail-Blazers*, who won 59 games and took the Lakers to seven games in the Western Conference Finals. Those Blazers held a 15-point lead in the fourth quarter of game seven (when 15-point leads were actually substantial). A great Kobe Bryant effort and Brian Shaw shooting clinic allowed the Lakers to advance and win their first Shaq & Kobe title.

[43] I had to think about this one. I think Kawhi, Rodman, Gary Payton, Walt Frazier, and Michael Cooper all deserve consideration. When I think about it more, Kawhi and Rodman both deserve to be in the top tier with Pippen and MJ. Kawhi limited peak-powers LeBron in the 2014 Finals', and like Rodman, also earned two Defensive Player of the Year awards. Rodman was primarily a perimeter defender while he played for Detroit, and grew into the ultimate defensive swiss army knife later in his career—to the extent that he actually gave early-Lakers Shaq problems. I'm still taking Pippen, but you know what the fucked up part is? RODMAN, PIPPEN AND MJ PLAYED ON THE SAME TEAM FROM 1996 TO 1998!!!!!!

best version of Michael Jordan. If you're wondering what the precedent looks like for being the second-best player on six championship-winning teams, there simply isn't one. Bill Russell's Celtics are the only team with more than six titles, and there wasn't a consistent second-best player on those teams throughout the run.[44] Yes, the gap between the first and second-best players during that Bulls run might have been wider than most championship teams (also, keeping in mind that Jordan won all six Finals' MVPs). But holy shit, just because he was the Bulls second option, let's not forget what hallowed ground Scottie Pippen's legacy stands on, having been that integral to *that many* championships.

Why He Belongs In This Tier? Despite a historically-great track-record of contributing to winning basketball, Pippen's peak efficiency numbers don't demonstrate to me that he could definitely be the best player on a championship team. Without evidence of that upside, I have him in Tier III. Pippen did receive legit Tier II consideration from me—His Greatness Index score is 12th all-time, and you just can't look past his contribution to *that many* championships. He's one of the five to seven greatest defenders of all-time, and there's overwhelming evidence of his style lending itself to historic team success.

---

[44] If you really squint, and pick out the most dynamic six of Havlicek's eight titles, you might say he would qualify. Sam Jones was probably the other notable member of the Russell Celtics that you could squint and consider, but impossible to say he was always the second-most important player—their system was truly egalitarian (around Russell). Pippen though, was unquestionably the second-best player on all of those Chicago championship teams.

Elgin Baylor

The Secret	Greatness Index	Ben Taylor Rank
92 /100	126.08 (38th)	37th

Playoff PER	Playoff Win Shares	Playoff O-Win Shares	Playoff D-Win Shares
21.83 (27th)	15.36 (42nd)	10.73 (31st)	4.63 (89th)

Elgin Baylor was your favorite player's favorite player's favorite player's favorite player. I have to harken back to the *500 Greatest Albums of All Time* list once more, and say that Elgin's inclusion here is in line with the underlining theory of that ranking—*reward influential characters early and often*. It's not like Elvis Presley's *The Sun Sessions* album comes in at #11 all-time because of its 're-playability'. In fact, hearing Elvis Presley's name conjures associations of a dusty era at the genesis of Rock 'n' Roll which no longer excites most of us. However, the album is important because your favorite artist's (Arcade Fire) favorite artist's (Bruce Springsteen) favorite artist (The Beatles) was Elvis Presley.[45]

Elgin Baylor grew up playing basketball in Washington D.C. By his senior season in 1954, he'd gained a reputation as one of the best players in the city—or at least within the black community, he had. A brutally unfortunate overtone in the stories of early black basketball stars was the constant, un-mitigated racism that they experienced throughout their careers. Elgin was no different. With the help of a brilliant *Deadspin* article by Dave McKenna in April, 2018, we get a very clear portrait of the segregation that was occurring in that era, even in the scouting and evaluating of young athletes. McKenna details how the *Washington Post* ran a whole page article when a star from the white Western High School, Jim Wexler, broke the city's single-game record by scoring 52 points in 1953. When Elgin scored 63 shortly after, it was only mentioned in a single-sentence, and hidden deep in a story that wasn't centered on

---

[45] In Bob Spitz's ridiculously detailed biography of The Beatles, he points out the first time John heard *Heartbreak Hotel*, and the first time George heard *Blue Suede Shoes* as watershed creative moments for both Liverpool lads. Spitz also quotes McCartney as saying 'That was the guru we'd been waiting for. The Messiah had arrived' – in regards to Presley. The Beatles swirled in a variety of British and American musical artists and styles into their music, but all signs point toward Elvis as being the most influential during their formative creative processes.

Baylor or his team. McKenna also posted this image, which reveals a citizen that is clamoring for *The Post* to pay closer attention to Elgin Baylor:

Dear Sports Editor:
This really is dedicated to the selectors of the All-High, All-Prep, All-Stars for the game in Uline Arena that is held each year.
I've seen just about all of them, with the Kernans, Georges, Sullivans, Kesslers, etc. All are good or better than good basketball players but before you do your selecting this year, go out and see Elgin Baylor of Spingarn. He is the greatest high school basketball player of all time.
So forget the unwritten rule and watch him play, so as not to do him the great injustice of leaving him off. Don't take anyone's word about him. See him yourselves, then if you can leave him off that's a different story. But please see him first. Thank you.
James A. Clay,
2026 4th St. NW.

You could probably imagine what the 'unwritten rule' was—black schools weren't covered or acknowledged. Organizers in the black community decided to pitch a game that would pit the white stars of the city versus the black ones. Directly from McKenna's article:

Bill McCaffrey, a senior at white Anacostia High, was tasked with getting white players. But when word got out about his recruiting efforts, principals from the white schools called his parents threatening suspensions, expulsions and pulling the letters from anybody who played, just a few months before graduation. McCaffrey got enough guys who would risk it just for the right to face the great Elgin Baylor, though he had to put himself in the lineup.

On March 12, 1954, a day before the All-High All-Prep game that Baylor wasn't invited to, the monumental race matchup was held at Terrell Junior High School. McCaffrey told me some years ago that 2,000 people, almost all of them black, bought tickets and jammed in a 1,200 seat gym, with 500 people turned away at the door. Baylor hit his first eight shots and scored 44 points on the way to a 25-point romp over the white team, who were given a tragically comic name: "The Scholastic All-Stars."

[Jim] Wexler, [whose city-scoring-record was glamorized in The Post] would go on to play minor league baseball in the Dodgers organization, told me in a 1999 interview that Baylor made him feel like a hoops fraud from tipoff to finish. "Here I am guarding Elgin Baylor one on one," Wexler said. "And he showed me basketball at a totally different level—

another world, head and shoulders above anything I'd ever seen. He could do everything. He was a scorer. He could jump out of the gym. He reverse-dunked on me! You have to remember: Nobody did that before Elgin Baylor. That's not how basketball was played before him."

Elgin's poor grades landed him at the College of Idaho[46] for one season, he then sat out a year to obtain eligibility at Seattle University, where he would play his final two seasons of college ball. He was dominant. He would get Seattle to their only Final Four in school history during his final season in 1958, even earning Final Four Most Valuable Player honors (despite losing in the title game to Adolph Rupp's Kentucky Wildcats). The Minneapolis Lakers drafted him first-overall in the 1958 NBA draft. The Lakers had also drafted him in 1956, as was allowed back then, but Elgin only decided to come play professionally in 1958. Minneapolis was owned by Bob Short at the time, and per ESPN's *Sportscentury* profile on Baylor by Larry Schwartz, Short would say this about how important Elgin was to his franchise:

> *If he had turned me down then, I'd have been out of business .. The club would have been bankrupt.*

Elgin was one of the best players in the league right away. He not only collected Rookie of the Year and First-Team All-NBA selections in his first season, but he'd lead that Minneapolis team to the 1959 NBA Finals' against the Boston Celtics. Bill Russell and friends would sweep the Lakers in that series, and after another dominant individual season which resulted in a postseason loss, Bob Short moved the franchise to Los Angeles for the 1960-61' season.

The Lakers had the second-overall pick in the 1960 NBA draft, and chose Jerry West. Baylor and West became running mates in pursuit of a Los Angeles championship for ten years together. The Lakers only won 36 games by the conclusion of the 1960-61' season, and then lost in seven games to Bob Pettit's St. Louis Hawks for the second season in a row. With the pace of the game peaking and defense being thought of as less important (except in Boston), the league saw a statistical spike from 1958 to 1962. In 1961-62' alone, you saw the following historic achievements that still get discussed today:

- Oscar Robertson's Triple-Double season (30.8 PPG, 12.5 RPG, 11.4 APG)
- Wilt Chamberlain averaging 50 points & 25 rebounds (50.4, 25.7)
- Despite only playing 48 games because of required military service, Elgin Baylor averaged 38.3 PPG and 18.6 RPG

In 1961-62', teams averaged 118 PPG, which is still the highest season average in the history of the league. For reference, amidst the current scoring bonanza, teams during the 2019-20' season averaged about 111.8 PPG. The Lakers jumped from 36 to 54 wins that season and earned a first-round bye (?) and a semifinal matchup against Detroit. A victory over the Pistons

---

[46] I couldn't find any pictures of Elgin in the Idaho jersey, which got me thinking—If you show up to a retro jersey party in a 55' College of Idaho Elgin Baylor Uni.. You win bro. You win.

in six games setup a Finals' rematch with Bill Russell's[47] Celtics for the 1962 championship. Those Finals' were an absolute bloodbath. The Lakers took a 2-1 series lead, and then a 3-2 series lead, but it would still come down to a seventh game to determine a champion. With the score tied in game seven, Laker Frank Selvy missed a jumper in the last five seconds of regulation, meaning the deciding game would require overtime. Boston edged Los Angeles by three points in the extra frame, and the Celtics were champions for the fourth season in a row. The following occurred during those Finals':

- o In game five, Elgin Baylor scored 61 points (still a Finals' record, and the second-most points ever scored in a playoff game)
- o Elgin averaged 40.6 points and 17.9 rebounds, Jerry West 31.1 points
- o Bill Russell averaged 22.9 points, 27 rebounds and 5.7 assists
- o In game seven, Bill Russell had 30 points and 40 FUCKING REBOUNDS (also still a Finals' record)

Yes, scoring was up and historical context brings those numbers back down to earth. But, as I read more into that series, it was clearly an epic battle over eleven days in April, 1962. Going forward, it's important to understand that Elgin Baylor had the profound misfortune of starting his NBA career one season after Bill Russell did. Little did anyone know at the conclusion of those 1962 Finals', with Boston already having won four consecutive titles, that until Russell would retire in 1969, only once would Boston not end the season as champions. Between Auerbach's revolutionary foresight into team-building and Russell's tireless will to win on the court, the Celtics unofficially embargoed winning from the other franchises of the NBA during the 1960s

The 1962 Finals', sadly for the Lakers, would prove emblematic of what the rest of the decade would look like—really, really good Laker Teams falling just short to the Boston war machine. In the bigger picture of Elgin Baylor's profile, his (and Jerry West's) thwarted efforts to win a championship in the 1960s hangs over whatever detail I'd like to attach to how good an individual player Elgin Baylor was. This table illustrates, for the remainder of Elgin Baylor's career, the playoff result for his Laker team every season after that epic defeat in the 62' Finals':

1963	L—NBA Finals'	Boston Celtics (2-4)
1964	L— West Semi Finals'	St. Louis Hawks (2-3)
1965	L—NBA Finals'	Boston Celtics (1-4)
1966	L—NBA FInals'	Boston Celtics (3-4)
1967	L—West Semi Finals'	San Francisco Warriors (0-3)
1968	L—NBA Finals'	Boston Celtics (2-4)
1969	L—NBA Finals'	Boston Celtics (3-4)

[47] Amid all of these outlying statistical achievements, Bill Russell won MVP in 1961-62'. Players voted on the award from 1955-1980. I have to think that is a better way to do it. It's become a totally narrative-driven award, and who drives a meaningless narrative quite like NBA writers who write entire books about meaningless narratives and subjective opinions?

1970	L—NBA Finals'	New York Knicks (3-4)
1971	L—West Finals'	Milwaukee Bucks (1-4)

So, for those doing the agonizing math at home, Elgin Baylor would retire a handful of games into the 1971-72' season without having won a championship. He would total *eight* Finals' losses,[48] *seven* of them to Russell's Celtics, and *four* of those Boston defeats coming in seven-game series'. If that's not heartbreaking enough, right after Elgin retired early in the 1971-72' season, the Lakers immediately proceeded to win 33 straight games, still an NBA record, en route to the first Laker championship in Los Angeles! They would reward Baylor's efforts with a 1972 NBA Championship ring, but I can't imagine he was too stoked receiving it after watching the 72' Lakers torch the rest of the NBA without him.[49]

I suppose this is the section where, despite a profile that suggests he couldn't get it done when it mattered, I will be convincing you that Elgin Baylor was great and deserves to be on this list because of _____. Yet, Elgin Baylor's influence on other NBA greats is ultimately why he's here. So, I think it's only right that the words of those that were so impacted by his play, be the ones to convince you why he was undeniably great.

> *He had an incredible instinct to score. But he also had an incredible instinct to rebound. I just marveled at him. He was truly a highlight film.*
> *--Jerry West*

> *What I'm going to really remember about Elgin Baylor is the fact that he still holds the NBA Finals' record for scoring 61 points in the Boston Garden. Do I have to go down the list of people who didn't do that? Including myself? Man, 61 points in the NBA Finals'? On the road?*
> *--Magic Johnson*

> *My biggest thrill came the night Elgin Baylor and I combined for 73 points at Madison Square Garden. Elgin had 71 of them.*
> *--Rod Hundley*
> *(Laker Teammate 58-63')*

> *Personally, I'd like to thank you because I've stolen so many of your moves, it's not even funny. That rocker step. The changing to the left rocker step, the hesitation. The elevating to the basket, putting your shoulder into the big and finishing with contact. I got all that from you, my brother.*
> *--Kobe Bryant*

---

[48] His 0-8 Finals' record is by far the most appearances without a title.

[49] Bill Simmons and his friend Dave Cirilli have been credited for coining the *Ewing Theory*—which attempts to explain why teams inexplicably enjoy more success when their megastar player leaves the team, or is injured and unable to play. The theory was galvanized when Patty Ewing tore his Achilles in game two of the 99' ECF, and miraculously the Knicks won three of the next four to make it to the Finals'. But, as Bill would say, *are we sure it shouldn't be called the Baylor theory?*

Let me tell you about what being great is. Ever heard of Elgin Baylor? Never mention his name, do we? Great basketball player.
--Oscar Robertson

When you listen to guys like Magic Johnson and Dr. J and Jordan talk about the greats, your name always came up. So finally, I Googled you. Let me say, you were a bad man.
--Shaquille O'Neal

I remember November 15th, 1960 I was thirteen years old, in the eighth grade. I went to Madison Square Garden to see the Lakers play, and Elgin got 72 [actually 71] points against the Knicks that night. Elgin really set a standard that I thought maybe I could catch up to. In my 20-year career, I never got close.
--Kareem Abdul-Jabbar

I remember he was the first guy I saw grab the rebound, bring it in transition and then play-make from the top of the key. He was a playmaker, he was great one-on-one, he was great using airspace … he was just ballet in basketball. And that opened a lot of doors for young players, myself in particular, to try that stuff. Suddenly it was like, 'Wow. This can actually work.'
--Julius Erving

Why He Belongs In This Tier? Influence. While claiming the 3rd-highest PPG and 10th-highest RPG (only he, Wilt Chamberlain and Bob Pettit are top-ten in both), it's clear that he was a truly dynamic player. Eight Finals' berths, granted they were all losses, is still a huge indicator of his style lending itself to winning basketball. Just not winning-enough to beat Russell. He was considered to be left off of the list, but throughout my research, love letters about how influential he was from high-profile NBA personalities were popping up too often. When I set out to really read into his case, I was enamored with his unofficial status as the league's first 'superstar'. He's a Tier III guy who lacks any personal hardware to give him consideration for Tier II.

Chris Paul

&

Isiah Thomas

	The Secret	Greatness Index	Ben Taylor Rank
Chris Paul	83 / 100	135.56 (33rd)	21st
Isiah Thomas	100 / 100	97.65 (54th)	Not Ranked

	PIPM	O-PIPM	D-PIPM	Peak	Wins Added
Chris Paul	+5.50 (4th)	+4.52	+0.97	+7.88 (8th) [2016-17']	204.05 (13th)
Isiah Thomas	+2.51 (56th)	+2.04	+0.47	+4.97 (56th) [1984-85']	124.25 (29th)

	Playoff PER	Playoff Win Shares	Playoff O-Win Shares	Playoff D-Win Shares
Chris Paul	24.16 (10th)	16.52 (33rd)	12.51 (20th)	4.01 (113th)
Isiah Thomas	19.80 (53rd)	12.55 (59th)	5.48 (98th)	7.07 (35th)

Part One

You're not wrong to think Chris Paul or Isiah Thomas was a greater player than the other, but either way you lean, your opinion reveals something about how you measure player performance. Belonging to each player are powerful legacies that look dramatically different. Chris Paul, aka *The Point God*, has one of the best advanced statistic profiles in the history of the NBA. He's also enjoyed a substantially longer career[50] than Isiah Thomas did, and has accumulated substantially more individual accolades along the way. However, CP3 has enjoyed very little relative team success and has never reached the NBA Finals'. Isiah Thomas, aka *Zeke*,

---

[50] Shit, as of 2020, Chris Paul's fifteenth season, CP is capable of dragging an Oklahoma City roster of misfit toys toward a legitimate playoff seed. Behold, The Point God.

imprinted an average statistical footprint over his thirteen NBA seasons, especially when measured against the canon of historically significant point guards. However, Isiah was the captain of two teams that won NBA Championships in an era of the NBA that's historically and nostalgically revered. Where does that leave us?

Personally—I think Chris Paul is the greater player in a catastrophic landslide that claims thousands of lives. But.. I do love *Zeke*—it's hard to deny the narrative claim he has to Tier III, as being a player that battled some of the best and most admired teams in NBA history, only to emerge on the other side as the best player (albeit marginally) on two consecutive NBA Championship teams.

I have to admit that I'm also thoroughly embarrassed by Isiah. I do appreciate the moment he and Bill Simmons shared in which he revealed that *The Secret* to basketball and doing all you can to prevent your teammates from wanting more money, playing time, notoriety etc. However, is there any other player in history more desperate to retroactively raise the profile of their own legacy? During his career, and especially after, the guy just could not get out of his own way in seemingly *every pursuit he chose*. He says he never had 'a Pippen', or 'he never gets enough respect', or he's pissy that he was left off of the *Dream Team* in 92'. Dude! Just shut the fuck up! He's been operating on the 'Kevin Durant-level' of self-aggrieved delusion for decades now! For someone that seemed to acknowledge what *The Secret* was to keeping a locker-room close during his career, after his career, Isiah seems doomed to be eternally ungrateful for the things his teams *were* able to accomplish.

This is especially embarrassing to me when his statistical profile suggests a very large pool of point guards could have been the point guard on those Piston teams and they still would have won championships. If you had to guess, in Isiah's thirteen-year career, all of which he played in Detroit, how many seasons would you say that he led the team in Win Shares?[51] At least a couple, right? Negative—only one time, and it was before they were competing for championships:

1981-82' Pistons	Kelly Tripucka (7.5)
1982-83' Pistons	Bill Laimbeer (8.5)
1983-84' Pistons	Bill Laimbeer (10.8)
1984-85' Pistons	**Isiah Thomas (11.2)**
1985-86' Pistons	Bill Laimbeer (9.2)
1986-87' Pistons	Bill Laimbeer (10.5)
1987-88' Pistons	Adrian Dantley (9.4)
1988-89' Pistons	Bill Laimbeer (9.0)
1989-90' Pistons	Bill Laimbeer (10.1)
1990-91' Pistons	Joe Dumars (9.9)
1991-92' Pistons	Dennis Rodman (12.6)
1992-93' Pistons	Joe Dumars (9.1)

---

[51] Generally, a good measure of who the best player is on the team for that particular season. LeBron has led his teams in Win Shares for 15 of his 17 seasons. Jordan led the Bulls in Win Shares during each full season he played in Chicago. Steph Curry has led the Warriors in Win Shares 6 times. Chris Paul has led his team in Win Shares 10 different times.

This got me thinking about just how much we've floated his status as *the best player on two championship teams* over the years. I can conclude with confidence that we've applied this quite liberally. When the Pistons finally won the title in 1988-89', it was Joe Dumars, not Isiah Thomas, that won Finals' MVP. Which of these two players do you think was more deserving of winning the Finals' MVP in the 1989 NBA Finals':

	PPG	FTA	FTM	FT%	FG%
????	27.3	33	38	86.8%	57.6%
????	21.3	19	25	76.0%	48.5%

The bottom player is Isiah Thomas, and the top player is Joe Dumars. The next season, when the Pistons won the 1989-90' championship, Isiah Thomas *was* awarded Finals' MVP, but Joe Dumars and Dennis Rodman were the only two Detroit players selected to an All-NBA team that season. How positive are you that Isiah was the best player on either *Bad Boy* Piston team that won a championship?

I know what you're thinking—*will I say anything positive about Isiah?*—Yes—well, maybe—we'll see—but I have to work through some things first. I've heard a lot in the last year about how underrated Isiah was, and I'm starting to think he might just have one of the most misinterpreted profiles in the history of the NBA. There are things attached to him like *the only guy to beat Bird, Magic and MJ*—which is painfully misleading.

The Pistons only beat Bird in 1988 after the Celtics ran out of gas.[52] The Pistons beat Magic's Lakers in the 1989 Finals' when Magic got hurt in game one, only played 29 minutes in game two, and just 5 minutes in game three. To the Pistons credit, they did hold down MJ for three consecutive postseasons in 1988, 1989 and 1990. But we're crediting that to Isiah? When it was either Rodman or Dumars who defended him? Or Mahorn or Laimbeer that roughed him up?

At the same time, is there any way Isiah's legacy isn't appreciably more valuable if the Pistons do close out Magic's Lakers in game six of the 1988 Finals'? The Pistons were up 3-2, and trying to close out in Los Angeles. Trailing early in the third quarter, Isiah put the team on his back, scoring 14 points in the first 8 minutes of the quarter. At which point, he suffered a high-ankle sprain that looked like it would keep him from playing the rest of the series. Isiah checked back in 35 seconds later and scored 11 more points before the end of the quarter—giving him a cool 25 in the third—*still* a Finals' record—and 11 on one fucking leg. The Pistons were narrowly edged out 103-102 in game six. Isiah was less than 30 seconds (and a bogus Laimbeer foul on Kareem) away from the most heroic playoff performance ever. But they lost that game, and then they lost the championship in game seven.

Okay .. I'm ready to say nice things. The bottom line is that Isiah stuck with Detroit until they built a really deep team around him, and he was the perfect pesky asshole to draw the ire of opponents, as well as keep the notoriously-tough team together from a chemistry standpoint. Wading into intangible qualities like grit and leadership can be a slippery slope, but

---

[52] They might have beat the Celtics in 1987 if Isiah hadn't thrown Bird that inbound pass in game five!!!

Isiah was never lacking in either category. In an era where you didn't really have a choice but to take a loss to a great team on the chin and try to get better before you saw them the next year, Isiah kept fighting as the Pistons gradually rounded out a championship caliber roster by the late 80s. It's also worth saying that those Piston teams were uniquely constructed to allow many players to flourish on any given night. But across all these great players that allowed Detroit to be granite-solid 1 through 9—Mahorn, Laimbeer, Dumars, Rodman, Salley, Aguirre, Johnson and Edwards—Isiah was the leader, even if he wasn't the dominant number one option that we expect from most championship teams.

Isiah was picked second-overall in the 1981 NBA Draft by Detroit. There were several years of buildup to their eventual championships, but Detroit planted the title seeds during that 1981-82' season by also acquiring Vinnie Johnson and Bill Laimbeer via mid-season trades. The team took their next substantial step forward in 1983-84',[53] the first season with Chuck Daly as their head coach, when they reached the playoffs for the first time in seven seasons. Detroit added Joe Dumars and Rick Mahorn for the 1985-86' season, then 1986-87' was the rookie season for both Dennis Rodman and John Salley.

The team was nearly complete, and a very narrow loss to the Celtics in the 1987 Eastern Conference Final put the franchise into the championship picture for the first time since the Fort Wayne Pistons made the NBA Finals' in 1954-55' and 1955-56'. Detroit charged to the 1988 NBA Finals' and missed out on the championship by a whisker. During the 1988-89' season, the final piece to the championship puzzle was secured by way of a mid-season trade that shipped out Adrian Dantley and brought in Mark Aguirre. The team was fully realized and dismissing Dantley established a truly one-for-all, all-for-one ethos—during the regular season, and excluding Dantley, the Pistons had nine players averaging at least 22 minutes per game and at least 7 points per game (with no players averaging more than 18.2 points per game). Detroit only lost two games in the 1989 playoffs (both to MJ's Bulls in the Eastern Conference Finals), and raised the first NBA championship in franchise history.

Detroit replicated that model for success during the following season when they returned all nine players from their 1989 playoff rotation. Detroit experienced more resistance during the 1990 playoff push, including a seven game rock fight against MJ in the ECF, but the Pistons won another championship using their team-oriented formula—across the 20 games of the 1990 postseason, seven Pistons averaged at least 9.5 points per game with no players averaging more than 20.5 points per game (Isiah). *Zeke* played four more seasons for the Pistons before a torn Achilles coerced him into an earlier retirement than he might have wanted. By that point, Detroit had gradually receded back into NBA mediocrity anyway.

At the conclusion of the 1980s, the headline of the Detroit story was their success in gradually adding layers to their championship viability, until their time came. The secondary headline of Detroit's story centered around their point guard, who'd persevered through all manner of setbacks to raise up the credibility of the franchise that drafted him. It's easy to overlook how difficult it is to transition a franchise not known for winning into, not just a competitive team, but a perennial championship contender. Isiah Thomas gets the lion's share of credit for that accomplishment. That's not quantifiable, and it doesn't bare out in any statistical profile, but it definitely matters.

---

[53] Isiah finished fifth in MVP voting during this season, the only time he finished in the top five for League MVP.

Part Two

When it does come to quantifying Isiah's career, there's seemingly been an understanding that Isiah deliberately took a huge step back stylistically (and/or statistically), to allow for Detroit's team-first concept to flourish. I think we need to revisit that narrative. Between 1983-84', the only season Isiah was voted top five for League MVP, and 1989-90', the second Detroit championship season, his shot attempts per game and overall usage within the offense stayed basically the exact same. The notion that Isiah could have been successful as a more traditional 1A star within a different team configuration doesn't really have any evidence to back it up, and that really boils down to Isiah not being an especially efficient player.

	FG%	3P%	FT%	TOV
Chris Paul	47.0	37.0	87.0	2.4
Isiah Thomas	45.2	29.0	75.9	3.8

Illuminating Isiah Thomas' relative inefficiency in a binary comparison versus Chris Paul isn't exactly 'fair', but we're going to do it nonetheless. If the conventional thinking has been that Isiah could have ramped up his individual volume as a scorer and assumed the heliocentric catalyst role for a different team, all we can say is that that team probably wouldn't have been any fucking good. His **FG%** is fine, but lower than you'd want. His **3P%** is very low, but he played in an era where the three-point shot wasn't really utilized. His **FT%** is low, especially for a guard, and a signal that a spike in his offensive usage wouldn't necessarily mean a spike for his team's offense overall. The **TOV** is a major problem—*Isiah has the seventh-most turnovers in the history of the NBA, driven by the fact that he averaged the second-most turnovers, per game, in the history of the NBA.* Yikes. The hits keep coming for Isiah when we open up the regular season advanced stat profile for each player.

	PER	TS%	USG%	WS	WS/48	BPM	VORP	PIPM	Ortg
Chris Paul	**25.1**	.582	23.9	**180.3**	.243	+7.6	86.0	+5.50	122
Isiah Thomas	18.1	.516	25.3	80.7	.109	+2.6	41.6	+2.51	106

I'm guessing there are unfamiliar metrics here for many of you, so I'd like to also use the comp between these players as a crash-course in basketball analytics.[54] If you're savvy with advanced stuff, sit back, relax, and behold, *The Point God.*

---

[54] All definitions pulled from *Basketball Reference* (except for PIPM). You may want to dog-ear these couple of pages if you're fairly new to advanced stats, as I'll be using many of these throughout the book.

- **PER** [Player Efficiency Rating] *A measure of per-minute production standardized such that the league average is 15.*

  - The highest career average is 27.91 (Michael Jordan). The highest single regular season rating is 31.86 (Giannis Antetokounmpo, 2019-20'). The highest rating for a single postseason is 37.39 (LeBron James, 2009).[55]

	PER
CP3	**25.1**
Zeke	18.1

    - Chris Paul's 25.1 is the ninth-best-ever career average, and he's the first point guard to appear on the list. Isiah's rating is good for 150th all-time.

- **TS%** [True Shooting Percentage] *A measure of shooting efficiency that takes into account two-point field goals, three-point field goals, and free throws.*

  - Players with really high TS% are usually either very accurate guards—Steph Curry has the fifth-highest career mark at .623—or rim-running big men who mostly dunk the ball—DeAndre Jordan has the second-highest career mark at .639.

	TS%
CP3	**.582**
Zeke	.516

    - Chris Paul's career mark of .582 is very good, but falls short of historically elite. Isiah's .516 is low, even for his era that generally put less emphasis on shooting percentage.

- **USG%** [Usage Percentage] *An estimate of the number of team plays used by a player while he was on the floor.[56]*

  - Basically, the percentage of team plays that a given player either shoots, goes to the free throw line, or turns the ball over. It's a helpful marker in knowing what type of role, volume-wise, a player has or had in an offense. The highest career average is 33.26% (Michael Jordan). The highest single regular season rating is 41.65% (Russell Westbrook, 2016-17'). The highest average for a single postseason, with at least two playoff series' played, is 38.03% (Michael Jordan, 1993).

	USG%
CP3	23.9
Zeke	25.3

    - Isiah and CP3 had identical offensive roles, but Isiah's is inflated by an unusually high turnover rate that brings his USG% up a little bit higher.

---

[55] Technically Hakeem posted a 38.96 in the 1988 postseason, but that was across just four games during a first-round exit. We'll use a minimum of two playoff series' played during this exercise (LeBron played in 14 games across three playoff series' in 2009 when he posted that 37.39).

[56] We only have USG% dating back to the 1977-78' season, otherwise Wilt Chamberlain would hold every record.

- **WS** [Win Shares] *An estimate of the number of wins contributed by a player.*

  - A cumulative stat that is usually graded on a per-season or per-career total. The metric can be spliced to isolate solely a player's Offensive Win Shares [OWS] or Defensive Win Shares [DWS]. The highest career total is 273.41 (Kareem Abdul-Jabbar). The highest single-season total is 25.37 (Kareem Abdul Jabbar, 1971-72'). The highest total for a single postseason is 5.94 (Tim Duncan, 2003).

	WS
CP3	**180.3**
Zeke	80.7

    - Tough look for my guy, Isiah. This illuminates how unproductive he was in his first two seasons and his final four. Chris Paul has racked them up by being a one-man, walking, (trash) talking, elite offense.

- **WS/48** [Win Shares Per 48] *An estimate of the number of wins contributed by a player per 48 minutes, with league average being around .100.*

  - It's basically the rate at which a player accumulates Win Shares. The highest career average is .250 (Michael Jordan). The highest single season rating is .339 (Kareem Abdul-Jabbar, 1971-72'). The highest single postseason rating is .399 (LeBron James, 2009).

	WS/48
CP3	**.243**
Zeke	.109

    - Chris Paul's career average is the fourth-highest rating of all-time. Isiah's doesn't register on *Basketball Reference's* top 250, and his figure is by far the lowest of any of the upper-echelon historic point guards.

- **BPM** [Box Plus/Minus] *A box score estimate of the points per 100 possessions a player contributed above a league-average player. Translated to an average team.*

  - This stat can also be spliced into Offensive Box Plus/Minus [OBPM] and Defensive Box Plus/Minus [DBPM]. On a per-season-basis, these markers are helpful: +10.0 is all-time elite (LeBron or MJ) +8.0 is MVP-level +6.0 is All-NBA-level +4.0 is All-Star level +2.0 is good starter-level +0.0 is decent starter-level -2.0 bench player-level. The best career average is +9.22 (Michael Jordan). The best ever rating for a single season was +13.24 (LeBron James, 2008-09'). The best ever rating for a single postseason was +17.53[57] (LeBron James, 2009).

	BPM
CP3	**+7.6**
Zeke	+2.6

    - Chris Paul has the third-best-ever career average. Isiah's rating suggests he was a fringe All-Star-level player for his

---

[57] lolololololol

career. Isiah's rough first two seasons and final four
seasons sink this rating noticeably as well.

- o **VORP** [Value Over Replacement Player] *A box score estimate of the points per 100 team possessions that a player contributed above a replacement-level player, translated to an average team and pro-rated to an 82-game season.*

  - Similar to Win Shares, this is a cumulative stat that is usually measured either in a per-season or per-career figure. The highest career total is 133.67 (LeBron James). The highest single season total is 12.47 (Michael Jordan, 1987-88'). The highest single postseason total is 3.40 (LeBron James, 2018).

	VORP
CP3	**85.6**
Zeke	41.6

  - o In comparing Chris Paul and Isiah Thomas' careers versus one another, this shows the cumulative value of CP3's career above league-average point guards. My thought was always that Isiah was closer to league average than people wanted to admit.

- o **PIPM** [Player Impact Plus-Minus] *A plus-minus impact metric that combines luck-adjusted plus-minus data with the value of the box score and a handful of interaction terms to estimate a player's value over the course of a season.*

  - Similar to BPM in how ratings are analyzed—scores can be measured in real-time over the course of a season, and players have a career average. PIPM combines playoff and regular season data, the only metric listed here that does so (the rest have to be broken out by a player's regular season or playoff figure). The highest career average is +6.14 (David Robinson). The highest single season rating is +9.83 (LeBron James, 2009).

	PIPM
CP3	**+5.50**
Zeke	+2.51

  - o Chris Paul has the fourth-highest career average in the PIPM database. His peak was +7.88 (2016-17'), the 8th-highest peak in the database. Isiah's peak figure was +4.97 (1984-85'), the 56th-highest peak in the database.

- o **Ortg** [Offensive Rating] *An estimate of points produced per 100 possessions.*

  - Offensive Rating (and Defensive Rating) are generally used as a team metric, and it shouldn't usually be used to rate individual players. It also becomes more viable as the sample size grows larger.

	Ortg
CP3	**122**
Zeke	106

○ Using this tool to compare Isiah and CP3 makes sense because they were both point guards who handled the ball more than anyone on their teams, making them primarily responsible for the proficiency of the offense. Each player's career is also a big enough sample for the stat to be viable. Chris Paul has the highest Offensive Rating ever for an individual player.[58] Isiah's career average doesn't register on *Basketball Reference's* top 250.

I'm picking on Isiah by using career averages. In fairness, every player is held to that standard, but Zeke's first couple seasons and his last few really bring down his efficiency stuff. If we look at the season where each player peaked, in terms of broad efficiency, Chris Paul still holds strong, but not by the same margin:

	PER	TS%	USG%	WS	WS/48	BPM	VORP	PIPM	Ortg
Chris Paul 2008-09'	**30.0**	.599	27.5[59]	**18.3**	.292	+11.0	9.9	+7.0	124
Isiah Thomas 1984-85'	22.2	.529	24.0	11.2	.173	+6.3	6.5	+5.2	115

To isolate more relevant seasons between each player we can also look at their postseason numbers. Chris Paul's playoff numbers dip marginally in efficiency but are still historically-elite. To Isiah's credit, his efficiency does improve in the playoffs, which cannot be claimed by a lot of players including many heavy-hitter all-time greats:

	TS%	PER	WS/48	PPG
Zeke Regular Season	.516	18.1	.109	19.2
Zeke Postseason	**.520**	**19.8**	**.143**	**20.4**

	TS%	PER	WS/48	PPG
CP3 Regular Season	**.582**	**25.1**	**.243**	18.5
CP3 Postseason	.581	24.2	.195	**20.9**

Player versus player comparisons are always sticky. It's hard to not manipulate the data you have to subjectively support your opinion. The aspiration should always be to project how the player would fare if they had played with the situational circumstances that the other player experienced. I don't think Isiah had the 'floor-raising' ability to raise up the level of the teams Chris Paul has played on. He sure as hell wouldn't have been *so much better* than Paul that he could have lifted the 2008-2011 New Orleans or 2012-2015 Los Angeles teams to a championship—and if that's true, what exactly are we talking about here? Conversely, Chris

---

[58] Even more, CP3's Clipper teammate of six seasons, DeAndre Jordan, boasts the third-highest Offensive Rating in history, just because he played so many minutes with Chris Paul! Chris Paul sits atop this stat by a full point over the player in second-place. One full point is enough to encompass the players in second through sixth place on the list! Ladies and gentlemen, behold, *The Full-Point God.*

[59] Chris Paul's most efficient season coming on what was his highest-volume season—*very good.*

Paul as the point guard of the *Bad Boy* Pistons? Had CP3 been the point guard on that team, there's nothing to suggest that don't they still win titles. Quantifying defense is more challenging, and it doesn't shine through especially well in many of these metrics, but Chris Paul's made nine All-Defensive teams, and Isiah never made one. So, on top of all the evidence we have of Chris Paul being a superior offensive player, are you ready to say that those Detroit teams aren't appreciably better with the best ever defender of the point guard position?

Maybe Isiah's leadership and perseverance overcome the vast statistical disadvantage he has in this comparison, but don't expect me to buy into that. My best friend Zach and I have this debate all the time and it never goes anywhere. We're stuck at the separate poles of how we should value a player's profile. For me, I agree with Alonzo Harris in *Training Day*: *It's not what you know, it's what you can prove.* For Zach, he just asks me to count the rings.

If the numbers don't do it for you, just keep in mind the difference in the ownership situation that each player played under during the years which their legacies were defined. Piston ownership during their 1980s ascent was hands off in the best way. Whereas Clipper ownership during their mid-2010s ascent, under Donald Sterling's leadership, was hands off in the worst way.

Part Three

The Clippers were poised to compete for a championship in 2013-14'. The *other* Los Angeles basketball team won a franchise record 56 games in 2012-13' and were bringing back their surging core. Plus, they brought in Doc Rivers to coach, adding an additional layer of championship legitimacy. Chris Paul, eager to forget a first-round loss to the *Grit-N-Grind* Grizzlies, was intent on a deep playoff run which had, so far, eluded him in his career. Fueled by an offense that led the league in Offensive Rating, the Clippers earned 57 wins and a three-seed in the extra-competitive Western Conference. A hard-fought seven-game victory over the also-surging Golden State Warriors setup a second-round matchup with the peaking Oklahoma City Thunder. With the series tied at two games apiece, the conclusion to the pivotal game five is now deeply entrenched in the conversation of Chris Paul's legacy.

Everyone recalls this as a colossal Chris Paul meltdown. But I stand before you a man that has watched the tape like the goddam Zapruder film, and this was more of an officiating debacle than it was a Chris Paul catastrophe. With 49 seconds left in the game, Chris Paul hits a jumper to give the Clippers a 104-97 lead. An implausible, contested Kevin Durant three at the shot-clock buzzer, and an easy transition bucket off of a fortuitous rebound, led to the Clippers inbounding with 18 seconds left with a trimmed 104-102 lead.

That's where things go off the rails. With the Thunder needing to foul, Chris Paul makes his only *real* mistake of this sequence by not waiting for an intentional foul, and instead looking ahead and jumping to attempt a pass and/or draw a foul. This created an opportunity for Paul's defender, Russ Westbrook, to make a pristine defensive denial that could lead to a deflection, which it did. Reggie Jackson[60] pounced on the loose ball, raced to the hoop, but had his shot

---

[60] I hated watching this guy when he still had a future ahead of him. I was so stoked when the Pistons snared him. He played one really good season in Detroit, but after enduring a little bad press about his leadership, he proceeded to pout and/or be 'injured' for the remainder of his time as a Piston. Good riddance. Wanna know how

attempt blocked out of bounds on the baseline, with the ball staying with Oklahoma City. They review this play, and it is *painfully clear* that Jackson directs the ball out of bounds after the initial block. Alas, they uphold the initial decision—Thunder Ball, down 2, 11 seconds left. They inbound on the baseline to Russ Westbrook, who curls to the three-point line, and in vintage Russ fashion, chucks an ill-advised, perfectly contested, situationally-suicidal three-point shot. Right after the shot bricked terribly, a whistle sounds, indicating a foul, but none of the referees physically signal a foul! The referees huddle and uphold a three-shot foul on the Clipper who defended Russ perfectly—Chris Paul. Steve Kerr, not yet with the Warriors and doing color commentary for the broadcast, said of the play:

> *Boy, I didn't see much of a foul. This is a horrible shot,[61] I mean, there's plenty of time, Westbrook needed to go to the rim. Maybe he got him on the arm on the follow-through, but I didn't see much. Doc Rivers can't believe what he's seeing right now.*

Meanwhile, on the Los Angeles bench, Doc Rivers is having a thorough and complete meltdown. Still upset about the review that allowed this foul to happen, Doc is repeatedly yelling *That is our ball!* Russ makes all three foul shots (the ball lied) and the Clippers advance the ball and inbound with 6.4 seconds left, now down 1 point. Prior to the play, Steve Kerr had this to say:

> *Paul has got to attack the rim. The officials have been berated by Doc Rivers. They're only human—they know that they've had a couple of calls going Oklahoma City's way. If I'm Chris Paul, I'm going to attack the rim.*

Chris Paul takes the inbound, and looked intent to follow Kerr's advice. Blake Griffin flashes a screen which gets Ibaka on Paul. CP3 begins to attack the right side of the paint when Reggie Jackson reaches in, clearly hits Chris Paul's arm, which causes him to lose the ball. Knowing his hand was caught in the cookie jar and verifying the foul, Jackson did the 'hide the guilty hand behind his back' move. Yet, no foul was called, Ibaka scoops the ball up, game over. Doc Rivers is at half-court, and by now has lost all his marbles. Kerr comments:

> *He's saying 'that was our ball', he's talking about the review when it looked like it went off Reggie Jackson's hand, that's what Doc[62] keeps repeating over and over again.*

Maybe the Clippers still lose that series with a win in this game. Even with a win in this series, the San Antonio Spurs had unfinished business with the Miami Heat waiting for them in the

---

I knew the Clippers would blow it in the 2020 bubble playoffs? Because they thought 2020 Reggie Jackson could be part of a championship rotation!!!!

[61] I laughed out loud the first time I re-watched this, because of Kerr's emphasis on the word *horrible*.

[62] Can we talk for just a minute about Doc Rivers' role in the Clippers meltdowns? I have a comp for all of my Mad Men peeps—Doc Rivers is the Duck Phillips of the NBA. Riding on the success of a campaign that many people have forgotten about, he continues to receive chances to re-create that success, and keeps failing.

Finals', and getting through Duncan in the Western Conference Finals would have been murder. Yet, the confluence of unfortunate events during this game's conclusion has come to be a defining pillar in the historical conversation of Chris Paul's legacy, rightly or wrongly.[63]

One year later, after another season of historically efficient offense, The Clippers entered the 2015 playoffs eyeing a championship. In the first round, Los Angeles beat defending-champions San Antonio in a brutal seven-game series.[64] Houston awaited in the second round, and heading into game six, with the series 3-2 in their favor, the Clippers had an opportunity to close out the two-seeded Rockets at home, and advance to the Western Conference Finals. At that point, the Clippers championship narrative was clearly in focus—LA had slain the Duncan-dragon in the first round, were making mince-meat of the Rockets, and would now receive a Western Conference Finals series in which they would be the favorite to advance to the Finals'.

What happened in game five was another cosmic, legacy-altering switcheroo that no one can really explain or define. With 2:16 left in the third quarter, the Clippers not only had built a commanding lead (89-70), but had seemingly broken the will of their opponent. Houston subbed James Harden out of the game, and the team looked collectively listless and ready for summer vacation. If ever there were a cosmic moment to diminish Chris Paul's legacy, it would be spearheaded by Josh Smith and Corey Brewer, right? Those two jokesters combined for 30 points in the fourth quarter as the Rockets improbably, so nearly impossibly, made this comeback to tie the series 3-3. The Rockets prevailed in game seven, capping off the rare 3-1 series comeback. The Clippers, and Chris Paul, would enter the offseason with more questions than answers. On one hand, Chris Paul was the leader of this team, and simply cannot allow a 3-1 comeback to occur. Especially in 2015, when the Clippers had a stranglehold on the Rockets, and a very reasonable path to the Finals' (with either the untested Warriors or beatable Grizzlies waiting for them in the Western Conference Finals). Yet, I'm also sympathetic for Paul in both scenarios—CP3 played at a really high level for both of those series', so it's not as if his play was directly complicit in the gut-wrenching losses.

Regardless of the weight you apply to those playoff losses with the Clippers, Chris Paul is invariably one of the best point guards of all-time. He was drafted by New Orleans in 2005, and they immediately jumped from 18 wins to 38 wins his rookie year. That's a bigger jump, by 2 wins, than LeBron managed with the Cavs during his rookie season, with Paul playing in the tougher Western Conference. Like LeBron, CP3 raised the floor of his team so quickly that his team lost the luxury of high draft picks, resulting in a struggle to acquire young talent for the duration of Paul's New Orleans tenure. New Orleans' first-round draft picks (that weren't dealt) during the CP3 'era':

- o (2006) 12th—Hilton Armstrong
- o (2006) 15th—Cedric Simmons

---

[63] PS .. During JJ Redick's podcast on 3/8/2019, JJ asked if the 2018 Warriors loss was more painful than the 2015 Rockets collapse. Paul mistakenly thought he was referencing the nightmare Thunder sequence, and proceeded to recollect, without hesitation, his failed attempt to draw a foul (which led to the Reggie Jackson turnover) and the subsequent phantom foul on Russ Westbrook. Pretty clearly a few plays that haunt him with some regularity.

[64] Because of a Chris Paul game-winning shot with 1 second left in game seven.

- (2007) 13th—Julian Wright
- (2009) 21st—Darren Collison

The 2006 draft would have been the moment to snare a star near the age of CP3, given the pair of picks they had. Unfortunately, 2006 was probably the worst draft in the history of the modern NBA, and even though New Orleans missed on their picks, the star wasn't even present after their selections. Alas, David West and Paul would be joined in 2007 by Peja Stojakovic and Tyson Chandler, which yielded a successful 56-win 2007-08' campaign. Despite posting a 30.70 PER during that 2008 postseason, good for the fifteenth-best-ever PER for a postseason, Chris Paul and the Hornets would fall in seven games to the Spurs in the second-round. That felt like the first of what would be many seasons that New Orleans was competing in the Western Conference, but it turned out to be the peak of the Paul era, and Chris Paul was moved to the Clippers a few seasons later. The lesson that seems to continually be un-learned—surround your young star with another compatible star (or two) ASAP.

Chris Paul's first season with the Clippers in 2011-12' was the shortened season, but Los Angeles saw an increase in winning percentage from .365 to .606 (the equivalent of going from 32 wins to 50 wins). Their Offensive Rating also jumped from twenty-second to fourth. The Clippers group with Paul, JJ Redick, Blake Griffin and Deandre Jordan peaked during the years that ended in those aforementioned heartbreaks, and injuries would continually haunt the team until all four players moved on before the 2018-19' season. Paul's first season in Houston saw the Rockets advancing to Chris Paul's first Conference Final. In fact, Houston grabbed a 3-2 series lead over the seemingly invulnerable Warriors. Yet, in a truly cruel twist of fate (and hamstring) CP3 sustained an injury in the final moments of game five that prevented him from playing in the Rockets two attempts to close out the defending champs. There's no telling what would have come of those two games, and perhaps we would have seen another spectacular meltdown for which he'd be blamed, but at that point I couldn't help thinking that this guy can't catch a break.

CP3 has managed to come up on the wrong side of a few high-profile postseason situations, which seems to shape the discourse when appropriately placing his legacy. I'd like to look past a horrifically officiated playoff game, a cosmic Corey Brewer & Josh Smith intervention, and the most unfortunate hamstring strain in the history of the NBA, to present a new lens through which we should be viewing CP3—most efficient point guard ever. Stockton and Paul are the only two players in history to average 13 assists and 3 steals, per 100 possessions. In that virtuosic 2007-08' season, Chris Paul became the only player in history to rack up 900 or more assists, while committing fewer than 220 turnovers. *The Point God's* 47/37/87[65] career shooting splits might not be directly flirting with the mythical 50/40/90 threshold, but they're definitely making eyes with them from across the room. Amazingly, Chris Paul only stands 6', 175 lbs. Given his frame, you can claim the following about his career—he's the best 6-foot-and-under player in NBA history, one of the three or four most efficient point guards in history, and in the subtext of the most efficient player ever conversation.

As it stands, Chris Paul is the NBA's Mike Trout. If your Chris Paul legacy begins and ends with his failures in the 2014 and 2015 playoffs, I want you to explain to me why the

---

[65] FG%/3P%/FT%.

Oklahoma City Thunder were a playoff team in 2019-20'. The franchise sold off both of their primary assets in Paul George and Russell Westbrook—the gesture explicitly suggested the Thunder would then be re-building. Stranded in Oklahoma City, Chris Paul re-fashioned a roster of players that, like him, weren't really a part of anyone's plan, and he did what Chris Paul always does—win fucking games, earn a 5th seed in a competitive Western Conference, be the maestro of an efficient offense (especially in the clutch), and defend the point guard position historically well.

In closing, I'd like to quantify Chris Paul's status as a 'winning player' and a 'clutch player', as he's been repeatedly classified as someone who is neither of these things. NBA.com has a very comprehensive 'clutch' stat dashboard that goes back to 1996-97'. The baseline framework is to aggregate stats from games that are within five points in the final five minutes of a game—broadly speaking, it draws from games that are in the balance. Using only postseason games, Chris Paul's efficiency remains stellar in this framework, and he's still won more games than he's lost.

	FGA	FGM	FG%	FTA	FTM	FT%	TS%	W	L
Chris Paul Clutch Stats	38	84	45.2	51	58	87.9	.610	26	22

Why They Belong In This Tier? The sketch of Chris Paul's career has created quite a conundrum for advanced metric enthusiasts, as he has an incredible profile from that perspective, but lacks the universally-galvanizing accolades—championships, MVPs, Finals' MVPs. To me, despite his unique and complicated profile, it's actually pretty easy to place him. His meteoric efficiency makes him one of the 30 best players of all-time, no question. But, his inability to turn one of those Clippers seasons into a championship run, and the lack of a single MVP prevent him from Tier II consideration. Hypothetically, had he earned a championship in 2015 or not gotten hurt in 2018 and pushed the Rockets over the top, the weight of a championship would feel very heavy on his profile, maybe pushing him up a tier. But that's not the game. And with him likely to ride out the remainder of his (painfully) expensive contract nursing injuries, it's unlikely he will add any appreciable layers to his existing legacy. Isiah is here because of what his success represented. He endured so many heartbreaking moments that would have otherwise crushed a lot of weaker players. Isiah pushed his team forward and he wasn't afraid to take the heat on his teammates behalf if something hadn't gone right. He was truly a leader of men, and I suppose it's important to note that he was the best player on two championship teams (kind-of).

Karl Malone

The Secret	Greatness Index	Ben Taylor Rank
88 / 100	200.97 (15th)	14th

PIPM	O–PIPM	D–PIPM	Peak—1996-97'	Wins Added
+3.58 (25th)	+2.91	+0.67	+6.03 (25th)	248.66 (6th)

Playoff PER	Playoff Win Shares	Playoff O-Win Shares	Playoff D-Win Shares
21.12 (35th)	22.99 (15th)	11.35 (28th)	11.64 (9th)

There really wasn't anything Karl Malone couldn't do on the basketball court. Only Kareem scored more regular season points than *The Mailman*. Per Ben Taylor, Malone is one of 14 players in history to post a scoring rate above 30 points per 75 possessions, and one of five players to do it twice (Shaq, MJ, Russ, LeBron). He was an excellent passer out of the high-post. He was a very good defender, utilizing his historically-rare combination of speed and strength to earn four All-Defense selections. Malone was also metronomically durable—he ranks fifth all-time in games played. Of his 19 seasons in the NBA, he played 80+ games 17 times, and played all 82 games 10 times. His profile as a player really is immaculate. Karl Malone was as skilled a big man as has ever played in the league, and he did so tirelessly for nearly two decades. Yet, his mantle reads, despite a brilliant career—one of the greatest players to never win a championship.

When I think about great players who never won a championship, I seem to experience a similar psychological distinction when considering that player's historical profile. Their ring-less-ness is one my first thoughts, and from there I quickly cast them aside from being evaluated with players that *have* won championships. When my brain thinks about Karl Malone, this grouping of thoughts pop up:

>Second All-Time Scorer<

>Never Won a Championship<

>Stellar Wristband Game<

Chris Paul, Elgin Baylor,[66] Karl Malone and one other player (to be profiled shortly) are the only four players on my list to have not won a championship. Truly great players in their own right, but be honest about the first things you think about when Chris Paul comes to mind:

>One of the Best Point Guards Ever<

>Never Won a Championship<

>Please Stop Making State Farm Ads<

I'm not proud of this pattern, but I can't imagine that I'm alone in this psychological sorting exercise, and I'm confident that it's a conditioned behavior. I'm sure as hell not breaking down any barriers by talking about how Karl Malone never won a championship. But, it was in consideration of his profile that I acknowledged how truly different I view players who never won an NBA title.

You better believe that former and current players evaluate their peer group through a 'champion versus non-champion' lens. These guys are so damn competitive. They can play nice for TV and public appearances, but behind the scenes, they know damn well who has won it all and who hasn't. That competitive fire burns forever, and for those that never won, those flames burn unsatisfied into all their post-NBA endeavors. Over time, players can find peace in the success they *did* have, even if they never won a championship. However, if you had some of these guys open up to you, I mean really open up, they would admit that they're haunted by the moments that they were closest to championship glory. You're telling me Chris Paul doesn't think about the 2015 collapse against Houston? Elgin doesn't think about those game seven losses to Boston? You better fucking believe Karl Malone thinks about game five of the 97' Finals'.

Is Malone's ring-less-ness justified, or should his play, and postseason play specifically, have yielded him a title? To me, it seems like Karl Malone and his Jazz teams always topped out at really good, bordering on really, really good in 97' & 98'. Drafted in 1985, it was clear that Malone would be a prominent player early on, but his Jazz were far from situated to compete against the Detroit, L.A. and Boston juggernauts of the mid-to-late 80s. By the time Malone led Utah to 50 wins in 1988-89', there were plenty of teams in the West that were already lining up to lose to MJ in the Finals over the coming years. The Jazz wouldn't manage to ascend out of that fray to ceremoniously lose to MJ before he retired for the first time in 1993. Utah peaked with a Western Conference Final loss to the Trail Blazers in 1992. Malone's Jazz then lost to the eventual champion, Houston Rockets, in both postseasons of the seasons without MJ[67] (1994 & 1995). Utah would make the Western Conference Finals in 1996, but lose a tough seven-game

---

[66] Refresher—Elgin Baylor played a few games of the 1971-72' season before retiring. The Lakers went on to win the title that season and awarded Elgin a ring. But that doesn't realllily count, right?

[67] Jordan came back late in the 1994-95' season, but wasn't quite MJ yet.

series to the Kemp/Payton Supersonics. Finally, in 1996-97', after outlasting the other contenders in the West, Malone had put the Jazz in position to lose to MJ in the Finals'.

    In the first 12 years of his career, Malone amassed a score of individual accolades. When he was finally set to take on MJ in June of 1997, he had made 10-consecutive All-Star appearances, 9-consecutive All-NBA First-Team selections, and just that year had been awarded his first of two league MVP trophies. Yet, if you look at the pattern of playoff results that I just ran through, those are clearly disappointing seasons when your team is led by such a decorated player. It's not as if Jordan really impeded the Jazz' ability to compete for titles, clearly the Jazz couldn't get through the West during Malone's prime athletic years. With the Finals' tied at two games apiece, game five was played in Utah. This game really looks like Karl Malone's biggest blown opportunity at a championship. Most people will remember this as Jordan's iconic 'Flu Game' where he battled the 'Flu'[68] en route to 38 points and a pivotal Finals' victory *on the road*. From Malone's perspective .. you just have to win that game! You would have to go to Chicago for games six and seven,[69] but you had to have that game five at home, especially if Jordan wasn't at full strength. Alas, Chicago erased a 16-point deficit in the second quarter, much of which came with Malone sitting due to foul trouble. The Mailman simply did not have a good game. He totaled 19 points and 7 rebounds, but just 6 of his points came in the second half, and he had this all-time-nightmarish sequence to close the game:

1:03 (UTA 85-84 CHI) Malone forces an awful long two-point jumper that he airballs
:45 (UTA 85-85 CHI) MJ draws a foul and makes the first FT to tie the game
:44 (UTA 85-85 CHI) MJ misses the second FT, Malone blows the box out, CHI retains the ball
:25 (UTA 85-88 CHI) MJ drains a clutch three ball on the extra possession
:15 (UTA 87-88 CHI) Stockton gets Oostertag a dunk on a drive and kick
:06 (UTA 87-90 CHI) The Jazz attempt to press the Bulls on the ensuing inbound. After pressuring the first dribbler, Malone looks lost and eventually blows the coverage that gets Luc Longley an uncontested dunk for Chicago.

Ouch. That's how quickly it happens sometimes. Instead of Utah's best player rising up and leading his team to a win that they absolutely had to have, you might have been better without him on the court (?). Props to MJ—this is an awesome game to re-watch because Jordan is physically exasperated, probably hallucinating and definitely operating on sheer will to win. In a lot of ways it was a career-defining performance for Michael Jordan. Sadly, I think it also served as a referendum on Karl Malone's shortcomings as well.

    Chicago would clinch the title in game six. The Jazz won 60+ games for the second season in a row during 1997-98' and met the Bulls again in the Finals'. In the most pivotal game of the series, with Utah down 3-2 entering game six, Malone would actually shine and get his team in position to win with a sterling line of 31 points on 11 of 19, 11 rebounds and 7 assists, plus the clutch assist on a Stockton three-pointer that gave the Jazz a three-point lead with 41 seconds left. Up 1 point and with the ball, Malone was stripped by MJ with 20 seconds left, setting up MJ's timeless 'Bryon Russell' jumper. Those are the breaks, especially when you're

---

[68] More to come on that game. This may be surprising to you, but Michael Jordan does appear on my list.
[69] The Finals' 2-3-2 format ran from 1985 to 2013.

trying to beat Jordan. Sometimes really, really good isn't good enough, which leads me to conclude that Karl Malone seemed to lack the '6th gear' or 'championship gear'. I know that's harsh to say of such a multi-faceted, otherwise mega-talented player. But the proof is in the pudding! Malone reached the Finals' one last time, during his final and only season not in a Jazz uniform—the 2003-04' season where he attempted to ride the Shaq and Kobe express to that elusive championship.

Only to be foiled by the greatest defensive team ever—*the 2003-04' Pistons, baby!!* After Malone's retirement, we have to ask ourselves if he was deserving of a championship. His counting stats would suggest that his play from the regular season translated well to the playoffs. But, the advanced numbers confirm what we already knew—Malone's style was substantially less efficient in the playoffs:

	PER	BPM	WS/48	TS%	FTr^
Regular Season	**23.9**	**5.4**	**.205**	**.577**	**.504**
Playoffs	21.2	3.6	.140	.526	.458

^Free Throw Rate—the number of free throw attempts per field goal attempt. Malone owns the regular season record for both free throw attempts and free throws makes (both by a wide margin). But wasn't quite as good during the postseason at drawing fouls.

We just looked at CP3 and Isiah's efficiency split under this same microscope, and it really illuminates how much worse Malone was in the playoffs. Isiah's pretty good numbers came up a little bit going into the playoffs, whereas Chris Paul's historic numbers came down just a touch. Malone's efficiency split getting the 'James Harden' treatment tells me everything I need to know.

Ben Taylor theorizes that Malone's low release point on his shots around the rim made it easier for defenders to block his shot, especially in the playoffs, when the game slowed down and he wasn't getting quick cuts to the basket for easy buckets. It makes a lot of sense—Malone would have to drive his shoulder into the defender first and flip the ball up throughout his career. So, was Karl Malone deserving of a championship? I would have to say no. He was unable to make it out of the West early in his career, and when MJ provided an opening, Malone wasn't able to take advantage. Was he a great player? Yeah, Karl Malone was a truly great regular season player, who was unable to replicate that level of success consistently in the postseason. Malone holds the record for most playoff losses—95—and despite all of the awards and recognition, this record seems the most fitting and representative of his greatness profile. So, what do I think about now when I think of Karl Malone?

>Punishing Dunker In Transition<[70]

>Second All-Time [Regular Season] Scorer<

---

[70] Looking at tape of this MF when he was younger was probably my favorite part of doing his profile. This dude was a mean dunker when he was a young man.

>Probably Didn't Deserve a Championship<

>Stellar Wristband Game [Irrefutable]<

>Most All-Time Playoff Losses<

Why He Belongs In This Tier? He has a *Scrooge McDuck*-level treasure chest of NBA accomplishments, which leads me to believe that if he could have beaten MJ in either of those Finals', he would garner serious Tier II consideration. However, relative lack of success in the playoffs prevents him from being considered for that party.

Dirk Nowitzki

The Secret	Greatness Index	Ben Taylor Rank
98 /100	135.39 (34th)	18th

PIPM	O-PIPM	D-PIPM	Peak—2002-03'	Wins Added
+3.89 (22nd)	+3.22	+0.66	+7.13 (11th)	241.24 (7th)

Playoff PER	Playoff Win Shares	Playoff O-Win Shares	Playoff D-Win Shares
23.82 (11th)	23.13 (13th)	17.99 (9th)	5.14 (67th)

Dirk Nowitzki broke my heart in June 2011. My frail LeBron-fan ego was sure that the first championship was imminent, and that Mavericks triumph broke my back. However, I was never mad at Dirk, and I was glad to see a few of his teammates win a championship as well. Additionally, even then in that sunken place, his seizing of that 2011 championship felt especially theatrical or dramatic. Maybe it's just me, but didn't Dirk hoisting the Larry O'Brien Trophy feel like Luke Skywalker receiving The Medal of Bravery at the end of *A New Hope?* Or Simba roaring triumphantly atop Pride Rock at the end of *The Lion King?* Maybe Dirk playing in a Dallas uniform his whole career[71] made his story seem more heroic, I'm not sure. But the closer I looked at the archetypal 'hero arc' in popular storytelling, the more I began to believe that we've all witnessed the *Hero's Journey* of Dirk Nowitzki.

In 1949, Joseph Campbell published *Hero with a Thousand Faces*, a work of comparative mythology, which explored the archetypal structure of the 'hero/heroine' within worldwide mythology. He imported a confluence of previous work to theorize the existence of a similar fundamental structure that constitutes a *Hero's Journey*. In the introduction, Campbell summarizes this 'Monomyth' as such:

> *A hero ventures forth from the world of common day into a region of supernatural wonder: fabulous forces are there encountered and a decisive victory is won: the hero comes back from this mysterious adventure with the power to bestow boons on his fellow man*

---

[71] Dirk is the only player in NBA history to play for the same franchise for 21 seasons.

The book introduced a 17-stage process which traced the experience of many heroes throughout their journey. Joseph Campbell's work was well-received, and many storytellers have credited his work in their process. For instance, George Lucas has revealed Campbell's influence in constructing Luke Skywalker's arc, and the *Star Wars'* universe at large.

Christopher Vogler, a highly-sought-after Story Development Executive in Hollywood, has worked on numerous high-profile Hollywood films, but might be best known for his time working for Disney and contributing to *Mulan, Hercules, Aladdin and The Lion King*. He was heavily influenced by Joseph Campbell, and even introduced a more succinct 12 stage arc within his own book, the aptly titled *The Writer's Journey: Mythic Structure For Writers*. In fact, that 12 stage arc has become the more refined and widely accepted version of the *Hero's Journey*. It feels appropriate to exemplify Vogler's work with a film he contributed to—the best animated film of all-time, and one of the best stories ever told, *The Lion King*. If you haven't seen *The Lion King*, I don't know what to fucking tell you .. Maybe, 'what's it been like living under a rock in Estonia for the last 30 years?'

Hero's Journey (Vogler)	*The Lion King*
1) Ordinary World	*Simba is heir to the throne of the Pride Lands*
2) Call To Adventure	*Scar kills Mufasa and blames Simba*
3) Refusal Of The Call	*Simba retreats into the desert*
4) Meeting With The Mentor	*Rafiki determines that Simba is still alive*
5) Crossing The First Threshold	*Simba embraces new experiences*
6) Tests, Allies and Enemies	*Timon & Pumbaa, rendezvous with Nala*
7) Approach To The Inmost Cave	*Rafiki leads Simba to a magical pond*
8) The Ordeal	*Mufasa appears and reminds Simba of his identity*
9) Reward	*Simba knows he must return to Pride Rock*
10) The Road Back	*Simba crosses the desert to return*
11) The Resurrection	*Simba approaches and defeats Scar*
12) Return With The Elixer	*Simba reclaims Pride Rock as its rightful King.*

So, for those that I haven't lost yet, I now present you—*Dirk Nowitzki: A Hero's Journey*.

Ordinary World
Our young hero was born June 19th, 1978 in Wurzburg, Germany. He had a fairly normal childhood, outside of being a foot taller than his peers. He played soccer, handball and tennis, but his height wasn't ideal for these sports.

Call To Adventure
The Nowitzki family was very athletic. The old man was an elite handball player, which along with soccer, were regarded as the more macho sports. His Mother was a professional basketball player who also represented West Germany in international play. His sister excelled at track & field, and was also a professional basketball player. Dirk started playing basketball at

the relatively late age of 13, and was quickly an impactful player in pickup games at a local gym, even though he'd never really played the game before.

Refusal Of The Call

Soon after Dirk began playing basketball, he was catching shade from his old man for choosing that sport. A *Sportsday* article from October 2012 by Eddie Sefko has some great quotes by Dirk's family, including this gem from his old man:

> *My wife and daughter used to play basketball,* Jorg-Werner said this week from Germany. *So, I teased my son when he wanted to get into a 'women's sport'.*

Dirk's father was obviously just poking fun at his son. Buuuut it may have given the freakishly tall German 'tweener' some pause.

Meeting With The Mentor

As Dirk continued to excel, he attracted the attention of German Basketball great, Holger Geschwindner. In a 1998 *Sports Illustrated* profile by Jackie MacMullan,[72] Holger says this of the first time he saw Dirk play:

> *But then one day in 1994, I watched this boy who instinctively was doing all the right things without knowing the game,* says Geschwindner. *I was fascinated. So, I asked him, 'Who practices with you?'*

> The boy, Dirk Nowitzki, then 15, answered quickly: *'Nobody.'*

Dirk had already been playing for DJK Wurzburg, a second-division German professional team. His training with Holger would take his game to another level, and it was the beginning of a lifelong friendship/partnership. Holger used unconventional methods of coaching Dirk that excluded weight training and emphasized shooting and passing drills. Holger also insisted Dirk not drop out of school to focus on basketball, and encouraged him to develop his personality by playing musical instruments and reading as much as possible.

Crossing The First Threshold

Our hero was careening for a prominent career in professional basketball, but where would he choose to play? He would gradually earn a more prominent role on his German Club team each season, and by his final season in 1997-98', he'd garnered buzz that permeated the international basketball community. Dirk would have to fulfill required service in the German Military from September 1997 through June 1998, but he was allowed to play for his club team and some international competition. Leading up to the 1998 NBA draft, Dirk's buzz went nuclear at the Nike Hoops Summit in San Antonio. In a match between the top American high-

---

[72] A genuine inspiration to me, and one of the best to ever do it.

schoolers and the top international talent, Dirk improbably led the international team to a 104-99 victory. In the effort he dropped 33 and 14 on 6 of 12 from the field, and 19 of 23 from the line. The tape was immediately being reviewed by every front office in the NBA, and Dirk had become a premier NBA draft prospect overnight. Larry Bird, then Pacers Head Coach, from Jackie Mac's piece:

> *If you went by that tape alone, you'd think he was the best ever.*

Some vintage Bird sarcasm, nonetheless, Dirk had a choice to make—continue playing in Germany for a team that would invariably pony up millions to sign him, accept one of the numerous collegiate scholarship offers he had from prominent American programs, or enter the NBA draft[73] and test his skills on the biggest stage.

Dirk's choice to pursue a career in the NBA immediately crossed a variety of thresholds. He barely understood the English language, and his unique skill set would require re-calibration within the rugged NBA.

Tests, Allies and Enemies

Thanks to a draft-night trade, both Steve Nash and Dirk Nowitzki would wind up on the Mavericks for Dirk's rookie season. A kinship was born of their parallel struggle to cement themselves in the league, despite Nash having a two-season head start on Dirk. They would be teammates from that 1998-99' season through 2003-04', and Dallas thoroughly rejuvenated their franchise over that period. However, Dirk's integration into the fabric of the NBA was challenging. In February of 2001, Mike Wise of *The New York Times* wrote an article that encapsulated the Mavericks rise, but also illuminated some of the early struggles for our German hero:

> *Shoot-around is like a rehearsal,* Gary Trent, a teammate, told him [Dirk].
>
> The rookie nodded his head knowingly before looking back at Trent, somewhat puzzled.
>
> *What's a rehearsal?*
>
> Becoming fluent in English and fluid in the National Basketball Association has taken time. Language barriers, quicker and bigger players and unrealistic expectations had to be overcome.

The team, and its pair of young stars, would spend the first two seasons coalescing. But the Mavericks would really start clicking in 2000-01'—They won 53 games, and won their first

---

[73] Technically, he could have been drafted and chosen to keep playing in Europe before coming over.

playoff series since 1988. That *New York Times* article perfectly summed up Dirk's then state of development:

> *Nowitzki was also close to becoming the third European to play in the All-Star Game, after Detlef Schrempf, his countryman and three-time All-Star, and the Dutchman, Rik Smits. With Lakers' center Shaquille O'Neal ailing, Nowitzki may yet be named as a reserve. In his last 18 games, he has averaged 23.1 points and 10.4 rebounds in almost 40 minutes a game. Against Orlando on Jan. 18, he had a career-high 38 points and 17 rebounds.*
>
> *Ambidextrous and a multi-position player, he shoots 46.3 percent from the field and 84.2 percent from the free-throw line. Despite being 7 feet, he has made 83 3-pointers this season. 'The young man in the corner may have the best stroke I've seen since Bird,' Rick Pitino said in his final days as the Boston Celtics' coach. 'He's a terrific basketball player.'*

Both Nash and Dirk made their first All-Star teams in 2001-02', and would then earn another playoff series' victory in the 2002 playoffs. In 2002-03', the Mavericks won 60 games and made it all the way to the Western Conference Finals, before being bounced by the eventual champion Spurs.[74] After just five seasons in the NBA, Dirk was boasting this sterling line during that 2002-03' campaign:

PTS	REB	PER	TS%	3P% (5 3PA PG)	FT% (7 FTA PG)
25.1	9.9	25.6	.581	37.9	88.1

Needless to say, this was an unprecedented confluence of skills for a 7-footer. Shit, in the Data-Ball bonanza of 2020, most GMs would be going from six-to-midnight thinking about a stretch-big with that kind of efficiency. In 2003, the NBA community was scrambling to contextualize Dirk's ability, but to no avail—his game was as unique as the story he was writing. Dallas might have been a twisted knee away from the Finals' in 2003, but they certainly planted a flag as contenders going forward.

Approach to the Inmost Cave

Steve Nash chose to leave Dallas in favor of Phoenix after the 2004 playoff exit. In retrospect, it was a move that favored both parties—Nash would flourish with Mike D'Antoni in Phoenix,[75] and the Mavericks would build on the 52 wins in 2003-04', by winning 58 and 60 in 2004-05' and 2005-06'. The 2005 playoffs brought an uncomfortable loss to Steve Nash and the Suns,

---

[74] Dirk twisted his knee in game three, and wouldn't play another minute of the series. They were only down 2-1 after that game, and would still pull out another victory without Dirk. If he plays, I have to think they at least force a seventh game.

[75] It was the perfect pairing .. a coach who would rather find the perfect talent and let them play instead of micro-managing, and the perfect talent who was beginning to access the full breadth of his abilities. A real Roger Sterling-Don Draper relationship.

but the 2005-06' Mavericks were ready to climb the mountain. Jason Terry and Jerry Stackhouse were entering their second seasons with the team, and coupled with Josh Howard and Marquise Daniels taking leaps in their third NBA seasons, there was magic in the air.[76]

The Ordeal

This is the part in many great stories where the hero has seemingly paid their dues, and are ready for the validation of their hard work. As our hero would find out, he still had many a mountain to climb. The Mavericks were excellent that season—60 wins, first in Offensive Rating and first in defensive rebounding. After an easy sweep of the Grizzlies in the first round, they outlasted Duncan's Spurs over seven games in the second round. Dallas found validation of their not signing Steve Nash in the form of a six-game Western Conference Final victory over the Phoenix Suns.

This was the moment, right? All the training, the difficult integration into the NBA, the countless practices with his teammates (and/or Holger[77])—the next step is a championship and eternal glory, or so we've come to understand the next step. The 2006 Finals' against the Miami Heat certainly started off in the direction of that narrative. Dallas dominated the first two games of the series and took a 2-0 lead. Dwayne Wade was stifled and inefficient, and Dallas was playing great team basketball. As the matchup traveled to Miami for the third, fourth and fifth games, so did the Maverick's momentum (and apparently their ability to get to the line). These Finals' have been remembered as the Finals' where *Dwayne Wade shoots free throws for half the game*. Wade attempted 73 free throws in the Heat's four consecutive victories, and the total free throw disparity over those four games would be 156 free throws taken for Miami and 104 for Dallas. Don't look at me, pal, I'm not saying anything about the sanctity of that series, *I'm just sayin'*. It was a crushing defeat for the Mavericks, and Dirk has cited[78] it as his most difficult loss on several occasions.

Reward

Dirk, my friends, is a resilient chap. He sparkled in the 2006-07' campaign—the Mavs won 67 games and Dirk won his first (and only) league MVP award. Alas, another major disappointment came with an improbable first-round playoff exit to the Warriors in the 2007

---

[76] Want a few more throwback names?? Keith motha-fuckin' Van Horn played his final NBA season on that 2005-06' Dallas squad. Erick motha-fuckin' Dampier was in the second season of a *seven-year, $73 million-dollar contract* that he somehow swindled Dallas into. Finally, Devin motha-fuckin' Harris was playing his second of thirty-seven seasons he would play for Dallas.

[77] Throughout Dirk's career, Holger would travel to the US three times per season. The final stretch would occur at the end of the season, and last until the end of the postseason campaign.

[78] On Zach Lowe's podcast 3/27/2019, he had Howard Beck on to discuss his feature article, *The Ballad of Dirk and Dwayne,* which had come out the same day and illuminated the symmetry of the two players' careers. Beck quotes Dirk regarding the 06' Finals': *probably the most frustrated I've been in my career. It was almost a feeling of emptiness. You don't want to get up in the morning, don't really know what's coming.* An even more juicy detail that re-emerged from the article was the frostiness between Dirk and Dwayne that ostensibly began when Dwayne said this when detailing why he believed Dirk cost Dallas the championship: *because he wasn't the leader that he's supposed to be in the closing moments.* Yikes. Going back to the Lion King parallel, think of Dwayne Wade as *Scar* in Dirk's character arc.

playoffs.[79] After the season, Dirk did what a lot of people do when they've hit their bottom professionally and/or personally —he got the fuck out of dodge. On 2/1/2019, Zach Lowe had Dirk on his podcast and asked him about that offseason:

> *Lowe: 2007 you win the MVP and lose in the first round. That's the summer of the Australian Outback, right? I've always wanted to ask you about that. What's the day-to-day on the Australian Outback? It's you and Holger right? [Dirk-'yeah'] Are you in a pickup truck? Are you isolated in the wilderness with animals and no one else around?*
>
> (Dirk explains that Sydney was their main hub for the 5-6 weeks they were there, and that they'd take different excursions to The Great Barrier Reef, Darwin etc. Then Dirk explained the purpose of the trip)
>
> *Dirk: I just wanted to get away as far as I could. I was proud of the season, but I was embarrassed about the playoffs and, at the time, the first 1-seed that had lost to an 8-seed. I didn't play well in the playoff run. I just wanted to get away as far as I could, and it was really refreshing. Back to the roots, outdoorsy. That summer I played [for the] national team and got focused again, but I needed a few weeks to get away.*

Those losses in back-to-back years clearly affected him enough to require a step back from his normal routine. What you have to love about Dirk is that he was a) competitive enough for those failures to really dig at him and b) he possessed the wherewithal to know that he needed to go to Australia for a minute to re-calibrate.

The Road Block

As is often the case with most heroic arcs, things get a little worse before they reach the triumphant crescendo, and Dirk's story was no different. Dallas would continue to win at least 50 games in the 2007-08', 2008-09' and 2009-10' seasons. But, would lose in the first round during two of those three seasons, as the Lakers clamped down on the Western Conference. Things in Dallas were starting to get a little stale—perennially earning a good playoff seed, but scaring exactly no one entering the postseason. Even more, our hero would embroil himself in a weird, mostly-online engagement to a categorically crazy woman. Luckily, the engagement ended, but uncertainty was in the air in Dallas, especially as Dirk's contract was up at the end of the 2009-10' season.

---

[79] At the time, it was the first time an 8-seed had beaten a 1-seed in a seven-game series. Since then, Memphis beat San Antonio in 2011, and the 2012 Sixers upsetting the Bulls (aka the series during which Derrick Rose first hurt his knee).

The Resurrection

He is our No. 1 priority—period.

Donnie Nelson, Mavericks' President of Ops since 2002, wasn't mixing up his words going into the summer of 2010. Nelson was in Germany visiting Dirk the moment free agency began, and he got that deal done. Dirk took less money than he would have likely earned on the open market, which would save the Mavericks money on their luxury tax bill and give them additional roster flexibility. If you recall, the 2010 free agency was a *fairly* memorable one, in which many premier players were available. Dallas had aspirations of going big-game hunting once Dirk had returned to the fold, but a few of the major free agents took their talents to South Beach and despite rumors of him being available, the Hornets did not move Chris Paul. The Mavericks' front office did make one trade, which seemed like a consolation at the time, but cemented a firm piece of their championship puzzle—Dallas acquired Tyson Chandler, a big whose style contrasted Dirk's so much that he immediately became the perfect compliment. Amidst other under-the-radar moves, Dallas had built a sneakily well-balanced roster around Dirk. You know who definitely thought that the Mavericks were looking good that offseason? Jason Terry—who was entering his seventh season with Dallas. You know how I know he was feeling confident? He got a tattoo of the Larry O'Brien trophy on his arm, and proclaimed that the Mavericks would win the 2011 NBA Championship. I guess it's only crazy if it doesn't happen, right?

Our courageous hero was about to embark on his fiercest challenge, which would yield his greatest accomplishment. The Mavericks had an up-and-down regular season which saw them race out to the league's best record early, slow down, and then hit the gas again in the spring when they won 18 of 19 games from January into March of 2011. During the season, Dallas endured a nine-game Dirk absence due to an injury, and the Mavericks also lost key contributor Caron Butler for the season on January 1st. Still, the team rallied to the franchise's eleventh consecutive 50-win season and was hopeful about a long playoff run.

Despite some pushback from the Brandon Roy-led Blazers, Dallas would get out of the first-round after six games. Next up was the defending champion Lakers, who looked poised to make another run. However, the Mavericks stifled everything Los Angeles wanted to do, and despite Los Angeles coming into the matchup with home court, they would see their championship window slammed shut across a four-game sweep to Dirk and the Mavs. The Maverick's Western Conference Finals opponent was the upstart Oklahoma City Thunder. Dirk struck a groove in game one that lasted for the remainder of the playoffs—he scored 48 points and set the tone for a five-game series victory over the inexperienced Thunder.

The stage was now set for a rematch against Dwayne Wade and the Miami Heat in the Finals'. Dallas entered the series as the underdog, with just cause, as Dirk would have to go through

Wade,[80] Bosh and LeBron to conquer his demons and avenge the many disappointments that he'd endured amidst his journey.

Game one was not an ideal start—the Heat dominated on their way to a victory, and Dirk tore a tendon in his finger. Dirk wouldn't allow the injury to be an excuse and never even mentioned that he might miss time because of it. Game two basically went the same way as game one, until the 6:50 mark in the fourth quarter.

Down 15 and staring down the barrel of an 0-2 deficit against a historically talented Miami team was not a great place to be. Like any great story, the hero has to go all the way to their bottom, where hope is all but choked out, to push forward toward eternal glory. Dallas charged back in the game's final minutes, led by 9 clutch points from Dirk. Somehow, the Mavericks stole game two and shocked the Heat, who thought the game was over.

After dropping game three, the Mavericks faced another must-win contest in game four at home. Dirk was running a temperature of 102 degrees at the time of tip off, but was unwilling to consider sitting out a pivotal game for his team. Dirk willed his way to 21 points, including a couple clutch buckets in the fourth quarter, and the Mavericks again tied the series at 2-2.

During game four, LeBron and Wade could be seen mocking Dirk's flu-like symptoms, something he would never let go of. Dirk wouldn't allow the Mavericks to look back from that point—they won the next two games, and despite the finger, the flu and everything in between, Dirk Nowitzki finally won a championship, and earned Finals' MVP honors to boot. It was a genuinely triumphant moment.

Return With The Elixer

Once you bring home a title for the team you've stuck with for so long, it's unrealistic to think you can re-create anything half as special after that pronounced triumph. Dallas continued to compete for the remainder of Dirk's career, but Dirk would never see the second round of the playoffs again. But hey, who cares? When you win a title that carried that amount of weight, the rest is gravy!

One last beautiful chapter in Dirk's story was the opportunity he had to mentor young European players that were acquired by Dallas (Luka Dončić via the 2018 draft, and Kristaps Porzingis via a 2019 trade deadline deal with the Knicks). While 2018 and 2019 is a much different environment for European NBA players, Dirk was given the opportunity to impart his experiences on brilliantly talented players just embarking on their own NBA journeys.

Why He Belongs In This Tier? Dirk's career shows us how important it is to win a championship. I basically spent 3,000 words bashing Karl Malone for his profile, and you just read through about 5,000 words of me, literally, glorifying Dirk's career. Sadly, the

---

[80] Just keep thinking of Dwayne Wade as Scar in this story. I suppose that makes LeBron and Bosh the hyenas? I'm good with that.

championship, and the context of that championship, is the difference. As far as specific placement is concerned, Dirk is a famously efficient basketball player—Like Chris Paul, he flirts with career 50/40/90 numbers (47/38/88). Dirk is also a historically prolific scorer who has unequivocally been linked to highly successful basketball teams in Dallas—11 consecutive 50-win seasons. The totality of his numbers, success in the playoffs, and yes, the eternally glorious 2011 playoff run, all point toward a player who fits firmly in this tier.

Jerry West

The Secret	Greatness Index	Ben Taylor Rank
98 / 100	214.25 (14th)	17th

Playoff PER	Playoff Win Shares	Playoff O-Win Shares	Playoff D-Win Shares
23.06 (15th)	26.75 (10th)	21.34 (5th)	5.41 (56th)

Jerry West is still the only player to win Finals' MVP in a losing effort, and let me tell you, it was not a welcome consolation. In the award's inaugural season, 1968-69', West averaged 38 per game in the 1969' Finals' versus Boston, including 42 points, 13 rebounds and 12 assists in a narrow game seven defeat. West had still yet to bring a championship to Los Angeles and it was the *sixth* time West had fallen short to Boston in the Finals' over the previous *eight* years. As Russell's C's celebrated at the conclusion of game seven, Russell went to West, who was crushed, to provide his admiration. Later, the award painfully (for West) took Russell's name. 50 years after the 69' Finals', the Lakers haven't lost a game seven on their floor since. Brutal. That was the last game Russell would ever play, ostensibly opening the door for a Laker championship. Only the Lakers would lose in seven games to a great Knicks team in the 1970 Finals'.

At the conclusion of the decade, West was 0-7 in the Finals'. Fellow Tier III player and Laker teammate, Elgin Baylor, was now 0-8. For the abuse that West endured in the Finals', he is often referred to as a tragic figure in the NBA lexicon. But we're not going to put more tread on that tired narrative. The 60s Lakers, like the rest of the NBA, were at the mercy of the Boston war machine. The engine of which will receive due acclaim within a higher tier in this ranking, but until then, let's not speak of Jerry West as if he resides in the shadow of Bill Russell, but celebrate the mighty silhouette that West himself cast since stepping foot in the NBA.

West was an incredible collegiate basketball player during his three seasons at West Virginia. The highlight of which occurred at the conclusion of his second season when his Mountaineers earned a chance to play for the 1959 National Championship. West Virginia fell short to Cal 71-70, but West was awarded the Final Four's Most Outstanding Player—some brutal foreshadowing for another loss that West would endure a decade later (where he'd go home with a trophy that wasn't the one he wanted). Alas, two years after the title game defeat, West was a heavily accomplished player entering the 1960 NBA draft. He was selected second-overall by a Laker team that had moved to Los Angeles over the summer. The Lakers reached the Finals in 1959 with another outstanding young player, Elgin Baylor. Between these two players, the 1960s were beginning with an earned sense of optimism for the Los Angeles Lakers!!!

Yikes. Before finally winning a title in 1972, West, Baylor and their Laker teammates would do a lot of winning from 1960 to 1971—seven Finals' appearances in eleven seasons is a stunning accomplishment, but failing to win even a single title makes the Buffalo Bills ineptitude in the Super Bowl seem normal. Fuck! Sorry, we're not going to do the 'tragic figure' thing. Let's take a look at West's most impressive accomplishment for each of his first eleven seasons in the league:

- **1960-61'**—In his rookie campaign, Jerry West helped the Lakers win eleven more games during the regular season, and averaged 23 points, 9 rebounds and 6 assists on 49% shooting during the 12-game playoff run (up from 17 points, 7 rebounds and 4 assists on 42% during the regular season).
- **1961-62'**—Known for his devotion to improving his game, West leaped forward appreciably in virtually every recordable metric during his sophomore season. Most impressive to me was not only doubling his free throw attempts (from 6 FTA to 12 FTA per game), but also increasing his free throw percentage from 67% to 77%.[81]
- **1962-63'**—Down 3-2 in the Finals', West gave everything he had in game six, totaling 32 points, 9 assists and 7 rebounds in the narrow 112-109 defeat.
- **1963-64'**—This season marked the beginning of Elgin Baylor's knee problems, but despite shouldering a larger role, West posted career best (up to that point) efficiency numbers (24.2 PER and .562 TS%).
- **1964-65'**—Five minutes into game one of the conference final, Elgin Baylor suffered a season ending (and career-altering) knee injury. West would go '2015 Finals'-LeBron' and score 49, 52, 44, 48, 43 and 42 during the six-game series victory. For that series, Jerry West averaged 46 points, 7 assists and 6 rebounds on 45% from the field, plus he hit 86 of his 95 free throws (91%).
- **1965-66'**—Los Angeles lost to Boston by two points in game seven of the 66' Finals'. West was now firmly the number one option, and he averaged 34 points, 6 rebounds and 5 assists during those Finals' (on 51% shooting).
- **1966-67**—West completed two seasons in a row hitting 86%+ from the free throw line. He came into the league shooting 67% on 6 attempts per game, and was now hitting 88% on 10 attempts per game.

---

[81] Per the profile on Elgin Baylor, the 62' Finals' were a bloodbath that initiated the Celtic-Laker rivalry. At the end of game five, with the series tied at two games apiece and only three seconds left, Jerry West stole the Boston inbound and cashed in a game-winning layup to give Los Angeles a 3-2 series advantage .. an advantage which they would, of course, relinquish. But, Mr. Clutch indeed!

- 1967-68—Despite a six-game loss to Boston in the 68' Finals', West would shine from an efficiency standpoint during the 68' playoff run. Over the Lakers' 15 games that postseason, West would lead all NBA players in PER (25.1), Win Shares (3.6) and Win Shares Per 48 (.278) [and finish 3rd in True Shooting at .596].

- 1968-69—The first season with Wilt in Los Angeles was a challenge from a chemistry standpoint (as was customary for any group absorbing the massively talented and massively self-absorbed superstar). But the Lakers won a ton of games, and after taking a 2-0 lead in the Finals' against Boston, it seemed like a championship was finally coming. Alas, they relinquished the lead and Boston won the title once again. West was awarded MVP of those Finals', and as I mentioned above, is still the only one to ever win the trophy in a losing effort. It was the end of the Russell era, and West was holding a devastatingly appropriate trophy. Sigh.

- 1969-1970—In game three of the 70' Finals', the Knicks took a two-point lead with three seconds left. West proceeded to receive the inbound and nail a 60-footer to tie the game and send the game to overtime[82] (where West sprained his wrist, missed all five of his shots, and the Lakers lost). West posted 38 points and 18 assists in the game four Laker victory to tie the series. Knicks' star, Willis Reed, would suffer an injury in game five that should have ruled him out for the series. The Lakers couldn't capitalize, and lost game five, but evened the series' with dominant West and Chamberlain' performances in game six. Having injured his other hand in game six, West entered game seven with both hands having received injections prior to tip-off. However, his injuries would be lost in the sands of time when Willis Reed famously hobbled onto the court for game seven and gave his team a massive lift. For the second season in a row, the Lakers would lose in game seven of the Finals'. Sighhhhhh.

- 1970-71—West received his second-consecutive selection to First-Team All-Defense[83] (he'd be selected First-Team two of the following three seasons as well).

The 1971-72' Lakers were one of the great all-time NBA teams. They ripped off a 33-game winning-streak (still a record), on their way to winning 69 games total (then a record). New coach Bill Sharman united the group and got Wilt to be content with just 14 points per game. West took a small step backward in scoring, but led the league in assists at 9.7 per game.

---

[82] The three-point line wasn't introduced until the 1979-80' season.

[83] The NBA started announcing All-Defensive teams in 1968-69', so it's reasonable to think that West would have racked up quite a few more through the 60s, had the distinctions been around. The real victim of the NBA waiting so long to start tracking All-Defensive teams? Bill Russell .. who would be named to the First-Team in his final season (but probably would have been selected every season of his career).

After sweeping the Bulls in the first round, and vanquishing the defending-champion Bucks[84] in the second round, the Lakers drew the Knicks in the 72' Finals'. Ironically, West would play poorly in those Finals' (by his standards) but the Lakers would defeat the Knicks in five games, regardless. Jerry West, at long-last, was an NBA champion. The Lakers lost to the Knicks in the 73' Finals', and West then called it quits after the 1973-74' season.

In his 14 NBA seasons, West made 14 appearances in the All-Star game. When he retired, he had amassed the most playoff points all-time. His career averages of 27, 6 and 7 were quite LeBron-ish. His eleven-consecutive seasons of at least 8 free throw attempts per game were a little Harden-ish. His (assumed) wingspan of 6'9", which allowed him to block, deflect and steal from the guard position, was very Wade-ish. His ability to hit a high percentage of difficult jump-shots, which previously had been considered bad offense, was a *whole lot* Steph-ish. Jerry West was a dominant all-around player. He had the rare distinction of being both a high-volume *and* efficient scorer, waaaay before anyone gave a damn about efficiency.

Jerry West may have found it agonizingly difficult to win championships as a player, but as an executive, this MF is tripping over championship rings! His fingerprints can be found on no fewer than 10 championships. My player ranking only takes into account what a guy did on the basketball court, but it's definitely worth looking at what West did off the court, after his playing days were over:

- *Los Angeles Lakers GM (1982-2000)* His office would oversee Los Angeles winning championships in **85'**, **87'** and **88'**. In the summer of 96', West acquired Kobe Bryant in a draft-night trade, and signed Shaquille O'Neal via free agency. In the summer of 99', West oversaw the Lakers signing Phil Jackson to coach the team. The Lakers would win championships in **00'**, **01'** and **02'**. West resigned his position after the 2000 championship, but he was unquestionably the architect of that three-peat. **[6 Championships]**
- *Memphis Grizzlies GM (2002-2007)* Memphis would go from 23 wins in 2001-02' to 50 wins in 2003-04'. Never, ever forget that Memphis was a coin-flip away from getting LeBron in the 2003 draft.[85]
- *Golden State Warriors Executive Board Member (2011-2017)* West was brought in when new owners, Joe Lacob and Peter Guber, took over the franchise.
  - Just one month into his role with the team, West pushed very hard to draft Klay Thompson with the eleventh-overall pick. In 1987, during his tenure with the Lakers, West's office had acquired Klay's father, Mychal, and was confident in Klay's ceiling as an NBA player.
  - In the summer of 2014, Jerry West reportedly threatened to resign his position with the team if they went through with a proposed trade that would send Klay to Minnesota in exchange for Kevin Love. The

---

[84] Young and dominant Kareem paired with aging, but still savvy Oscar.
[85] Instead, the Top-1-protected pick was relinquished to Detroit, and Memphis was left with nothing to show.

conclusion of the following season saw the Warriors winning the **15'** title over the team that *did* make the trade for Love (only Love missed the majority of the playoffs due to a shoulder injury).

- In the summer of 2016, West famously called Kevin Durant to coerce him into joining the Warriors in free agency. Reportedly, West emphasized the agony he experienced in the 8 times he lost in the Finals', and that Kevin had the chance to avoid similar disappointment by joining a ready-made championship squad. Durant joined the Warriors, and Golden State won titles in **17'** and **18'**. West resigned his post after the 17' title, but again, was integral in the construction of the team and at least partially responsible for the creation of the culture that cultivated dynastic-championship success. **[3 Championships]**

  o *Los Angeles Clippers Consultant (2017-)* West jumped at the chance to work with a dynamic owner and up-and-coming organization. In a short amount of time, the Clippers have gotten off bad money, and accumulated a ton of valuable draft assets since West arrived (all while still competing as the roster flipped over continuously). It's unclear what role, if any, Jerry West played in the Kawhi Leonard-Paul George midnight heist during free agency in 2019, but I'll let you be the judge. If West's presence is any indication, the Clippers are entering a prosperous stretch for the franchise.[86]

In 2011, Jerry West and best-selling author Jonathan Coleman worked together to create West's memoirs entitled *West by West: My Charmed, Tormented Life*. Many of the pages reveal personal struggles that West encountered throughout his life, having nothing to do with basketball. Yet, West's embrace of the profound personal and professional loss that he's encountered reveal an acceptance that only comes with time (and maybe being the primary architect for 10 championships as an executive). Nevertheless, we too can accept that West was an incredible player, years ahead of his time, and easily one of the 30-best players ever. But also accept that, like the rest of the NBA in the 1960's, just couldn't beat Russell.

Why He Belongs In This Tier? Because he's a top-five shooting guard of all-time. One that had the playmaking ability to lead the league in assists if he needed to. Rebounded and defended his position extremely well. As harsh as it is, he needs to break down the Russell-wall just once or twice to truly be considered for the next tier. I do think there's a case to be made for him as a Tier II player, especially when you start to rank Russell-era players. Yet, when he played in a league that only had between 8 and 14 teams, he had to figure out a way to a) win a few MVPs (West never won one) and/or b) come away with another title or two.

---

[86] Despite the epic 2020 collapse amidst their status as everyone's pick to win the championship.

Dwayne Wade

The Secret	Greatness Index	Ben Taylor Rank
92 / 100	146.89 (26th)	24th

PIPM	O-PIPM	D-PIPM	Peak—2005-06'	Wins Added
+2.58 (53rd)	+2.58	+0.20	+7.24 (11th)	142.25 (30th)

Playoff PER	Playoff Win Shares	Playoff O-Win Shares	Playoff D-Win Shares
22.37 (25th)	21.63 (17th)	12.29 (22nd)	9.33 (17th)

I was in the unenviable position of rooting against Dwayne Wade in the 2005 and 2006 playoffs. In the 2005 Eastern Conference Finals, Wade posted 40 points in game two and 36 points in game three.[87] As Miami took a 2-1 lead in that series, I was too awestruck by what felt like the next MJ, to be angry that Detroit was now in a dogfight battle for a chance to return to the Finals'. He was so impactful on both sides of the ball that as long as he stepped on the court, Detroit losing felt like a foregone conclusion. Turns out, it would take Wade missing the fourth quarter of game five, all of game six and playing noticeably hurt for game seven for Detroit to escape with a series victory. However, less than a year before that 2005 ECF, my Pistons, an all-time great defensive team, had handled the Lakers in the Finals' over just five games. How the hell was a *second-year* NBA player gashing one of the league's all-time great defenses?[88] The following season, Detroit would pay the piper. Miami and Detroit again met in the ECF, except Miami won in six games, and Wade posted 27 PPG, 6 APG and 5 RPG (on a preposterous .684 True Shooting %). Wade proceeded to dominate in the Finals', and claimed a championship for Miami. By winning a title as his team's best player in just his third season,

---

[87] Keep in mind, scoring was waaaaaaay down—Miami averaged 88 PPG and Detroit averaged 91 PPG in this series.
[88] Never Forget! Scoring was down, there's no doubt about it. But, Ben Wallace won four of five DPOY awards from 2002-2006 (First-Team All-Defense each season). In 2005 and 2006, Chauncey and Tayshaun would both make Second-Team All-Defense, giving the Pistons 3 All-League defenders in the same starting lineup for back-to-back seasons (the only time that's happened since the merger in 76'. Eric Bledsoe, Giannis and Brook Lopez all made All-Defense teams for the 2019-20' season, but it was the first time since those Pistons, in 2005-06', that three teammates had made the cut.

Dwayne Wade immediately joined very exclusive company—only seven players[89] have ever won a championship as their team's best player, with three or fewer seasons under their belt in the league—Russell, Kareem, Walton, Magic, Bird, Duncan and Wade. In the fifteen years since he scared the shit out of me in that 2005 ECF, Wade continued to flash supernova ability over stretches of his career. That sheer downhill force that he erupted onto the NBA stage with was also likely to blame for nagging injuries that consistently sidelined him throughout his career. But when he was right, especially in the postseason, Dwayne Wade was as good a two-way player as I've ever seen play the game.

Wade presents an interesting case when it comes to his historical profile. He's a three-time champion and was either the best or second-best player on all three of those teams. Yet, not only does he not have an MVP, he only finished in the top five for MVP voting twice. He also had the benefit of playing on championship level teams during two different phases of his career. He maximized those opportunities and was a force during the first run with the Heat (w/ Shaq). Then was a worthy co-pilot for LeBron and the *Flying Death Machine* Heat. As the Heat's best player during the 2005 and 2006 playoff runs, his numbers looked like this over those 37 games:

PTS	REB	AST	STOCKS^	PER	TS%
27.9	5.8	6.2	2.9	25.6	.577

^ Per Bill Simmons—Steals + Blocks = Stocks

Wade's shining moment will always be those 2006 Finals'. He proved that at his peak ability, he could lead a team to a championship. Wade's numbers over those six Finals' games in 2006:

PTS	REB	AST	STOCKS	PER	TS% (Usage)
34.7	7.8	3.8	3.7	33.8	.572 (36.9%)

It's hard to imagine Wade making this list without the 2006 Finals' performance—but when you turn up the dial to *'MJ Status'*, even for just one Finals' series, you'll always be historically rewarded and remembered. After those playoff runs, Wade experienced a few injury-plagued and largely irrelevant seasons before teaming up with LeBron and Chris Bosh in the summer of 2010.

I was a LeBron 'truther' from 2010ish to 2016ish—as in, I always felt like I had to convince people of his greatness. So, I was naturally stoked when LeBron would finally play with All-NBA talent in 2010. Rooting for Wade, opposed to living in fear of his abilities, was a pretty nice thought. I watched Wade very closely during the four LeBron years, and my appreciation of his game only grew during that time. I have to admit, he would really piss me off, at first, with the degree of difficulty on a lot of his shots. It took some serious adjusting to realize that bad shots for the vast majority of the league, were rhythm shots for Dwayne Wade. But overall, his sense for the game, both offensively and defensively, was truly a treat to watch during that stretch. As the Heat's second-best player during the 2011-2014 Finals' runs, Wade's playoff numbers looked like this over those 86 games:

---

[89] Post Russell being drafted in 1956. I only kind-of acknowledge basketball before then. Sue me!

PTS	REB	AST	STOCKS	PER	TS%
20.3	5.2	4.4	2.6	21.4	.539

There are two things to consider 1) his efficiency began to wane in the third and fourth *Flying Death Machine* seasons as he regressed out of his physical prime, and 2) he was playing alongside the best player in the world at the time, and one of the great players of all time (during the *meat* of their prime). Someone he'd frequently have to cede opportunity to, at the cost of his own stats. Given those qualifiers, those are damn fine numbers.

Given how much time Dwayne Wade missed during the regular season throughout his career, it's kind of remarkable that he was able to take the court for such a large percentage of the postseason. I mentioned that he missed that game six of the 2005 ECF against Detroit due to an injury—while that absence seemed emblematic of how Wade's story would always seem linked to untimely injuries, shockingly, that was just the first of two playoff games Wade missed during his entire postseason career.

Postseason	Team Games	Games Wade Played
2004 (Miami)	13	13
2005 (Miami)	15	14
2006 (Miami)	23	23
2007 (Miami)	4	4
2009 (Miami)	7	7
2010 (Miami)	5	5
2011 (Miami)	21	21
2012 (Miami)	23	23
2013 (Miami)	23[90]	22
2014 (Miami)	20	20
2016 (Miami)	14	14
2017 (Chicago)	6	6
2018 (Miami)	5	5

Considering Wade played in just 81% of his team's regular season games throughout his career (1,054 of 1,296), it is fucking-other-fucking-worldly that he would play in nearly 99% of his team's playoff games (177 of 179)![91] That, of course, requires playing through several injuries during the playoffs, and in all likelihood, taking off more games during the regular season to make sure he was right come the postseason. But still! We can conclude here that this explains why, for the talent he possessed, he received a relatively small number of regular season accolades (no serious MVP consideration, plus he would likely have exceeded 8x All-NBA and 3x

---

[90] Beside the 2005 ECF game six, the only other playoff game that Dwayne missed was the fourth game in a first round sweep of the Milwaukee Bucks during the 2013 playoff run.

[91] In fairness, Wade was the king of the nagging injury. He's since transferred that distinction to my guy Anthony Davis, but while he may have played in a really high percentage of games, he was nursing something or other during many of them.

All-Defense had he been on the court 5-10% more often). However, this sterling playoff attendance record explains why he is a historically prolific and efficient postseason performer.

I was a teenager when I first watched Wade terrorize the Pistons in the mid-2000s. My evaluation process for player effectiveness was rather un-nuanced back then. Since, and with the aid of countless evaluation metrics, we have a lot more tools to determine how effective a player really is. His PIPM peak was that 2005-06' season, and good for the 11th highest peak ever, which seems just about right. Yet, as endlessly dumb as I was at 18, I didn't need math to figure out that Wade was going to find a way to beat Detroit or Dallas or fucking whoever was standing between him and a championship. For all we know, maybe the guy has been *Belichicking* us all along by floating through regular seasons and dialing it up for the games that we all remember most—who knows? Either way, he's a dude that performed when the lights were on, and always brought an uncanny variety of ways to impact a basketball game.

Why He Belongs In This Tier? Best player on a championship team upside, coupled with a historically significant body of postseason work. He'll have less regular season markers than nearly everyone on the list, but as we discovered, was always ready come playoff time. Had he been sturdier during the regular season, and had Miami not blown the 2011 Finals', perhaps we could talk about Wade as a Tier II guy. Alas, we're not especially close to that discussion. Similarly, we're not especially close to the rear-wall of Tier III. Wade firmly belongs in this Tier.

Steve Nash

The Secret	Greatness Index	Ben Taylor Rank
88 / 100	79.61 (68th)	19th

PIPM	O-PIPM	D-PIPM	Peak—2007-08'	Wins Added
+2.17 (78th)	+3.40	-1.23	+4.62 (69th)	130.13 (37th)

Playoff PER	Playoff Win Shares	Playoff O-Win Shares	Playoff D-Win Shares
19.84 (52nd)	11.87 (60th)	11.74 (26th)	0.13 (N/A)

The 50/40/90 club is an exclusive group reserved for some of the finest shooters the league has ever seen. A player qualifies by making at least 300 field goals, 82 three-point shots and 125 free throws in a season—all while hitting 50% from the field, 40% from three, and 90% from the free throw line. It's the basketball efficiency equivalent of being knighted, and some of our best, most efficient shooters are represented. It's easy to see that Nash is not only a member, but the chairman, treasurer, and probably the guy who mops the floor after the club is done meeting:

50/40/90 Club	Year
Larry Bird	1987, 1988
Mark Price	1989
Reggie Miller	1994
Steve Nash	2006, 2008, 2009, 2010
Dirk Nowitzki	2007
Kevin Durant	2013
Steph Curry	2015
Malcolm Brogdon	2019

The best part is Nash missed joining the club in 2007 by exactly *one made free throw* (.899 FT% that season). So, he's the only one to do it three times, as well as the only to do it four times, and was a grey Mike D'Antoni hair away from being the only player to do it five times. Yeah, we're talking about one of the all-time efficient point guards the game has seen, and while we're at it, let's look at a few other clubs he's in:

- *The Multiple MVP Point Guard Club*—Nash, Magic Johnson and Steph are the only point guards to have won more than one MVP.
- *The Back-To-Back MVP Guard Club*—Nash, MJ, Magic and Steph are the only guards to have won back-to-back MVPs.
- *The Back-To-Back MVP Club*—Nash, Magic, MJ, Russell, Wilt, Kareem, Moses Malone, Bird, Duncan, LeBron and Steph are the only players to win back-to-back MVPs.
- *The 90% Free Throw Club*—Nash, Mark Price and Steph are the only players to have career free throw percentages north of 90%.
- *The 5x Assist Leader Club*—Nash, J Kidd, Stockton,[92] Oscar and Bob Cousy are the only players to lead the league in assists five times or more.

Alright, Danny, we fucking get it—Steve Nash was a really good point guard. Somehow Nash's greatness was hiding in plain sight during his career, and I was kind of blown away digging into his statistical markers. However, he's a player that wasn't especially feared when it came to the postseason, and to say he was a liability on the defensive side would be like saying Fredo was a liability to the Corleone Family Business. We'll get to his defensive ineptitude, but he was the maestro of historically significant and efficient offenses, so should we care that his teams never *truly* contended for a championship?

Nash's career began in Phoenix in 1996, was traded to Dallas in 1998, elected to go back to Phoenix in 2004, then finally was traded to the Los Angeles Lakers in 2012 (but let's pretend the proposed Laker super team with him, Dwight and Kobe never happened). Nash's legacy was written during that second stint with Phoenix, and it yielded the lofty stats that allowed him to join a few exclusive clubs. The pivot point for Steve Nash is obviously his decision to leave Dallas for Phoenix, and I think it's worth zooming in on. However you feel about him choosing Phoenix, it didn't take long for Nash to feel validated in his decision—in one of the all-time rapid franchise turnarounds, the Suns went from terrible to title contender in one offseason. Let's dig into the numbers behind that turnaround, and just for funsies, let's round out the top-five biggest single-season turnarounds in league history:

2003-04' Suns		2004-05' Suns
29-53	W-L	**62-20**
101.4 (21st)	Offensive Rating (League Rank)	**114.5 (1st)**
105.5 (25th)	Defensive Rating (League Rank)	**107.1 (17th)**
-2.94 (21st)	SRS[93] (League Rank)	**+7.08 (2nd)**
Nash in, Marbury out, Stoudemire rising, 5 players average 14+		

---

[92] John Stockton led the league in assists nine seasons in a row, from 88' to 96'. Holy Smokes.
[93] SRS-Simple Rating System-Team metric that mitigates a team's average point differential and strength of schedule, with zero being average.

2006-07' Celtics		2007-08' Celtics
24-58	W-L	66-16
103.2 (28th)	Offensive Rating	110.2 (10th)
106.9 (16th)	Defensive Rating	98.9 (1st)
-3.70 (25th)	SRS	+9.30 (1st)
Garnett in, Allen in, Rondo rising, Historic team defense		

1988-89' Spurs		1989-90' Spurs
21-61	W-L	56-16
100.9 (23rd of 25)	Offensive Rating	107.7 (15th of 27)
107.5 (13th of 25)	Defensive Rating	104.2 (3rd of 27)
-7.45 (22nd of 25)	SRS	+3.58 (7th of 27)
David Robinson in, League subsequently put on notice[94]		

1978-79' Celtics		1979-80' Celtics
29-53	W-L	61-21
101.6 (19th of 22)	Offensive Rating	109.4 (2nd of 22)
106.4 (19th of 22)	Defensive Rating	101.9 (4th of 22)
-4.78 (21st of 22)	SRS	+7.37 (1st of 22)
Bird in, Planet Earth subsequently put on notice		

2000-01' Nets		2001-02' Nets
26-56	W-L	52-30
100.0 (24th)	Offensive Rating	104.0 (17th)
105.5 (23rd)	Defensive Rating	99.5 (1st)
-5.30 (25th)	SRS	+3.67 (5th)
J Kidd in, Marbury out,[95] Jefferson in, 7 players averaging 9+		

The epic turnaround was punctuated by Nash winning league MVP in 2004-05', and the Suns earning a berth in the Western Conference Finals. The success continued as Phoenix won at least 54 games in four of the next five seasons, while winning at least one playoff series' three times over that same stretch. However, they failed to reach the Finals', and it's probably because immediately after Nash's arrival, Phoenix would demonstrate an institutional master class on *how not to get over the championship hump, despite having all the assets to do so.*

Reading through the chronology of missteps by the Suns, beginning with the 2004 draft, reads basically like the spiraling downfall of bad advice that Tyrion Lannister provided Daenerys Targaryen over the last few seasons of *Game of Thrones*.[96] Each step compounding the prior mistake. Listen, I don't like doing the revisionist history thing, because all of the men who made these choices are smarter than I'll ever be. But, the misfires in the valuation of their draft

---

[94] The 1997-98' Spurs are the honorable mention on this list—Duncan's rookie year when he and Robinson combined for 97 double-doubles, capping an all-time successful (and sneaky) tank-job the prior season.

[95] Stephon Marbury's departure from two different teams in his career resulted in two of the top-five biggest single-season turnarounds in league history—Yikes.

[96] After Jorah kidnaps him, he finds himself promoted to Daenerys' Hand of the Queen. Which seemed like a slam dunk hire for Daenerys—think New Orleans hiring David Griffin—yet it quickly started feeling Isiah Thomas in New York-ish. A) Tyrion botched an agreement with the masters of Slaver's Bay, failing to understand the political and cultural implications of the region, needing Dany to bail him out via dragon fire. B) When the Yara Greyjoy / Olenna Tyrell / Ellaria Sand / Daenerys super team held all the strategic cards during their summit at Dragonstone, somehow Tyrion's plan to split their forces between Casterly Rock and King's Landing played out like LeBron's performance in the 2011 Finals', and they quickly lost their supreme advantage. C) Tyrion's preposterous plan to capture a white walker and bring it to King's Landing, in so doing, demonstrating the threat the Army of The Dead posed to Cercei, was the worst idea anyone's ever had in the history of fiction. It cost Dany a dragon, who would subsequently begin fighting for the Night King. I still think the Suns' draft strategy in the mid-2000s was worse.

picks between 2004 and 2007 were so bad, and Phoenix was so close to competing for a title during that stretch, that it has to be part of the conversation with Nash's legacy.

2004 Draft—The Suns held the seventh-overall pick and took Luol Deng, but quickly moved him to Chicago for a future first-round pick and Jackson Vroman. If Jackson Vroman doesn't ring a bell, it's because he didn't play long enough in the NBA to ring any bells. As for the future first-round pick, it conveyed as a twenty-first-overall pick in the following year's draft.

2005 Draft—The Suns took Nate Robinson with that pick, but quickly packaged him and Quentin Richardson in a trade to the Knicks for Kurt Thomas and Dijon Thompson.[97] The thinking was to bolster their exposed defensive shortcomings, which had presented in the 2005 WCF loss to the Spurs. But it also shipped Q Richardson, who now under contract, was the rationale for not holding onto Luol Deng. They would also trade their fifty-seventh-overall pick, Marcin Gortat, to the Magic for cash considerations. The trend here is Phoenix throwing away actual assets for theoretical ones, and it only gets worse.

2006 Draft—The Suns struck a deal to send their twenty-first-overall pick (which became Rajon Rondo), Brian Grant and cash considerations to the Celtics for a future first-rounder. Phoenix may have already had a point guard, but Rondo would have cushioned their depth—a crucial ingredient to the championship equation. Revisionist middling draft pick stuff is low-hanging fruit, but it supports my narrative, so we're moving on. As for the future first-rounder acquired, it once again would convey as a worse pick.

2007 Draft—The Suns used the twenty-fourth-overall pick, acquired from the Rondo trade, to select Rudy Fernandez, whose shooting would space the floor for the running-and-gunning that Phoenix preferred to do. However, they shipped Fernandez to Portland for cash considerations. Cool. Shortly after the draft, in what was labelled a financial move, the Suns got off of Kurt Thomas by attaching their own 2008 and 2010 first-round picks in a deal with Seattle in which they received back, and this is not a fucking typo, a conditional second-round pick. On one hand, Phoenix created an 8M$ trade exception by doing so, and continually cited that they were content staying the course with their core. On the other hand, Phoenix used that second-round pick in 2009 to take Emir Preldžič, who spent less time in the NBA than the time it took me to insert those dumb letters/characters in his last name (Sorry, Emir). Seattle/Oklahoma City used their first-round picks to take Quincy Pondexter and Serge Ibaka.

Teambuilding is really hard, and when you have a perennial 50-win team, maybe it's easier to stay focused on your core, stay the course, and hope things swing your way as the postseason chips fall. Over this window, the General Manager duties transitioned from Bryan Colangelo to Mike D'Antoni (doing the infamous coaching/front office double-duty), and then to Steve Kerr, who was getting his feet wet in the NBA front office world. By all accounts, these are NBA characters with favorable approval ratings, and conservatively speaking, credible basketball thinkers by-and-large.[98] However, time and again, we've seen championship contenders succeed, at least in part, through their utilization of the draft. It's one thing to

---

[97] Not even sure which joke to make—a mustard one, or one about how little Dijon played in the NBA. Let's just say that Dijon failed to Ketchup to the pace of the NBA game.

[98] Not to mention, Amin Elhassan and David Griffin were in the organization during this whole stretch as well—without question some of the brightest basketball thinkers around.

swing and miss in the draft, which the greatest of talent evaluators have done countless times. It's another to knowingly choose not to use the draft as a means for bettering your team— Which Phoenix did immediately after acquiring Steve Nash in the summer of 2004. Success is relative, and the Phoenix Suns enjoyed basketball and commercial success during Nash's 2004 to 2012 tenure that would be the envy of most fanbases and front offices alike. As we've come to conclude again-and-again, winning a championship is the ultimate exemption from guesswork and conjecture. Therefore, when a group this talented falls short of a championship, or even a Finals' appearance, I feel a bit less guilty for pulling out the rear-view magnifying glass on their draft strategy.

So, why didn't Nash stay in Dallas? Primarily, Mark Cuban was in salary cap hell, and he was being told that Nash's rambunctious style of play would result in a bad investment were he to extend a lofty contract to the Canadian point guard. There is definitely some 'He said vs. He said' elements to what exactly went down, but in the end, Cuban wasn't willing to untie his purse strings like the Suns were, and Nash chose Phoenix. I discourage you from viewing Cuban in a *Scrooge McDuck*, unwilling to part with his swimming pool of gold, type of way. The long-time Mavericks owner detailed his thoughts on the totality of the situation with granular specificity in a July 3rd, 2004 blog post (which, as of fall 2020, can still be read in its 4,000 words of glory). My main takeaway was that Cuban is a great owner, who understands his business— he highlighted the complexities of taking on bad money in a luxury-tax NBA. He drills home how Nash's contract would extend past where the existing CBA was in place, and with the NBA in a much more precarious financial position than it is now in 2020, offering Nash a deal that approached a max would be a seriously risky investment. We know now that Nash would defy Cuban's concerns to become a historically efficient point guard who avoided injuries until his late 30's, but Cuban wasn't wrong to be concerned about extending a pseudo-max deal to a 30-year-old player who often played harder than his body allowed him to. I highly recommend reading Cuban's perspective—it's a rare peak under the hood of the decision-making process of a truly invested, intellectually curious and competitive NBA owner.

So, what if Nash had stayed with the Mavericks? I know the *Shoulda, Coulda, Woulda* game is often times a fruitless effort, but it's especially fascinating in Steve Nash's case. I've gotta say, I think he *Shoulda* stayed. We know that he and Dirk were bros fo sho, and having your two premier players get along is a big advantage already. Plus, everything pointed toward their best basketball being in front of them—Nash was 30 when he left for Phoenix, and Dirk was 25. Nash wasn't exactly young, but keep in mind he ripped off his most impactful seasons between the age of 30 and 36 in Phoenix, and *Coulda* done the same in Dallas. In the two seasons leading up to Nash's departure (2002-03' & 2003-04'), Dallas led the league in Offensive Rating. From when Nash left for the Suns, through when his body started breaking down (2004-05' through 2010-11'), the Mavericks averaged fifth in Offensive Rating, which is still pretty damn good. Furthermore, the Mavericks averaged 57 wins over that same stretch— so, how much could Nash have impacted a perennially successful team? I'm confident he finds a way to improve the Maverick's efficiency within this window. Nash was a very unselfish player, and never once in his career did his usage exceed 23%. He was spectacular at setting the table for others in Phoenix, and his co-star *Woulda* been appreciably brighter in Dallas. It's very possible that Nash's MVPs in 05' and 06', and Dirk's MVP in 07' would have gone to others, as the two would cannibalize MVP votes on the same squad. Meaning Nash may have forgone his entry into a few of the MVP clubs that we mentioned at the top. But as far as team success goes? It's hard to imagine they don't find their way to an additional Finals', on top of the two appearances accredited to the Dirk-led Mavs. Now, what happens in the Finals'? That's up to the Basketball Gods.

So, maybe he would have enjoyed more team success in Dallas, and perhaps the Suns front office brutally undervalued their draft picks during the crucial team-building phase of their contending run. One thing is for sure, Nash was a lia-fucking-bility on the defensive side of the ball. At 6'3" 200 lbs, it's not as though he was tragically ill-equipped to defend his position, but time and again over his career, opposing teams would seek him out and force him to be on the defending side of their actions. Nash's IQ and competitiveness drove him to be a solid rotator, and above average at securing position to draw charges. But as far as the defensive counting and impact stats go, he might as well have been an open door. It took me about 10 minutes to scroll down far enough to find where he ranked in D-PIPM. His -1.23 rating is good for 3,233rd among NBA players in the PIPM database.

I went back and forth on whether I thought he belonged on the list, given his defensive shortcomings, but eventually concluded that the offensive floor-raising was just too elite. As a shooter, his percentages and appearances within the 50/40/90 club speak loudly toward what he could have done with more championship caliber players around him. As a leader, there isn't any available writeups that suggest he was anything less than a fierce competitor who always earned the respect of his teammates. As a passer, there is plenty of evidence that Nash was as precise and accurate a passer as there has ever been in the league. Ben Taylor, who's done as much or more exploration on precision passing than any NBA statistical paleontologist, is confident saying that:

> Nash delivered more quality passes, per possession, than anyone I've ever researched on film.

Why He Belongs In This Tier? Considering he never played in the Finals', and owns a very poor reputation as a defender, admittedly Nash was a fringe addition to the Tier III for me. I'm uneasy adding any player that wasn't at least adequate as a two-way player. But, Nash's Mozart-level-offensive conducting has to be celebrated in the NBA universe, and it most definitely is by our more analytics-driven appraisers of greatness. Had he played on even marginally better teams over that 2005-2011 stretch, he likely would have reached the Finals' and his shortcomings would have become less a part of his narrative.

Moses Malone

The Secret	Greatness Index	Ben Taylor Rank
76 / 100	139.01 (31st)	26th

PIPM	O-PIPM	D-PIPM	Peak—1982-83'	Wins Added
+2.01 (96th)	+2.14	-0.13	+4.42 (79th)	134.49 (35th)

Playoff PER	Playoff Win Shares	Playoff O-Win Shares	Playoff D-Win Shares
21.40 (31st)	13.67 (52nd)	8.78 (45th)	4.88 (73rd)

My friends, I struggled mightily with this profile. I would be driving in my car, in social settings where I was clearly ignoring people, or even in the heat of a yoga class .. deep into my Triangle pose .. and all I could think about was whether Moses Malone was overrated, properly-rated or underrated. While my *Namastes-Above-Replacement* (NAR) was in the 98th percentile while I was writing this up, I still couldn't identify the right statistic to make sense of the contextual puzzle that Moses Malone's legacy presented to me. For instance, Moses positioned himself into a few historically, ultra-elite clubs—at 9th all-time in career points and 5th in career rebounds, just Moses Malone, Elgin Baylor, Kareem, *Karl* Malone and Wilt are top-ten in both categories. Moses also won three league MVPs—the only players to do so are him, Kareem, Russell, MJ, Wilt, LeBron, Bird and Magic. Then, on a more direct level, Moses smoked Kareem Abdul-Jabbar like a 4 lb. brisket both times they met in the playoffs!

But on the other hand..

As the greatest offensive rebounder of all-time, by a wide margin, was Moses a one-trick-pony, so-to-speak? He played for a lot of different teams, which tends to refract our perception of players,[99] should we hold that against him? Malone's longest tenure was with Houston, which coincided with probably the strangest stretch in the NBA's history—despite the success he

---

[99] This wasn't worthy of a full-on theory because I think it's universally accepted, but your brand and how you're remembered depreciably suffers every time you're seen in another uniform. A player's greatness is far more digestible when we can only picture them in one jersey.

enjoyed during that time, should he or could he have had more? Should we asterisk his accomplishments that occurred between 1977 and 1982 in that backwards, cocaine-fueled NBA? Fuck if I know, man. But let's try to do this thing together.

Moses Malone *is indeed* the greatest offensive rebounder of all-time. There is a triumvirate of players that could all make a case in the conversation—Moses, Andre Drummond (kill me), and Dennis Rodman—these three cement that status by holding the top three career offensive rebounding percentages, as well as rounding out the top three for most seasons having led the league in total offensive rebounds:

	Career ORB%^
1) Dennis Rodman	17.21%
2) Moses Malone	16.39%
3) Andre Drummond	16.35%

^ORB%—Offensive Rebound Percentage is an estimate of the percentage of available offensive rebounds a player grabbed while he was on the floor.

	League-Leading Seasons in Total Offensive Rebounds
1) Moses Malone	8
2) Dennis Rodman	6
3) Andre Drummond	6

In fact, of the 20-best seasons all-time by offensive rebounding percentage, these three players claim 13 of them—Rodman (6) Moses (5) Drummond (2). Rodman was a fucking animal on the boards, however, on sheer consistency and prolific-ness, Moses takes the cake. By a wide margin, Moses owns the record for most career offensive rebounds—1) Moses Malone (6,731) 2) Robert Parish (4,598) 3) Buck Williams (4,526). Considering the back-breaking nature of conceding offensive rebounds and subsequent second-chance points, it's actually a highly valuable distinction to have to your name. Fundamentally, if a player on your team is grabbing nearly 20% of your team's misses, that significantly improves your offense, and chances of winning. Any skill that doesn't need to be integrated into a team's game plan is 'found money' in a way—if Malone's teams didn't need to draw up plays for him to exhibit his most dynamic skill, his ridiculous offensive rebounding served as highly valuable connective tissue in the way of his team's success.[100] For that same reason, this skill is highly transferrable, and allowed Malone to be successful on the number of different team's that he played for during his career.

Moses played for nine different organizations during his twenty-one seasons as a pro. My immediate feeling on players with that kind of background is 'nobody wanted to play with this guy (or) nobody wanted to coach this guy (or) nobody wanted this guy in their organization'. However, I couldn't find any glaring evidence of that being the case with Moses. Plus, his first two franchises were in the ABA—which had the institutional stability of three

---

[100] Andre Drummond is working his way toward being the greatest offensive rebounder ever, and trust me, his play does not transfer to winning basketball. In fairness, Moses was a better player with the ball in his hands. Probably by a wide margin.

fourth graders standing on each other's shoulders in a trench coat, attempting to provide the appearance of a man (or a professional basketball league).

After the merger in 1976, as the NBA was making up rules about rights to players in real-time, Moses would find himself a Buffalo Brave for just two games before he was moved to Houston where he would play for six seasons. Moses thrived in Houston to the tune of two league MVPs (1978-79' & 1981-82'), and an NBA Finals' appearance (1980-81' 4-2 loss to Bird's Celtics).[101] However, Malone's tenure as a Rocket coincided, almost perfectly, with a myriad of challenges for the NBA, which created a very strange window of time for the league:

Cocaine—The drug was deeply entrenched in American culture, and NBA culture wasn't exempt. Some of basketball's most talented players of the late 70's and early 80's were irrefutably limited by their problems with cocaine use—David Thompson, Michael Ray Richardson, Spencer Haywood, Bernard King, John Lucas and many others.

Fighting—On December 9th, 1977, during a scuffle between The Lakers and Rockets, Laker Kermit Washington landed a brutal punch on Rocket Rudy Tomjanovich. Tomjanovich's head violently bounced off the canvas, and the damage almost killed him. It was the boiling point[102] for the fighting issue which the NBA was already struggling with—Kareem, the league's biggest draw at the time, broke his hand fighting earlier in the season. Kermit was suspended for the remainder of the season, without pay, on top of a $10,000 fine (the biggest in the history of pro sports at the time).

Ratings & Attendance—Both figures had been trending downward since the merger, and 1979 was when alarm bells started going off. *There's An Ill Wind Blowing For The NBA* by John Papanek—a vaulted *Sports Illustrated* article from February 26th, 1979, demonstrated the totality of the NBA's challenges through the use of some glaring statistics that surely kept then league commissioner, Larry O'Brien, up at night. A few of the revelations:
  o In February 1979, national TV ratings were down 26% from the season prior.
  o All four major NBA markets—New York [Knicks](-11%), Chicago (-31%), Philadelphia

---

[101] That 1980-81' Houston team has to be the most improbable Finals' team in NBA history—they're the only regular season team with a negative SRS (-0.20) and a losing record (40-42), to reach a Finals'.
[102] It didn't help that Kermit was black and the image of him clocking the white Tomjanovich was broadcast to an unsurprisingly terrified white America.

(-19%) and Los Angeles [Lakers] (-11%) were all significantly down in attendance.[103]

o   As of 1979, 75% of the league was black, as compared with ten years prior when the number was 60%—Simply put, white America was less comfortable tuning into the league as it became blacker and blacker.

Image—All of the above factors resulted in the biggest problem—the image of the league, its very brand and concept, was materially flawed from the perspective of far too many Americans for the league to have a stable future. The merger definitely needed to happen for the advancement of pro basketball in America, but it also contributed to a de-stabilized period for the NBA from 1977-1982. On top of the listed factors, integrating the more individualistic style of ABA players made for sloppy, disjointed play (as did the cocaine). More importantly, you didn't have traditional markets dominating until Bird & Magic (both rookies in 1979-80') came on the scene—Portland won the championship in 77',[104] Washington in 78', and Seattle in 79'. Fortunately, Bird & Magic would lift the NBA back up by the mid-80's.

All of this to say—the first eight seasons of Moses's professional basketball career were split between the messy conclusion of the ABA (2 seasons) and the also messy post-merger NBA (6 seasons). It seems to me that this instability prevented the league from properly showcasing the talents of a player like Moses during this stretch—and with so many of his prime years, at least physically, having come during this unusual window, it seems to have colored his legacy negatively. Weird to say, considering he competed for a title and won a few MVPs, but conversely, had he come into a more stable league, perhaps we'd remember him differently.

Alas, Moses enjoyed one undeniably great, fully appreciated and recognized moment in the sun during his career—Philly's virtuosic 1982-83' season—Malone's first season as a Sixer after leaving Houston. Naturally, Moses led the league in rebounding and was fifth in scoring, on his way to his third league MVP in five seasons. I was rather surprised how well his advanced profile matched his counting stats—he led the league in PER (25.1) Win Shares (15.1) and Win Shares Per 48 Minutes (.248) during that 1982-83' triumph. It's also not surprising that his PIPM peak occurred during this season.

Philly won 65 games that year, and their 'big four' of Andrew Toney, Julius Erving, Maurice Cheeks and Moses were poised to make a deep playoff run. As the postseason approached, Moses famously said the Sixers would sweep each round of the playoffs when he

---

[103] Well before the internet, major media markets actually had an enormous impact on the popularity ceiling of the league. After the Ewing-Knicks runs of the 90s, why did we care about the Knicks and all of their bullshit? My guess is because, for a long time, the viability of the New York Knicks was actually meaningful to the success of the league, and that mindset never fully dissolved despite their wretchedly terrible play/front office decisions.

[104] Make no mistake—the 1976-77' Blazers were a historically good team, but their potential run ended the following season when Walton suffered the first of a string of career-altering foot injuries. Coincidentally, they had the rights to Moses prior to their championship season in 1976-77', but chose to walk away from him because they felt Jerry Lucas and Moses had redundant skill sets. We can always trust Portland to make great choices when it comes to big men.

proclaimed his *Fo Fo Fo* prediction. He wasn't too far off as the Sixers beat the Knicks in *Fo*, the Bucks in *Fi*, and then decisively smacked the Lakers in *Fo* during the 1983 Finals'. The significance of which can't be overlooked—the Lakers weren't in full Showtime form yet, but they led the league in offensive rating and were third in SRS during the season. Not to mention, Kareem was a spry 35 and Magic was flirting with his peak powers. Still, Moses kicked their ass. The Sixers had lost to the Lakers in the 1980 and 1982 Finals', with Kareem's size and ability spearheading those victories. Moses' arrival made things tough on Kareem, and unquestionably was the reason Philly was able to get over the hump. Moses' stat line from the 1983 Finals':

Points	Rebounds	Stocks^
25.8	18.0	3.0

^Stocks—Combination of blocks and steals.

This was the second and last time that Moses would face Kareem in the playoffs—both were convincing victories by Malone's team. In these 1983 Finals', Moses had more offensive rebounds total (27), than Kareem had defensive rebounds (25). Moses was too big and strong for Kareem. The other playoff matchup was in the first round of the 1981 Western Conference Playoffs—Malone's Rockets won the three-game series 2-1, which was their first step on their massively improbable run to the 81' Finals'. Moses was the best player in the series, and posted 31 & 18, including a Wilt-ish 38 & 23 in game one. Moses had anywhere from 20-30 pounds on Kareem, and was not shy about throwing his weight around—Kareem's in a higher tier than the one I'm writing in now, but he was vulnerable to bruising bigs, and younger Moses was the perfect foil to aging Kareem.

Moses played three more seasons for the Sixers, but they'd never reach the Finals' again. Malone spent his final two seasons in Philadelphia mentoring their 1984 draft pick, Charles Barkley. Chuck still speaks fondly of Moses, as he took Barkley under his wing and pointed him in the direction of NBA greatness. Prior to their relationship, Chuck's compass was perpetually guiding him toward Burger King and playing himself out of the league a few years after being drafted. Moses played for five more teams over the remaining nine seasons of his career, none of which were especially meaningful, and images of him in a dozen more jerseys probably diluted his legacy a little more.

Why He Belongs In This Tier? He has the credentials for Tier II consideration, given the MVPs and the accumulation of top ten all-time sums in both rebounds and points. However, despite the impressive breakthrough during the 1982-83' season, there isn't enough evidence of him always leading a team to high-level success. There certainly weren't any holes in his rebounding or interior scoring, and by all accounts, two selections to the All-Defense team indicates he was an above-average defender. But because he lacked as a creator, his skills will always seem like mercenary efforts to me. His most dynamic skills were definitely allowing his team to win, but he was rarely making teammates better and/or promoting any flow within an offensive scheme. I had to keep asking myself whether or not Andre Drummond could have had the same success as Moses if he'd played within the same era and circumstances. The fact that that answer might actually be 'yes', prevented me from leaning toward placing Moses in

Tier II. Lastly, I have a hard time over-rewarding a player who played many of their prime years during such an off-kilter stretch for the NBA. There were so many moving pieces for the NBA post-merger, and if Moses had Tier II upside, he would have figured out a way to raise his team to the top of a shifting league, which was begging for a legitimate Tier II player to come along and drag the league into the Bird & Magic era.

Dennis Rodman

The Secret	Greatness Index	Ben Taylor Rank
92 / 100	143.22 (28th)	Not Ranked

PIPM	O-PIPM	D-PIPM	Peak—1991-92'	Wins Added
+0.87 (271st)	-0.46	+1.34	+2.29 (339th)	73.42 (126th)

Playoff PER	Playoff Win Shares	Playoff O-Win Shares	Playoff D-Win Shares
12.30 (N/A)	11.74 (64th)	2.19 (N/A)	9.55 (15th)

I know. I know, I know, I know, I know, I know .. I know.

Let's just talk about this for a minute.

Every championship team in history had at least one of the following—a crazy guy, a historically-versatile defender or a historically-prolific rebounder. Five different championship teams were lucky enough to have a player that checked all three boxes. Rodman is the prototype for the hustle guy/rebounder/defensive swiss army knife, and I have to admit I have a weakness for those guys .. so here we are.

Rodman's cumulative rebound numbers won't blow you away, mostly because his NBA career didn't start until he was 25, and his 14 years in the league is a modest tenure compared to some of the prolific giants on the all-time rebounding list. But his rebounding efficiency numbers make it clear that he's one of the best to ever do it. This table reflects all of his statistics regarding rebounding, with his all-time rank in parenthesis:

	Regular Season	Playoffs
Rebounds Per Game	13.12 (**11th**)	9.92 (**52nd**)
Total Rebounds	11,954 (**23rd**)	1,676 (**12th**)
Offensive Rebounding Percentage^	17.21% (**1st**)	15.01% (**1st**)
Defensive Rebounding Percentage*	29.57% (**4th**)	26.20% (**10th**)
Total Rebounding Percentage+	23.44% (**2nd**)	20.50% (**3rd**)

^ ORB%—Estimate of the percentage of available offensive rebounds a player grabbed while he was on the floor.

*DRB%--Estimate of the percentage of available defensive rebounds a player grabbed while he was on the floor.

+TRB%--Estimate of the percentage of total available rebounds a player grabbed while he was on the floor.

****Rebounding Percentage became available after Russell's career, and for just the last few seasons of Wilt's career, or they would own all of those numbers.

Of the top fifteen players on the all-time rebounds per game list, only three played in the post-1984-modern era—Dennis Rodman, Andre Drummond, and Dwight Howard. Of the 22 players with more all-time rebounds than Rodman, no player is shorter than him at 6'7", and based on *Basketball Reference's* provided weight, he is also the lightest at 210 (safe to say his playing weight as a Bull was a little higher than that). Rodman's greatest rebounding feat was clearly carrying the rebounding title for seven consecutive seasons—not even Wilt did that. In fact, Wilt's eleven rebounding titles are the only cumulative mark higher than Rodman's seven.

Most Consecutive Seasons Leading League in RPG		Years
Dennis Rodman	7	1991-92'—1997-98'
Moses Malone	5	1980-81'—1984-85'
Wilt Chamberlain	4	1959-60'—1962-63'
Wilt Chamberlain	4	1965-66'—1968-69'
Kevin Garnett	4	2003-04'—2006-07'

Most Total Seasons Leading League in RPG	
Wilt Chamberlain	11
Dennis Rodman	7
Moses Malone	6

Rodman's preposterous 18.7 rebounds per game in 1991-92' was the most per game since Wilt, twenty years prior in 1971-72'. The following season, in 1992-93', Rodman missed twenty games, and still led the league in total rebounds (1,132) and RPG (18.2)!

Okay, he was an elite rebounder, maybe in the conversation for best-ever. So is Andre Drummond,[105] and I know better than anybody else that his ass isn't contributing to winning basketball. However, Rodman was truly one of the best defenders the game has ever seen. From 89' to 96', this is where he finished for Defensive Player of the Year—3rd, 1st, 1st, 2nd, 4th, 6th, 5th, 7th. With two DPOY trophies to his name, he joins the following list of players to have won the award more than once—Sidney Moncrief, Mark Eaton, Hakeem, Dikembe, Alonzo Mourning, Ben Wallace, Dwight Howard, Kawhi Leonard and Rudy Gobert. At seven First-Team

---

[105] One of the great tragedies of this NBA archeological dig for me has been coming to grips with Andre Drummond actually, truly, being one of the best rebounders ever. Through research for this and the Moses Malone profile, Drummond's rebounding figures are all but impossible to ignore. Bummer he has no other redeemable basketball qualities!!! Good Riddance.

All-Defense selections, only Bobby Jones, Pippen, Duncan, Gary Payton, MJ, Garnett and Kobe have more.

Rodman came to Detroit in 1986-87', played in 77 regular season games, and all 15 playoff games his rookie season. He then played in every single regular season and playoff game for the Pistons over the next five seasons. The Pistons fell in the Eastern Conference Finals to Bird in 1987 (Bird stole the ball (..sigh..)). Detroit then fell short in the 1988 Finals' to the Lakers (Isiah's miracle quarter on a high ankle sprain ruined by Laimbeer's phantom foul (..super sigh..)). The Pistons broke through to win back-to-back titles in 1988-89' and 1989-90'. In fact, Detroit lost a total of one game combined in the 1989 and 1990 Finals', against the Lakers and Blazers respectfully. Their real challenge in each of those postseasons was getting through Chicago in the Eastern Conference Finals. Someone had to guard MJ, and Rodman was the right guy for the job.

I'd love to give you an admonishing stat line from MJ that demonstrates how good Rodman was on him, but it's Michael Fucking Jordan. Think what Kawhi did in the 2014 Finals' and Iguodala did in 2015 Finals'—not exactly slow down LeBron, but make things hard on him, and wear him down enough to give their teams a chance to win. That was Rodman in the 1989 and 1990 Eastern Conference Finals, and in six and seven games respectively, the Pistons advanced to become champions. Without Rodman on MJ, are we sure they advance?

The ecosystem in Detroit apparently kept in check the restless, unusual side of Dennis Rodman, and as the team began to break up in the early 90's, we started seeing the stuff that we can't forget about Rodman—the hair, the piercings, the wedding dresses, the Madonna thing, all that shit. But he could still play, and he'd be productive, despite the weirdness, for the Spurs during the 1993-94' and 1994-95' seasons. Rodman was displeased in San Antonio, and he was traded to the Bulls just prior to the 1995-96' season. He then became an essential ingredient to another multi-championship run. The 1995-96' Bulls are included in any discussion about the greatest team ever, and Rodman was integral to their success. The Bulls won 72 games that season, and Rodman extended his rebounding title streak to five seasons, grabbing 14.9 per game. The Bulls lost only one game during their run through the Eastern Conference in the 1996 playoffs, but faced a legitimate challenge in the 1996 Finals' against Seattle. Look at how badly out-shot the Bulls were in those Finals':

Bulls		Supersonics
41.6%	FG%	44.5%
26.3%	3P%	31.4%
75.7%	FT%	85.1%

The Bull's FG% was the worst for a Finals' winner since the 1963-64' Celtics. Pippen was 34% from the field—good for the third-worst percentage of his 43 career playoff series'. MJ shot 41.5% from the field, the worst of all his Finals' performances, and good for *his* third-worst percentage of his 37 career playoff series'. Rodman to the rescue—he not only was the game-high rebounder in all six Finals' games, but he totaled 41 fucking offensive rebounds in this series! That's 7 per game! Rodman made countless hustle and momentum-swinging plays that allowed Chicago to overcome historically poor shooting. On top of that, he guarded Shawn Kemp during this series, preventing him from playing hero in, what the shooting stats would indicate, was the possible vanquishing of the 'unbeatable' Bulls. Kemp was still very good, and even earned 3 Finals' MVP votes at the conclusion of the series. MJ won Finals' MVP with 6 of the 11 votes, but fucking Rodman earned the 2 remaining votes! Are we sure the Bulls win the 1996 Finals' without Rodman? Totally sure?

The 1997 and 1998 Finals' triumphs over the Jazz are justly attributed to the greatness of Michael Jordan, and the seasons which MJ's legacy strutted into unprecedented territory. Rodman was damn good, serving as Chicago's primary rebounder, and exclusive annoyer of Karl Malone (to legitimate success). After the Chicago three-peat, Rodman would play sparingly for the Lakers and Mavs before retiring.

If I'm being honest, I only half-believed he should be here when I began writing the profile itself. Pritch, my stepdad, who's primarily responsible for my love of the NBA, insisted on Rodman's inclusion because of his contribution to winning, and eventually I couldn't deny the arguments he always made when we debated the claim. I kept writing it into existence, and eventually I actually started believing he belonged too.

A much different conversation than the ranking I'm making my way through here, and one that my stepdad and I have had a dozen times, is putting together the best starting five of all-time—choosing any player from any era. Pritch has always, every single time, included Dennis Rodman on his all-time starting five team. I scoffed at this for years, while I foolishly selected ball-dominant players who would never function well together (MJ, Kobe, Vince, Shaq, Hakeem—or something dumb like that). I get it now. The bottom line is that players who rebound and defend at a high level are crucial to winning championships. Rodman was a poor shooter, he was erratic, and was certainly not a talent that you would build a team around. But, he's one of the best examples of a player who does everything else for a team, wasn't concerned with receiving credit, and cared about winning on a psychopathic, nearly-MJ-esque level. You need those guys too.

Why He Belongs In This Tier? I stand by it. Surely, peddlers of impact and weighted box score stats will want my head for this, but you simply have to have players like this to win championships. Let's be clear here though, Rodman was not a run-of-the-mill hustle guy, and don't let his non-basketball noise color (no pun intended) what is undeniably true—any possible way you'd like to dissect the conversation, he's one of the best defenders of all-time, and he's one of the best rebounders of all-time.

Draymond Green

The Secret	Greatness Index	Ben Taylor Rank
86 / 100	108.06 (46th)	Not Ranked

PIPM	O-PIPM	D-PIPM	Peak—2015-16'	Wins Added
+4.89 (7th)	+1.58	+3.31	+9.75 (2nd)	97.99 (69th)

Playoff PER	Playoff Win Shares	Playoff O-Win Shares	Playoff D-Win Shares
16.92 (118th)	14.02 (50th)	6.10 (79th)	7.92 (28th)

If we'd been prepared for the pace-and-space revolution that tipped off during the 2014 Finals', teams would have been drafting accordingly—seeking out players with fewer weaknesses, instead of continuing to put more energy into hiding blemishes. None of us could have known, looking at Draymond Green coming out of Michigan State, that he'd become the prototype for what a big should be by the end of the 2010s. If I'd told you that this fringe NBA player/prospect would make two All-NBA teams, win a Defensive Player of the Year award, and be a key contributor on three championship-winning teams, you'd ask me if I'd taken my meds that day and suggest that a higher dose might be required. What if I told you he'd become the evolutionary version of Bill Russell, and the second-most important player on the greatest team of all-time? Before you kindly ask me to *Get The Fuck Outta Here*, just answer me the following question. As you know by now, I'm big on clubs or lists that players belong to—I went pretty deep on Nash's profile in this direction. Riddle me this—how many bigs in the history of the NBA are a perennial threat for Defensive Player of the Year, and also perennially leading their team in assists?

I really should hate Draymond. I grew up, and still am, a big supporter of The University of Michigan football and basketball teams. I grew up in metro-Detroit, but was far too dumb to even apply to U of M, and settled for Western Michigan. But just like the dumber kids around the United States who go to smaller schools, you tend to have a bigger in-state school that you root for, and of course, one that you root against. That's been Michigan State for me, and boy did I hate Draymond Green in college. Cocky, loud and obnoxious, Draymond was almost too easy to dislike. Like most people (and NBA front offices), I figured he would fizzle out as an NBA player.

Lucky for Draymond, The Warriors, the NBA and for basketball itself, Draymond found himself drafted in 2012 by a team that was incubating something special. After two seasons of calibrating his game for the professional level, the fuse would really be lit during the 2014-15' season. This was Steve Kerr's first season as coach, and he started experimenting more with Draymond at center—Kerr deployed variations for 200 minutes of the regular season:

	Minutes	Def. Rating^	Net Rating*
Steph, Klay, Iggy, Harrison Barnes, Draymond	102	91.9	+21.8
Livingston, Klay, Iggy, Harrison Barnes, Draymond	30	91.1	+22.0
Steph, Livingston, Klay, Harrison Barnes, Draymond	27	92.1	+38.1
Steph, Livingston, Iggy, Harrison Barnes, Draymond	21	79.2	+68.3
Steph, Livingston, Klay, Iggy, Draymond	20	83.3	+20.0

^Defensive Rating—Measures the number of points surrendered per 100 possessions.
*Net Rating—Measures a team's overall point differential per 100 possessions.

These Warriors posted similar efficiency numbers with Andrew Bogut at center during the 2014-15' season, but knowing they could unleash Draymond at center could prove immensely important in the right playoff matchup. Sure enough, when the Warriors found themselves down 2-1 in the 2015 Finals', with Hercules-mode LeBron eyeing another championship, Kerr's brain trust[106] moved to start Draymond at center for games 4, 5 and 6 (all victories). The success of this strategy for Golden State is surely in part to the historically efficient shooters they have. However, the main liability you assume in trotting out a smaller lineup is the potential for glaring mismatches on the defensive end. But with Draymond, The Warriors had someone who could defend 3's, 4's and 5's at an all-league level, and more-than-capably defend guards on a switch. Oh yeah, he could also control the tempo of the game with the ball in his hands, and run your offense from the center position.

The revolution was in full swing during the 2015-16' season. The Warriors won their first 24 games of the season, and posted an NBA-record 73 wins. This is recent enough to where most of us remember it, but it's still ridiculous to wrap your head around. This was the first of a three-season window for Draymond that paints a vividly clear picture of his impact on the Warriors dynastic success:

	Points	Rebounds	Assists	Blocks	Steals
2015-16'	14.0	9.5	7.4	1.4	1.5
2016-17'	10.2	7.9	7.0	1.4	2.0
2017-18'	11.0	7.6	7.3	1.3	1.4

---

[106] Nick U'Ren, who Kerr has referred to as his 'chief of staff', is credited with the original idea to start Iguodala instead of Bogut for game four of the 2015 Finals'. The credit belongs to Kerr for being flexible enough to embrace the ideas of everyone around him.

I have another exclusive club that Draymond belongs to .. are you ready for this? Seven times in the history of the NBA has a player averaged at least 7 assists, 7 rebounds, 1 block and 1 steal over the course of a season—three of those seasons belong to young LeBron in 2007-08', 2008-09' & 2009-10', one of those belong to Scottie Pippen in 1991-92', *the other three belong to Draymond Green in the seasons listed above!* 2015-16' for Draymond was truly a triumph, and created one of the most unique statistical profiles ever put together. Check out where Draymond ranked league-wide in this hodge-podge of stat categories for that season:

- Minutes Played (11th)
- Rebounds Per Game (13th)
- Assists Per Game (7th)
- Defensive Win Shares (6th)

- Box Plus/Minus (9th)
- Win Shares Per 48 (15th)
- Effective Field Goal % (17th)
- Total Blocks (16th)

The Warriors assaulted the playoffs and found themselves with a 3-1 lead over the Cavaliers in the Finals'. Bummer is, Draymond would exceed the flagrant fouls threshold in game four, and infamously be suspended for game five.[107] The Cavs evened up the series, and despite Draymond having the best game of his career in game seven (32 points, 15 rebounds, 9 assists on 11-15, 6-8 3P), Golden State lost to LeBron and Kyrie's heroics.

Two weeks later, Kevin Durant committed to joining the Warriors. With the exception of a few stressful minutes against Houston in 2018 during their Western Conference Final matchup, Golden State would largely breeze through the league on their way to back-to-back championships. Because, well, they were a 73-win team that added the best scorer in the league. Draymond continued to Draymond, but was a little less Draymond-ey when the Warriors elected to grant iso-possessions to their prized small forward. Injuries plagued the Warriors throughout the 2018-19' season, and spiked in the Finals' against the Raptors when Klay and Durant went down. Nonetheless, no team has made five consecutive Finals' since Russell's Celtics, and there's no way it was possible without Draymond Green.

I'm serious, I really should hate the guy—the Michigan State stuff, on top of the fact that the Warriors continued to beat LeBron in the Finals'. When you're the second-most important player on a dynasty as prolific as the Warriors have been, you need to be appropriately rewarded. Now, I know you might scoff at that assertion, especially after watching how good Durant made the Warriors in those fateful 11 minutes he played against the Raptors. But, none of this happens without Draymond. He has Predator-level defensive instincts. I'm not exaggerating—Draymond's advantages defensively equate to others using their normal sight, while he has night-vision, and body-heat sensors to know what the offense is doing next. He's the walking-talking exception to the rule that some players are 'too *this*' to play this position, or 'too *that*' to play another position.

---

[107] Way too many people cite this suspension as a means of discrediting Cleveland's comeback, and subsequent championship. The Cavs still had to win twice at Oracle (where Golden State had lost a total of five times in the previous two seasons), and plenty of other things had to happen for the Warriors to lose. Like LeBron going 41, 16 and 7 / 41, 8 and 11 / 27, 11 and 11. Just sayin'. Kyrie was superb also—I'll never forget his 17-24 shooting dissertation in game five.

What we have to appreciate about the Warriors is that all of their players embraced a spread-out, team dynamic. The nucleus of Steph, Klay, Draymond, Iggy and KD—in addition to their lesser players, Livingston, Bogut, Barbosa, West, Ezeli, JaVale—they all accepted the uniform goal of championships. As great as those players in the nucleus are/were, no one required the disproportionate attention or admiration that would typically accompany them on basically every other team in history. When the buzz around KD leaving for New York swirled to the point where he began behaving as if he were above that singular uniform goal, he was swiftly called out by Draymond.[108]

I think a fair criticism of Draymond's profile was the good fortune he's had in playing with such dynamic shooters and offensive players. Would his multitude of skills be as relevant if he'd not played alongside Steph, Klay and Durant? No. But, it's because Golden State agreed to such an egalitarian state of mind that allowed all of their players to maximize their individual skills, and if you were to pull out one of the players from their nucleus, the team's dynastic upside would suffer substantially. If the lower body of the Warriors dynasty is the unprecedented shooting of Klay and Steph, the upper body is KD and Iggy, that would make Draymond the core. The connective tissue that allows the different parts to operate at their full potential. The muscle group that does all of the little things, but can also take on a bigger role when it's required. Draymond's been referred to as *the heart* of the Warriors success, but I think that lazy assertion is too often reserved for the guy who tries the hardest, and usually lacks playmaking skills. Draymond is the core strength of the Golden State dynasty—allowing the weapons to be weapons, picking up the slack when necessary, on top of doing all the cliché little things required for championship success.

Because so many NBA teams are trying to find their hyper-versatile defensive stopper, I hear a maddening number of aspirational Draymond-comparisons when NBA prospects are being appraised. It truly does make me mad, because Draymond's skill set is that unique. Even in the Zion profile, I heard several draft experts describing him as a possible 'Draymond-esque' defender. I like Zion to be a massively impactful NBA player, but let's get a grip. It's disrespectful how often this comparison is made, to a player whose defensive profile is as unique and impactful as anyone in history.

Speaking of impact—I think Draymond's historically high PIPM score is a testament to how important advanced metrics are. Do I think Draymond's impact on the game is worthy of the metric's seventh-best-ever score? No. But do counting stats measure the totality of Draymond's impact on a basketball game? Not even close. Draymond's PIPM rank is the numerical argument for why he is on this list—his seventh-overall defensive rating might be pretty accurate, factoring in his versatility. I also found the cumulative postseason Offensive Win Shares very telling, among the Warriors nucleus players—Steph (12.31 / 21st all-time) Draymond (6.10 / 79th all-time) Iggy (5.93 / 84th all-time) Klay (4.70 / 121st all-time).[109]

It never seemed like Steph needed a Pippen, given Golden State's democratic, all-for-one ethos. But, he did. Klay Thompson is an amazing shooting guard. Kevin Durant is one of

---

[108] This might be my favorite Draymond moment. It really says everything about Draymond and the original core of the Warriors. Dismissing the fact that KD was a top-three player in the world, Draymond called him a 'Bitch', and didn't relent from reminding Durant what they'd accomplished before his arrival. Amazing.

[109] Excluding Durant, because he's played most of his postseason career on a different team. Plus, Iguodala had played a lot of playoff games before coming to the Warriors (41).

the ten best scorers of all-time. Andre Iguodala is a marvel of versatility in his own right. But, if not for Draymond's variety of skills, we never would have seen these players showcase their abilities on the highest stage. Without Draymond setting the table, is Golden State attractive enough for Durant to come? Does Iguodala ascend and slow down LeBron in the 2015 Finals'? Is it even possible to count how many open looks the above players got because their 'defensive stopper' turned a defensive rebound into a fast break?

The air-tight orbit that a defender has to maintain around Steph Curry makes defending him on an island an excruciating effort. Couple that required effort with the defensive no-win situation of the Draymond Green-Steph Curry pick-and-roll—[guard high on Steph, Draymond short-rolls and feasts on a short-handed defensive formation **OR** honor Draymond, and tempt the greatest shooter of all-time on a shot he could make with his eyes closed]—now you've uncovered Steve Kerr's ultimate trump card, and perhaps the most unstoppable play in modern NBA history. The peanut butter and goddam jelly of the Warriors success. And it's all because their center, an all-time defender, passes like a point guard, runs like a wing, and wants to win more than he wants to breathe.

Why He Belongs In This Tier? Because he's the second-most important player to one of the great NBA dynasties. He doesn't walk, talk or play like a Pippen, but in concept, he is absolutely a Pippen. Actually, he does play a little like Pippen, but you know what I mean! Dynasties aren't built by one player, and while I acknowledge that the Warriors, to their credit, built theirs on more balanced contributions than the traditional model of championship success (usually, it's one or two players, surrounded by other guys). But, I refuse to believe that outside of Steph, there isn't a more integral player to Golden State's success than Draymond.

David Robinson

The Secret	Greatness Index	Ben Taylor Rank
96 / 100	166.56 (19th)	15th

PIPM	O-PIPM	D-PIPM	Peak—1991-92'	Wins Added
+6.14 (1st)	+2.28	+3.86	+8.43 (5th)	215.65 (11th)

Playoff PER	Playoff Win Shares	Playoff O-Win Shares	Playoff D-Win Shares
23.02 (16th)	17.52 (29th)	7.83 (49th)	9.69 (14th)

Bill Simmons once likened David Robinson's physique, posture and overall build to that of an aircraft carrier elegantly marauding its way through the ocean—I've never been able to get that out of my head. Seemingly forged intricately out of molten lava at the base of an erupting volcano, David Robinson's frame was on another level during his playing days. But Simmons' comparison wasn't just admiration of the still aesthetic of David Robinson's build, it was mostly illustrating how well a 7'1" 240 pound man could move around and run without the clunkiness of posture that's typically observed from big men who play basketball. He was truly a seven-foot Greek statue that could easily get up and down the court. *The Admiral*, a nickname stemming from his service as an officer in the Navy, utilized his stellar frame to bruise and punish opponents for the entirety of his career. What a lot of people don't know about Robinson is that he also boasts a bruising and punishing advanced statistical profile.

One of the great joys in my life is looking up a player's *Basketball Reference* profile, scrolling to their Advanced breakout, and seeing a preponderance of statistics in bold type—indicating that the player led the league in that figure for that season. The Admiral is the first profile in my ranking where there is a filthy amount of bold type in their *Basketball Reference* Advanced breakout. I was truly shocked to find that Robinson led the league in PER for three straight seasons from 1993-94' through 1995-96'.[110] He led the NBA in VORP over that same

---

[110] Fun bar trivia question—only seven players have ever done it, can you name them? George Mikan, Bob Pettit, Wilt Chamberlain (7 out of 8 seasons from 60' through 68', Kareem (did it twice, and 8 of 10 seasons in the 70's), MJ (7 seasons straight from 87' through 93'), Shaq (5 seasons straight 98' through 02'), LeBron (6 seasons straight 08' through 13').

three-year window, and holds the tenth-best VORP figure of all-time. In the eight seasons from 1993-94' through 2000-01', he had the league's best WS/48 five separate times, and maintains the second-best all-time WS/48 (only MJ has a higher figure). In the eight seasons from 1991-92' through 1998-99', Robinson had the highest BPM six times, and holds the fifth-best all-time BPM figure. Defensive Rating isn't always a great individual measurement, except when you lead the league in the figure five separate times, like David Robinson did, helping him to claim the fourth-best individual Defensive Rating figure of all-time (95.65). Did I mention that he's number one all-time in overall PIPM? Yeah. In the land of the immortals, David Robinson emerges with the *best ever* PIPM score. The metric really rewards hugely impactful defenders who have any semblance of an offensive game, and Robinson had more than that. He had a back-to-the-basket game, a nice face-up jump shot and was an excellent finisher. David Robinson .. advanced statistic darling .. a thing like that?

He has the conventional counting stats covered too, my friends. He's unquestionably one of the great shot-blockers of all-time, holding both the fourth-best Blocks Per Game figure (2.99), and sixth-most total blocks (2,954). Because of his propensity to block a lot of shots, he occasionally threatened to record a quadruple-double[111]—which he ultimately did, February 17th, 1994, against my Detroit Pistons (34 points, 10 rebounds, 10 assists & 10 blocks). A few months later, Robinson scored 71 points against the Clippers, joining the exclusive list[112] to have scored at least 70 points in an NBA game. What's kind of crazy, as I continue to rattle off stats and you all try not to fall asleep, is that he didn't accumulate numbers that illuminated just one or two aspects of his game—his stat profile illustrates a hugely versatile and powerfully capable NBA player.

Remember in *The Office* when Michael promised a bunch of third graders he would pay for their college, then only told them he would *not* be able to pay for their college *after* they graduated high school [S6:E12—*Scott's Tots*]? Classic.

David Robinson actually did this! In 1991, he visited a group of 94 fifth graders at Gates Elementary school in San Antonio, and promised them a $2,000 scholarship each, if they were able to graduate from high school. In 1998, when 50 members of the group made good on graduating, he surprised them by presenting an $8,000 scholarship to each graduate. Dude actually pulled the *Scott's Tots* move! Unreal!

The NBA Community Assist Award started as a monthly award for the 2001-02' season, then became an annual award for the 2011-12'. As you could probably guess, the league awards players whose community service efforts go above and beyond. So, what does it say about David Robinson's community service efforts that each recipient also receives a plaque in David Robinson's name? Inscribed on the plaque—*Following the standard set by NBA Legend David Robinson, who improved the community piece by piece*. The Admiral has always cared about giving back, and it's not to say that he gets extra points for it here, but there isn't an especially long list of NBA players who genuinely care about community service (apart from the positive optics it provides their brand).

---

[111] Another fun bar trivia question—only four players have ever done it, can you name them? The Admiral (94'), Hakeem Olajuwon (90'), Nate Thurmond (74') & Alvin Robertson (86'). Again, steals and blocks only started being tracked in 1973-74', so Wilt and Bill Russell alone probably had a shit-load of un-recognized quadruple-doubles.
[112] *Another* fun bar trivia question—only six players have ever done it, can you name them? The Admiral, Elgin Baylor, Wilt Chamberlain, David Thompson, Devin Booker & Kobe Bryant.

Robinson's rookie year[113] of 1989-90' was pretty fucking ridiculous. The Spurs won 56 games, and Robinson got 24 points, 12 rebounds and 3.9 blocks—Christ. The next four seasons would see the Spurs enjoy relatively static success (55 wins, 47 wins, 49 wins, 55 wins & falling short of the Western Conference Final in each postseason). David Robinson continued to hang preposterous numbers.

1994-95' was a little different. The Spurs acquired Avery Johnson before the season, who gave them much better play from the point than they had been getting. It would be (MY GUY) Dennis Rodman's second season in San Antonio—he was now fully comfortable in his role, and in the heart of his seven-season-long reign as the league's top rebounder. As with every team that acquired Rodman's services, it allowed them to be flexible in their lineups, and opened up David Robinson to absolutely crush his opponents. The Admiral got 27 points, 10 rebounds and 3 blocks (on .602 True Shooting, 29.1 PER and .273 Win Shares Per 48), and took home the league MVP for his efforts. The Spurs also won 62 games, and finally broke into the Western Conference Final, where Hakeem's defending-champion Rockets awaited them. The Spurs would not only be outmatched as a team, but admittedly, David Robinson was also outmatched. Hakeem Olajuwon, at his peak, which is conceivably this very 1995 Western Conference Final, was a world-*ender* in every facet of the game. Robinson's numbers vs. Olajuwon's numbers in that 1995 Western Conference Final:

	Points	Rebounds	Assists	Blocks	TS%	USG%
Robinson	23.8	11.3	2.7	2.2	.553	28.5
Olajuwon	35.3	12.5	5.0	4.2	.590	36.8

Hakeem ate his lunch in this series, and would get 39, 17 and 5 blocks in the game six close-out game. The Rockets had a better team, and were championship-hardened when this series tipped off. Does it matter that Robinson was out-dueled, in his MVP season, by a player who played the same position as him? Not really. The consensus is that Hakeem was a greater player overall, and I would tend to agree. The outcome of this series was relatively predictable, and says as much about Hakeem as it does The Admiral. It also matters that Hakeem had a Clyde Drexler, a quality second star, and Robinson was still lacking one. The Spurs won 59 games in 1995-96' with the same strategy, but lost in the second round. Then, an injury-riddled, lost season in 1996-97' forever changed the trajectory of the Spurs franchise.

Up to this point, David Robinson had led the Spurs in Win Shares each season since he entered the league. But a pair of injuries would limit him to just six games in 1996-97'. This resulted in the Spurs only winning 20 games, and Will Perdue taking over the Win Shares lead for the Spurs (Yeeeesh).[114] What a year to bottom out[115]—the Spurs owned their own pick, and while their 20 wins were third-worst in the league, they still won the lottery and held the first

---

[113] The Spurs actually drafted Robinson first-overall in the 1987 draft, but had to wait two years for his active duty to play out, which San Antonio was fully aware of at the time. Let that sink in for a minute. How good a prospect must *The Admiral* have been for the Spurs to be like *Eh, we'll blow our first overall pick on a guy, even though he won't be available for the next two full seasons..* WTF! No way that happens today. Amazingly, David Robinson was fully worth the wait.

[114] Putting to bed the classic barstool argument of what would happen if Will Perdue had his own team.

[115] A lot of worthy speculation suggests the Spurs bottomed-out on purpose—I'll leave that up to you.

pick. It's kind of incredible, because it was a pretty flat draft overall. Only five players ever exceeded 10 VORP in their career and become truly meaningful NBA players—Tim Duncan (1st pick), Chauncey Billups (3rd pick), Tracy McGrady (9th pick), Derek Anderson (13th pick) & Stephen Jackson (42nd pick). Duncan was a generational prospect, and the Spurs didn't blink in their appraisal of him. New coach Greg Popovich had taken over mid-way through the 1996-97' Tank-a-thon/Will Perdue showcase. Popovich immediately connected with Duncan, and the Spurs were already a formidable team in 1997-98'—they won 56 games, which meant that they'd pulled off two of the great all-time single-season turnarounds in less than a decade. San Antonio would sputter and exit the playoffs in the second round, but the team's new duo had both averaged 20 & 10 for the season, and the future looked very bright.

The Spurs absolutely dominated in Duncan's second season. They held the league's best record during the lockout-shortened regular season, and only lost two games throughout their stellar championship-winning 1999 postseason run. They smoked young KG in five, swept the *almost-ready* Lakers in round two, swept a really good Portland team in the Western Conference Final, then finally whooped the New York Knicks in five before hoisting the Larry O'Brian trophy for the first time in franchise history. Tim Duncan was a revelation, and indisputably the 1A star on this title team. David Robinson served as a legitimate 1B, and proved vital to their dominance. Duncan earned Finals' MVP honors over the course of a rock-fight[116] of a Finals' against the Ewing-less Knicks. But David Robinson was a champion, and a twenty-year run of excellence from the San Antonio Spurs franchise was officially underway.

All of the Popovich-isms that we've come to admire—team dinners, signing the perfect mercenary veteran at the perfect time and playing them at their perfect position, finding international gems in the draft, adapting team philosophy to maximize player effectiveness, unprompted yet timely and tasteful liberal-leaning talking points, winning 50 games at a death & taxes-level frequency, conjuring and sustaining a culture with foundational roots in selflessness and commitment to excellence—they were all birthed during the Twin Towers-era Spurs. Duncan was the perfect young and talented understudy to bring these principles into the future for San Antonio. However, it was Robinson who established and owned what it meant to commit yourself to excellence. How to demonstrate tangible and intangible habits that permeate positively throughout his teammates, coaches and front office. Remember in *The Wire* Season One when D'Angelo tried to school Poot, Wallace and Bodie about how the game was to be played? D'Angelo was a rather tragic character who was stuck in the game and was just realizing it before it was too late. But, you could tell that passing on the best practices to the young-ins, particularly Bodie, who obviously possessed the most potential, really energized him. It wasn't that David Robinson wanted out of the league (like D'Angelo), but taking Duncan under his wing and teaching the other young players about how you were to conduct yourself as a professional certainly re-energized his career. Not to mention, would be one of the key ingredients to the Spurs institutional success of the past twenty years.

Unfortunately for the Spurs, the Lakers were officially 'ready' come the next season, and embargoed Western Conference Championships for the 1999-00', 2000-01' and 2001-02' seasons. Kobe & Shaq won three straight championships and eliminated the Spurs in two of

---

[116] Talk about how far we've come in the NBA—neither team exceeded 100 points throughout the series, and only the Spurs in game four broke 90 points!

those three postseasons. The Spurs were really, really good—winning 53, 58 and 58 games in the seasons of those Laker titles, and Duncan ascended to MVP status in 2001-02' behind a stat line of 25.5 points, 12.7 rebounds and 2.5 blocks on .576 True Shooting and 27.0 PER. But the Lakers were too good and too deep. Robinson's minutes and stat lines were taking gradual steps back each season, but he remained a formidable player, and the Spurs had one more run in them.

With a new generation of talent to support Duncan and Robinson, the Spurs were dominant in 2002-03'. Duncan repeated as MVP, Manu Ginóbili was fantastic off the bench, and 20-year-old Tony Parker was manning the point like a crafty veteran. They earned 60 victories in the regular season, and entered the playoffs as the overall first-seed where they vanquished a gauntlet of quality teams to reach the Finals' again.

- o 1st round – defeat Garnett's Timberwolves, on the eve of KG's MVP season
- o 2nd round—defeat the Lakers and end their championship run
- o 3rd round—defeat a really good Mavs team (less Dirk after game three)

In the 2003 Finals', San Antonio out-muscled the New Jersey Nets for their second championship. Tim Duncan dominated, and David Robinson gave them efficient minutes. Hampered by a persistent back issue, and now a two-time champion, David Robinson decided to call it quits after the 2002-03' championship campaign. He played 14 NBA seasons, all with the Spurs, and retired with a bevvy of accomplishments. He'd serve as an integral character in the establishment of the *San Antonio Way*—eventually joining the likes of the St. Louis Cardinals, New England Patriots & Pittsburgh Penguins as the NBA's model franchise that always seemed to get it right, year after year. If that intangible fluff doesn't do it for you, Robinson boasts a statistical resume for the ages. I elaborated on his advanced stuff, but riddle me this my friends—how many players in the history of the NBA have all of the following to their name (?):

- o Total Rebounding Title (1990-91')
- o Defensive Player of The Year (1991-92')
- o Total Block Title (1991-92')
- o Scoring Title (1993-94')
- o League MVP (1994-95')
- o NBA Champion (1998-99' & 2002-03')

Exactly one player.

Why He Belongs In This Tier? David Robinson was a massively impactful NBA player. Traditional numbers reflect it, advanced numbers reflect it, and the tape not only reflects an aircraft carrier of an athletic specimen maneuvering around the basketball court, but also a really smart and skilled player. He was missing a move or two around the hoop, which manifested during the postseason when having high-percentage, go-to shots is appreciably more important. It might have also been nice to have another star captain the go-to scoring role, a role into which Robinson was miscast. Robinson also wasn't as prolific as some of his historical contemporaries. Nevertheless, Robinson has one of the best profiles in Tier III. I flirted with moving him up, but concluded that without the cosmic acquisition of Tim Duncan in 1997, Robinson probably doesn't have a championship. Duncan was also definitely the best player on both of Robinson's championships. Despite a simply menacing statistical profile, and you know how I feel about that, it's just not quite enough to get into Tier II.

John Havlicek

	The Secret	Greatness Index	Ben Taylor Rank
	99 / 100	255.81 (9th)	32nd

Playoff PER	Playoff Win Shares	Playoff O-Win Shares	Playoff D-Win Shares
17.51 (101st)	19.27 (26th)	10.94 (29th)	8.34 (25th)

"He was the best all-around player I ever saw"

Bill Russell

Take it for what it's worth—John Havlicek *was* Russell's teammate from when he was drafted into the dynasty in 1962-63', until Russell retired in 1968-69'. They'd win six championships in their seven seasons playing together. Havlicek's multitude of talents gave fresh legs to the tyrannical stranglehold Boston held over the league in the 1960's. As great as Bill Russell was, he far from won all of those championships by himself, and it's my estimation that Havlicek was the second-most important ingredient to their dynastic success. Further proof of Havlicek's greatness was his integral role in 1974 and 1976 Celtic championships, long after Russell had retired. You might be fatigued by profiles of Russell-era players. So, before you check out of this one, let me be clear in saying that John Havlicek—an 8-time NBA champion, 74' Finals' MVP, the Celtics all-time leader in points, minutes and games played, was also *8-and-fucking-0 in the NBA Finals'*. In short, when Russell made that seemingly bold proclamation about Havlicek, he wasn't giving a soft compliment to a long-time teammate and friend, he might have been making a pretty honest assessment.

Auerbach didn't really know what he had with Havlicek when he arrived in Celtics camp in 1962. The Ohio State product was also an NFL draft pick of the Cleveland Browns, and even had a future as a pro baseball player, after garnering favor from some of the prominent clubhouses of the era. The weird thing about being drafted by Cleveland, is that Havlicek didn't play a down of football in college! That's right, Paul Brown, one of the great football visionaries of all-time, drafted John Havlicek to play wide receiver despite the last time Havlicek had played a down of football was when he was quarterbacking his high school team! Now, I know there is a fairly modern trend of basketball-oriented athletes being drafted to play tight-end or some kind of receiver, but even for the era, this was pretty epic. Apparently Woody Hayes, then Ohio State football coach and certifiable crazy guy, hounded Havlicek throughout college to play football. Havlicek relented as an undergrad, but he would accept Paul Brown's challenge and try out for the Cleveland Browns.[117] Despite being cut, it was a testament to his athleticism that he'd been afforded the opportunity. He narrowed his focus to basketball and his obligation to the Boston Celtics. What would follow was a brilliant NBA career, largely fueled by his exceptionally well-rounded athletic profile.

Red Auerbach built the Russell-era Celtics dynasty on pace, defense, cohesion and versatility. From the center position, Russell's very basketball DNA is woven together with these principles. From the wing position, and from when he first stepped foot in the league, Havlicek embraced and excelled at those same principles. Through the 60s, *Hondo* (his nickname, which stemmed from a John Wayne flick) fully embraced the role of the sixth man, while continually being among the team's leaders in minutes and points. In this way, think of what Manu Ginóbili was able to do for the Spurs for almost two decades. Because Havlicek was such a tireless athlete on both ends of the court, he'd obtain the reputation for wearing out his opponent. Red was a firm believer in the importance of a versatile[118] and athletic sixth man. After Boston's leading scorer in just his second season, Havlicek quickly grabbed sole possession of the spot, and would remain there until Russell retired and a starting role was required.

Unlike Manu, who was assigned the sixth man role in part because his style of play would lend itself to injuries, Havlicek would both play heavy minutes, and remain impossibly durable. He played 80+ games 11 times in his 16-season career. He'd never play fewer than 71, and he played all 82 on 5 separate occasions. He would finish his career averaging 36 minutes per game, despite coming off the bench the first half of his career. In the 1970-71' and 1971-72' post-Russell seasons, this guy would play 81 and 82 games respectively, and average 45 minutes per game! Load management be damned!

Havlicek was a really good defender, as evidenced by his 8 All-Defense selections. What makes those especially interesting and of consequential value is that they came in seasons 7 through 14, of his 16-season career (All-Defensive teams weren't selected prior to the 1968-69' season). Even factoring the context of the era, it's impressive that he was a perennial all-league defender during the second half of his career—definitely not a common trend, even among the best defenders of all-time. Furthermore, I mentioned earlier that it was only in the 1973-74' season that steal and block numbers began being tallied. In the first two seasons of those numbers being available, Havlicek's 12th and 13th in the NBA, he would average about 1.5 steals

---

[117] An amazing side note was that the NFL continued to try and get Havlicek to drop basketball for Football. In 1966, Art Modell would again try to pry Havlicek away from basketball with a lucrative contract offer. Hondo enjoyed winning championships too much to leave Boston, but it creates an amazing question—how many times in history has inter-sport tampering been a problem?? My guy was such a good athlete that other professional sports leagues wouldn't leave him alone!

[118] Havlicek's playoff Win Shares (19.27) don't stand especially high all-time (25th). However, the fact that they're so evenly balanced between the offensive and defensive contributions is very telling of his versatility. He'd be an excellent player in the modern era, where weaknesses are routinely played off the court in the postseason.

per game. Conservatively expanding those numbers back into his physical prime would suggest really high steal-rates for a player who was, by all accounts, a relentless defender.[119]

So far we're talking about a secondary or tertiary contributor to dynastic success, someone who's a little Manu-ish, a little Pippen-ey in his dynamic versatility. Maybe even just a sprinkle of Draymond-esque in the way his conditioning allowed him to control the tempo of a game. But what about what he was able to do on his own?

I mentioned Russell retired after the epic 1969 Finals' (which will probably be mentioned 100+ times before the book's conclusion), but *Hondo* played almost another decade for the Celtics beyond the Russell-era, and he was really good during that time. After a few rebuilding years post-Russell, Havlicek and MVP-level center, Dave Cowens, pushed the Celtics back into title contention during the 1972-73' season—they won 68 games and forced the eventual champion New York Knicks to a seventh game in the Eastern Conference Final. Havlicek separated his shoulder in game three, and after sitting out a game, gutted out the final three games with barely any function in his right arm. Different times, amirite? The narrow seventh-game defeat would provide ample motivation for the Celtics the following season.

Despite a less dominating regular season, Boston would make their way to the Finals', where a young Kareem and a mostly-cooked Oscar awaited them. A brutal seven-game series ensued, and despite a masterful Kareem performance, the Celtics had more answers than the Bucks. In 1973-74', Havlicek led the team in scoring during the regular season, during the playoffs, and again in the Finals', and was justly awarded his first and only Finals' MVP trophy. With the merger pending and the NBA sputtering a bit, the Celtics remained highly competitive and were able to win another championship at the conclusion of the 1975-76' season—Havlicek was still an important contributor to this title, having logged the third-most points and minutes during their Finals' victory over the Suns, but he was definitely regressing athletically. These two titles are important though. He was the best, or second-best player on the 74' title team, and was an important contributor to the 76' title team—long after the Russell dynasty had ended, and legitimate evidence of his skills yielding championship-level success.

John Havlicek, Tom Sanders and K.C. Jones were all members of the Russell dynasty, and all three went 8-0 in the NBA Finals'. They're tied for the most Finals' victories without a loss (Bill Russell, that bum, went 11-1). Behind them—Robert Horry (7-0), MJ (6-0), Pippen (6-0), and several at 5-0. The difference, and I know I'm kicking the shit out of this horse, is that Hondo was the only one of his three Boston teammates to win titles without Russell on the roster. Before you scoff at what an uncompetitive landscape the league was in, let me just say that three of Havlicek's Finals' victories came in seven-game series', and another three of them came in six-game series. Not to mention, en route to many of these Finals' series, Boston had to vanquish historically great players and teams on their own side of the bracket—Oscar's Cincinnati Royals pushed Boston to seven games in the 1963 playoffs, Wilt's 76ers lost an iconic

---

[119] Steals aren't a perfect measure of a player's defense, of course, but I'm just trying to say that he was a more comprehensive defender, whose play likely yielded steals within the confines of his team's defensive scheme. Opposed to a Monta Ellis or late-years Kobe, who would sell out disproportionately for steals.

seven-game series[120] to Boston in the 1965 playoffs, then again in the 1968 playoffs[121] Boston would outlast Wilt's 76ers in a grueling seven-game set. On top of that, Boston had to go through Jerry West and Elgin Baylor in five separate Finals' victories. That's why I'll always stand up for the Boston dynasty—they didn't always roll through their competition, but they were virtually always the last ones standing.

Put a pin in that one, as we'll dive even deeper when Bill Russell comes up. But for now, let's agree that Havlicek was integral to that success. Bob Cousy was also important in the late 50s and early 60s titles, but he didn't win any championships until Russell arrived. Sam Jones was the most consistent offensive player across the Russell dynasty, but there is no evidence of him winning outside that dynamic, and he wasn't the overall player *Hondo* was. Havlicek carried the torch for Boston and bridged the gap until Boston's second-greatest player arrived in 1979.

Why He Belongs In This Tier? He's the ultimate example of a winning player, and when thrust into primary or secondary creator status, he still succeeded at a high-level. There's an argument out there for him to be upgraded to Tier II given the historic championship numbers, but I think the rational move is to dilute many of those successes and attribute them to the common denominator of the Celtic's success in the 60s. Some people may go the other way on his profile and say that he wasn't required often enough to take the reigns of his team. Furthermore, his primary individual successes came in the mid-70s, a pretty weird decade overall for the league. However, I think he demonstrated skills that come at a premium, regardless of the era they're being showcased in. The league has gone through so many trends over the years, but somehow the principles that built the first great dynasty always re-surface. There might not have been a three-point line back then, but moving the ball, competing on both ends, and sacrificing individual accomplishments for winning will always be tenants of championship-level success in the NBA. Havlicek rode those principles to unprecedented success, even after the league's greatest dynasty had ended.

---

[120] If you're not 60+ years old, your only association with John Havlicek might be the famous radio call from long-time Boston announcer Johnny Most, in which he yells in ecstasy 'HAVLICEK STOLE THE BALL'. Which described Havlicek's iconic steal of an inbounds play, with five seconds left in game seven of this 1965 Eastern Final against Wilt and the 76ers.
[121] Havlicek led all players in the 1968 postseason in both points and assists.

Kevin Durant

The Secret	Greatness Index	Ben Taylor Rank
68 / 100	175.27 (17th)	23rd

PIPM	O-PIPM	D-PIPM	Peak—2009-10'	Wins Added
+3.75 (23rd)	+3.88	-0.13	+6.15 (23rd)	149.79 (25th)

Playoff PER	Playoff Win Shares	Playoff O-Win Shares	Playoff D-Win Shares
24.42 (7th)	23.09 (14th)	16.67 (10th)	6.42 (43rd)

I've found it exceedingly difficult to properly rate Kevin Durant's legacy—so I figured it would make a doozy of a profile to close out Tier III. It's clear to me that Durant is a guy who has grappled with his own self-image, and that self-perception gets blurry through the lens of celebrity—and then intensely magnified under the pressure of growing your legacy as an NBA player. After nine seasons with a franchise that watched him grow up, he had the chance to leave. He opted to join the ready-made, championship-contending Golden State Warriors, believing all-but-guaranteed championships would validate his greatness. There wasn't a precedent for a player that good going to a team that good, so he took some shit for it. But he won some trophies, in fact, he became one of just 12 guys to have won 2 Finals' MVPs. Yet, many people, myself included, have a hard time not asking—*are we sure the Warriors wouldn't have won back-to-back titles without him?*

In *Game of Thrones'* second season, after nine years with the Stark family, and on the behalf of Robb Stark, Theon Greyjoy returns to his home of Pyke, in hopes of striking an agreement with his father, Balon Greyjoy. Theon, a character who fought his own battle with the complexities of self-identity, was eager to impress his father. Upon appraisal of his son's clothing, Balon asks if Theon had paid the *Golden Price* for the extravagant attire, or the *Iron Price*. He was essentially asking if he'd paid for the clothing (*Golden Price*), or had he taken it for himself (*Iron Price*):

The golden bauble around your neck, did you pay the Iron price or the Gold? Did you pull it from the neck of a corpse you made, or did you buy it? Iron or Gold?

Kevin Durant paid the Golden Price for his trophies. By succumbing to the very voices that kept him up at night, he purchased a route to adding prominent layers to his legacy. It also shouldn't come as a surprise to KD that the trophies didn't quell what was ailing him—what we've always believed was missing from Durant's personality was an ability to accept himself, and especially to accept what people have to say about him. For most great players, that pivot requires bottoming out and having to build yourself back up.[122] From the perspective of his professional basketball career, I don't think he ever reached a valley low enough, early in his career, to necessitate a re-calibration of what was important to him. His star kept ascending, and he was universally pretty popular until he left Oklahoma City. He may have believed the backlash received from his 2016 free agency decision to be his bottom, but no player's basketball low-point occurs when you're holding trophies at the end of the season.

But, looking ahead, I'd say—a) Ripping your achilles in the NBA Finals'—b) Watching your team lose the championship from a hospital bed in New York City—and finally, c) Stomaching how close you were to attaining the 'unquestioned greatest player in the world' status, only to have the designation transfer to a player on the team which vanquished yours .. all kind of feels like bottoming out.

In *Game of Thrones'* third season, Jaime Lannister, perhaps the finest swordsman in the realm, has his primary sword-wielding hand cut off. Jaime had been born into one of the wealthiest families in Westeros, and had been on an upwards trajectory his whole life as the family's handsome, talented and capable heir. His ability as a swordsman was integral to his own positive self-image, and when he lost his primary hand, he was forced to dig deeper within himself than he had previously. So, maybe there's an opportunity for KD to bypass the version of himself inherently restricted by how much he cares what outside voices have to say about him—the Brooklyn move certainly felt like a choice made using a compass calibrated with that in mind.

I promise you that we'll get to how great a player Kevin Durant is, but I've been waiting to get some of this off my chest since July 4th, 2016. Let me assure you, only in the mid 2010s would the consensus take on an MVP-level, top three player in the league, leaving a winning situation to join a 73-win team, be—'He's earned the right to make his own decisions'. Am I taking crazy pills?[123] It's not to say that Durant didn't hear criticism, but he would have been absolutely buried in every other era of the NBA. I'm big on precedent here—as you've come to know—and there is positively no precedent for that quality of a player, leaving a quality team, and electing to join such an established, great team. Maintaining the concept that the modern game began after the 1983-84' season, with the qualifier that true unrestricted free agency

---

[122] A recurring theme—LeBron being the sterling example.

[123] For all my fellow 90's kids—In *D2: The Mighty Ducks*, this would have been like Gunnar Stahl leaving Iceland to play for the Ducks (making the *Flying V* the equivalent of playing Draymond at center?). INCONCIEVABLE.

didn't begin until 1988,[124] these *would have been* the closest 'ring-chasing in your prime' moments:

Free Agent	Prior Year Team Result			Prospective Team Result		
	Team	Record	SRS^	Team	Record	SRS^
Shaq 1996	**1995-96' Magic**	**(60-22)**	**+5.40 (5th)**	**1995-96' Bulls**	**(72-10)**	**+11.80 (1st)**
MJ 1996	1995-96' Bulls	(72-10)	+11.80 (1st)	1995-96' Sonics	(64-18)	+7.40 (2nd)
Kobe 2004	2003-04' Lakers	(56-26)	+4.35 (7th)	2003-04' Spurs	(57-25)	+7.51 (1st)
LeBron 2010	2009-10' Cavs	(61-21)	+6.17 (2nd)	2009-10' Lakers	(57-25)	+4.78 (5th)
LeBron 2014	2013-14' Heat	(54-28)	+4.15 (7th)	2013-14' Spurs	(62-20)	+8.00 (1st)
Durant 2016	**2015-16' Thunder**	**(55-27)**	**+7.09 (3rd)**	**2015-16' Warriors**	**(73-9)**	**+10.38 (1st)**

^Simple Rating System—A team rating that takes into account average point differential and strength of schedule. In parenthesis is the team's league-wide rank in SRS for that season.

The closest hypothetical, to me, would have been Shaq joining the 1996-97' Bulls—given the 1995-96' Magic lost to that Chicago team in the 96' Eastern Conference Final, and Chicago had enjoyed a historically dominant season. The difference being, Kevin Durant was the only one who *actually* left a really good team to join a historically dominant team, one that had also eliminated him in the prior season . Enough of the hypotheticals though, let's look at the players who come closest to Durant in the competition for best player to leave a good team, and join an established, great team:

	Prior Year Player Stats			Team Player Chose		
	PER	TS%	Sum PPG/RPG/APG	Team	Record	SRS
Shaq	**26.4**	**.570**	**40.5**	**1995-96' Lakers**	**(53-29)**	**+4.21 (6th)**
Chauncey Billups	17.6	.555	20.8	2001-02' Pistons	(50-32)	+1.69 (10th)
Rashard Lewis	20.7	.587	31.4	2006-07' Magic	(40-42)	+0.35 (11th)
Steve Nash	20.5	.590	26.3	2003-04' Suns	(29-53)	-2.94 (21st)
Ray Allen	14.8	.607	19.7	2011-12' Heat	(46-20)	+5.72 (4th)
Kevin Durant	**28.2**	**.634**	**41.4**	**2015-16' Warriors**	**(73-9)**	**+10.38 (1st)**

It's incredible how few examples there are of high-level players joining high-level teams. Why not LeBron? Because the 2009-10' Heat gutted their roster when Bosh and LeBron came. The 2013-14' Cavs won 33 games, and the 2017-18' Lakers won 35 games. Love it or hate it, but since LeBron left Cleveland the first time, his environment has invariably become a product of him, and not vice-versa. Steve Nash and Rashard Lewis helped yield big turnarounds for their teams upon their arrival, but their teams were bad before they signed in Phoenix and Orlando, respectively. Ray Allen was well past his prime when he joined the Heat, but he does get points

---

[124] In May of 1988, The NBA Players Association and the NBA agreed on a new CBA which included terms for the first version of unrestricted free agency. The player prerequisites were that the prospective unrestricted free agent player had to of played at least seven years in the NBA, and completed at least two contracts. Furthermore, if the player's team wished to retain the prospective free agent, they were required to offer, at minimum, a 25% raise on the previous year's salary. Prior to this, teams basically, perpetually had restricted free agent rights on their players—so at the conclusion of their player's contracts, they retained 'right of first refusal' rights, which meant they could match another team's offer, or sign that offer sheet and subsequently trade that player. Tom Chambers' departure from Seattle for Phoenix is famously looked at as the first big unrestricted free agent move.

in the 'back-stabb-ey' category—his 2011-12' Celtics lost to the Heat in the Eastern Conference Finals immediately before he left Boston for Miami. Chauncey is an unlikely third-place finish here, as I'd forgot that Detroit won 50 games before he arrived. However, Chauncey was signing onto his sixth team in six seasons, and hadn't established himself in the league before joining the Pistons. Ironically enough, where Shaq *actually* chose to go in the summer of 1996 is the runner-up for best player to join a good team. It's still not close though—the Lakers weren't contenders yet, and wouldn't be for a few more seasons. So, yes, Kevin Durant's choice was the biggest 'ring-chasing in your prime' moment of all-time, and it's not even close to being close .. to being close.

The real loser was my man, Sam Presti. He built those Thunder teams from the ground up, and there's plenty of evidence that shows that they're the most unlikely team to have not won a title in the modern NBA. After Durant chose Golden State in the summer of 2016, Todd Whitehead wrote up one of the most brilliant basketball articles of all time—*How Free Agency Changed NBA Teambuilding*, for Fansided.com. I'll surely butcher any attempt at a synopsis, and greatly undercut how well-thought-out the article was, but it centers on how the 1988 CBA allowed for a dramatic shift in player movement, and the subsequent adjustment NBA teams had to make in crafting their rosters. Largely, championship teams became less constituted of players which the team had drafted, as you could imagine. To illuminate, Whitehead put together the top fifty teams (since the 1988 CBA was introduced) with the most total VORP[125] from players drafted by that same team. In this context, the individual VORP scores (from the players drafted by that same team) are added together:

	Team	Sum of VORP From Drafted Players (% Total Team VORP) [Players]
1	1991-92' Bulls	22.3 (93%) [Jordan, Pippen, Grant, Perdue]
2	1990-91' Bulls	20.9 (96%) [Jordan, Pippen, Grant, Perdue, Armstrong]
3	2015-16' Thunder	19.5 (99%) [Durant, Westbrook, Adams, Roberson, Collison, Ibaka, Payne]
4	1992-93' Bulls	18.9 (95%) [Jordan, Pippen, Grant, Perdue, Armstrong]
5	2015-16' Warriors	18.4 (79%) [Curry, Green, Thompson, Barnes, Ezeli]

Effectively, the OKC team that Kevin Durant left was one of the most expertly crafted teams of all-time, and so was the GSW team he arrived on—and both squads were built the old fashioned way—through the draft. In fact, not surprisingly, you'll find the 2011-12', 2012-13' and 2015-16' Thunder teams—with the 13' and 16' teams having the unfortunate distinction of being the only teams in the top-ten to have not reached the Finals'. Presti built an excellent team around Kevin Durant. Unfortunately, Kevin Durant didn't think so, and unintentionally revealed as much via a fake Twitter account in September 2017. In an unforgettable document of Durant's lack of gratitude for the people he spent time with in Oklahoma City, and in an attempt to clap back at someone who questioned his leaving the Thunder, he Tweeted via his actual account, but thinking it was from a fake account:

> *he didn't like the organization or playing for Billy Donovan. His roster*
> *wasn't that good, it was just him and russ*

---

[125] Actual *Basketball Reference* definition—A box score estimate of the points per 100 team possessions that a player contributed above a replacement-level player.

What a shame Durant had to play with so many versatile, athletic, capable players, which Sam Presti had neatly cocooned around his blossoming star. But, you know what they say—*you can bring a horse to water, but the horse has to close out the 2016 Western Conference Finals when you've built a 3-1 lead*. Unfortunately, this horse went 32 of 81 (.395) from the field during the three unsuccessful close-out games, and the Thunder blew it to Durant's future teammates. But, you know what they say—*if you can't close 'em out, join 'em*.

Do you know how many truly great players in NBA history would have given years of their prime, just to play with a supporting cast as good as Durant's in OKC? In the modern era alone, early 2000's KG certainly would have, and you better believe middle-to-late 2000's LeBron and CP3 would have sacrificed to be surrounded by that much talent. My God, I mean, Presti had to trade away Harden because they had *too much* talent on the team?![126]

A few of those versatile, athletic and capable Thunder players also happened to be elite defenders—Roberson and Ibaka have both made All-Defensive teams, and Steven Adams has always defended his position ruthlessly. Care to take a stab at who has *never* made an All-Defense team? In Tier III, only Nash, Dirk, Elgin and Durant do not have an All-Defense selection to their name—Elgin is exempt because the vast majority of his career was played before All-Defensive teams were selected (the 1968-69' season was the first time the NBA selected All-Defensive teams). He was surrounded by long and switchable defenders in Oklahoma City, and joined a Warriors team with historically-proficient defenders. A few years before Klay Thompson made his first All-Defensive team in 2018-19', he was freezing out Kyrie Irving in the 2017 Finals'. Iguodala has made two All-Defense teams in his career, but I'd say his pinnacle achievement defensively was winning a Finals' MVP for his efforts in slowing down peak-powers LeBron in the 2015 Finals'. Then, I suppose playing next to Draymond Green, the preternaturally instinctive reincarnation of Bill Russell, has to help your individual defense, right?

Listen—Kevin Durant is not a poor defender. His D-PIPM hovers around neutral, he's in the top-100 for cumulative Defensive Win Shares in his career, and his length and effort has always yielded good block figures. But, if I have to hear 'how underrated' his defense is one more time, I'm going to rip my TV off the wall, and break it in two over my knee. I'm not

---

[126] Rant Engage. Way too many people put on their rear-view goggles and kill Presti for moving Harden, when, I'm sorry, it was absolutely the move at the time. Of Durant, Russ, Harden and Ibaka—coming into the 2012-2013 season—you absolutely build your franchise around KD, Russ and Ibaka. KD (no doi). Russ had just thrown up a 43-7-5 (on 20-32) in a pivotal road Finals' game while James Harden peed his pants on the bench and nursed a hangover. And Serge Ibaka? He led the league in blocks the year before on his way to the first of three consecutive First-Team All-Defense selections. Oh, and he looked like the evolutionary version of Dikembe— protecting the rim, spacing the floor and occasionally giving the Mutombo finger-wag (for good measure). Even if you thought Harden had MVP upside then, do you divest from Ibaka and leave yourself with Perk, Nick Collison and Cole Aldrich at the big spots? C'mon man. More things had to go wrong than go right for OKC to not get a title in the Durant era, and that's what happened—Pat Beverly's foul in 13', Revenge-Driven Duncan in 14', Durant's Fifth Metatarsal in 15' and Klay's Game 6 in 16'. In most NBA universes, they win a title over this stretch and no one questions Presti, but that's not always how it goes. Fact remains, moving "Big (regular season) Game James" Harden was the right move, and no fewer than 26 NBA franchises would be lucky to have Presti calling the shots. Rant disengage.

actually strong enough to do either of those things—but—he's played in ecosystems that have masked any and all defensive shortcomings he's had—am I wrong?

The exaggeration of his contribution to defensive basketball brightly illuminates my frustration with how we've adjusted Kevin Durant's legacy in the last couple years. All of this venom is sourced from the same location—somehow we normalized that Kevin Durant joined a historically dominant team, but have celebrated his achievements as if they'd come from the same degree of struggle which other players have had to endure. It was endlessly stunning to me that we were on the brink of anointing Durant the 'best player in the world' status before he got hurt in the 2019 playoffs. How could we award him that status when he was tripping over versatile, complimentary, all-time great teammates? What did we learn about Kevin Durant in his time with the Warriors that we didn't already know?

Durant was legitimately breath-taking for the 11 playoff games he did play, before getting hurt in game five of the 2019 Western Conference Semi-Finals' [32, 5 & 5 on 51%FG / 44% 3P / 90% FT]—but, if his teammates were able to get a win in that game five during which he got hurt, then close out the Rockets on the road in game six *without him*, what are we talking about? And then the Warriors sweep the Western Conference Finals' *without him?* Not to mention, The Warriors were six Klay-Thompson-less quarters in the Finals' short of, at minimum, a game seven in Toronto for the championship? What are we even talking about here?

In his three seasons as a Warrior, when KD was out of the lineup, but Steph did play, Golden State was 35-8   ..   just let that sink in for a minute   ..   how many players on this list, in their prime, would watch their team enjoy such success without them in the lineup? .. Are you still thinking about it? It's zero! The answer is zero other players on this list have played in an environment where their team were still favorites to win the championship without them in the lineup.[127]

Durant wasn't necessarily the weapon that made the Warriors go, but he was the element that made them unfair to defend. All I'm asking is that he pay the toll on the detour he selected to winning championships. Some will say he paid the tax already, in fact, maybe the majority of the NBA landscape would say that. I'm just here, dying on this hill, to say that the NBA landscape got this one wrong. Does that mean I would have preferred Mike Breen, Jeff Van Gundy and Mark Jackson savage Durant on national TV, and refuse to acknowledge his accomplishments as a Warrior? Or that I would have preferred a three-year news cycle, from July 2016 to July 2019, that relentlessly attacked Durant's legacy?[128] No, but the next time I'm having a barroom conversation with someone who, in defending Durant, reiterates how few guys have won two championships & two Finals' MVPs, I want them to remember that Durant paid the *Golden Price* for them. I also want them to remember what paying the *Iron Price* looks like—Steph in 15', LeBron in 12', Dirk in 11', KG in 08', David Robinson in 99', Hakeem in 94', MJ

---

[127] I love Bill Simmons and there's no way this book happens without him .. but .. I have to call him out for a hot second. In *Basketball: A Love Story*, he's quoted chastising LeBron's 'Decision' in the summer of 2010—*The thing that bothered me as a basketball fan and as somebody who's overcompetitive in general is that he's supposed to be trying to beat Dwayne Wade. Bird wanted to beat Magic. Russell didn't want to be on Wilt's team. [Dave] Cowens didn't want to play with Kareem, he wanted to beat him*—buuuuut, that felt rather hypocritical when Bill wrapped both of his arms and one of his legs around Kevin Durant when Durant joined the Warriors.
[128] No .. Yes.

in 91', Isiah Thomas in 89', fucking Jerry West in 72',[129] Oscar in 71'—it's a disservice to these dudes when Durant comes up in top-fifteen, even top-ten conversations, when his inclusion is predicated on the trophies he won when he played for the Warriors.

I promised I would talk about what a great player KD is—I just didn't know I had 3,500+ words to work through before I got there. In fairness, he did ruin my Fourth of July in 2016. Anyway, when you're talking about pure scorers, in the history of the NBA, you don't have to squint too hard to conclude that Durant is invariably on the shortlist.

- o **Volume.**
    - ▪ **6**th all-time in regular season PPG (27.03).
    - ▪ **4**th all-time in postseason PPG (29.09).
    - ▪ **31**st all-time in career regular season points (22,940).
    - ▪ **10**th all-time in career postseason points (4,043).
- o **Efficiency.**
    - ▪ **88.3%** from the free throw line is good for 15th all-time.
    - ▪ **[49/38/88]** career shooting splits (totally preposterous).[130]
    - ▪ **.217** Win Shares Per 48 is good for 12th best all-time.
    - ▪ **.613** True Shooting percentage is good for 11th all-time.

For five consecutive seasons, from 2009-10' through 2013-14', KD led the NBA in points scored and free throws made—no player in NBA history has accomplished both of those over a five-year stretch. Not to mention, even if Durant stays healthy for the rest of his Brooklyn contract, he'll find himself flirting with the top-ten in regular season points scored, and the top-five for postseason points scored—which would basically start to level out his hyper elite per-game averages to the cumulative averages, which are usually reserved for hyper-prolific players.

I think Durant's ability to create for others is average, but there is one continuity aspect that I have to give him credit for—my (long) preamble about Durant joining the Warriors glossed over his ability to assimilate into an established, high-efficiency machine. I initially scoffed at this being a credit to Durant, but I've softened to how difficult it can be to not interrupt high-level basketball, particularly when you're a scorer of Durant's quality. I think that speaks to Durant's assassin-level scoring ability—he's so efficient that he can make just about any team better. I don't love relying on the brilliant work of Ben Taylor too often, but he sheds light on just how difficult it is to appreciably improve an already historic team:

Slotted next to two of the best shooters ever — Thompson and Curry — Durant helped Golden State improve from one of the best full-strength teams ever to the best ever, playing at a mind-bending 73-win pace when healthy (14.4 SRS). Durant missed 19 games, and the otherwise

---

[129] Has anyone ever paid a steeper cumulative price for a championship than Jerry West?
[130] [FG%/3P%/FT%] Don't forget, he's also one of just eight players in the 50/40/90 club.

healthy Warriors "only" played at a 67-win clip (10.4 SRS). This might sound minimal, but adding 4 points to an all-time level team, as a scorer, is incredibly difficult due to the diminishing returns on scoring.

14.4 SRS is *God-Mode* basketball. The problem with throwing a bunch of great players together is the fear that their individual contributions will fall short of the sum of all their parts. Golden State leveling up to *God-Mode*, and stretching the sum of their historic parts is a credit to the institutional brilliance of the Warriors, but unquestionably also indicative of Durant's ability to blend in unobtrusively. If you look at Durant's splits between his tenures with OKC and GSW, it's incredibly impressive that he sustains nearly the volume, on less usage, with appreciably higher efficiency:

	PPG	USG%^	TS%*	FG%	PER
(9 seasons) OKC Durant	27.4	30.5	.605	48.3%	25.0
(3 seasons) GSW Durant	25.8	29.1	.640	52.4%	25.8

Durant was a historically dynamic scorer for the decade before he joined the Warriors, and continued his high-volume/high-efficiency dominance, whilst playing within a much different team dynamic. Which leads me to another credit that my preamble dismisses—Kevin Durant could have continued pursuit of more MVPs and further individualistic success, had he not chosen to go to the Warriors. Playing with Curry meant that the two would cannibalize one another's chances at more MVP trophies, as well as undercut each other's individual stats. It has to be recognized that Durant willingly sacrificed individual accolades for the opportunity to win championships. I bash Harden all the time, and mostly because I don't know that he cares about titles. He likes stats, and thinks that they legitimize him as a player. Maybe Durant cut some big corners on the path to winning championships, but at least he willingly sacrificed contention for individual trophies to do so.

In the ninth episode of *Game of Thrones'* first season, aka Ned's last episode, we're introduced to one of the most enduring lessons from the series—*only death pays for life.* A desperate Daenarys recruits the blood magic of a witch to save the life of her dying husband, Khal Drogo. The decision placed a curse on Daenarys, one that she would struggle with for the duration of the story. Were the Warriors cursed after they agreed to absorb a player as dynamic as Kevin Durant? Did Bob Meyers engage in blood magic to construct such a ridiculous accumulation of talent?

The confluence of factors that resulted in the Warriors being able to sign Durant were so unusual, that they might be interpreted as blood magic—the $24M cap spike in 2016, plus the Warriors improbably blowing their 3-1 2016 Finals' advantage, and having Jerry West at their employ to close the deal on any doubts Durant had. But no, to my knowledge, no blood magic was expended. What it did was truly throw the competitive balance for the league way out of whack. I remember thinking when Durant chose Golden State that the Basketball Gods would smite such an event with unprecedented fury. But, after the Warriors smoked the league and earned their 2017 and 2018 championships,[131] I resigned myself to their dominance, and to the idea that perhaps the Basketball Gods had softened on what was allowed (much like the rest of the NBA world). Come the 2019 playoffs, the Warriors were poised for a three-peat, and Durant was looking better than ever .. right up to when he got hurt.[132]

The league has always had a certain balance, and somehow the *Red Wedding*-esque 2019 NBA Finals' for the Warriors, followed by Kawhi choosing the Clippers over the Lakers, brought balance back to the league. When something so completely unprecedented occurs to disrupt the power balance of the league, perhaps an equally meteoric shift was inevitable for the NBA. It's rather unsavory on my part to say that the injuries to Klay's knee and Durant's achilles were locked into some sort of NBA justice, offsetting the injustice of KD's arrival in Golden State.

However, there could be a much more tangible, less cosmic explanation for a rash of untimely injuries to the two-time-defending champs—acquiring KD was going to limit the Warriors' ability to add depth, which peaked during the 2019 season. After four consecutive seasons playing in the Finals', the Warriors asked huge minutes of their premier players (including (gulp) Klay Thompson and his knees), and in a more infamous, more heart-breaking way, the desperate Warriors asked Kevin Durant to return from an injury before he was ready. So, all blood magic aside, perhaps the Warriors signed up for this fate without realizing it. By refusing to regress from the championship success they'd grown accustomed to, it's conceivable that the lack of depth they would inevitably encounter, in absorbing Durant, came back to bite them. *Only death pays for life*—amirite?

As far as Kevin Durant goes, the struggles that he avoided in joining the Warriors, which I labored to exaggerate, are coming for him soon. If a few things go their way, it's completely reasonable that, upon return of a 90%-of-himself-KD, the Brooklyn Nets could win a championship. But the days of a tailor-made, all-time great supporting cast around Durant are way behind him now. His Nets will not go 35-8 without him, and only with him, and a lot of other things going their way, will the Nets be favorites to win a championship. The sad part for me, is that Durant had an opportunity to change the narrative on himself after the injury in the 2019 Finals'—ironically, by staying with the Warriors. Having lost, and in such heart-breaking fashion, he could have pursued the role of an underdog—'rehabbing a catastrophic injury in pursuit of a championship for the team that always supported him through the criticism he endured from June 2016 through June 2019. But truthfully, Durant chasing the narrative with the biggest common denominator led to critics like me savaging him. He wants to go play with his boys, and maybe bring a championship to New York City? I'm with it. Yes, I believe that when it's time for Durant to retire, that we need to apply a just tax on some of the figures he

---

[131] For my money, the 2016-17' Warriors are the greatest team of all-time. Aside from the tangible talents of Steph, Durant, Klay and Draymond, you have to factor in one of the most powerful forces in the history of championship-winning basketball—the revenge factor. Losing the 2016 Finals' in such brutal fashion, to LeBron, at Oracle Arena in game seven, was quality motivation for a group who hardly needs motivation anyway. On top of that, weigh-in Durant's hunger for his first title, and you had the perfect ingredients for an absolutely unbeatable NBA team. The 2017 Cleveland team, that the Warriors beat over five games in the 2017 Finals', was a historically-dynamic team! But the super-team to end all super-teams dismantled them.

[132] He literally made the shot during which his calf was injured.

accumulated. However, Durant being one of the best scorers we've ever had, and indisputably one of the best 30 overall players, is *duty-free* my friends.

Why He Belongs In This Tier? For me, Durant winning a title while in Brooklyn, which will be ostensibly the last years of his prime, would go a very long way. It would be the championship that I chided him for not being able to win. Some people may think he has Tier I upside, but I'm lightyears away from that suggestion. While I do give him credit for the ability to assimilate into multiple team dynamics and substantially enhance their odds at a championship—he hasn't yet won a championship with a normally proportionate amount of pressure on him. The teams in Oklahoma City were good enough to win, and they didn't. Props again to Ben Taylor who, in far more eloquent and analytical fashion, explained that despite Durant's 2017 and 2018 trophies, *he is not a player well-rounded enough to perennially transform a weaker roster into a contender.* A Brooklyn championship will be my prerequisite for his Tier II application. We can revisit at that point.

Tier III Recap.

As the great British philosopher Mick Jagger once said—*I see a red door and I want it painted black, no colors anymore, I want them to turn black.*

Believe it or not, I was not listening to *Paint it Black* on repeat while I wrote Kevin Durant's profile, but I do feel a little lighter.

Ladies and gentlemen, we've reached the conclusion of Tier III. We're about to engage the two most prestigious tiers of NBA greatness, but before we move into Tier II, I wanted to reflect on some of the choices I made in constituting Tier III. With so many players from so many different eras to choose from, there was inevitably going to be some deserving players left out. To honor the players I considered for Tier III, but ultimately decided against, I've put together a hypothetical 'Tier IV'. I then sub-divided those 20 players into groups of how seriously I was considering them for a selection. Those sub-divisions are as follows, and each respective player's Greatness Index score is in parenthesis:

Most Screwed Over	Considered .. Kinda	No Chance
Charles Barkley (44th)	Elvin Hayes (63rd)	Patrick Ewing (76th)
John Stockton (43rd)	Willis Reed (56th)	Bob Cousy (16th)
Manu Ginóbili (42nd)	Rick Barry (61st)	Reggie Miller (85th)
Kawhi Leonard (21st)	Kevin McHale (30th)	Bill Walton (70th)
Walt Frazier (27th)	George Mikan (23rd)	Gary Payton (41st)
Giannis Antetokounmpo (74th)	Jason Kidd (22nd)	Bob Pettit (24th)
Sam Jones (20th)	James Worthy (60th)	Allen Iverson (92nd)

I did Barkley pretty dirty—there are very few lists that *don't* have him as a top-30 guy. Despite winning an MVP and being a meaningful player for a long time, I can't get my head around a guy who had to be nudged so hard to get in shape. I also think he was a poor defender and relatively one-dimensional (sorry).

Stockton, to me, is a *prolifically very-good player*. His peak occurred during a watered-down stretch for the league, which allowed him to sustain and put off playing the 'Tommy Lee Jones in *No Country For Old Men*' role—with a lack of incoming, dynamic talent, he persevered as a premier point guard .. by default.[133]

---

[133] That feels like a drive-by shooting on John Stockton, but am I wrong? Honestly though, Stockton is my honorable mention Tier III player if there were one—most assists all-time, most steals all-time, and he was usually the one making winning plays for those Jazz teams while Karl Malone tried not to pee his pants.

I love Manu Ginóbili, and a lot of impact stats suggest that his inclusion wouldn't have been crazy. But, I feel like he was living a bit of a charmed life coming off the bench, and he wouldn't have held up physically if he would have played full-time—still, one of the most clever, multi-talented, maniacally-competitive dudes to ever play basketball.

Speaking of living a charmed life, Manu's once-upon-a-time teammate Kawhi Leonard very nearly made Tier III. He probably has the best overall case of anyone that was left out. His profile is interesting given his championship success, yet we have such a limited sample of him being one of the best players in the league. Kawhi could very possibly move into Tier III, but the favorable team environments he continues to find himself in—which he deserves some credit for, in fairness—and the absolute collapse against the Nuggets in the 2020 playoffs[134] will keep him out for now. Another championship could very possibly bump him into Tier III, but by the same token, if the injury he's been managing for almost five seasons rapidly degrades his dynamism, he may never get there.

Walt Frazier is a guy that just continued to hover around the research I was doing on other players. I also have a soft spot for elite defenders. The downside was that those great early-70s Knick teams were fairly egalitarian in their own right, and no single player really stood out enough, statistically or otherwise, to jump into Tier III. Most people are taking the guy who won the Finals' MVP for their 1970 and 1973 championships, Willis Reed. For me, I'm taking Frazier.

Giannis is lurking. He'll be in soon.

I gave Sam Jones some serious consideration. He won 10 championships as the most important offensive player to the 60s Celtics, but I ultimately couldn't get myself to include two Russell teammates, especially when I thought that Havlicek was an appreciably better overall player than Jones.

As for the other current players most likely to make the jump into Tier III during the 2020s? Klay Thompson has a good chance—assuming his cumulative three-point numbers begin to line up with his insane averages. A lot of people will rally for James Harden, but Harden will have to prove to me that he's *not* James Harden to make this list. A guy who's impact substantially depreciates during the postseason, while he continues to just play the same way, hoping for a different result? And is so bad on defense that his team has to strategize around how bad he is? No thanks. If Harden leads a team to a championship, I'll have to consider him, but that will never happen. Harden's pal, Russell Westbrook—Pass. If Anthony Davis continues to stay healthy, and perennially continues to sniff around a championship, he'll likely make Tier III at minimum—he's simply an unprecedented conglomeration of skills, but I fear that human bodies built like that aren't built to last. Jokic has Tier II upside, given his historically diverse range of skills, but we'll have to see how it goes in Denver. Plus, he looks like a bouncer who hasn't actually exercised in a decade—that has to

---

[134] I won't be soon forgetting Kawhi's 6-22 no-show in game seven of this series.

catch up to him at some point, right? Luka Dončić will be here one day, it's just a matter of which Tier he'll land in.

I should also identify the players most likely to get bumped by surging Tier III candidates. The plan beyond publishing this book will be to keep the Tiers as they are—Tier III (16 members), Tier II (10 members), Tier I (4 members). Members of Tier III and Tier II will be vulnerable to losing a spot as greater players eventually come along. Tier I spots are lifetime memberships and not vulnerable to relegation.[135] I will say, like *Rolling Stone's 500 Greatest Albums of All Time* list, it's going to be hard to unseat most of these insanely influential and iconic players throughout Tiers II & III. If I had to rank current Tier III players by their likelihood to get bumped, it would look like this:

Hot Seat	Comfortable	Straight Chillin'
Steve Nash	Dennis Rodman	Dirk Nowitzki
Elgin Baylor	John Havlicek	David Robinson
Isiah Thomas	Draymond Green	Kevin Durant
Karl Malone	Moses Malone	Scottie Pippen
	Julius Erving	Jerry West
	Chris Paul	
	Dwayne Wade	

There are three active players here, and only Durant can realistically move into Tier II. Even a few more years of Draymond Draymond-ing at a high-Draymond level would be unlikely to push him into Tier II—short of him adding a reliable three-point shot and/or procuring an ability to control the ball with his mind.

Before we step into Tier II, I'd like to acknowledge a rivalry that existed between players within Tier III. There are plenty of Tier III players that have clashed, but the one I wanted to zoom in on was the Dirk & Wade saga that has always intrigued me. Their careers had a unique symmetry, with each player's greatest achievement coming at the other's expense—Wade's virtuoso 2006 Finals' over Dirk's Mavericks, and Dirk's 2011 Finals' triumph over Wade's Heat. If my feet were to the fire, I'd probably go with Dirk. Dirk played 5 more seasons than Wade, and maintained a more efficient statistical profile, on substantially less usage:

	Career	Games	USG%	PPG	PER	TS%	WS/48^	Career Win Shares
Wade	2004-2019	1,054	31.4	22.0	23.5	.554	.162	120.7
Dirk	1999-2019	**1,552**	26.5	20.7	22.4	**.577**	**.193**	**206.3**

As far as postseason success goes, Wade won two more rings than Dirk, courtesy of the Bosh/LeBron/Wade trio. Wade was great for those four years, and sometimes gets overshadowed by the insanity that was LeBron at his peak. But, I'm pretty sure you could drop me on a team with 2010-2014 LeBron James, and my PER would be 14.5, minimum. Plus, Dirk not only beat that team, *but ripped their heart out.* It's still a tough call between these two

---

[135] I'll explain further in the Tier I recap. You can find my UP-TO-THE-MINUTE rankings, in perpetuity, at strainofdiscourse.com.

players, because Wade was appreciably more impactful defensively, and you know how I love two-way guys! That sounds weird, but I'm keeping it in. Bottom line, to me, is that Dirk was more efficient. He was on winning basketball teams for virtually his entire career,[136] all while the Mavericks shuffled-in and shuffled-out dozens of players around him. Regardless of the team dynamic, Dirk always stood out as the team's best player, and did not need to be overly-ball-dominant to do so. Had you dropped apex LeBron in his lap, he'd probably had dynastic championship success as well.

Legendary basketball coach, Tex Winter, popularized the quote 'Everything turns on a trifle'. It was originally a Napoleon quote, but Winter's intended context was within the basketball world. That quote tells you everything you need to know about the margins that define and collapse many player's legacies. Everything can turn on a barely missed shot, a loose ball that goes the wrong way, or even a freak injury. This can serve to delegitimize the accomplishments of certain players if you think about it for too long—to know how close they were to not winning a trophy, considering that trophy ultimately serves to validate their greatness. However, great players don't get defined by an unfortunate moment, or a game that got away from them. Great players keep knocking on the door, because it's the only way to be on fortune's side of the turning trifle when your number is called.

I think this is why we need to start thinking of this conversation, in its totality, in the framework of a tiered system. If it's challenging to draw a line in the sand between larger groups of players, as I've experienced with this project, what does that say about drawing lines between individually listed players? You're compounding the subjectivity each time you place a player above another one. The number of players in each of my tiers, or who I selected to fill the tiers with, might not be perfect. I can live with that. What I'm trying to get us to is a place where we can just accept that we don't know if Dwyane Wade or Jerry West was a better player. Individually ordered rankings are always going to be arbitrary. Let's get away from that.

Next up are the 10 players of Tier II—the 14th through 5th greatest players ever—depending on how you see it.

---

[136] 11 consecutive 50-win seasons for the Mavericks between 2000-01' and 2010-11'.

Oscar Robertson

The Secret	Greatness Index	Ben Taylor Rank
84 / 100	134.95 (35th)	12th

Playoff PER	Playoff Win Shares	Playoff O-Win Shares	Playoff D-Win Shares
20.99 (37th)	13.65 (53rd)	10.17 (34th)	3.47 (138th)

If Oscar Robertson is a name that only vaguely registers because it was thrown around while Russell Westbrook bastard-ized and de-legitimized[137] the triple-double over the past few years, let us quickly reset why you should care about Oscar Robertson's basketball career:

- After leading the United States to a Gold Medal in the 1960 Rome Summer Olympics, *The Big O* was drafted first-overall in the 1960 NBA draft by the Cincinnati Royals.
- Famously, Oscar averaged a triple-double during the stat-padded 1961-62' season, but few people know that he basically averaged a triple double for the first five seasons of his career. He'd also average at least 30 PPG in six of his first seven seasons:

	PTS	REB	AST	PER
1960-61'	30.5	10.1	9.7	25.9
1961-62'	**30.8**	**12.5**	**11.4**	**26.0**
1962-63'	28.3	10.4	9.5	24.6
1963-64'	31.4	9.9	11.0	27.6
1964-65'	30.4	9.0	11.5	26.7

---

[137] When you look at the players with the most triple-doubles ever—1) Oscar 2) Russ 3) Magic 4) J Kidd 5) LeBron—you have four players whose individual play generated systemic team success .. and then Russell Westbrook. I really appreciate Russ for the firestorm of benevolently entertaining inefficiency that he is. I think stylistic diversity is important, and we need dudes like that. He's just not as effective as his numbers suggest.

1965-66'	31.3	7.7	11.1	25.2
1966-67'	30.5	6.2	10.7	25.5

- o Robertson won league MVP for the 1963-64' season, which was especially significant for two reasons:
  - He was the only player not named Russell or Chamberlain to win an MVP from 1960 to 1968. Winning the award speaks to the individual greatness of the *Big O,* when super greats like West and Baylor were unable to snag even one MVP during that window.
  - He beat out Wilt Chamberlain, who averaged 37 points and 22 rebounds during the 1963-64' season.
- o In the 1967-68' season, Oscar became the first player to ever lead the league in scoring and assists (and still only one of two players ever—Tiny Archibald in 1972-73').

The 1963, 1964, 1965 and 1966 postseasons were the closest the Royals would come to championship competition. Three of those were losses to Russell's Celtics,[138] who won the title every season from 1959 to 1966. The Royals were highly productive offensively with Oscar at the helm, but sub-par defensively during their championship window, and downright bad defensively outside of that window:

	Off. Rating^ (Rank)	Def. Rating^ (Rank)
1960-61'	95.6 (1st of 8)	98.4 (8th of 8)
1961-62'	98.3 (1st of 9)	96.9 (8th of 9)
1962-63'	**99.4 (1st of 9)**	**98.3 (7th of 9)**
1963-64'	**98.9 (1st of 9)**	**94.5 (4th of 9)**
1964-65'	**98.0 (1st of 9)**	**96.0 (7th of 9)**
1965-66'	**97.5 (3rd of 9)**	**96.5 (7th of 9)**
1966-67'	98.4 (2nd of 10)	98.6 (8th of 10)
1967-68'	101.1 (2nd of 12)	101.8 (12th of 12)
1968-69'	100.2 (1st of 14)	101.1 (14th of 14)
1969-70'	98.0 (10th of 14)	100.4 (10th of 14)

^Quick Refresher—Offensive Rating is the team points scored per 100 possessions. Defensive Rating is the team points allowed per 100 possessions.

The median opinion about Oscar's defensive ability is that he was 'adequate'. There is room for criticism here, while it might feel like Oscar's preposterous offensive statistics might feel a little

---

[138] 1963—Held a 3-2 series' lead but lost in seven. 1964—Lost in five. 1966—Held a 2-1 series lead in the five-game series' but lost in five. Keeping in mind there were only nine NBA teams during this stretch, the conferences were referred to as divisions, and only division Finals' and NBA Finals' would be seven game series'. Woof .. format changes are exhausting.

James Harden-ey[139] if they never translated to consistent championship contention. However, it wasn't Oscar's defense that prevented his Royals' tenure from yielding a championship—to me, it was the lack of a Pippen, a Wade or a Draymond (if you will) that was the missing ingredient here.

I told myself that I wouldn't lean too heavily on Ben Taylor's work throughout the book, but he came up with a stat that was so telling about Oscar's Cincinnati teams, that I have to include it—the 1963-64' and 1964-65' Royals were the only two NBA teams of the 1960s to not have a player taller than 6'8" log a single minute throughout an entire season.[140] Having a bigger player to limit Russell, Pettit or Chamberlain certainly would have helped, but determining exactly why Cincinnati was well below average defensively as a team remains a bit of a mystery to me (and anyone else that feels like trying to figure that out via the internet in 2020).

However, the best I could do was evaluate the best players around Oscar during his time in Cincinnati—forward Jerry Lucas, center Wayne Embry and small forward Jack Twyman. Twyman was a scorer, and Lucas, despite legitimate stature and rebounding ability, is generally described as 'stretchy' for a forward of the time. Wayne Embry is especially puzzling for me, as he's categorized as the rim-protector for those teams, and wasn't especially small at 6'8" and 240 pounds. Without any defensive stats, much less advanced stats, or any nuanced analysis of these players, it's hard to make any sharp judgements about their defensive abilities. With all that said, and I probably could have just skipped to this part—it's safe to conclude that the Royals of the mid 60s were very good, but not good enough (largely because of poor defenses), to beat Russell's Celtics. Join the fucking club.

Bob Cousy, Celtic legend (player from 1950-1963), took over the Cincinnati coaching responsibilities during Oscar's final Royals' season. Cousy's attempt to re-shape the landscape of the team resulted in a blockbuster trade immediately after the 1969-70' season. The trade shipped *The Big O* to Milwaukee for Completely Forgotten NBA Player 1[141] and Completely Forgotten NBA Player 2.[142] According to the *New York Times* article reporting the trade on April 21st, 1970, Oscar had his choice of a few different teams, after it was concluded that he would be moved based on how expensive he was, and perhaps because he and Cousy had butted heads. Whatever the case, Oscar made a great choice because the Bucks had just finished their first season with a player named Lew Alcindor, who had the potential to completely dominate the league.

Oscar's time in Cincinnati leaves us asking how good they might have been with another premier two-way player. We'll never know, and we'll be left to speculate. But what happened immediately to the Bucks after they acquired Robertson indicates that Oscar, past his prime when the trade occurred, was still more than capable of quarterbacking dominant NBA teams.

---

[139] I'm sorry, but I'm done hearing the media ramp up James Harden's profile during the regular season, only to watch Harden, lifeless and exhausted, fail to grasp the most important moments of his career during the playoffs. He's the new Karl Malone, and at least Malone was a two-way player.

[140] With Cincy boasting the most efficient offense for both of those seasons with such a small lineup, I can't help but think that this was early evidence of small ball's effectiveness. The *14 Seconds or Less* Royals!

[141] Flynn Robinson—All Star in 1969-70' for Milwaukee, and a champion with the epic 72' Lakers.

[142] Charlie Paulk—Charlie had missed the prior season due to his serving a tour of duty in the Vietnam War. He would only play 120 NBA games in his career.

Take a look at what Milwaukee looked like the season before Oscar's arrival, and the first season with him:

	Off. Rating (Rank)	Def. Rating (Rank)	MOV^ (Rank)	Record
1969-70'	102.1 (2nd of 14)	98.1 (6th of 14)	4.6 (2nd)	56-26
1970-71'	**103.9 (1st of 17)**	**93.1 (1st of 17)**	**12.3 (1st)**	**66-16**

^Margin of Victory

Milwaukee was really good in Alcindor's rookie season, but they were one of the most dominant teams of all-time in 1970-71'. Their 12.3 Margin of Victory in the regular season is tied with the 72' Lakers for the best of all-time.[143] The Bucks didn't slow down once the postseason began, and faced little resistance before claiming the 1971 NBA Championship— five-game blowouts in the first two playoff rounds, and a four-game sweep in the Finals' over the Baltimore Bullets.[144] In Fact, Milwaukee's 14.5 Margin of Victory during the postseason remains the best cumulative playoff margin of all-time.

To me, Oscar's prominent role on such a dominating team served as evidence that the historically significant individual stats that he hung in Cincinnati were not empty calories, but representative of the *Big O's* ability to contribute to championship-winning basketball. Oscar's numbers came down to earth playing alongside Alcindor,[145] as he ceded plenty of opportunity to the rise of one of the league's all-time most dominant and prolific players. But, Milwaukee's leap in efficiency and overall dominance was clearly a result of their new point guard, not the maturation of their third and fourth best players, Bob Dandridge and Jon McGlocklin.

Milwaukee followed up their championship season with another dominating 63-win season in 1971-72'. They battled to a six-game series defeat against the great 1971-72' Lakers—spearheaded by Jerry West and Wilt Chamberlain. In Oscar's final two seasons, 1972-73' and 1973-74', Milwaukee won 60 and 59 games, respectively. The 1973 playoffs were a first-round exit for the Bucks, but the conclusion of the 1974 postseason was an epic seven-game Finals' between the Bucks and the Celtics. Oscar was mostly cooked from injuries at that point, and only managed a 2 for 13 shooting performance in a fairly uncompetitive game seven loss to the Boston Celtics.

Like the profiles of many NBA greats, we're left to wonder what might have been had a certain player been surrounded by a better compliment of talent or been in a more favorable situation overall—Oscar Robertson is no different. But the success he enjoyed in the twilight of

---

[143] Because of league expansion in the early 70s, coupled with ABA interference, it makes sense that powerful teams in the early 70s were poised to dominate depleted competition. It's still fucking impressive. Regular season point differential is actually quite indicative of historically great teams. The top ten teams by regular season point differential—1) 71' Bucks 2) 72' Lakers 3) 96' Bulls 4) 17' Warriors 5) 72' Bucks 6) 16 Warriors 7) 97' Bulls 8) 16' Spurs 9) 92' Bulls 10) 08' Celtics. With some variation, present are a handful of the widely-regarded greatest teams of all-time.

[144] The great Kevin Pelton, brilliant NBA writer and analytical interpreter of NBA trends, has done some great work on quantifying the 50 greatest NBA teams of all-time. The fundamentals of the list are based around regular season and postseason point differentials, combined with those of the observed team's playoff opponents. He updated the ranking in June 2018, and the 71' Bucks ranked as the 7th best team ever on the list.

[145] Lew Alcindor publicly changed his name to Kareem Abdul-Jabbar shortly after Milwaukee's 1970-71' championship.

his career, albeit next to an all-time big man, proved that he was a winning player with historic stats, not just a historic stats guy who also enjoyed some team success.[146]

It would be unfair to gloss over Oscar Robertson's contributions off the court. Per the Hall of Famer's own website, Robertson served as President of the National Basketball Players' Association from 1965 until he retired in 1974—still the longest tenured president of the NBPA to this day, and the first black president of any national sports or entertainment labor union. In 1970, he filed a class action anti-trust lawsuit on behalf of his colleagues, which sought the prevention of an NBA merger with the ABA. The suit halted the merger until player rights improved, specifically regarding the reserve clause and the current stipulations of the NBA draft (both hugely impeded the freedom of current and incoming NBA players). The suit wasn't resolved until 1976, and its conclusion that became the 'Oscar Robertson Rule' granted players a rudimentary version of free agency, making the NBA the first sports league to encourage player movement. Over the six years that the suit was being settled, Robertson was hurled a vast amount of criticism for what owners, spectators and some players thought would destroy the game. Conversely, the conclusion of the suit was partially responsible for ushering in an era of unprecedented prosperity for the league, and laid the groundwork for the player empowerment movement of the 2010s. Eat your heart out, LeBron.

On a more discouraging note, racism is the constant subtext for the black players of the NBA, especially those from the first few eras of the league. Oscar, fellow black basketball players, and all black Americans have endured routine hatred and discrimination for a long time. Shit, until The Civil Rights Act in 1964, it was still *legal* to discriminate against whoever you wanted, for whatever reason you felt like. But after the legislation was passed, everything got better and racism died off almost immediately. Sigh. The role racism plays in this story is the hardened exterior that high-profile black basketball players developed as a defense and shielding mechanism against an onslaught of bigotry and hatred. Oscar was hard on his teammates and those around him. Like Russell, Oscar seemed to channel a good deal of his frustration onto his teammates and opponents on the basketball court. The reason for including this is to confront the narrative that Oscar, and other black players of his era, were inherently unhappy, ornery or mercurial personalities. I believe time and proper rationale has ironed out the truth behind their, at times, abrasive exteriors. But if your personal life included, in Oscar's specific case, receiving threatening letters from the Grand Wizard of the KKK, sleeping apart from his teammates because hotels wouldn't allow blacks, and in the very city he went to college and played professional basketball, being disallowed from entering more than half of Cincinnati's restaurants and theatres .. you might just bring all that shit to work with you too.

Why He Belongs In This Tier? He's one of the most complete basketball players ever, and despite playing in an era that continues to lose tread, his reputation never does. Most serious lists have *The Big O* in Tier II territory, based on his ocean of historic stats and his singular blend of talents. In comparing Oscar versus the other Russell-era players, I think Oscar's 1963-64' MVP speaks volumes to the level of player he was. He was a player away from being able to

---

[146] Knock, Knock. Who's there? Russell Westbrook.

beat Russell in the playoffs, but he maximized his lesser roster and pushed Russell to the limit two different times. Oscar was the first true heliocentric star of the NBA—capable of scoring or facilitating from the perimeter, and it was up to the defense what they would prefer to give up in trying to defend him. In the historic floor-raisers that have come after him—Bird, LeBron, CP3, Luka—we see a glimmer of Oscar Robertson always positioning his team to win, regardless of the team construction.

Kevin Garnett

The Secret	Greatness Index	Ben Taylor Rank
90 / 100	175.26 (18th)	8th

PIPM	O-PIPM	D-PIPM	Peak—2003-04'	Wins Added
+4.53 (13th)	+1.81	+2.72	+8.06 (7th)	261.11 (3rd)

Playoff PER	Playoff Win Shares	Playoff O-Win Shares	Playoff D-Win Shares
21.12 (36th)	16.42 (35th)	7.10 (54th)	9.32 (18th)

KG was a two-way monster—a preternaturally instinctive yet forceful defender, he also possessed a historically proficient set of offensive tools.

Kevin Garnett never flew under anyone's radar, but being stranded in Minnesota for so long definitely diluted our perception of how impactful he was. There's a certain explainable phenomenon that occurs when teams draft a generational player who then makes them competitive so quickly that they're unable to add meaningful value to their team via the draft. In many cases, the franchise compounds the isolation of their superstar by bungling the acquisition of complementary talent through other means. In Kevin Garnett's case, *Bungled* would be the perfect title for a documentary about the first 12 seasons of Garnett's career in Minnesota. That or you could simply remake *Castaway*—with KG in the Chunk Noland role .. and Wally Szczerbiak guest-starring as Wilson.

I'm convinced that Minnesota's bungle of their draft rights to Kevin Garnett resulted in him becoming the most underrated player in NBA history. I've watched enough film of Garnett's T-Wolve' years to know that he was a viciously-impactful player that was stuck with a rotisserie of poor supporting talent. But how could I quantify just how bad Garnett's teammates were in a broader context, and maybe put a magnifying glass to other inadequate supporting casts that surrounded other stranded superstars?

There were a lot of different approaches to the experiment, but I decided to use Jacob Goldstein's PIPM database to quantify the play of prominent teammates adjacent to the most stranded players in modern NBA history (after 1983-84'). To start, I had to determine who those stranded players were, and this was the list I came up with:

	Stranded Window	Years Stranded
LeBron James	2003-04' through 2009-10'	7
Chris Paul	2005-06' through 2010-11'	6
David Robinson	1989-90' through 1996-97'	8
Hakeem Olajuwon	1984-85' through 1991-92'	8
Kevin Garnett	1995-96' through 2006-07'	12

There were a few close calls here—Allen Iverson and Anthony Davis' lonely tenures in Philadelphia and New Orleans, respectfully, narrowly missed the cut because their individual impact stats weren't in line with the rest of the group. Wilt Chamberlain and Oscar Robertson are in the conversation, but building statistical profiles for their teammates from the 60s would fall very short of the detail we can provide for more modern players.

Next, to determine each player's stranded window, I started with their rookie season, and extended the window through when I deemed them to have finally been playing with decent surrounding talent. For example, LeBron James' window starts with his rookie year and extends through when he took his talents to South Beach. Chris Paul's window starts with his rookie year and extends through when he was traded to the Clippers. David Robinson's window starts with his rookie year and extends through when the Spurs lucked into drafting Tim Duncan. Hakeem's window starts with his rookie year and extends through when Houston started getting serious about building a contender. Garnett's window starts with his rookie year and extends through when he was finally, mercifully moved to the Boston Celtics.

Next, to determine the players who played the most around each stranded star, I researched the five players who played the most minutes for the star's team across their stranded stretch. For example, I measured which five players played the most minutes for the Cavaliers, besides LeBron, in the seasons between LeBron's rookie year, 2003-04', and the last season of his first Cleveland tenure, 2009-10'. By taking the top five players by minutes played, I'm grabbing starter-level teammates, and in theory, the teammates that were most responsible for supporting the franchise's stranded superstar. Let's start there, with LeBron, and the Career PIPM for the five players he played with the most during his stranded stretch:

LeBron James – Cavaliers – 2003-04' through 2009-10'

Most Total Minutes Played by Cavaliers During that Stretch (Excluding James):	Career PIPM			
	O-PIPM	D-PIPM	PIPM	Wins Added
1) Zydrunas Ilgauskas	-0.35	+1.20	+0.85	56.71
2) Drew Gooden	-0.77	-0.50	-1.27	17.35
3) Anderson Varejão	-0.29	+1.73	+1.44	44.20
4) Eric Snow	-0.80	+1.04	+0.24	47.61
5) Mo Williams	+0.06	-0.88	-0.82	28.29
Cumulative	**-2.15**	**+2.59**	**+0.44**	**194.16**

Pretty brutal. LeBron and Big Z had great chemistry in Cleveland, but you'd want the big fella as maybe the third or fourth option on a title team, right? Drew Gooden as young LeBron's number three is pretty harsh. Harsher still is how reliant those Cleveland teams were on Andy Varejão, while *unironically* trying to win a championship. LeBron did benefit from less turnover in personnel than some of the other contestants—he may have had crumby teammates, but at least they were consistently similar crumby teammates!

The PIPM results are probably to be expected—the Cavs had some really effective defensive teams during LeBron's first seven years. But, the lack of secondary or tertiary offensive players, capable of getting their own shot adjacent to LeBron, is the primary reason the team failed to truly compete for a championship.

Chris Paul – Hornets – 2005-06' through 2010-11'

Most Total Minutes Played by Hornets During that Stretch (Excluding Paul):	Career PIPM			
	O-PIPM	D-PIPM	PIPM	Wins Added
1) David West	+0.47	+0.74	+1.21	80.43
2) Rasual Butler	-1.40	-0.33	-1.73	8.38
3) Tyson Chandler	-0.34	+1.58	+1.24	84.89
4) Peja Stojaković	+2.02	-1.27	+0.76	65.99
5) Desmond Mason	-0.48	-0.60	-1.09	18.93
Cumulative	**+0.27**	**+0.12**	**+0.39**	**258.62**

At first glance, this looks like a much more capable group of support players. Championship-level group? Probably not. More capable than Andy Varejão & Drew Gooden? Yes. Were Desmond Mason and Rasual Butler brutal? Yes. Were Rasual Butler's career averages 7.5 points and 0.8 assists, per game, on 40% from the field? Yes. Was there a secondary creator getting substantial minutes alongside Chris Paul during the first stretch of his career? No. But, at least *The Point God* began his career with NBA players that had a pulse. Behold, *The Point God's* (lousy) teammates.

David Robinson – Spurs – 1989-90' through 1996-97'

Most Total Minutes Played by Spurs During that Stretch (Excluding Robinson):	Career PIPM			
	O-PIPM	D-PIPM	PIPM	Wins Added
1) Sean Elliott	+0.06	-0.48	-0.42	35.03
2) Avery Johnson	+0.18	-0.26	-0.08	45.86
3) Willie Anderson	-0.51	+0.11	-0.40	22.04
4) Vinny Del Negro	-0.02	-0.80	-0.82	21.48
5) Terry Cummings	+0.75	+0.05	+0.80	74.80
Cumulative	**+0.46**	**-1.38**	**-0.92**	**199.21**

Considering Robinson is one of the greatest defensive players of all-time, this compliment of mostly positive offensive players rounds out a 'not brutally awful' supporting cast. But Terry Cummings certainly isn't an acceptable second option in pursuit of a championship. Cummings and Sean Elliott were solid wings playing alongside Robinson, each made two All-Star games in their career. However, Cummings' best basketball was behind him before playing for the Spurs, and Elliot wasn't quite the star required for true championship contention.

If we remember back to the Steve Nash profile, we looked at the biggest turnarounds in NBA history—Robinson's arrival into the league resulted in the Spurs winning *35 more games* in his rookie season (also Sean Elliott's rookie season). The Admiral was unquestionably one of the most immediately impactful NBA players of all-time, and there's also no question that he lacked a championship-level supporting cast—until Tim Duncan fell into the Spurs' lap in the 1997 draft.

Hakeem Olajuwon – Rockets – 1984-85' through 1991-92'

Most Total Minutes Played by Rockets During that Stretch (Excluding Olajuwon):	Career PIPM			
	O-PIPM	D-PIPM	PIPM	Wins Added
1) Otis Thorpe	+0.17	-0.34	-0.17	60.73
2) Rodney McCray	+0.13	-0.19	-0.06	38.28
3) Sleepy Floyd	+0.96	-0.80	+0.16	42.98
4) Buck Johnson	-1.36	+0.13	-1.23	8.83
5) Ralph Sampson	-0.72	+1.20	+0.48	25.79
Cumulative	**-0.82**	**+0.00**	**-0.82**	**176.61**

Hakeem's candidacy was the most complicated, and I almost pulled him out. In his second season, Olajuwon was the best player on a team that made a run to the 1986 Finals'. It also wasn't just any Finals' run—they smoked the Showtime Lakers in five games during the Western Conference Finals, and despite losing to the Celtics in the Finals', they took two games from the 1985-86' Celtics—a team on the shortlist for greatest teams of all-time. It's clear the Rockets had a lot of immediate promise and success with Hakeem .. so why include him here?

Because the contender that portended to be a perennial threat in the West for the remainder of the 80s evaporated as quickly as it had materialized. Ralph Sampson would never be healthy after that 1985-86' season, and we can see that his career Wins Added is 4th best among this group of Rockets. Even with Sampson's positive contribution to cumulative PIPM, Hakeem's teammates compile a negative cumulative PIPM figure (-0.82, yikes), similar to the -0.92 figure that Robinson's teammates add up to. Hakeem's teammates notably also have the lowest total Wins Added so far.

The Rockets would gradually add pieces into the 90's (Kenny Smith, Vernon Maxwell). But it wasn't until they missed the playoffs in 1991-92', and were awarded the 11th overall pick, that they would really upshift into contending-mode. They used that pick to select Robert Horry, and in Rudy Tomjanovich's first full season as coach, the team won 55 games. Jordan retired in 1993, opening the door for the Rockets to win back-to-back championships in 1993-94' and 1994-95'.

And then .. there were Kevin Garnett's teammates.

Kevin Garnett – Timberwolves – 1995-96' through 2006-07'

Most Total Minutes Played by T'Wolves During that Stretch (Excluding Garnett):	Career PIPM			
	O-PIPM	D-PIPM	PIPM	Wins Added
1) Wally Szczerbiak	+0.85	-0.80	+0.04	37.19
2) Sam Mitchell	-0.88	-1.13	-2.01	6.01
3) Anthony Peeler	-0.44	-1.22	-1.66	11.78
4) Tom Gugliotta	-0.49	+0.32	-0.17	36.18
5) Rasho Nesterović	-1.62	+1.67	+0.05	32.83
Cumulative	**-2.58**	**-1.16**	**-3.75**	**123.99**

I don't even know where to begin with this one. Garnett's teammates in this experiment provide the worst cumulative O-PIPM, overall PIPM, and Wins Added. Previous to this breakout, Hakeem's poo-poo platter of Rocket teammates compiled the worst cumulative Wins Added—(176.61). The cumulative figure for Garnett's teammates is a brutal 123.99.

The cumulative overall PIPM figure for Garnett's teammates is -3.75—ouch. For perspective, -3.75 is exactly Boston Celtic draft pick Semi Ojeleye's career PIPM figure—the 3,479[th] ranked player in the entire PIPM database, and a fringe NBA player in 2019-20' at the age of 25.

Don't forget that Garnett spent *12 years* in Minnesota before being traded, which dwarfs the stranded stretch for the other players we've talked about—LeBron (7) Chris Paul (6) David Robinson (8) Hakeem (8). Without question, the opening stretch of Kevin Garnett's career showcased the most stranded we've ever seen a superstar.

Minnesota's organizational let-down can't be put on just one person, event or decision—failing to get more talent around Garnett required the Holy Trinity of unfortunate franchise happenings—bad fortune, bad timing and bad decisions. I really don't like highlighting the mistakes of basketball-thinkers who are smarter than I'll ever be, but seriously man, 12 years? Wally Szczerbiak? What the hell happened here?

My buddy Pat is a long-time Minny native, and I asked him where the real failure occurred. He suggested the Stephon Marbury situation as a pivot point, and it seems like investing in Marbury was a primary organizational failure. In Pat's words:

> *They [KG & Marbury] seemed to have a really good thing going in 97'-98', and had the Sonics on the ropes in the playoffs but were edged out. Seemed like they could have been the young dark horse team on the way to being elite. Season after was the lockout year, and Marbury demanded a trade. He had the talent they were looking for, but he didn't like being #2 to Garnett. Thinking back on this makes me realize how far the organization has fallen.*

No kidding, brother. Unquestionably, Minnesota betting on Stephon Marbury becoming a franchise cornerstone was a crucial mistake.

The team drafted KG in the 1996 draft, and they held the fifth pick in the 1997 draft. They used the pick on Ray Allen, but swapped it on draft night for the rights to Marbury.[147] Marbury's skill on the court was immediate, and Minnesota began shaping their future around him. We didn't know Marbury was terminally malignant as a personality yet, so you can't fully blame Minnesota. But they would let Tom Gugliotta walk to free up cap space (and satisfy his displeasure playing with Marbury),[148] in an attempt to utilize it on a massive contract for Steph.

In the lockout-shortened 1998-99' season, after that narrow loss to the Sonics in the playoffs, Marbury forced his way out via in-season trade. Rough. He was the most talented player KG would play with in Minnesota, however brutal a personality he was. In the offseason after the lockout-shortened season, Minnesota would engage highly sought-after free agent Joe Smith in an illegal contract that would come at a large cost. Reportedly, Minnesota had worked out a deal with Smith to sign him to three straight, one-year contracts for very little money, so they could obtain his Bird Rights,[149] then sign him to a huge deal going into the fourth season.

The league came down hard on the circumvention of the salary cap, and the T'Wolves eventually lost their 2001, 2002 and 2004 first-round draft picks. Owner Glen Taylor was suspended for a year, and VP of Basketball Operations, Kevin McHale, was forced into a year-long, unpaid leave of absence. Rough. Also, not great:

o As part of their haul for Marbury, Minnesota received the sixth pick in the 1999 draft. They used it on Wally Szczerbiak—who was an alright NBA player—but as we learned earlier, became the player who played most alongside KG. Not great. The 7th, 8th, 9th and 10th picks in that 1999 draft? In order—Rip Hamilton, Andre Miller, Shawn Marion, Jason Terry. Not. Great.
o Malik Sealy died in a car crash in November 2000. He wasn't a star for the team, but a solid contributor, nonetheless. Really not great.
o Chauncey Billups broke through in the 2001-02' season, his second for the Timberwolves, but bolted for the Pistons in free agency after the season, and become a perennial All-Star, All-NBA caliber point guard, and 2004 Finals' MVP'. Effectively Chauncey used his two seasons in Minnesota to rehab his career. I'm a Pistons fan, so I'm not mad, but *super not great* for the T'Wolves.

---

[147] Not to mention, they threw in a future first-round pick to get off of Ray Allen and acquire Stephon Marbury. Just brutal.

[148] On September 2nd, 2018, Patrick Reusse of the *Star Tribune* (Minnesota's biggest newspaper), published an interview with Gugliotta. This priceless quote from Gugliotta told you everything you needed to know about Marbury—*Steph looked at Allen Iverson as his rival, even if no one else did. Some nights, Steph passed. Other nights, he tried to be Iverson.*

[149] Bird Rights, in short, allow a player to earn more when they go to sign contracts, and allow the team to exceed the salary cap when signing deals with players who have them. A player obtains Bird Rights after three seasons with one team.

Despite the frequent turbulence during KG's Minnesota tenure, they still made the playoffs seven straight seasons from 1996-97' to 2002-03'. Determined to get over the hump, the organization went 'all-in' for the 2003-04' season. The team added Sam Cassell, Latrell Sprewell and Michael Olowakandi who all contributed to a dominant team that won 58 games in the regular season. The T'Wolves won the first two rounds of the Western Conference playoffs but ran into the Lakers in the Western Conference Finals. Had it not been for a Sam Cassell injury that severely limited him during the series, perhaps the T'Wolves would have reached the Finals', but alas, they lost in six games to Los Angeles.

That season, which also saw Garnett hoist his only League MVP trophy, stands as the golden moment for the Minnesota Timberwolves franchise. In part, because the glory would soon fade. The T'Wolves failed to reach the playoffs in the three following seasons, before finally agreeing to move Kevin Garnett in the summer of 2007. Minnesota spent 12 years with a historically great NBA player, but just one of those years saw the team go beyond the first round of the playoffs.

Context is endlessly important in this exercise, and I thank you for enduring 3,000+ words of me trying to properly contextualize just how bad Kevin Garnett's situation was to begin his career. I admit that you have to squint to reveal Garnett's candidacy for Tier II, but once you get a glimpse of it, it's impossible to look away. Watching Kevin Garnett on tape is legitimately thrilling. Defensively, he truly never stopped moving, and was seemingly never out of position. Offensively, he had an array of post-moves, and was perhaps the greatest front-court creator in the history of the game. I highly recommend watching as much Garnett tape as possible, because his impact was undeniable in every facet of the game. If logging serious YouTube time isn't in the cards, well then, we've now encircled why advanced stats are so important—contextualizing someone's impact versus someone else takes far more than comparing a box score, and when you don't have the ability/time/desire (or League Pass) to actually watch a certain player, we have a rapidly expanding reservoir of advanced metrics that show us that which we don't always have time to see.

From my perspective, Kevin Garnett's profile is one of the best arguments for why advanced statistics matter. We've covered why it was that Garnett was unable to bolster his all-time profile with playoff success and/or championships for the first two-thirds of his career (and the majority of his prime). The question then becomes 'Is there evidence to suggest greater team success, given he'd played through the meaningful portion of his career with appreciably more capable teammates?'. Because of the nuance, balance and variety of situational factors baked into advanced statistics, the overwhelming answer is 'You bet your sweet ass there is'.

In terms of his standing in the PIPM model—Garnett comes in as the 13th-highest rated player ever, claims the 7th best ever peak for his virtuoso 2003-04' season, and stands 3rd all-time in Wins Added. Outside of PIPM, KG is 9th all-time in Win Shares, holds the 15th-best Box Plus/Minus figure, and accrued the 4th-most VORP in the history of the NBA.[150] Blah, blah, blah—I get it, I get it—enough with the goddam NERD marathon. Alright, if the monster

---

[150] 1) LeBron James 2) Michael Jordan 3) Karl Malone 4) Kevin Garnett.

statistical profile doesn't float your boat, how about the fact that the moment he actually had a real team around him, he won a championship? [151]

After the 2006-07' season, *just when LeBron thought his vanquishing of the Pistons meant Eastern Conference supremacy for years to come*, Boston acquired Ray Allen and Kevin Garnett in the 2007 offseason, further deterring the title odds for LeBron's Cavs, and monumentally increasing their own. They now boasted a core of Rondo, Garnett, Allen and Pierce—all of whom, like Garnett, were hungry for their first championship. The 2007-08' championship season for Boston is worth zooming in on for obvious, and maybe less obvious reasons. It was Garnett's lone championship, and one he contributed massively toward. It was also the only season he'd be fully healthy with Boston, and in that way, to me, was the marker for the end of his prime. The Celtics absolutely dominated the league in 2007-08'—they won 66 games, and regardless of who you ask, were one of the three best defensive teams of all-time. How did Garnett integrate into his new ecosystem? He managed to lead the league in defensive rating (94),[152] and despite lower usage numbers, increased his shooting efficiency numbers while ceding possessions to Pierce and Allen.

Play slowed down for the Celtics when the postseason began, as it tends to do, and it took them seven games to win both their first and second round matchups.[153] They beat the past-their-best Pistons in six games, before meeting the Lakers in the Finals'. The Celtics prevailed in six games over Kobe & Pau's Lakers, marking the first championship for the franchise since the 1985-86' season. Pierce was awarded Finals' MVP for his efforts versus the Lakers, but Garnett was unquestionably Boston's most important player throughout the season. He finished third in league MVP voting, and during the playoff run led all Celtics in Defensive Win Shares, Offensive Win Shares, BPM, VORP, Usage, Total Rebounding Percentage, and held a huge advantage over his teammates in PER (KG 23.0, Allen 14.9, Pierce 17.4, Rondo 15.8). I'm glad KG was able to prove that he was capable of being the best player on a championship team, because it's clear he did it in the nick of time.

I'll spare you the Ken Burns-level detail regarding the remainder of KG's career, but the overhead view would show that he played with the Celtics until 2013, was moved to Brooklyn in that heist of a trade by Danny Ainge, got moved less than two seasons later (back) to Minnesota, where he would end his playing career. Garnett, who was ruggedly durable early in

---

[151] Just like Oscar Robertson. Oscar's lonely tenure in Cincinnati, followed by his immediate success in Milwaukee is actually a fascinating parallel to KG's career. Jacob Goldstein created a faux-PIPM for players who played prior to 1973-74', and I'm going to do a faux-Oscar Robertson profile for the experiment we did earlier in this profile for stranded players. The five teammates who played the most minutes during the first ten years of Oscar's career in Cincinnati, followed by their career PIPM —1) Jerry Lucas [+1.73] 2) Adrian Smith [-0.83] 3) Wayne Embry [-0.81] 4) Jack Twyman [+0.90] 5) Bucky Bockhorn [-1.96]. The cumulative PIPM for these five guys is -0.97. It's not as accurate as the other guys I profiled, but Oscar's early career symmetry to KG was noteworthy, nonetheless.
[152] Always a better team stat than an individual one. But, I'd say it's valuable in large sample sets, or say, when a player spearheads maybe the greatest defense of all-time.
[153] Including the classic in game seven of the second round versus the Cavaliers—aka Pierce v. LeBron—during which Pierce scored 41 (on 13 of 23) and LeBron had 45 (on 14 of 29). Too bad LeBron's starting five was him, Wally Szczerbiak, a washed Ben Wallace, a 32-year old Big Z, and Delonte West. There are no typos in that re-interpretation of the starting five which pushed the 2007-08' Celtics to the brink—I REPEAT—NO TYPOS WHATSOEVER.

his career,[154] was never the same after a knee injury during the 2008-09' season. Despite the rapid aging of their core, the Celtics remained a threat in the Eastern Conference for the remainder of Garnett's tenure with the team.

Garnett proved to be the chess piece against the Cavs that they had no counter for. In fairness, their counter was always Antawn Jamison, super-old Shaq, J.J. Hickson or Andy Varejão, but I guess that's a different story. Their vanquishing of Cleveland in the 2010 Eastern Conference Finals would pit them against the Lakers in the NBA Finals' again, and perhaps force LeBron James to make a really difficult, legacy-defining decision. They lost those Finals' by a Ron Artest goatee hair, but it was an impressive run, nonetheless. At 35, Garnett finished second in Defensive Player of the Year voting for the 2010-11' season. Then in his last season as a Celtic, Boston pushed LeBron's Heat to the brink during the 2012 Eastern Conference Finals, before eventually losing in seven. Garnett then middled on the Nets, before playing on flat-out bad Timberwolves teams to end his career (how fitting).

Garnett was kind of like the princess who was trapped in the highest tower of a castle for so long, that by the time he was finally rescued, he'd already lost a good deal of what made him so desirable. Don't get me wrong, when he was paraded through the village, he still turned a lot of heads, but was clearly past his prime. All gender-confusing metaphors aside, what we have here is the story of the most tragically under-utilized superstar in the history of (at least) modern professional basketball. If figuring out the best players of all-time were a science, which it absolutely is not, you would hypothetically publish Garnett's profile as ground-breaking evidence that evaluating players is much more nuanced and complicated than picking from the teams who win the most often. I'm of the firm belief that Garnett had the skills, ferocious attitude and physical build to be one of the greatest, if not the greatest player of all-time, had he not been in such a shit situation for so long.

All of the things he did best were immediately transferrable across any team dynamic—help-side/rotation defense, passing, defensive rebounding, tirelessly running the court from a frontcourt position, and spreading the defense with a very reliable jump shot. The impact stats back up what we thought we were seeing with Garnett, it just took a little longer for the math to catch up, and re-interpret the effectiveness of his time in Minnesota—and let's just be honest with ourselves, none of us were watching a ton of Garnett in Minnesota.

Why He Belongs In This Tier? Given just his one championship and one MVP award, making the case for Garnett in Tier II would seem like a long shot. But, I think we now know how bad things were in Minnesota, and the conclusion his advanced metric profile tends to suggest is that he might even be *further* underrated. I think it's safe to say that we're talking about a player who has been majorly mis-appropriated in the all-time-great player hierarchy, until the last few years. There are a lot of really dynamic big men profiles that are coming for the remainder of this tier (you can probably guess, at least, a few). A lot of whom have been penciled into their respective places on the hierarchy for a long time. I can't help but think if Garnett had swapped team situations with a lot of these guys, the consensus on how great Garnett was, would definitely be appreciably higher. Beyond that, Garnett's greatness

---

[154] He played at least 81 games during the eight seasons from 1997-98' through 2004-05' (including all 47 games of the lockout-shortened 1998-99' season).

transcended the era he played in. To me, there's no question that his variety of skills would have been heavily dynamic in any era of NBA basketball—just watch his tape. Or, if you don't have the time, be prepared to concede what little statistical precedent there is for a player like Garnett, and how fingerprints like his, throughout history, always yield winning basketball.

Wilt Chamberlain

The Secret	Greatness Index	Ben Taylor Rank
48 / 100	238.38 (11th)	9th

Playoff PER	Playoff Win Shares	Playoff O-Win Shares	Playoff D-Win Shares
22.75 (21st)	31.46 (6th)	15.65 (12th)	15.81 (4th)

Matthew Weiner's *Mad Men* portrays themes and events from the chaotic, fascinating, amazing and terrifying American experience during the 1960s. The show is an unprecedented achievement in terms of historical detail, yet in seven seasons of the show, and to the very best of my knowledge, they only make three references to the NBA. Each one involves a specific NBA player, for a specific purpose. Two of the references involve guys who played for New York Knicks,[155]—the hometown team for the majority of the characters on the show. But one reference was to an NBA player that wasn't in the New York media market, meaning that player must have transcended regional popularity.

It was Wilt Chamberlain who found his name written into *Mad Men's* precisely written script. I didn't think much of the first few times I watched the episode, but his inclusion, of all possible NBA players of the era, makes perfect sense and strangely explains a lot. Pete Campbell, the *Mad Men* character who makes the reference to Wilt's physical size,[156] is not a

---

[155] In S6:E3, one scene opens with Pete Campbell staring blankly at a television set. From the TV you can hear a basketball game and the announcer says 'Willis Reed with 16 points tonight' before commotion in the scene forces Campbell to turn the TV off. The episode was set in late December, 1967—Willis Reed was helping the middling Knicks ramp up toward championship contention in 1967-68'. In S7:E2, Don is at lunch with Dave Wooster from a rival firm, Dave suggests that they take in a Knicks game soon. In one of my *favorite-ever* Don Draper lines, he responds 'Bradley's having a hell of a season'. Don Draper, who's made no other mention to basketball throughout the entire series whatsoever, is all of sudden all about Bill Bradley's box score! *Yes!* This episode takes place in mid-February of 1969—it makes sense that Don was celebrating a white Knicks player, and the ever-so-gradual integration of Knick references in the show is in line with the Knicks becoming competitive toward the end of the 1960s, and eventually winning championships in both the 1969-70' and 1972-73' seasons.
[156] Pete Campbell makes this reference during S5:E5 of the show. Given the other historical events mentioned during that specific episode, the episode was likely to have taken place during August of 1966.

person that had any interest in basketball. Yet, he knew about Wilt Chamberlain, not for his technique protecting the rim or his rebounding ability, but because Wilt had achieved the status of a spectacle during the 1960s.

Wilt's frame was north of 7-feet tall and 250 pounds, flanked with unprecedented agility and speed for that size—which made Wilt *truly* a spectacle. So why does it matter that Pete Campbell is dropping Wilt's name? Simply put, it made me realize that Wilt's 'human spectacle' status began prior to his being talked about in cosmopolitan Manhattan social circles in 1966. Long before that, he was a nearly 7 foot, 14-year-old kid in the 1950s—which to me suggests that Wilt was internalizing his status as equal parts spectacle and human being for the majority of his life—a complicated self-image that explains a ton about his basketball and non-basketball lives.

It's hard to grasp just how imposing and unprecedented Wilt's skill set was when he was becoming a professional basketball prospect. While in high school, Red Auerbach—architect of the Russell and Bird-era Celtics—acknowledged Wilt's potential to completely change the game and attempted to strike up a relationship with the kid from Philadelphia. In fact, in the summer of 1954, Red Auerbach arranged[157] for Wilt to play a 1-on-1 game with a prominent collegiate star basketball player—B.H. Born, Most Outstanding Player of the NCAA Tournament in 1953. Born was recently the 22nd pick in the NBA draft and was told by his coach to go easy on the youngster. Wilt was so dominant in the 1-on-1 game (which Wilt won 25-10), as well as traditional pick-up games that they played with others and against each other, that Born decided not to pursue a professional basketball career, and instead became a tractor engineer! He's quoted as saying:

> He turned me inside out. I'd never seen college guys do some of the
> things he did, dunking, blocking, running along with the speediest little
> guys … it was almost terrifying. Go easy? Several times I just wanted to
> save my life. I think he got something like 29 off me, and I was supposed
> to be able to play defense.

So yeah, while in high school, Wilt Chamberlain was so good that he demoralized legitimate NBA prospects to the point where they decided to not play basketball anymore. In his three high school seasons, his team went 56-3 and he averaged a modest 37.5 points per game. Every university in America that had a basketball program tried to recruit Wilt. Writer Robert Cherry did the definitive biography on Wilt (*Larger Than Life, 2004)* and he states that Wilt wanted to get away from Philadelphia (and thus NYC) for his college ball. He also apparently wanted to avoid the south because of segregation (smart), which left the Midwest as an attractive choice. After visiting The University of Kansas, and striking a connection with coach Phog Allen, Wilt decided to become a Kansas Jayhawk.

This might come as a surprise to you, but he flattened everyone in college. He was forced to play for the freshman team his first year, but was elevated to the varsity squad for the 1956-57' and 1957-58' collegiate seasons. He dominated individually, but the team would fall

---

[157] It was common for prominent prospects and draft picks to gather in the Catskills in New York to showcase their skills, providing prominent figures in the basketball community to evaluate young talent.

short of the championship in both seasons **{put a pin in that {1}}**. One serious difference between my pre-research appraisal of Wilt and my post-research conclusion was how truly gifted he was as an athlete. I'd always visualized him as a plodding, methodical player who simply over-powered the competition, and that just couldn't be further from the truth. While at Kansas, Wilt competed in track and field all three years—he would clock a personal best 100-yard dash at 10.9 seconds,[158] he triple-jumped more than 50 feet, and won the high jump at the Big Eight track and field championship all three years at Kansas. Despite falling short of a championship in basketball, Wilt had already achieved spectacle status by the time he was ready to leave Kansas. When it was time for professional basketball, he'd already been featured in *Life, Look, Time* and *Newsweek* (NBD by 2020 standards, BD by 1958 standards).

Wilt wasn't allowed to jump to the NBA after just three collegiate seasons at that time—a player would have to wait for his undergraduate class to graduate—so Wilt Chamberlain decided to play for the Harlem Globetrotters for the 1958-59' season. Wilt's celebrity status made him a very cohesive fit into the basketball circus that the Globetrotters were famous for. The Globetrotters made history by doing a tour of the USSR in 1959. If the timing of that seems strange, it's because the USA was deeply entrenched in the Cold War with our Soviet adversary. The Harlem Globetrotters performed in front of Nikita Khrushchev himself, against whom Kennedy would square off during the Cuban Missile Crisis just three years later. All international tensions aside, The Globetrotters were received very well during their sold-out tour of the USSR. Wilt always spoke fondly of his time with the team, and would even return to The Globetrotters later in his career during the offseason from his NBA responsibilities. In 1959 though, it was time for Wilt to take his talents to the NBA and compete against the best in the world.

Wilt immediately became the league's highest paid player when he joined his hometown Philadelphia Warriors for his rookie season of 1959-60'. The stats from his first three seasons would suggest that he also immediately became the league's best player. Wilt won rookie of the year and league MVP in that first season, and notched records in the first three seasons of his career that haven't even been approached. Just to name a few—PPG during a season (50.2 in 1961-62'), total points during a season (4,029 in 1961-62'), and most consecutive 30-point games (65 from 1960-61' into 1961-62') will all never be broken, full stop. Wilt was an immediate force to be reckoned with (and game planned around) from when he first stepped foot in the league.[159] One of the approaches from his opponents was to foul him, and to foul him very hard. In fact, Wilt even considered walking away from the NBA in those

---

[158] I don't know track and field, but I read that the 100-yard dash has largely been replaced by the 100-meter dash. Stupid metric system. But for context, Usain Bolt's best 100-meter dash was 9.58 seconds (9.14 in the first 100 yards). So Wilt, at over 7 feet and 230 pounds, ran less than two seconds slower than that. That's pretty fucking wild.

[159] The weight of this fact deserves more than a literal footnote, but I have to include it, nonetheless—Wilt was so dominant that he forced the league to make rule changes. 1) Because Wilt's teammates discovered they could inbound the ball over the basket from the baseline and have Wilt just dunk the ball, the league outlawed that. 2) Because Wilt developed the strategy of rebounding his own missed free throws for dunks (or jumping and missing on purpose), the league outlawed crossing the free throw line until the ball hit the rim. 3) Because Wilt was legitimately unstoppable on the block, the league outlawed his parking himself so close to the basket by widening the paint area. 4) Because Wilt was so dominant on the offensive glass, the league outlawed offensive goaltending. All of these measures significantly impacted the game going forward.

first couple years because of the omnipresent double and triple-teams he was facing, on top of the brutally hard fouls he routinely endured. Boston Celtic legend, Tommy Heinsohn, who played against Wilt throughout the 60s, is quoted as saying:

> *Half the fouls against him were hard fouls .. he took the most brutal pounding of any player ever.*

Wilt's Philly Warriors had high hopes for the postseason in those first three seasons, but would fall short of the Finals' each year, with two of the three defeats coming to Russell's Celtics **{put another pin in this one {2}}.**

The team moved to San Francisco after Wilt's third season and became the San Francisco Warriors prior to the 1962-63' season. Because many key players either decided to retire or play for teams closer to their home in Philadelphia, the Warriors sucked that year and missed the playoffs. The franchise had yet to bring in a coach that could get through to Wilt, so they brought in a new coach for 1963-64'—Alex Hannum—an ex-military guy that was a little more heavy-handed. That would be Wilt's fourth coach in five seasons **{PIN {3}}**, but coupled with the addition of future hall-of-famer Nate Thurmond, the Warriors would have a successful season that yielded Wilt's first trip to the Finals'. Unfortunately for Chamberlain, he'd face off against Russell in the Finals', and Boston sealed their sixth consecutive championship in five games over Wilt's Warriors. In 1964-65', San Francisco got off to a miserable start, and ended up shipping Wilt back to Philadelphia (in 1963, the Syracuse Nationals became the Philadelphia 76ers). The Warriors owner had this heartwarming remark after shipping Wilt back to Philly:

> *Chamberlain is not an easy man to love .. the fans in San Francisco never learned to love him. Wilt is easy to hate .. people came to see him lose.*

Wilt joined a very talented Philly team for the remainder of the 1964-65' season, and despite some chemistry issues and Wilt crossing wires with the coach, the squad began to mesh by the time the postseason came around. They'd knock out Oscar Robertson in the first round, setting up another matchup between Wilt and Russell in the Eastern Division Finals. The series was an absolute battle that was forever immortalized when, down one point with five seconds left in game seven, the 76ers' Hal Greer had his inbound pass stolen by the Celtics to secure a Boston series victory (*HAVLICEK STOLE THE BALL*).

Before we start on the 76ers' 1965-66' campaign, and because I haven't used a single table yet in Wilt's profile, let's just pause to admire the numbers that Wilt had hung up to this point in his career:

	PPG	RPG	PER	WS/48
1959-60'	**37.6**	**27.0**	**28.0**	**.245**
1960-61'	**38.4**	**27.2**	27.8	**.240**
1961-62'	**50.4**	**25.7**	**31.7**	**.286**
1962-63'	**44.8**	**24.3**	**31.8**	**.264**

1963-64'	**36.9**	22.3	**31.6**	**.325**
1964-65'	**34.7**	22.9	**28.6**	.219

Repurposing the *Basketball Reference* bold print strategy here—the bold stats represent a category which Wilt led the league in—don't avert your eyes, it's basically all of them. He couldn't get past Russell and the Celtics (yet), but he was an unstoppable force otherwise. This also necessitates another important conversation about the role of pace and possessions per game in the processing of statistics in the NBA. We've talked about that 1961-62' season several times now, but let's try to put into context why the numbers blew up so much. Over the course of the NBA, a combination of rule changes and league trends have resulted in varying ranges of scoring averages. This graph charts the variance in the amount of points per game that teams have scored over time, as well as the correlative figure of team field goal attempts per game:

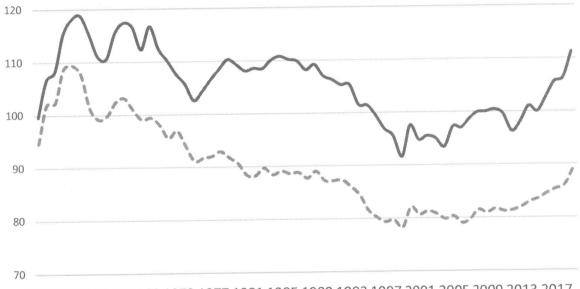

—— Team PPG   --- Team FGA Per Game

I chose to use PPG and FGA per game because possessions per game stats only date back to 1973-74'.[160] If you look at the first spike on the graph, you'll see that PPG crests at 118.8 in that 1961-62' season—the highest scoring season in the history of the NBA. You can stretch this data to assume that more points, more shots and more possessions meant vastly increased individual statistics for points and rebounds. Conversely, you can see that these numbers bottom out in 1998-99' (a lockout-shortened season) at 91.6 PPG, and again during 2003-04' at 93.4 PPG—because 2003-04' was a full season, it is considered the lowest scoring season in the

---

[160] Granular and nerdy sidenote—all Offensive Rating and Defensive Rating figures from before 1973-74' are estimated, but still pretty reliable.

history of the NBA.[161] When it comes to Wilt, does this historical context mean that we shouldn't appreciate those bonkers numbers? Absolutely not. He was genuinely that physically dominant and skilled, even if the numbers are exaggerated. But, now we know that they didn't occur in a vacuum.

The 1965-66' season for the 76ers was a pretty familiar storyboard—Wilt individually dominated (winning his second league MVP), he pissed off his coach, and they lost to Russell's Celtics in the playoffs. Wilt's stubbornness was reaching new bounds at this point, as he was living in New York City and commuting to Philly for his team responsibilities—this forced the team to practice later in the day, which made everyone unhappy. During the series with Boston, while Wilt played superb during the games, he skipped several practices and refused to integrate with his teammates. Not great. Philadelphia brought in Alex Hannum as the coach after this season (he had coached Wilt in San Francisco when they went to the 1964 Finals'). The hope was that Hannum's more assertive style would rein Chamberlain back into a team-oriented framework—a seemingly far-fetched prospect, but it would actually work out better (and faster) than anyone would have expected.

The 1966-67' Philadelphia 76ers were one of the greatest teams of all-time. Per Cherry's biography on Wilt, there was a very tense meeting between all members of the team before the season which established the dynamic that drove them to such a successful season. Hannum called out Wilt for being selfish, and allegedly several team members had to separate the two from a physical altercation (that would have been terribly one-sided). Legend has it that Alex Hannum's approach yielded respect from Wilt Chamberlain, and accomplished the unthinkable in the process—convinced Wilt to adjust his style of play to potentially produce greater team success. The result was an incredibly balanced and dominant basketball team that got off to a 46-4 start, and would ultimately go 68-14 (which was then a record for wins). Wilt saw his numbers dip significantly as Hannum implored him to focus more on the defensive end, allowing the other effective offensive players to balance out the Philly attack. During Wilt's nuclear 1961-62' season, he took 35% of his team's shots, but only took 14% during their 1966-67' campaign. That focus on efficiency, instead of volume, led Wilt to break the record for field goal percentage at the time (68.3%). Philly matched up against Boston once again in the Eastern Finals, with Boston now the eight-time defending NBA champions (not a typo). This script did not go the way it had gone the previous five times Wilt had lined up against Russell, and the 76ers actually bruised the Celtics on their way to a convincing five-game series victory. In the 1967 Finals', Wilt and Hannum thwarted the efforts of their former team, the San Francisco Warriors, to win the NBA championship. It's a pretty remarkable feat to convince a player of Wilt's stature to adjust his approach and get him to buy into winning.

Philadelphia was nearly as dominant in their 1967-68' campaign. They won 62 games, following the more egalitarian script that had earned them a title in the previous season. Once again, they would find themselves pitted against Boston in the Eastern Finals, and even

---

[161] Five players belong to the 20-5-5 club—reserved for rookies who notch 20 PPG, 5 APG and 5 RPG—Oscar Robertson (1961), Michael Jordan (1985), LeBron James (2004), Tyreke Evans (2010) and Luka Dončić (2019). While these are all significant achievements for each player, LeBron's has to stand out considering what we just learned about the variance in scoring environments. When all of the other player's hit that mark, scoring was way higher than LeBron's rookie season—Big O (118.1 PPG), MJ (110.8 PPG), Tyreke (100.4 PPG) and Luka (111.2 PPG) hit 20-5-5 in far more fertile scoring environments than LBJ (93.4 PPG).

amounted a seemingly insurmountable 3-1 series lead. Bill Russell and John Havlicek (remember him?) collectively demanded that someone 'hold their beers' as they completed the first ever comeback from a 3-1 deficit to upset Wilt's 76ers.[162] Alex Hannum walked away from the team, and coupled with the unresolvable issues Wilt had with 76ers management, Chamberlain demanded a trade. He was shipped to the Los Angeles Lakers, where he would play out the final chapter of his career.

Wilt wasn't an immediate fit into the Laker's system, which by then had been spearheaded by Jerry West and Elgin Baylor for a decade. Still, they'd utilize their indisputable amount of talent to notch 55 wins in the regular season, work their way through the Western Conference playoffs, and arrange the legendary 1969 Finals' matchup against .. you guessed it, the Boston Celtics. I've already touched on this series several times, and it won't be the last time either. The storylines and melodramatic series of events that occurred during this series is more than overdue for its own *30 for 30*. For Wilt's part, it was a similar role—matchup against Bill Russell, who was playing in his final season, and had shown plenty of signs of wearing down. The Lakers grabbed a 2-0 series lead, and seemed poised for their first championship in Los Angeles. Boston evened the series, then the teams would split the next two to set up probably the most iconic game seven in the history of the NBA. Famously, the Lakers hung balloons in the ceiling of the Forum which Russell and the Celtics cited as extra motivation to claim their eleventh title in the Russell era.

Boston carried a fifteen-point lead into the fourth quarter, but Los Angeles would cut into the lead gradually. Wilt twisted his knee and infamously left the game with just a few minutes left. The Lakers got to within just one point in the final minutes, but ended up losing by two points in Bill Russell's final game. Wilt took an ocean of criticism for sitting the final few minutes of the game, and it didn't help that Wilt didn't play an especially good series, and his historic durability failed him in the worst possible moment. Or perhaps it's as good an example as there is of the difference between the different cloth from which Russell and Wilt were each cut from. Or there are those that believe that the Lakers coach prevented Wilt from re-entering the game because he vindictively wanted to cap the championship without Chamberlain.[163] Wilt had clashed with Lakers coach Butch Van Breda Kolff from the very start of the season, as he'd criticized Wilt for being lazy, egotistical and overly concerned with statistics (crazy, I know). Van Breda Kolff resigned, and Wilt had yet another coach to contend with going forward.

---

[162] 24 hours before the tip of this series, Dr. Martin Luther King Jr. was assassinated. It's hard to contemplate the fallout of such an event by today's measure. Game two of the series was postponed to honor what then president, LBJ, proclaimed a national day of mourning. Russell, who'd been continually outspoken throughout his career regarding the civil rights movement and numerous political topics, was reportedly so distraught that he didn't sleep for several days in the early part of this series.

[163] I've read a ton on this controversy, and it's actually unclear to me exactly what happened. I will say that there is a crystal-clear video of the fourth quarter of this game on YouTube, and I demand that you all go watch it. In support of the coach, the Lakers actually crested a wave a momentum after Wilt exited the game, and perhaps he was betting that he could ride that to a victory. One thing is for sure, when Wilt sustained the injury, his mannerisms were identical to how a 10 year old would act if they were hurt and trying to exaggerate their injury—even if he were in a good deal of pain, Wilt was exhibiting melodramatic gestures worthy of an Oscar. LeBron would have been jealous!

In the 1970 NBA Finals', the Lakers lost in seven games to Don Draper's New York Knicks.[164] Los Angeles then fell short of the Finals' in the 1970-71' season, when they ran into that historic Oscar-Alcindor Milwaukee Bucks squad. After that season, Wilt Chamberlain challenged Muhammad Ali to a fight. I couldn't possibly make that up. The plans had been formally drawn up for the fight to happen, and footage of the special which announced the fight, is available online. Wilt ultimately backed out, based on his father's apprehension that Chamberlain could be seriously hurt. However, Wilt's off-court endeavors (including in-bedroom endeavors) were part of his constant pursuit to prove that he was capable of things that other people simply weren't **{let's put another pin here {4}}**.

The 1971-72' Los Angeles Lakers season played out much like the historic 1966-67' Philadelphia season had—The Lakers brought in coach Bill Sharman, who was able to rein in Chamberlain's talents, while illuminating those of other teammates. Applauded as another of the great teams of all-time, the Lakers won 69 games, including a record 33-game winning streak (still a record). Come the playoffs, Chamberlain was supremely challenged again by a rematch with Lew Alcindor and the Milwaukee Bucks. Milwaukee had bested the Lakers the year before, but Wilt played one of his all-time great series', and drove the Lakers to a six-game victory and a berth in the 1972 Finals'. The Lakers capped off the season with a revenge-fueled championship performance over the New York Knicks. It was the first championship for the Lakers since moving to Los Angeles, who had been continually suppressed by heart-wrenching losses over the previous 10+ years. Wilt was named Finals' MVP as the exclamation point on one of the great team seasons in the history of the league.

The following season would be Wilt's final campaign, which was riddled with injuries, and despite again reaching the Finals', would end in a loss to those same New York Knicks. The NBA was forced to say goodbye to one of its biggest and most polarizing stars. At the end of his career, Wilt would hold more than 100 individual records, on top of being the 7x scoring champ, 11x rebounding champ, a thirteen-time all-star, 4x MVP and without question, the most physically dominant player of all-time.

Okay, so by my count, we have four different topics that we need to expand upon.

{Stats vs. Winning Stuff} From pretty early on, there was a consistent pattern for Wilt's approach to the game—*it's all about me, and how can you dispute my play if I achieve such lofty statistics.* Without question, Wilt Chamberlain has the most dominant counting[165] statistic profile of all-time. He averaged 30 points and 23 rebounds per game for his career. During that *wild west* season of 1961-62', Wilt averaged 50 points and 25 rebounds—in fact, in March of that season, Wilt famously scored 100 points in a game. I've mentioned several times that blocks and steals weren't officially tallied until the 1973-74' season, the season after Wilt retired. But, conservative anecdotal evidence suggests that Wilt probably averaged anywhere from 5 to 8 blocks per game. Wilt even led the NBA in assists (8.5 APG) during the 1967-68'

---

[164] Hobbled Willis Reed tries to play in game seven, which rallies his teammates to a victory.

[165] I don't think I ever clarified what I mean when I say counting stats—this means conventional stats like points, rebounds, assists, steals, blocks. The common compliment to a player's counting stats profile is their advanced stat profile—true shooting percentage, PER, offensive and defensive rating, PIPM, shit like that.

season. That unprecedented statistical footprint, all things being the same, should put him in the running for best ever, right?

But.. All things weren't quite the same when comparing Wilt to other all-time greats. To stilt up those lofty career averages, Wilt routinely sucked up the air of his team's offense, and seldom allowed teammates to snag defensive rebounds. For Wilt to average 50 during that 1961-62' campaign, he took *40 fucking* shots *per game!* During the game he scored 100 points, he took 63 shots to get there![166] Wilt was indeed an elite rim-protector, but would often sell-out for a block and be willing to goaltend *very often.* While the block stats would have helped to boost his legacy, if turnover stats had also been tracked during his career, his propensity to commit a lot of them would have also been a demerit.[167] As for Wilt leading the league in assists, that was a publicly-acknowledged pursuit from the big fella—he made it known that it was an achievement he coveted, and his team had to adjust their offense to reflect that Wilt was totally selling out for assists. Stat-chasing is a theme throughout Wilt's career, and a rather tough one to grapple with. Almost all NBA players keep a conscious relationship with their stats within a game,[168] but Wilt really took that to a different level. There was no question that Wilt perceived a basketball player's value to be explicitly correlative to the type of stats they compiled. So, he deliberately compiled a lot of stats, but usually to the overall detriment of the offenses within which he played. We lost Wilt in 1999, and I can't stop thinking about what an advocate he'd have been for advanced stats (namely, his own advanced stats). YOU KNOW he would have started a podcast called *Wilt's Stat Corner,* during which he would just read off his own Win Shares Per 48 and PER stats.

The exceptions to his self-centered approach are painfully obvious, and we've already covered them at this point—his willingness to emphasize winning for the 67' & 68' 76ers was clearly a deliberate decision, along with the approach he had with the 72' Lakers. I think it's too easy to just ask why he couldn't have embraced this attitude more often during his career, and it gets to the heart of what I mentioned at the top—Wilt bought into the notion that he himself was a spectacle. Sure, two different coaches were able to wedge themselves between Wilt and his pursuit of being superhuman, but he was always going to revert to believing he was bigger than the game, bigger than others judgement of him, and bigger than compromising his role as the biggest draw on any given night, regardless of the jersey he was wearing.

{**Chamberlain vs. Russell Stuff**} In all, Russell and Chamberlain faced off eight times in the postseason, with Russell's Celtics advancing or winning the championship in seven of those meetings. Their 'rivalry' serves as an effective case study for those wanting to illuminate the virtues of embracing a team concept versus executing a strategy of attempting to win on your

---

[166] His 36 makes and 63 attempts from that game both stand as the record for an individual game. Somewhere, James Harden just murmured *challenge accepted.*

[167] Not to mention usage stats. Totally conceivable that Wilt, especially his first ten seasons, is the highest usage player of all-time. Somewhere, James Harden feels slighted.

[168] Wilt never fouled out of an NBA game. An absolutely stunning statistic given larger players propensity to commit fouls. As you might expect though, this was a deliberate venture on the part of Chamberlain. For whatever reason, he thoroughly enjoyed that he could make this unprecedented claim. It's easy to speculate how this intentional effort would leave him playing less aggressive on defense at the end of countless games—a perfect example of how his pursuit of statistics superseded the importance of pursuing winning.

own. It wasn't exactly that simple, but I think that's a fair assessment. Wilt cited many times in his career that Russell wasn't required to shoulder his team's offensive load the way Chamberlain often was, allowing Russell to focus on defense and team continuity. Wilt's not totally wrong there, and Boston almost always had the more balanced team when the two faced off against one another. However, there is so much evidence that Wilt was rarely capable of grasping what it meant to be a good teammate, and when he did, it was still on his terms.

It's clear that Russell continually used Wilt's lack of self-awareness against him. Kind of like the married guy who will continually endure his single, similar-aged friend brag about his bachelor lifestyle, when maybe, deep-down, the friend knows that he too wishes he was living a more thoroughly connected life. Maybe I'm off on that, but I've spent a lot of time thinking about their relationship ever since I read Bill Simmons' 10,000-word manifesto in *The Book of Basketball* that lays out, in granular detail, why Russell should be lauded as the greater player than Wilt. Russell knew Chamberlain had the physical edge all 143 times they played against each other, but Russell was cerebral enough to know that allowing Wilt to dominate individually would cap his team's collective ability to win. If you're really looking to determine who the greater player was, you just have to look at what their peers thought of them. Up until the 1980-81' season, the league MVP was determined by a player vote. While Wilt secured more first-team All-NBA selections than Russell (7 to 3), you have to remember that those selections were determined by media members. Russell obtained more MVP awards (5 to 4), and those were selected by fellow players. Think about it this way, in that crazy 1961-62' season where Wilt went 50 & 25, Oscar averaged a triple-double, and Elgin averaged 38 & 19, *Bill Russell won the MVP award*. Where credit must be awarded though, is that Wilt was the only player to penetrate the fortress of the great Boston dynasty. His convincing championship in 1966-67' marked something that Oscar, West & Baylor failed to do during the 1960s—knock off the Celtics. And while Russell may have grabbed more MVP trophies overall, it's also significant that Wilt won multiple MVPs during the Russell era. No player outside of Bill Russell and Wilt Chamberlain won multiple MVPs during the 1960s.

It's not surprising to me that Russell and Chamberlain were friends throughout their careers. Despite one being socially conscious and politically outspoken, and the other more of a free-wheeling playboy who loved the limelight, they both were uniquely positioned to share experiences with one another. They both endured radical acts of racism, and while Wilt may have achieved a higher level of 'spectacle' status, they both lived very unusual lives that only a small number of people could relate to at that point.

{**Serial Coach-Killer Stuff**} With the exception of Alex Hannum and Bill Sharman, none of Wilt's coaches could get through to him. It was actually exhausting trying to keep up with how many coaches Wilt had during his career—in Wilt's 14 NBA seasons, he had 8 different coaches: Neil Johnston (60', 61'), Frank McGuire (62'), Bob Feerick (63'), Alex Hannum (64', 65'), Dolph Schayes (65', 66'), Alex Hannum (67', 68'), Butch Van Breda Kolff (69'), Joe Mullany (70', 71'), Bill Sharman (72', 73'). You can interpret this however you want, and you have to calculate that he was traded twice as well. But given what we've learned about Wilt here, it's probably fair to say that the number of coaches that shuffled in and out of his NBA life had more to do with him, than the circumstances beyond his control. I'll leave it up to you, but it's not a great look.

{Off-Court Stuff} Mercy—how much time do you have? Wilt Chamberlain's on-court exploits succeeded in building a legacy. But his hardwood accomplishments are only part of that story. We already covered that he actually was going to box Muhammad Ali.

In his memoirs later in his life, Wilt claimed to have had sex with more than 20,000 women. Now, I know what you're thinking—*they say he died of congestive heart failure, but it must have been all of his sexually transmitted diseases blending together to create an ultra-virus, kind of like when all the Power Rangers combined all their vehicles together to form Ultrazord.* That's probably true actually, but to me I just had to crunch the numbers here. Wilt was 63 when he died. Let's say he began his sexual experiences at 16, and was sexually active right up to when he passed away. That comes out to about 425 women slept with per year, and about 1.2 women slept with per day for the entirety of his sexual life. Considering, I'm sure, plenty of his sexual experiences involved multiple women, that is a totally conceivable number, and if it's true, that's like a sexual PER of 45—a totally unattainable metric of sexual efficiency.[169] The truth is, whether the 20k number is true or not (which it's probably not), it was supremely important to Wilt that the public believe that it was. It's kind of like when someone that claims to be rich, brags about how rich they are, when we all know that the truly rich aren't saying a word and instead are spending their energy on ways to become more rich—you know what I mean? But again, this is Wilt building the legend.

Among Wilt's post-playing career activities, the big fella started his own film production company, and starred versus Arnold Schwarzenegger, in *Conan the Destroyer*. He became a board member of the International Volleyball Association shortly after retiring from basketball, and his promotion and passion for the sport led to his induction into the Volleyball Hall of Fame. He formed a track & field club in southern California that actually cultivated a culture of high-level achievement in the sport. Andre Phillips, Alice Brown and Jeanette Bolden were all members prior to their Gold Medal performances. Three-time world champion Greg Foster was a member, as well as Florence Griffith (the only name I recognize). Wilt would maintain his status as a public figure via advertisements for TWA, American Express, Volkswagen, Foot Locker and many others.

All-in-all, you have one of the NBA's all-time most intriguing characters. When we ran down the bio on his playing career, I wasn't intentionally coloring him as a dick, that's just how a lot of his biography reads. I have to proceed with caution, however, and remember that the sheer amount of attention that Wilt Chamberlain was receiving throughout his career is something that so so so so few people can actually relate to. When I say attention, I mean all manner of attention—positive attention from fans wanting a piece of him—negative attention from people chopping him down for not winning more championships—really brutal negative racist attention because he was one of the first black mega celebrities, and like many of the star black athletes of the era, some of which we've talked about, they became the source of discomfort

---

[169] Truthfully, his methodology for arriving at the 20,000 mark was totally ridiculous. Allegedly, the number comes from the extrapolated data from a 10-day sample of his sexual exploits—over a 10-day period, he slept with 23 different women, so he then halved that number (to be conservative) and extrapolated it out over the course of his sexual life. He wasn't exactly Nate Silver over at *538* in that regard, and it really makes that number look like a sham. Also, can we talk about the fact that only one person came out and claimed to be his child—c'mon man—if we're talking about 20,000 women, he would have at least 25 (UNMISTAKABLY TALL) kids walking around.

for a lot of whites as they ascended beyond many white stars. Interestingly enough, I think Wilt and all of his antics would have been very popular in the 'me me me me me me me me' moment of 2020—people would have eaten him up. Maybe I'm overthinking the fact that *Mad Men* wrote him into its script, but maybe Wilt Chamberlain's life as a human spectacle was perfectly encapsulated into a seemingly innocuous reference.

Why He Belongs In This Tier? Wilt had an enormous leg up on the competition (pun intended). He was granted a physical advantage over the players guarding him that is incomparable to any other player in history. While he utilized that advantage to the ceiling of his own individual success, his knowing refusal to play within a winning team dynamic for so much of his career prevented him from the things that could have nudged him into Tier I—another championship or two over Russell. I can hear the case for him being in Tier I, and given how much I weight stats into all these different player's profiles, maybe I'm being a little hypocritical. But, when you have such an obvious advantage over your competition, and 'only' come up with two championships in your 14 years of playing, that's just not going to be enough for me, plain and simple.

Kobe Bryant

The Secret	Greatness Index	Ben Taylor Rank
82 / 100	332.78 (5th)	13th

PIPM	O-PIPM	D-PIPM	Peak—2008-09'	Wins Added
+2.33 (66th)	+3.23	-0.66	+4.83 (62nd)	184.99 (14th)

Playoff PER	Playoff Win Shares	Playoff O-Win Shares	Playoff D-Win Shares
23.40 (24th)	28.26 (8th)	20.97 (6th)	7.29 (31st)

      1/26 started as a pretty lovely Sunday morning. My wife and I got up slow, made coffee, and I actually put the finishing touches on one of the profiles I'd been working on for this book. I checked my phone and had a message on Google Hangouts from my friend Quinn—it's a chat with my college friends which doubles as the fantasy football thread amongst the same group. The message was just a link with a few searing words when you read them in logical order https://www.tmz.com/2020/01/26/kobe-bryant-killed-dead-helicopter-crash-in-calabasas/. In that single, indelible moment, the NBA was never the same, but that was far from my reaction at exactly that time. The rest of that day, as it was for everyone reading this right now, was spent in refusal that it was true. In fact, I was waiting for Kobe to walk through the door for the whole week following the helicopter crash. Losing Kobe was way more than a loss for the basketball community, and the outpouring of love following his death represented the incredible resonance he had with generations of people around the world. Unapologetically, he couldn't understand why everyone around him wasn't as obsessed with greatness as he was. He chose basketball, or maybe it chose him, but regardless of the pursuit, he would have willed his way to the top of his field. Tragically, he was just scratching the surface of the impact he would have had across numerous disciplines. His resonance traversed continents, cultures and language—for instance, he was so popular in China, that is was legitimately unsafe for him to be on Chinese soil. I'm a basketball fan who cares deeply about the history, precedence and context of the NBA. But on a human level, we only get a finite number of people that are wired this way, and they're worth celebrating.

Beyond a shadow of a doubt, Kobe was one of the most prolific players we've ever had. He played twenty seasons in the league, all with the Lakers. During which, he logged the seventh-most minutes in NBA history. Kobe made 18 All-Star games and earned 15 All-NBA selections during his career.[170] Kobe also stands third in field goal attempts, sixth in field goal makes, fourteenth in games played, seventh in playoff games played, and fourth in playoff points. Kobe also won five championships, either as the best or second-best player on the team—a massively impressive achievement in any context.

Less the very end of his career, Kobe was able to be a highly productive player across a very long stretch of time in the NBA. That shit was not a happy accident. Kobe played very hard for a very long time, and while he was the recipient of a bevy of physical gifts, he was a psychopathic worker behind the scenes. We've heard both quantifiable and anecdotal evidence of how hard Kobe worked on his body and his game during his career. On Jim Rome's show, I recall him telling a story of bumping into Kobe during the offseason, and Kobe declining a request to go out with Rome and his friends because Kobe insisted that he needed to get back to the gym. These tales fuel the Kobe mythology and are so common, that to his credit, they're less mythology and actually serve as realistic evidence of how his wildly successful career was fueled. I'm very quick to debunk reputational exaggerations related to Kobe's profile, but how hard Kobe worked is not one of those exaggerations. I'm going to spare you a drawn-out list of stories about his work ethic, or about how he was always the first one in the gym, or what a tireless worker he was. Make no mistake, you'll find glowing testimonials that attest to all of these claims from the likes of Tyson Chandler, Jay Williams, Metta World Peace, Jerry West, Michael Jordan, Byron Scott, John Celestand,[171] Shaquille O'Neal, Rick Reilly, Gary Payton, Deron Williams, Robert Horry, Caron Butler, Ronnie Turiaf, and many more. What I am going to do is focus on a cluster of stories about Kobe Bryant that genuinely had a profound impact on the world of basketball.

I've come to love watching USA basketball crush their opposition in international tournaments. USA should always win in basketball, but there's something especially gratifying about watching my country dominate my favorite sport. All of the counter-narratives, melodrama and bullshit that tends to accompany high-profile NBA stars during their league season doesn't apply here—just win, and preferably by a wide margin. In September of 2014, I had quit my job and decided it was a good idea to go to Spain for a month. I had completely forgotten that Spain was hosting the FIBA World Cup, and I was in perfect position to go to the semifinal in Barcelona and final in Madrid.

Conservatively put—we arranged a roster of very talented young players to counter what was a fairly weak FIBA field—Steph Curry, Klay Thompson, Derrick Rose, Kyrie Irving, DeMarcus Cousins, James Harden, Anthony Davis and Andre Drummond,[172] among others. We

---

[170] Only Kareem has more All-Star game selections (19). Kareem, Duncan and Kobe are tied for second place in most All-NBA selections (15). LeBron has the most (16) and the most First-Team All-NBA selections (13).

[171] Celestand was the Laker's thirteenth-overall draft selection in the 1999 draft. Even as a rookie, he prided himself on being early to the gym, but could never get there before Kobe. Kobe broke his wrist prior to the season beginning, and Celestand was elated that he might finally beat Kobe to the gym the morning after the injury had occurred. He arrived that morning to the sound of a bouncing ball in the gym—it was Kobe, with a cast on his right hand, in a full sweat, getting shots up with his left hand.

[172] I only included him here to let you know that I was heckling him the whole time.

had Lithuania in the semis and Serbia in the final—we won those two games by a total of 65 points. We scored *twenty* more points per game than any other team in the tournament, and allowed the third-fewest points per game—the tourney was a bloodbath. My friend Jake and I had a blast at these two games, and especially at the parties afterward. We saw it fitting that we drink *twenty* more beers per bar we visited after each game, in honor of Team USA. Dizzy Spanish mornings aside, up until the travesty that was the 2019 FIBA Team USA debacle,[173] for more than a decade USA Basketball had made a point to always bring a dominant roster to FIBA or the Olympics.

Beginning with *The Dream Team* in 1992, the USA won the gold medal at the Summer Olympics in 1992, 1996 and 2000. The World Championships in 2002, however, saw the beginning of an embarrassing slide for USA Basketball—we finished sixth in the tournament and suffered three losses—the first three losses Team USA had conceded in international play for the decade since beginning to roster NBA players. The slide would get way worse during the 2004 Olympics, where we lost three games again and ended up with a bronze medal—including an unforgettable loss to Puerto Rico in the opener—*Puerto-Freaking-Rico*. USA Basketball appointed Jerry Colangelo[174] as head of the program, granting him full autonomy in putting a team of players and coaches on the court. Colangelo's attempt to re-shift the culture couldn't prevent another semifinal loss at the 2006 World Championships, but the organization was focused on an intense redemption at the 2008 Olympics in Beijing. That's around where our story picks up.

Kobe Bryant had missed the World Championships in 2006 because of offseason knee surgery. Kobe began honoring his commitment to Colangelo and USA Basketball in the summer of 2007, ahead of the August FIBA Tournament of the Americas. Colangelo held a camp for prospective team members in July—It was Kobe's first appearance in a Team USA jersey, and from when the practices tipped off, his dedication was obvious to everyone involved.

Jerry Colangelo: His [Kobe] first day of practice when that team got together that summer, he set the tone. The ball was up in the air, it hit the floor, and he dove for a loose ball, and there it was. That was the beginning.

Kevin Durant: His [Kobe] work ethic, approach and how he appreciates the game is infectious. He's someone who loves to play so much. He's competitive when he steps in between those lines. He wants perfection.

The camp's defining moment was a now legendary scrimmage that drew a crowd of 15,000+ in Las Vegas.

---

[173] I've never been so frustrated. I was up at 5am to watch it take a miracle for us to beat Turkey in group play—including watching Furkan Mother-Fucking Korkmaz, aka guy who can barely make an NBA roster, get 16 points on 6 of 11 from the field. Fucking stab me. Then the game against France .. no redemption in the Tokyo Olympics will erase me having to watch Evan Fournier's stupid French face (sorry, Evan, it's not personal) celebrate the first time anyone had beaten the USA in 58 fucking games. That is laser-etched on my psyche. NEVER AGAIN.

[174] One of the greatest sports executives of all-time, and at the time of his appointment to head of USA Basketball, was one of the most respected high-level basketball thinkers in the world. The perfect hire.

Chris Sheridan (Basketball Writer): Bryant hit the game-winning shot over Tayshaun Prince[175] with 6.6 seconds left to give the blue team a 105-104 victory over the white team. Bryant freed himself of Prince with a pump fake before hitting a jumper from 19 feet away to put his team ahead by one. After a timeout, Bryant defended LeBron James on the game's final possession and forced him to miss wide right on a short jumper from the lane that would have won it. Bryant finished with 26 points on 10-for-22 shooting, including 4-for-9 from 3-point range [plus 5 assists and 5 steals]. Blue squad teammate Carmelo Anthony led all scorers with 28. One of the more impressive performances came from rookie Kevin Durant, who shot 9-for-14 for 22 points for the blue squad.

Kevin Durant would be left off of the FIBA roster, but the USA brought a dominant squad that swept the competition in emphatic fashion[176]—giving Team USA their first victory at a major international competition in seven years. Colangelo's sweeping vision of bringing USA Basketball back to dominance was under way, and Kobe's tangible and intangible fingerprints were all over it. The Following summer, on June 23rd, 2008, USA Basketball announced their 12-man roster for the Beijing Olympics—Carmelo Anthony, Carlos Boozer, Chris Bosh, Dwight Howard, LeBron James, Jason Kidd, Chris Paul, Tayshaun Prince, Michael Redd, Dwayne Wade, Deron Williams, and Kobe Bryant. Mike Krzyzewski was named head coach, with Jim Boeheim, Mike D'Antoni and Nate McMillan named assistant coaches. A few days later, the team would convene in Las Vegas for three weeks of training before flying to China for a few exhibition games before the Olympics got under way. Kobe's focus was apparent from the squad's first meeting and practice.

Chris Bosh: We're in Las Vegas and we all come down for team breakfast at the start of the whole training camp, and Kobe comes in with ice on his knees and with his trainers and stuff. He's got sweat drenched through his workout gear. And I'm like *'It's 8 o'clock in the morning, man. Where in the hell is he coming from?'*

Dwayne Wade: Everybody else just woke up. We're all yawning, and he's already three hours and a full workout into his day.

Chris Bosh: You never forget stuff like that. I felt so bad. I'm like 'what is he trying to prove?' But he was just doing his normal routine. We're all supposed to be big-time NBA players, Olympians and stuff. And then there's Kobe, taking it to another level from Day 1.

Nate McMillan: Kobe sat right behind the coaches at a table by himself. It looked kind of weird. Kobe was sitting at the first table as if he didn't know the other guys.

---

[175] Too bad Kobe couldn't figure out how to get past Tayshaun in the 2004 Finals'!!!!!!!

[176] The first game of the tournament was against Venezuela—Team USA was up 40 in the second half, but it didn't stop Kobe from pressing Venezuela's guards full court. Said Jim Boeheim—*He doesn't fuck around. He doesn't care if it's summer, winter, fall or spring. He does not take any prisoners. That's what you're looking for as a coach. He's a killer. He comes out to kill people. He was up 40 points pressing some poor kid from Venezuela.*

Jerry Colangelo: In some ways, he was a little bit of a loner. People didn't really have a good read on him. People looked at him in a particular way and just kind of put him in a box.

Nate McMillan: Kobe is a guy that doesn't allow himself to be that close with opponents. All of those guys, even though they played in All-Star Games against each other—and some of them together—he didn't know them like that. He knew them, but he didn't know them in a sense.

This isolation Kobe was exhibiting early on in camp comes as a surprise to none of us. Kobe has always been about the work, and until Kobe perceived that the group was trying to work as hard as he was, he'd continue to keep his distance.

Chris Bosh: You saw that focus and how much he pushes himself. He beat me to the gym, and he had just finished playing[177]—I had been off for three months. That showed me this guy really wants to be the best.

Kobe Bryant: He [Dwayne Wade] met me in the gym at five, and then LeBron started showing up at five, and then they all started showing up at five. And then next thing you know, most of the guys were in the gym at five getting some work in. In that time, we were all in the same hotel, generally the same schedules. That's when I got to know guys a little bit more.

Chris Bosh: I thought I was working hard. Now I have to get back into the gym.

Carlos Boozer: We all clung to it. It soon became our workout, not just his workout.

Kobe, the second-oldest player on the roster, was genuinely leading by example. Throughout the camp, he forced the rest of his team to raise their level of preparation much further than they'd been accustomed to. In 2008, you didn't have players Instagramming their workouts for millions to see—for all of the other members of Team USA, this was their first exposure to Kobe's work ethic off the court, which previously had only been mythologized. The group arrived in China already playing in high gear. As soon as they arrived, many of Team USA's budding stars were able to witness what it meant to be an international superstar—even at that time, it was genuinely unsafe for Kobe to be in China, because he was so monumentally famous. As the preliminary games got underway, Kobe's cachet and international popularity was palpable amongst opposing teams as well.

Kobe Bryant: I don't really know how to explain it to be honest with you. I think it's my fifth time in China. I've been popular here since 99', but this summer, I didn't know I was this big!

Tayshaun Prince: Out of anybody on our team, those international guys, no matter who we played against, all them dudes wanted to guard Kobe. That was their guy. They looked up to him, and every time he got the ball, there were two or three guys around him.

---

[177] Kobe's Lakers had narrowly lost in the Finals' to the Celtics just a few weeks prior.

For guys like LeBron, Wade, Bosh and Melo, they could see first-hand the impact that Kobe had on the international basketball community. A status that clearly became aspirational, particularly to the rapidly-ascendant-megastar, LeBron James. From the beginning of camp, there had been questions about how LeBron and Kobe would mesh, and whether or not there would be a coherent chemistry.

Jason Kidd: The talk was always gonna be between LeBron and Kobe. Can they get along? Can the two alpha dogs coexist?

Chris Bosh: Kobe was obviously on top,[178] and Bron wanted to get there. We all wanted to get there.

Jim Boeheim: They were in the card games. They were always together. There was no mistaking the leader of that next generation. LeBron's combination of basketball ability and IQ commanded respect not just from his peers but everyone on the roster. When he spoke, they listened.

Tayshaun Prince: His [Kobe] mentorship was going out, playing hard all the time, putting in the work, and letting you see it.

Jim Boeheim: I don't know if LeBron would say this, and I'm not going to put words in his mouth, but I felt Kobe raised the level of everybody, especially on the defensive end. If we had a weakness in 2006, it was on the defensive end. We weren't committed. In 2007 and 2008, we were much better there, and I think Kobe was responsible for a lot of that.

Tayshaun Prince: Even though Coach K made Jason Kidd the captain, LeBron was pretty much a captain as well. Because whether it was trying to do a breakfast in the morning or go work out at the gym before practice or any of that stuff, LeBron was the guy who was calling everybody and saying 'hey, I'm doing this, man, if we all want to get our chemistry together and try to get this thing rolling the right way'. He was the guy setting things up so everybody could be together. For him to be doing that at his age, at that time, it was impressive.

Ben Rohrbach (Basketball Writer): Where Kobe was a killer, LeBron was a unite-er.

Chris Bosh: It started with those two. Just the competitive spirit with Kobe being so serious, Bron starts being serious, and then it's like *'oh, ok, damn, I've gotta get serious'*.

Mike Krzyzewski: They developed a great relationship. They both did things to make it easy for their teammates to see and for me to see that they were going to get along and do what was necessary to help win the gold.

---

[178] On top of the three rings Kobe had won earlier in his career, Kobe was also the reigning NBA MVP in the summer of 2008.

After smoking their first three opponents in group play, Team USA matched up against Spain, which pitted Kobe against his Lakers' teammate, Pau Gasol. In the opening minutes of the game, Pau attempted to set a screen on Kobe, which prompted Kobe to bulldoze through Pau as if he hadn't been there. Kobe let the world know in bold print that nothing was standing in the way of an American gold medal.

Nate McMillan: That sent a message to everybody. It was a message to Spain and it was a message to us—Pau is in a different uniform. We're not teammates.

Kobe Bryant: He [Pau] knows me, man. I don't play, and for us, it was important to send that message, too. We had just come off losing to the Celtics, and I wanted to send Pau a message as well in *'this is what you have to be willing to do in order to win titles'*. So, it was kind of a dual message, one for our team and USA and winning this game, winning this medal, but also for Pau in understanding this is the line that you have to cross in order to be a champion.

LeBron James: It was one of the first plays of the game. I was like 'this guy's all about winning and whoever he's playing for or who he's playing with that point in time'. He really forgot Pau was his teammate. Like, he really forgot that he was about to see him in like three weeks in L.A. I swear. It was crazy.

Team USA throttled Spain in that game, closed out group play 5-0, proceeded to smoke Australia and Argentina, resulting in a rematch with Spain in the gold medal game. The 2008 gold medal game is widely considered the greatest international basketball game ever played. Spain's roster consisted almost entirely of players who were playing, or who would eventually play in the NBA. The game was a see-saw battle that saw Spain cut the lead to just two points late in the game. However, 13 points from Kobe Bryant in the fourth quarter helped to assure a gold medal for Team USA.

Pau Gasol: It was a very competitive game, it was back and forth a lot. They were throwing punches, but we were not backing down. It was really a fun game to play in until the last few minutes of the game and Kobe took over.

Carlos Boozer (reciting Kobe during a timeout): *This is the fucking moment when we squeeze them and we win the gold medal fucking right now! We squeeze them and we don't let go!*

Mike Krzyzewski: I would not have been the coach in Istanbul in 2010 if Kobe Bryant didn't step up there. But thank goodness that we had that type of team dynamic where he felt good and guys felt good about him stepping up. And he did.

USA Basketball was truly redeemed. As far as the players who helped make that happen, much of the success that they saw after the Beijing Olympics can be traced back to things they learned during their 35 days together in the summer of 2008. Kobe gave the other young stars an informal tutorial on what it took to be the best, what it looked like being the best, and how to perform when everything you'd worked for was in the balance.

163

Jason Kidd: I think for LeBron, he benefited from Kobe, and I think vice versa. I think you can look at Kobe and everybody got better. Everybody had great years that following year—Melo, Chris Paul, those guys got better seeing Kobe in that light.

Mike Krzyzewski: This whole thing wouldn't have started the way it did without him. That's why I'm still coaching. Believe me, I recognize those moments.

Jerry Colangelo: One of my great joys was watching him [Kobe] during the time with USA Basketball. He was a different guy, at least perception-wise. He led. That's how he fit in. It was different. If anyone had seen or known Kobe in his Laker days before all the Olympic stuff, that was one thing. I think the Olympic experience gave people a different opinion, viewpoint about Kobe. I think the experience helped Kobe going forward.

LeBron James (01/31/2020—during the press conference after the Lakers' first game following Kobe Bryant's death): I accepted an invitation to be a part of the Olympic team in 08', and those 37 or 42 days that we spent .. watching him from afar and you could see a lot of the clips from a lot of the practices .. me and Kobe was leading the gang, leading the troops. You could tell both of us were seeing which one was the alpha dog at the point in time, but at the same time so much mutual respect and so much grit and so much drive. I kinda just watched to see what he was able to do. Why he was great. Why he was successful in this league, and why he was one of the best players in the world year after year after year.

The more rocks I looked under surrounding the 2008 Olympics, the more certain I became that Kobe's participation changed basketball forever. LeBron became *LeBron*[179] after the 2008 Olympics. Dwight Howard led his team to the Finals' the following season (beating LeBron on the way). Chris Bosh, who's switchable defense was instrumental in Team USA's defensive scheme, continued dominating in Toronto. Chris Paul, Dwayne Wade and Carmelo Anthony would all continue to trend upwards on their Hall-of-Fame trajectories. In fact, researching Team USA in the manner I did yielded one result that was previously inconceivable—I actually gained more respect for Carmelo Anthony! He committed to Colangelo's plan, and instead of pretending to be a business mogul in his summer's off, Melo carved out a role for himself in USA Basketball history as one of our more important players.

Beyond maybe changing his sport forever, I love how positively *"Kobe"*, Kobe Bryant was in the 2008 Olympics. All of the bullet points we attach to Kobe's playing career, some of which I believe have been exaggerated over time, were on full display during the tournament. In Beijing, in the only instance where his team required him to step up, he was super clutch. After watching more tape on Kobe's defense than I'd like to admit, I can't help feeling underwhelmed and that his team would usually hide him on a lesser offensive threat—but in Beijing, Kobe was

---

[179] LeBron's 2008-09' season is the best ever season by a player to have not won a championship. Many statistical models use his performance from that season as a benchmark, as his efficiency from that year is unlikely to ever be replicated. Basically—there is a shit-load of bold-print statistics on his *Basketball Reference* page for the 2008-09' season!

watching tape on each opponent's best scorer, and demanded that he guard them. When it comes to leadership, Kobe's left a wake of Laker teammates alienated when they failed to reach the threshold of preparation and dedication that he required (amirite, Shaq?)—but in Beijing, he had teammates that were not just capable of leveling up their off-court preparation, but were skilled enough to step up capably when their number was called during the games. In so many ways, it was the perfect ecosystem for Kobe's approach to thrive.

I learned a lot doing this. Mainly, I get the dogmatic Kobe fanhood now. There's never, ever been a question about his dedication or whether or not he was putting in the work. As a fan, that's all you're looking for—to not be cheated, to know that you're attaching yourself to someone whose shortcomings won't be because they weren't prepared. That state of mind really connects with people—both the people who actually live their lives with that ferocity, and those who pretend to. Because Kobe performed a lot of MJ karaoke throughout his career, we may have given him more credit than he was due. Because he was so closely emulating the style, attitude and approach of the player generally considered to be the best ever NBA player, we started subconsciously moving him toward the MJ zone. I definitely think that's true.

The parallels are right there in front of us, shit, even MJ acknowledged as much in his book. In *Michael Jordan: The Life* by Roland Lazenby, MJ says: *Kobe had done that work to deserve the comparison. Kobe's the only one to have done the work.*[180] There are two important distinctions that have to be made going forward, and I'll elaborate on both further. Earmuffs for the Kobe legion:

1) Just because Kobe was a psychopathic worker and played with an unrelenting killer instinct, that does not exempt him from legitimate criticisms regarding his efficiency as a player.

2) Michael Jordan was a *far* superior player to Kobe Bryant in every facet of the game—and that separation should serve as worthy justification for them to be in separate tiers of historical significance.

1) Kobe Bryant was not a good outside shooter. The weird thing is that his shot was absolutely beautiful—it was like watching Leo DiCaprio smile, or listening to Paul McCartney sing a ballad, or watching Beyoncé do anything (because she's perfect). But the truth is that he was a 32.9% shooter from three for his career. That's well below average, my friends. In 16 of his 20 seasons, he shot less than 35% from three—not great! That would be okay, were he to have acknowledged it as a weakness in his game. But, he took the eleventh-most threes in the history of the game. In fact, of the 50 players to have shot the most threes in the history of the NBA, only Baron Davis and Antoine Walker have a worse career shooting percentage from three. When it comes to the playoffs, only 6 players have shot more postseason threes, but of the 25 players to have taken the most playoff threes, only Scottie Pippen has a worse playoff three point percentage than Kobe.

---

[180] There's so much to unpack in that MJ statement. I love Michael Jordan, but he may have the most advanced ego in the history of the human race. Let me translate what this statement really means—*Kobe is done playing and doesn't have a chance to surpass my legacy, but because he modeled his entire game after me, I'm going to allow soft comparisons to my game.* It's essentially a veiled shot at LeBron James, who can surpass his legacy, and that bums him out.

Given the nuclear volume that Kobe operated on—he averaged 20 field goal attempts per game in 13 of his 20 seasons—I'd say career shooting percentage of 44.7% is actually pretty good. However, there are a lot of misses across his career. When it comes to the record for most shots taken in a single game, six of Kobe's games can be found in the top ten. Oh yeah, there's also the thing about how Kobe missed more total shots than any player in the history of the NBA. It's pretty simple—missed shots are typically possessions for your opponent. When it comes to advanced stats, Kobe's statistical profile is essentially barren—effectively, there is no advanced stat that especially liked Kobe Bryant for any period of his career. On his *Basketball Reference* Advanced breakout, the only bold print statistics are Usage Percentage for three seasons, predictably. I don't need advanced stats to tell me that iso-heavy, ball-dominant, volume scorers are lacking from an efficiency standpoint. Killer instinct sometimes, maybe a lot of times, means killer-instincting/shooting your team out of games. Sorry.

That leads me to an uncomfortable conversation regarding Kobe's NBA career—earmuffs again for the Kobe legion—given his propensity for abrasiveness within a team dynamic, and a perpetually engaged *green-light*, I think Kobe needed really good teammates to succeed in the NBA. When the Lakers had middling talent around Kobe in the middle 2000s, his leadership style was wasted on players who weren't going to level up anyway. When the Lakers began to reload later in the 2000s, players like Lamar Odom, Metta World Peace, Andrew Bynum and Pau Gasol were all poised to level up around Kobe, and willing to, at minimum, emulate Kobe's level of off-court work. I get it, I'm not really providing anything dynamic—you need good players to win championships. What I'm getting at is Kobe is not a 'floor-raiser' like most of the players in his tier. Kobe was a weapon. A potentially catastrophic weapon. But to inflict maximum damage on the opponent, there was a prerequisite of his teammates knowing the instruction manual on the weapon inside and out.

1,000 makes a day, beating everyone to the gym in the morning, and accepting nothing short of excellence from your teammates every day, all make for good traits in a role model. Particularly if you're an aggressively wired human who is seeking attachment to a professional athlete who brightly illustrates all of the qualities you want to accept into your own life. That's all great, but I'm making a list of the greatest NBA players ever, and while Kobe's influence weighs in massively, I'm mostly interested in how effective a basketball player he was. The truth is there are much bigger holes in Kobe's profile, largely around his efficiency, than his sterling reputation would suggest. Don't get me wrong, I gained a lot of respect for Kobe throughout writing and researching this, but to the tune of *I think of him in the 10th-11th range all-time, instead of the 12-13 range where he'd previously been positioned for me.* After his passing, the temptation to juice his number again was difficult to ignore, but ultimately, I think he should be thought of in that fringe top-ten spot.

2) Alright, let's start this off by simply looking at Kobe versus MJ's normal counting stats for their respective careers, starting with their regular season breakout:

	Steals	Assists	Rebounds	Field Goal Attempts	Field Goal Percentage	Points
Kobe	1.4	4.7	5.2	19.5	.447	25.0
MJ	2.3	5.3	6.2	22.9	.497	30.1

Playoffs:

	Steals	Assists	Rebounds	Field Goal Attempts	Field Goal Percentage	Points
Kobe	1.4	4.7	5.1	19.5	.448	25.6
MJ	**2.1**	**5.7**	**6.4**	**25.1**	**.487**	**33.4**

Basically, Michael Jordan was a hyper-volume scorer, but did so in astonishingly efficient fashion. After we lost Kobe, there was a push to ignore some of his inefficiency, given he played in iso-heavy and less efficient iterations of the NBA. *Excuse me*, but what does that say about Michael Jordan's efficiency throughout the rock-fight 1990s? The full 5% better shooting from the field is a similar disadvantage for Kobe when compared to LeBron. The crazy thing is MJ took a bunch more shots, and still made way more of them, and averaged almost 8 more points per game in the playoffs. MJ was also a better playmaker, rebounder, and is one of just a few guards to have won Defensive Player of the Year[181]—an award Kobe was never in the running for. Let's look at the advanced stats, starting with the regular season breakout (their respective figure is followed by their all-time rank in that statistic).

	PER	Win Shares Per 48	BPM	VORP	PIPM
Kobe	22.9 (26th)	.170 (59th)	+4.55 (29th)	80.14 (12th)	+2.33 (66th)
MJ	**27.9 (1st)**	**.250 (1st)**	**+9.22 (1st)**	**116.08 (2nd)**	**+5.98 (3rd)**

Playoffs:

	PER	Win Shares Per 48	BPM	VORP	PIPM[182]
Kobe	22.4 (24th)	.157 (48th)	5.38 (23rd)	16.15 (5th)	+2.33 (66th)
MJ	**28.6 (1st)**	**.255 (1st)**	**11.14 (1st)**	**22.85 (2nd)**	**+5.98 (3rd)**

MJ's stranglehold on many advanced stat categories is another feather in the cap of analytics. No one was thinking about advanced stats while MJ was playing, but the numbers align with what we all were seeing when MJ was playing. The bottom line is MJ's profile is unassailable— the anecdotal stuff, the normal stats, the advanced stats, the hardware, it's all there. Kobe was on nearly the same number of championship teams, but the data would suggest he was the second-best player for the majority of his championships—which is fine!—but when you're being compared to MJ, that matters. Or as Omar Little would say—*When you come at the king, you best not miss!* All Tier I foreshadowing aside, no rational person is out there making the case that Kobe was greater than MJ, and to me, no rational person should be aligning them at the same lunch table and/or within the same tier and/or mentioning them within the same breath.

Any professional, regardless of their pursuit, seeks to be acknowledged by their peers above all else. Digging into the colossal impact that Kobe had during his time with USA

---

[181] Another fun bar trivia question—Can you name the five guards to have won DPOY? Sidney Moncrief (2x), Alvin Robertson, Michael Cooper, MJ and Gary Payton.

[182] PIPM doesn't separate playoff and regular season data, that's why the numbers are the same.

Basketball, particularly at the 2008 Olympics, truly adjusted my perspective on Kobe Bryant. I've been in a position where I've had to defend LeBron in LeBron vs. Kobe debates so many times at this point, that I'd begun to view Kobe as an adversary. I've been overlooking how much respect Kobe carries throughout the international basketball community, there's no question about that, and I'm glad to have re-calibrated Kobe's legacy closer to where it belongs. His ranking may not be close enough to the top for a lot of people, and for them I know the rings and the work will mask whatever criticisms come his way. I may not agree, but at least now I better understand where they're coming from.

Why He Belongs In This Tier? Saying Kobe Bryant is not a top-four player all-time is not a slight toward Kobe Bryant. He is irrefutably a great player, just not on par with the most sacred historical profiles—*also not a slight toward Kobe Bryant!* The tiered system which I based this book on is a subjective exercise that is open to pretty wide re-interpretation—I get that. However, within this self-generated construct, Kobe Bryant fits in Tier II like a glove. He's probably the player in this tier that would see the most variable placement depending on who you ask. But, if you think he's better than 5th all-time, you are delusional. However, if you think he's worse than 14th all-time, you're *also* delusional. Most importantly, if you feel Kobe needs to be at the front of this Tier, which would nominally make him a *'top-five'* player, then by all means, go for it. I just think you'll find that people that have really done the work on Kobe's contemporaries will agree on his placement being closer to a fringe top-ten guy, rather than a fringe top-five guy.

Hakeem Olajuwon

The Secret	Greatness Index	Ben Taylor Rank
88 / 100	215.8 (13th)	6th

PIPM	O-PIPM	D-PIPM	Peak—1992-93'	Wins Added
+4.70 (11th)	+1.22	+3.48	+7.03 (14th)	232.23 (8th)

Playoff PER	Playoff Win Shares	Playoff O-Win Shares	Playoff D-Win Shares
25.69 (5th)	22.60 (16th)	11.88 (23rd)	10.72 (12th)

1994 was a great year for Quentin Tarantino—*Pulp Fiction*, the film that would solidify him as one of our great filmmakers, hit theatres in September and was immediately accepted as brilliant work. Hakeem Olajuwon was having a year as well—in the 1993-94' season, he became the first (and only) player to win league MVP, Defensive Player of the Year, and Finals' MVP in the same season. Both people had given plenty of evidence of their greatness prior to that year, but it all came together in 1994 for two men that are now highly celebrated within their respective professions. Tarantino has directed 10 brilliant films over the course of his career, and *Pulp Fiction* was just his second directorial credit. The director's peak wouldn't occur for several more years and several more films. But, Hakeem's thorough dominance in 1994 represented the height of his peak—a peak that rests in air space that has been reached by only a few other players in NBA history.

I'd venture to say that Hakeem is somewhere between the 6th and 9th greatest NBA player of all-time, and Tarantino falls somewhere between the 6th and 9th greatest director we've ever had. Other than that, we're talking about people that don't ostensibly have anything in common. The thing is, outside of truly fanatical NBA followers, I'm not sure that most people realize how dominant Hakeem was. Nor do casual cinema-goers recognize the brilliance of Tarantino's universe of characters, and that the ten films he's directed have illustrated an encyclopedic, unprecedented understanding of film from a historic, contextual perspective. So, in an effort to illuminate the powerful greatness of Olajuwon's game, and the oft-subtle, ever-dazzling brilliance of Quentin Tarantino, I'm going to continue these subjective links by running down a very special top-ten list double-feature—simultaneously, I'll be counting down the top-ten greatest things about Hakeem Olajuwon's basketball career, and ranking in order of overall greatness, the ten films Tarantino has directed. Buckle your seat belts, and don't shoot Marvin in the face.

#10 Phi Slama Jama

Hakeem Olajuwon chose to play his college basketball at the University of Houston. He emigrated from Nigeria to play basketball, but wasn't a highly sought-after prospect. In fact, they didn't even know how tall he was until he was picked up at the airport in Houston. He redshirted his first year in Houston, as his eligibility with the NCAA was worked out. He played 18 minutes per game his redshirt freshman year, contributing a small amount to a team that lost in the NCAA Semifinal. That offseason, Hakeem was encouraged to work out with local Houston resident, then-reigning NBA MVP (and Tier III player), Moses Malone. Hakeem worked out with Moses extensively, and has credited that unofficial internship with Moses during the summer of 1982 as hugely important to his development. Hakeem was ready to be a main contributor to winning basketball heading into the 1982-83' season, but he had no idea that his University of Houston Cougars would spark a stylistic heel turn that reverberated throughout the basketball world.

Phi Slama Jama refers to the 1982 through 1984 University of Houston Men's Basketball team that smothered their competition with an up-tempo, flashy and free-flowing approach to the game. Spearheaded by Olajuwon, Rob Williams, Benny Anders[183] and Clyde Drexler, Houston reached the Final Four in 1982, and NCAA Title game in both the 1983 and 1984 NCAA Tournaments. Drexler left after 1982-83' for the NBA, but Hakeem led the team all the way back to the National Championship game, where they fell short to Patrick Ewing's Georgetown Hoyas. The teams went 67-9 over those two seasons. Their success through such a ground-breaking, high-flying style was heavily influential to future basketballers for generations to come. Hakeem was utterly dominant. He averaged more than 5 blocks per game in both seasons, and his blend of length, speed and strength was absolutely lethal for other teams to deal with—foreshadowing of the brewing nightmares that NBA teams would have trying to game plan around such a wildly versatile basketball talent.

#10 Death Proof (2007)

In 2012, The Hollywood Reporter held a fascinating 'Director Roundtable' which allowed a peek at the perspectives of six of the world's most notable directors at the time—David O. Russell, Ben Affleck, Gus Van Sant, Tom Hooper, Ang Lee and Quentin Tarantino. Each filmmaker was exposing really interesting insights into their process and mindset, but Tarantino was throwing 110 MPH for the whole thing, including this gem on how he feels about his 2007 film, *Death Proof*:

---

[183] One of the primary subjects of the great 30 for 30—*Phi Slama Jama*.

*To me, it's all about my filmography, and I want to go out
with a terrific filmography. Death Proof has got to be the
worst movie I ever make. And for a left-handed movie, that
wasn't so bad, all right? So, if that's the worst I ever get, I'm
good. But I do think one of those out-of-touch, old, limp,
flaccid-dick movies costs you three good movies as far as
your rating is concerned.*

Far be it from me to disagree with Tarantino, so here we are. I also love that he cares about where he lands historically in the all-time filmography discussion—but we'll focus on that a little further down the list.

Death Proof is not *not* a tough watch. It was a challenge to stay engaged when I first saw the film, and there's plenty of reasons why I've never sought out a re-watch until I went back for this. It's chock full of Tarantino-isms, like subtle reminders of the inter-connected universe his films take place in, an incredible soundtrack, and seemingly pointless, but excruciatingly deliberate dialogue and references. Tarantino likes to play around in different specific historical genres, often times constructing visual references to films that are so specific that he's categorized the practice as stealing. Stealing sounds strong, but in his own words:

*I steal from every single movie ever made. I love it—if my
work has anything it's that I'm taking this from this and that
from that and mixing them together. If people don't like that ,
then tough titty, don't go and see it, alright? I steal from
everything. Great artists steal; they don't do homages.*

Tarantino might be evoking the famous quote from artist Pablo Picasso which goes:

Good artists copy, great artists steal.

The vision Tarantino had for this movie was of a slasher film, intentionally constructed to look like the B-Level exploitation films[184] of the late 60's/early 70's. The film also showcased Tarantino's interest in movie stunt performers, with Kurt Russell's villain character playing a deranged stunt man who stalks two separate groups of women over the course of the film. The second group of women include Zoë Bell, who plays herself—a real-life stuntwoman who was the stunt double for Uma Thurman in the *Kill Bill* films. Tarantino is famously annoyed by the over-digitization of Hollywood in general, and attempted to create a real car chase scene, which he felt hadn't occurred since he began

---

[184] I didn't really know what the fuck that meant either, but apparently exploitation films are defined as low-budget movies that use sensationalist advertising to promote their lurid subject matter—specializing in sex, nudity, violence, gore etc.

making films. In that pursuit he succeeded, as the car chase scene at the film's climax is top-notch.

In fact, Tarantino succeeded overall in carrying out the hyper-specific vision he had for the film—*while toeing the line of female sexual empowerment and exploitation, he relied on numerous attractive, strong female characters to play out his foray into the retro exploitation-car chase-slasher-meta Hollywood commentary genre, all while maintaining an observable Tarantino-ness.* But his dedication to re-creating film elements that often come off corny .. led the film to feel .. a little corny. The unrelenting snappy dialogue between characters that usually crackles in his films, kind of popped and deflated in this one. He pulled off what he wanted to do, but I'm not sure that thing is terribly interesting, and it definitely feels like his worst film by a decent margin.

#9 Hakeem & The 1984 NBA Draft

It's truly wild re-imagining the results of the 1984 NBA Draft. Houston had the first pick and selected Hakeem, Portland then selected Sam Bowie, Chicago selected Michael Jeffrey Jordan, Dallas took Sam Perkins, and Philadelphia rounded out the top five by selecting Charles Barkley. It's the only draft in NBA history that yielded three MVP-winners in the first five picks.

Houston made out pretty well selecting Olajuwon, who had also played his supremely dominant college career at the University of Houston. But what if they coveted MJ? Would MJ have had nearly the career playing in Houston, ostensibly without Pippen & co., and having to battle the Western Conference the entirety of his career? No way Portland passes on Hakeem at that point, which would have re-united Olajuwon with college teammate and *Phi Slamma Jamma* broski, Clyde Drexler. Doesn't Portland compete for a title through the remainder of the 80s if Hakeem falls to them? Absolutely they do. Barkley to Philly was probably the reality that allowed Chuck to succeed—he was able to learn under Moses Malone before his penchant for off-court debauchery fast-tracked his way out of the league. The rest of the draft, including John Stockton at #16 to the Jazz, marked a massive influx of NBA talent—7 of the first 24 picks became All-Stars, and 15 of the first 24 played at least 8 seasons in the league. But the sliding door of those first three selections altered the way the league would shake out for at least 15 more seasons, as MJ was the best perimeter player of the 90s, and Hakeem was the best big man of the 90s.

#9 The Hateful Eight (2015)

After *Death Proof* in 2007, Quentin gave us four straight films that served as historical re-imaginings. In fact, this group of films make up the final phase of films by Tarantino, in what feels like three very definable phases of his directorial career:

L.A.-based Crime Films	Martial Arts / Exploitation	Historical Re-Imaginings
(1992) Reservoir Dogs	(2003) Kill Bill Vol. 1	(2009) Inglorious Basterds
(1994) Pulp Fiction	(2004) Kill Bill Vol. 2	(2012) Django Unchained
(1997) Jackie Brown	(2007) Death Proof	(2015) The Hateful Eight
		(2019) Once Upon a Time... in Hollywood

With very little exception, very bad people are the stars of Tarantino's universe. The nineteenth century American West feels like such a great setting for Tarantino films—a lawless expanse of territory with all manner of swashbuckling, morally compromised and violence-prone individuals trying to out-swindle one another at every turn. *The Hateful Eight* ranks fairly low within Tarantino's filmography, but the cast of ruthlessly deplorable characters allowed for a few majorly effective Tarantino-isms.

The enormity of the Civil War hangs over this film quite heavily. In all of Tarantino's historical revisionism, even though he takes liberties with what may have actually happened, the events in his universe have a particular relationship with real events. Seemingly, every character in this film, even though it takes place more than ten years after the Civil War, is somehow wearing the weight of the conflict.

Because the nefarious intentions of all these characters slowly gets teased out, the film unfolds like a *who-dunnit*, murder mystery—which most resembles the unfolding plot of *Reservoir Dogs*, but largely represents a foray for Tarantino into unchartered waters. Per usual though, the director creates his own genre throughout the production of the film—let's call it an *ensemble-heist-murder mystery-western*—the only one of its kind, but unfortunately one of Tarantino's least-great films.

#8 Olajuwon vs. Everybody

Losing to Georgetown in the 1984 National Championship was a brutal defeat for Hakeem, but fortunately he was able to exact revenge on multiple fronts throughout his career. Olajuwon entered the NBA one season before Ewing, and the two retired the same season, which created an undeniable symmetry.

One great thing about Hakeem's profile is that he went head-to-head against the other premier big men of his era in very high-profile situations, so when you're ranking him against Barkley, Malone, Robinson, Shaq and Ewing, you don't have to do a lot of speculating about who was better—you can just watch the tape! We've established in a couple different spots that the Rockets failed to surround Olajuwon with adequate talent to truly compete for a championship until the 1993-94' season. If we look at the back-to-back championship seasons of 1993-94' and 1994-95', Hakeem rolled through an almost impossible gauntlet of historically great big men on his way to two championships.

In the 1994 playoffs, he'd go through Barkley's[185] Suns in seven games during the Western Conference Semifinals, and then through Malone's Jazz in five games during the

---

[185] In the 1994 playoffs, Barkley was one year removed from his MVP season of 1992-93'.

173

Western Conference Finals. To cap off the championship run, Hakeem dominated Ewing's Knicks in the 1994 NBA Finals'—it was a brutal seven-game series that Hakeem bookended with 25 points, 10 rebounds and 7 assists in the clincher. Consider the debt paid against Patty Ewing. In the 1995 playoffs, it was an even more ridiculous run of triumphs over great big men, take a look:

Opponent	Round	Result	Hakeem Stat Line
Malone (Jazz)	WC 1st Round	W (3-2)	35.0 PPG 8.6 RPG 4.0 APG 3.4 SPG[186]
Barkley (Suns)	WC Semifinals	W (4-3)	29.6 PPG 9.0 RPG 3.7 APG 3.2 SPG
Robinson (Spurs)	WC Finals	W (4-2)	35.3 PPG 12.5 RPG 5.0 APG 5.5 SPG
Shaq (Magic)	NBA Finals'	W (4-0)	32.8 PPG 11.5 RPG 5.5 APG 4.0 SPG

Dude. Not only was Hakeem advancing past these teams .. *those stat lines, though!* Not only did Hakeem have his revenge on Ewing, he would explicitly, definitively demonstrate that he was the greatest big man of his era. [187] He was truly, in every sense, a mushroom-cloud-layin' motha fucka, motha fucka!

#8 Django Unchained (2012)

If Tarantino showed us anything, it's that he's not afraid to ruffle feathers and tackle brutally controversial subject material. QT tackled the Holocaust and Nazi-occupied Europe during *Inglorious Basterds*, and pivoted to the American slave trade in the middle of the nineteenth century for *Django Unchained*. *Django* is shockingly his most violent film, and probably the most cringe-worthy. Between the painfully accurate depiction of how African Americans were treated in 1858, and totality of the film's gun violence, it's a tough watch at times.

Anthony Hamilton, Rick Ross and John Legend all created original songs for the film (and all three are outstanding). The use of hip hop and rap in this film is a little jarring at first. As far-reaching and deliciously obscure as the music is in the Tarantino Universe, he sparingly uses hip hop or rap. I found it really effective in Django, especially the mashup of 2Pac's *Untouchable* and James Brown's *The Payback*, during the Candyland Massacre.

Tarantino elected to steal bits from spaghetti westerns[188] in this film, a genre that he obviously adores. The kinship between Django and Dr. Shultz makes the film feel like a pseudo-western-buddy flick with vivid imagery of the slave trade in the south. This is a great film, and my ranking here says more about how great the films are ahead of this one, than this classic landing at #8 of 10.

---

[186] SPG—Stocks per game—Combination of steals and blocks per game.

[187] In fairness, he got a pretty young Shaq in those 1995 Finals'. Call me crazy, but I'm still taking that peak Hakeem versus peak Shaq (99'-03' Lakers Shaq)

[188] Film genre about the American West, made cheaply in Europe, typically by an Italian producer and/or director.

#7 Hakeem Olajuwon—*American Hero!*

I could have sworn Hakeem was Nigerian! My bad, big fella! Not only is he American, but he won a Gold Medal with Team USA at the 1996 Olympics. In July of 1996, while covering the lead-up to those Olympics, Jerry Bembry of the Baltimore Sun wrote an article that quotes Hakeem clarifying his citizenship:

> *When I became a U.S. citizen [in 1993], there were some people in*
> *Nigeria who criticized me. But I've been here over 10 years, my home is*
> *in Houston and a lot of family is in the United States. It was just natural.*
> *I'm still a Nigerian and I'm proud of it, but I'm a U.S. citizen.*

There was a small hiccup in FIBA granting him to play for Team USA, as Hakeem had played for the Nigerian juniors team as a teenager. But, FIBA granted him availability to play for the United States, and I'm retroactively very grateful!

#7 Kill Bill Vol. 2 (2004)

It really would have been convenient for the sequel to have been a greater film, that way I could talk about the *Kill Bill* films sequentially. Unfortunately, it's just not. Per usual, there are a handful of scenes that are unforgettable. Namely, Beatrix' escape from the casket underground goes from nauseating, to utterly triumphant as she emerges from the dirt. I also forgot how fucking awesome Michael Madsen (Budd) was in this film. He is the first on Beatrix' *to-do list of murder* in the film, and until the Black Mamba[189] gets him, I found his character one of the best elements of the film. As Budd was preparing to bury Beatrix in the ground, I couldn't help but think about how, coupled with his performance as Mr. Blonde in *Reservoir Dogs*, this film marked the second time he had gruesomely tortured someone—nice! There was one other scene with him that I loved, but also represented the main issue I have with the *Kill Bill* series.

We get to see Budd go to his place of employment—a strip club, where he works the door—and we get to see his boss hassle him for his persistent tardiness. It's a very grounding, relatable scene that demonstrated to me that Tarantino was trying to have this film exist on two different planes—one plane where characters have to observe normal rules and societal nuances, and one plane of utter fantasy, where the rules are much more lax. I truly love both of the *Kill Bill* films, but I might rank them a little higher if they didn't feel a little incoherent. Beatrix' knife fight against Vernita Green (Vivica A. Fox) needs to

---

[189] Kobe Bryant [R.I.P.] actually has Quentin Tarantino to thank for his self-appointed nickname. It was Beatrix Kiddo's codename—*The Black Mamba*—that prompted Kobe to research the snake and start, I don't know, asking people to start calling him that (?). Not super clear on how you give yourself a nickname.

be paused because Green's daughter comes home, and they don't want to expose the child to the violence. But, as soon as Beatrix travels to Tokyo to exact revenge on O'Ren Ishii (Lucy Lieu), the story turns into an utterly fantastic, hyper-stylized, pseudo-graphic novel of a film. I fucking loved that, but what I found difficult was that Tarantino was concurrently trying to tell a story that was both based in reality and a blurred-reality fantasy. I think vacillating between the two can work, but it falls apart when the films, particularly Vol. 2, try to evoke compassion on a real human level.

At the end of Vol. 2, Beatrix arrives at Bill's house with the intention of finally getting her revenge. She's taken aback when she sees that the child we were led to believe had perished while Beatrix was in a coma, is alive, and has seemingly been raised by Bill. To me, the emotional punch of a plot twist like that was majorly softened when so much of the story had existed in a world with pretty soft rules on gravity, physics and overall plausibility. That in and of itself is pretty interesting because all of Tarantino's films take place in the same universe—so it's crazy to think that part of his world is portrayed in animation, and some people have what are basically superpowers when it comes to fighting. Keep in mind, this was his fourth film and *Reservoir Dogs*, *Pulp Fiction* and *Jackie Brown* had all existed in real-world metro-Los Angeles— where characters had to abide by normal earth rules pertaining to gravity, physics and a general platform of plausibility.

Despite lapsing between real and surreal, *Kill Bill Vol. 2* is an epic film. Beatrix' escape from under the ground felt like a Hitchcock scene. The battle sequence at Budd's trailer between Elle and Beatrix is fucking amazing—it provides us, by far, the best line from either film:

> *Elle: Now I'm gonna kill you too, with your own sword no less, which in the very immediate future will become my sword.*
>
> *Beatrix:* **Bitch .. You don't have a future.**

Uma Thurman is so overwhelmingly (yet subtly?) beautiful in this film, that it's difficult for me to appropriately measure her acting. But, I'll give her the benefit of the doubt and say that her portrayal is at least one of the most memorable heroines in the history of modern film, if not one of the best.

#6 Hakeem, The Late-Bloomer

If ever there was a case to be made for the benefits of developing athletes to play multiple sports, I'd say Hakeem Olajuwon is exhibit A. He didn't start playing basketball until he was 16 years old. Hakeem focused most of his energies on soccer and handball before the basketball coach at his high school in Lagos, Nigeria encouraged him to give hoops a try. There's no question that Hakeem's transition to basketball was made easier by the footwork, balance and timing required in soccer. We've heard many times how this same soccer background helped Manu Ginóbili succeed in basketball. Hakeem even credits soccer for the genesis of the *Dream Shake*:

> *The Dream Shake was actually one of my soccer moves, which I translated to basketball. It would accomplish one of three things—one, to misdirect the opponent and make him go the opposite way; two, to freeze the opponent and leave him devastated in his tracks; [and] three, to shake off the opponent and give him no chance to contest the shot.[190]*

#6 Kill Bill Vol. 1 (2003)

I'm going to have to go ahead and retract my assertion that Django was Tarantino's most violent film. Django's sheer uncomfortable-ness might be higher, but this film stylized graphic violence while putting up Wilt Chamberlain-level murder numbers during the *Showdown at the House of Blue Leaves*. That scene will likely be the one that people remember this film by, for good reason, but there are plenty of amazing things going on here.

Of the many choices in a deep pool, I'm certain this is my favorite soundtrack to a Tarantino film. The soundtrack was organized, produced and orchestrated by the RZA of the Wu-Tang Clan (who paired with Robert Rodriguez to perform the same duties in Vol. 2). Quentin is known for oversight of his projects, but seemingly RZA and Tarantino found a cohesive dynamic—from a 2003 interview:

> *It was more of a collaboration. He had an idea and a vision when he wrote the script. I think I was more of somebody that kept it in the guidelines of what he wanted. He was like, here go the eggs, the milk, the cake, the sugar, everything, and I'm going to stir it up. Put this in the oven, watch it, take it out in forty-five minutes.*

In the *Pitchfork* review of the soundtrack, they list 11 of the many genres that the score traverses. The Tarantino ability to find the '*perfectly placed eclectic song that will remind me of this scene forever*' is one of my favorite things about his films, and that's definitely on display in *Kill Bill Vol. 1*. Because it was a higher concept project than his previous films, the score needed to also include proprietary instrumentals to assist in narrating, and it most certainly did. Specifically, you hear plenty of Tarantino's trademark Spaghetti Western-themed music, which gives Beatrix Kiddo some John Wayne appeal. You also hear plenty of instrumental music designed to enhance the far-eastern imagery and aesthetic which visually constitutes the second half of the film in Okinawa

---

[190] All three of those things sound like pretty much the same to me!! 'Leave him devastated in his tracks' (!!!) Incredible quote from *The Dream*.

and Tokyo. Additionally, the song that precedes Beatrix battling the Crazy 88's, entitled *Crane/White Lightening*, is a masterful sample created by RZA that blends old-school kung-fu bits and video game tones in front of a hip hop backdrop beat.

This is an amazing film, and it marked the beginning of a brand-new era for Tarantino. The success of the first three films provided him the creative freedom to basically do whatever the fuck he wanted. He chose to do an amazing martial arts-western-revenge epic that spanned two movies and aren't we all glad he did.

#5 The Dream Shake

The Dream Shake was Olajuwon's series of low post pivots and up-fakes that kept his defenders off balance for the entirety of his NBA career. I naturally started thinking about the precedent for devastating signature moves throughout the history of the NBA, and several players came to mind—MJ's turnaround, Dirk's fall-away, Steph's 33-footer, Kareem's skyhook, Iverson's crossover, and so on and so forth. I won't subject you to a thorough breakdown of which ones are best, because there really are only two correct answers—Kareem's skyhook, or Hakeem's dream shake. You could say Kareem, because he rode that methodical hook shot all the way to the most points of all-time. You could say Hakeem, because the shake serves as the standard for low-post footwork and efficient scoring at the rim. It doesn't really matter to me, I guess I would give it to Kareem because no one has ever been able to re-create the skyhook with any measure of consistency. But, the dream shake lives and breathes, in part because Hakeem has worked with so many young players to help them emulate his devastating signature move.

#5 Jackie Brown (1997)

Every time I re-watch this film, I'm kind of blown away at how smoothly the story moves along, and how enjoyable the characters are. QT's aim was to revive the blaxploitation[191] films of the 70's—what better way than to cast the primary star of that era, as the star of your film? Pam Grier had played several title roles for films of that genre, and she's incredible in this role. Because *Jackie Brown* is a less glamorous character than those she'd played in the 70s, her swaggering, savvy demeanor feels more relatable and less fantastic.

Are we sure this isn't Sam Jackson's best performance? I think people probably look at Jules from *Pulp Fiction* as his best work. Jules was framed an anti-hero, in a more attractive way. Conversely, Ordell Robbie is just anti—he's

---

[191] Per Wikipedia (take it or leave it): blaxploitation is an ethnic subgenre of the exploitation film that emerged in the United States during the early 1970's. The films, while popular, suffered backlash for disproportionate numbers of stereotypical film characters showing bad or questionable motives, including criminals, etc. However, the genre does rank among the first in which black characters and communities are the heroes and subjects of film and television, rather than sidekicks, villains or victims of brutality.

a real gangster. A guy that actually prowled Compton in 1995. I'm not sure which is better, but Jackson's role in *Jackie Brown* is absolutely in the conversation for his finest moment.

Are we sure this isn't Tarantino's best film?? It might be hard to say this is Tarantino's best, but it's unique in his filmography for a few reasons. QT is stealing from many films throughout *Jackie Brown*, per usual, but all the pieces that he uses to construct the story seem to coalesce more naturally. For QT to piece together films based on devices, shots, aesthetics and music that he's stolen from other films, he lives with certain stretches of his films feeling disjointed. *Jackie Brown* flows easily from start to finish, without the abstract statements from the director that can occur in his other films. Many of those statements/references have become why we love Tarantino's films so much. But what I'm getting at is that this movie unrolls like a more 'normal' film. Tarantino is still splicing in the funky, soulful soundtrack and niche elements of blaxploitation films that satisfy him and are only picked up on by the nerdiest of film nerds. But, the result is a really interesting, cohesive and entertaining film. Additionally, the film ages really well, and perhaps it's because it feels less proprietarily a Tarantino film (but under the surface it absolutely is). In that way, even if this isn't his best film, it's as good a representation of his style of filmmaking succeeding as there is. Does that make sense?

The film succeeds triumphantly as a romance. Actors Pam Grier and Robert Forster were past their primes in more ways than one when they agreed to do this film—correlatively, so were both of the characters they were portraying in *Jackie Brown*—a symmetry masterfully captured and re-imagined by Quentin Tarantino during this film. Going down the path of the *'lovers from different sides of the tracks'* trope can be a slippery slope fraught with repetitiveness. But Jackie and Max's attraction and pull toward one another feels genuine and unique. In the tunnel of a commonplace storyline that almost always feels forced, this film's romantic development is as unique as Quentin Tarantino himself.

#4 Hakeem Olajuwon—An Army of One

Hakeem had poor teammates leading up to the years that the Rockets truly competed for a championship—we established during the KG profile that the other five players who played the most minutes for Houston in Hakeem's first eight seasons were Otis Thorpe, Rodney McCray, Sleepy Floyd, Buck Johnson, and a few seasons of Ralph Sampson. Not great. But if you look at the roster that finally broke through and won a championship in 1993-94', while there are certainly quality players, there is far less individual talent than is normal for a championship-winning team.

The five most important players on that Rockets team, besides Hakeem, were Kenny Smith, Vernon Maxwell, Robert Horry, Sam Cassell and Otis Thorpe. Let's take a look at how individually accomplished those guys were in their career:

	All-Star	All-NBA	All-Defense
Kenny Smith	0	0	0
Vernon Maxwell	0	0	0
Robert Horry	0	0	0
Sam Cassell	1x	1x	0
Otis Thorpe	1x	0	0

These are the accumulations for the entirety of these players' careers, not just the selections they'd earned by the time of the 1994 championship. Don't get me wrong, these are fine players in their own right, and perhaps the selfless approach limited them from contention for these selections. However, this is monumentally rare in the history of the game. History tells us you need two premier guys, if not three.

The past few years constitute a 'super team' moment, where teams might be more stacked than champions of the past. Still, just two combined All-Star appearances among Hakeem's supporting staff is the lowest total for a championship-winning team in the history of the NBA. Now, there's subjectivity there, as you're letting me determine each champion's most important player, and then their five most important supporting players. But c'mon, how much could we disagree there? In 1994-95', The Rockets would repeat as champions and Hakeem received reinforcements in the form of Clyde Drexler. In Drexler's career, he earned 10 All-Star game appearances and 5 All-NBA selections—however—by the time he came to Houston, he'd already gone to 8 of those All-Star games, and earned 4 of those All-NBA teams. Meaning, Hakeem dragged one of the weakest supporting casts to a championship in 1994, and repeated with a secondary star who was past his prime.

#4 Reservoir Dogs (1992)

As the saying goes—bands have 20 years to make their first album, and six months to make their second. There are endless examples of rock acts who were never able to re-create the magic, angst, passion and power of their first album or two ..

The Doors, Arctic Monkeys, Guns N' Roses, Van Halen, The New Pornographers, The Stone Roses, MGMT, Pearl Jam, Boston, The Killers, The Strokes, The Band, The Velvet Underground, Alabama Shakes, Interpol, Television, Neutral Milk Hotel.

There are good artists here, without question, and some created really great work. But the greats reinvent themselves after the initial momentum and reservoir of inspiration has depleted beyond their first few projects ..

The Black Keys, Radiohead, Bon Iver, Bruce Springsteen, The Hold Steady, Green Day, Oasis, Spoon, The Talking Heads, Sturgill Simpson, Yeah Yeah Yeahs, Wilco, Arcade Fire.

The legends not only reinvent their sound over time, they change the sound as we know it..

The Beatles, Led Zeppelin, Jack White, The Rolling Stones, David Bowie, Neil Young, Prince, Tom Petty, Bob Dylan, Pink Floyd, The Who, Elvis Presley.

Quentin Tarantino is a legendary filmmaker, whose implementation of nonlinear storytelling, irreverent dialogue, uncomfortable violence and unrelenting pop culture references have become the signatures by which we know his stories. But when *Reservoir Dogs* came out in 1992, no one was ready for an independent heist film to utilize all of those things. It was undeniably a powerful debut, and Tarantino's first film was already forcing us to ask what a movie should look like. When it comes to music and film, it's very easy to over-sentimentalize your favorite work, or work that you perceive to have been especially influential to you. For me though, without hyperbole, *Reservoir Dogs* marked a hard pivot in my perception of what films could be.

Realistically, from the first scene of QT's first film he was making a statement. Tarantino makes a cameo[192] in all of his films, and in the opening scene of *Reservoir Dogs* his character—Mr. Brown—espouses a super-hot take about Madonna's *Like a Virgin* essentially being about big dicks. *In the first scene of his first film.* That, folks, is the world-record for fewest fucks given in your directorial debut. Another major flex by Tarantino was to write and direct this film, which centers around an elaborate diamond heist, and virtually not show the heist whatsoever. Instead, the characters explain to us how things played out, and we're introduced to the very particular way that Tarantino players communicate with one another.

When she knew that I was starting to seek out classic films, including *Pulp Fiction*, my stepmom Teresa insisted that I watch *Reservoir Dogs*. Needless to say, we've been quoting it ever since, and when *Stuck in the Middle With You* came on at my wedding, we naturally danced around doing our best Mr. Blonde impersonations. I was going to sit and pretend I was being tortured but thought that might be over the line (?).

#3 Hakeem Olajuwon—Mr. April, May and June

There's one thing Hakeem did that is reserved for the greatest of the great. When the postseason came around, he managed to increase the quality of both his counting stats and his advanced stats. That doesn't sound that impressive, as maybe you think all great players improved their play during the postseason—you'd be wrong. Historically, when the pressure ratchets up and defenses dig a little deeper, numerous great players have struggled to replicate the success they've had during the regular season (much less increase their play).

---

[192] Kind of. He appears in some fashion in each of his films, with the exception of *Kill Bill Vol. 1*, although allegedly he was one of the dead Crazy 88's. Some of the appearances are very subtle voiceovers.

The inelasticity of Hakeem's impact throughout his prime is something exhibited almost exclusively by Tier I guys. The devastating array of offensive moves and strategy-altering defensive ability that made Houston a tough out on a Tuesday night in the regular season, made Houston an extremely tough out in the spring and early summer. Take a look at Hakeem's career advanced stats:

	PER	WS/48	BPM	TS%	USG%
Regular Season	23.6	.177	4.9	.553	27.1
Postseason	**25.7**	**.189**	**7.1**	**.569**	**28.9**

I'll use any excuse to bash James Harden, so let's look at the inverse of a player who performs better during the postseason. Mr. October through February himself, Mr. James Harden:

	PER	WS/48	BPM	TS%	Usage %
Regular Season	**24.8**	**.227**	**7.0**	**.611**	**30.7**[193]
Postseason	22.8	.178	6.7	.585	29.4

#3 Pulp Fiction (1994)

This is obviously the chalk take for Tarantino's best film—and it's not the wrong take. My thinking that there are two greater Tarantino films than this one is a testament to his filmography—not a demerit to the film—but more an acknowledgement that the last three films on this list are virtually perfect. As we covered at the beginning of this profile (which feels like forever ago), *Pulp Fiction* came out in 1994. *Reservoir Dogs* had made Tarantino a star overnight, and two years later when *Pulp Fiction* came out, he proceeded to become one of the most important directors we had.

When I re-watch this film, which I've done a lot in the past year, it's hard not to notice the erosion of the film's impact between the first time you saw it, and re-watching it years later. Don't get me wrong, the film is very rewatchable. The entire Jack Rabbit Slim's scene completely eats me alive every time I watch this movie—the tracking shot that immerses you into the restaurant, the verbal two-step between Travolta and Thurman's characters as they synergize, leading into the *physical* two-step dance sequence[194] that can

---

[193] Mr. Harden hit 40.5% usage during the 2018-19' regular season. That is fucking ridiculous. For perspective, LeBron was at 40.8% usage during the 2015 Finals'. MJ was at 41.2% usage during the 1998 Finals'. What a joke! I'm tough on Harden because he never seizes the moments in the postseason that seemingly continue to fall in his lap. Then, magically, everyone forgets how much less of a player he is in the playoffs when the regular season starts back up, and he's hanging Wilt Chamberlain numbers from the perimeter. Well, yeah, if you're going to hit 40-fucking-percent-usage, you better put up some stats, you bum!

[194] Every time I watch this film, I start off second-guessing why Travolta receives so much admiration for his role (he was nominated for Best Actor). I always remember why during the Jack Rabbit Slim's scene—he's remarkable.

only be categorized as iconic. I've calibrated the impact a film can have on me when I first see it, and then re-calibrate what percentage of that impact it can retain every time I re-watch it. Because of that, I've found *Pulp Fiction*, and more so *Reservoir Dogs*, while immensely important to the pop culture moment they profoundly impacted at their releases, to retain less of that impact than the films I ranked ahead of them. Now, I'm full of shit to some degree, because one of the films still to be ranked came out in 2019, and its ability to retain its impact is yet to be seen. I'm simply high enough on that film to place a big bet on it braving the test of time.

The films I perceive to be greater than *Pulp Fiction* also both came out within a cultural context that, I believe, was less prone to allow for a film to profoundly impact pop culture. The years in which the final two films on my list were released (2009 & 2019) were well into the internet age. In 2009 we were starting to get distracted, starting to splinter into more niche and less unifying artistic pursuits. In 2019, we have ten years of flying headfirst in all of those same directions. The point being, in 1992 and 1994, the landscape was far riper for dynamic, visionary films to be completely absorbed into the pop culture consciousness, with far fewer distractions distorting our perception. In 2019, the undisputed greatest film of all-time could be released, and everyone will have moved on to 20 other things on their phone the minute the film ends. Feel me?

#2 Back-to-Back Champion

In chronological order, MJ, MJ, Hakeem, MJ, MJ, Shaq, Kobe, LeBron and Kevin Durant are the only players in history to have won back-to-back Finals' MVPs. I already mentioned that Hakeem ran a mighty gauntlet through the Western Conference to earn those titles—gunning down all of his big men contemporaries in order, like Beatrix Kiddo crossing off every member of the Deadly Viper Assassination Squad. However, there is an emptiness to Hakeem's championships, in the view of some, because they occurred during MJ's hiatus. It's a valid point, and it would have been absolutely fascinating to watch the Rockets face Jordan's Bulls in the Finals'.

I'm not so sure that the Rockets don't still win. Regarding that Bulls team that won titles in 1990-91', 1991-92' and 1992-93', what has history taught us about locker rooms that play deep into June several years in a row? The chemistry starts cracking, and the weight of relentless media coverage and competitive pressure starts to yield fissures in even the most stable team environments. The 2011-2014 Heat and 2008-2011 Lakers are glaring recent examples of locker rooms that fell apart abruptly after repeated title chases. MJ is MJ, and it's totally conceivable that the Bulls win again in 1993-94' and 1994-95' if David Stern hadn't convinced him that he needed to take a break from playing, *I mean*, he decided to play Minor League Baseball for a couple years. I'm just saying that MJ taking a sabbatical (whatever the

---

Also—the dance they do is a nod to the 1963 Federico Fellini film, *8 ½*. Tarantino steals, nods and homages his way through the entirety of his films, and I could write a separate book by pointing all of them out.

underlying reasons) was the best thing that could have happened to the Chicago dynasty in the 90s. While it's conceivable that the Bulls would have continued to win if Jordan hadn't left, it's equally conceivable that Hakeem would have pounced on a vulnerable, worn-down Chicago group, and won those titles anyway.

#2 Once Upon a Time... In Hollywood (2019)

Quentin Tarantino has been splicing together movies with parts of other movies his whole career. His last movie is explicitly about the movies, and it's not only set in the town that serves as the epicenter for making movies, but the town where the director made his first movies. Quentin Tarantino is a movie nerd. He didn't go to film school. It's been well-documented that his education came from watching every movie he possibly could while working for the video rental store Video Archives in Manhattan Beach. Wherever you might rank his final film, it's hard to argue that it could have been a more perfect final signature. Tarantino's filmography has been a confluence of cryptic homages, splices and steals from his favorite films. To me, that created a few layers of intrigue and complexity to his films. But when I watched *Once Upon a Time... In Hollywood*, it was like watching the ultimate climax of a mystery flick, and all the intrigue and complexity melted away, revealing unbridled, brilliant, all-time filmmaking.

Holy shit do you get acting performances in *Once Upon a Time... In Hollywood*. *The Rewatchables* podcast has a segment called Apex Mountain in which the hosts determine whether or not the *rewatchable* film they're covering marks the peak for any of its actors (or behind the camera personnel). Conceivably you have numerous apexes occurring in this film. I've always liked the less secure, less glamorous Leo DiCaprio characters, which has generally led me to think his best performance was in *The Departed*. In this film, on the surface, he's playing a rather glamorous movie star—but under the surface, his character is woefully insecure, self-loathing, carries a noticeable speech impediment, and with his horrid smoker's cough, is rather unappealing. Leo fucking DiCaprio, unappealing .. inconceivable. He's truly incredible in this film. At bare minimum, this is in the short conversation for Brad Pitt's best performance. I also don't care what your pronoun is, *you felt something* when he took his shirt off on the roof. Don't lie to me. Margot Robbie is so preposterously, distractingly gorgeous in this film that I have the *Uma Thurman in Kill Bill Syndrome*, where I'm rendered incapable of determining how effective her acting is (but she gets the benefit of the doubt too). I've never liked Timmy Olyphant—I always thought he brought *Deadwood* down, despite my loving of the show—but I think this is my favorite performance by him. Madsen has like one line, and it's amazing. Only the film I have ranked higher than this one might have a greater totality of performances in the Tarantino-sphere.

The film leans heavily on the theme of identity. You see Rick go through the complexity of maintaining his own identity as he's caught between the characters he's currently playing, and nostalgically longing for the characters that provided him what he thinks he wants—notoriety, fame, and recognition. We explicitly see Rick struggle with this throughout the film, and it assists in creating one of the great, subtle masterstrokes of Tarantino's career. At the end of the film, after Cliff and Rick successfully fight off the Manson family members, Rick watches the police and ambulance drive away at the foot of his driveway. Jay Sebring (Emile Hirsch's character) recognizes him as Rick Dalton, movie star, and asks him what had happened:

> *Rick Dalton:* We don't know what the fuck they wanted. Were they robbin' me, I don't know. Were they freakin' out on some bummer trip, who knows? But, they tried to kill my wife and my buddy.

> *Jay Sebring:* Jesus Christ, are you serious?

> *Rick Dalton:* Yeah I'm fuckin' serious, my buddy and his dog killed two of em' and then well shit, I torched the last one.

> *Jay Sebring:* ..Torched?

> *Rick Dalton:* Yeah, I burned her ass to a crisp.

> *Jay Sebring:* How'd you do that?

> *Rick Dalton:* Believe it or not, I've got a flamethrower in my toolshed.

> *Jay Sebring:* From the *14 Fists of McCluskey?* [a well-known WWII film where Rick played Sgt. Mike Lewis]

> *Rick Dalton:* Yeah. [glowing and thrilled to be recognized for his work]

Jay is completely blown away that Rick (seemingly) stacks up to the badass persona that his film characters embody—literally torching intruders in his home with a flamethrower. But, we've spent the entire film watching how insecure Rick Dalton is, and even when he pulled out his flamethrower and scorched the hippie in his swimming pool, he was still finding a way to question himself.

Now, I don't know about you, but I'm very hard on myself, and I'm confident most people are (Rick Dalton sure as hell is). Thus, how we perceive our actions, our words, and our influence on the world around us is often met by speculation and self-critique. But to others, those ripples into our surroundings can appear profound, no matter how hard we are on ourselves. Rick used his flamethrower because it was the only thing he knew how to do, and it provided a practical resolution to his problem. But to anyone that knew Rick as Jake Cahill, or Sgt. Mike Lewis, or Nebraska Jim, or Mike Murtaugh, hearing that he'd torched someone that crossed him would appear to be confirmation that this movie star lives the way his characters act on screen.

To me, this film feels tonally connected to *Jackie Brown*. Both films unravel enjoyable, engaging, coherent, and dare I say sentimental (?) stories. Tarantino's films use music so brilliantly, and when he integrates it organically, like music coming out of Cliff Booth's speakers, that's when it's most effective. The music in *Once Upon a Time... In Hollywood* is unmistakably Los Angeles in August, 1969. In *Jackie Brown*, The Delphonics song *Didn't I (Blow Your Mind This Time)* repeats organically on record players and on the radio while serving as the subtle soundtrack to the film's romantic plot. Don't get me wrong, bad men doing bad things, anti-heroes, nefarious intentions and avoiding the cops are fine themes for movies. But every once upon a time, we want to feel good when we go to the movies—isn't that why we started going to the movies in the first place?

#1 Hakeem Olajuwon—The Greatest Defender of the Modern NBA

I'm confident that anyone else that's done the research would arrive at the same conclusion. When I watched tape of Hakeem, one of my first thoughts was how many shots he altered. He's already the greatest shot-blocker in the history of the block, but even when he wasn't getting the block, he fundamentally bent the game plan for his opponents. This then led me to really wish that we had the advanced defensive stats then, that we do now. Courtesy of Second Spectrum, NBA.com has stats for deflections, individual opponent shooting percentage, shots contested etc. Hakeem would have savagely torn those stats apart. Olajuwon operated around his own basket like a soccer goalie defending a hockey net. He was never more than a step and jump away from a weak-side block and was a living nightmare at disrupting passing lanes.

If we'd had the stats, it would help validate what we saw and it would serve as another layer on Hakeem's legacy. To me, it's also evidence that his colossal impact wasn't relegated to his era. But when we look at the stats we do have, you don't have to reach too far to realize that Hakeem is likely the greatest defender ever, with only Bill Russell licensed to take offense to the notion. I mentioned Hakeem's ability to break up passing lanes, which resulted in a shitload of steals for the big fella. His efforts there are likely the finest by a big man, as he stands ninth all-time in steals, and is the only forward or center in the top ten. Hakeem is also the only person that will likely *ever* be in the 2,000 steals-2,000 blocks club. His all-time block record of 3,821 is also unlikely to ever fall (second on the list is Dikembe Mutombo with 3,289). For five seasons in a row, from 1986-87' through 1990-91', Hakeem led the NBA in defensive rating. Let me repeat that—for five straight years, while his team wasn't even consistently competitive, opposing teams averaged the fewest points in the league when Olajuwon was on the court. No one in modern basketball has approached a five-year defensive embargo like Hakeem's.

I think there is a pull to overrate certain player's two-way-ability when they're so capable on both ends. Hakeem was a very potent offensive player, but if he'd had a Ben Wallace or Dikembe-esque offensive profile, he'd still be on this list. He moved around the paint on defense like he had a force field that offensive players had to constantly contend with. His instincts and recovery to help and contest was like having a 7-foot Draymond flying around. Hakeem Olajuwon was a historic problem on defense. In my opinion, no player has ever had the defensive impact he did. It might come in at #1 here, and was his most dynamic skill set, but it does get crazy when you think about what a compliment it was that he was an absolutely savage low-post scorer on offense too.

Why He Belongs In This Tier? I actually had to think twice about whether Hakeem deserved a Tier I spot or not. He was such a complete player, with such incredibly high upside on both ends of the court. At one point or another, he smoked all of the prestigious big man contemporaries of his era, and he definitely proved that he could be the best player on title teams. For him to have moved into Tier I, I think there would have had to be two substantial differences with his profile. He'd first have to have established himself as a better passer/creator. The other thing is he doesn't quite have the hardware to walk amongst the Tier I guys. Another MVP or two, another title or two and now we're talking. These are obviously nit-picky, but those are the margins.

#1 Inglorious Basterds (2009)

Before the credits roll, the last line of *Inglorious Basterds* is Lt. Aldo Raine proclaiming that his most recent work just might be his finest:

> You know something, Utivich? I think this just might be my masterpiece.

Many have speculated that this was Tarantino acknowledging, through this line, that he'd just completed his finest work. I obviously do not disagree, assuming that was an intentional choice by Quentin Tarantino. There's evidence to suggest that even if the director doesn't think it is his greatest film, it's probably the one he spent the most time thinking about before it actually was released. There are public quotes from Tarantino, 9 years before the *Inglorious Basterds* premiere, that show he'd been working on a 'man on a mission' WWII project in the overall theme of *The Dirty Dozen* or *The Guns of Navarone*. Whether or not this is truly his greatest film, and whether or not that is the opinion of the director himself, are both up for debate. Something not up for debate is that this is Tarantino's greatest accomplishment in the crafting of captivating dialogue.

Only about 30% of this film is in English, and in a spectacular flex by the director, necessitated subtitles don't inhibit the tension, posturing and speculation within the discourse by the film's characters. The opening scene[195] of this movie introduces the world to Christoph Waltz—who has since done

---

[195] The melody from *Für Elise*, probably Beethoven's most recognized piece of music, plays at the very beginning of the opening scene. This is directly sourced from the 1966 western *The Big Gundown*, as the same score welcomes the introduction to that film. Popular analysis indicates that Tarantino is taking this nod a step further *in Inglorious Basterds*—Beethoven, a German master composer, plays while Colonel Hans Landa, a German master manipulator in the Third Reich, arrives at the LaPadite farm. The opening shot is also a nod to the introductions of both *Unforgiven* and *The Good, the Bad, and the Ugly*, both in the way they're shot, and the setup of the scene.

several karaoke sessions of the character he plays in this film that somewhat diluted his breakout performance in *Inglorious Basterds*. In the moment the film came out though, I think I can speak for everyone and say that Waltz looked like the best actor we'd ever seen for his efforts as Colonel Hans Landa. His introduction takes place during a 20-minute conversation that demonstrates his character's duality of charm and purified evil. The scene is tense and gripping and thoroughly accomplishes the seizing of your attention for the duration of the film.

Waltz really is the centerpiece for why the film's dialogue works so well. Not only can he impressively speak English, German, French and Italian, but he is able to gesture and inflect perfectly in all of these languages. Apparently, Tarantino was very deliberate in working with Waltz to craft all of those verbal mannerisms that made Colonel Hans Landa unforgettable. Waltz' multilingual triumph makes every scene he's in captivating—it reminds me of how it felt whenever Heath Ledger was in a scene during *The Dark Knight*.

Ironically enough though, apart from the opening scene, the other best dialogue sequence in this film does not include Waltz. *Operation Kino*, the film's fourth chapter, stages a counter-intelligence effort from the allied forces, the goal of which is assassinating large numbers of the Nazi high command. Although the scene fits cohesively into the movie's plot, it stands on its own as a mesmerizing visual vignette packaged within the movie. Actors Michael Fassbender,[196] Diane Kruger, Gideon Burkhard and Til Schweiger are under cover as Nazis at La Louisiane tavern in the small French village of Nadine. They blow their cover in the presence of a very observant Nazi officer (actor August Diehl), and nearly everyone in the tavern loses their life in a brief and brutal shootout. But before the shots are fired, a bilingual chess match unwinds between all the actors—the tension, intrigue and precision of which is as well-crafted as you'll ever see on film.

I mentioned earlier that *The Hateful Eight* was created in a backdrop that works well for the things Tarantino likes to do—bad people out-tricking others and doing overall bad things. While some of the subject matter in *Inglorious Basterds* is undeniably controversial, to me, it's the picture-perfect setting for a Tarantino film. Indignity was par for the course in World War II, to say the very least, but it creates a very fertile framework for a Tarantino story, and for characters within that story to flourish. A great director is tasked with many of the same challenges that a football coach faces. It's hugely important to put all of your resources in positions to succeed. In this film, Tarantino sculpts a dynamo in the form of Hans Landa. He gets Brad Pitt in a role that ends up being probably his greatest performance. He brings in Fassbender off the bench for basically two incredible scenes. He has Mélanie Laurant work as a film projectionist for 10 days before shooting to prepare for her role as Shosanna (and she's brilliant in her complex role). It seems to me that every decision in this film, casting/writing/shooting, is so meticulously thought-out,

---

[196] Fassbender is a native German speaker, and his verbal dexterity clearly enhances the back-and-forth of this scene. Fassbender also tried out for Hans Landa, and would have been great, albeit different, in that role.

that it makes sense Tarantino was ruminating on the various aspects of this project for 10+ years. The way it turned out, it was not just as if he'd picked the perfect fantasy football team, but as if he'd caught all of his players at the perfect moment. *Inglorious Basterds* plays out like a fantasy football team with 2013 Peyton Manning, 2006 LaDainian Tomlinson and 2007 Randy Moss.

When I first saw this film in 2009, I cared much less about the second, third and fourth levels of Tarantino-sphere meta-analysis. I just wanted to see a cool flick—it passed that test then, and does so with flying colors every time since. But the reason it perseveres as what I believe to be his finest work, is because of the in-depth stuff. It's clear Tarantino poured all of himself into writing, casting and creating this film, as much or more so than any of his other films. Given some of the multi-lingual stuff, the framework and historical bylines required for *Inglorious Basterds*, it also stands as the project with the highest degree of difficulty.

However, I acknowledge the subjectivity in selecting which Tarantino film stands as his best. As a man who loves tiers, I've got some tiers for you. Realistically, starting with number five on my list, I think a case can be made for all films listed then and after as being Quentin Tarantino's best. It's kind of a cop-out after expending so much energy ordering them individually. But while I stand firmly by my list, I appreciate many re-orderings of his top five films. I'll leave it up to you, but hopefully at this point you can order your list with a little more knowledge on the films from quite possibly the greatest director of the last 30 years.

TIER III	TIER II	TIER I
10) Death Proof	7) Kill Bill Vol. 2	5) Jackie Brown
9) Hateful Eight	6) Kill Bill Vol. 1	4) Reservoir Dogs
8) Django Unchained		3) Pulp Fiction
		2) Once Upon a Time... in Hollywood
		1) Inglorious Basterds

Steph Curry

The Secret	Greatness Index	Ben Taylor Rank
100 / 100	131.33 (37th)	20th

PIPM	O-PIPM	D-PIPM	Peak—2016-17'	Wins Added
+5.31 (5th)	+5.48	+0.05	+8.32 (6th)	140.46 (33rd)

Playoff PER	Playoff Win Shares	Playoff O-Win Shares	Playoff D-Win Shares
23.00 (18th)	17.11 (30th)	12.31 (21st)	4.80 (77th)

On the day of Halloween 2012, Steph Curry inked his first prominent NBA contract. Beginning with the 2013-14' season, the extension guaranteed him $44 Million over four seasons—a pretty legit grab for a player who'd shown immense potential, but had missed the final 40 games of the 2011-12' season because of ankle issues, had surgery for the second consecutive offseason because of ankle issues, and who'd sprained his ankle again just days prior to the contract being signed. In that moment, it meant security for Steph and his family, and it demonstrated a calculated risk for newly promoted Warriors' GM, Bob Myers. What that contract meant in the grand scheme of things, however, was much bigger than any of us could have fathomed in our wildest dreams—the agreement marked the genesis and institutional roster framework of the Golden State dynasty.

Part 1: The Ankle-Breaker's Broken Ankles

Well before the Warriors started playing teams off the floor though, Steph Curry had to figure out how to merely stay on the floor in the first place. During a workout in July 2012, he revealed this to his personal trainer:

> I feel like I've been doing nothing but rehabbing for two years. I feel like I'm never going to be able to play again.

Steph played in 78 games during the 2012-13' regular season, but he was still hampered by ankle sprains and was noticeably more tentative. Warriors' teammate from the 2012-13' season, Brandon Rush, said this of his play during that campaign:

> *You could see when Steph didn't trust his ankle. He didn't try to make the moves he usually makes. He didn't finish and take contact like he usually takes.*

Still, Steph averaged 22.9 PPG and 6.9 APG on .589 TS% (not to mention shooting a bonkers 45% on 7.7 3PA per game). However, he rolled his ankle badly in both of Golden State's playoff series' during the 2013 playoffs (Steph's first postseason), and it was apparent that his ankles were going to be inexorably tied to his narrative if things continued that way.

In July of 2013, The Warriors hired Keke Lyles as Director of Performance. Lyles was/is an expert on body dynamics, strength and conditioning, and is an obsessive thinker in the way of tailored, individualized training plans to maximize an athlete's potential. As much as it sounds like Myers and Golden State just went out and got a new strength and conditioning guy, hoping a new regimen would yield a brighter future for Steph's ankles, Lyles was actually uniquely positioned to succeed when it came to the case of Steph's persistent issue. In high school, Keke Lyles was diagnosed with a hip condition called femoroacetabular impingement, which causes great pain stemming from extra bone growth. The condition sparked a fascination with the importance and potential of that region of an athlete's body. So, when Lyles eventually carved out a successful career in maximizing athletic performance, his expertise and emphasis on hip and core strength would become a calling card.

Lyles' initial assessment of Steph's body dynamics led him to conclude that Curry was already a world-class athlete in terms of changing direction. However, in doing so, he was applying a disproportionate amount of weight to his ankles:

> *Shiftiness is an ankle strategy, but power comes from the hips. We wanted to teach Steph how to load his hips to help unload his ankles.*

Steph bought in right away. He perfected his form on several yoga poses and deadlift variations during his first session with Lyles. The trainer raved that Curry's central nervous system was the best he'd ever worked with. Steph's physical intuitiveness and relentless dedication to training that summer did not go unnoticed. Klay Thompson, who had been with the Warriors two full seasons in the summer of 2013, marveled at Steph's commitment to self-improvement and overcoming his ankle issues:

> *The man was always in the gym. Steph just stuck with the routine. He works on his body just as much as he works on his jump shot.*

I get it—teammates talking up other teammates is patterned behavior in sports at all levels. But my thing is, how many guys on this list had to overcome an unrelenting, unforgiving physical barrier to maximize their potential? How many NBA players in totality have fundamentally pivoted their approach to physical training after several years in the league?[197] How many would be even *willing* to do so? Respectively—zero, only great players, and only the super great players. Lyles' strategy and Curry's work would quickly yield noticeable results when the 2013-14' season got underway. Steph was observably more confident, and his play leveled up in nearly every way, including a spike in efficiency:

	PER	TS%	WS/48
2012-13'	21.3	.589	.180
2013-14'	**24.1**	**.610**	**.225**

2013-14' was Draymond's second season with the team, Klay's third, and Iguodala's first, but it was Curry that spearheaded the dangerous Warrior squad that won 51 games. They played fast (fifth-highest pace in the league), they made a lot of threes (second-most in the league per game), and they shared the ball (seventh-most assists per game).

The league was flirting with a revolution, and it bubbled over during the 2014 postseason. The Warriors drew a brutal first-round matchup against a great Clippers team, and lost to Lob City in seven games. Much deeper in those playoffs though, during the Finals' between Miami and San Antonio, we all watched the pace-and-space revolution execute its launch sequence—the Spurs yanked Tiago Splitter from his traditional center position and their small lineup became increasingly adept at shooting threes, possessed a shut-down perimeter player, were all willing passers, and were defensively anchored by a switchable and historically-intelligent big man.

An inventory of the Warriors' assets in the summer of 2014 produced a roster immaculately prepared to replicate the San Antonio template—a roster full of willing passers, dynamic three-point shooters with Steph and Klay, an elite perimeter defender in Andre Iguodala, and while it may not have been unlocked just yet, Draymond had all the tools to be the switchable, defensive anchor that allowed everything else to work.

As far as Steph's ankles were concerned? He'd had minimal setbacks during the 2013-14' campaign, and into the second year of the new strength program, he was only getting stronger. At the beginning of the program, Steph was deadlifting 200 lbs. Into the second year of the more deliberately targeted strength strategy, he was up to 400 lbs., which was twice his body weight, and second only on the Warriors to Festus Izeli (who was 7-foot and 265 lbs.). Improbably, Steph had vanquished the ankle issues that were surely going to wash him out of the league just a year before.

---

[197] No question that Steph putting the ankle issues behind him should be accredited to the advancement of sports physiology, and plenty of players in the past may have overcome physical impediments had they the access to the resources available to Curry and players of the modern day. I'd just say that we should not hold that against Curry, which some of the dumber commentary seems to have, and remember above all else that Curry's work was the prerequisite for the turnaround in his career. Yes, the information was available, but he was the one putting in thousands of single-leg deadlifts, single-leg lunges and perfect trap deadlifts—right or wrong?

Part 2: Steph-Mania

{2014-15'} {Rubber Soul}

The bubbling basketball revolution in 2014 reminds me of the inevitable rock music revolution that was stirring back in 1965. Artists like the Who and The Rolling Stones were evolving their sound, Bob Dylan had gone electric and was re-defining folk music, and California-based artists like the Byrds, The Mamas and The Papas, Buffalo Springfield and The Beach Boys were further exploring where rock music could go. To say nothing of the powerful releases across the genres of jazz, R&B and soul that were reverberating the angst of the civil rights movement, if not directly articulating it—James Brown's *Live At the Apollo*, Nina Simone's *Pastel Blues*, The Supremes' *Where Did Our Love Go*, Otis Redding's *Otis Blue*, John Coltrane's *A Love Supreme* and Miles Davis' *Sketches of Spain* are just a taste of the historically great albums that were shaping the moment's sound. All the cross-pollination in the music industry yielded many great works of art by the end of 1965, but it was the four impossibly famous dudes from Liverpool that truly upped the creative ante. The Beatles blended the unprecedented number of popular musical styles and crafted a masterpiece that set the tone for the creative nuclear explosion of the late 1960s.

To me, the 2014-15' Golden State season was comparable to The Beatles dropping *Rubber Soul* into the fertile creative musical cauldron of December 1965. While there were plenty of other artists pushing the boundaries in that moment, many of which inspired and encouraged Lennon and McCartney to re-invent their sound, The Beatles managed to absorb all of that energy and put forth a record that changed the landscape forever. While traversing at least a handful of different musical traditions, *Rubber Soul* marked the official pivot for the Beatles themselves— away from more formulaic songs about love, and toward songs about the world around them, which was increasingly seen through the lenses of marijuana and LSD. *Rubber Soul* marked the first major spike in the Beatles' creative arc, but certainly wouldn't be their last. Heading into that 2014-15' season, and having added championship-savvy Steve Kerr as their head coach, The Golden State Warriors were ready to take what San Antonio (and Mike D'Antoni to an extent) had done, and notch a major spike in their own growth as a team, and re-shape the NBA as we knew it.

Remember in the first Jurassic Park when the cast is first introduced to the raptors? They lower a full-sized cow into the raptor pen, and all manner of chaos ensues as the raptors feed on the cow. Watching the 2014-15' Warriors, when they were creating that swirling, nauseating chaos, made me feel like Jeff Goldblum when he first saw the raptors feed. In fact, we were all Jeff Goldblum that season—every one of us—watching the Warriors rip apart their competition and initiate a forced extinction of immobile big men. With Curry serving as the master of the chaos, Golden State won 21 of their first 23 games. After that, they ripped off additional win streaks of 8 and 12 on their way to 67 wins. All of the impressive team-oriented stats from their previous season blasted off into rarified air (league rank in parenthesis):

	Wins	Offensive Rating	Defensive Rating	Pace	SRS
2013-14' Warriors	51	107.5 (12th)	102.6 (4th)	96.2 (6th)	+5.15 (4th)
2014-15' Warriors	**67**	**111.6 (2nd)**	**101.4 (1st)**	**98.3 (1st)**	**+10.01 (1st)**

Individually, Curry continued his meteoric ascent into the league's upper-most tier. Steph earned an All-NBA Second-Team selection in 2013-14', but found himself a no-brainer selection for the First-Team in 2014-15', as he would also see himself winning the MVP award in a landslide vote over James Harden. It was truly a triumphant season, and Steph was quickly establishing efficiency as his hallmark. It's unthinkable to massively level up your efficiency in two consecutive seasons, but Steph Curry is an unthinkable player:

	PER	TS%	WS/48
2012-13'	21.3	.589	.180
2013-14'	24.1	.610	.225
2014-15'	**28.0**	**.638**	**.288**

When the Beatles set out to record *Rubber Soul* with their legendary producer, George Martin, there was said to be a consistent culture of innovation, and an openness to unconventional ideas in the recording process. Similarly, with Steve Kerr as Golden State's producer, The Warriors welcomed unorthodox game plans, particularly in the postseason. Down 2-1 to the Grizzlies in the second round of the 2015 playoffs, Kerr instructed Andrew Bogut to guard the much smaller Tony Allen. The rationale was to dare Tony Allen to shoot, knowing he was a terrible perimeter shooter, and it would allow Bogut (an excellent defender) to provide extra help on the Grizzlies' bigs, who'd been feasting up to that point in the series. The Warriors won game four and took the next two to close out the series. After making short work of Harden and the Rockets in the Western Conference Finals, the Warriors skipped a step or two by making their first Finals' appearance. Again down 2-1, this time to Goliath-LeBron and the Cavs, Kerr made Draymond the primary center for the Warriors, and Golden State won the next three games to capture the 2015 NBA Championship.

Perhaps you're wondering why I started Curry's profile with him signing a contract that, at the time, was a bit of a bargain for the Warriors because of Steph's ankle issues. After Curry led the Warriors to the championship, and snagged a league MVP in the process, how did that contract look at that point? During the triumphant 2014-15' championship campaign, Curry was Golden State's *fourth-highest paid player*, with Iguodala, David Lee and Andrew Bogut making more money than him. The Warriors signed Klay to a big extension before the 2014-15' season, and gave Draymond a big deal after the championship. So, with David Lee coming off the books, that now meant that Steph would enter the 2015-16' season as the Warriors *fifth-highest paid* player. Coming off an MVP and a championship, Steph would have been well within his rights to demand a better deal—but he didn't—and if you don't like Steph, which seems like a fairly well-travelled position in NBA chatter, respect him for no other reason than he allowed the Warriors dynasty to happen by permeating a culture of selflessness, and valuing nothing over doing what was best for the team. Which, when the Warriors set out to defend their title, meant that Curry had to be okay with being paid well under what his value was.

{2015-16'} {Revolver}

Rubber Soul truly re-charted the Beatles' creative course, and *Revolver* confidently travelled further down the sonic path of introspection, recreational drug use and societal inquisitiveness. Following up a virtuoso creation is a hefty challenge for any artist, but the Beatles continued to ride the wave of percolating creativity into 1966. An unusual amount of time off in the early part of the year afforded each member of the group to pursue their interests and passions of the moment. The result was songs that picked up where *Rubber Soul* left off, but doubled down on echoing the booming principles of the counterculture, and saw each member of the group evolving their contribution to the sound. Armed with numerous concepts for quality songs, The Beatles would record *Revolver* from April through June 1966. In that small window, all-time historic records like Bob Dylan's *Blonde on Blonde*, The Rolling Stones' *Aftermath* and the Beach Boys' *Pet Sounds* would all be released. Raising the bar once again meant the Beatles would have to innovate not just in the construction of their sound, but push the boundaries of how the sound was recorded and delivered to the masses.

The band had become more and more involved in the production process over time, but during the *Revolver* sessions, Paul, John, George and Ringo established an environment of unencumbered innovation and collaboration with George Martin, the studio's engineers and recording technicians. For a particular vocal effect, the team re-wired the circuitry in the studio to have the vocals come out of a certain speaker, where they were re-recorded for the desired vocal sound. Many of the studio innovations were developed throughout the construction of the record's landmark track—*Tomorrow Never Knows*. It was the first track the team would attempt to record during the sessions and was continually adjusted throughout the process. Artificial Double Tracking, or ADT, was invented to necessitate adding texture to John's vocals on the track. The technique would completely refashion how vocals were recorded in popular music. *Tomorrow Never Knows*, a Lennon track through and through, exhibits existential lyrics and a sonic signature that dripped with innovation and upheaval. *Revolver*, and especially *Tomorrow Never Knows*, marked a paradigm shift in both the mass-popularization of psychedelia, and the transition from recording no longer serving as a means of simply putting out songs, but a new way of creating them.

Exactly 50 years later, Steph Curry and the Warriors were executing their own paradigm shift in the NBA, which also could be reduced to a singular '*Tomorrow Never Knows*'-moment for Curry. It was late February in 2016, and I was bartending in Detroit. Rarely does a regular season game in the NBA really matter or command universal attention, but I remember vividly when the entire bar stopped for an instant when Steph Curry pulled up from 37 feet for the potential game-winning shot against the Thunder. In the moments after the shot went down, and for the remainder of the night, it was all anyone could talk about. The energy from that moment felt like what it must have been like after Neil and Buzz stepped foot on the moon. Okay, maybe that's a stretch, but for those that don't remember, it was definitely an unforgettable moment.

195

That moment had been brewing all season for the Warriors, who had completely leveled up again during the 2015-16' campaign. Fueled by criticism that their improbable championship from the year prior was 'cheapened' by the health of their Finals' opponent, Golden State won their first 24 games of the season, and 35 of their first 39. By the time Curry nailed that 'Moon Landing' game-winner against OKC, Golden State was an unspeakable 53-5 on the season. The talk-show whispers of whether or not the team could approach the unapproachable 72 wins of the 96' Bulls were getting louder, and it seemed like the Warriors had a real shot at 73 wins. Deciding to keep the pedal down, Steph and the Warriors proceeded at full speed, as they openly pursued the record. They hit that mark, and I don't think we should ever lose sight of how utterly absurd it was. Bill Simmons had the Bulls 72-win mark as one of the records least likely to fall in *The Book of Basketball*, and for good reason. If the question was 'how to level up from a 67-win, championship-winning season', I guess the answer is 'break an un-breakable record':

	Wins	Offensive Rating	Defensive Rating	Pace	SRS
2013-14' Warriors	51	107.5 (12th)	102.6 (4th)	96.2 (6th)	+5.15 (4th)
2014-15' Warriors	67	111.6 (2nd)	101.4 (1st)	98.3 (1st)	+10.01 (1st)
2015-16' Warriors	**73**	**114.5 (1st)**	**103.8 (5th)**	**99.3 (2nd)**	**+10.38 (1st)**

As for Steph Curry .. well .. this was probably the most efficient, high-volume, statistical season in the history of the NBA. Curry was rewarded with his second-consecutive league MVP (in an unprecedented, unanimous vote). The virtuoso campaign was the apex of an impossible, unparalleled, simply preposterous ascent in efficiency over four consecutive seasons:

	PER	TS%	WS/48
2012-13'	21.3	.589	.180
2013-14'	24.1	.610	.225
2014-15'	28.0	.638	.288
2015-16'	**31.5**	**.669**	**.318**

On top of leading the league in all three of those markers, he'd also lead the NBA in Box Plus/Minus, Value Over Replacement Player and total Win Shares. In a statistical crunch of Curry's 2015-16' season, Tom Haberstroh came up with the following, barely-believable facts— Curry's 3.5-point increase in PER between MVP-winning seasons is the largest jump by a repeat MVP. Bird stands second when he bumped up 2.3 points in his repeat MVP campaign of 1984-85'—Curry averaged 50.4 points per 48 minutes during the 4th quarter, the highest mark since the stat became available in 1996—Curry made 51.6 percent of his shots from between 28 feet and the half-court line (47 feet). The rest of the league hit 20.8 percent of those shots. *Guys ..* he made more than half of his shots that were *beyond* 28 feet. The man is an astronaut.

The conclusion of this season, however, would render the team with the tag 'greatest team to not win a title' instead of 'greatest team ever'. A 3-1 Finals' lead crumbled with the convergence of numerous factors, to me, none more impactful than LeBron James providing his own version of jumping up a level and snatching a championship away from Golden State. A loss rendered in such dramatic fashion left the media pointing a lot of fingers at why the Warriors didn't clinch the championship. Draymond's suspension for game five still gets a lot of play. LeBron (and Kyrie) going nuclear probably doesn't get enough tread—(did I already mention that?). The Warriors being tired from a long, fast-paced season probably contributed to some of their sluggish close to the Finals'. Perhaps Steph's unspectacular play in the Finals' validated the fringe idea that jump-shooting teams weren't built for championship contention. Whatever the equation that resulted in an improbable Warriors' loss, it should not be lost how great that team was. They put the league on notice, and it hasn't been the same since. Remarkably though, their best, most complete, most dominant team was still yet to come.

After the loss to Cleveland, Golden State re-captured the headlines by signing Kevin Durant less than one month after the defeat. With Durant's contract on the books, Curry would enter the 2016-17' season as the Warriors' *fourth-highest paid player*. As the league's two-time-defending MVP, Curry not only honored his contract that left him historically underpaid, but his singular focus on winning allowed for acquiring a mercurial mercenary like Durant. Curry would have been well within his rights to shut down a move like that for any number of reasons—a) from an intangible standpoint, Durant coming in would irrefutably take some shine off of Steph's star-status throughout the league b) tangibly, it would mean fewer shots for Steph, and a forced adjustment for the Warrior style of play c) Steph's stake in Under Armour would take a hit when a Nike goliath like Durant comes to town d) maybe most concerning, Durant would surely take away from the credit for winning that Steph was already having a hard time receiving while he was the only superstar on the Warriors. Take your pick at the issue that would have driven any number of superstars to collapse the chemistry on their team in pursuit of their individual goals. Leave it to a historically great leader like Steph Curry to shoulder all of it and remain focused on winning basketball games. This was Bill Russell shit. Steph dramatically sacrificing individual advancement for himself and his family meant that the Warriors were able to, and did, put together maybe the greatest team of all-time.

{2016-17'} {Sgt. Pepper's Lonely Hearts Club Band}

Shortly after *Revolver* was released in August of 1966, the Beatles decided that they would no longer perform live for audiences. For years, their unprecedented popularity made live appearances a security nightmare that often resembled a military operation to get them in and out of venues. The shows they played in 1966 were also accompanied by death threats, and Lennon's assertion in a March 1966 interview that the Beatles had become *more popular than Jesus* stirred up many a protest among offended Christians. Additionally, their music was becoming increasingly difficult to perform live, given all of the sonic enhancements they were applying in the studio. The group said enough was enough when, at the beginning of July, they unintentionally caused an international incident in Manila.[198] The Beatles finished out a tour of

---

[198] The First Lady of the Philippines, Imelda Marcos, wife of dictator Ferdinand Marcos, perceived the band to have snubbed her when they no-showed a breakfast meet-and-greet. The band had to high tail it out of the country the

the United States, to which they were previously committed, and officially gave up touring at the end of August 1966. Without the stress of touring on the horizon, each member was free to explore their own lives before they came together for their next project. Before the Beatles reconvened in November of 1966, George spent more time in India honing his sitar skills and immersing himself in Hindu philosophy. Ringo spent time with his family, John further entrenched himself in London's booming artistic scene, and Paul went for holiday in Kenya.

On Paul's flight back to Britain, he had an idea for a song that would eventually become the concept of their next record. The idea was to create a fictional, alter-ego band that would release them from their requirement of being 'The Beatles', freeing them to experiment even further with different sounds and recording techniques. Creating a record around such a narrow concept was absolutely radical for the time, but eventually the group signed off on the idea, and from November 1966 through April 1967, the Beatles poured themselves into the creation of *Sgt. Pepper's Lonely Hearts Club Band*. The desire to keep pushing the envelope in the studio space picked up where *Revolver* left off but without the deadline that came with *Revolver*, the exploration was reaching new heights. Album by album, the Beatles and their team were spending dramatically more time in the studio refining their sound:

	Studio Time
Rubber Soul (1965)	80+ hours
Revolver (1966)	200+ hours
Sgt. Pepper's Lonely Hearts Club Band (1967)	400+ hours

However, the Beatles perceived the industry and their competition to be catching up to them, particularly Brian Wilson's own innovative sonic experimentation on *Pet Sounds*. In response, the Beatles, with McCartney in the creative driver seat, set out to blast off into musical airspace that not only hadn't been previously explored, but hadn't been previously deemed conceivable before the release of *Sgt. Pepper's*. While citing *Pet Sounds* as inspiration during production of the record, McCartney and his band mates knew that they could bring a more avant-garde, abstract approach to their own offering that would render *Pet Sounds* toothless and lacking creative bravery. Paul's sonic vision for the project, in his own words:

> Do a bit of B.B. King, a bit of Stockhausen, a bit of Albert Ayler, a bit of Ravi Shankar, a bit of Pet Sounds, a bit of The Doors.

When the record was finally released in late May of 1967, *Sgt. Pepper's* immediately, and forever, placed the Beatles in their own tier of sonic achievement. The album showcases a variety of different songs that still come together cohesively within the project's conceptual framework. From its initial release, the album has been critically rewarded over and over again for being perhaps the first concept album. In the wake of their accomplishment were the

---

following day, and many in their group have attested to the fact that all of their lives were legitimately in danger. The government pulled away their security detail and they were under siege as they left their hotel all the way to when they boarded their plane out of the country. Yikes.

Beatles' perceived competitors who were then forced to grapple with how they were going to respond. McCartney's pursuit of what began as a small idea and concept, had manifested into what is largely considered the Beatles' creative apex, and perhaps the most influential album of all-time.

The group's decision to stop touring, and an overall departure from their angelic image, had then resulted in a much lower universal approval rating for the Beatles. McCartney's concept that drove *Sgt. Pepper's* allowed for the Beatles to hide behind the guise of a fictional band and take a breather from being 'The Beatles', which was a welcome reprieve. The Warriors on the other hand, had nowhere to hide from the negativity they brought aboard after agreeing to take on Kevin Durant. They too would see a precipitous drop in universal fan approval, as they would now be tagged as a villainous super team in the greater NBA discussion. However, in June 2017, the Golden State Warriors were raising another Larry O'Brien trophy. In their wake were a lot of perceived competitors, but no one that could genuinely challenge the team that they had assembled. They could now look back on a season that had been theirs to conquer, with very little resistance from what would have normally been formidable opponents.

During Oscar's profile, we did a brief aside into what are generally considered the greatest single-season teams of all-time. That discussion is very open, and given the era-specific variables, it will generally be widely open to interpretation. For what it's worth though, in my opinion, the 2016-17' Warriors were the greatest team in the history of the NBA. When you take a nucleus that is capable of winning 73 games in a season—a truly turn-key, championship-hungry team—and you add a fairly ball-dominant score-first superstar to the equation, logic would push you toward thinking that the sum of all of these individual parts may not result in a greater team output. But somehow, in this singular NBA occurrence, they did for the 2016-17' Warriors. Durant granted the Warriors dynamic isolation scoring when it was required, but Golden State was still free to mostly play their wide-open, controlled-chaos brand of basketball. A team that had continually demonstrated a willingness to change their style according to their opponent, now had a tool for every conceivable matchup problem that could arise. They sustained league-leading team efficiency numbers while they jogged to a modest 67 wins:

	Wins	Offensive Rating	Defensive Rating	Pace	SRS
2013-14' Warriors	51	107.5 (12th)	102.6 (4th)	96.2 (6th)	+5.15 (4th)
2014-15' Warriors	67	111.6 (2nd)	101.4 (1st)	98.3 (1st)	+10.01 (1st)
2015-16' Warriors	73	114.5 (1st)	103.8 (5th)	99.3 (2nd)	+10.38 (1st)
2016-17' Warriors	**67**	**115.6 (1st)**	**104.0 (2nd)**	**99.8 (4th)**	**+11.35 (1st)**

As a brief reminder, SRS, or Simple Rating System, is a team measurement that combines point differential and strength of schedule. The Warriors' +11.35 mark is good for the fourth-highest figure of all-time. To explain why I believe this was the greatest team ever, as briefly as possible, I have to say that I don't think any of the teams we generally grant greatest-ever status to—96' Bulls, 72' Lakers, 01' Lakers, 71' Bucks—could have dealt with the Warriors' offensive flexibility, nor could they score with all of the defensive options that filled out the 2016-17' Golden State roster. Simply put, none of the historically-dominant teams from other eras could deal with the shooting of Klay, KD and Steph on the court at the same time. The Warriors' popularization of pace and space was the toothpaste coming out of the tube in terms of how basketball is supposed to be played. The game has always been about finding open space, passing and movement, but egos and reputations cloud that model with the allure of individual, 1-on-1 glory. If the 2015-16' Warriors made the compelling argument that pace and space was a more efficient way to play basketball, the 2016-17' Warriors proved that pace and space with 3 of the 10 best shooters ever was an unbeatable recipe for championship success. I don't think any team in history could guard this team,[199] and I highly doubt that any team could keep pace with them on the other end of the court.

I had a rooting interest in LeBron winning the title at the conclusion of the 2017 postseason, as you now know, and continually found cheering against that Warriors team to be a futile effort. As the Warriors continued to sweep every round in the Western Conference playoffs, it started to feel like you were rooting against the snow falling in the winter, or the rain falling in the spring, or for an MVP-caliber performance from James Harden for just one postseason—all things that were just never going to happen. When it came time for the Finals', I foolishly held out hope that LeBron could figure it out. But the Warriors trounced a *truly great* Cleveland team in the Finals'. Klay Thompson erased Kyrie Irving on the defensive end, Cleveland's inability to double Durant allowed him to casually put up monstrous stat lines, and the Warriors' inevitable championship was achieved after a relatively uncompetitive five game series.

In the vast landscape of popular music, the Beatles raised the bar to unthinkable heights when they released *Sgt. Pepper's,* and the album's legacy of innovation and creative brilliance shines to this very day. Something tells me that the roster flexibility, raw collection of talent, selflessness and sheer dominance that the Warriors demonstrated in 2016-17', reset the bar in the NBA for generations to come.

None of that happens without Steph Curry. Steph, as one could imagine, ceded a lot of touches, shots, and narrative attention to the construction of such an unbeatable team. His counting stats fell off a bit, and his efficiency profile took a significant step back, marking the end of his historic efficiency ascent:

	PER	TS%	WS/48
2012-13'	21.3	.589	.180
2013-14'	24.1	.610	.225
2014-15'	28.0	.638	.288
2015-16'	31.5	.669	.318
2016-17'	**24.6**	**.624**	**.229**

---

[199] Maybe MJ, Pippen and Rodman from the 96' Bulls .. maybe .. but they weren't as mobile as they'd once been during the 1995-96' season, and guarding out to 25 feet, which was required against the 2016-17' Warriors, would be an adjustment they would not be ready for.

Curry couldn't have cared less after the Warriors hoisted another trophy. He'd again put his money where his mouth was in selflessly allowing the creation of this super team, and the championship was reward enough.

I'm going to spare you continuation of this comparison to the Beatles' arc, although, trust me, it totally continues to work.[200] To show how the rest of the NBA began emulating the Warriors, look at this chart of a few more team-oriented stats from the Warriors' five-year run of Finals' appearances (again, with league ranks in parenthesis):

	Wins	Pace	3-Point Makes PG	3P%	APG
2014-15' Warriors	67	99.28 (1st)	10.8 (2nd)	39.8 (1st)	27.4 (1st)
2015-16' Warriors	73	100.24 (2nd)	13.1 (1st)	41.6 (1st)	28.9 (1st)
2016-17' Warriors	67	100.37 (4th)	12.0 (4th)	38.2 (3rd)	30.4 (1st)
2017-18' Warriors	58	**100.35 (5th)**	**11.3 (8th)**	39.1 (1st)	29.3 (1st)
2018-19' Warriors	57	**101.73 (10th)**	**13.3 (3rd)**	38.5 (3rd)	29.4 (1st)

While Golden State continued to lead the league in assists, notice in bold what had been revolutionary three-point make and pace figures a few year prior, were now becoming normal within the league toward the end of the run. In trying to mimic what the Warriors were doing, other teams were playing faster, spacing the floor and taking way more threes.

The Beatles arc between *Rubber Soul* and *Abbey Road* was a singular creative occurrence, not replicable by any other artist, but instead serves as an unapproachable North Star for other artists to strive for in producing their own contributions to the musical landscape. The Warriors dynasty, similarly, is a singular (ongoing) event that NBA front offices attempt to re-create, but will inevitably continue to fall short of.[201]

The Golden State dynasty and stylistic revolution doesn't happen if its central figure doesn't overcome a debilitating, complicated physical flaw in his body dynamics. A dynasty that wasn't just built on the savvy draft strategy and financial maneuverings of Myers and his team, but largely built around a central superstar who was willing to be the third, fourth or fifth-highest paid player on his team *while he was winning MVPs and changing the fundamental mathematics of the sport.* A leader who, in the heart of the player empowerment era, decided that an exclusive focus on winning and team camaraderie was more important than earning every cent he was worth.

---

[200] {2017-18'} {Magical Mystery Tour} The Beatles do karaoke of themselves, and while the music is ground-breaking and brilliant, the competition is catching up, and the record lacked the raw creative genius of the previous album. The Warriors continue to dominate the league in the same fashion, but lack the edge that pulled them together for their historic run the season before. {2018-19'} {The White Album} The Beatles offer another incredible collection of songs, but the band's chemistry is noticeably cracking, the album dramatically lacks cohesion, while still demonstrating, in moments, the brilliance they were still able to achieve. The Warriors' chemistry is also noticeably cracking, and while they're still able to hit the highs that defined the two prior seasons, there was glaring evidence that there was a timeline on their current construction.

[201] Give me a phone call the next time the same team makes five Finals' appearances in a row.

Part 3: The Mathematician's Superstar

Free Throw Shooting—I've already mentioned it a few times, but without any real challenge, Steph Curry is the best free throw shooter in the history of the NBA. He boasts the highest career regular season free throw percentage at 90.5%. During the 2018-19' postseason, Steph went 148 for 157 from the free throw line (94.2%), which is the highest postseason percentage ever from a high-volume player (minimum 100 free throw attempts). Lastly, in one of the most underrated streaks of all-time, Steph Curry did not miss a free throw in the fourth quarter or overtime of a Finals' game from *June 16th, 2015 through May 20th, 2019*—an absolutely ridiculous 81 consecutive made free throws.

RAPTOR—In October of 2019, FiveThirtyEight introduced the world to their groundbreaking, weighted plus/minus model, titled RAPTOR (Robust Algorithm [using] Player Tracking [and] On/Off Ratings). The model's dynamic attribute is the incorporation of player tracking data, which the league has been keeping track of since the 2013-14' season. The model includes historical data, but lacks the tracking data prior to 2013-14'. This makes PIPM still a better metric overall, to me, but I find the tracking data fascinating because it is calculating extremely precise data from the beginning of the pace and space era. Naturally, Steph Curry is rewarded a very high rating from RAPTOR—his +8.7 offensive rating, coupled with a respectable +0.9 defensive rating, results in a combined +9.5 RAPTOR rating. That is good for the best overall rating from any player, dating back to the 2013-14' season. Additionally, Steph's 2014-15' and 2015-16' seasons measure as the two best individual seasons within the model.

PIPM—In case you missed it at the top, Steph is rated very highly in PIPM. His overall career PIPM rating of +5.31 is good for the 5th-best career average in NBA history .. His +5.26 O-PIPM rates him as the most impactful offensive player of all-time .. Is that good?

Clutch—It seems to me that Steph Curry gets an unfair shake when it comes to his play in the clutch. As is usually the case, this is commonly a reputation versus reality conversation, so let's use the NBA.com clutch breakout to look at just how clutch Steph has been in the playoffs. I pulled data from the Warriors five consecutive Finals' runs (2014-15' through 2018-19'). I also used the basic clutch framework from NBA.com,[202] which pulls data from any game that was within five points with five minutes or less remaining in the fourth quarter.

FGM	FGA	FG%	3PM	3PA	3P%	FTM	FTA	FT%	TS%
42	98	42.9%	24	54	44.4%	42	43	97.7%	64.2%

These are really good numbers. People get all *up-in-arms-ey* when it comes to clutch stuff because I think one bad, usually memorable, missed shot in the clutch can color your perspective on a player for good. The truth is .. these are fairly representative of Steph's career averages. I think even the most ardent anti-Steph truther has to concede that the

---

[202] The same framework used for the clutch stats compiled at the end of Chris Paul's profile.

aforementioned streak regarding Steph's postseason fourth quarter and overtime free throw shooting has to get him a seat at the table for the 'most clutch free throw shooter of all-time' conversation. That shit really matters too. For the Warriors to have an ice-box, frosty closer like that at the line has been a huge advantage for them. Anecdotally, I was rooting against Golden State in a lot of those games and rooting for Steph to miss a free throw was like rooting for James Harden to not blow it at the end of an important playoff game—it's just not going to happen.

Three-Point-Shooting—Are you ready for this? Steph Curry has hit at least 10 threes in a single game 15 different times in his career—by far the most by any player in the history of the league. The player closest to him? His fellow Splash Brother, Klay Thompson, has hit 10 threes in a single game 5 different times. Steph Curry's 121 career threes in the Finals' is by far a record. Steph Curry's 470 career playoff threes is by far a record. Steph Curry currently sits third in all-time regular season threes, but is likely to supplant Ray Allen by the conclusion of the 2021-22' season. Curry's injury in 2019 ended the greatest streak in the history of three point shooting—he made at least 200 threes in seven consecutive seasons between 2012-13' and 2018-19'. [203]

Are you sitting down? Good. This final table really illuminates just how ridiculous Steph Curry was over the Warriors' five year run to the NBA Finals'. This table combines all of Steph's shots in the regular season and playoffs that were taken between 27 feet and 47 feet. The majority of the NBA three-point line is at 23.75 feet but goes down to 22 feet in the corners. So, this table shows Steph's shooting percentage when he took *ridiculous* threes:

	3PM (27-47 feet)	3PA (27-47 feet)	Percentage
2014-15'	74	169	43.7%
2015-16'	83	177	46.8%
2016-17'	66	166	39.7%
2017-18'	36	90	40.0%
2018-19'	108	278	38.8%
	367	880	41.7%[204]

Steph Curry is an astronaut. Any NBA player that routinely attempts three-point shots should strive to hit nearly 42% of them—shit, if you shoot 42% on your threes, it's a safe bet that an NBA team will pay you $11 Million per year to just do that. The fact that Steph, over the course of his basketball apex, was able to hit almost 42% of his threes from 27 feet through the half-court line (47 feet), is totally inconceivable, even after he accomplished it! When a player has unlimited range, it puts immeasurable pressure on a defense, creates very fertile spacing for an offense, and quite literally, changes the game.

---

[203] James Harden will likely equal that mark at the conclusion of the 2020-21' season, but that's because his team's abhorrent philosophy is for him to hog the ball every possession.
[204] Dude .. what?

Why He Belongs In This Tier? Appraisal of Steph Curry's profile was one of the biggest challenges I faced in the writing of this book. There's not really a comparison for the way he impacted the game, thus there is very little room for contextualizing his impact. My profile of Steph is a very positive one, and that's largely in response to what I perceive to be apprehension from others to place Steph amongst all-time greats. Steph has two things that really work against him in this conversation 1) Steph doesn't physically impose his will on his opponents, which either directly has drawn criticism, or indirectly confuses people when it comes to appraising Steph as an all-time player. It's obvious that toward the top of this list you'll find pretty freakish athletes, all of whom have been able to utilize physical characteristics to their advantage more than Steph has been able to 2) Steph is not a traditional floor-raiser—a player that has the ability to lift teams of middling talent toward championship contention—like the majority of players he's grouped with. When it comes to his size, I simply don't think this matters. We're trying to use an outdated model of what effectiveness is when appraising a player whose effectiveness doesn't require a physically-imposing frame. Points are points, Offensive Rating is Offensive Rating, and championships are championships. My theory on this is that as we continue to travel further and further down the pace and space rabbit hole, we'll continue to appreciate Steph's profile more and more. When it comes to Steph not possessing the ability to floor-raise like nearly every player around him, I do see this as a demerit. If basically every player in his tier and in the tier ahead of him could turn chicken shit into chicken salad, Steph not being able to has to be criticized. However, I do want to say that there is monumental value in a player who, with requisite talent around him, can take a good team and make them a historically great team. Steph's skill set allowed a Draymond to become a Draymond. Steph's skillset allowed Klay to do what he does best, so when it's game six in 2016 versus Oklahoma City, he's not afraid to fire away. That's what Russell did. Allow the pieces around you to be the best version of themselves, and don't let your vanity and pursuit of individual glory impede the team's chance to win. That's Steph Curry.

If you're still not sold, try wrapping your head around this—he's the best three-point shooter of all-time, he's the best free throw shooter of all-time, he's the best off-ball player of all-time,[205] and he's on the short-list for best ball-handler of all-time. C'mon man.

---

[205] I didn't even touch on this, but the way Steph moves when he doesn't have the ball is a huge part of what's made the Warriors so hard to guard. It's also a huge part of why Steph Curry's advanced stats on the offensive side of the ball are fucking inconceivable.

Shaquille O'Neal

The Secret	Greatness Index	Ben Taylor Rank
82 / 100	269.24 (8th)	5th

PIPM	O-PIPM	D-PIPM	Peak—1999-00'	Wins Added
+4.48 (14th)	+2.93	+1.54	+6.79 (16th)	229.29 (9th)

Playoff PER	Playoff Win Shares	Playoff O-Win Shares	Playoff D-Win Shares
26.13 (4th)	31.08 (7th)	20.12 (8th)	10.96 (11th)

There are a lot of names on this list that were just names before I chose to write this book. The broad challenge has been to merely inform you (and myself) about the accomplishments and the impact each player has had—especially if they were just a name for you (or me). For this guy—you kind of know this guy, right? Maybe you remember him entering the league like a hurricane in Orlando—breaking backboards and beating MJ in the playoffs during just his third NBA season. You probably remember him in purple and gold—pulling off the league's most recent championship three-peat and cementing his all-time-great status. Or maybe you remember his run to a title next to Dwayne Wade in Miami. Perhaps you remember his brief tenures in Phoenix, Cleveland and Boston, where he racked up more nicknames than unforgettable moments.

So, what can I tell you about Shaq that you don't already know? Well, if I'm being honest, I think Shaq's legacy is disproportionately clouded because of the stuff that doesn't necessarily involve his basketball profile. Clouded with his movies, his rapping career, the nicknames, the antics, his charming personality, the Kobe stuff, his law enforcement career, his success in business, the numerous products he serves as the spokesman for (to this day), his meme-able moments working with Ernie, Kenny and Charles—he's been singularly, uniquely present in our lives for so long, that it seems to have clouded just how *viciously* dominant he was as a basketball player.

But, maybe you haven't forgotten. Maybe you were one of many people who, during Shaq's most surreal statistical stretch with the Lakers, were in a fantasy basketball league that outlawed acquiring him, because it was *that* unfair to have him on your squad.[206] Maybe you look at Joel Embiid and see flashes of the raw, unstoppable power that Shaq demonstrated throughout his prime. But then you remember that Shaq brought that *every night* .. well .. *most* nights, and it becomes clear that Embiid is a watered-down version of Shaq. Maybe you already know that Shaq's physical dominance in the low post is really only rivaled by Wilt Chamberlain's, yet, Wilt emerged when there were only a few players in the league that he couldn't roast into barbequed chickens, and Shaq made barbeque chicken out of everyone, *every night* .. well .. *most* nights. Maybe you already know how un-fucking-believably-dominant Shaquille O'Neal was. But in case all of Shaq's non-basketball head-fakes have diluted your memory of his playing career, let's cut right through that and re-iterate why his greatness on the court made everything off the court more interesting, and not vice-versa.

Ben Taylor has Shaq as the fifth-greatest player of all-time. I've had difficulty grappling with that throughout this process because of how highly Taylor generally rewards more mobile and versatile big men—Garnett—eighth[207], Duncan—seventh, Olajuwon—sixth. Shaq desperately lacked the horizontal defensive versatility of these players, and his offensive game was a little more 'one-dimensional' than those three as well. So why place Shaq above these guys?

As Taylor's brilliant work illuminates, much more eloquently than mine—it's irrefutably clear that if Shaq was on your team for the first 15 seasons of his career, he was going to cause historic defensive disadvantages for your opponent that were so glaring, that your team would perpetually be in the mix for a championship. Shaq's size—7'1" and 320 lbs—would already create a mismatch for a team attempting to defend him. But throw in the physicality and ferocity with which Shaq fought for post position, rebounds and put-backs, and you now have an unstoppable force in the game of basketball.

The gravitational chasm that Shaq's size, skill and downright nastiness created for a defense, routinely forced his opponents to re-direct what they wanted to do, and put more resources into answering the question—*how the hell do we stop that guy?* With Shaq's rangier Tier II contemporaries, much of their greatness lied in subtleties that might not be grabbed by the casual fan, or even absorbed by any advanced metric—Garnett's interior passing, or Hakeem's contests on shots that he *didn't* block, which resulted in countless opponent misses. With Shaq, he was bigger, stronger and meaner than his opponent, all of which are attributes that casual eyes acknowledged, and so did the stats.

Shaq's arrival in Orlando represented an immediate pivot for the Magic franchise. The team progressed from really bad the year before he arrived, to immediately competitive during Shaq's rookie year, to really good in his second year, to making a run to the Finals' in his third year, to nearly replicating that dominance in his fourth year. League rank is in parenthesis, keeping in mind there were only 27 teams in the NBA during this five-year stretch:

---

[206] That's a real thing. I was unable to dig up another player, in any fantasy sport, where there was significant evidence of them being outlawed because they created such an unfair advantage.

[207] Taylor was the first person—that I came across—that was really pushing for KG to be included in top-ten conversations, despite his comparative lack of hardware. He's said on multiple occasions on his podcast (*Thinking Basketball)* or in his conversations with Nate Duncan on his podcast (*Dunc'd On Basketball)* that perhaps he's still underrating KG. When I look at clips of prime KG, I have to wonder that myself.

	Record	SRS	Off Rating	Def Rating
1991-92' Magic	21-61	-6.52 (24th)	103.5 (25th)	110.5 (22nd)
1992-93' Magic	**41-41**	**+1.35 (11th)**	**108.5 (13th)**	**107.1 (12th)**
1993-94' Magic	50-32	+3.68 (8th)	110.8 (3rd)	106.7 (15th)
1994-95' Magic	57-25	+6.44 (3rd)	115.1 (1st)	107.8 (13th)
1995-96' Magic	60-22	+5.40 (5th)	112.9 (3rd)	106.9 (12th)

O'Neal was the NBA player of the week.. *his first week playing in the NBA.* During his rookie year, he brought two different NBA backboards down to the canvas, forcing the league to re-engineer and reinforce the construction of their hoops across all of their arenas. Shaq was an All-Star for all four seasons he spent in Orlando and was an All-NBA selection each season except his rookie year. Orlando's success was spearheaded by historically-efficient scoring from Shaq, and the Magic's 115.1 Offensive Rating in 1994-95' stands as the tenth-highest figure in NBA history—monumentally impressive, given the climate for scoring was drastically worse than nearly every team ahead of them on that list. Penny Hardaway joined the Magic one season after Shaq did, and initiated one of the more interesting through-lines in any career of a player that landed on my list. Teambuilding is a rather inexact science, heavily dependent on a team's circumstances and present assets. One of the more subtle testaments to Shaq's greatness was how much he simplified the fraught process of team-building by creating a very simple equation for winning. This is pretty gaudy stuff, and I apologize for going over your head, but the equation was as follows:

<u>Shaq + Talented Wing Scorer + Some Other Guys = Championship Contention</u>

S + TWS +SOG = CC .. It was really that simple. Orlando unlocked that complex equation beautifully, as Penny Hardaway quickly blossomed into one of the more potent wing scorers in the league. The degree of said potency derived *because of* the attention Shaq demanded every night, well, I'll let you be the judge of that. Either way, the tandem (along with some other guys, Horace Grant, Dennis Scott and Nick Anderson) deflated the energy of MJ's return to the NBA during the 1995 playoffs, by implausibly defeating the Bulls in the Eastern Conference Semis. The Magic made the Finals', but were swept by Hakeem's wizardry and a hungry Rockets squad. The following season went similarly, except MJ wasn't having it this time around, and eliminated the Magic before they could return to the Finals'. Shaq saw greener pastures in Los Angeles, and the ever-alluring whispers of Jerry West encouraged Shaquille O'Neal to relocate his dominant impact to the west coast. In the wake of Shaq's controversial decision was an Orlando team that would win 15 fewer games and substantially fall off in other team metrics after Shaq left the equation:

	Record	SRS	Off Rating
1995-96' Magic	60-22	+5.40 (5th)	112.9 (3rd)
1996-97' Magic	**45-37**	**-0.07 (16th)**	**105.6 (16th)**

The Lakers acquired Kobe Bryant and Derek Fisher in the same summer they lured Shaq into the purple and gold, but it would take a few years for the Lakers to adequately figure out the equation. People in the organization knew that they had their TWS in Kobe. But Kobe was raw, and began his career coming off the bench for the veteran-heavy Lakers squad. In the three seasons before the Lakers' 1999-00' runaway-train season, Shaq was posting dominant numbers:

	PPG & RPG	Off Rating	WS/48	TS%
1996-97'	26.2 & 12.5	110	.224	.556
1997-98'[208]	28.3 & 11.4	113	.255	.587
1998-99'	26.3 & 10.7	115	.283	.584

In early June of 1997 *and* 1998, Michael Jordan grabbed two more titles (while smashing the hopes and dreams of every resident in greater Salt Lake City, Utah).[209] in heartless fashion. Then in June of 1999, Tim Duncan rescued David Robinson's legacy and raised the Larry O-B after the lockout-shortened season of 1998-99'. *The Twin Towers* crushed their opposition on their way to that championship, including a second-round sweep of the Los Angeles Lakers.

It's hard to imagine now, but patience was now being tested with the Lakers group as constructed—they hadn't reached the Finals' in three seasons with Shaq, and despite being a force on the court, he'd had a few injuries that cost him substantial time. Some speculated that the group would be broken up with another disappointing season in 1999-00'. Enter Phil Jackson into Shaq's life. The two connected early on, and Shaq has suggested on many occasions that Phil served as a father figure to him. Coming into the season, Phil was able to come in and unlock the best possible version of the Shaq equation:

Shaq + TWS [Kobe] + SOG [Rice, Harper, Green, Shaw] = Championship Contention

The Lakers fire-bombed the league during the 1999-00' season. They won 67 games behind a league MVP campaign for Shaq—29.7 PPG, 13.6 RPG, 30.6 PER and a 95 Defensive Rating. The Lakers won their first 'post-Magic and Kareem' championship that season, and it was the beginning of one of the best runs in NBA history:

	Playoff Result
1999-00' Lakers	Championship
2000-01' Lakers	Championship
2001-02' Lakers	Championship
2002-03' Lakers	Lost, WC Semis
2003-04' Lakers	Lost, NBA Finals'

---

[208] 1997-98' marked the first of five consecutive years that Shaq would lead the league in both PER and field goal percentage. Is that good?

[209] I was living in Salt Lake while I wrote the majority of this book. I learned to appreciate how knowledgeable and passionate Jazz fans are—but they're all clearly *still* suffering from Post-Traumatic-MJ-Disorder.

Making four Finals' in five seasons is very rare. The list to have done that? Mikan's Lakers, Russell's Celtics, Magic's Lakers, Shaq's Lakers and Steph's Warriors. Shaq took home all three Finals' MVPs from their championship seasons. The list to have won three consecutive Finals' MVPs? MJ, (MJ) and Shaq—*that's it.*

Toward the end of this run, Kobe and Shaq were signaling that there was a conflict between them, the sole resolution for which was a change of scenery for one of the superstars. Historically speaking, the Kobe and Shaq feud was fairly predictable if you look at the strain that generally occurs for teams that are repeatedly playing into June. Fundamentally, that familiarity with each other magnified the familiarity of one another's shortcomings, and unfortunately resulted with each player losing sight of the bigger picture. Kobe could only focus on Shaq's inability to consistently be in shape. Shaq could only focus on what an asshole Kobe was. The final straw occurred prior to the 2003-04' season.

Shaq was understandably mad when Kobe named him as paying hush-money to women. While Kobe was talking with detectives in Eagle, Colorado, during the investigation of his own inappropriate behavior regarding a female, Kobe revealed that he should have 'just done what Shaq does and pay women off'. Shaq was set to begin his first season with the Miami Heat in September of 2004 (when the ESPN article detailing that quote was released), but the thing is, Shaq found out about this in September of 2003, one year before the story publicly broke. So, it's safe to say that Kobe and Shaq played the entire 2003-04' season, their final season together in Los Angeles, absolutely hating each other.

It's probably the most high-profile feud in the history of the league, especially for teammates. What I will say is that it was simpler than most people remember, as it seems to be re-litigated from time to time—Kobe was mad that Shaq didn't share his maniacal approach to improvement, and Shaq was mad that Kobe wouldn't let him live. The hate was real though—this is the quote from Shaq, about Kobe, after Los Angeles chose Kobe as their future and shipped Shaq to Miami:

> *This whole situation is ridiculous. I never hang out with Kobe, I never hung around him. In the seven or eight years we were together, we were never together. So how this guy can think he knows anything about me or my business is funny. And one last thing—I'm not the one buying love. He's the one buying love.*

Ouch. Shaq landing in Miami gives another direct glimpse into what another team looked like after Shaq left their equation, during his prime. The Last season Shaq was in Los Angeles, and the first without him:

	Record	SRS (League Rank)	Result
2003-04' Lakers	56-26	+4.35 (7th)	Lost in NBA Finals'
2004-05' Lakers	**34-48**	**-2.32 (22nd)**	**Missed Playoffs**

Similarly, Shaq was immediately impactful for the Heat during the 2004-05' season, powering them to 59 wins in his first season, and breaking through for a championship in his second season:

	Record	SRS (League Rank)	Result
2003-04' Heat	42-40	-0.13 (15th)	Lost EC Semis
2004-05' Heat	**59-23**	**+5.76 (4th)**	**Lost ECF**
2005-06' Heat	52-30	+3.59 (6th)	Championship

We wouldn't have guessed at that point, but that 2005-06' championship would be a hard bookend on the prime of Shaquille O'Neal. The 2006-07' season would be lost because of injuries to both Shaq and Wade. Shaq would then play for four teams over his final four seasons before retiring, the tenures of which weren't especially interesting or noteworthy. However, that 13-year prime stretch was as good as any in league history. From Shaquille O'Neal's 1993-94' season with the Magic, through his 2005-06' season with the Heat, every single one of his teams won at least 50 games.[210] Shaq also led the league in field goal percentage 9 of those 13 seasons. Did I mention he was an all-star in 12 of those 13 seasons? All-NBA in 12 of those 13 seasons? Including seven consecutive First-Team All-NBA selections from 1999-00' through 2005-06'? My God.

As for the team building equation that kept repeating itself throughout Shaq's prime, the extent to which Shaq increased the effectiveness of his score-first guard counterparts will be argued in perpetuity. All three of them were paired with Shaq when they were very young—Penny's first three seasons in the league, Kobe's first eight seasons in the league, and Wade's second, third and fourth seasons in the league. All three were irrefutably benefited by less defensive attention than they would have otherwise received, and the confidence they gained from such early success allowed each talented wing player to blossom into great players well before most players do. As for which element of the equation was more instrumental to team success, between Shaq and the Talented Wing Scorer, keep these things in mind:

- The Magic won 20 more games the year he was acquired, and won 15 fewer games the season after he left for the Lakers.
- Los Angeles won 3 more games (56) in their first season with Shaq (despite drastically flipping their roster), won at least 50 games for eight straight seasons *with* Shaq, then won 22 fewer games the season after Shaq left for Miami.
- The Heat won 17 more games in Shaq's first season with the team.

All I have to say is that Penny, Kobe and Wade should be grateful for having played alongside a big man with such gravity, and I'll leave it at that.

Why He Belongs In This Tier? When you start looking at historically-great players, I find myself instinctively picking apart what they didn't do well, and use that to gradually disqualify them from contention for higher tiers or consideration. Shaq was a dreadful free throw shooter. In fact, him and Wilt are the worst high-volume free throw shooters in NBA history. His inability

---

[210] During the lockout-shortened 1998-99' season, Shaq's Lakers won 31 of 50 games—which was a 51-win pace—so I'm counting that as a 50-win season too. Deal with it.

to consistently convert at the stripe encouraged opponents to invent the *Hack-a-Shaq* method of trying to slow down Shaq's teams. But here's the dirty little secret—it didn't really work. It didn't prevent Shaq from racking up a Scrooge McDuck-sized pile of individual accomplishments, on top of historically consistent team success. It speaks loudly to Shaq's dominance and greatness that such a glaring deficiency failed to meaningfully take away from his overall effectiveness. Similarly, Shaq's relative lack of ability (and/or willingness) to move horizontally on defense didn't bring down his defensive profile too much. This shortcoming is a little more interesting to me. I kind of fell in love with the ability of Hakeem, Garnett and Duncan (to an extent) to cover ground on defense, and that skill set scales so well across any different team environment. Additionally, teams never punished Shaq enough via pick-and-rolls—getting him away from the basket, and out of his comfort zone. Were he playing today, you best believe teams in the pace-and-space era would make Shaq work on defense. Ultimately, it's unclear what percentage of Shaq's effectiveness would translate to an era unsuited to his strengths, and his prime correlated closely with some of the slowest, lowest-scoring seasons the league has ever had. Still, the case rings loudly that Shaq's physical dominance plays in any style of basketball. But for me, this weakness was ultimately the one that pulled him from contention for the first tier. Hakeem, Garnett and Duncan were not the offensive dynamo that Shaq was. But their ability to anchor perennially awesome defenses put them in the same range as Shaquille O'Neal.

Larry Bird
&
Magic Johnson

	The Secret	Greatness Index	Ben Taylor Rank
Larry Bird	96 / 100	254.49 (10th)	11th
Magic Johnson	86 / 100	295.89 (6th)	10th

	PIPM	O-PIPM	D-PIPM	Peak	Wins Added
Larry Bird	+4.39 (15th)	+2.94	+1.44	+5.91 (29th) [1985-86']	176.52 (18th)
Magic Johnson	+4.57 (12th)	+3.98	+0.59	+6.01 (27th) [1988-89']	178.10 (17th)

	Playoff PER	Playoff Win Shares	Playoff O-Win Shares	Playoff D-Win Shares
Larry Bird	21.41 (30th)	24.83 (11th)	13.78 (16th)	11.05 (10th)
Magic Johnson	22.95 (19th)	32.63 (5th)	23.10 (3rd)	9.53 (16th)

In *The Wire*, McNulty needed Avon to do his best policework. In *Harry Potter*, Harry needed Tom Marvolo Riddle. In *The Matrix,* are you going to tell me that Neo didn't need Agent Smith? In Christopher Nolan's *The Dark Knight*, one of the most predictive and important films of the young century, Heath Ledger's Joker character alludes to how he needs Batman around for him to remain energized:

> *Oh, you—you just couldn't let me go, could you? This is what happens when an unstoppable force meets an immovable object. You truly are incorruptible, aren't you? You won't kill me out of some misplaced sense of self-righteousness. And I won't kill you because you're just too much fun. I think you and I are destined to do this forever.*

We spend a lot of energy projecting who might serve as an appropriate 'Robin' for someone we perceive to be Batman. We don't spend nearly enough energy ensuring the presence of an appropriate Joker figure to bring the very best out of the Batman for which we're centering our attention. MJ had the *Bad Boys*, then Drexler, then Penny, then Payton, then Malone. LeBron had the *newer Bad Boys*, then Garnett, then Duncan, then Steph, then Kawhi. Magic Johnson had Larry Bird, and Larry Bird had Magic Johnson, and the symmetry and importance of their rivalry can never be overstated.

People have tried like hell to overstate their rivalry, though. Even in my own appraisal, choosing to do Bird and Magic's profiles together felt cheesy and overdone—how many documentaries have we seen, how many ESPN montages have we watched, how many books have we read about how *Bird and Magic changed the game and saved the league in the process*? It's diluted the dynamic qualities of each player, and strips their individuality when their legacies are forever tied.

But, in fairness, their story is compelling enough to rise above the mark of over-saturation. They really were the portrait of the change the league wanted (and needed) to see. During their rise, the NBA hit its stride and would never look back. Also, yeah, they absolutely saved the NBA from a myriad of unique challenges that appeared insurmountable in the late 1970s. All the overplayed narratives are worthy of their over-exposure. Re-fashioning the importance of Larry Bird and Magic Johnson's rivalry is essential in telling any story about the NBA, and we shouldn't ever get sick of it. To fully understand it though, we have to zoom back in on where the league was just prior to Magic and Bird's entry.

After a decade of competing against one another, the NBA absorbed four ABA teams via the merger in the summer of 1976. This was a good thing for the NBA—they were able to absorb the talented stars that became a draw for the ABA (Dr. J, Moses Malone, Artis Gilmore), and the NBA no longer had any competition. There seemed to be immediately positive results when the merger's crown jewel, Julius Erving, led his Philadelphia 76ers to the 1977 NBA Finals', where they would meet Bill Walton's Portland Trailblazers. You had marketable stars and one of the league's biggest media markets represented in the Finals'—this all looked pretty good. However, there were numerous negative undercurrents. Cocaine was being regularly used by as many as half of the league's players. Perhaps correlatively, fighting was also becoming more and more commonplace during games. The league had a serious image problem on their hands, and while the NBA-ABA merger would eventually be a positive for the league, it created unique problems for the NBA in the early going.

One downside to the merger was the biggest influx of stylistic diversity the NBA had seen to date. Stylistic diversity is generally a positive in basketball—different perceptions on the best way to play the game is ultimately a good thing for the sport. However, integrating the ABA's style of play into the NBA in 1976 was like taking a bunch of guys who played like (White Chocolate) Jason Williams, and expecting them to play like Matt Dellavedova. The NBA had never been more boring by the mid-70s, and they were attempting to absorb a league in the ABA that had popularized the slam dunk, the three-point shot, and a much more free, open and creative interpretation of the game. Coaches struggled to corral rosters of historically un-like-minded teammates, with historically wide-ranging skillsets. Players continually disagreed over how the game should be played, and factions formed between players who came up in the ABA versus those who had been in the NBA before the merger. Teams struggled to sustain consistency amid all the stylistic and interpersonal inconsistency, and the result would be three different NBA champions in 1976-77', 1977-78' and 1978-79'.[211]

Integrating the ABA also meant a dramatic increase in the number of black players in the NBA. By 1979, 75% of the league was black, which was a 15% increase from 1969. The league was attempting to sell their product to a majority-*white* audience, so attendance and ratings figures were plummeting by 1979. All four major media markets (Philly, NY, LA, Chi) were down at least 11% in ratings from the year before, and the national broadcasts were down 26%. White America had a definable threshold of 'blackness' in professional basketball that they found acceptable, and the NBA had now crossed the line. Sometimes the truth hurts, and it's uncomfortable to say, but the NBA needed a white megastar in the absolute worst kind-of-way. When I think about this conundrum the league was in, I can't help but think about rock n' roll pioneer Sam Phillips. In the early 1950s, Phillips, the founder of Sun Records, started recording black artists like B.B. King and Howlin' Wolf in his Memphis studio. He loved the blues, and he saw the musical tradition as a potential bridge between white and black cultures. He quickly learned that marketing records to the black demographic had a very definable ceiling for profits, which encouraged him to give this very poignant and controversial quote:

> *If I could find a white man who had the negro sound and the negro feel,*
> *I could make a billion dollars.*

Shortly after Phillips said this, an 18-year-old kid named Elvis Presley walked into his studio. For a few years after that Sam Phillips got a glimpse at the upside of a white megastar contributing to, if not forwarding, a majority-black tradition.

Larry Bird was born in West Baden Springs, Indiana on December 7th, 1956. He was a tremendous high school basketball player and accepted a basketball scholarship at Indiana University. Bird was a Hoosier for less than a month when he determined that Bloomington was too big-time for him—he moved back to his home of French Lick, Indiana, and enrolled at Indiana State University before the 1976-77' season. Bird put the Sycamores on the map during his three seasons[212] at Indiana State. They immediately jumped from 13 wins to 25 wins during Bird's first season, and by Bird's third season, they put together a perfect record (33-0) leading up to their berth in the 1979 National Championship game against Michigan State.

Earvin Johnson Jr. was born in Lansing, Michigan on August 14th, 1959. Earvin transformed into Magic during high school, when a triple-double performance encouraged a local sportswriter to nickname the 15-year-old 'Magic', based on his preternatural ability on the court. Like Bird, Magic decided to stay close to home for his college ball—Magic was a Michigan State Spartan when the 1977-78' season tipped off. Magic lifted Michigan State

---

[211] Parity might be aspirational in some professional sports, but it's historically not gone well for the NBA. The league has always been at its best with a few different teams in contention for the Larry O'Brien Trophy.
[212] *The Legend* averaged 30.3 PPG, 13.3 RPG and 4.6 APG at Indiana State.

immediately, and they made a run to the Elite Eight during his freshman season. During Magic's sophomore season, the Spartans made a run all the way to the 1979 National Championship game, where Larry Bird and the Indiana State Sycamores awaited them.

A writer's room of Damon Lindelof, David Simon, Richard Price, Aaron Sorkin and Louis C.K. couldn't have story-boarded the 'Larry and Magic' show any better than it actually played out, including the show's incredible pilot episode. The 1979 NCAA Basketball National Championship game, through the 2019-20' season, remains the highest-rated college basketball game ever played. The tens of millions of people that tuned in for the 75-64 Michigan State victory were seeing a glimpse at the next decade of NBA basketball, they just didn't know it yet. The nuclear rating from the game demonstrated something that had been missing from basketball for many years—excitement! Be it the supremely confident white dude in baby blue, or the historically talented black dude in green and white, America was interested, and the NBA had reason for genuine excitement at a time that was preceded by very little good news.

In the same way that we overrate the importance of finding the ideal Robin, perhaps we also undervalue the power of a painful or tragic origin story. The story doesn't have to include the hero witnessing the mugging and murder of their parents, but in the cases of both Bird and Magic, it wasn't too far off. Bird's parents split while he was in high school, and his father committed suicide shortly after. Basketball was Bird's sanctuary and coping method as a teenager. That passion, competitiveness, edge and straight-up swagger that we've come to love from Larry Bird was forged in very hot fire as he dealt with tragedy as a very young man. As a middle schooler, Magic Johnson couldn't wait to play for Sexton High School—the school was just five blocks from his home and along with being predominantly black, it had a storied lineage of high-level basketball, which Magic was eager to be a part of. Instead, shortly before his high school career began, Magic was informed that he would be bussed across town to Everett High School—the predominantly *white* school on the other side of town that his older siblings had also been bused to, and experienced harsh bigotry and racism the year prior. Magic joined the basketball team, only to be ignored and never passed the ball. He eventually gained the respect of his teammates and was grateful later in his life for the exposure to the interiority of white culture early in his life. The ferocity, competitiveness, fearlessness and straight-up swagger with which Magic played the game was born of the forced mitigation of complicated racial tension by a very young man.

Bird and Magic entered the NBA the same season, but arrived in two very different ways. Magic's entry was more conventional—he played two seasons at Michigan State, declared for the draft, and was the first-overall pick[213] to the Los Angeles Lakers in the 1979 NBA draft. Bird was drafted the year before by the Celtics, but rules allowed him to play out his final season of NCAA eligibility if he couldn't come to terms with the NBA team that drafted him—so that's what Bird did. After Bird's virtuosic 1978-79' Indiana State season, Boston was forced to pony up an enormous contract or Bird would re-enter the draft, where he probably would have been the first overall pick (even ahead of Magic Johnson). It was an all-time savvy move by Red Auerbach to draft Bird 6th in the 1978 draft, as all five teams ahead of them

---

[213] The fourth-overall pick in the 1979 draft was my guy, Greg Kelser! Magic's Michigan State teammate, but more importantly, the long-running color commentator for the local Detroit Pistons broadcast. Special K!

weren't willing to possibly lose out on Bird if he refused to sign. It was then an all-time savvy move by Bird to leverage the biggest rookie contract ever out of the Boston Celtics. Despite their varied paths of entry to the NBA, Magic was in Los Angeles, Bird was in Boston, and shit was about to go down.

It's a little strange reading about two budding superstars who enter the NBA and immediately enjoy high-level team success. With the best talents going to the worst teams in the modern NBA, we've grown steadily captive of the 'isolated superstar' narrative, while the likes of Anthony Davis or Karl Anthony-Towns toil away for mediocre teams while we speculate about their appropriate Robin, and guess when the point-of-no-return will come and the franchise will have to move them. In the late 70s and early 80s, it was easier to swindle other franchises, and a witty, aggressive front office could pull one over on an opponent before they knew it was happening. Red Auerbach and the Celtics had been fleecing the rest of the league for decades already, and after Bird's rookie season, a season in which Boston won 61 games, Red traded the Celtic's first-overall pick for the third-overall pick and Robert Parish. Red selected Kevin McHale with the third pick, and the front line of Bird, Parish and McHale was prepared to dominate the NBA for years to come. The Lakers swindled their way into the first-overall pick that became Magic Johnson. Years earlier, in the summer of 1976, the New Orleans Jazz signed Gail Goodrich away from the Lakers, but under current rules, owed the Lakers compensation. That came to Los Angeles in the form of a few draft picks, which included the Jazz' 1979 first round draft pick. Naturally, the Jazz were bad in the years following the Goodrich signing, and that 1979 pick became the first-overall pick. This allowed the Lakers to pair Kareem Abdul-Jabbar, who they'd acquired in 1975 and still had plenty of mileage left, with young Magic Johnson. The pairing made hay immediately, and the Lakers won the NBA championship in Magic and Bird's 1979-80' rookie season. Magic is the only player to win the NCAA Final Four Most Outstanding Player award and an NBA Finals' MVP trophy in consecutive years. Shit, Magic is still the only player ever to win Finals' MVP as a rookie.

At the conclusion of Bird and Magic's rookie season, there was league-wide clarity around the promise and potential of the two young megastars. Both players led their teams to 60+ wins during the regular season. Bird won Rookie of the Year and was selected First-Team All-NBA. Magic improbably steered Los Angeles to their first championship in eight seasons. When Bird, now with McHale and Parish flanking him, powered the Celtics to a championship the following season, the rivalry was officially galvanized. After Boston beat Moses Malone's Houston team in the 1981 Finals', Bird and Magic each had a championship, and America was gifted a powerfully compelling binary rivalry. Magic versus Bird, on its face, was simply the two most promising NBA prospects pitted against one another—which is pretty compelling on its own. Maybe it didn't feel like it in the moment, but it was much deeper than that. The nation picked their side of the rivalry based on much deeper insights, whether they realized it or not. It was the glitz and glam of Los Angeles versus the lunchpail, everyday American appeal of Boston. It was east coast versus west coast. Finally, and let's just be honest, it was black versus white. Everyone agreed that Magic was incredible, maybe even an unprecedented talent. But the league had landed their Elvis Presley—a demographic crossover megastar that white America could really get behind. The sky was now the limit for the NBA.

Trading hands throughout the 1980s, between the Boston Celtics, Los Angeles Lakers and later in the decade, the Detroit Pistons, was one of the most potent motivators throughout the history of the NBA—revenge. Watching Magic win a championship in his rookie season fueled Bird to new heights on his way to the Boston championship in 1980-81'. Watching Bird win a championship fueled Magic and the Lakers to another championship in 1981-82', defeating Dr. J's Sixers in the Finals' for the second time in three seasons. Already with an enormous stack of chips in front of them, the rich would get richer when the Lakers' 1982 draft pick conveyed as the first-overall pick. Los Angeles acquired the pick in a 1979 trade with the Cleveland Cavaliers—naturally, Cleveland had been terrible in the interim, and tied for the worst record in the league during the season which the pick would convey. Ultimately, the Lakers entered into a coin flip with the San Diego Clippers, the winner would claim the first-overall selection in the 1982 NBA draft—naturally, Los Angeles won the toss and selected North Carolina super-stud, James Worthy.[214] Neither Bird or Magic would win the championship in 1982-83', as Dr. J finally broke through with the help of Moses Malone. However, the addition of Worthy for Los Angeles gave legs to the Los Angeles championship window in a way that Boston was ultimately unable to match. But we're not quite there yet.

The Celtics and Lakers again exchanged championships in 1983-84' and 1984-85', with the added narrative benefit of head-to-head Finals' matchups between the teams, which had yet to happen up to that point. The league was thrilled for two consecutive seasons to conclude in a showcase of its two most valuable assets. Prior to the 1984-85' season, David Stern became league commissioner, and the modern NBA as we know it was taking shape. The coalescing of many factors defined this pivot for the league, many of which we've discussed, like the introduction of a 'soft' salary cap, harsher penalties for drug use, and perhaps more important than anything else, a deliberate emphasis on marketing the league's most important brands. In that moment, the Laker and Celtic brands were selling themselves. America was fully invested in the Bird and Magic saga. It wouldn't be long before the league would transition into marketing the individual brand potential of Michael Jordan, but in the middle of the 1980s, selling the team-oriented brands was bringing the NBA back into prominence.

By the beginning of the 1985-86' season, Magic's Lakers had claimed three championships, and Bird's Celtics had claimed two. Bird, however, had enjoyed more individual success, and was the league's two-time-defending MVP—Magic had yet to win an MVP award. Bird's Celtics evened the championship score by the conclusion of the 1985-86' season, and their thorough dominance that year has earned the 1986 Celtics as a first-ballot candidate in any debate about who was the greatest NBA team of all-time. Boston had acquired Bill Walton, who played an instrumental role in Boston's 1985-86' success. It was another brilliant, albeit risky, maneuver by Auerbach (given Walton's long history with injuries). Despite the championship triumph, there existed an underlying issue for Boston—the need for a younger player, as Los Angeles had done with Worthy, that would lighten the hefty load that Bird was shouldering. Don't get me wrong, Bird was still at his peak, and had even notched another MVP award in 1985-86', joining only Wilt and Russell as the players to have won three consecutive

---

[214] In fact, the Los Angeles Lakers earned the rights to the first-overall picks of both James Worthy *and* Magic Johnson by way of literal coin-flips. Two different coin flips that changed the Lakers' fate immeasurably—talk about turning on a fucking trifle.

league MVPs.[215] However, and as hard as it was to see in that moment, Boston needed another major piece to extend their championship window.

That piece appeared to be on its way in the form of Len Bias. Red had fleeced another team when he traded holdout-starter Gerald Henderson to Seattle in 1984, for their 1986 first-round pick. Once again, the team that traded their pick was terrible in the year the pick conveyed, and Boston was sitting on the second-overall pick in the 1986 draft—just weeks after winning a championship and having the championship core well intact. Having a legitimate championship-favorite roster and being afforded the luxury of adding a blue-chip prospect is a benefit that few teams in history have enjoyed. Imagine the Bulls claiming the rights to Chris Webber in the 1993 draft, the Lakers claiming the rights to Yao Ming in the 2002 draft, or the Spurs claiming the rights to Anthony Davis in the 2012 draft—inconceivable, especially by today's standards. That was the enviable position that Boston had configured for themselves, and Red was salivating over the mega-talented forward out of Maryland, Len Bias. The multi-talented Bias looked like a game-changer on tape, and projected to be the perfect player for the Celtics. As Bird aged, Boston could now slowly pass the torch to the youngster, and with the championship count tied at three versus magic's Lakers, the Celtics could now envision an advantage in the rivalry that would allow them to amass more titles going forward. Except, Boston wouldn't win any more titles in the Bird era, in large part to the tragic and sudden death of Len Bias, *just two days* after being drafted by the Boston Celtics. In the canon of the Bird and Magic saga, this plot twist was certainly the most unexpected, and the ripples of that tragic event permeated the future of the NBA for decades.

The ghost of Len Bias immediately haunted the Boston Celtics, as injuries that were ostensibly the yield of heavy minutes for their championship core, piled up during the 1986-87' season. Despite a mildly depreciated version of Bird, and McHale playing on a broken foot, Boston would escape the 1987 Eastern Conference Finals with a narrow victory over the Detroit Pistons. I have to warn you that this is where the Detroit Pistons began to emerge as title contenders, and I'm admittedly emotionally compromised when it comes to the results of the 1987 Eastern Conference Finals. I say 'escape' because game five of that series concluded with the iconic steal by Bird of an Isiah Thomas inbound pass, which implausibly flipped the result of that game, and ultimately the series. In Detroit, we haven't forgotten, trust me. Anyway, Bird's Celtics faced Magic's Lakers for the last time in the 1987 Finals'. It was a competitive six-game series in which Magic's Lakers, with vintage Kareem performances, prevailed for their fourth championship in the Magic era. Effectively, the Boston run was over, as the Pistons got over the hump and beat the Celtics in the 1988 Eastern Conference Finals. Bird's back was getting worse, McHale's decision to play through his broken foot late in the 1986-87' season rapidly put a cap on his longevity, and as we've covered, there wasn't a younger cavalry riding to the front of the battle to relieve the beleaguered Boston core. On the other side of the battle, not only was Magic flanked by a Kareem with just enough juice for another run or two and a peaking James Worthy, but Magic Johnson was three years younger than Larry Bird, and fundamentally had more in the tank. The Lakers followed up the 1987 championship by escaping the 1988 NBA Finals' with a narrow victory over the Detroit Pistons. I have to warn you that this is where

---

[215] They remain the only players to have accomplished three consecutive MVPs. Don't hold your breath waiting for anyone else to join that club. Giannis could do it in 2021, but my guess is the voters find a new narrative.

the Detroit Pistons are in arm's length of an NBA championship, and I'm admittedly emotionally compromised when it comes to the results of the 1988 Finals'. I say 'escape' because game six of that series includes the legendary 25-point Isiah Thomas third quarter, only to have a last-second, phantom Bill Laimbeer foul rob the Pistons of the 1988 NBA championship. Ask me if I'm still upset. Anyway, the Lakers *allegedly* won the 1988 championship, their second consecutive title. The NBA title was the fifth and last championship of the Magic era.

In the battle for the 1980s, Los Angeles outlasted Boston. By the end of the decade, the Lakers had represented the Western Conference in the NBA Finals' 8 out of the possible 10 seasons, and the Celtics had represented the Eastern Conference 5 of the 10 seasons. As the league ventured into the 1990s, popularity was humming along with the villainous Detroit Pistons carrying the torch, and before long, the MJ era would deliver unprecedented popularity for the NBA. The prosperity and promise the league was enjoying was built on the storybook rivalry between Magic Johnson and Larry Bird. The rivalry illuminated the capacity that professional sports had to tap into the consciousness of an American audience. It's irrefutably a bummer that we needed a white guy to be the best player in the league for the league to become wildly popular again, but if that's what it took for us to get to a place where the league could be massively popular during the 1990s with a cast of exclusively black superstars, then I guess it was worth it. If we required a white megastar to bring the league to new heights of popularity, I suppose that makes the Bird and Magic rivalry the rivalry we needed, and not necessarily the one we wanted, but we're grateful nonetheless.

The narrative story of Bird and Magic really is an amazing one, and I encourage you to cough up that ESPN+ dough and watch the ESPN Films 30 for 30 series—*Best of Enemies*—which visually portrays the story in much greater granular detail than I chose to include. The question now, is how do these players fit into *this* story? It's true that their paths are inexorably tied, which is why I decided to do their profiles together, eliminating the need to constantly refer to one another's profile. But when it comes to comparing their true basketball impact versus other all-time greats, where do we start?

I think you have to start with an acknowledgement that each player possessed a collection of attributes that has rarely ever been seen. Each player had the unique ability to not only raise the floor of their team's potential, but bump up against the championship ceiling of their team's potential. Very few players in history have been able to do both. At the same time, both players were fortunate to have championship supporting casts essentially as soon as they entered the NBA. Kareem was league MVP during Magic's virtuoso rookie campaign, and McHale and Parish fell into Bird's lap after just his first season. We've already discussed how rare that is, and what an enviable reality that is for the likes of LeBron James, Chris Paul, David Robinson, Hakeem Olajuwon and Kevin Garnett, who were all trapped on bad teams early in their careers. Ultimately, there was never any doubt that each player was a comfortable fit in Tier II. Despite bringing historically unique individual profiles, they shined brightest among teammates who also shone brightly and were able to carry the load if need be. By my measure, the primary criteria I've used to evaluate players thus far are as follows:

- o Counting Stat Profile (Points, Rebounds, Assists, etc.)
- o Advanced Stat Profile (PER, True Shooting, Win Shares, etc.)

- Team Success (Championships, Near Championships)
- Individual Accolades (MVPs, All-NBA, All-Star, etc.)
- Unique Intangible Narratives (A player's reputational legacy)

This isn't a definitive list of the criteria I've used, and I fully admit that I've used and mis-used different profiles based on the narrative I'm pursuing. But as we sit on the brink of the most prestigious tier of all-time NBA greats, most of the evaluating we've done so far can be sorted into one of these camps. So, let's do this—let's go through each of these profiles as it pertains to Bird and Magic, and determine which player has the advantage within each profile:

Counting Stats

I think it makes sense to first look at each player's cumulative career numbers, then to glimpse at each player's peak season for counting stats, and finally take a look at their playoff split.

	Regular Season			
	PPG	RPG	APG	SPG[216]
Larry Bird	24.3	10.0	6.3	2.5
Magic Johnson	19.5	7.2	11.2	2.3

	Peak Regular Season			
	PPG	RPG	APG	SPG
Larry Bird (1984-85')	28.7	10.5	6.6	2.8
Magic Johnson (1986-87')	23.9	6.3	12.2	2.2

	Postseason			
	PPG	RPG	APG	SPG
Larry Bird	23.8	10.8	6.5	2.7
Magic Johnson	17.7	7.0	11.2	2.0

I think this has to be Bird. He was definitely a better individual shooter and scorer, but also always boasted high assist numbers as the conduit for really efficient offenses. Additionally, his numbers were incrementally better during the postseason, but higher volume didn't mean higher efficiency, as we'll soon see. *Advantage—Bird.*

Advanced Stats

	Regular Season			
	PER	TS%	WS/48	USG%
Larry Bird	23.5	.564	.203	26.5
Magic Johnson	24.1	.610	.225	22.3

---

[216] Stocks—combination of steals and blocks = stocks.

	Peak Regular Season			
	PER	TS%	WS/48	USG%
Larry Bird (1984-85')	26.5	.585	.238	28.5
Magic Johnson (1986-87')	27.0	.602	.263	26.3

	Postseason			
	PER	TS%	WS/48	USG%
Larry Bird	21.4	.551	.173	24.8
Magic Johnson	23.0	.595	.208	21.2

Has to be Magic, with very little case to be made for Bird. The one thing that really stands out is how low their usage was, especially during the postseason. In the heliocentric 2020 moment of the NBA, we've grown accustomed to superstars ordinarily eclipsing 35%+ in terms of usage. I think this speaks to the more team-oriented approach by both Bird and Magic, but also the fact that they had reliable supporting players around them to get buckets. I'm truthfully disappointed with Bird's advanced profile. The postseason split especially is relatively average. *Advantage—Magic.*

Team Success

This is a pretty open-and-shut case, as Magic's five championships stand tall over Bird's three. I really love Bird, and I feel compelled to re-litigate what Len Bias would have meant for Boston's team success between 1987 and 1991, but I'll let it go.[217] We're safe in saying that Magic gets the nod in team success, and is actually validated in the narrow edge that Magic enjoys on the list of all-time winning percentage[218] amongst NBA players to have played at least 250 games:

		Win Percentage	Record
1)	Kawhi Leonard	75.37%	352-115
2)	**Magic Johnson**	**73.95%**	**670-236**
3)	**Larry Bird**	**73.58%**	**660-237**
4)	Draymond Green	73.36%	391-142
5)	KC Jones	73.08%	494-182
6)	Michael Cooper	72.85%	636-237
7)	Tommy Heinsohn	72.63%	475-179
8)	Danny Green	72.10%	447-173
9)	Manu Ginobili	72.09%	762-295
10)	Sam Jones	72.06%	624-242

---

[217] For now.
[218] This table is only accurate through the 2018-19' season, and only includes regular season games.

This is actually a fascinating list that, with the exception of Magic and Bird, is primarily a list of supporting players that were part of other historic winning traditions—K.C. Jones, Tommy Heinsohn and Sam Jones of the Boston/Russell dynasty. Danny Green, Kawhi and Manu of the San Antonio/Duncan dynasty. Draymond as the heart of the Golden State/Steph dynasty, and Michael Cooper, the longtime teammate of Magic's on the Lakers. *Advantage—Magic.*

Individual Accolades

Let's lay all of these out, and then work our way through them.

Bird		Magic
3	League MVPs	3
2	Finals' MVPs	**3**
9	First-Team All-NBA	9
12	All-Star Selections	12
1	All-Star MVP	**2**
3	All-Defense Selections	0
1979-80' Rookie of the Year	Miscellaneous	4x Assist Champ, 2x Steals Champ

This is pretty tight, and I'm not sure there's a real winner here. My leaning is toward Bird because of his selections to the All-Defense team, but Magic buoys that advantage with another Finals' MVP and having led the league in assists and steals for several seasons. Too close to call. *Advantage—none.*

Individual Legacy Narrative

This is inevitably subjective, but I will say that Bird has a less complex and more easily metabolized legacy. Larry Bird wasn't especially eager to speak with the media or provide many non-basketball stories for the world to sink their teeth into. Magic Johnson was less apprehensive about the perils of being an *actual* celebrity, not just a basketball celebrity. Bird's legacy is competitiveness, confidence, and keeping to himself (while at the same time wanting to rip your heart out). I think it's fair to say that Magic's legacy can claim all of those things, with the exception of keeping to himself. To me, I'd prefer the guy who leads quietly and with the way he plays versus the guy who has a hard time keeping his mouth shut—but that's me.

Does that mean that I would take Bird over Magic? Not necessarily. If I had to start a team with a player that did not have requisite talent around them, I'd take Bird. If I had to pick a player for a team that already had reliable supporting players, I'd probably take Magic for his ability to get the most out of them. If I had to pick a player to get me a bucket when it mattered, perhaps the most crucial question here, I'd have to side with the opinion of Pat Riley[219]:

---

[219] Keeping in mind that Pat Riley was *Magic Johnson's coach* from 1982 through 1990.

> *If I had to choose a player to take a shot to save a game, I'd choose Michael Jordan. If I had to choose a player to take a shot to save my life, I'd take Larry Bird.*

Advantage—Bird.

Final Tally—Bird-2, Magic-2

How fitting.

Why They Belong in This Tier? Neither player has the advanced profile for a compelling Tier I case. Magic's five championships and three MVPs present a glimmer of a case for Tier I, but I don't think I'm being unfair in saying that he was tripping over really talented teammates for the entire duration of his career—the core of the Showtime Lakers was three different first-overall draft picks. Including the metronomic offensive production that Kareem Abdul-Jabbar provided, which continually raised the floor for the Lakers, even as he aged into the late 1980s. Scientifically, we don't even really have data on Magic playing for bad teams, which leads me to believe that his career played out as virtually the best it possibly could have, given his set of skills. Conversely, both of these players were far too great, from every perspective, to be in consideration for Tier III. Each player fits comfortably in Tier II and it's unlikely that they'll ever be bumped.

Tim Duncan

The Secret	Greatness Index	Ben Taylor Rank
100 / 100	399.52 (4th)	7th

PIPM	O-PIPM	D-PIPM	Peak—2000-01'	Wins Added
+4.97 (6th)	+1.80	+3.17	+7.12 (12th)	284.78 (2nd)

Playoff PER	Playoff Win Shares	Playoff O-Win Shares	Playoff D-Win Shares
24.28 (8th)	37.84 (3rd)	20.46 (7th)	17.38 (2nd)

There are four players that forced me to consider a fifth position in Tier I—Shaquille O'Neal, Hakeem Olajuwon, Kevin Garnett and Tim Duncan. Shaq was really a once-in-a-lifetime talent, but Hakeem and Garnett appear to be part of a traceable lineage of players. Those two were so unbelievably switchable, fast, long, and smart on defense. Plus, they coupled that with really strong, albeit varied, offensive profiles, forcing me to conclude that they represent an incredibly rare and hyper-effective archetype in the lineage of the NBA—The Bill Russell Model—big men that are wickedly-athletic and super-competitive defenders, whose offensive skillsets compliment, if not create, efficient offense.[220] Not only are their attributes scalable across different team environments, I also think it's clear that this archetype travels well through different eras of the NBA, and subsequently across various styles of play. Garnett's peak (2003ish-2008ish) came during a very slow and defensively minded NBA, but his preposterous switchability, length and shooting[221] would probably look best, well, in 2020, right? Olajuwon was the best player on a team that pushed the freaking 1985-86' Celtics to six games during the 1986 Finals' (during a season where the average team scored 110.2 PPG), and

---

[220] You probably hated me putting Draymond into Tier III, but he was the spiritual torch-bearer of this archetype.

[221] In Ben Taylor's *Great Debates* series on his podcast, *Thinking Basktball*, he and Andre Snellings broke down the legacies of Duncan versus Garnett. In attempting to extrapolate what Garnett's three-point viability would have been had he peaked in the three-point explosion, Taylor made a really poignant example out of Brook Lopez's three-point development. In the five years before Lopez started shooting threes, Lopez was a 43% shooter on long two-point shots. Across Garnett's peak—2003 through 2008—he shot just under 47% on long two-point shots. That's just a shade under Dirk's percentage from that range, over Dirk's best five-year stretch. The point being, were Garnett asked to step out to the three-point line, the data suggests he would have been excellent.

then was the best player on back-to-back championship teams in 1993-94' and 1994-95' (during seasons where the average team scored 101.5 and 101.4 points, respectively).

Where the comparison between those two players and Duncan gets tricky is when you start to realize that the three players comprise a spectrum of the varying team success an immensely talented big can have. Garnett, as we discussed in agonizing detail, was stuck with awful teammates for the first twelve seasons of his career. Somewhere in the middle of the spectrum, Hakeem challenged for a title in just his second season (1985-86'), and eventually was cocooned with talented, complimentary players by the mid-90s. Duncan had good teammates his *entire* career, to say nothing of a savvy front office and a Belichick & Brady-level connection with his coach, Gregg Popovich. This highly fortunate confluence of factors yielded *twenty straight* 50+ win seasons[222] and five championships. As much as I love Garnett and Olajuwon, their legacies and their consideration for a higher Tier II ranking, or Tier I spot, are largely hypothetical. I look at those guys and am forced to project team success, had they been flanked by higher-level players more consistently. We're not playing that game with Tim Duncan—he had good players around him, and whether or not Tim Duncan was the chicken or the egg, he also played in a very secure institutional environment. Maybe Kevin Garnett would have won more than one ring if he'd played on better teams, and maybe Hakeem Olajuwon would have more than two championships if Ralph Sampson had stayed healthy, or his reserve cavalry would have arrived before the mid-90s. But, we know what Duncan was capable of, were the right things around him. While there are very legitimate cases for Hakeem and Garnett as greater players, we have to reward Duncan for enjoying the metronomic team success that the other two *might* have had.

Bob Dylan's most critically acclaimed albums found their way into my orbit over the years—*Blood on the Tracks, Blonde on Blonde* or *Time out of Mind*—but it never felt like I had a feel for the guy. Don't get me wrong, The Beatles, Rolling Stones and Led Zeppelin, all massively important bands to me, have their fair share of cryptic music and mysterious contours that outline their respective profiles. But Dylan seems to have existed on his own track in the pantheon of all-time rock acts—staying close enough to stand aside those others in genre, but standing alone on his winding path through music and life over the last 65 years. For example, Bob Dylan spent half a century being so flippant and irreverent to the media, that he's become a primary reference point when describing a public figure who's uncooperative with the press. I mean, the guy was awarded a fucking Nobel Prize for Literature[223] in October 2016, and didn't even respond to the announcement until April of 2017. Throw in the fact that he's made like a thousand albums spanning six decades, and you have one of the more confounding catalogs to unpack in the history of rock music. Intent to get a better feel for the man and his music, I embarked on the arduous chronological journey through Dylan's discography. In total,

---

[222] The Spurs' run of 20-straight 50-win seasons dwarfs the second and third longest runs, which are predictably held by the Lakers (12-straight, 1980-1991) and the Celtics (10-straight, 1959-1968).

[223] And then only agreed to accept the award and give the customary speech *so long as no members of the media were present!* This book has taken me in a lot of directions, but I certainly didn't expect to be researching the Nobel Prize for Literature, but here we are. Apparently, it's been awarded every year since 1901, and Bob Dylan was the 2016 recipient. If you desire feeling especially unsophisticated, I encourage you to read the list—I only recognized a handful of names, and you bet your ass there aren't any other rock musicians on the list. In fact, the only other songwriter was this Indian dude—Rabindranath Tagore—who won the award in 1913.

between the years of 1962 and 2019, there are 38 studio albums, 13 live albums, 7 soundtracks (which he served as the primary contributor), and Dylan's *Bootleg* series, which consists of 15 (large) volumes. It was a hell of a lot of music, but a worthwhile effort that yielded a better understanding and appreciation for, probably, the most prolific musician of the twentieth century.

Throughout the process I kept drawing parallels to the most prolific NBA player of the twenty-first century, Tim Duncan. Admittedly, there might have been a little 'Jim Carrey in the movie *23* going on'—conjuring parallels that probably, but almost definitely, did not exist. Sure, each guy enjoyed a long, storied career, but plenty of musicians and athletes can claim that. I guess where I first saw a connection was the ability to go years in between masterpieces. Duncan's Spurs won titles in 1999, 2003, 2005, 2007 and 2014—winning championships fifteen years apart as a primary contributor is very nearly unprecedented.[224] Timmy would also never dip below a 21.3 PER over that stretch, and made an all-defensive team 14 of those 15 seasons. Dylan's six best albums constitute a similar pattern—*Highway 61 Revisited (1965), Blonde on Blonde (1966), Blood on the Tracks (1975), Desire (1976), Street-Legal (1978),* and *Time Out of Mind (1997)*—his best work is mostly spread across two clusters from the early stretch of his career, but he then pops up several years later with *Time Out of Mind.* Okay, maybe I'm grasping at Tim Duncan-sized straws, but stay with me. Where I really believe there to be a connection is how these two guys are generally regarded versus their peers. How each's unique demeanor, and intentionality toward the people around them, represented inverse traits versus the people generally selected as greater than them. If the only guys ranked above Duncan are the Zeppelins, Rolling Stones and Beatles of the world, maybe the only reason that we don't think of him in that regard is because he acted nothing like them.

For many years, I've heard many 'what if KG had gone to the Spurs instead of Duncan' takes, and while it's a fun hypothetical to latch onto, I'm not so sure that it goes as well for Garnett. Listen, if KG plays out his career as a Spur in Duncan's place, his over/under for championships is 3.5. But for all of the deep KG, Manu and Tony Parker playoff runs we might have been gifted, I think we have to agree that many of those runs would include some legendary emotional meltdowns and/or technical fouls in pivotal moments by Kevin Garnett.[225] The more interesting hypothetical to me is the one where we try to place the legacy of a player with Tim Duncan's accomplishments, but behaved more like Kevin Garnett. God Bless Duncan and his methodical attempt to bore us to death over the years with his personality. Don't get me wrong, I've always loved guys that don't get too up or down—in Detroit, we loved Chauncey for this quality. Furthermore, I think Duncan's demeanor was the ideal intangible centerpiece to permeate consistency and togetherness across that insane Spurs run. However, his lack of swagger and bravado clearly holds his legacy back in conversations about the very greatest players of all-time. If I've learned anything, it's that we overvalue hyper-masculine, swaggering,

---

[224] Kareem Abdul-Jabbar was the best player on Milwaukee's 1971 virtuoso championship squad, then was the second or third best player on Los Angeles' 1987 title team—a remarkable 16 years between titles. Kareem was also instrumental in the Lakers' heist of the 1988 championship from my Detroit Pistons, but I'm emotionally incapable of assigning credit to anyone in that series (other than referee, Hugh Evans, for making the worst call in the history of the NBA).

[225] Garnett is #7 all-time in technical fouls. Above him? Dirk Nowitzki—6th, Dennis Rodman—5th, Gary Payton—4th, Rasheed Wallace—3rd, Charles Barkley—2nd, and Karl Malone—1st.

MF-dropping superstars. For a contemporary example, try to imagine a player with Joel Embiid's personality winning and enjoying the success that Tim Duncan had. It's hard for me to visualize that reality and us not campaigning for that player to be considered perhaps the greatest player of all-time. But because of Duncan's quiet personality, I think we've undervalued him in this sense, and it's reminiscent of our feelings toward another heavily prolific all-timer who wasn't exactly a crowd-pleaser.

"Contemporary Kareem Abdul-Jabbar" is the mantle that I couldn't get away from when studying Duncan's profile. Never hampered by substantial injury, each player afforded their team a mark of consistency and relevancy by simply showing up each game. Defensively, there is little to be parsed between each player, also keeping in mind that we don't have much advanced stuff on Kareem, which is especially helpful in unravelling defensive effectiveness. I'm inclined to give Duncan the edge because a) his 'death zone', or area where offensive players only dare attempt shots, was a little wider than Kareem's, and b) the Spurs dynasty was a defensive one, and Duncan was not just the straw that stirred the drink, he was the glass, he was the sweet vermouth, he was the bitters, and he was at least one part of the whiskey. Offensively, Kareem has a definitive advantage. Kareem probably possessed the most unstoppable signature move/shot in the history of the NBA—which largely drove him to being the NBA's all-time leading scorer (by a wide margin). Duncan was a strong offensive player, primarily looking to body his opponent in the post, but was also able to step out a few feet, where he established his own signature shot—the face-up bank shot. I think I'm okay saying that Duncan was a marginally better defender, and Kareem was a meaningfully better offensive player—a player you could actually build a highly-proficient offense around—something you can't say about Duncan.

Where I do feel the players are especially similar though, is that while they were always able to keep their team in the mix for a championship, they were susceptible to players who turned it up to 10 in the playoffs. If Duncan and Kareem gave you an 8.9 out of 10 every single night, that's truly something to be treasured. But when players came along that were peaking at 9.7 during certain playoff series', Kareem and Duncan seemed incapable of the sixth-gear to match those players going nuclear. Kareem got bodied by Moses Malone in the 1981 and 1983 playoffs, like legit bodied, including the Lakers getting swept in the 1983 Finals'. Duncan's Spurs bookended the Lakers' three-peat with titles in 1999 and 2003, but were swept by Shaq's Lakers squad in the 2001 playoffs, and lost in five games to Los Angeles in the 2002 playoffs.

Just like Bob Dylan's early-80s gospel and Christian-rock phase, Tim Duncan has this noticeable blemish on his legacy. Duncan's version of those dreadful Dylan albums—*Saved* (1980), *Shot of Love* (1981), *Infidels* (1983) and *Empire Burlesque* (1985)—are some odd playoff exits, mostly between 2008 and 2012. To me, it seems like Duncan's Spurs were so consistently competitive, that in the absence of really dominant teams, they were always just kind-of 'there', waiting to fill the vacuum. But in the presence of a few dominant teams, it's hard to ignore the instances of the Spurs falling short. On top of the examples above, the Spurs lost in five games to the Lakers during the 2008 postseason—which was weird because Los Angeles had acquired Pau Gasol just a few months prior, were effectively still 'figuring it out', and were seemingly vulnerable. San Antonio was swept by Phoenix in the 2010 postseason—also not a great look. Most puzzling of all, being inexplicably bounced by the Thunder in the 2012 playoffs, when San Antonio held a 2-0 lead and looked unbeatable.[226] It raises interesting questions about why the Spurs approach proved to be less effective in the face of really dynamic teams. I think Pop's focus on doing the little things—not fouling, handling conflict in-house, not turning the ball over, frequent team dinners—provide a lesser competitive advantage during the playoffs than they do on a Tuesday in February against the Suns. But the other part is that they seemed to lack a dynamic go-to scorer, not named Manu, for the tense pivot points in playoff games. Duncan, despite being able to get reliable, consistent offense, wasn't routinely able to create a chasm in his opponent's defensive strategy (a la Shaq or Wilt), and that deficiency contributed to a few peculiar playoff exits.

Let's be real though, Duncan's Spurs also beat some really great teams in the postseason. In both 2005 and 2007, San Antonio bounced 60-win Steve Nash Phoenix teams. Duncan faced the Kobe-Shaq Lakers five times, and despite getting bodied in the aforementioned 2001 and 2002 matchups, he did pretty damn well across all five times they matched up in the playoffs:

Playoff	Matchup Versus Shaq-Kobe Lakers	Eventual Champion (Finals' MVP)
1999	W (4-0) Western Conference First Round	San Antonio (Tim Duncan)
2001	L (0-4) Western Conference Final	Los Angeles (Shaquille O'Neal)
2002	L (1-4) Western Conference Semi-Final	Los Angeles (Shaquille O'Neal)
2003	W (4-2) Western Conference Semi-Final	San Antonio (Tim Duncan)
2004	L (2-4) Western Conference Semi-Final	Detroit (Chauncey Billups)

Duncan wasn't able to win the early 2000s battle for the Western Conference versus those great Laker teams, but two out of five isn't bad against that Los Angeles juggernaut. What he, Pop, Manu and Tony were able to do was outlast them—happy to fill the Western Conference power vacuum after the Shaq and Kobe breakup, Duncan's Spurs won two out of the next three titles in 2005 and 2007. Outlasting is an important overall theme. San Antonio's drumbeat consistency allowed them to outlast Nash's Suns, Dirk's Mavs, Kobe's Lakers, and shit, LeBron's Heat, to capture that last glorious title in 2014.

The totality of Duncan's individual accolades is not easy to ignore. On sheer volume of accomplishment, Tim Duncan's profile is as distinguished as anyone—5 Championships, 3 Finals' MVPs, 2 League MVPs, 15-time All-Defense,[227] 15-time All-NBA, 1,392 career regular season games (tenth-all-time), 251 career playoff games (third-all-time), 206.38 Win Shares (seventh-all-time), 37.84 Postseason Win Shares (third-all-time), 284.78 PIPM Wins Added (second-all-time), 50+ wins in all 19 seasons (never ever ever ever ever ever happening

---

[226] For what it's worth, during the broadcast for game two of this series, Marv Albert said the 2011-12' version of the Spurs 'reminded him of the early 70's Knicks and some of the Russell-led Boston teams. They rode a 20-game win streak to that 2-0 lead versus OKC, and the media was largely asking if they could sweep the playoffs, but implausibly proceeded to drop four-straight to KD, Harden and Russ. Crazy.

[227] Insane. 15 is the most all-time. In fact, the players tied for 2nd—Kobe Bryant and Kevin Garnett—each have 12 selections. Based on where current players stand on this list, it's not really possible for anyone to pass Duncan in the next decade, and unlikely anyone ever eclipses that mark.

again).[228] *Slightly light* Kareem Abdul-Jabbar feels appropriate in making sense of that award profile. Duncan doesn't boast a divine advanced profile like LeBron, MJ, Kareem, David Robinson or Chris Paul, but it's pretty damn good, and as you could probably guess, paints the portrait of a historically consistent player. Jacob Goldstein's PIPM has him as the sixth-most impactful player of all-time. Defensive Rating isn't a viable individual stat most of the time, especially in samples less than a full season—but when a player has a career defensive rating of 95.6, good for the third-best all-time mark, I'm comfortable rewarding them with a mantle like 'irrefutably, one of the best defenders of all-time'.

My deep dive of Dylan's music yielded some buried treasure, and I found Dylan's *The Basement Tapes Complete* collection to be a gem of gems. A motorcycle crash in June 1966 cut short production of probably Dylan's best work, and forced him to discontinue touring for a while. When he was ready to start making music again, the band that had been backing him on the road, The Hawks, would join him for sessions[229] between May and October of 1967. The sessions yielded much of the brilliance heard on his landmark work during 1965 and 1966, but the music was emotionally richer and more genuine than any music Dylan ever created. The best cuts from that session would be trimmed and polished into a 1975 release, simply titled *The Basement Tapes*. But the beauty is in the raw sessions, which were released in 2014, and really capture the energy of Dylan during one of the most interesting moments of his life. The collection exists as one of the most valuable documents in rock history, and as such was described as follows by rock writer and rock n' roll archeologist, Jim Beviglia:

> *Music fans having access to the complete archives of The Basement*
> *Tapes is somewhat akin to historians being presented with the tapes of*
> *the meetings of the Continental Congress or art buffs who receive a*
> *videotape of Da Vinci's entire process of painting The Last Supper.*

The collection has a 99 rating on Metacritic, which I genuinely didn't think was possible, but I can't really disagree. The songs capture a version of Bob Dylan that was a bit hobbled and disillusioned by how the public had viewed him over the past couple years. Dylan burst into the public eye with acoustic protest songs in the early 1960s. By the mid-60s, his voice had become a vital one for the swelling counterculture. Uncomfortable with being anointed 'the voice of his generation', or being pigeonholed as being any one thing, Dylan zagged when everyone expected him to zig—he built out his sound with electric instruments (seen as a sell-out move), and produced music that wasn't addressing the political unrest of the moment. People were pissed and he heard boos in every auditorium he played during the tour that led up to his motorcycle accident in July of 1966. When Dylan took to the basement of a big pink house in

---

[228] During the 1998-99' lockout-shortened season, the Spurs played at a 50-win pace, so I'm counting that like I did before. But seriously, 50+ wins for each season of his 19-year career is the most insane stat of Duncan's legacy. It never happened before him, and it's never ever ever ever ever ever ever ever happening again. The guys in 2nd, 3rd, and 4th place? Tony Parker—16, Manu Ginobili—15, Shaquille O'Neal—13.

[229] Many of those musicians would soon form The Band, who released their landmark debut album, *Music From the Big Pink*, in 1968. The 'Big Pink' refers to the big pink house, in the basement of which, the *Basement Tapes* sessions occurred. A Bob Dylan painting also serves as the album's cover art.

upstate New York during the summer of 1967, he wanted to play music with his friends again, but he also wanted to prove that hard losses wouldn't define him.

Tim Duncan's finest moments aren't as difficult to pinpoint, but they were also frequently fueled by particularly difficult playoff losses. After getting abused by Kobe and Shaq, the Spurs pieced together one of the great championship runs in NBA history. Between **2002-03' and 2006-07'**, the Spurs won three out of five championships, which has only been accomplished by Mikan's Lakers, Russell's Celtics, Magic's Lakers, MJ's Bulls, (MJ's Bulls), Shaq's Lakers, Duncan's Spurs and Steph's Warriors. Individually, this was also Duncan's apex—2002-03' was the second of back-to-back league MVPs, and he was well within the conversation for best player in the league during this stretch. The **2012-13' and 2013-14'** seasons are the other cluster of Duncan's career worth zooming in on. Miami and San Antonio would trade titles at the conclusion of both of these seasons, but it was San Antonio's revenge-fueled triumph in the 2014 Finals' that really punctuated the Spurs dynasty. Losses don't get any tougher than what happened to San Antonio in game six of the 2013 Finals'. They were up five points with less than thirty seconds to go in the clinching game six. League officials had wheeled the Larry O'Brien trophy onto the court—*the championship was right there*. A few missed free throws and a Ray Allen three-point shot for the ages flipped the series in Miami's favor. A gutting loss on its own, but it was just the most painful disappointment in what was a stretch of disappointing playoff exits between 2008 and 2012. Ever resilient, the Spurs locked in the following season and reaped their revenge during the 2014 Finals'. That was Duncan's fifth and final championship, and at least partially validated the many recent disappointments the Spurs had weathered.

Why He Belongs In This Tier? I feel as though I litigated Duncan's case throughout his profile more than I usually have with other players. I genuinely struggled with Duncan's case as a Tier I player, but eventually found him (and Garnett, and Olajuwon), to be a definable degree below the four players to be named shortly. Tim Duncan is one of the most prolific and consistent players of all-time. While 'prolific' and 'consistent' aren't the sexy attributes that we'd engineer our ideal superstar to have, if your franchise aspires to win 50 games for an unfathomable two decades, those are exactly the attributes you want to see in your centerpiece. You might also want to look for a defensive-minded center with the wingspan of a pterodactyl, and the steadiness and calm of a Buddhist monk.

Tier II Recap.

As the great British Philosopher Mick Jagger once said—*I'm giving you a piece of my mind, there's no charge of any kind, try a very simple test, you should just retrace your steps.*

Let's retrace our steps, shall we?

As we stand ever closer to the summit of all-time NBA greatness, we're now distancing ourselves from the variance of Tier III. The line between Tier II and Tier III is much more defined (to me) than the divider between Tier III and the vast player pool beyond that. As such, there were only a few players in Tier III that I actually considered for Tier II:

Most Screwed Over	Considered.. Kind of	No Chance
David Robinson	Kevin Durant	John Havlicek
	Jerry West	Dennis Rodman
	Dirk Nowitzki	Steve Nash
	Karl Malone	Draymond Green
	Scottie Pippen	Julius Erving
	Moses Malone	Dwayne Wade
		Chris Paul
		Elgin Baylor
		Isiah Thomas

The Admiral has a pretty legit Tier II case. His first ten seasons in the league were massively impactful, and his advanced stat profile is amazing—he has the highest career average in PIPM, and is second-all-time in career Win Shares Per 48. Ultimately, as we covered before, Duncan's San Antonio arrival somewhat bailed out his legacy. It's really unlikely he wins a title if the Spurs don't swindle their way into the first-overall pick in the 1997 draft—a very rough draft beyond Duncan as the slam dunk first-overall pick. Hypothetically, would Robinson have a Tier II case if it weren't for the two titles he'd won as a compliment to Duncan? Probs not, totes probs not.

I suspect that Chris Paul will be playing for a contender or pseudo-contender by the start of the 2021 season. While I feel a very special way about Chris Paul's profile, would a hypothetical championship in the twilight of his career be enough to bump him into Tier II? Probs not, my friends.

You know I'm hard on Durant, and I discount his success in Golden State for the unabashed 'ring-chasing in your prime' that it was. But a title as Brooklyn's best player, and the level he'd need to be to playing at for that to occur would create a persuasive Tier II case. Even for me, the President of the anti-Kevin Durant club. Yet, we shouldn't be holding our breath for a Brooklyn championship—Kyrie will continue to get hurt,[230] and KD will continue to be an injury risk in his own right, on top of the fact that he'll have basically not played NBA basketball for two years when he picks back up in 2021. Most of all, I don't think there are any real adults/leaders on that roster. Not to mention any defensive players? Jarrett Allen and Taurean Prince are going to spearhead a championship defense? Steve Nash is going to coach up their team defense? Even if everything swings in Brooklyn's direction and they somehow capture a championship, I'll never forget how we, collectively, began thinking of Kevin Durant with such reverence. He's the same mercurial guy that blew a 3-1 lead in the 2016 WCF until I'm presented compelling evidence otherwise.

The only other players that could break into Tier II in the relatively near future are players that havn't even cracked Tier III yet—Giannis Antetokounmpo and Luka Dončić. If Giannis keeps adding layers to his profile at the rate he currently is, he could be primed to present a Tier II case before you'd think. My man just put up the highest single season PER of all-time in 2019-20'. He'll probably ditch his current franchise after the 2021 season and take his talents to one that is ready to steer him toward a championship—like say, Toronto :)

For Luka, the sky's the limit. He's the best 20-year-old basketball player of all-time[231]—a basketball prodigy, through and through. I have concerns about the Mavericks' financial commitment to Kristaps Porzingis, and how that could lower Luka's championship ceiling. On the other hand, Luka possesses an intangible quality that no young player in the league has, and it's something players usually have to build over several years—he's not afraid of *any* moment. He's already played in countless high-stakes, pressure moments against grown men. We won't have to watch him incrementally improve year-over-year in postseason crunch time situations—he's literally ready *right now* to win a championship, so long as the Mavericks can improve their roster by 12% before the 2021 season. A season during which I'm 100% sure Luka will win his first league MVP.

The wild thing is Giannis could conceivably make his way to Dallas to form an unstoppable duo.

It would take a lot to relegate any of the existing Tier II players, but if KD, Giannis and Luka could conceivably push their way into Tier II sooner than later, who would be the players most likely to get relegated to Tier III—let's take a look:

---

[230] Maybe eat some meat, bro.
[231] I was profoundly disrespected by all of the LeBron comparisons that Luka's first two seasons necessitated, but I've softened in the interim. Luka is *that* special.

Hot Seat	Comfortable	Straight Chillin'
...	Steph Curry	Tim Duncan
	Kobe Bryant	Kevin Garnett
	Wilt Chamberlain	Hakeem Olajuwon
	Oscar Robertson	Larry Bird
		Magic Johnson
		Shaquille O'Neal

I just don't think any of these players are especially vulnerable. I'll re-evaluate as necessary.

If Steph continues to have injuries for the rest of his career, and effectively adds zero layers to his profile, I still think his case is appreciably more compelling than Durant's. Am I going to swap Kevin Durant into Tier II in place of the player who created the ecosystem for which Durant's case even exists? Probs not. *On top of that,* If the Warriors five year run to the NBA Finals' was the equivalent of The Beatles dropping *Rubber Soul, Revolver, Sgt. Pepper's Lonely Hearts Club Band, Magical Mystery Tour* and the *White Album* into the public consciousness, that means that they still have one last masterpiece in their system—one last *Abbey Road*-ish reminder that even though they're outside of their peak window that will ultimately define them, they're still capable of a final triumph.[232]

It's almost time for the four selections of Tier I—*four players who can all make a legit claim to greatest-ever status.* Before we untangle that conversation, there is a player comp I'd like to do. Last time we convened in-between tiers, I ran through a head-to-head comparison that felt pertinent to my Tier III selections. Because I tackled a few of these head-to-heads within different Tier II profiles—KG vs. Hakeem vs. Duncan *or* Bird vs. Magic—I only have one comparison for you, and it looks a little different.

There's a player in Tier II that has a very vocal, passionate and fiercely loyal fanbase that will not be happy about his not being in Tier I. Doubly upset is that fanbase that a player he is oft-compared to has, ostensibly, been selected to a higher tier of greatness than he. Tragically, we lost this brilliant player/person early in 2020, and at 41 years of age, we lost him way earlier than we were supposed to. Losing that guy meant each and every one of us had to grapple with how important he was to the game, and what his legacy meant on a personal level.

Alas, that player's career began to fade as another player ascended to the top of the mountain, and the battle over who was a greater player has been waged for many years now, on many fronts, and for some people, the quarrel remains unresolved. With all due respect to the life and many achievements of this player whom we all treasure, it's time that we finally, collectively acknowledge that LeBron James has been a more impactful, greater NBA player than Kobe Bryant. Don't get me wrong, there was a time where imagining a reality in which LeBron would have a greater historical legacy than Kobe seemed legitimately impossible. To really appreciate how inconceivable this reversal has become, let's return to my NBA sunken place, aka June 2010.

---

[232] Reminder—you can visit strainofdiscourse.com, in perpetuity, to see my up-to-date Tier III, Tier II, and Tier I players.

LeBron had just pulled his famous David Copperfield routine in a pivotal game five against the Celtics, leading to a game six elimination and another early exit from the playoffs. Meanwhile in Detroit, Joe Dumars gave panic contracts[233] to Charlie Villanueva & Ben Gordon the summer before, yielding only 27 wins in 2009-10' and kicking off what would be a shit decade for my Pistons. To make things worse, Kobe just completed back-to-back championship campaigns for the Lakers, and I was hearing it from the many Kobe/Laker fans in my life. Kobe's 5 rings (and now 2 Finals' MVPs) towered over any conversation that pitted LeBron versus Kobe. In this dark place, I couldn't reasonably picture a convergence of events that might result in LeBron becoming a greater player than Kobe. But .. if such an unlikely sequence of events were to occur, I suppose The Lakers would have to fall off fast, and Kobe would fail to add any prominent layers to his legacy.

Kobe was only 32 heading into the 2010-11' season, and with conservative extrapolation of stats and success, Kobe might have had a shot at drawing lasting MJ comparisons. With Kobe the oldest of the Pau/Bynum/Odom/Artest core, it was reasonable to think that they could win another title, right? In 2010-11', LA earned 57 wins, a two-seed, and looked poised for another deep run. However, the fatigue that often accompanies three straight Finals' trips caught up to the group, and a full-on *Jesse Pinkman Tossing Stacks of Cash Out The Window*-level meltdown ensued. Dirk's Mavs *swept* Kobe's Lakers, and the only memorable moment was 7-foot-285-pound Andrew Bynum laying a flying elbow for the ages on 6-foot-185-pound JJ Barea.[234]

Phil Jackson walks away, but the Lakers manage a three-seed in the shortened 2011-12' season, only to lose in five games to the Thunder in the second-round. Finally, a Kobe-less flameout in the 2012-13' playoffs, via the collapse of the proposed Kobe/Nash/Dwight super team, kicked off a seven-year playoff drought that would have to be ironically rescued by .. LeBron. Kobe really had stellar individual seasons in 2011-12' and 2012-13' (27.6 points, 5.5 rebounds, 5.3 assists, First-Team All-NBA both seasons), but would only play 41 total games in 2013-14' and 2014-15' combined, before gutting out his farewell tour in 16'. Well, I suppose if all of that happens, all LeBron James would have to do between 2010 to 2020 was:

- ✓ Lead his teams to four championships (Collecting all 4 Finals' MVPs—2 more than Kobe)
- ✓ Grab his third and fourth League MVPs (3 more than Kobe)
- ✓ Clock the best Finals' performance by a single player in the history of the NBA (2016)[235]

---

[233] It wasn't until spring 2014, a year after the Josh Smith mega-panic contract, that Joe would step aside from the big job.

[234] Equally violent and shocking every time you watch it. I actually think this is the dirtiest live-ball foul I've ever seen. I love Isiah Thomas, but Karl Malone's infamous December 1991 elbow looks like a basketball play to me—Zeke goes up high with the ball, Malone goes up to play the ball, and Isiah brings the ball down to absorb the contact and draw a foul. Listen, it was a brutal foul and truly frightening moment—Isiah lost a lot of blood and ended up with 40 stitches. But honestly, I'd say Laimbeer's retaliation and his mid-air takedown of Bird were both dirtier plays. In fact, the list probably goes something like this: 1) Bynum's elbow 2) 18 fouls from Bill Laimbeer's career 3) McHale's 1984 Rambis clothesline 4) *Metta World Peace's* 2012 hurricane elbow on Harden 5) Dexter Pittman's 2012 elbow on Lance Stephenson.

[235] Only once in the history of the NBA playoffs has a player led a playoff series in points, rebounds, assists, steals and blocks. That player accomplished this while simultaneously completing the only 3-1 comeback in the history of

- ✓ Cement himself as the best basketball player in the world for a *full* decade
- ✓ Go to 8 straight Finals'
- ✓ Transition his brand from 'unmet expectations' to 'maybe the best player ever, global icon, and role model for an entire generation'
- ✓ Pioneer the player empowerment movement across all major professional sports
- ✓ Become one of the most influential human beings on the planet

Kobe Bryant was a tenacious competitor with a vast array of offensive tools, complimented by a devout commitment to defending at a high level. His determination to improve his game was the first, second and third priority during his basketball career. Win at all costs, leadership through ferocity and an omni-present alpha state—those principles resonated *so* strongly with *so* many people. He embodied the way a lot of people wanted to approach their lives—to bring that relentless, hyper-competitive, *Mamba Mentality* to everything they do. The problem is, in the context of this conversation, that trait or series of attributes doesn't always make you a better basketball player. It was how MJ approached the game (and his life), but somehow, we've largely come to believe that pinnacle greatness can't be achieved without employing the maniacal asshole approach. As if somehow, not only did MJ set the bar for his play on the court, but he's made us also believe that to be greater than him requires the abrasive, psychopathically competitive personality that drove his success. So, when Kobe did MJ karaoke by acting brash, being hard on teammates, resistant to coaching, and generally acting like a dick sometimes, is it possible we gave him extra points for that? I'm not sure, but probably. I believe the fan connection to that ethos is the main reason for the discrepancy of where many fans place Kobe, and where he rightly belongs in the historical league hierarchy. For any other great NBA player, being considered, at very worst, a top-14 player ever, would be a validating accomplishment. The issue comes when claiming that Kobe belongs anywhere other than the top-5 of all-time players. That inevitably becomes an affront to Kobe Bryant's legacy.

Zach Lowe did a podcast June 15th, 2018 with Howard Beck that I believe to be one of the most measured discussions of all-time NBA power dynamics on record. Lowe is better known for granular dissections of the modern game, but Beck had recently written an article for Bleacher Report that had former players weigh in on the current state of LeBron's legacy—*Kobe Bryant, NBA Greats Get Lathered About LeBron's Legacy*, and the podcast would be a further discussion of the article itself as well as the questions that naturally arise when player's historical legacies are up for debate. The format of the article basically has Beck posing a question related to LeBron's legacy, and the panel of former players give their response. However, the pattern rapidly became—'*Well thought out, intelligent responses by the panel, and glaring self-important remarks from Kobe Bryant*'. For instance:

Beck: Is legacy only about rings? LeBron has been to eight straight Finals'— no one has done that since the 1960s Celtics. Doesn't that mean something?

---

the NBA Finals'. That player's opponent also happened to win an NBA record 73 games that season. No further questions, your honor.

Vince Carter: When he starts training camp, guess what he says? My season is going to the middle of June, every year. For eight years. I can't knock somebody like that when I, who's standing before you today, have not been there one time. I think it's amazing.

Jon Barry: That's an accomplishment in itself, regardless of whatever [outcome].

Chauncey Billups: That means a ton. Absolutely. Just the level of excellence and commitment and dedication, every single year.

Isiah Thomas: He's been able to dominate this era, going to the Finals' for nine of the 15 years. In my lifetime, I've never seen this. And I've played against Kareem Abdul-Jabbar, played against Michael Jordan. I don't think any of us have ever seen anything like what we're witnessing.

Paul Pierce: I mean, yeah, it puts him up there. But not 'there'.

Kobe Bryant: You've known me long enough to know what my answer is.

Beck: LeBron has three rings. He's been to more Finals' than any player in modern times. But he's 3-6 after this series. Does that matter to his legacy?

Paul Pierce: When you're talking about being the greatest, yes. You're already in the top five. But we're talking about being at the top of the throne, the top of the mountain; yes, that number does matter when you're talking that.

Isiah Thomas: I think it all matters. You also have to take into account again the teams that he's lost to. He's been to the nine Finals', and in seven of the Finals' his team has been the underdog.

Chauncey Billups: I'm not charging LeBron for some of those losses in the Finals'. He wasn't the favorite every time. He's rarely the favorite in the Finals'. So how can you expect him to really win? It's the NBA Finals'. It's the two best teams in the world.

Dennis Scott: The 3-6 [record], I don't buy into it, because Jerry West is the logo and he was 1-8 in the Finals'. And we still revere him as Mr. Clutch, right? I want to let LeBron finish doing what he's doing.

Jon Barry: I think it's very unfair to put it solely on LeBron James, six Finals' losses. In 2011, I think he had a lot to do with that [loss]. But all the other ones, he got a lot of inferior teams to the NBA Finals'. It's not his fault that the Eastern Conference was as weak as it was.

Vince Carter: At the end of the day, he's given himself an opportunity to win nine times. Everybody can't say that. I salute him. That's an unbelievable feat.

Kobe Bryant: All I thought about as a kid personally was winning championships. That's all I cared about. That's how I valued Michael. That's how I valued [Larry] Bird. That's how I valued Magic [Johnson]. It was just winning championships. Now, everybody's going to value things differently, which is fine. I'm just telling you how I value mine.

If I'm Bron, you got to figure out a way to win. It's not about narrative. You want to win championships, you just gotta figure it out.

Hilarious, Kobe. I suppose the helpless Cavs in 2007[236] should have figured out a way against the hardened Spurs. Or, when Kevin Love and Kyrie were both injured in the 2015 Finals', I suppose you just figure out a way to win with Timofey Mozgov as your second-leading scorer, and Matt Dellavedova as your starting point guard. Anyway, Beck would backup Kobe's 'count the rings' ideology during Lowe's podcast by saying:

Kobe's been consistent since the day I met him in 1997, all the way before he won championships, after he won the three, after he won the next two, in between. Kobe has always been in the count the rings camp, always, that's who he is.

So, in fairness, dismissing context and counting the rings has been Kobe's barometer for measuring NBA power dynamics prior to him winning his own rings. Lowe then described the 'count the rings' argument perfectly:

Maybe it's his fault, maybe this entire strain of discourse is actually not Michael's fault, but Kobe's fault.

There's no way I could craft a better definition, so why not let the best NBA writer do it for me. Without question, championships need to be considered when evaluating a player's historical legacy. Karl Malone scored the second-most points ever, but without a ring no one is getting him anywhere near their top ten. Dirk Nowitzki wasn't touching anyone's top thirty until his 2011 triumph, and now he's somewhere in the upper teens on most lists.

---

[236] The Finals' starting five for Cleveland—LeBron, Boobie Gibson, Sasha Pavlovic, Drew Gooden and Zydrunas Ilgauskas. With all due respect to my guy, Big Z, but it might as well have been—LeBron, Daffy Duck, Bugs Bunny, Air Bud and Teen Wolf. Although, Teen Wolf got almost all of his points at the rim—he truly was efficient beyond his years.

But it's tricky when it comes to Kobe. He came into a league in 1996 that would soon experience a greatness vacuum after Jordan retires in 1998. Duncan and Shaq were poised to take the mantle, especially with the immediate impact, and subsequent success, Duncan had. Kobe came to Los Angeles at the same time as Shaq, which is unquestionably a fortunate landing spot for a young wing coming into the NBA. Not to mention being drafted by a franchise with a high bar for success, the operations of which were being controlled by someone as savvy as Jerry West. Until 2009, that greatness vacuum would suck up many players to hold the 'best in the league' mantle—Iverson, Duncan, Shaq, Nash, Dirk, KG and Kobe.

How different does it look if Kobe's not traded on draft night and plays for Charlotte, or Denver, or Toronto, or .. Cleveland? Pretty fucking different. As it stands, it's unclear for how long Kobe was actually the best player in the league. Scouring the web, to include a few subreddits, leads me to believe that he was probably the best player in the league for two to three seasons (2006-2008). Which compared to just about any NBA player, is a legitimate feather in the cap of Kobe Bryant. Except when Kobe's compared to a player that was the undisputed best player in the NBA for at least a full decade. Don't take my word for it—in a Thomson Reuters article from May 18th, 2009, NBA Legend Jerry West claimed that LeBron was a better player at that point. Jerry West, the executive that drafted Kobe Bryant, is quoted saying:

> *But even though it's hard for me to be objective, because I brought Kobe to Los Angeles, I do think LeBron has surpassed Kobe as a player.*

LeBron sealed the greatness vacuum in 2009, and it's just now opening back up in 2020 (kind of?). So realistically, what is the rational argument for Kobe as a greater player than LeBron if Kobe was only the best player in the league for one to three seasons?

1.
"Kobe was a better scorer"

We've all seen Kobe hit shots from every spot on the floor that made us gasp. To his credit, there's no question that Kobe was both a difficult shot taker and shot maker. However, making a relatively higher percentage of unnecessarily difficult shots doesn't constitute quality or effective offense. It will however, as it did in the case with Kobe, inflate the reputation of a player's relative scoring ability. All-time regular season points per game:

1. Michael Jordan (30.12)
2. Wilt Chamberlain (30.07)
3. Elgin Baylor (27.36)
4. LeBron James (27.07)
...
13. Kobe Bryant (24.99)

Baked into those averages you'll find the inherent dip Kobe had in scoring during the twilight of his career, something LeBron will soon experience (maybe?). So, what about playoff average, where LeBron's averages are less likely to dip, given that April through June will be the only months LeBron gives 100% for the remainder of his career?

1. Michael Jordan (33.45)
2. Allen Iverson (29.73)
3. Jerry West (29.13)
4. Kevin Durant (29.09)
5. LeBron James (28.81)
...
12. Kobe Bryant (25.64)

Adjusting for pace and offensive fluctuations in the league, LeBron still has higher scoring averages when you compare regular season and playoff points per 100 possessions:

	PP100	Playoff PP100
LBJ	**36.6**	**37.2**
KB	35.8	34.2

Let's drill down on how efficiently each player arrived at those scoring averages. This is ultimately why LeBron is a greater scorer—he's shot nearly a full 5% better from the field for the entirety of his career. C'mon, man:

	FG% (Reg Season)	FG% (Playoffs)[237]	3P% (Reg Season)	3P% (Playoffs)
LBJ	**.504**	**.491**	**.344**	**.335**
KB	.447	.448	.329	.331

There is one absolute scoring advantage Kobe had over LeBron—free throw shooting. I'll concede this one. However, if your case for Kobe standing as a greater scorer is centered around an appreciable, albeit not huge, advantage in free throw shooting, you might want to go back to the drawing board:

	FT% Regular Season	FT% Playoffs
LBJ	.739	.743
KB	**.837**	**.816**

I suppose you might say that Kobe's expansive range of offensive skills permeated his teammates, thus cultivating better offense overall. Which might, in turn, encourage someone to make the argument that:

---

[237] LeBron's shot, for his career, a full 5-6% better from the field. Just try to fathom how many awful missed shots lie in the 5-6%? Or how many long rebounds that turned into easy points for Kobe's opponents?

2.
"Kobe was a more complete offensive player"

Let's compare some career offensive figures that don't necessarily involve scoring:

	Usage	Assists Per Game	Offensive Rating	Offensive Win Shares	Offensive Box Plus/Minus
LBJ	31.5%	**7.4**	**116**	**168.5**	**8.9**
KB	31.8%	4.7	110	122.1	4.6

(Playoffs)

	Usage	Assists Per Game	Offensive Rating	Offensive Win Shares	Offensive Box Plus/Minus
LBJ	32.1%	**7.2**	**117**	**38.1**	**10.2**
KB	31.0%	4.7	110	21.0	5.4

Zero in on the Usage numbers for me, because it allows us the most succinct way to contextualize each player's overall offensive impact. Their Usage figures are virtually identical—which, broadly speaking, demonstrates that each player used about the same number of offensive possessions for their respective teams. What the other numbers brightly illuminate is how much more efficient LeBron has been with his possessions on offense—we already know that he scores more points, but now we see that he also gets way more assists, his teams score 6 or 7 more points per 100 possessions, and his offense contributes way more to team success than Kobe's.

I think we've demonstrated that LeBron has been a greater scorer, and I can't imagine even the most fanatical Kobe fans suggesting that Kobe was a better passer and/or playmaker—passing and/or playmaking is a quantitative and qualitative advantage LeBron has over all of his historical contemporaries, including Kobe Bryant.

With respect to Kobe, LeBron carries a higher turnover rate. I'll concede this one. However, if your case for Kobe standing as a greater offensive player is centered around a marginally smaller turnover rate, you might want to go back to the drawing board:

	TO (Reg Season)	TO% (Reg Season)	TO (Playoffs)	TO% (Playoffs)
LBJ	3.5	13.2%	3.7	12.9%
KB	3.0	11.6%	2.9	11%

Alright, LeBron is a greater offensive player in just about every way, but ..

3.
"Kobe was a better defender"

Peak

As a sample for each player's peak window, I'm going to use the first season each guy was top-ten in Defensive Player of the Year voting, through the final year they were voted top-ten in Defensive Player of the Year voting. Resulting in a peak for Kobe from 1999-00' through 2007-08' (9 seasons), and LeBron from 2008-09' through 2012-14' (6 seasons).

Spreading out such elite defensive seasons in that manner is already an advantage for Kobe, as he finished fifth in DPOY voting in 1999-00', and fifth again in 2007-08'. However, LeBron finished in the top-ten for DPOY voting all six years of this peak, including second-place finishes in 2009 and 2013. Kobe totaled four top-ten DPOY finishes during his nine-year peak window.

I sifted through all of their defensive-minded stats, and I'm going to spare you, for now, from more tables. In summation of the numbers, and I'm not sure how else to say this, but during their peak defensive years, LeBron, while committing far fewer fouls, managed to block more shots, and was a much better defensive rebounder. He was also responsible for more team wins because of his defense, and his teams, while he was on the court, held opposing teams to substantially fewer points. During the playoffs within their peak windows, LeBron stole the ball and blocked the ball at an even higher rate than Kobe. And while continuing to commit substantially fewer fouls, he was still responsible for a much higher percentage of team wins based on defense, and his playoff teams, with him on the court, held teams to a full 5 fewer points per 100 possessions.

I was really struck by the Defensive Rating Numbers, and I think they paint us a pretty clear picture. The league was shooting substantially more threes, and scoring was up by more than a few points at the end of Kobe's peak and the beginning of LeBron's. Yet, LeBron's teams still manage to hold their opponents to 4 and 5 fewer points per 100 possessions compared to Kobe's teams.

There's an argument out there for the eye-test being that overwhelmingly impressive for Kobe's insane on-ball defense, especially during this really high peak. I just don't think anyone wants to try and get into an 'eye-test' competition with LeBron James from 2009 to 2014 .. ? As good as Kobe was at his absolute peak defensively, LeBron was the anchor of terrifying defensive teams in Miami. Going back to the fact that LeBron finished as DPOY runner-up twice—in 2009, Dwight Howard won in a landslide, but in 2013, LeBron only lost by a few votes to Marc Gasol.[238] Kobe was never in serious consideration for DPOY, and I think that tells us everything we need to know—at their respective peaks, LeBron was flirting with being the best defender in the game because of his versatility, while Kobe was always appreciated as one of the league's best defenders of his position.

Peak Advantage—LeBron.

---

[238] While LeBron made First-Team All-Defense and Marc Gasol made Second-Team (?) [?] {?} <?>

Consistency

All six of LeBron's All-Defense selections occurred during that six-year peak that we just covered, which is an impressive run—First-Team selections 2009 to 2013, and a Second-Team selection in 2014. The problem is, Kobe Bryant was selected to *twelve* All-Defense teams. Between 2000 and 2012, there was only one season (2005) in which Kobe didn't make an All-Defense team. In fact, only KG and Tim Duncan have been selected to as many or more All-Defense teams:

	Total	First-Team	Second-Team
1) Tim Duncan	15	8	7
2) Kevin Garnett	12	9	3
3) Kobe Bryant	12	9	3
4) Kareem Abdul-Jabbar	11	5	6
5) Scottie Pippen	10	8	2

Kobe's 9 First-Team selections also put him in a tie for most all-time with MJ, Gary Payton and KG. Is that good?

I'll shortly bang on statistics to illuminate how different Kobe's reputation and Kobe's realistic defensive profile are, but I believe we've walked in on a battle where Kobe's reputation affords him an advantage. He probably made the last two teams based on that reputation, as he was fishing for steals more than playing real team defense (Phil Jackson knows what I'm talkin' about). But, he guarded his position as well as anyone ever has. He also did it at an all-league level for more than a decade. LeBron, because of his frame, was able to max out at a higher level for a substantial number of years. But those physical advantages became disadvantages as his lateral speed began to leave him (especially in a league that required more running, switching, closing out etc.).

Most of the time, I don't want to hear about 'Mamba Mentality' and the flock of Kobe clichés about his work ethic. But the bottom line is if you're a guard in the NBA between 1999 and 2011, you are not looking forward to playing the Lakers—whether it was a November night in Portland, or a pivotal game four at Staples, that asshole was going to be bothering you on the perimeter all night.

Consistency Advantage—Kobe.

Versatility

The fifth game of LeBron's Laker tenure saw Los Angeles hosting Denver. Down late, and tired of watching 250 pounds of Nikola Jokic bully Javale McGee, Luke Walton elected to put 250 pounds of LeBron at the five to stop the bleeding. Sure enough, LeBron froze out Jokic on back-to-back possessions, Lance Stephenson hit a couple threes and the Lakers squeezed out a victory. We've established that LeBron was well past his prime defensively, in fact, he was electing to play defense less than half the time during that doomed 2018-19' season. But, even as a shell of his former self, his frame and IQ will continue to provide defensive versatility to his team until he retires.[239]

LeBron just has more clubs in his bag than Kobe. LeBron's frame *is the prototype*—agile and quick enough to guard smaller players, but also long and strong enough to challenge post players. It gets crazy when you realize that the two signature plays of LeBron's defensive profile both come from *help-side* efforts—The chase-down block, and the 'out-of-nowhere' pick-six that leads to an uncontested hammer-dunk.

Defensive versatility has become a highly sought-after attribute in today's switch-happy, pace-and-space bonanza. The statistics are beginning to catch up, as NBA.com introduced their incredible Box Score Matchup breakout, and trust me, it is a great a way to lose four hours of your life. But the module only calculates intricate Player vs. Player statistics for the 2017-18' season going forward—providing no help for us in comparing the totality of Kobe and LeBron's defensive versatility. However, the NBA had been tracking the info since 2013. In fact, In September 2016, the league hosted its first Hackathon[240] in New York City, and the team that took second place[241] used the data to create a defensive versatility module. So, we'll surely see more polished defensive versatility statistics over the coming years. More concisely, they'll be interpretable by morons like me that can't do math. Until we have broader sets of data, we'll have to use what we've seen for the sake of this debate.

It wasn't difficult for me to think of a few times LeBron notably guarded outside of his position at a high level—I've watched 95% of his games in the last decade—not a typo. My challenge was always going to be researching comparative examples for Kobe to make sure I was walking a straight line. I scoured subreddits, dozens of articles, standard message boards and too many

---

[239] 2019-20' showed that he could still be a premier defender, especially during the playoff run.

[240] Sidebar on the NBA Hackathon. It's a very forward-thinking concept the NBA borrowed from Silicon Valley, with the aim of staying at the forefront of both Business Analytics and Basketball Analytics. By answering a few basketball analytics-driven questions, undergraduate, graduate or PhD students are able to apply individually, or as 2-4 person teams. If accepted, they're invited to New York City for a day in September to attend the all-day Hackathon. The morning of the event, the league poses a few complex questions, or 'prompts', that these *NERDS* come up with answers to. For instance, in 2016, participants could choose from the following prompts: 1) Develop a new method for evaluating defensive performance 2) Develop a new method for evaluating the effectiveness of timeouts as an offensive or defensive strategy 3) Build a model to predict the outcomes of shots attempted 4) Open topic—participants can pursue a creative, original topic. The league then provided the teams with a massive five gigabyte file which contained hyper-detailed raw data for *every single play* in the NBA since 2013. The teams then use the data to create a model which addresses one of the prompts provided. A panel of judges, one panel each for Basketball and Business, then vote on the top three models. The details change a little each year, but without question the event is a brilliant, low-risk venture for the league.

[241] Senthil Natarajan & Chris Pickard comprised Team Nylon representing the brilliant website, Nylon Calculus (which I highly recommend). Their model re-categorized offensive players by their offensive tendencies, rather than the position-normative trends of the box-score position they play. The model, **D**efensive **R**ange **A**daptabilit**Y** score, or DRAY, was aptly named as an homage to the league's most versatile defender—Draymond Green—who rightly held the highest overall score. LeBron, KD, Steven Adams, and Serge Ibaka also scored well, illuminating how good OKC's defense had been when they nearly made the Finals' the summer before.

YouTube videos. I waded through layers of Dogmatic Kobe-fanhood, and yet, after reading thousands of ludicrous opinions from users like KB24Forever, Mamba4LYFE, Kobe81Mindset and Kobe5LeBron0, I didn't find one specific example in support of Kobe's defensive versatility. It's not exactly what he's known for, and the majority of his era was pretty iso-heavy, so perhaps that was an unrealistic expectation. I was still a little shocked that even the Kobiest of Kobe fanatics weren't pointing to one series where either *Frobe* or *Vino* went to another level to freeze out another premier player, much less one that was outside of Kobe's position.

I eventually went to *the source* for information—my buddy Roger.[242] Remember when I said that the Laker fans in my life wouldn't stop giving me shit when Los Angeles won championships in both 2008-09' and 2009-10'? That was Roger. When I asked him for some examples of Kobe's defensive versatility, he pointed toward the Finals' game seven win in 2010 over the Celtics, and battles with the Spurs over the years. I'd always looked at that game seven victory over the Celtics as a Lakers win *despite* Kobe's effort to shoot them out of it, so I re-watched the game and catalogued every defensive Kobe possession:

- o Boston had 82 total possessions in that game, with a staggeringly low 7 fast breaks.

- o Kobe guarded Rajon Rondo for 53 of those, Ray Allen for 27, and Tony Allen just 2.

- o With Rondo having absolutely no jump shot back in 2010, Kobe played 6 to 10 feet off of the Boston point guard on every possession.[243]

- o Ray Allen and Paul Pierce were the tougher assignments, and with the bulk of those being handled by Derek Fisher and Ron Arte .. *I mean, Metta World Peace,* it was obvious they were trying to preserve Kobe.

I have a lot of data from the game that I could very well use to admonish Kobe's performance— for instance, players he was guarding were 7 of 7 from the field and tallied 8 assists. But at the end of the day, in that game, Kobe Bryant's defense was simply .. okay. It was fine. Hiding him on Rondo assured that he wouldn't expend a ton of energy, and it allowed him to cheat off and grab a lot of rebounds.

He basically had two defensive plays that I found really impressive—chasing Ray Allen off a pin-down just in time to deny a three-point try in the third quarter, and on the final play of the game, he was part of a really fluid switch from Ray Allen to Paul Pierce to deny Boston from getting a quality look. Metta World Peace was obviously their best defender, and considering the stakes, probably had the best game of his career—20 points, an enormous three-point make with 1:01 left in the game, and 5 steals. Like I said, Kobe was fine.

---

[242] Roger is not only one of the sane Kobe fans, he's a champion of men. Not only did he provide essential advice while I was writing the book, he read this chapter and still wanted to be my friend.
[243] Not an exaggeration. Go watch it.

In fairness, it was his *fourteenth* NBA season and he was obviously past his physical peak. For all intents and purposes, we can say Kobe's finest examples of defensive versatility were during his battles with the Spurs. Kobe faced the Spurs six times in the playoffs—San Antonio advanced in 1999 and 2003, with the Lakers advancing in 2001, 2002, 2004 and 2008. Don't worry though guys, I didn't go back and watch all 30 playoff games between Kobe and the Spurs. OH WAIT, I TOTALLY DID.

1999 WC Semis / Spurs 4-0

- Kobe's primary assignment was Sean Elliott—his season averages versus this series:

	PPG	FG%	3P%
1999 SEASON	11.2	.436	.328
1999 WC SEMIS	13.8	.444	.400

- Kobe also guarded Jaren Jackson (Senior!) and Antonio Daniels.

- *Overall Thoughts*—Kobe cheats a lot. Like a lot, a lot. He was technically guarding Elliott most of the time, but more appropriately, he's basically rim-protecting. He gives up a lot of open looks.

2001 WC Finals / Lakers 4-0

- Kobe's primary assignment was Antonio Daniels—his season averages versus this series:

	PPG	FG%	3P%
2001 SEASON	9.4	.468	.404
2001 WC FINALS	19.0	.407	.235

- Kobe also guarded Terry Porter and Sean Elliott

- *Overall Thoughts*—Daniels was a much more aggressive challenge for Kobe, but Kobe largely played him very well, albeit still cheating a lot. More than that, The Spurs were atrocious from three in this series. While shooting .407 as a team during the 2001 season, they shot 13 of 59 in this series (.220). Props.

2002 WC Semis / Lakers 4-1

- Kobe's primary assignment was Bruce Bowen—his season averages versus this series:

	PPG	FG%	3P%
2002 SEASON	7.0	.389	.378
2002 WC SEMIS	9.2	.450	.500

- Kobe also guarded Terry Porter and Antonio Daniels

- Overall Thoughts—It's truly amazing watching how unsophisticated offenses were compared to 2020. Bowen sat in the corner the whole series, allowing Kobe to play 12-15 feet off of him (not exaggerating).

2003 WC Semis / Spurs 4-2

- Kobe's primary assignment was Bruce Bowen—his season averages versus this series:

	PPG	FG%	3P%
2003 SEASON	7.1	.466	.441
2003 WC SEMIS	11.2	.558	.654

- Kobe also guarded Manu Ginóbili, almost exclusively in crunch time.

- Overall Thoughts—I think the strategy was to preserve Kobe for offense, by not forcing him to chase Manu around the whole game. Mostly, it's Bruce Bowen sitting in the corner and Kobe playing off of him by a truly insane distance.

2004 WC Semis / Lakers 4-2

- Kobe's primary assignment was Bruce Bowen—His season averages versus this series:

	PPG	FG%	3P%
2004 SEASON	6.9	.420	.363
2004 WC SEMIS	4.7	.286	.368

- Kobe also guarded Manu Ginóbili, again, almost exclusively in crunch time.

- Overall Thoughts—A lot more of the same. Manu had already become a primary creator for the Spurs, and the Lakers (maybe smartly) elected to hide Kobe on Bowen until crunch time, instead of wearing himself out chasing Ginóbili down.

2008 WC Finals / Lakers 4-1

- Kobe's primary assignment was Bruce Bowen—His season averages versus this series:

	PPG	FG%	3P%
2008 SEASON	8.2	.420	.403
2008 WC FINALS	7.2	.556	.545

- Kobe also guarded Manu Ginóbili, again, almost exclusively in crunch time situations.

- Overall Thoughts—The Lakers were really good after acquiring Pau this season. With Kobe more than ten seasons into his career at this point, the 'hiding him on Bowen' strategy finally kind-of makes sense.

None of this data[244] represented any examples of Kobe guarding outside of his position, much less guarding at a high-level doing so. All it really confirmed for me was that hiding Kobe on minor offensive threats was a trend throughout his playoff career. Alright, I know, I've treaded well into vindictive waters at this point. But honestly, and I don't feel great about savaging him, but to me watching all those games made it clear that Kobe's defense is overrated by nearly any measure. He could really get into his stance on any given possession and make life hell on an offensive player with the ball. But his team rarely asked him to do that, and the era he played in didn't require him to absorb complex switching and matchup-fishing techniques that have become commonplace by 2020.

For LeBron, the example at the front of most people's minds would be his work in taking Derrick Rose out of the 2011 Eastern Conference Finals. Erik Spoelstra elected to put LeBron on Rose (league MVP that season) in crunch time of games four and five, and it gave Miami a substantial advantage. When guarded by LeBron, Rose went 1 for 15 from the floor with 3 turnovers.

Another important showcase of LeBron's defensive versatility came when Chris Bosh went down in game one of the 2012 Eastern Conference Semis against Indiana. Bosh was ruled out for the rest of the series, and LeBron's ability to switch became crucial to Miami advancing. Not only did he do well on his two primary assignments—Paul George (36.5 FG% / 10 PPG / 50.4 TS%) and Danny Granger (37.7 FG% / 13.3 PPG / 48.6 TS%)—but he was routinely switching onto Roy Hibbert, David West, or onto the guard tandem of George Hill and Darren Collison. LeBron had a Defensive Rating of 95 for that series, again a messy individual stat, but it was 4 points better than any other Miami starter. Bron also committed just five fouls for the entirety of that series![245]

LeBron's crowning achievement defensively, and truest exposition of defensive versatility, will always be the 2016 Finals' triumph over the Warriors. Adjusted for what was at stake, the comeback effort of those last three games all have to be included in LeBron's greatest games. His defensive numbers that series, against what was then the most efficient scoring team ever, are absolutely ridiculous:

DRB	STL	BLK	DRtg	PF
9.3	3.0	3.0	93	1.7

---

[244] I have three takeaways from watching all of these Lakers-Spurs games. 3) Combing through all those grainy games makes me truly appreciative of HD television. 2) I forgot how incredibly stupid Derek Fisher looked with the 'headband-over-the-ears' look. 1) Sweet mother of Moses is Kobe Bryant a cheating MF! Throughout all of these games, he's playing WAY off of every single guy he's assigned to! The game was much different and three-point shooting was nowhere near the threat it is in 2020, but holy shit! If that's what elite defense looked like in the 2000s, we are giving Kobe Bryant way too much credit. You don't have to take my word for it, go watch the tape! I challenge you to watch all of those grainy-ass awful Youtube videos, look me in the eye, then tell me that you see elite-level defense from Kobe Bryant. There's no way, Jack.

[245] Game four of that series is probably LeBron's least-heralded achievement. Down 2-1 in the series, Miami had to go to Indy for game four without Bosh—LeBron had 40 points, 18 rebounds, 9 assists, 2 blocks and 2 steals (to say nothing of Wade's 30, 9 and 6).

LeBron was primarily drawing assignments of Harrison Barnes or Draymond Green, but was required to switch continually per the Warriors motion offense. With less than two minutes left in game seven, and the score nodded at 89, LeBron sprinted 89 feet[246] to pin Andre Iguodala's shot against the backboard. *The Block* has become the signature play of LeBron's career. It might be, adjusted for the stakes of the moment, the greatest defensive play of all-time, and a play that only LeBron (or fucking Batman) could have pulled off.

I cut Kobe some slack for his performance in game seven of the 2010 Finals'—that was his fourteenth season in the league, and he shouldn't reasonably be expected to be a pristine defender at that stage of his career. Conversely, let's please applaud LeBron James for delivering *The Block* and Cleveland's 2016 comeback during his *thirteenth* NBA season. In the 2015 Finals', LeBron became the first player to ever lead both teams of a playoff series in all three major statistical categories—points, rebounds and assists. In the 2016 Finals', LeBron became the first player to ever lead both teams of a playoff series in all five major statistical categories—points, rebounds, assists, <u>steals</u> and <u>blocks</u>. Well past his peak defensively, LeBron's versatility allowed him to be the best defender in a tightly contested NBA Finals'.

In any Chess set, the Knight piece is often the most treasured of the collection, and commonly the most creatively detailed. When it comes to playing the game, the Knight is often the favorite, and also the most unpredictable piece in the game, with many games being decided because of the high-risk, high-reward maneuvers of the Knight. The Queen on the other hand, is the most dangerous and versatile piece on the board. Like the Knight, the Queen is most valuable when they're in the center of the board, as they have the widest range of motion there. The difference is that the Knight is restricted to a more specific, narrow move set. The Queen can move wherever she damn pleases.

Versatility Advantage—LeBron.

<u>*Greater Defender—LeBron.*</u>

Maybe none of that matters because ..

4.
"Kobe was more clutch"

With the help of the insane Clutch statistical breakouts on NBA.com,[247] my challenge was to create fair measurements for each player's clutch performance. I knew that I wanted to exclusively use playoff data—the games matter much more and I believe legacies should be

---

[246] Per John Brenkus of ESPN's *Sport Science*. LeBron clocked the first 60 feet of the sprint in 2.67 seconds, with a top speed of 20.1 MPH. Because Iguodala released the ball so close to the backboard, it created just a .2 second window for the block to occur, and LeBron pinned the ball 12 feet off the ground while he was 35" off the court.
[247] Which we used during Chris Paul and Steph Curry's profiles.

forged in the postseason.[248] Also, because making and missing largely defines who is clutch and who is not, I wanted the stats to be centered around Field Goals, Three Point Field Goals and Free Throws. However, I also wanted to integrate the Usage dashboard available from NBA.com to demonstrate how often Kobe and LeBron were being utilized as their respective team's primary clutch player.

Most importantly, the temptation to bend the stats to fit my narrative would simply be too juicy. So, I was going to have to choose breakouts, record the data and live with the results. Basically, I couldn't pull a Bunny Colvin from Season Three of *The Wire* and boast a city-wide crime reduction of 14%, if I had merely been juking the stats and quarantining the crime to the vacant homes near Vincent Street![249]

I decided to use three specific data sets, with a matching alternative data set for each. These are the three I chose:

- o *Crunch Time*—Last 5 minutes of playoff games that are within 5 points
- o *Super Crunch Time*—Last 60 seconds of playoff games that are within 3 points
- o *Threat Level Midnight*—Last 10 seconds of playoff games that are within 3 points

The first breakout is what has become the common understanding of what 'clutch' time is—that is in large part, if not exclusively because of, this landmark stat breakout that NBA.com has developed. Which, super lucky for us, dates back to the 1996-97' season (Kobe's first playoff appearance). Because NBA.com allows you to drill down to more granular clutch windows, I wanted to provide a second data set that gave statistics for when the game was truly in the balance with less than a minute remaining. Then finally, the actual 'game-deciding' clutch stat which would track undecided games with less than ten seconds left. Many of those last-second shots we can remember—Kobe's game-tying three against the Pistons in game two of the 2004 Finals', or LeBron's pair of buzzer-beaters during the 2018 playoffs.

The alternative data set that I will apply to each primary set stems from a personal belief of mine that being truly clutch is when your team is behind in the game. After discovering that you could adjust the data to give results specific to the score of the game, I then collected samples for the aforementioned time constraints, but specific to when LeBron or Kobe's teams were behind, or tied, in a given game. I understand this was a personally driven addition I wanted to throw in, but in fairness, I think most people would agree that it takes a bigger set of cojones to perform when your team is down or tied than when your team is winning and your performance then wouldn't immediately jeopardize your team's chance to win the game. So, in total, the three breakouts plus their alternate results will give us six different breakouts.

---

[248] Sure, Kobe has plenty of signature clutch moments in the regular season. But LeBron has four League MVPs and Kobe has one—are you sure you want to do the regular season thing?

[249] I'm still pissed Rawls and Burrell dropped him to a Lieutenants' pension after the *Hamsterdam* situation. You so badly wanted the institutions to accept that 'alternative' policing and celebrate Colvin instead of condemning him. But that narrative illuminates one of the many lessons The Wire was telling us throughout its run—the system never changes, there are just different characters.

Crunch Time (Less than 5 minutes, score within 5 points)

For this breakout, there is a sample of 132 games for LeBron and 112 for Kobe. Over the 519 minutes LeBron has played within these constraints, and the 419 that Kobe did, this is what their raw stats look like:

	FGM	FGA	FG%	3PM	3PA	3P%	FTM	FTA	FT%
LBJ	138	338	**.408**	36	102	**.352**	155	204	.759
KB	107	270	.396	15	64	.234	149	179	**.832**

	True Shooting %
LBJ	**.546**
KB	.542

LeBron holds a narrow edge in overall Field Goal Percentage, and a substantial edge in three-point shooting, yielding a narrow advantage in True Shooting % overall. The advantage Kobe has in free throw shooting can't be overlooked because those points certainly matter. Ultimately though, the marginal advantages LeBron has here are amplified by the fact that his sample of *Crunch Time* games is much larger, and thus, sturdier. Let's now look at each player's Usage profile within this data set, and there are a few new stats that I've defined for you:

	USG%	FGM%	FGA%	PTS%
LBJ	40.3%	41.3%	40.4%	41.6%
KB	36.2%	38.8%	38.3%	40%

FGM% = Percentage of team field goals made by a specific player.
FGA% = Percentage of team field goal attempts by a specific player.
PTS% = Percentage of team points scored by a specific player.

This *Crunch Time* data set is the broadest we're going to be looking at. It's telling us that LeBron shoots a better percentage from the field, and that he's been a higher usage player within his team's offenses—accounting for more field goals made, field goals attempted, and a higher portion of total points scored.

Crunch Time (Alternate Result)

Let's put the screws to these numbers and look at the alternate result—which again, only pulls numbers from games in which each respective player's team was *tied or trailing by 5 points or less, in the last 5 minutes of a playoff game*. This creates a set of 88 games and 252 minutes played for LeBron, 79 games and 201 minutes for Kobe.

	FGM	FGA	FG%	3PM	3PA	3P%	FTM	FTA	FT%
LBJ	82	184	**.446**	27	66	**.409**	62	84	.738
KB	56	148	.378	12	46	.261	49	57	**.860**

	True Shooting %
LBJ	**.573**
KB	.500

Given the game circumstances that this data is drawing on, Kobe's stats are pretty damn good. LeBron's are just really good—.573 True Shooting, almost 41% from three, and almost 45% from the field overall. LeBron was also a substantially more prominent scorer in the context of his team's play across this breakout:

	USG%	FGM%	FGA%	PTS%
LBJ	41.4%	42.7%	40.4%	42.7%
KB	33.9%	33.2%	37.4%	34.2%

It's not a coincidence that LeBron's usage numbers are higher, because he's been the number one option for his teams throughout his career[250]—I did anticipate higher usage numbers on Kobe's line, but I suspect they'll go up as the breakouts drill down.

Super Crunch Time (Less than 1 minute, score within 3 points)

This is a much narrower sample, and the shot-taking/shot-making becomes more important as this stage of the game is typically very iso-heavy. LeBron has played in 84 games that qualify for these parameters, to Kobe's 74.

	FGM	FGA	FG%	3PM	3PA	3P%	FTM	FTA	FT%
LBJ	30	74	**.405**	5	18	**.277**	32	44	.727
KB	21	62	.339	3	20	.150	46	55	**.836**

	True Shooting %
LBJ	.519
KB	**.528**

Kobe edges LeBron in True Shooting for the first time because of the volume and percentage of free throws made—given the game circumstances baked into this breakout, I'm guessing there are a lot of intentional fouls included here. LeBron continues to shoot way better from the floor across a larger sample.

	USG%	FGM%	FGA%	PTS%
LBJ	39.7%	41.1%	42.4%	43.7%
KB	49.8%	35.5%	54.4%	43.5%

---

[250] Less a brief power struggle with Dwayne Wade in 2011, which ended in Wade publicly declaring he would defer to LeBron, as to not impede his undeniable greatness. My words, not his.

Enter the hyper-spike in Kobe usage at the end of the game, right on cue. Kobe starts taking an enormous number of his team's possessions (almost 50% USG, 54% of his team's field goal attempts), but still makes a lower percentage of his team's field goals, and a lower overall percentage of team points (despite all of those made free throws). The crux of my hypothesis in digging into all of this was that Kobe took a lot of shots, and sure, was not afraid to, but also missed a lot more than his reputation would suggest. I expected LeBron to also take a lot of them, just to make a higher percentage of them. The results appear to be shaping up to be the true on both of those guesses.

Super Crunch Time (Alternate Result)

So, let's take a look at the alternate result, which will also collect stats from the final minute of games within three points, but only games where either player's team was *tied or trailing by 3 points or less, in the last minute of a playoff game.* This even narrower sample gives us 55 games for LeBron and 51 for Kobe.

	FGM	FGA	FG%	3PM	3PA	3P%	FTM	FTA	FT%
LBJ	22	45	**.489**	4	9	**.444**	10	13	.769
KB	13	45	.289	3	18	.167	15	19	**.789**

	True Shooting %
LBJ	**.572**
KB	.412

Both of the Alternative Results have now been highly favorable to LeBron. 49% from the field on 57% True Shooting when your team is losing by a possession or tied? C'mon, man—that's nasty stuff.

	USG%	FGM%	FGA%	PTS%
LBJ	37.0%	42.0%	39.5%	38.0%
KB	52.5%	31.1%	52.8%	44.5%

Kobe accounts for 6.5% more of his team's points within this sample, but on a bonkers 52.5% Usage, that's an expected result. Because Usage numbers get really noisy when we drill down to the last 10 seconds of games, this is the final Usage breakout and we can conclude what the numbers have been suggesting—LeBron's overall usage and the percentage of his scoring in the team context remains static, while Kobe begins using way more of his team's possessions for his own scoring as the game gets closer to the end. Trouble is, Kobe increasingly takes way more and misses way more. He spikes up to nearly 53% of his team's field goal attempts, but only nets 31% of his team's made field goals. LeBron was responsible for at least 41% of his team's made field goals across all four of these breakouts, while Kobe failed to make it over 39% in any of them.

Threat Level Midnight (Less than 10 seconds, score within three points)

Did Secret Agent Michael Scarn back down when Goldenface threatened to blow up the NHL All-Star game? Of course not. Now we'll find out how Kobe and LeBron fared when the clock hit _Threat Level Midnight!_—when the game was truly on the line and the ball was in their hands.

The first breakout will demonstrate stats from when Kobe or LeBron's teams were winning or losing by three points or fewer. Understanding that, situations where their teams were winning would typically be situations that the opposing teams would intentionally foul, so the vast majority of field goal attempts would come from go-ahead or game-tying situations.

	FGM	FGA	FG%	3PM	3PA	3P%	FTM	FTA	FT%
LBJ	10	27	**.370**	2	7	**.286**	12	16	.750
KB	6	24	.250	1	9	.111	11	11	**1.00**

	True Shooting %
LBJ	**.499**
KB	.416

Three of Kobe's six makes are truly 'game-winning' shots, including one buzzer-beater:

- ○ 2000 Western Semis Game-Winner (2 secs left) in game two vs. PHX
- ○ 2002 Western Semis Game-Winner (5 secs left) in game four vs. SA[251]
- ○ 2006 Western Quarters (OT Buzzer-Beater) in game four vs. PHX

The other makes:

- ○ 2000 Finals', game four, put-back layup (5 secs left) increased lead from 1 to 3 vs. IND
- ○ 2004 Finals', game two, three-pointer (2 secs left) forced overtime vs. DET
- ○ 2006 Western Quarters, game four, layup (.7 secs left) forced overtime vs. PHX

Eight of LeBron's ten makes are truly 'game-winning' shots, including five buzzer-beaters:

- ○ 2006 Eastern Quarters Game-Winner (5 secs left) in game three vs. WSH
- ○ 2006 Eastern Quarters Game-Winner (.9 secs left) in game five vs. WSH
- ○ 2007 Eastern Finals Double-OT Game-Winner (2 secs left) in game five vs. DET
- ○ 2009 Eastern Finals (Buzzer-Beater) in game two vs. ORL
- ○ 2013 Eastern Finals (OT Buzzer-Beater) in game one vs. IND

---

[251] This is just a sick play. Kobe goes up about as high as he possibly can (very high for Kobe Bryant in 2002), snares the rebound from a Derek Fisher miss and puts back the game-winner. _The Mamba!_

- 2015 Eastern Semis (Buzzer-Beater) in game four vs. CHI[252]
- 2018 Eastern Quarters (Buzzer-Beater) in game five vs. IND
- 2018 Eastern Semis (Buzzer-Beater) in game three vs. TOR

The other makes:

- 2007 Eastern Finals, game five, dunk (9 secs left) forced overtime vs. DET
- 2007 Finals', game three, layup (6 secs left) cut lead from 3 to 1 vs. SA

This window of time where we were made to believe that Kobe Bryant reigned supreme—the *most* clutch moments—we can actually see that LeBron has simply hit way more game-winning shots. Like .. *way* more. LeBron's five-to-one advantage in buzzer-beaters is a fairly un-nuanced or context-rich comparison, but isn't that the inverse of the result we would have expected, given Kobe's long-standing reputation in these end-of-game situations? As far as the percentages are concerned, given what we've learned from the breakouts leading up to this statistical conclusion, we know that LeBron is a more efficient scorer and these clutch situations aren't a departure from that advantage over Kobe.

Threat Level Midnight (Alternate Result)

We're going to look at the final breakout, the *Threat Level Midnight* alternate result, which will not look much different from the original sample. However, I believe this breakout to be enormously important in this experiment. The first breakout (*Crunch Time*) gave us broad data on how each player performs within a window that is now most-commonly accepted as 'clutch' (less than 5 minutes left in a game, and the score within 5 points). I believe that breakout and this breakout are equally important, and tie for being the most important breakouts that we've looked at. This one is vitally important because we're stripping away games in which either player's team was winning, we're talking about shots on game-tying or go-ahead attempts with less than 10 seconds left in playoff games—*a framework that has long been considered the barometer for clutch performance.*

	FGM	FGA	FG%	3PM	3PA	3P%	FTM	FTA	FT%
LBJ	10	24	**.435**	2	6	**.333**	3	4	.750
KB	5	22	.227	1	9	.111	2	2	**1.000**

	True Shooting %
LBJ	**.485**
KB	.284

---

[252] People forget about this one. The Cavs were down 2-1 in the series, and this game was in Chicago. Even more, LeBron sprained his ankle badly in this game. When Bill Simmons had David Griffin on his podcast in May 2018, Griff recalls going to the bench and asking LeBron's long-time trainer, Mike Mancias, if he was going to be okay—Mike responded 'Does he have a choice?'. They taped it up and LeBron banged home a filty Buzzer-Beater to tie up the series.

The spotlight is firmly on both players when they had the most pressure on them, and it's fairly clear who performed at a higher level. I think we're done here.

Do stats tell us everything in basketball? Absolutely not. Do stats tell us whether a player is more clutch than another player? Yeah .. they kind-of do. The basketball world has created an ocean of nuance in how we evaluate players, but being clutch is mainly about making and missing. LeBron hitting twice as many game-winning shots, and five times the number of buzzer-beaters is pretty staggering. Those facts alone could have made the case for LeBron in this clutch argument, so providing the more comprehensive breakouts ostensibly would be favorable to Kobe .. but they're not.

I'm far from the first to second-guess Kobe's unassailable 'clutchness'. Henry Abbot—basketball media OG, Mr. Truehoop, and brilliant basketball thinker—wrote a piece for ESPN on January 29th, 2011 entitled *The Truth About Kobe Bryant in Crunch Time*. At the time, Kobe's reputation as a clutch hero was firmly entrenched into the NBA lexicon. Naturally, his article ruffled the feathers of bloggers from Santa Ana to Santa Clarita, and the totality of the Kobe legion around the world. Abbott's conclusion shouldn't have been revolutionary, but after the article was released, he was treated like Carl Bernstein and Bob Woodward unraveling the *Watergate* scandal.

With ESPN Stats & Info at his disposal, Abbott drilled down to a data set that included all shots taken by Kobe Bryant in the last 24 seconds of games in which the Lakers were tied or trailing by two points or less (1996 through 2010). Using regular season and playoff data, this totaled 115 shots. Kobe made 36 of those shots.

So ultimately, Kobe was 31% from the field in the most clutch moments, over the course of the meaningful portion of his career (as we mentioned earlier, after the 2010 title, things mostly unraveled in LA). The article proved that Kobe's clutch performance had been league-average, at best, up to that point in his career. This segment from Abbott really drives it home better than I ever could:

> Bryant's absolutely the best in the world at the game of winning the hearts and minds of crunch time. A lot goes into it: creating shots against any defense, staying calm, ignoring fear and more. It's about who most has the rest of the league by the throat. In that game, it's cowardly to pass the ball, and misses are merely the cost of doing business. In that game, degree of difficulty counts. That game, though, is not basketball.

Kareem Abdul-Jabbar

The Secret	Greatness Index	Ben Taylor Rank
96 / 100	408.68 (3rd)	1st

PIPM	O-PIPM	D-PIPM	Peak—1976-77'	Wins Added
+4.09 (17th)	+2.41	+1.68	+7.36 (9th)	210.38 (12th)

Playoff PER	Playoff Win Shares	Playoff O-Win Shares	Playoff D-Win Shares
23.01 (17th)	35.56 (4th)	21.82 (4th)	13.74 (6th)

Ferdinand Lewis Alcindor Jr.

"Lew" was born on April 16th, 1947 in Harlem but was raised in the Inwood section of Manhattan. He was a good kid—obedient, curious and shy, he mostly kept to himself—which became exponentially difficult as he shot up to 5'8" by the age of nine. The brutal racism of the time wasn't lost on Lew, and from a very early age he began accumulating painful realizations of the difference between white America and black America. Time at an all-black boarding school also illuminated the in-fighting and anger within the interiority of the black community in New York City. Lew preferred to blend into the background—listen to his jazz records, play chess with a friend or read more about the world around him. It just so happened that the world around him was New York City in the late 50s/early 60s—an epicenter for the growth, change and ultimate discomfort that the US was experiencing, especially if you were black.

It wasn't long before the adults in Lew's life corralled him onto a basketball court, where he (obviously) excelled. My man was 6'8" in eighth grade and 6'10" by the time he was ready to play high school basketball. Lew chose number 33 because of New York Giant hero, Mel Triplett, the fullback who scored the opening drive touchdown of the 1956 NFL championship.[253] Lewis Alcindor would eventually transform Power Memorial Academy into a nationally dominant basketball institution, but before Lew was known as *the Tower from Power*, he had to mitigate the awkwardness of being a freshman in high school .. when you're damn near 7-feet tall, surrounded by uneasy white people, and despite having an advantageous physical profile, didn't know how to sculpt it into something great .. yet. Prior to the first varsity game, coach Jack Donahue, surprised Lew with a number 33 jersey and a spot on the varsity squad—a monumental gesture to the youngster, which earned Lew's trust for several years to come. Power won that first game, but despite the excitement, the school's star center prospect was continuing to struggle with identity issues, and race was at the heart of it. For now, Lew had begun building himself a barrier from these things that angered him or he did not understand—or perhaps was beginning to understand, but having a hard time fully acknowledging:

> *I'd been hurt enough times to be wary of people, and that icy wariness*
> *could have been as much a barrier as my skin color. I was discovering*
> *that racism was like a disease, and one of the side effects was that it*
> *made the victims withdraw from anyone who looked like the victimizers.*

But basketball was good. As it's done for numerous players on this list and beyond, it provided Lew an even playing field, even though his booming skills were beginning to stack the deck heavily in Power's favor. The completion of a very promising freshman year came as a relief for Lew. He liked basketball but found practice and training to be a linear, predictable and somewhat mundane endeavor—he still preferred the intellectual stimulation of reading or the creative efforts of his favorite jazz artists. Without the rigid parameters of the basketball season, Lew and his friends had time to seek out pick-up games throughout New York City, where they were exposed to a harder, more individualized expression of the game. In that summer of 1962, the legendary Rucker Park[254] tournament was holding its 13th annual competition, and Lew figured it was worth checking out. This was the first time that Lew saw Wilt Chamberlain in person, and to Lew's great surprise, Wilt knew who he was. Wilt said this to Lew, after Lew had summoned all his courage and approached the larger-than-life NBA star:

> *Oh yeah, I heard of you—you're the young boy that plays for the*
> *Catholic school. Supposed to be getting good.*

It was thrilling and shocking for Lew that Wilt was aware of him. This was *Wilt freaking Chamberlain*, fresh off his monumentally dominant 1961-62' season—the one during which he scored 100 points in a game and averaged 50 PPG and 25 RPG for the entire season. Within Wilt's profile, we circled what a spectacle Wilt was for the people around him, and Lew wasn't

---

[253] Mel Triplett was an especially revered figure in the black community—someone the black community could put their arms around, which weighed into Lew's decision to rock his number.

[254] At 155th and Fredrick Douglass Blvd in Harlem, there's a legendary basketball court within Holcombe Rucker Park. For decades and decades, it's been a proving ground, as well as a showcase, for some of the best basketball players on earth. More than 100 NBA players have competed there, including Allen Iverson, Kobe Bryant, Julius Erving and Wilt Chamberlain.

exempt of feeling that way, but this first meeting with Wilt provided a glimmer of what Lew's future could look like if he continued to dominate in basketball. The Jedi-Padawan relationship between Lew and Wilt was a hugely important one in Lew's development, and this was merely the first chapter.

Basketball was very good. Power Memorial won their first of three consecutive New York City Catholic championships during LA's sophomore year. Lew helped spark a winning streak during that season that would span 71 games and carry into his senior year. His local notoriety was matriculating outside of New York City, and collegiate offers elevated from a trickle to a steady stream by the time Lew was a junior. Coach Donahue did well to keep Lew away from the press, and even kept the tuition offer letters away from his star center, allowing (or forcing) him to devote his attention to the game. Coach and player had established a very good relationship—Lew wanted to play hard and get better to please his coach, who was notoriously difficult to please. Coach Donahue protected and cared for Lew as best he knew how to protect and care for an unprecedented basketball prospect of Lew Alcindor's status.

Their relationship irreparably changed during halftime of a game during Lew's junior season, against rival Demantha Catholic High School. After a lethargic first half performance from his team, Coach Jack Donahue, a white man, in an attempt to fire up his All-American center, accused him of 'playing like a nigger' in front of the whole team. In a horrifying moment, their relationship lost all the goodwill and trust that had been built. To Lew, Coach Donahue had exposed himself to be just as prejudiced as the people Lew had tried so hard to distance himself from. Most painfully, Coach Donahue didn't realize how hurtful his language had been, and they wouldn't speak about the incident until decades later.[255] But the remainder of Lew's time at Power Memorial Catholic High School, he no longer trusted his coach, and was that much more troubled by how differently America looked, dependent upon the color of one's skin.

The summer between Lew Alcindor's junior and senior season was transformative for many reasons. The first time Lew felt comfortable in his skin was when he landed a spot in the heritage teaching program for the Harlem Youth Action Project. He was accepted into the journalism workshop as a reporter at a salary of $35 a week. He was there exposed to volumes of black heritage and culture he felt he'd been kept from—previously he'd been relegated to history books, teachers and superiors that had accentuated the accomplishments of white Americans in history, and in one way or another, denigrated or buried the exploits of African Americans. In his own words, walking into the Schomberg Center for Research in Black Culture was like:

> walking across the burning desert and being handed a glass of ice
> water. I hadn't even known how thirsty I was until I saw all of the books
> on black history.

The program director, Dr. John Henrik Clarke, quickly became an intellectual mentor for Lew. Dr. Clarke was formerly John Henry Clark, and changed his name in honor of a Norweigen

---

[255] Lew's college coach, the great John Wooden, arranged for Lew and coach Donahue to mend their fences many years after the incident. But his coach's words stung Lew's psyche for a very long time.

Playwright. This was the second person Lew had come across who'd changed their name—the first was jazz musician Art Blakey who also went by Abdullah Ibn Buhaina after becoming a Muslim. Their relationship permitted the widening of Lew's intellectual aperture, to now include a grander perspective on black and white relations:

> *I had been a little too comfortable being the young basketball star, a little out of reach of the kind of dangerous racism that others faced on a daily basis. Ironically, it was Coach Donahue who, by immersing me in basketball, kept me insulated from that real world—and it was Coach Donahue who reminded me that such insulation was a fantasy that could be shattered whenever he wanted to. That was all over now. Dr. Clarke encouraged us to explore our own past as well as what was going on in the streets around us.*

The second reason the summer between Lew's junior and senior season was so transformative was the cementing of the relationship between LA and Wilt Chamberlain. The program's offices that Lew had immersed himself in were located at the Harlem YMCA, where Wilt would often work out in the summer of 1964. Lew would intentionally 'run into' Wilt during many of Wilt's workouts, and Lew began to see a portrait of the work required to be a premiere big man in the NBA. Maybe more importantly, their relationship allowed Wilt to demonstrate how glamorous the lifestyle of a premiere NBA big man could be. As Lew's senior year of high school got underway, Wilt would frequently invite Lew to accompany him and Wilt's entourage to some of the hottest clubs in New York. Wilt even brought Lew to a horse track, where they watched a Wilt-owned horse compete against other horses. Lew's connection with Wilt over that period was an informal internship in what it was like to be a celebrity. The two had polar opposite personalities—Wilt relished being the life of the party, and didn't internalize things the way Lew's introspective approach did—but the friendship was instrumental in Lew's development.

I couldn't help but think of the way another quiet(er) generational prospect looked up to another brash, swaggering, established superstar. LeBron looked up at Kobe the same way Lew looked up at Wilt. After passing Kobe on the all-time scoring list, and tragically, the night before we lost Kobe, LeBron told this story to the press:

> *I believe I was playing [a high school game] in New Jersey and the [NBA] All-Star game, if I'm not mistaken, and you all can correct me, was in Philly. That Saturday, me and Maverick [Carter] drove to the Intercontinental [hotel] in downtown Philadelphia, and he gave me a pair of shoes which I ended up wearing that following night. It was the red, white and blue Kobe's. I was a [size] 15 and he was a 14 and I wore them anyways. I sat and just talked to him for a little bit. He gave me the shoes, and I rocked them in the game and it was the same night we played Oak Hill against 'Melo [Anthony]. Then, I saw what he was able to do the next night winning [All-Star] MVP here in Philly that following night.*

As we covered during Kobe's profile, Kobe's mentorship of LeBron peaked during those six weeks they spent together for the 2008 Olympics, which encouraged LeBron to fully unleash his compliment of skills. As for Lew, his world was getting bigger thanks to some important influences. He dominated again during his senior season, but was conflicted that the success was shared by Coach Donahue and Power Memorial at large. He left the school as the most sought-after basketball prospect since .. Wilt Chamberlain. Lew was thrilled to get to the next stage of his basketball and intellectual progression, and he virtually had free range to choose whichever college he wanted to attend. After much deliberation, it was the California sun and an immediate connection with John Wooden that made UCLA the clear choice for Lew Alcindor. Lewis Alcindor arrived in Los Angeles on a Saturday, and skipped catholic mass the next day for the first time he could remember. The Los Angeles version of himself would make his own choices about what to believe.

Basketball was very good. NCAA rules for that 1965-66' season prevented freshman from playing on the varsity team. Unfortunate for UCLA, as their incoming freshman class had five high-school All-Americans. Lew was accompanied by a few other incoming freshman players when he went to the UCLA practice court for the first time. It just so happened that they met up with a handful of the varsity players when they arrived, and they all decided to play a few games of 'freshman vs. varsity'. UCLA had won the national championship in 1964-65' and the tenured varsity players were confident approaching the pickup games against a handful of kids that were brand new to Los Angeles. The freshman kids, anchored by Lew, won all three games against the varsity players.

Lew and his freshman teammates were very eager to start working with John Wooden. Many players, including Lew, had foregone full scholarships elsewhere to play at UCLA and soak up the precise teachings that Wooden was famous for. When it came time for the freshman to have their first session with John Wooden, he immediately began handing out lessons on the importance of being detail-oriented—the basketball legend's signature hallmark:

> *Good morning, gentleman. Today we are going to learn how to put on our socks and sneakers correctly*

> [the players, anticipating a powerful opening speech from the mentor for whom they'd sacrificed so much to merely be sitting in front of, watched in surprise and horror as Wooden removed the shoe and sock from one of his feet]

> *We are going to talk about tug and snug. Tug. And. Snug.*

> [the unprecedented collection of young basketball talent had no clue where this old man was going with this]

> *As Benjamin Franklin said, 'for want of a nail' ..*

> *For want of a nail the shoe was lost,*

For want of a shoe the horse was lost,
For want of a horse the rider was lost,
For want of a rider the battle was lost,
For want of a battle the kingdom was lost,
And all for the want of a horseshoe nail.

You want to learn about basketball, read Benjamin Franklin.

[the players were still lost, and Wooden might as well have been speaking mandarin]

If you do not pull your sock on tightly, you're likely to get wrinkles in them. Wrinkles cause blisters. Blisters force players to sit on the sideline. And players sitting on the sideline lose games. So, we are not just going to tug. We are going to also make it snug.

[he demonstrated his proper sock etiquette, and the players followed suit, having now grasped at least some measure of what Wooden was attempting to convey]

I don't drink and I don't smoke, and the only reason you have to be up beyond nine or ten o'clock at night is if you're studying. Number one in your life is your family. Number two is the religion of your choice. Number three is your studies—you're here to get an education. Number four is to never forget that you represent this great university wherever you are, whatever you are doing. And number five, if we have some time left over, we'll play some basketball. Questions?

There weren't any questions, and the tone had been set. Each player, just as players before them had done, adjusted to the maniacally detail-oriented program that Coach Wooden orchestrated. Lew was fascinated by Wooden's approach from the very beginning and articulated it beautifully in *Becoming Kareem:*

> *Sometimes he would climb to the very top level of the Pauley Pavilion and watch us play from up there, where we must have looked like a bunch of beetles scurrying around. Other times he would be courtside, walking along with the players like a shadow.*
> *I had never seen a coach think like that before. I had heard coaches talk about seeing the Big Picture before, but Coach Wooden saw the game in 70 mm Panavision. Yet he saw it on a microscopic level, too.*
> *Every morning he scribbled on those note cards, with drills for the team and customized drills for individuals. I had never met anyone with such an eye for detail and such commitment to his players as names rather than numbers.*

Sometimes my teammates and I would laugh a little about how focused he always seemed to be. Secretly, we also felt relief that he took our playing that seriously and wasn't willing to settle for anything less than our best. He saw his job as helping us find out how far we had to go to reach out best. Turned out it was farther away than any of us imagined. And a lot harder to get to.

Basketball was good for Lew and his overqualified freshman teammates. They went 21-0 against other schools' freshman squads, winning by an average margin of 57 points. Their smallest margin of victory was 28 points, with their largest margin of victory being 103 points.

Toward the end of Lew's freshman year, John Wooden invited Lew to dinner. Coach Wooden wanted to connect with the player he perceived to have the capability to be the greatest college player ever. Lew was cool with a free meal. They had a pleasant dinner and Coach Wooden had a chance to warn Lew about what the media attention might be like in the coming years, as he would soon leave the cocoon of the freshman team and step into the national spotlight on a team that was expected to win a national championship. In the parking lot, an elderly white woman approached Lew and looked him up and down as if he were an alien. In her amazement, she asked of Coach Wooden:

Woman: How tall is that boy?

Coach Wooden: Seven foot two inches, ma'am.

Woman: I've never seen a nigger that tall.

The woman had no concept of how ignorant her phrasing had been. For Lew, it was exactly the same way that Coach Donahue had used that word—utterly failing to grasp how hurtful it was, and in Donahue's case, destroying their relationship in one sentence. John Wooden was also horrified but was unsure of what to say. Needless to say, it made for an awkward ride home for Lew and Coach Wooden. The event didn't prevent the coach and player from having a very close relationship that would extend well beyond Lew's time at UCLA, but in that moment a few different worlds clashed. Despite John Wooden's singular abilities as a basketball coach, and as a life coach to a similar degree, he didn't have the right club in his bag to communicate one-to-one with Lew on that subject.

In 1966, Lew read *The Autobiography of Malcolm X*—a book that *was* able to speak directly to his frustrations as a black man of that moment. Beyond that, Lew points to that text as igniting a spiritual awakening that yielded a fascination with Islam, and ultimately encouraged Lew to begin studying the Quran. Lew Alcindor had come a long way to improve his basketball and intellectual profiles in Los Angeles. And while he was being reminded frequently that the battle for equality was being fought on both the east and west coasts, he was determined to find his own unique role—one of his deliberate choosing.

Basketball was very good from the exact moment Lew Alcindor tipped off his sophomore season at UCLA. In his first varsity collegiate game, Lew scored 56 points—a school record by a whopping 14 points—*in his first game!* UCLA went 30-0 and won the national championship in 1966-67'. Shortly after the season, an opportunity presented itself for Lew that might have been even more thrilling than winning a championship. Jim Brown, football star, Hollywood star and important civil rights voice, asked Lew Alcindor to join a group of black athletes who were convening to solve a complex issue that had far-reaching judicial and financial implications for the black community—whether or not Muhammad Ali should indeed skip the selective service draft for the Vietnam War, or take a deal that wouldn't require him to fight, but would contract him to visit military bases and put on boxing exhibitions for active soldiers. The Cleveland Summit, as it's commonly known, took place on June 4th, 1967.

Muhammad Ali, whom Lew had met on two separate occasions since moving to Los Angeles, needed support in that moment. He had divisive popularity among white *and* black Americans since changing his name, joining the Nation of Islam and proclaiming loudly that he wouldn't go to Vietnam. It said a lot that otherwise popular athletes—Bill Russell, Jim Brown and Lew Alcindor were willing to even posture positively toward Ali. There were financial stakes in the balance as Ali's saga unfolded as well. Many in the boxing industry would prosper if Ali were able to continue fighting, which he would not be, given his boxing license had been revoked amidst his draft-dodging charges.[256] Muhammad Ali faced a lot of hard questions on that day in June, but never relented from his opposition to involvement of any kind in the Vietnam War. A press conference had been pre-arranged to take place at the summit's conclusion, during which Ali proclaimed that there was 'nothing new to say'. Bill Russell said this of Ali, after Russell's involvement in the summit:

> *I envy Muhammad Ali. He has something I have never been able to attain, and something very few people possess: he has absolute and sincere faith. I'm not worried about Muhammad Ali. He is better equipped than anyone I know to withstand the trials in store for him. What I'm worried about is the rest of us.*

At just 20 years old, Lew was the youngest athlete in attendance of The Cleveland Summit. Before that day, despite all the reading he'd done, and passion he'd poured into the subject, Lew felt as though he'd been on the sidelines of the civil rights movement. After that day, he became a prominent voice for social and political issues involving African Americans. Lew Alcindor was very proud of his friendship with Muhammad Ali and looked up to him a great deal. At this point, Lew already had numerous prominent influences in his life, but maybe none as meaningful as Ali. Wilt Chamberlain, for instance, showed him what it was like to be a celebrity. Muhammad Ali demonstrated for Lew what it meant to be an internationally recognized black megastar, whose advocation for equal rights might just cost him everything. Additionally, Muhammad Ali represented the third African American in Lew's life that had changed their name, and by far the man with the highest profile who'd done so. Lew found

---

[256] Two weeks after the summit, a jury quickly found Ali guilty of draft evasion. He was exiled from boxing for years because his application status of 'contentious objector' to the war—stemming from his anti-war, Muslim beliefs—was rejected leading up to his conviction. The Supreme Court reversed the ruling in 1971—Clay v. United States, Ali's appeal to his conviction, found that: *Ali's beliefs are founded on tenets of the Muslim religion as he understands them.* Ali was then allowed to box again.

Ali's bravery awe-inspiring and in Lew's own words, Ali's use of his platform opened up the possibilities of what Lew could do with his own:

> *I'd had plenty of coaches teaching me how to win. Muhammad Ali was the first to teach me what to do with winning.*

Ali was hugely inspirational to Lew, but Ali remained a massively controversial figure around the country. John Wooden, for example, was heavily critical of Ali. Decades prior, Wooden left his family and prosperous life to join the cause against the Axis powers. Wooden served as a physical education instructor for four years during World War II, and just before he was scheduled to ship out to the Pacific Theatre, appendicitis prevented him from going. He was replaced by a friend and fraternity brother who would soon thereafter die from a Japanese kamikaze attack. Knowing that Lew was close with Ali, Wooden wouldn't overtly dump his feelings into the open on the subject. But he would make pointed comments every once in a while, which was especially unusual to hear from the legendarily respectful Coach Wooden. Lew described the paradox as an 'irritant' between he and his coach. As Lew was dipping his toes in the water of becoming a political figure, he was learning that it often came with personal consequences.

Basketball was very good at the start of Lew's junior season, but it was clear that America's honeymoon period with him was over. He began receiving criticisms from the press for not smiling enough or not giving the press more availability. Lew's proximity to Ali and the movement likely made him less attractive to white America, but realistically, Lew didn't care for talking about himself, and still preferred to pass his limited free time reading a book or spinning jazz records. Prior to the 1967-68' season, the NCAA also banned the slam dunk, largely because Lew Alcindor had weaponized it to the degree that it was deemed unfair to his competition. Lew was understandably upset, especially when he found out that Coach Wooden was one of the people who had voted to make the dunk illegal. Lew's frustration subsided, and the NCAA ruling necessitated Lew to work on his hook shot. Coach Wooden originally viewed the hook as a selfish move, but relented when he saw the world-ending potential that the move possessed in the hands of Lew Alcindor.

On January 20th, 1968, UCLA played The University of Houston. UCLA handled Houston in the 1967 NCAA semifinal, but this matchup was building up to be one of the great basketball games ever played, and it didn't disappoint. The game was arranged to be the first ever nationally televised, prime time, regular season NCAA game. To spice up the drama, Elvin Hayes, standout Houston forward had publicly taken shots at Lew Alcindor—he claimed that Lew wasn't tough on defense, hadn't been aggressive rebounding the ball and wasn't as good a player as he'd been hyped up to be—bold words, my man! 53,000 people jammed into the Houston Astrodome for the showdown, which basically doubled the previous record for the number of people to watch a college basketball game live. Lew hadn't been able to practice leading up to the game because of an eye injury, and he ultimately played poorly by his standards. Elvin Hayes put down two last-second free throws to secure a 71-69 win for Houston. The loss ended a 47-game winning streak for the UCLA Bruins. Suddenly, the words of Elvin Hayes might be ringing as fact across America, and perhaps Lew Alcindor *was* overrated. *Sports Illustrated's* cover image for their January 29th, 1968 edition was an image of

Hayes scoring over Alcindor. Lew ripped off the cover of that issue and hung the image in his locker for the remainder of that season. They again faced Houston in the NCAA semifinal a few months later, but this time UCLA won 101-69. John Wooden rolled out a Box + 1 on Elvin Hayes, which resulted in him scoring just 10 points (when he'd been averaging 37 for the season).

After winning a second consecutive national championship, Lew Alcindor figured to be the centerpiece of the American effort toward a Gold Medal at the 1968 Summer Olympics in Mexico City. Professionals weren't allowed to compete yet, and Lew was expected to compete for his country. However, Lew couldn't help but think about how Muhammad Ali had been treated after securing an American Gold Medal at the 1960 Olympics. After earning the medal at the Olympics in Rome, Ali returned to his hometown of Louisville and expected to be treated heroically. He attempted to eat at a 'whites-only' restaurant in Louisville, to test whether or not the country viewed him any differently after claiming a Gold Medal in the name of the USA. Ali was still refused service and asked to leave.

Lew perceived his potential participation in the 1968 Olympics as an endorsement that 'everything was okay' in America, which he was unable to do. Fresh on his mind, and psyche, were the assassinations of Dr. Martin Luther King Jr. and Robert F. Kennedy. King had been the most important singular voice in the advancement of civil rights, and Kennedy, a leading presidential candidate, had been running on a platform of equality that unified millions of people with vastly different demographic profiles. Lew Alcindor sat out the 1968 Olympics,[257] and received harsh criticism for doing so, almost exclusively from white American citizens.

Lew Alcindor, up to this point in his young life, had been fortunate to have numerous dynamic and high-profile influences[258]—many of whom we've already talked about. For Lew, it was the summer of 1968 when he really stepped out of being someone who would do what was expected, and proceeded to live in a manner that represented a clearer portrait of his ideals:

> *I had many influences: what my parents wanted, what my teachers*
> *wanted, what my religion wanted, what society wanted, what my peers*

---

[257] There's a direct line to Colin Kaepernick here. White Americans were so pointedly offended by Kap's gesture, but most of them were misplacing their anger. Opposers saw the gesture as an afront to the military or to American exceptionalism at large, and the criticisms that were hurled at Kap were the same ones that have been directed toward civil rights activists for more than 50 years. Lew was repeatedly asked why he wasn't grateful to be a prominent athlete, on the cusp of making life-changing money .. by people that largely took for granted the opportunities that white America presented them. People that have never seen the injustice that Kap was kneeling for also asked him to be more grateful of his advantageous professional situation. Kareem Abdul-Jabbar wrote an editorial focused around Kaepernick for the Guardian in December of 2019, in which he said: *the tactics used to discredit the former quarterback are how conservative America has always treated black athletes who speak out.*

[258] Did I mention that he became friends with Bruce Lee and claims Bruce's teachings had a profound impact on his life and conditioning? It's kind of unreal how many huge figures from the 1960s crossed paths with Kareem, and how many huge events were somehow adjacent to his young life. Shit, the way Kareem seemed to wind his way around so many uniquely American storylines in the 1960s felt, for lack of a better comparison, a little *Forrest Gump*-ish.

wanted, and what my coaches wanted. There were so many that I had to examine each one to figure out which ones were what I wanted.

Kareem Abdul-Jabbar

It was in the summer of 1968 that Lew intensified his studies of the Quran, and officially converted himself to the Sunni sect of Islam. He inherited his new name, Kareem Abdul-Jabbar, as part of his conversion, but was apprehensive to tell the world about his new identity:

> *My reluctance to proclaim my new name wasn't just shy-ness or the need for privacy. Part of me recognized a contradiction. I was on a spiritual quest to define who I was and what I believed in—to forge my own identity. I had chosen my political positions. And I had chosen my religion. But in neither case had I chosen my name. My parents named me Lew, and a slave owner in Haiti indirectly named me Alcindor. Now my Muslim teacher named me. I was still too naïve and too new to the religion to argue about my name, but I knew that my journey of growing up was still not quite over.*

Basketball—for those wondering—*still very good!* Kareem returned to UCLA's campus for his senior season, and the team picked up right where they'd left off. UCLA won their third-consecutive national championship, and Kareem Abdul-Jabbar became the first (and still only) player to earn the Final Four Most Outstanding Player award in three consecutive Final Fours. Kareem Abdul-Jabbar left UCLA after three seasons with a record of 88-2. Power Memorial Catholic High School's record in Kareem's four seasons there included only 9 losses, meaning he'd now lost a total of eleven organized basketball games in eight years.

Kareem Abdul-Jabbar was an unprecedented NBA prospect. His skill level was poised to immediately transform any franchise into a championship contender. Two franchises were vying to contract his skills—The Milwaukee Bucks of the NBA had won a coin toss with the Phoenix Suns for rights to the first-overall pick in the 1969 NBA draft, and The New York Nets had secured the first-overall pick in the 1969 ABA draft. Ultimately, it would be up to Kareem to decide which franchise he would like to sign with. KAJ requested a single meeting from each organization, during which they would make him an offer, and he would decide which one he preferred.

Milwaukee went first and made him a generous offer that would make Kareem a millionaire. The Nets' meeting included the presence of then ABA commissioner and NBA all-time great player, George Mikan, as well as the Nets' representation. Their offer was much lower, a great disappointment to KAJ, as he had looked ahead to a future where he could play for and represent the city he grew up in. Alas, Kareem took Milwaukee up on their offer, and he was to be a Milwaukee Buck for the 1969-70' season. Shortly after Kareem committed to Milwaukee and the news was fanned out to the press, the ABA came back with an offer that tripled the Bucks' offer. As enticing as it was, Kareem declined the offer respectfully, claiming he'd already given his word to Milwaukee's representation, and going back on his word would be unjust.

Coming into the 1969-70' NBA season, the Milwaukee Bucks were in just their second season of existence. Kareem Abdul-Jabbar was a Buck for six seasons, and he immediately made them both financially viable and extremely competitive across the NBA landscape:

	Record	SRS (League Rank)	Result
1969-70' Bucks	56-26	+4.25 (2nd of 14)	Lost-Eastern Division Final[259]
1970-71' Bucks	66-16	+11.91 (1st of 17)	Won NBA Championship
1971-72' Bucks	63-19	+10.70 (2nd of 17)	Lost-Western Conference Final
1972-73' Bucks	60-22	+7.84 (2nd of 17)	Lost-Western Conference Semifinal
1973-74' Bucks	59-23	+7.61 (1st of 17)	Lost-NBA Finals'
1974-75' Bucks	38-44	+0.25 (8th of 17)	No Postseason Play

The weird thing about Kareem's basketball profile, is the number of championships he won (6) starts feeling like the floor of output he could have had in his career. If you look at this opening stretch to his career, he and Oscar Robertson did break through in 1970-71' for an NBA Championship. But, he also kept the Bucks knocking on the door for at least another two titles. In Kareem's rookie year, the all-time great *Garden of Eden* Knicks knocked out the Bucks when they had a real shot at the title. In Kareem's third year, it was the virtuoso 72' Lakers squad (including Kareem's mentor, Wilt Chamberlain) that prevented Milwaukee from reaching the Finals'. In Kareem's fifth and final competitive season as a Buck, Havlicek and Cowens' 1973-74' Celtics team narrowly edged Milwaukee in seven games during the 1974 NBA Finals'.

Kareem struggled with his adjustment to the NBA and found Milwaukee to be a little lonely without family, friends, or a prominent Muslim community. But he played really hard for the Bucks before politely requesting a trade at a dinner with team management in October 1974. His numbers[260] from that Milwaukee stretch are downright savage:

	PPG	PER	TS%	WS/48
1969-70' Bucks	28.8	22.5	.552	.187
1970-71' Bucks	**31.7**	**29.0**	.606	**.326**
1971-72' Bucks	**34.8**	**29.9**	.603	**.340**
1972-73' Bucks	30.2	**28.5**	.580	**.322**

---

[259] After the 1969-70' season, Milwaukee was moved from the 'Eastern Division' to the 'Western Conference', as the NBA re-organized their structure to a framework much more similar to that of today's NBA.

[260] Keeping in mind that PIPM and other advanced metrics began tracking in the 1973-74' season. Even without his first four seasons, Kareem rates very high in PIPM. However, without his first four seasons—which are arguably his most dominant—we're definitely missing part of the puzzle. Jacob Goldstein created a model for calculating PIPM prior to 1973-74' which I chose to omit for Russell-era players, as to not grade on a curve. I busted out that model during KG's profile to include Oscar Robertson in the stranded players conversation, and it seemed appropriate to also look through the model to see how it rated Kareem's first four seasons. Kareem was by far the most impactful player in the model—he boasted a +6.47 PIPM for the four seasons, claiming a huge advantage over the player positioned in second place within the model, Wilt Chamberlain (+5.03). Goldstein also predicts an additional 80.91 Wins Added from his first four Milwaukee seasons, which if they'd been part of his total in the main PIPM database, would move him up from 12th all-time in Wins Added to 2nd all-time.

1973-74' Bucks	27.0	24.4	.564	**.250**
1974-75' Bucks	30.0	**26.4**	.550	.225

Bold Type—Led the NBA in that specific stat for that season

A broken hand, and having one foot out the door, led to a disappointing team season in 1974-75' (but still led the league in PER). Kareem was granted the trade he sought, and to an NBA market for which he was both excited about personally, and one he already knew very well—Los Angeles. Kareem played four seasons for Los Angeles on low-talent rosters, within the infamous post ABA-NBA merger vortex of the late 1970s. It was a goofy time for the league, as the merger had violently shaken the snow globe of the NBA, and the pieces were only slowly falling back into a semblance of order into the 1980s. But Kareem was absolutely the best player in the league during his first four seasons with the Lakers, but with only one conference final appearance to show for it in the way of team success, it might not seem like it in retrospect:

	PPG	PER	TS%	WS/48
1975-76' Lakers	27.7	**27.2**	.567	**.242**
1976-77' Lakers	26.2	**27.8**	.608	**.283**
1977-78' Lakers	25.8	**29.2**	.589	**.257**
1978-79' Lakers	23.8	**25.5**	.612	**.219**

Bold Type—Led the NBA in that specific stat for that season

Not only did Kareem lead the NBA in PER and WS/48 during this stretch, but also led the league in Box Plus-Minus (BPM) and Value Over Replacement Player (VORP) for the same window. Only MJ and LeBron have led the league in those breakouts for that many years in a row. The Lakers finally paired Kareem with another star via the 1979 NBA draft, and it happened to be a star of stars. But gazing backward across Kareem's first ten years in the league, it's hard not to fathom how Kareem Abdul-Jabbar didn't win more championships. That window has to be the most unlikely championship outcome for any stretch of *any* superstar's career. Even LeBron's first seven seasons in Cleveland had a rather narrow window for true championship contention.

Perhaps the Basketball Gods intended to repay Kareem during the second decade of his career. In the ten seasons that Kareem and Magic played together for Los Angeles, which happened to be the exact duration of the 1980s, the Lakers made the NBA Finals' 8 times, and secured 5 championships. Astonishingly, that run coincided with the decline of Kareem's individual ability. But unlike many historically great big men, Kareem's decline was incrementally gradual, and he was able to provide championship-level contributions right up until he decided to retire after the 1988-89' season. He played at least 74 games during 19 of his 20 NBA seasons, to the great pleasure of his *Snug and Tug* mentor, John Wooden. It's an especially remarkable feat of longevity when you consider how much of Kareem's game was predicated on mobility and agility. Wilt Chamberlain, for example, was a historically great, prolifically durable, NBA big man. But contrary to the finesse and movement of KAJ's game, Wilt relied much more on brute force, and much of his patterned movement on the court was sauntering from one block to another block. KAJ credits John Wooden's emphasis on cardiovascular ability for his staying power (and dynamism) in the NBA:

I always felt the conditioning regimen I was put through at UCLA was a primary reason I was able to play at a high level in the NBA far longer than players like Wilt Chamberlain. Wilt was dedicated to being stronger than anybody else, but he wasn't able to run the court and he wasn't flexible. As he got older, things that required quickness and agility grew further and further beyond his reach.

Throughout his NBA career and beyond, Kareem Abdul-Jabbar continued to be outspoken on political and social issues for African Americans and oppressed peoples at large. President Barack Obama presented KAJ with the Presidential Medal of Freedom, the highest honor an American civilian is eligible for. President Obama showered Kareem in compliments during the ceremony, mostly for his work in the arenas of civil rights, cancer research, science education, and social justice. This quote from President Obama stuck with me, and sums up why I have come to find Kareem's life to be so fascinating:

Physically, intellectually, spiritually—Kareem is one-of-a-kind. An American who both illuminates our most basic freedoms and our highest aspirations.

It's weird to think about it this way, but Kareem had a longer Los Angeles tenure than Magic Johnson did, to say nothing of the dominance he displayed during his years in Milwaukee. The leadup to Kareem's NBA career is inexorably tied to the era with which it occurred, so trying to put Kareem's ability in a vacuum is hard. However, a player of his skill level, if circumstances had been only marginally more favorable for that first decade, should have conservatively won 8 championships for his career. It speaks so loudly to Kareem's greatness that the Lakers were able to achieve so much team success during the 1980s, given their first or second-most important player for that window was outside of his prime.

Why Is Kareem The Greatest Player Ever? Because he had KG's interior passing and Kevin Love's outlet passing. He had the most devastating and indefensible signature move in the history of the sport. He protected the rim like Gobert and thwarted offensive game plans like Hakeem. His advanced stat profile lives in a neighborhood that only has three properties—the KAJ, MJ and LBJ residences. He won a staggering, and record-breaking, 6 league MVP trophies. He won 6 championships. He amassed more points than any player in history and managed to be a high-level player, even at the very end of his 20-year career. He carries the hyper rare distinction of having been able to both raise the floor of his poorer teams, and also possess the capability of being the best player on one of the best teams of all-time (1970-71' Bucks). Why is Kareem *not* the greatest player ever?

Bill Russell

The Secret	Greatness Index	Ben Taylor Rank
107 / 100	295.28 (7th)	4th

Playoff PER	Playoff Win Shares	Playoff O-Win Shares	Playoff D-Win Shares
19.40 (62nd)	27.76 (9th)	6.00 (82nd)	21.76 (1st)

There are few players in this book that I disrespected more than George Mikan. If you're unfamiliar, Mikan was a Minneapolis Laker 1948-49' through 1955-56', and was a dominant force during the NBA's early days.[261] He won five championships in that short window and was so physically overwhelming that he forced the league to make several different rule changes. With all due respect to that infant stage of the NBA .. it bores me. With the exception of Bob Cousy's dribbling and passing style, the game drastically lacked stylistic diversity. It wasn't until Russell's 1956 NBA draft, and a historic heist by Red Auerbach and the Celtics, that the league would quickly need to adjust to a different way of playing.

I recognize the challenge that lies before me, because unless you're an NBA junkie, Bill Russell may not mean a whole lot to you. You probably know he played for the Celtics. You probably know that he won a ton of championships. Yet, because he played in an era that's lost tread in our collective NBA consciousness, and one that we all perceive to have been disproportionately uncompetitive, I'm guessing that you tax his unfathomable number of championships pretty heavily. I mean, Bill Russell won 11 championships in his 13 seasons in the NBA—if we weren't taxing his championships, he'd irrefutably be the greatest player of all-time .. right?

The reason I go to bat for Russell in this discussion boils down to a single stat, and it happens to be the best statistic in this book. There's a misconception that Russell's Celtics always blew away their competition—shit, when you score 11 rings in a 13-year career, it's a safe assumption that other teams didn't have a chance. In reality, only two of those

---

[261] 1946-47' was the NBA's inaugural season. The biggest pivot during this pre-Russell stretch was the implementation of the shot clock in 1954.

championship campaigns came with minimal resistance in the postseason, while the vast majority of them hung in the balance at one point or another. In Russell's playoff career, he played in 10 game sevens .. and he won all 10 of them:

		Opponent (Notable Players)[262]
1957 NBA Finals'	W (4-3)	St. Louis Hawks (Bob Pettit)
1959 Eastern Division Finals	W (4-3)	Syracuse Nationals (Dolph Schayes)
1960 NBA Finals'	W (4-3)	St. Louis Hawks (Bob Pettit)
1962 Eastern Division Finals	W (4-3)	Philadelphia Warriors (Wilt Chamberlain)
1962 NBA Finals'	W (4-3)	Los Angeles Lakers (Elgin Baylor & Jerry West)
1963 Eastern Division Finals	W (4-3)	Cincinnati Royals (Oscar Robertson)
1965 Eastern Division Finals	W (4-3)	Philadelphia 76ers (Wilt Chamberlain & Hal Greer)
1966 NBA Finals'	W (4-3)	Los Angeles Lakers (Elgin Baylor & Jerry West)
1968 Eastern Division Finals	W (4-3)	Philadelphia 76ers (Wilt Chamberlain & Hal Greer)
1969 NBA Finals'	W (4-3)	Los Angeles Lakers (Baylor, West & Chamberlain)

10-and-fucking-0 in game sevens. Russell's Celtics also won a 'do-or-die' game five against Oscar Robertson's Cincy Royals in the 1966 Eastern Division Semis—making him a preposterous 11-0 in 'series-deciding' games.

If you're in the business of discounting Russell's profile, how do you explain that stat? Russell and his teammates lucked into an 11-0 record in the dynasty's most important games? Circumstantial advantages inherent to that era allowed Russell's teams to always win do-or-die games and not their opponents? Bullshit.

If there were 11 different times that this 'invulnerable' Boston juggernaut was pushed to the brink, that actually suggests that the league was more competitive than in many other eras—MJ only played in 5 series-deciding games (4-1), Kareem played in 9 (4-5), and LeBron has played in 8 (6-2). Common appraisals of Russell's profile are invariably distorted by our quickness to weaponize Russell's era against him. It's time to re-route that line of thinking because this bad motherfucker went 11-0 in series-deciding games, and that's resistant of era-specific criticism.

Regardless of how different the NBA looked in the late 50s and throughout the 60s, game sevens have always represented the same occurrence throughout the course of NBA history—two teams were so evenly matched that they needed a deciding game to determine a winner. It's one thing if those Boston teams had just steamrolled everyone, and it was clear that they held disproportionate, era-specific leverage over their opponents. The leverage they held in so many of these narrow championship victories was Bill Russell—a basketball player with a bevy of tangible basketball skills, and a man whose reluctance to ever allow another player or team to impose their will over him allowed Boston to establish the greatest dynasty in the history of North American sports.

---

[262] We've met most of these guys. Bob Pettit—2x League MVP and led the St. Louis Hawks to the 1957-58' championship over Russell's C's. Dolph Schayes, other than having an incredible 1950s white-guy name, was 12x All-NBA and won a championship in 1954-55'. Hal Greer was the second-best player on that virtuoso 1966-67' Philly team, and was 7x All-NBA himself.

Part I

As a boy in West Monroe, Louisiana, Bill Russell's grandfather told him that—*a man has to draw a line inside himself that he won't allow any man to cross.* Russell lived his life on that hard-edged principal. Regarding the modern NBA, there's a mindset that we seem to have completely resigned ourselves to, that I have come to completely reject—the notion that modern players have definable advantages over players from previous eras because of the advances in medicine, exercise science and the overall creature comforts that come with life in the twenty-first century. Indisputably, the science of injury prevention, treatment and recovery allows modern players to spend much more time on the court, and ultimately prolongs the careers of the modern professional basketball player. Where this idea loses me is when we pretend that the modern professional basketball player is as tough of a human being as those we had in the 1960s. Those were harder men, and no one will convince me otherwise. It's easy to lose sight of how important toughness is to the game of basketball, particularly nowadays when there is less contact and dramatically more spacing.

In late 2019, my buddy Kenny suggested the *Move the Sticks* podcast episode that included an interview with the great college football coach, Urban Meyer. As a University of Michigan supporter, it's an understatement to say I was apprehensive. Despite my resistance, I did give it a listen and I was really glad I did. The guy just has a next-level approach with talent evaluation and development. The main thing I zero-ed in on, as you would probably guess, is that he routinely would seek out and recruit football players that also played basketball. Apparently, it was really common for Urban Meyer (while he was coaching) to attend the basketball games of high school players of which he was actively recruiting to play football. The reason being, he deeply believes basketball to be a pristine showcase for how tough a person is.[263] I tend to agree, and I think NBA players were tough as nails for decades before the pampering, pandering and bloated contracts of the twenty-first century player.

Bill Russell's family moved from West Monroe to Oakland, California when he was nine years old. Shortly after the move, Russell was playing outside when five kids ran by, one of whom slapped him across his face. He ran back into his family's apartment and explained what happened to his mother. Now, let's just be honest about what many mothers would have done, were this in 2020, and not in 1943—track down the parents of the rambunctious kids, and ensure they were properly disciplined (or something of the sort). That's not what Katie Russell did. She *did* track down the five boys, and her son identified them as the ones that had messed with him. The difference being, Bill Russell's mother then forced her son to fight each boy individually, one after another, before he was able to return home.

That story is detailed in the autobiographical *Red and Me*, which Russell wrote as a tribute to the unique and special bond he had with Red Auerbach. Russell claims he won two of the five individual bouts—not bad (?) The book really speaks to Red Auerbach and Bill Russell's

---

[263] All of the hockey people/football people/rugby people/lacrosse people that are now losing their minds because they think basketball is soft—relax. Yes, of course basketball is not as physical as many other sports. But if you believe basketball is a leisurely exercise that doesn't require toughness or physicality .. well .. you've just exposed the fact that you've never played basketball.

connection, on and off the court. Their bond was the driving force for that Boston dynasty, and it began with Red's absolute theft at the 1956 NBA draft.

A little refresher on Red Auerbach—Red became Boston's coach and general manager before the 1950-51' season. He eventually relinquished his coaching duties (to Bill Russell) before the 1966-67' season. Auerbach would continue to be a voice in Boston's front office decision-making up until his death in 2006—he's credited as the primary architect for all 16 of Boston's championships (prior to their 17th title in 2007-08'). During the 1950s, Red was envious of the dominance that Mikan displayed for the Lakers, and wanted his own dominant center—but preferably one able to run the up-tempo variety of basketball that Red preferred Boston play, but didn't have the personnel to pull off at a high level. Well before the 1956 draft, it was obvious that Red coveted Russell, and envisioned him as the unicorn up-tempo center of his dreams.

> *If I had the chance to, I'd grab Russell.* Red told the Boston Globe's Clif
> Keane in January, 1956. *He'll no doubt be the no. 1 selection.*

Russell was a genuinely superb NBA prospect, but well before teams had endless hours of tape on any potential draft pick. In fact, they didn't have any tape on the standout University of San Francisco product. Red had to exclusively rely on word-of-mouth to evaluate Russell's skillset. Among other opinions, Red asked Don Barksdale, who played with the Celtics in 1953-54' and 1954-55', and was living in Oakland, CA at the time of the 1956 NBA Draft. Barksdale insisted that—*this is the Guy you need*—so, Red started crafting a plan to draft Russell, despite a draft table that would make the acquisition difficult. There were basically three considerations for Auerbach to mitigate, which he would combine cleverly to pull off the caper of the century:

1) Territorial Draft

Between the 1949-50' and 1964-65' seasons, the NBA had a draft provision that granted franchises the opportunity to forego their first-round pick for the ability to select local (within 50 miles) collegiate players, before other franchises were able to pick them. The thinking was an established regional star would be a good draw for the professional franchise from a financial standpoint.[264] Boston held two first round draft picks in that draft (keeping in mind there were only 8 teams)—predicting that neither pick would be high enough to select Russell, Red decided to forego one of them and use their territorial pick to select Tommy Heinsohn

---

[264] Wilt Chamberlain in the 1959 draft and Oscar Robertson in 1960 were territorial draft picks by Philadelphia and Cincinnati, respectively. I had to start digging into a rabbit hole when I saw Wilt here, because I know that Wilt attended The University of Kansas, and I was curious how Philly managed to still snag him. Apparently, and per *basketball.fandom.com,* the Philadelphia Warriors successfully argued that because Wilt had achieved so much of his fame at Overbrook High School in Philadelphia, they still should be allowed to claim him as being within their territory. I dug even further into the rabbit hole when I started thinking about what would have happened if Philly hadn't won that appeal—Wilt would have gone to Cincinnati as the first-overall pick in the 1959 draft, and Cincinnati would have likely still claimed Oscar as their territorial pick in the 1960 draft! Mother of God! Oscar and Wilt playing out their primes together!? I mean, granted they wouldn't have murdered each other, that would have been an absolutely unreal pairing! I need a cigarette.

from Holy Cross. This allowed the 'white-catholic-Boston-white' demographic (aka all of Boston) to wrap their hands around a white-catholic-Boston-white kid, much the way the city had done with another Holy Cross product, Bob Cousy. It also helped that Tommy Heinsohn projected as a really good pro. But again, this was just the first domino in Red's plan.

2) Ed Macauley

Red had made a deal with 'Easy' Ed Macauley, to try and get him closer to his home in St. Louis, where McCauley had a sick son at home that he wanted to spend more time with. The St. Louis Hawks happened to hold the second-overall pick in the draft. Red sent Macauley, Boston's best shooter and one of their primary scorers, along with their other first round pick (seventh-overall), in return for the second-overall pick. Red was close to ensuring he could secure Russell's services but needed to work out a deal with the team holding the first pick—the Rochester Royals.

3) Ice Capades

Yeah .. this is where it gets weird. Walter Brown, who founded the Celtics in 1946 and owned the team from 1950 until his death in 1964, was also a prime stockholder of the Ice Capades at the time of the 1956 NBA draft. The Ice Capades were a travelling entertainment show featuring theatrical ice-skating maneuvers. At the behest of Red Auerbach, Brown got on the horn with the Rochester Royals' ownership and made them an unusual offer. Brown ensured the Royals' ownership group that if they were to pass on Bill Russell with the 1st overall pick, the Ice Capades would book a two-week residency at the Rochester arena, which would be highly lucrative for the ownership of the Royals. Rochester emphatically agreed,[265] and Boston was free to draft Bill Russell with the second-overall pick. Boston then took K.C. Jones a few picks later, and somehow Red had acquired the rights to Heinsohn, Jones and Russell in the same draft—all three would eventually make the Hall of Fame, but in the short term, they would power the first wave of the great Boston dynasty.

Bill Russell entered the NBA as someone who had not trusted his college coach at all. If I've gathered anything about Bill Russell, it's that he's an inflexibly principled guy, and always has been. He played a certain way, especially on the defensive end, and despite the disapproval from every coach he'd had, his style of play always translated to winning. At the University of San Francisco, Russell routinely bumped heads with his coach, but his approach to the game was validated when the team won back-to-back NCAA championships in 1954-55' and 1955-56' (including a 55-game win streak). In Russell's own words, the conflict he had with his collegiate coach:

---

[265] I can't help but imagine a present-day leadership group for an NBA franchise jeopardizing their draft position to ensure *Sesame Street on Ice* would perform in their arena for two weeks. I'm imagining Sacramento, let's be honest.

Our main point of conflict was that he wanted me to play exactly like his center had played the previous year. In that era, virtually every coach in the country subscribed to the conventional prototype of how a center should look and play: lumber to a spot under the basket and plant himself for layups and rebounds—basically an offensive-oriented game. The accepted wisdom of the day on general defensive strategy was this frozen idea—a good defensive player never leaves his feet—well, that mindset eliminated me off the bat. I had invented most of my game on the playgrounds, and I approached it from a defensive premise that was largely vertical. I left my feet a lot.

Things would be different with Red Auerbach, but Russell certainly didn't expect them to be when he showed up in Boston. Russell's commitment to the 1956 US Olympic team meant that he missed both training camp and the first 25 regular season games of his rookie year in Boston. It wasn't exactly a smooth transition to the pro game, and Russell was nervous. On December 22nd, 1956, as Bill Russell walked down the corridor toward the Boston Garden floor where'd he'd shortly be introduced for the first time as a Celtic, his coach sensed his nerves and approached him. Because, again, there wasn't tape on college prospects, Russell's strengths and weaknesses were all relayed by word-of-mouth. One of the books on Russell was that he couldn't shoot.

Red—*I heard you can't shoot. Are you worried about shooting?*

Russ—*Not much. But it's been on my mind.*

Red—*Well I'll tell you what, let's make a deal today, right now. When we talk contract down the line, I will never discuss statistics. All I'll discuss is if we won and how you played. That's all I care about. Don't worry about being a big scorer—I don't give a damn about that. All I want you to do is what you've always done. Play your game. And I won't tell you how to do that. Just play the way you know how.*

This might not have been the *exact* exchange, but whatever was said left an indelible mark on Bill Russell and opened the door for his first positive relationship with a coach. From the book, Russell cites three reasons for why this was the exact moment that allowed their relationship to flourish:

1. *He was doing away with the accepted, preconceived notions of what a center, in general, was expected to do.*
2. *Instead of trying to bend me to do what he expected me to do, like other coaches, he was allowing me to do what I expected myself to do.*
3. *He not only trusted that I knew what I was doing, but he freed me to do the one thing nobody else had let me do since high school: play my own game.*

Part II

I want you to do me a favor. Whip out your phone or tablet or whatever, pull up your Spotify or YouTube or whatever, and queue up the song *Please, Please, Please* by James Brown. I can already hear you grumbling—just do it, bitch! It's literally never been easier to access literally any song ever! I grew up listening to James Brown, among so many other things, and he never sounded like a revolution to me—he sounded like a maniac. He proclaimed to be a sex machine in many of his songs, which was utterly confounding for my young ears. Much later on, my desire to contextualize the American popular music lexicon led me to appreciate James Brown enormously. *Please, Please, Please*, James Brown and The Famous Flames' very first single and breakout hit in 1956, follows the doo-wop chord progression in 3/4 time that defined so much of that era's popular music. Under the hood of this song though, you'll find a much more unconventional confluence of influences for that moment in music. You can notice that Brown changes the lyric at the end of each phrase, a direct nod to the jazz tradition of doing so. The 'call-and-response' vocals that reach out to his backup vocalists is a pillar of gospel music. The stopping and starting with the tight breaks is fresh off the Chitlin' Circuit, and consistent with the R&B showmanship of acts like Little Richard or Ray Charles (the other pillars of soul music). It's pretty stunning that this was James Brown's early work, and he would not only proceed to massively influence the music industry from a sonic standpoint, but completely revolutionized what a live performance was supposed to look like. James Brown's powerful, theatrical and downright sexual live performances have a direct link to (seemingly unrelated) artists that came later like Led Zeppelin,[266] Iggy Pop and Prince. Genre bending and blending styles is so commonplace now, but there was a time at the genesis of popular music when blending styles could synthesize new genres—that's what James Brown did.

Bill Russell was composing a revolution of his own in 1956. Red's Celtics had been playing fast for years, with dribbling and passing maestro Bob Cousy pushing the pace at every available opportunity. With Russell now in the fold, not only could the team continue to play fast, they immediately became the best defensive team in the league. Pace being the estimated number of possessions per 48 minutes, and defensive rating being the number of points allowed per 100 possessions:

	Pace (League Rank)	Defensive Rating (League Rank)
1954-55' Celtics	108.6 (1st of 8)	93.0 (8th of 8)
1955-56' Celtics	114.5 (1st of 8)	91.7 (6th of 8)
1956-57' Celtics **(with Russell)**	118.0 (1st of 8)	**84.0 (1st of 8)**

Despite Russell missing so much of the beginning of his rookie year, the Celtics would re-organize around their generational center quickly and claim Boston's first-ever NBA

---

[266] On Zeppelin's 1973 record, *Houses of the Holy*, there is a song called *The Crunge*. The majority of James Brown's early recordings were done with little or no rehearsal, and he would bark out instructions to his band in real time. In the Zeppelin song, a sonic tribute to James Brown's trademark funky sound, Robert Plant is also continually asking about 'the bridge' of the song (in a similar, if not parody-ing version of how James Brown would shout out various segments of the song). I'm glad I eventually made this connection, because that was always one of the weirder Zeppelin songs without context!

championship. The revolution really tipped off in Bill Russell's sophomore season, when Boston played even faster, and the league started to mimic what Boston was doing. The NBA's first major shift in style was sparked by Bill Russell's devotion to, and Red Auerbach's enabling of, a revolutionary approach to defending, and its transference to fast-break offense. These shifts have happened time-and-again over the course of the NBA, and it's amusing to watch how the league always tries to adapt to a way of playing, when in actuality, there tends to be virtuosic player at the heart of the change. While plenty of teams tried to play fast as the NBA crossed into the 1960s, only Boston had a Bill Russell to both eradicate their opponent's scoring strategy, and also ignite fast-break attacks going the other way. It's kind of like how plenty of contemporary teams are trying to play fast, shoot a bunch of threes and be seamlessly switchable on defense, when in actuality, only the Warriors have Steph Curry and Draymond Green. Look at how league scoring skyrockets into the 1960s, yet Boston's Defensive Rating stays impossibly static:

	League Average PPG	Boston Defensive Rating (League Rank)
1956-57'	99.6	84.0 (1st of 8)
1957-58'	106.6	83.6 (1st of 8)
1958-59'	108.2	84.5 (1st of 8)
1959-60'	115.3	84.9 (1st of 8)
1960-61'	118.1	84.5 (1st of 8)
1961-62'	118.8	85.1 (1st of 9)
1962-63'	115.3	87.4 (1st of 9)

That's fucking wild. Whether these style pivots were good for the league or not, both of these changes played directly into the hands of Russell's Celtics and Steph's Warriors. Given the rise of the three-ball, Golden State's era was much more difficult to defend, but their defensive dominance between 2013-14' and 2016-17' is representative of their dynasty not having been exclusively an offensive one:

	League Average PPG	Golden State Defensive Rating (League Rank)
2012-13'	98.1	105.5 (14th of 30)
2013-14'	101.0	102.6 (4th of 30)
2014-15'	100.0	101.4 (1st of 30)
2015-16'	102.7	103.8 (5th of 30)
2016-17'	105.6	104.0 (2nd of 30)
2017-18'	106.3	107.6 (11th of 30)
2018-19'	111.2	109.5 (13th of 30)

From that first game in December of 1956, all the way through the waning moments of that iconic game seven of the 1969 Finals', Russell was a historically-unrivaled defensive force. Boston effectively blanketed the rest of the NBA for the duration of Russell's career, and the limited data and film we have confirm his defensive impact. It's a crying shame we don't have weighted plus-minus data from this era to really illuminate Russell's importance, but the historic ownership he has over Defensive Win Shares gives us a pretty good idea of his defensive value. I usually don't look into the granular construction of advanced metrics, I just tend to know what a good score is for the buffet of stats that we have now. As Bill Russell happens to be the king of Defensive Win Shares, and it doubles as one of the only publicly available advanced bodies of data we have for him, I figured I would take a deeper look at the metric.

I've gotta be honest, it's a simple concept that *Basketball Reference* translated from Bill James' famous baseball model, but it's pretty brilliant, and looks pretty fucking accurate on a big picture scale. It translates across eras well because of inelastic, baked-in data like defensive rating and the ratio of player minutes played versus team minutes played. Russell led the NBA in Defensive Win Shares for 11 of his 13 seasons,[267] including his final season. Where most player's defensive value tends to diminish as their athleticism does, Russell was an unbelievable defender for the entirety of his career. Win Shares really tend to favor higher-end prolific players, but Russell racked them up during a dramatically shorter career than most historically-revered big men. The top five for all-time regular season and postseason Defensive Win Shares:

Regular Season	Defensive Win Shares
1) Bill Russell	133.64
2) Tim Duncan	106.34
3) Kareem Abdul-Jabbar	94.49
4) Hakeem Olajuwon	94.47
5) Wilt Chamberlain	93.92
Postseason	
1) Bill Russell	21.76
2) Tim Duncan	17.38
3) LeBron James	17.18
4) Wilt Chamberlain	15.81
5) Scottie Pippen	14.12

It's probably important to remember that blocks and steals weren't recorded until a few years after Russell retired. Russell basically *invented* the block, and tea leaves from the era suggest that he averaged anywhere from 7 to 9 blocks a game. In fairness, we have to remember how many more possessions there were per game during the Russell era, which bring those numbers into focus around 5 to 7 blocks per 100 possessions—still an unbelievable figure, and good or better than the most elite rim-protectors in the history of the game.

When it comes to watching Russell's defense on tape, he looks a hell of a lot like the players I've already compared him to earlier in the book—Hakeem, Garnett and Draymond. His ability to flash into weak-side blocks or contests looks just like Hakeem, and his ability to capably survey, switch, re-position and command the entire defensive end of the court was very Garnett and Draymond-ey.

---

[267] Russell also led the league in postseason Defensive Win Shares for each of his first 10 postseasons.

For the stretch covering 1956-57' through 1962-63', only the 1957-58' season[268] was not an NBA championship campaign for Boston, but they made the Finals' all seven seasons. Usually we have to zoom in on championship seasons and stretch them out, but welcome to Bill Russell's profile, where we have to yada-yada-yada a seven-year stretch where the player won six championships! 1962-63' was John Havlicek's rookie season and Bob Cousy's final season. By Havlicek's sophomore season, he was already second on the team in minutes played, and was ready to carry the torch, along with Sam Jones, as the perimeter drivers of Boston's up-tempo winning machine. The second half of Boston's dynasty saw an equal volume of winning—five championships in six seasons—and was similarly driven by consistently devastating defense, while the league's scoring environment[269] remained unusually fertile:

	League Average PPG	Boston Defensive Rating (League Rank)
1963-64'	111.0	83.8 (1st of 9)
1964-65'	110.6	84.2 (1st of 9)
1965-66'	115.5	88.3 (1st of 9)
1966-67'	117.4	91.0 (1st of 10)
1967-68'	116.6	92.4 (2nd of 12)
1968-69'	112.3	89.1 (1st of 14)

If you're keeping track at home, this means Russell led his Boston teams to the best defensive rating in the league for 12 of his 13 seasons—totally ridiculous, absolutely the only time that's ever happened, and will never, ever happen again. Steph Curry, with the backing of Draymond Green, capitalized on the league inefficiency regarding utilization of the three-point line, and Russell market-corrected the basketball world on how important defense was.

Offensively, Bill Russell was a fine player, but certainly not a player that dynamic offenses could be built around. Russell was substantially more dynamic on the fast break than he was in the half court. The film we have makes it pretty clear that Russ was not afraid to hammer down one-handed and two-handed dunks, especially in transition. He was a willing and able passer, and there is evidence that he had pretty dynamic vision, especially for a big man of that era. From a transition scoring standpoint, it's impossible for me to not think of Draymond Green—getting a rebound, quickly starting a fast break, and using his above average ability to finish at the rim as leverage while he surveys the passing lanes taking shape in the open court. From a scoring standpoint in the half court, Russ kind of reminds me of .. Draymond Green—reluctant to seek out his own offense (unless there is a glaring advantage), a very capable finisher, and a very competent passer in the presence of defensive vulnerabilities. Again, Russ was not a player that prolific offenses were built around, in fact, Russell's Celtics tended to be below average in terms of offensive efficiency.

Splitting up the dynasty (arbitrarily) into halves once again, this graph shows the Offensive Win Shares for Boston's relevant offensive players between 1956-57' and 1962-63':

---

[268] Russell badly sprained his ankle in the 1958 Finals' against Bob Pettit's St. Louis Hawks, and Boston lost in six games. Bill Russell has grumbled about how lucky St. Louis was on several different occasions over the years.
[269] For reference, the modern NBA is generally categorized as a 'high-scoring' era within the history of the NBA, and the league averaged around 111 PPG in 2019-20'.

	Sharman	Cousy	Ramsey	Heinsohn	Jones	Sanders	Havlicek	Russell
1956-57'	**7.0**	4.0	1.9	3.0				*1.6*
1957-58'	**5.8**	0.8	6.4	1.9	1.0			*3.7*
1958-59'	4.5	3.3	2.5	2.5	2.6			***4.7***
1959-60'	**5.4**	1.9	2.0	3.0	3.2			*4.9*
1960-61'	2.7	0.9	2.7	1.4	**3.9**	0.5		*1.7*
1961-62'		0.7	3.9	3.7	**4.9**	2.2		*3.9*
1962-63'		0.1	0.8	2.5	**5.0**	2.3	1.6	*1.0*
	25.4	**11.7**	**20.2**	**18.0**	**20.6**	**5.0**	**1.6**	***21.5***

Bill Sharman was Boston's most important offensive player over those first couple years—he was an excellent scorer and led the league in FT% for 7 of the 9 seasons between 1952-53' and when he retired after the 1960-61' season. Cousy's overall impact quickly slid downhill, and while his scoring waned (and proportionately, so did his Offensive Win Shares), he was still a valuable ball handler until he retired after 1962-63'. Frank Ramsey and Tommy Heinsohn were reliable scorers throughout their time in Boston. Sam Jones, as the chart perfectly illustrates, was just ramping up his critical offensive role within Boston's dynasty. In terms of Offensive Win Shares, the second 'half' of Boston's run with Russell looks like this:

	Ramsey	Heinsohn	Jones	Sanders	Havlicek	Siegfried	Nelson	Howell	Russell
1963-64'	0.5	0.8	**3.7**	1.5	1.6	-0.3			*1.3*
1964-65'		-0.5	**7.3**	1.9	-0.1	1.0			*2.4*
1965-66'			**6.1**	1.8	0.1	3.1	2.3		*0.3*
1966-67'			4.4	1.3	4.2	3.7	1.5	**8.0**	*3.0*
1967-68'			4.5	1.5	2.7	2.2	3.6	**5.6**	*0.4*
1968-69'			1.9	1.3	1.0	1.2	4.2	**6.4**	*1.0*
	0.5	**0.3**	**27.9**	**9.3**	**9.5**	**10.9**	**11.6**	**20.0**	***8.4***

Sam Jones, who played with Russell for 12 of his 13 seasons, was by far the most consistent and important offensive player for Russell's Celtics. While Frank Ramsey and Heinsohn finished out their Boston careers, Satch Sanders and John Havlicek[270] provided steady offensive value before the cavalry of Siegried, Donny Nelson and Bailey Howell arrived. In total, of the 11 most-notable offensive contributors to the Russell dynasty—Bill Russell included—the players with the largest sum of Offensive Win Shares is as follows:

	OWS
Sam Jones	48.5
Bill Russell	29.9
Bill Sharman	25.4

---

[270] My only big surprise in totaling all of the Offensive Win Shares was how poorly Havlicek showed up for several of the years, despite having good counting stats and minutes played.

Bailey Howell	20.0
Frank Ramsey	19.7
Tommy Heinsohn	17.7
Satch Sanders	14.3
Bob Cousy	11.7
Donny Nelson	11.6
John Havlicek	11.1
Larry Siegfried	10.9

Early in Russell's career, at the height of his athleticism, we see his highest offensive impact. For someone whose offensive game wasn't as polished as the offensively-minded superstars of the era, having that extra quickness meant easier buckets for Russell. Seeing his offensive impact, at least in terms of this metric, go up and down over time, speaks to his ability to ramp up his offense when the team needed it.

Part III

When Russell left the NBA, he also left Boston. Viewing it from a wide-angle lens, with Russell having brought so many championships to Boston, he could have bought a quiet house in Andover, MA and allowed his retirement to be a continual celebration of his greatness in the Boston area. When you zoom in though, you realize that Boston never really embraced Bill Russell. Turns out that for most Boston residents during the 1960s, closeted (and overt) prejudice was a more powerful emotional draw than accepting Russell as one of their own. Even though the Boston Bruins were fucking awful across the same stretch that Bill Russell was a Boston Celtic, the Bruins dwarfed the Celtics' attendance figures:

	Average Attendance	Results
1956-57' through 1968-69' Celtics	8,399	11 NBA Championships
1956-57' through 1968-69' Bruins	12,212	5 Playoff Appearances

The Bruins missed the playoffs every single season between 1959-60' and 1966-67', and still killed the Celtics in ticket sales each of those seasons. The Boston Garden, where both of the franchises played all of their home games during this stretch, had a capacity of 13,909 up until 1968, and at least 14,933 after 1968. That meant that most Celtic games, during the best run in the history of fucking sports, were played in barely half-full arenas. That also resulted in the majority of those game sevens (that the Celtics always won) being played in front of thousands and thousands of empty seats. There's a non-zero number of Boston residents that simply preferred hockey over basketball, but there's a *larger* non-zero number of Boston residents that preferred to not support a sport that was increasingly becoming more synonymous with African Americans. If you don't believe me, the Boston fans clearly voiced their opinion coming into Russell's final 1968-69' season—in the summer before the season, the results of a fan survey concluded that more than 50% of Boston fans identified 'fewer black players' as the *number one thing* they would like to see changed with the franchise. Did I mention that Boston 'fans' broke into Bill Russell's home, smashed his trophy case, spray-painted racist slurs on his walls and shit on his bed? Russell chose to have his number retired in an empty arena, in a private ceremony surrounded by his teammates. Can you blame him?

Even though Russell was clearly the driving force behind the success of the first 'half' of the Boston dynasty. The fans that *did* care about the Celtics were still tripping over themselves to proclaim Bob Cousy as Boston Basketball's savior. Cousy had certainly hung around in Boston long enough to become a fan favorite, justifiably, but as we just looked at through the lens of Offensive Win Shares, he was only a primary contributor to the first championship in 1957-58'. But we all know that Cousy had a certain trait that Russell lacked, and unjustifiably, Russell did not receive his due from the city he gave so much for. It also never sat right with Bill Russell when the city of Boston elevated Larry Bird to God-status during his 1980s run, despite enjoying a fraction of the success Russell's Celtics had. Russell certainly had the last laugh when the dynasty continued to thrive post-Cousy, but the savage racism he experienced while in Boston left him wanting to do anything but smile.

That first generation of black NBA stars in the 1950s and 1960s had a rough go. The political turbulence of the 1960s put a broad target on the black public figures of that era, which uncomfortable white Americans could easily identify and vent their frustrations through. Russell embraced his role in the civil rights movement, and his efforts yielded a few signature moments.

On October 17th, 1961, the Celtics were in Lexington, KY for an exhibition game. Shortly after arriving at their hotel, Satch Sanders, K.C. Jones and Sam Jones were refused service at their hotel restaurant. As they were returning to their room, they informed Russell of what had transpired, and Russ phoned Red to tell him that they would be flying home. Red arranged a dinner with the hotel owner to smooth things over, but Russell still insisted he and his black teammates were going home. Red respected their decision and even accompanied them to the airport. To his black teammates that were involved in the incident, Russell was effusive that they not make a big deal out of the incident, insisting that they would not be embracing a role that resembled victimhood. Their refusal to play in the exhibition game spoke volumes without speaking a word. Per *Red and Me,* Years later, Russell was approached by Baseball Hall of Famer Joe Morgan at a public event. Morgan, an African American, told Russell that his choice to not play that game in Lexington was endlessly meaningful to not just himself, but to the black community at large.

In 1950, Red Auerbach was the first executive to draft a black player when he took Chuck Cooper. Red had established a culture that was much more free of prejudice than any other franchise in the league. On December 26th, 1964, the Boston Celtics started an all-black starting five for the first time in NBA history. Institutionally, the Celtics had been at the forefront of integrating African Americans into the NBA for a long time, but this was a massive, previously unimaginable leap forward in that regard. A few years after that, Bill Russell became the first black head coach in the history of American professional sports—and he hadn't yet retired from playing. That's right, for the final three seasons of Bill Russell's career, he was the Boston Celtics' 'player-coach'. Prior to the 1966-67' season, Red had consulted Russ during every step of the coaching search (after Red had decided to step down from coaching), and after not being able to agree on any candidates, Russell decided to take the job.

Russ and Red's relationship was one to be treasured, and I could have spent a hell of a lot more time leaning in on their friendship. I refuse to dismiss the poetic way a short Jewish dude from Brooklyn and a 6'10" black dude from the desperate poverty and savage racism of 1940s rural Louisiana found a way to be life-long friends. Red enabled Russ to play his game, and knew that it would be good for his own career if the Celtics did well. But he also cared about Russell, a devoutly private and sensitive person, on a human level. When he had something to tell Russ, he did so in private, instead of around teammates, which Russell detested. One trend in Russell's career that I haven't touched on was how little he practiced. Very early in Bill Russell's career, he concluded that because he expended so much energy scrimmaging in practice (because he was incapable of not playing insanely hard whenever he played), he'd be better off barely practicing or not practicing at all. A totally insane concept that literally every other coach in the league would have rejected .. except for Auerbach. In the book, Russell shares a story that Red had shared with him before Red passed away in 2006. At the beginning of a practice during Russell's first few years in the league, Red announced that Russ would not be practicing. The news, which relayed a frequent occurrence, was met with some grumbles from teammates. Red snapped back at his team:

> listen, listen, listen—there are two sets of rules on this team. One set of rules for Russell and another set of rules for the rest of you guys! Period!

This suggests that the approach may have ruffled some feathers, but by every account available, everyone fucking loved Bill Russell as a teammate. Realistically, this was a savvy move by Red—for basically their whole time together, Red played Russ 40+ minutes every game. This encouraged Russ to completely wear himself out while fully unleashing Russell's 'Frenzy'—Bill Russell's self-described *heightened intensity, a metaphysical state of synchronicity between my mind and body, and the game.* Red put all of his chips on Russell succeeding, and Russell gave him everything he had in return. Their partnership changed the NBA and transformed the Celtics into a power player within the professional basketball landscape. Boston didn't appreciate Bill Russell like they should have, I'll sure as hell never make that same mistake.

Why Is Russell The Greatest Player Ever? I wrote Bill Russell into the profiles of Elgin Baylor, Jerry West, Oscar Robertson and Wilt Chamberlain because Boston's dominance prevented their legacies from carrying more weight historically. Every one of those players, with the exception of Oscar, was present in Russell's final moments as an NBA player, and poetically, they were all showcasing signature principals of their individual legacies. In the fourth quarter of the iconic 1969 NBA Finals', as the Lakers were desperately mounting a comeback to try and finally get over the hump against Boston, Jerry West was defying double-teams to still knock down super clutch jumpers. Elgin Baylor was attacking the rim whenever he got the chance. Wilt Chamberlain, who'd played a quality game with 18 points and 27 rebounds, endured an injury with a few minutes left and suspiciously sat out the conclusion of the game. And then there was Bill Russell—commanding the defense, coming up with a huge block when the game was in the balance, and despite the best efforts of three of the five best players from that era on the other team .. winning the game. Russell is a stone-cold lock for Tier I because he's the best defender of all-time, the winningest player of all-time, and perhaps the best-ever example of how a teammate should conduct himself. I wrote earlier about how we have to tax some of Bill Russell's accomplishments, and I think that's a just exercise, but what is the appropriate tax rate? He won 11 championships, so if we think the era he played in forces us to deduct three of those championships, is he still not in the running for best player ever if he won 8 championships in a more modern era? If you think the appropriate tax is *five* championships, and he has the equivalent of six 'more modern' championships, *isn't he still in the conversation for best ever!?*

LeBron James

The Secret	Greatness Index	Ben Taylor Rank
94 / 100	441.81 (2nd)	2nd

PIPM	O-PIPM	D-PIPM	Peak—2008-09'	Wins Added
+6.00 (2nd)	+5.07	+0.93	+9.83 (1st)	322.32 (1st)

Playoff PER	Playoff Win Shares	Playoff O-Win Shares	Playoff D-Win Shares
28.41 (3rd)	55.27 (1st)	38.09 (1st)	17.18 (3rd)

The great American philosopher Kanye West once described himself as a *Hood Phenomenon* and *The LeBron Of Rhyme,* which, for Mr. West, subsequently made it hard for him *To Be Humble When You're Stuntin' On A Jumbotron.* If anyone could empathize with the plight of a prodigal talent mitigating the fraught realities of hyper-stardom, it might be Kanye.

I know it sounds crazy, but there was a time where we all loved and needed Kanye. After nearly a decade in the music industry behind the scenes, Kanye was introduced to the majority of us in 2003 and 2004. Popular music was looking pretty bleak at that point. The New York City rock resurgence was mostly beneath the surface, with brutally sub-mediocre rock acts like Maroon 5, Three Doors Down and Evanescence topping the charts. We were also pretending that 50 Cent and Lil' Jon were capable of carrying the rap torch from Nas, Jay and Em. Kanye already had cache from rap purists for his work on Jay's *The Blueprint* in 2001, but his debut album checked every box up and down the popular music checklist. When *The College Dropout* came out in February 2004, there were 15 different reasons to love the album and we all got to choose the one that made sense for us.

As an Akron phenomenon rapidly became a national phenomenon in 2002 and 2003, LeBron James came into our lives around the same time as Kanye. The contours of the NBA landscape upon LeBron's arrival were unknown—the league was wondering how to follow up the popularity of the Los Angeles dynasty, and it sure as hell wasn't the lockdown defensive ideology being preached in Detroit and San Antonio. Born into the lowest scoring season in the history of the NBA, 2003-04', LeBron began checking so many boxes that we had to re-think what our checklist should look like.

I know it sounds crazy, but there was a time where we all loved and needed LeBron. Despite being on the outside of the championship picture for his first few seasons, Bron was creating the template for what it meant to be a superstar in the internet era. He re-fashioned the model for how a premier player should handle his business and image, and when he shocked the NBA by driving a clown-car of supporting talent to the 2007 NBA Finals', it felt like anointing him *The Chosen One* wasn't actually far-fetched.

Kanye West continued his rapid ascent to the forefront of the popular music lexicon over the years following *The College Dropout*. He put out *Late Registration* shortly after his debut album and followed that with *Graduation* in 2007. *Late Registration* carries more weight for rap purists, but both albums were constructed with the same ingredients as Kanye's debut—each album was a mosaic of songs that gave fans of every musical genre countless entry points into enjoying his music. All at once, Kanye was giving us songs we could dance to, songs we could work out to, songs we could have a contemplative moment to, songs that black people could feel proud of, and songs whites didn't feel excluded from. There was an equal expanse of reasons to like early-Cleveland LeBron James—he was an unprecedented mixture of speed, size, strength and skill, and his rags-to-riches ascent to NBA superstardom was easily metabolized by every version of basketball fan. As the 2000s became the 2010s, both geniuses faced individual challenges that would ultimately yield their best work, but the trials they endured yielded far fewer people appreciating those signature moments.

Say what you will about Kanye's 2008 record, *808s & Heartbreaks*, but it's a massively influential album and it marked a hard pivot in Kanye's creative arc. The album was the product of an emotionally turbulent stretch for Kanye, during which he unexpectedly lost his mother and ended a long-term romantic relationship. Sadly, on a personal level, we can also pinpoint this stretch as where Kanye West's behavior became much more erratic. The album's strength is in its rawness and vulnerability, but it marked the beginning of the era where many longed for Kanye to return to the template that constituted his first three records. Reflexively, Kanye resented the notion that the record was a step backwards, and from that point forward deliberately pursued creative innovation at the cost of his own mass popularity. LeBron's pivot from mass popularity to stratifying himself as a divisive figure came when he decided to play for the Miami Heat in the summer of 2010. Two consecutive playoff exits when the stakes were 'championship-or-bust' forced LeBron to re-shuffle his legacy cards. Right or wrong, Bron taking his talents to Miami irreparably damaged his reputation in perpetuity. Everyone felt validated when LeBron choked away the 2011 Finals'. The depths of that failure conjured the very best of LeBron's ability, and propelled him on a warpath through NBA precedents for another decade.

Embracing the villain role, LeBron won championships in 3 of the following 6 seasons and reached the NBA Finals' in each campaign. Bron muscled his way back into the favor of anyone with a modicum of ability to analyze statistical data, but even after his 2016 triumph in the NBA Finals', it was clear that he had lost the favor of the masses for good. Despite embodying the traits we said we wanted in a global-icon-level professional athlete, and gifting us the storybook narrative of returning to Cleveland and sealing a championship, Bron remained a heavily-divisive figure. That's where Kanye and LeBron's legacies truly intersect. The people that support them are evangelical in the belief of their ability (no pun intended regarding Kanye's transition to Christian-oriented music). Those with deep-seated resentment for any of Kanye or LeBron's shortcomings, refuse to acknowledge their 'post-pivot' achievements, no matter how profound. In fairness, Kanye has made it much easier for us to paint him as a villain. Shortly after *808s & Heartbreaks,* Kanye rushed the stage of the VMAs and infamously grabbed the microphone out of Taylor Swift's hand to proclaim that Beyoncé was more deserving of the award Taylor was holding. That was really the beginning of countless erratic gestures from Kanye, and even as someone who loves the guy's music, his behavior over the last ten years has been routinely indefensible. That is with a notable exception—the genius-level, hyper-innovative creative choices embedded within his work since 2010.

Kanye followed up *808s* with *My Beautiful Dark Twisted Fantasy* in 2010, and the Jay-Z collaboration, *Watch the Throne,* in 2011. MBDTF and WTT are Kanye at the peak of his prodigal powers as a producer and arranger, but it was just the beginning of his prime. *Yeezus* in 2013 really drew a line in the sand—defenders of Kanye would tell you it was creative exploration in the vein of *Sgt. Pepper's Lonely Hearts Club Band* or Radiohead's *Kid A.* Across the aisle were a hardened group of scorned former-fans who nostalgically beckoned for 'the old Kanye'. I'm out on the self-aggrandizing version of Kanye that *Yeezus* ushered in, but I'm in for the creative choices throughout the record. After *Graduation* in 2007, the easy creative decision for Kanye was to make 15 diluted versions of *Late Registration* and steer into the pursuit of popularity. But Kanye, as we've now grown accustomed to him doing, steered in a different direction. Kanye *confronted* people with *Yeezus,* and most people prefer to be *comforted* by the work of their favorite artists. As brave as the album was, it wasn't until *Life of Pablo* in 2016 that Kanye figured out how to harness his desire for sonic experimentation and package it with the hooks, melodies, idiosyncratic samples, and A-list features that made up so much of his earlier work.

LeBron and Kanye each authored their finest work in 2016, but a disproportionate percentage of basketball and rap fans had their backs turned anyway. Don't get me wrong, LeBron was finally able to enjoy an unassailable approval rating for a few weeks after the 2016 Finals', before the Warriors re-loaded and LeBron's narrative regressed back into apprehensive appreciation. *Life of Pablo's* February 2016 release .. and then re-release .. and then re-mixed re-release at Madison Square Garden was definitely a moment, but probably the final unifying Kanye moment.

Since each guy's respective peak, we've received bright glimpses of their individual ability. Kanye flexed his chops on 2019's *Jesus Is King* when he unironically integrated a Kenny G saxophone solo into what I believe to be one of his best all-time tracks—*Use This Gospel.* We recently witnessed LeBron's best post-peak moment when he raised a pair of trophies at the conclusion of the 2019-20' NBA season. But, are we sure LeBron's best post-peak moment wasn't unironically integrating Dwight Howard into a championship-caliber team?

On April 23rd, 1910, Theodore Roosevelt gave one of the most famous speeches of all-time. America's 26th President had left office one year earlier and spent that year hunting in Central Africa (dope). The speech occurred in Paris, which was one of the many stops on an engagement tour of events and speeches for Teddy. Within the very long speech, Teddy voices his displeasure for people who habitually criticize other people that are in positions for which they have no reference point:

It is not the critic who counts; not the man who points out how the strong man stumbles, or where the doer of deeds could have done them better. The credit belongs to the man who is actually in the arena, whose face is marred by dust and sweat and blood; who strives valiantly; who errs, who comes short again and again, because there is no effort without error and shortcoming; but who does actually strive to do the deeds; who knows great enthusiasms, the great devotions; who spends himself in a worthy cause; who at the best knows in the end the triumph of high achievement, and who at the worst, if he fails, at least fails while daring greatly, so that his place shall never be with those cold and timid souls who neither know victory nor defeat.

The Man in The Arena has been a co-opted metaphor by several public figures in the last century, including LeBron James.

Bron keeps a copy of this segment of the speech in his locker, and you can see him write the moniker on his sneakers prior to nearly all of his games. LeBron's always seen himself as the man in the arena, and it exposes a certain loneliness that he's burdened with. Very few people can understand the scrutiny and strain that a public figure of LeBron's gravity encounters. Sure, other NBA players are plenty famous, and yeah, Bron has a tight circle of support between family and friends that help him mitigate such a unique human experience, but the guy is famous on a level that few people can comprehend.

It's the level of fame, or at least recognizability, that's always accompanied by having a certain number of people dislike you, regardless of your choices. Like how a politician expects there to be x percentage of the voting base that will never, ever in a million years vote for them. He has, of course, endured self-inflicted PR wounds along his path toward the goal of being the best basketball player ever. Bron has also had to stomach brutal losses on the court, that justly, we'll never let him off the hook for. But, LeBron's reluctance to back down from his goal not only benefits his case for a higher position within conversations like this, but a by-product of his pursuit of basketball greatness has been his omnipresent status at the forefront of NBA culture, and thus, popular culture.

Given LeBron's accumulated fame over twenty 'internet-magnified' years, he's now one of the most famous people on earth. As of October 2020, the NBA personality, past or present, with the second-most Instagram followers is Steph Curry (31.5 million followers). LeBron James has 73.9 million followers. Speaking of politicians, the most culturally accepted President of all-time, Barack Obama, has less than half the Instagram followers of LeBron James. This leads me into the first of my three LeBron-oriented theories.

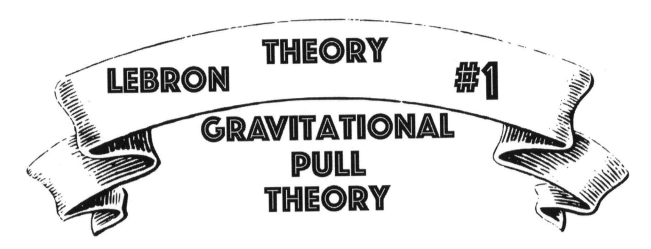

LEBRON THEORY #1

GRAVITATIONAL PULL THEORY

As a certified and accredited LeBron-ologist, I've noticed and been frustrated by our collective inability to grip exactly what it means to play or work alongside LeBron James. There is a definable difference between not wanting to be around LeBron from a chemistry, team-dynamic standpoint, and not wanting to get sucked up into the gravitational pull of the media, hype and expectations that come with a player of his singular basketball ability, international fame, and surging cultural influence.

LeBron has been the sun for every solar system he's been a part of. He can't help being the sun and without exception, the team's solar system is way better off with him as the sun. There have been other massive planets, like planet Wade, planet Kyrie,[271] planet AD, and from the management side, planet Riley. There is always space for that other large planet, but Bron's ability and popularity, at least through 17 seasons, hasn't left room for two suns. Planet Wade learned that pretty quickly. Planet Kyrie, for all its potential, is floating through various solar systems in perpetuity. Planet AD may have the first opportunity to relegate the LeBron star to supernova status—scientists are predicting this process to unfold as early as the year 2021 (we'll see). While they're all worthy of being the centerpiece of their own solar systems (more or less), the gravity of LeBron's greatness and notoriety was always going to reshape the solar system to work around him and not vice-versa.

We shouldn't blame LeBron for being one of the four best players ever, or for being internationally hyper-famous, but there are certainly exceptions where teammates are more likely to have a negative experience playing with LeBron. Because of the ever-present expectations, younger planets do not thrive in a LeBron solar system. Mature, fully-formed planets that understand their exact orbital path are far more likely to succeed.

On September 3rd, 2019, teammate of LeBron's from 2014-2018—Kevin Love—was a guest on HBO's *The Shop: Uninterrupted,* along with Kevin Hart, Rob Gronkowski, CJ McCollum, Charlamagne tha God, Lil Nas X, Paul Rivera and LeBron's longtime business partner, Mav Carter. Charlamagne, Kevin Hart and Gronk were discussing whether or not players in the conversation for 'greatest of all-time' are born or made. Mental health is an undercurrent of the episode's tone, and Carter and Love reiterate the mental toughness required to play alongside LeBron:

---

[271] Woof, what a despicable place that would be.

Charlamagne: So you don't think there's a g.o.a.t. gene?

Kevin Hart: No!

Kevin Love: See, I personally do think that the g.o.a.t. gene is always there, and it doesn't have to be in your body [he points to each of his temples] Tom Brady is right here, LeBron James is right here.

Mav Carter: You see Tom Brady, you see LeBron James, to your point [to Charlamagne] you think it's just genetics, when he [Love] talks about mentally locked in, and when he talks about Tom Brady and LeBron as here [points to his temple], I 100% agree with that. It's here, but you have to work on that and lock in. LeBron always says this thing to me— he says about a player 'he's good, but he can't lock in'.

Kevin Love: It's the attention to detail that the great ones have .. That's trust—can't lock in, can't trust him. Can't lock in, can't trust him.

LeBron has played in the NBA Finals' at the end of more seasons than he hasn't. As a teammate, coach, or collective front office, you're either capable of locking in and rising above the incredible noise that comes with perpetual championship contention, or you're not going to be part of the equation for long. Playing with LeBron since 2010 has meant that your season is not only 'championship-or-bust' but 'championship-or-catastrophe'. LeBron isn't blameless in the construction of those nuclear expectations—but let's be real here—since 2010, the media and particularly ESPN, have been exploiting his divisiveness across the viewing public. LeBron has been a win-win for ratings because the clicks and views don't fluctuate whether his losses are being hate-watched, or his victories are being soaked in by millions of losers like me.

My friend Nate texted me about LeBron during the 2018-19' regular season. Nate is extremely thoughtful, measured and dissects sports and life with an open mind. Nate reached out and suggested to me—the LeBron-ologist—that George Hill's improved play for Milwaukee might be evidence of LeBron's diminished ability to improve the play of his teammates (as Hill had largely struggled to make an impact with LeBron's Cleveland team the year before). He wasn't wrong to hypothesize this, but this exemplified to me that LeBron-adjacent players harbor enough residual gravity that they, at least temporarily, lose the ability to carry their own narratives and become part of LeBron's.

The truth is George Hill was *good but couldn't lock in*. He'd only sparingly played competitive basketball in the three seasons preceding his year with the Cavs, and had never played in a Finals' game before he came to Cleveland. He wasn't able to lock in by the 2018 NBA Finals', and that's why he missed a free throw that would have won a Finals' game. But .. when he was traded to Milwaukee the next season and was playing at a higher level, it certainly seems that his better play would be somewhat attributed to getting experience at a higher level than he'd previously experienced .. right? It takes a certain player to play in a LeBron James solar system, and it doesn't have much to do with their tangible basketball skill set—can they lock in, and can they be trusted—to rise above all the other noise to perform in the most pressure environments.

High-Mass Stars go through three main stages in their life cycle—*Main Sequence, Red Supergiant* and *Supernova*. Bron entered the *Red Supergiant* phase when he left Cleveland in 2010, and he's been an unprecedented gravitational force ever since. The impact on your peers when you're the best player in the league is one thing. That level of cache and respect has observable precedent. What doesn't have a precedent is a player making 8 straight NBA Finals'—something that won't ever happen again—while also being the person Drake reaches out to for advice when Kanye West directs a diss track at him. It's one thing to be the player of your generation, and it's another to be the player of your generation who's also famous enough to universally popularize the 'dad hat'.[272] Do you want to know what gravity looks like? It looks like NFL and English Premier League athletes mimicking LeBron's signature celebration. How many inter-professional sports celebrations, on a global scale, can you remember? Pretty soon, LeBron's on-court gravity will diminish as he's begun drifting into the *Supernova* phase where his basketball accomplishments will be presented in the past tense, but he's only just begun embracing his role as a leading voice for the advancement of African Americans and establishing more opportunities for his fellow professional athletes.

I've thrown a lot at you, and maybe you're still asking what I'm trying to convey with this theory.[273] For years I've watched the media, and ultimately uninformed Sportscenter-level basketball fans perpetuate false narratives about what a poor teammate LeBron James is, and what a chemistry disaster so many of his teams are. I'll spare you the first-hand player accounts of what an incredible leader and teammate LeBron James is and leave you with this.

From the standpoint of someone who plays in the NBA, it's one thing to be around the greatest player of your time, and another to be around the Muhammad Ali of your time. So— buckle up and lock in—or you're out.

---

[272] *Sub-Theory*—at minimum, LeBron was present at the forefront of making the dad hat cool, and he might be the actual epicenter of the movement. My guy is pictured in dad hat's as early as 2013—well before the movement got underway. The now controversial fictional character, Frank Underwood, once said: *Money is the McMansion in Sarasota that starts falling apart after 10 years. Power is the old stone building that stands for centuries.* To me, the true definition of power is popularizing the fucking dad hat—the most maligned article of clothing in the history of fashion.

[273] Any player that wants to step into LeBron's shoes and own the NBA narrative for a decade during the internet era—good luck. The amount of attention, pressure and scrutiny presents a mental challenge to that player that they can't begin to prepare for. Giannis, Zion, Luka—it's coming for you if you want it. I think Luka is the best prepared for what's coming, and I foresee a Luka-Giannis power struggle throughout the 2020s.

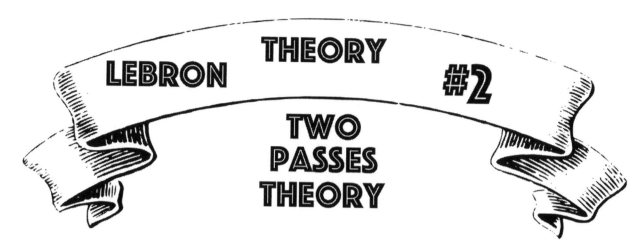

LEBRON THEORY #2

TWO PASSES THEORY

LeBron is the greatest forward in the history of the game, but are we sure he's not also the greatest point guard? I've been saying for years that when you watch LeBron play—like *really* watch—he's going to make at least two passes every single game that leave you asking a hard 'HTF'. How the fuck did he see that opening (!?), or how the fuck did he thread that needle (!?). He's a devastating distributor in transition, a maestro in the pick-and-roll, and his ability to pass out of the post because of his size yields statistically very efficient offense. The passing aspect of his game has never been overlooked and he's often lauded for his passing ability. I appreciate all that, but I'm not sure it's enough. In 2019-20', the only season that LeBron's played point guard full time, he led the league in both assists per game (10.2) and assist percentage (49.7%).[274] What should it say that he was the best point guard in the league that season—his *seventeenth* season in the league?

There are basically two levels to this, and the first is how LeBron matches up against the other greatest point guards of all-time. With respect to Bird, MJ and Jokic, LeBron is the greatest non-point guard playmaker of all-time, and the assist numbers back it up. The assist is a flawed measurement to a certain degree. Depending on the era, what counted as an assist has varied quite a bit. Additionally, it's a stat that's notoriously guilty of correlative variance with where league average scoring was at a given point in time. However, it's the conventionally understood metric for rating point guards, and passing ability at-large, and all of the players we generally deem to be the best playmakers are consistently represented at the top of the all-time assist chart.

1)	John Stockton	15,806
2)	Jason Kidd	12,091
3)	Steve Nash	10,335
4)	Mark Jackson	10,334
5)	Magic Johnson	10,141
6)	Oscar Robertson	9,653
7)	Chris Paul	9,607
8)	**LeBron James**	**9,346**

---

[274] In fairness, LeBron wasn't routinely asked to defend the other team's point guard (a qualifier for actually playing point guard to many observers). But for all intents and purposes, LeBron was the Laker's point guard in 2019-20'.

9)	Isiah Thomas	9,061
10)	Gary Payton	8,966

Not only is LeBron the first 'non-point guard' to show up in the midst of point guard royalty, but it's not until the thirty-first player on this list that the next 'non-point guard' clocks in. LeBron's place in the all-time playoff assist pantheon:

	All-Time Postseason Assists:
1)	Magic Johnson	2,346
2)	**LeBron James**	**1,871**
3)	John Stockton	1,839
4)	Jason Kidd	1,263
5)	Tony Parker	1,143

We can agree that LeBron's sheer volume of minutes played, both in the regular season and postseason, have a lot to do with his inclusion on these cumulative all-time assist rankings. Regardless, if we use this broad assist data as a marker for where a player ranks in the point guard pantheon, LeBron would come in as a top-ten point guard ever. When you look at the gap between LeBron and the top of the heap in all-time assists, we have to remember that the margin is filled by possessions where LeBron was in pursuit of the mantle for greatest scorer ever. It's hard to argue he's actually the best scorer ever, but he's conservatively in the top five, highlighted by the fact that he's the most efficient finisher at the rim in the history of the game.[275] The threat he poses to score exponentially increases the value of his passing ability because defenders always have to honor both.

LeBron entered the NBA with an elite ability to create opportunities for his teammates. Out of necessity, it was his scoring profile that evolved in a much more profound way—for the first seven years of his career, Cleveland failed miserably to partner LeBron with an elite scorer to whom he could defer. If LeBron spent more of his formative years deferring and ultimately developing his table-setting skills, you bet he'd sit in a better spot on these assist tables, and it would sound less crazy to consider him a point guard. What I'm trying to say is if he'd been drafted by a team that already had, say, Kareem Abdul-Jabbar in MVP form, not only would he have had more team success early on, we also would likely see him as more of a point guard.

The second level to this is how LeBron stacks up against the *actual* greatest point guard of all-time, Magic Johnson. So much of Magic's dynamism, compared to his point guard contemporaries, was how much bigger he was. At 6'9" 215 lbs., Magic had a clearer view of the court, was always big enough to at least not get killed on defense and could post smaller point guards to create his own offense or distribute from the block. These are all advantages Magic

---

[275] Thanks to Kirk Goldsberry's incredible Instagram (@kirkgoldsberry) we know that LeBron had the best field goal percentage in the restricted area for the entirety of the 2010s. He used 500 FGA as the qualifier for jump shooting zones on the court and 2500 FGA in the paint. Steph, Kyle Korver and Danny Green owned the three-point line, while Dirk, Nash and CP3 owned the mid-range. At the rim? LeBron shot 69.5%, good enough for the best of the decade, and coupled with what we've all witnessed anecdotally about LeBron's capability around the basket, he's positioned comfortably in the conversation for best-ever finisher at the rim.

has over every point guard to ever play the game, but they're all disadvantages in a comparison with LeBron James. At 6'9" 260 lbs., LeBron also possesses an elite vantage point of the court. Defensively, as of his seventeenth season, his frame still prevents him from being a liability. If you look at the totality of each player's career, LeBron was an appreciably better defender, and it's not really close—LeBron made 6 All-Defensive teams, including two seasons where he finished 2nd for defensive player of the year, while Magic was never selected to an All-Defense team. Like Magic, LeBron is an accomplished passer out of the post, but his substantially bigger frame and heightened scoring efficiency around the rim make him a more dynamic player with his back to the basket. Per Kirk Goldsberry, during the 2019-20' season, LeBron's post-ups yielded 1.24 points per possession—which led the league—and that efficiency is derived from the unprecedented dual-threat that LeBron presents when he quarterbacks from the block.

I've been watching LeBron put at least two ridiculous passes per game into the breadbasket of teammates for fifteen years. Peak LeBron's ability in the open court is second to none, and maybe he doesn't have the same volume of passing numbers as Magic on the fast break because LeBron was busy punishing the rim as the game's best ever finisher. When it comes to passing out of the post and dissecting vulnerabilities in a defense, having watched LeBron for as long as I have, I'll hear nothing of Magic's superiority when LeBron is bigger, faster and a far better scorer.

It wasn't until LeBron partnered up with Kyrie, ten years into his career, that he played with a consistently dynamic scorer on his level.[276] Conversely, Magic's first ten seasons were played with the NBA's most reliable scorer of all-time. It's true that the 80s were when Kareem experienced his gradual decline, but KAJ won his final league MVP during Magic's rookie season, and he was a constant scoring threat from there on out. Before Magic's fourth season, the Lakers procured the first-overall pick and added James Worthy to the list of talented scorers who were capable of being on the business end of Magic Johnson assists.

Let's be fair, Magic made Kareem and Worthy better. Magic made all of his teammates better, but these two primary scoring forces of the Lakers dynasty were both first-overall picks and had the scoring upside to prevent Magic from needing to consistently be the number one scoring option throughout his career. The two best scorers that LeBron had for the first seven seasons of his career were Mo Williams and Zydrunas Ilgauskas[277]—so, you could probably understand why LeBron escalated his scoring during his developmental years in Cleveland.

I'm very open-minded when it comes to different interpretations of the greatest-ever hierarchy. This book is merely a log on the fire of that conversation, and even if my structure or the players I chose are completely off-base, I'm just trying to get to a more sophisticated way of appropriately placing players from an all-time perspective. With that being said, it's *fucking nuts* to me when basketball observers pick Magic Johnson to have been a greater player than LeBron James.

Remember when we all liked saying that LeBron was 'more Magic than Michael'? Man .. we were so clever, and honestly, it didn't upset me to hear this early in LeBron's career—Bron's ability to create was thrilling to watch, and it made his profile uniquely dynamic. But to

---

[276] Maybe Wade for the first two Miami seasons..

[277] Big Z, to this day, and probably for good, is the player to have received more assists from LeBron than any other player LeBron has played with—that's a stunning indictment on how bad LeBron's early-career teammates were.

trumpet that comparison now is ruthlessly insulting to LeBron James. The totality of Magic Johnson's game comprises only part of LeBron's—gifted with the same quarterbacking mindset, in a bigger and faster frame, LeBron James is every bit the creator Magic Johnson was[278] (when he chooses to be). LeBron's a dramatically superior defender, and he's a far-more accomplished individual scorer than Magic ever was. My friends, it's time we start saying that Magic was 'more LeBron than Michael'.

---

[278] The difference being .. LeBron's shit sandwich Cleveland teams demanded that he progress as an individual scorer, while Magic, as great as he was, was flanked by a pair of first-overall picks with diverse individual scoring profiles of their own.

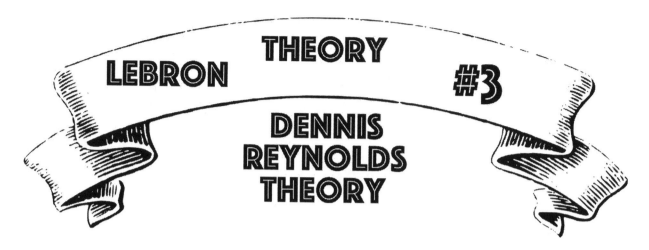

LEBRON THEORY #3

DENNIS REYNOLDS THEORY

LeBron James D.E.N.N.I.S.-systemed the Cleveland Cavaliers.[279] In S5:E10 of *It's Always Sunny in Philadelphia*, the show's best character, Dennis Reynolds, introduces his systematic approach for psychologically manipulating women. Behold, the D.E.N.N.I.S. System:

D—Demonstrate Value
E—Engage Physically
N—Nurture Dependence
N—Neglect Emotionally
I—Inspire Hope
S—Separate Entirely

Dennis, a narcissist and sociopath, used this methodical process to bed women and quickly get rid of them. LeBron, not a narcissist or sociopath, used the D.E.N.N.I.S. system to get everything he wanted from the Cavs, and maybe to fuck with Dan Gilbert in the process. Observe:

D—Demonstrate Value
In June of 2003, Cleveland drafted LeBron James and he immediately provided immense value. The Cavs were so fortunate to be in his presence and were certain he would never leave.

E—Engage Physically
In May of 2007, Cleveland and LeBron consummated their relationship when he improbably beat the Pistons. The Cavs had never felt that way, nor had they ever reached the NBA Finals'.

N—Nurture Dependence
During the 2008-09' and 2009-10' seasons, the Cavaliers were entirely dependent on LeBron to fuel their 60-win regular season and postseason runs. The Cavs were nothing without him.

---

[279] Reddit user u/c2darizzle published this theory on February 1st, 2018, but I thought of this utterly independent of their post, and had the idea written down in my OneNote since November 2017. I once went as Dennis Reynolds for Halloween and had the D.E.N.N.I.S. system embroidered on my shirt. I'm something of an expert on the system (in theory, not in practice).

N—Neglect Emotionally

In July of 2010, LeBron rejected Cleveland's love for him and decided to play for the Miami Heat. The Cavs were emotionally crushed.

I—Inspire Hope

In July of 2014, LeBron announced he would come back to Cleveland and play for the Cavaliers. The Cavs had hope that LeBron would never leave them again.

S—Separate Entirely

In July of 2018, LeBron decided to play for the Los Angeles Lakers. The Cavs were ghosted by LeBron for good.

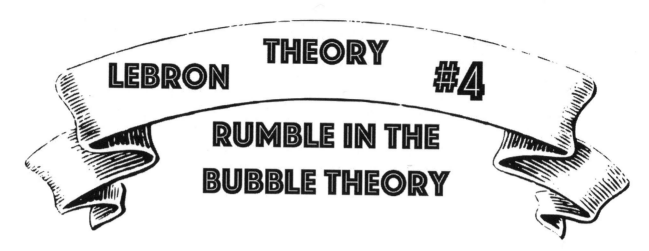

LEBRON THEORY #4

RUMBLE IN THE BUBBLE THEORY

I guess if I had to describe my emotions after LeBron's championship victory at the conclusion of the marathon 2019-20' season .. I'd say that it felt like the saxophone solo from *Jungleland* was playing triumphantly in my head for a month straight. It was glorious. The championship felt like an inevitability for many people by the time Los Angeles captured it, but in my celebration of the accomplishment, the number of other teams who were picked to win the championship were at the front of my mind.

The championship felt to me like LeBron's *Rumble in the Jungle*. Well past his prime, Muhammad Ali was picked by most to lose the fight against George Foreman in Kinshasa, Zaire on October 30th, 1974. Ali provoked Foreman by throwing a ton of risky right crosses early. George Foreman eventually punched himself out trying to make Ali pay for his provocations, and Ali rope-a-doped his way to another improbable Heavyweight championship.

Past what people deemed his prime, LeBron endured everyone picking the Clippers or Bucks to win the championship in 2019-20'. LeBron engaged Denver by squeaking out a narrow game two victory, and further provoked the Nuggets by conceding a game three loss. The Lakers went up a level and LeBron delivered a game five TKO in the stream of a 38, 16 and 10 closeout of the Western Conference Finals.

When the Lakers got to the NBA Finals', many prominent basketball media members still doubted that a LeBron championship was imminent.[280] The narrative was Jimmy Butler's leadership. The narrative was Heat Culture. Boy, what a great leader *Jimmy Butler* is. Boy, that *Heat Culture* just continues to turn out stud young players. The Lakers rope-a-doped the Heat by providing openings in games three and five, but Jimmy Butler and that Heat Culture tumbled to the canvas just like Foreman.

---

[280] 8 out of 17 ESPN NBA contributors picked the Heat to beat the Lakers before the Finals'. Bill Simmons took the Heat in six. Amin Elhassan took the Heat in six. In *The Athletic's* Finals' preview, 3 of the 6 NBA contributors that they polled took the Heat, one of whom predicted Duncan Robinson would be Finals' MVP. Flagrant disrespect.

So, what happens when the superlatives that I'd been ascribing to LeBron since 2009 begin to be the mainstream narrative of his legacy? That's the weird existence I've found myself in over the past few years. Really smart basketball thinkers and popular culture surveyors alike have been coming out of the woodwork to anoint LeBron as the greatest player of all-time. Shit, this is the introduction to Wikipedia's profile on LeBron:

> *LeBron Raymone James Sr. is an American professional basketball player*
> *for the Los Angeles Lakers of the National Basketball Association.*
> *Widely regarded as the greatest basketball player of all time, which has*
> *resulted in frequent comparisons to Michael Jordan.*

It's Wikipedia, I get it, but it still made me do a double take. In the lexicon of all-time NBA greats, LeBron has inexplicably bullied his way to the top of the food chain. It's certainly rewarding when the thing you've been fighting for, more or less, comes true. However, even for a LeBron fan of my commitment, I'm not all the way *there*. Don't get me wrong, there are days where LeBron's 'greatest of all-time' candidacy comes to me with 20/20 clarity, but I'm still very torn about signing off fully on the completion of the *Chosen One* prophecy. I never imagined his legacy would approach Mike's. But I admit, and I think we all should admit, that we were mistakenly using MJ's profile as a measuring stick. Bron might just be the greatest player ever, but he didn't do it emulating Mike and trying to 'out MJ, MJ'—love him or hate him, both on and off the basketball court, LeBron James has imprinted his own legacy that rests in the shadow of no one else.

We're not talking about MJ and LeBron .. yet. LeBron James is in Tier I because he has a case as the greatest player that ever lived, isolated from comparison to anyone else. It's difficult to ignore that there are good, bad and ugly headline components to LeBron's legacy. For the duration of LeBron's profile, which many of you are mercifully praying for a conclusion to, I'm going to work my way through them with all the objectivity that I'm able to muster.

{Scoring Stuff}

Currently, LeBron has the third-most points in the history of the NBA (34,241). Before Bron retires, he has a decent chance to pass Kareem Abdul-Jabbar (38,387) for the most points all-time. LeBron has the most career playoff points in the history of the NBA by a wide margin—LeBron stands at 7,491 points, MJ has the second-most with 5,987. It's unlikely anyone ever passes LeBron in playoff points. When it comes to PPG, LeBron stands at fourth all-time in the regular season (27.07), and fifth all-time in the postseason (28.81). These raw stats strongly suggest that LeBron is a top-five scorer in the history of the league, but when you drill down on the efficiency, the evidence positions him closer to first than to fifth.

The best granular research on pure scoring was done by none other than the world's foremost expert on NBA archaeology, Ben Taylor. The very first episode of his *Thinking*

Basketball podcast ranked the 10 best scorers in NBA history, and he re-fashioned the list with more specific data for the 50th episode of his podcast, which aired March 24, 2020. The clearest way Taylor defined the list was 'which players created the most value or championship equity by virtue of their scoring alone'. On-ball vs. off-ball scoring, skill vs. effectiveness, and finishing vs. dependency were all large considerations in compiling the list. At the heart of the list was Taylor's mitigation of the eternally complicated relationship between volume scoring and efficient scoring. As a measure for volume he used Adjusted Scoring Rate, and for efficiency he used Real Scoring Percentage:

- Adjusted Scoring Rate—Points per 75 possessions,[281] adjusting for the pace of the era and for the quality of the defenses played against. Next level shit.
- Real Scoring Percentage—Using a variety of efficiency markers (True Shooting %, Free Throw Rate, Free Throw %, etc.), Taylor determined how many percentage points a player was above league average scoring. The metric also factored in turnovers that were a function of attempted scoring possessions for a player. Next fucking level.

As is common with much of Taylor's work, he used specific windows of time to evaluate players—it represents sustained performance in a given statistic—in this case it was three-year playoff runs where a player played a minimum of 1,000 minutes across, at least, that three-year window.[282] To create a qualifying list of players that would weigh heavily on the final ranking, Taylor drilled down his volume and efficiency metrics to include the top 100 scoring postseasons in NBA history by volume (at least 27.7 in Adjusted Scoring Rate) and +5% above league average in Real Scoring Rate. This yielded 14 players total that have ever met this criterion.

Six players accomplished it once:
- Amar'e Stoudemire (2005-2008)
- Kawhi Leonard (2017-2019)
- Steph Curry (2015-2017)
- Dirk Nowitzki (2009-2012)
- Elgin Baylor (1960-1963)
- Reggie Miller (1992-1995)

Five players accomplished it twice:
- Hakeem Olajuwon (1986-1988, 1993-1996)
- Kevin Durant (2010-2014, 2017-2019)
- Dwayne Wade (2005-2007, 2009-2011)
- Jerry West (1963-1965, 1966-1968)
- Kobe Bryant (2001-2003, 2006-2010)

---

[281] His thinking with Points Per 75 Possessions was the thought that a star player typically plays 36-40 minutes every playoff game.
[282] As you'll see, there are several players that qualify for the thresholds across four or five postseasons, but the experiment is specifically targeting isolated three-year playoff runs.

Three players accomplished it three times:
- o Michael Jordan (1986-1990, 1991-1993, 1995-1998)
- o Shaquille O'Neal (1996-1998, 1999-2001, 2002-2004)
- o LeBron James (2008-2011, 2012-2015, 2016-2018)[283]

After getting these results, Taylor decided to drill down his volume and efficiency thresholds to see how many players would still qualify (while maintaining the same minimum three-year postseason run qualifier with at least 1,000 minutes played across that run). He went from 27.7 in Adjusted Scoring Rate to 29, which zoomed in from the top 100 scoring postseasons from a volume standpoint, to the top 50. He then bumped the Real Scoring Percentage qualifier from +5% above league average to +6.5%. Wade, Elgin, Kawhi, KD, West, Dirk and Reggie Miller all still hit the mark for one three-year postseason window. MJ and Shaq still hit the mark across two different windows. LeBron James was the only player to still qualify across three different three-year playoff runs. Using that data and other criteria, Ben Taylor concluded that the top ten scorers in the history of the NBA are as follows:

- o 10) Steph Curry
- o 9) Dwayne Wade
- o 8) Kobe Bryant
- o 7) Kevin Durant
- o 6) Jerry West

- o 5) Kareem Abdul-Jabbar
- o 4) Shaquille O'Neal
- o 3) Dirk Nowitzki
- o 2) LeBron James
- o 1) Michael Jordan

{8 Straight Finals' Stuff}

The objective counterpoint to LeBron's perfect 24-0 record against the Eastern Conference between 2011 and 2018 is the lack of real competition he faced. The most damning evidence lies in how many more All-NBA players were concentrated in the Western Conference during this stretch. In the 8 seasons between 2010-11' and 2017-18', there were 120 total All-NBA selections—just 38 of them (31.7%) were players from the Eastern Conference.

While the East was irrefutably leaner on premier talent, I encourage you to not lose sight of what is in many ways an unprecedented achievement. LeBron embargoed the East from reaching the NBA Finals' much the way that Jordan did between 1991 and 1998. Just like MJ, LeBron outlasted more playoff-hardened Detroit and Boston teams until it was his time. When it was their time, and with the power mostly consolidated in the West, neither player allowed teams[284] in their conference to slip by and earn the confidence that comes with an NBA Finals' trip. On its own merit, and from a comparative standpoint, this is arguably LeBron's greatest achievement. No one in the modern NBA has come close to this streak (with the

---

[283] Translated—LeBron hit those markers for 11 consecutive postseasons. Mother of God.

[284] The Bulls lost to the Magic in 1995, shortly after Mike came out of retirement, and we can agree that didn't really count. For the six full seasons that MJ played between 1991 and 1998, he didn't lose a single series in the Eastern Conference.

exception of LeBron's Remora Fish, James Jones). Realistically, given a more universally competitive and forward-thinking NBA environment, it's highly unlikely any player ever reaches 8 consecutive NBA Finals' again. The only players to ever approach this mark were Bill Russell-adjacent Boston Celtics .. and James Jones:

	Consecutive NBA Finals'[285]	Seasons Covered
Bill Russell	10 (1957-1966)	1957-1966 Celtics
Sam Jones	9 (1958-1966)	1958-1966 Celtics
Tommy Heinsohn	9 (1957-1965)	1957-1965 Celtics
LeBron James	8 (2011-2018)	2011-2018 Heat & Cavs
Frank Ramsey	8 (1957-1964)	1957-1964 Celtics
K.C. Jones	8 (1959-1966)	1959-1966 Celtics
Bob Cousy	7 (1957-1963)	1957-1963 Celtics
James Jones	7 (2011-2017)	2011-2017 Heat & Cavs

The weight of this accomplishment compounds when you factor how little relative resistance the Celtics encountered on their way to the NBA Finals'. Across the 1957 through 1966 Boston run of 10 consecutive Finals', during which all of the listed Celtics achieved their respective streaks, there were only 8 or 9 teams in the NBA. Even more, during only one of those ten postseasons was Boston required to win multiple playoff series' prior to reaching the NBA Finals'—again, in 9 out of those 10 postseasons, the Celtics *only had to beat one other team* before reaching the NBA Finals'. In each season of LeBron's streak (and James Jones' streak in fairness), the NBA had 30 teams. Even more, for LeBron to reach the Finals' during each postseason of his 8-year run, he had to win three seven-game series' before doing so.

Try to think of it this way. LeBron is 14-0 in the first round of the playoffs—Carmelo Anthony has seen the second round of the playoffs twice in his career. LeBron is 11-3 in the second-round of the playoffs—11 trips to the Conference Finals' is the combined number of Conference Final berths earned by Giannis Antetokounmpo, Kawhi Leonard and Steph Curry in their careers. LeBron is *10-and-fucking-1* in the Conference Finals. I don't care who the opponent is, if you need help determining why that is a preposterous figure, I don't know how to help you.

{The Championships With Different Teams Stuff}

The Los Angeles Lakers are now the third franchise that have won a championship with LeBron James as their best player. Combined with marking both LeBron's fourth Finals' MVP and fourth title overall, he's now generated an unprecedented argument in the greatest-ever discourse. We're going to talk about the ballad of Michael Jordan and LeBron James soon, but I can't help but think that LeBron now has a chip stack equal to that of MJ's. I know the raw numbers are still missing a few figures in the category of 'championships won', so let me

---

[285] Yeah, yeah, yeah, Andre Iguodala has now made 6 straight appearances. He won't make 7 and he sure as hell won't make 8. LeBron made 8 straight Finals' as his team's best player—something only Russell can say.

explain what I mean—I believe four championships as the best player for three different franchises is a commensurate accomplishment to winning six with the same franchise.

I didn't hear much of this specific dialogue after the Lakers won the championship in 2019-20', so I'm guessing that other basketball observers aren't seeing this the same way I am. I'm surprised by that, but it won't stop me from shooting this shot.

If we've learned anything from watching teams attempt to build a championship contender, we can agree on the fact that it's very hard to do. The eternal challenge of teambuilding in the NBA is to align the interests of players, coaches, front office and support staff in the uniform direction of a championship—much more difficult than it looks.

We now have evidence of a player that is great enough to allow their franchise to bypass the micro-decisions and micro-directives of teambuilding. A player so great that he could relegate Dwayne Wade to secondary status in Miami, Florida. A player so great that he could rescue Cleveland twice. A player *so great* that he could bail out a floundering Los Angeles franchise at its darkest hour. A player so great that he's bigger than teambuilding—that's fucking *wild.*

Sometimes it takes a generation of efforts from everyone in an NBA organization to win a championship. Look at how much respect the Dallas Mavericks organization has around the league. They've reached that status where any move they make is perceived as golden and made with keen foresight.[286] Yet, the credibility of a franchise with that much cache rests on the fact that they threw everything at the championship wall through the 2000s, and something happened to stick in 2011. Encapsulated within an acquisition of LeBron James across this decade-long run of play is his ability to take a process that can take a franchise as long as a decade, and get them there in a year or two.

Championships were not happening in Cleveland. LeBron didn't have a Horace Grant and Scottie Pippen arranged for him early in his career .. and that's why he *had* to hit the road. You can be mad about how he announced he'd be playing for Miami, but it's probably time we stop treating him like he announced that he was opening a nationwide chain of puppy mills that night.[287] After becoming the greatest player in Miami Heat history, he returned to Cleveland and cemented his status as a second different franchise's greatest-ever player. He chose to play in Los Angeles in an attempt to have his cake and eat it too, where LeBron indeed was able to enjoy both more time with his family and championship success.

We're not talking about MJ and Bron .. yet. But there's a scientific advantage to LeBron's case in that experiment which Jordan just can't match. If Jordan had been forced to play in different uniforms, there's a pretty great chance that he'd have been able to eliminate the need for teambuilding as well. But we don't know. If LeBron is the control in that experiment, the result is championships for the franchise he chooses. We can't say that about anyone else in the history of the NBA on the scale that LeBron has now demonstrated, and it's now the most potent weapon in his battle for greatest-ever supremacy.

---

[286] Except giving Kristaps the max .. yikes. They need to get off that money ASAP. Maybe a dumb team like Detroit would take him.

[287] In reality, a nationwide announcement of where he intended to play rose to the level of how his free agency had been covered by the media—it was the highest profile free agency in the history of sports, just as widespread internet use was tipping.

{Advanced Stat Stuff}

When you look at LeBron's profile on *Basketball Reference*, his traditional box score stats only have a few figures in bold—indicating that he led the league in that statistic for that specific season. One bold figure is his Points Per Game in 2007-08' (the only season he led the league in scoring), and the other bold figure is his Assists Per Game in 2019-20' (the only season he led the league in assists). Conversely, peruse a little further down his *Basketball Reference* page to his Advanced stat and Playoff Advanced stat profiles, and you'll see a flurry of bold print across a broad collection of metrics.

VORP—Value Over Replacement Player

- LeBron led the league in VORP between 2005-06' and 2012-13'. No other player in history has led the league in VORP for 8 straight seasons.
- LeBron has accumulated the highest total VORP in NBA history by a wide margin.
- Of the 14 postseasons LeBron has participated in, he's led the league in VORP for 9 of those playoff campaigns. That's resulted in an even wider lead in all-time postseason VORP.
- LeBron claims 3 of the 5 most valuable postseasons by VORP, including the highest ever figure by the metric during the 2018 playoffs:

		VORP	Postseason
1)	LeBron James	3.40	2018
2)	Tim Duncan	3.15	2003
3)	LeBron James	3.12	2012
4)	LeBron James	2.99	2013
5)	Larry Bird	2.95	1984

PER—Player Efficiency Rating

- LeBron led the league in PER between 2007-08' and 2012-13'. Leading the league in PER for 6 straight seasons has only been done one other time in NBA history—Jordan's 7 straight seasons between 1986-87' and 1992-93' is the only longer streak.
- Similarly, LeBron's career regular season PER figure (27.49) is second all-time to MJ's 27.91.
- LeBron holds the record, by a wide margin, for the highest PER in a single postseason (37.39—2009 postseason).[288]
- The top five players all-time by career postseason PER are as follows:

---

[288] The qualifier being that the player had to have played in at least two playoff series' during the playoff run. LeBron's Cavaliers made it to the Eastern Conference Finals' before being bounced during their 2009 playoff run (three playoff series').

		PER
1)	Michael Jordan	28.60
2)	George Mikan	28.51
3)	LeBron James	28.41[289]
4)	Shaquille O'Neal	26.13
5)	Hakeem Olajuwon	25.69

BPM—Box Plus/Minus, Version 2.0[290]

- o LeBron led the league in BPM between 2007-08' and 2012-13'. Only he and Kareem have led the league in BPM 6 seasons in a row, second only to MJ's 7 seasons in a row (and 9 out of 10) between 1986-87' and 1996-97'.
- o In both the regular season and postseason all-time figures, Jordan is first and LeBron is second.
- o LeBron's 2008-09' season does hold the record for both the highest single regular season figure (+13.24) and single postseason (+17.53).[291]
- o When *Basketball Reference* and BPM creator Daniel Myers released BPM Version 2.0, Ben Taylor released a podcast with a synopsis of the update's strengths and weaknesses, as well as a ranking of the top ten playoff peaks within the metric. Using a minimum 5-year playoff peak window, he determined the best postseason BPM peaks were as follows:

- o 10) Larry Bird (1982-1986)
- o 9) Magic Johnson (1986-1990)
- o 8) Tim Duncan (1999-2004)
- o 7) Dirk Nowitzki (2006-2010)
- o 6) Dwayne Wade (2006-2011)

- o 5) Kawhi Leonard (2014-2019)
- o 4) Kareem Abdul-Jabbar (1974-1980)
- o 3) Chris Paul (2013-2017)
- o 2) LeBron James (2008-2012)
- o 1) Michael Jordan (1987-1991)

PIPM—Player Impact Plus-Minus

- o LeBron's career PIPM rating of +6.00 is good for second-best all-time, while MJ's +5.98 is the third-best all-time rating.
- o LeBron sits atop the 'Wins Added' component of PIPM—The top three players within PIPM by Wins Added:

		PIPM Wins Added
1)	LeBron James	322.32
2)	Tim Duncan	284.78
3)	Kevin Garnett	261.11

---

[289] Bron's 30.2 PER during the 2019-20' championship run actually *brought up* his career figure. This motherfucker's historic PER average *increased* after his 14th postseason. Bend the knee, y'all.

[290] The metric was re-calibrated and updated in February 2020. All BPM data in my book reflects the 2.0 iteration.

[291] +17.53 lolololololol

BAD

{Free Throw Stuff}

A career percentage of 73.4% (74.1% in the playoffs) might not seem like the end of the world, but it's hard to overstate just how important it is to have an icy free throw closer at the end of crucial games—and my man's played in a lot of crucial games. Compared to other Tier I and Tier II players, LeBron's playoff Free Throw Percentage is definitely on the low end, which is a tough look for my guy when he's been expected to be his team's closer for the entirety of his career:

	Playoff FT%		Playoff FT%
14) Wilt Chamberlain	46.5%	7) Kevin Garnett	78.9%
13) Shaquille O'Neal	50.4%	6) Kobe Bryant	81.6%
12) Bill Russell	60.3%	5) Michael Jordan	82.8%
11) Tim Duncan	68.9%	4) Magic Johnson	83.8%
10) Hakeem Olajuwon	71.9%	3) Oscar Robertson	85.5%
9) Kareem Abdul-Jabbar	74.0%	2) Larry Bird	89.0%
8) LeBron James	**74.1%**	1) Steph Curry	90.6%

Like all great scorers, LeBron was able to find a rhythm when it mattered most, and his Free Throw Percentage gets a bump in his 8 career game sevens to 77.9%. It's obvious though, that being trapped in the low to mid 70s as a free throw shooter has held him back in more ways than one. LeBron has taken the fifth-most regular season free throws and the most playoff free throws in the history of the league. While hitting 10% better from the free throw line wouldn't have added any trophies to his shelf, necessarily, the volume of misses serve as his profile's biggest opportunity cost, and should Bron fall short of Kareem's all-time points mark, that will assuredly be the reason. Perhaps LeBron's greatest ability is assessing the best course of action in nearly every circumstance. When there is a rather significant aspect of his game that he's unable to fully trust, especially at the end of important games, it lessens the totality of his powers by a measurable degree.

{The Overly Ball-Dominant Stuff}

Give LeBron the keys to your team, with at least a few usable pieces around him, and there's a better chance than not that you'll be playing in the Finals'. However, there's plenty of evidence that when you tie yourself to a 'point-LeBron' system, yes, you might just be riding off into the sunset, but you might also be going down with the ship.

For years, we've speculated what the perfect complement of players around LeBron really looks like. Shooters are essential, and per Kirk Goldberry, LeBron has led the league in corner-three assists, statistically the most efficient three-point shot, since the 2014-15' season. Rim runners tend to thrive around LeBron because of his ever-present ability to flip a defensive vulnerability into a lob before the defense knows what's happening.[292] The prevailing wisdom has told us that those two components around LeBron are the recipe for a trip to the NBA Finals'. However, and this is a conclusion that came further into focus during the 2019-20' season, smart teambuilding around LeBron starts with contracting a stop-gap creator to 'LeBron' the team while LeBron takes a breather. In essence, when you build a system around all the things LeBron can do, your team also needs someone that can do 80% of what he can do when he's not in the game, and that's not an easy team to build!

The most team success LeBron has enjoyed was in Miami when there was another apex predator that the Heat could stagger LeBron with to mitigate the minutes he wasn't in the game. But it's not enough to say that to win with LeBron that you need another superstar, because in fairness to LeBron James, 95% of past NBA champions have needed multiple star-level players to win a championship. The beauty of what the Heat had was options. LeBron could do his 'Queen of the chessboard' thing and spread the defense out because of his dual threat to score or pass, but they could also create via Wade. Because of the basketball synergy and personal friendship they had, they were able to succeed with two apex predators. This worked but to a lesser degree with Kyrie, to whom LeBron was able to defer scoring responsibilities, but Kyrie lacked the overall ability to generate team cohesion (both schematically and from a chemistry standpoint). LeBron and AD definitely make a cohesive pair together, but because AD is not a perimeter creator by nature, it leaves an even bigger void for the Lakers when LeBron rests.

It's not necessarily a criticism of LeBron to say that his team's have, at times, been overly reliant on him. The problem is that the best way to build around him is to partner him with someone that does a lot of the things he does—a tall ask for a front office. The answer to the eternal question of who fits best around LeBron might just be another LeBron.[293]

{The 4-6 Stuff}

Whether it's fair or not, LeBron's historic ability to reach the Finals' will usually be overshadowed by his inability to raise a trophy at the conclusion of the majority of those series'. Using raw winning percentage, a blunt tool by any estimation, but one that the public tends to use in appraising LeBron's Finals' record, LeBron is just ahead of Wilt across all Tier I and Tier II players:

---

[292] There's no better example of this than what Chris Andersen was able to do during the 2012-13' postseason. He finished the playoffs with an NBA record for field goal percentage (80.7%), including a stretch between games 1 and 4 of the Eastern Conference Finals where he went a perfect 15-15. He deserves credit on his own accomplishments, but there are a hell of a lot of easy lob dunks from LeBron mixed into that insane 80.7% mark.

[293] Frank Vogel and The Lakers figured this out in the form of a rejuvenated, three-point-shooting, Rajon Rondo. During the championship run, Rondo ran the offense when LeBron was sitting or needed an on-court reprieve from his offensive duties. Who saw that coming?

	Finals' Record (Win %)		Finals' Record (Win %)
14) Wilt Chamberlain	2-4 (33.3%)	7) Kareem Abdul-Jabbar	6-4 (60.0%)
13) LeBron James	**4-6 (40%)**	6) Hakeem Olajuwon	2-1 (66.6%)
12) Oscar Robertson	1-1 (50.0%	5) Shaquille O'Neal	4-2 (66.6%)
11) Kevin Garnett	1-1 (50.0%)	4) Kobe Bryant	5-2 (71.4%)
10) Magic Johnson	5-4 (55.5%)	3) Tim Duncan	5-1 (83.3%)
9) Larry Bird	3-2 (60.0%)	2) Bill Russell	11-1 (91.6%)
8) Steph Curry	3-2 (60.0%)	1) Michael Jordan	6-0 (100%)

However misleading that figure is, it will continue to be kill switch evidence for a huge percentage of basketball fans that LeBron should be prevented from discourse about him as the greatest player ever. Here's why that's bullshit:

1) When the 2006-07' Cavs improbably upset the Pistons in the 2007 Eastern Conference Finals', they found themselves staring down a championship-hardened and veteran-laden San Antonio Spurs team. As you could probably guess, LeBron and a supporting cast of Drew Gooden, Daniel Gibson, Sasha Pavlović, Zydrunas Ilgauskas, Anderson Varejão and Larry Hughes were no match for Tim Duncan, Tony Parker, Manu Ginóbili, Bruce Bowen, Michael Finley and Robert Horry. The Spurs swept the Cavs with little resistance.

   How is a loss in those Finals' considered a demerit to LeBron's legacy? He didn't have a puncher's chance to win that series. This seems to be the beginning of where LeBron is punished for pulling a weaker team into the NBA Finals'.

2) When the 2014-15' Cavs reached the Finals', they were narrow underdogs to the 67-win 2014-15' Warriors. The Cavs started the Finals' without Kevin Love because of a first-round injury that shelved him for the remainder of the playoffs. After the game one Finals' overtime loss to the Warriors, the Cavs would also be without Kyrie Irving because of a cracked kneecap. That left LeBron with Timofey Mozgov, J.R. Smith, Tristan Thompson, Matthew Dellavedova, Iman Shumpert and James Jones (who, at 34 years old, played an unimaginable 113 minutes of those NBA Finals'). As you could probably guess, that wasn't a match for Steph Curry, Klay Thompson, Draymond Green, Andre Iguodala, Harrison Barnes and Leandro Barbosa. LeBron did go down fighting and earned 4 Finals' MVP votes, but the Warriors won in six games.

   How is a loss in those Finals' considered a demerit to LeBron's legacy? For the second consecutive postseason, LeBron had lost in the Finals' and the recipient of the Finals' MVP won the award for how well they'd defended him. Don't believe me? Across the 52 different recipients of the Finals' MVP award, Kawhi Leonard (2014) and Andre Iguodala (2015) hold the two lowest usage rates for a Finals' MVP winner:

	USG%
48) Larry Bird 1984 Finals'	*23.7*
49)Chauncey Billups 2004 Finals'	*22.5*
50) Larry Bird 1986 Finals'	*22.0*
51) Kawhi Leonard 2014 Finals'	**20.5**
52) Andre Iguodala 2015 Finals'	**18.7**

They won because they were defending the only player capable of making either of those series' competitive. MJ had Grant and Pippen healthy for all three of the 91'-93' Finals', and he had Rodman and Pippen healthy for all three of the 96-98' Finals'. We're going to hold LeBron's legacy hostage for the 2015' Finals loss, when Cleveland's second and third-best players were both injured? It feels like we're better than that.

3) When the 2017-18' Cavs reached the Finals' on the legs of a historic LeBron playoff run, they were massive underdogs to the 2017-18' Warriors. LeBron did have the services of Kevin Love for those Finals', but the rest of the cast was filled out by J.R. Smith, George Hill, Tristan Thompson, Larry Nance and Jeff Green. As you could probably guess though, they had no chance against Steph Curry, Kevin Durant, Klay Thompson, Draymond Green, Andre Iguodala and Shaun Livingston. The Cavs were swept handily, with the exception of a tight game one. [294]

How is a loss in those Finals' considered a demerit to LeBron's legacy? LeBron may have had a better supporting cast than he did in 2007, but his odds of being able to pull off an upset were even worse in 2018 because of how much better the opponent was. If his team had no chance to win in the 2018 Finals', are we really saying that a loss is worse than having made the Finals' in the first place?

History will wash over those defeats as merely notches in the loss column for LeBron's Finals' record, but even ardent LeBron detractors have to acknowledge that the likelihood of LeBron's team winning any three of these series', without an injury to the opposing team, was next to zero. Conversely, there is one Finals' defeat LeBron suffered that was his fault. A lost championship that his legacy won't ever recover from.

---

[294] LeBron's heroic 51 points on 19 of 32 from the field in game one was spectacularly ruined by the two-headed knuckleheadery of a missed game-sealing free throw by George Hill that was impossibly out-knuckleheaded by J.R. Smith running out the clock in regulation with the score tied. I'm still mad, can you tell? Alas, even if the Cavs had pulled off a game one upset, the Warriors still would have won this series regardless of how you slice it.

UGLY

{The 2011 Finals' Stuff}

The way the 2011 Finals' played out for LeBron James survives as the most high-profile, legacy-damning loss that any premier NBA player has ever endured. The years preceding the 2011 Finals' between the Heat and Mavs were pretty tough on LeBron, but with the Heat figuring out their roster during the 2011 postseason, it seemed like Dirk's Mavs were going to be circumstantial victims to the inevitability of LeBron's first NBA championship. Dallas took a very famous full timeout with 7:14 left in the fourth quarter of game two. Miami had won game one convincingly and held a 15-point advantage when the timeout was called. I think that timeout was when LeBron's legacy changed course forever.

I've written at length about how important this loss was in developing LeBron's ability to quiet the outside noise, and ultimately, synthesize the finest version of himself. However, there's a chance that LeBron could have skipped the necessity to block out all the noise by simply jumping on the more direct path to greatest of all-time status—through winning that 2011 championship. There's definitely an observable precedent for the confidence a premier player earns by winning their first championship. There's a reality where LeBron just wins that 2011 championship and supercharges his momentum toward MJ's legacy. In 2020, LeBron doesn't need that championship for a lot of people to already think he's the best ever. However, without it, it will be hard for a lot of people to bend the knee for LeBron's legacy as the greatest-ever with such a high-profile meltdown on his resume. The tragedy for Bron was not just the loss itself, but the brutal choke job that he managed to display in full 1080p.

During that timeout, LeBron mentally claimed the 2011 championship. Effective immediately after that timeout, for the remainder of the series, LeBron was uncharacteristically awful. He let go of the rope for the remainder of game two, during which the Mavericks went 9 of 10 from the field, and the Heat only managed 1 of 10 in an impossible 2-point loss. The Heat won game three and seemingly stabilized what seemed to everyone a championship that was theirs to lose. But lose they did the next three games, as the Mavericks successfully exploited whatever was going on between LeBron's ears. The Mavs held LeBron to 8 points on 3 of 11 in game four, and LeBron was spinning his wheels for the remainder of the series trying to decipher the different coverages and matchups Dallas continued to throw at him. For the series, LeBron only averaged 17.8 points, the lowest for any series in his entire career.

John Steinbeck's *East of Eden* is far and away my favorite novel. It's a powerful story about a handful of Americans around the turn of the century, and focuses sharply on the wide range of tendencies that combine to form different personality-types. Central to the story's symbolism is a disputed Bible translation from the fourth chapter of Genesis—the story of Cain and Abel. For those as un-religious as I, Cain and Abel were brothers and the first children of Adam and Eve. Each made an offering to the Lord, and the Lord respected Abel's offering and did not respect Cain's. Cain then killed his brother. When the Lord came to Cain, there is a dispute over how exactly the Lord said that Cain should move forward from this sin. In the King

James version of the Bible, the Lord *promises* Cain that he will conquer sin—'thou shalt' (rule over sin). In the more modern New Standard Version Bible, the Lord *orders* Cain to conquer sin—'do thou' (rule over sin). But in the original Hebrew text of the Bible, the Hebrew word timshol is used, which translates to—'thou mayest' (rule over sin).

Thou mayest rule over sin. *That's Goddam right.* It's not pre-determined that you'll conquer your fears, vanquish your demons or move past your losses—that's on you .. and it's on me .. and it was on LeBron in the summer of 2011. From *East of Eden*:

> *Thou mayest! Why, that makes a man great, that gives him stature*
> *with the gods, for in his weakness and his filth and his murder of his*
> *brother he has still the great choice. He can choose his course and fight*
> *it through and win.*

No one was promising or commanding LeBron to rule over his high-profile losses. LeBron alone refused to succumb to the sting of his embarrassment. He chose to strive forward and live with the results of his dedication. If you focus on the yield of that dedication—the results of the seasons since the Dallas loss—it's easy to lose sight of why LeBron is now in Jordan's airspace. The true glory of LeBron James' legacy is in his reluctance to allow loss and negativity to triumph over him. As the great American philosopher Kanye West once said—*Went from most hated to the champion-God-flow, I guess that's a feeling only me and LeBron know.*

Why Is LeBron The Greatest Player Ever? Bron is the greatest player ever because, in a vacuum, if you had to choose one player in the history of the NBA to start a franchise with, and would give you the best chance to compete for a championship for two decades—you'd choose LeBron James. The regular season is about a player's strengths, and the postseason is about a player's weaknesses. There's never been a player in history with as many strengths and so few weaknesses.

Michael Jordan

The Secret	Greatness Index	Ben Taylor Rank
94 / 100	447.28 (1st)	3rd

PIPM	O-PIPM	D-PIPM	Peak—1987-88'	Wins Added
+5.98 (3rd)	+4.87	+1.11	+8.49 (4th)	258.59 (4th)

Playoff PER	Playoff Win Shares	Playoff O-Win Shares	Playoff D-Win Shares
28.60 (1st)	39.76 (2nd)	27.32 (2nd)	12.44 (7th)

23.

Opportunities of a lifetime very rarely present themselves, and it's even more rare when they're acknowledged as such in the moment. 1962 was going to be a wildly successful calendar year for The Beatles, but it began with a massive disappointment for the lads and a colossal missed opportunity for Decca Records. The Beatles' manager, Brian Epstein, had struck out with every major record label in London up to that point. However, Decca had sent a representative up to Liverpool to watch The Beatles play at The Cavern Club, and he was impressed enough to invite the Beatles down to London for a test at Decca studios. On January 1st, 1962, John Lennon, Paul McCartney, George Harrison and Pete Best played 15 songs for Decca A&R man, Dick Rowe. Unimpressed by the tryout, Decca allowed the Beatles to record again but at full cost to the band. Decca eventually signed another band that auditioned that same day—Brian Poole and the Tremeloes—in part because they were local and the label could cut travel costs versus what they would incur if they signed the Liverpool-based Beatles. Legend has it that Decca informed Brian Epstein that 'guitar groups are on the way out' and 'The Beatles have no future in showbusiness'. Later that year, EMI subsidiary, Parlophone records, signed the Beatles after producer George Martin heard serious promise on the Decca demos.[295] The Beatles quickly ascended within the popular music industry, and would eventually become the greatest band of all-time.

In the 1984 NBA draft, two different NBA franchises managed to pass on the opportunity to draft Michael Jordan. The Houston Rockets had the first-overall pick and took Hakeem Olajuwon. This is forgivable as Hakeem is a top ten player of all-time. Shit, just two years after the 1984 draft, Houston was in the NBA Finals' giving the freaking 86' Celtics all they could handle. The Portland Trailblazers held the second pick and their decision to pass on MJ lives on as a much tougher look for the franchise. Portland grabbed Clyde Drexler in the draft one year before Jordan's draft, and were content enough with his rookie year to feel they were set at Jordan's position.[296] Portland Coveted 7-foot center, Sam Bowie, from the University of Kentucky. The league still valued big men higher than perimeter players at the time, but Portland's appraisal process of Bowie is beyond perplexing to this day. Just a few years earlier, Portland had to finally move on from Bill Walton, their generational big man talent who was plagued with chronic lower body injuries. Sam Bowie had the same red flags—after completing productive freshman and sophomore seasons at Kentucky, *Bowie missed two full collegiate seasons because of lower body injuries* before completing a fifth-year-senior season leading up to the 1984 NBA draft. Dr. Jack Ramsay, then Trailblazers coach, and an otherwise heavily respected figure in the basketball community, said over the years that Jordan was never in their draft plans. The Blazers took Bowie, and the Chicago Bulls selected Michael Jeffrey Jordan. Brian Poole and the Tremeloes, I mean *Sam Bowie*, was an okay pro who battled leg injuries for many years. Michael Jordan quickly ascended as one of the league's best players, and would eventually become the greatest basketball player of all-time.

22.

Remember when we did the Kobe-LeBron thing and I defined their defensive peak as the seasons between when they were first and last top ten in Defensive Player of the Year voting? Let's play that game with MJ to demonstrate what a different planet Jordan was on in regard to the recognition of his defensive ability. LeBron finished top ten in DPOY six times—all six seasons of his peak between 2008-09' and 2013-14'. Kobe finished top ten in DPOY four times—across select seasons between 1999-00' and 2007-08'. With the exception of his rookie year, Mike finished in the top *eight* for DPOY during *each full season of his Chicago Bulls career*:

- o   1984-85' [rookie season]
- o   1985-86' [broken foot, only played 18 games total]
- o   1986-87' [8th]
- o   1987-88' [1st]
- o   1988-89' [5th]

---

[295] You can hear some of the tracks from the Decca demo on The Beatles' *Anthology 1*. To some degree, there are differing accounts of what actually transpired between Decca and Brian Epstein regarding The Beatles audition on New Year's Day 1962. It's been said that The Beatles weren't at their best during the session, but It does seem pretty clear that Decca had The Beatles in their pocket if they wanted them .. and they let them go.

[296] LOL. Put a pin in the MJ-Drexler stuff.

- 1989-90' [5th]
- 1990-91' [7th]
- 1991-92' [3rd]
- 1992-93' [2nd]
- 1993-94' [baseball]
- 1994-95' [baseball, only played final 17 games]
- 1995-96' [6th]
- 1996-97' [5th]
- 1997-98' [4th]

Get the actual mother fuck outta here! Not only is he one of a very small number of perimeter players to ever win DPOY, but to be consistently in the running as a guard is utterly inconceivable in any era.

21.

I think we all know why MJ came back to the NBA and played for the Wizards, but I try not to think about it. Someone as competitive as Mike couldn't stay away for too long, and I'm sure in his own mind he actually thought he could will that zombie Wizard roster to a title. I think it sucks we had to bookend his career with a diluted reunion tour in a jersey that wasn't black, red and white. It sucks that we saw Emmitt Smith in a Cardinals uniform, Hakeem Olajuwon in a Raptors jersey, Jerry Rice play for the Seahawks, Tony Parker play for anyone but the Spurs and I'll throw my TV out the window before I see Tom Brady in a fucking Buccaneers jersey. The common thread is that successful athletes commonly want to keep competing after it makes business sense for the brand that forged their aesthetic to keep them around. That wasn't really the case with Jordan—he chose to walk away after hitting that famous jumper over Bryon Russell, but the itch to compete brought him back a few years later. His two seasons with the Wizards are a net neutral to his legacy, and in some ways his ability to still play high level basketball at the tender age of 38 and 39 are additive to his legacy in the opinion of some basketball thinkers. To me, keeping your legacy to one metropolitan city and within a singular color scheme is always for the best. I wish Mike would have corralled his competitive tendencies and rode off into the sunset in June of 1998, but that's not the way that dude is wired.

20.

Which is why there's no way in hell that we know the full truth behind why Michael Jordan left the NBA on October 6th, 1993. Just imagine an alien has come to earth for the first time and you're supposed to lay out for them the version of events we're supposed to believe when it comes to why Michael Jordan left basketball at the apex of his cache and ability:

> **Earthling:** Here on earth, we like to participate in recreational, athletic activities to pass the time. If you're good enough at one of those activities, in rare cases, that can be your means of making a living on

our planet. My favorite game is one called basketball where participants work as a team to get a round object into a net more times than the other team. So, one time, this basketball player, Michael Jordan, he became the greatest basketball player on earth, and he liked nothing more than beating everyone else at basketball. Then one day, when he was by-far the best basketball player on earth, he decided that he didn't want to play basketball anymore.

Alien: Seems like you're not telling me the whole story.

On October 6ᵗʰ, 1993, Michael Jordan decided to walk away from basketball because he didn't have anything left to prove. Given MJ's towering status as a global icon, the public was prone to digest this narrative. He was the most dominant two-way player that anyone had ever seen. His marketability not only brought him landmark sponsorships with Gatorade and Nike, but the NBA discovered through Michael that there was dynamic commercial potential in deliberately marketing individual players versus the teams themselves. Throw in the fact that MJ's father had been murdered just two months prior, and quite frankly, we were eating out of Michael's hand in that moment—Mike could have said that he was starting a grunge rock band, and the tour would have sold out before the October 6ᵗʰ, 1993 press conference was over.

During that presser that officially announced his retirement, he also provided this very believable proclamation for why he might want to step away from the game—*I've always stressed to people that have known me, and the media that has followed me, that when I lose the sense of motivation and the sense to prove something as a basketball player, it's time for me to move away from the game of basketball.* That sentiment was good enough for just about everyone in 1993. MJ could do no wrong, and we took him at face value.

I don't think I'm crossing any lines by saying that we didn't know then what we know now about Michael Jordan. That press conference, which is on YouTube in its hour-long glory, is about the strangest thing I've ever watched. The broadcast is from the metro-Chicago NBC affiliate, so naturally, the gravity around the situation was not just heightened because a local network was covering Chicago's prodigal son, but also the broadcast team was especially amenable to believe every word that came out of Jordan's mouth.

Watching through that presser, I couldn't deny the duality of personas I was forced to make sense of. The version of MJ that I've come to understand, and make no mistake, have also come to devoutly appreciate, is a ruthless, savage competitor. Someone that not just relishes winning, but embarrassing and demoralizing his opponents in the process. Someone that would pay off a baggage handler in the baggage claim area of the Portland airport to ensure his bag would come out first, allowing him to swindle his *Dream Team* teammates on a wager of whose bag would come out first.[297] The version of MJ that I've come to understand had a

---

[297] That's a real story. On the way back from the 1992 Olympics, MJ paid off a baggage handler at the Portland airport to make sure his bag came out first. Waiting for the bags to come out, MJ whipped out a $100 bill and

gambling habit that was just as much a part of him as was his basketball habit—without Mike's unchained desire to gamble on everything you could feasibly gamble on, you don't get Michael Jordan, top-of-the-food-chain basketball player—they're inexorable from one another.[298] In front of all the microphones on October 6th, 1993 was a version of Michael Jordan that was saying with a suspiciously straight face that he didn't have anything left to prove in basketball, that his father's murder had no bearing on his decision, and that he was looking forward to 'watching the grass grow' and 'relaxing' in retirement. Every icon-level athlete learns to sanitize their media responses and to project the most digestible, politician-esque portrait of themselves during interviews. I just don't buy it. It runs against every single point of data we've gathered on Mike over the years. In 1993, maybe we were blinded by the sheer glare of his celebrity and overwhelming basketball ability, but if we've learning anything about Michael Jordan over the years, it's that there's no way in hell he walks away from the game at the absolute crest of his basketball and cultural influence.

I knew I was going to touch on Michael's first retirement, and god dammit if I didn't fall all the way down the rabbit hole after trying to tip-toe around it. When MJ took the podium to retire in the fall of 1993, there had already been huge red flags about both the type of people his gambling led him to associate with, and the stunning commitment he was routinely making just to gamble. The public was going to believe whatever Jordan said that day because he was such a beloved figure. Whether or not his retirement was part of a spectacular conspiracy or not, there was a darker figure that existed within the plastic, wholesome, camouflaged version of Jordan that expected everyone to believe that 'the thrill was gone'. To me, the simple fact that he was capable of embodying such drastically different characters is what breathes life into such a conspiracy. Far be it from me to pass judgement on the guy for the activities that make up his private life, but don't expect me to take my medicine when the version of MJ that we all familiarized ourselves with would die before handing over the keys that drove the fast-paced life style he was addicted to. So, here's the other narrative:

On October 6th, 1993, Michael Jordan announced his retirement in accordance with a secret agreement struck with then NBA Commissioner, David Stern. Sitting to Michael's left during that press conference was his wife, Juanita, to whom he was married from 1989 to 2006. To her left was David Stern. Jordan wasn't the only majorly impactful NBA figure to begin their tenure in 1984—David Stern also took over as NBA commissioner. They always had a close relationship during Michael and NBA popularity's correlative ascent. If such a nefarious and secret pact could have been struck, their relationship had the equity to conceivably do so. At the end of the public announcement, Jordan was asked if he would ever return to the NBA, to

---

openly wagered to his teammates that his bag would come out first because 'he was the biggest star'. He got nine undisclosed members of the Dream Team to take him up on the bet, and sure enough his bag came out first.

[298] There's a shot I just have to shoot here. I couldn't help but make a Don Draper comparison. Don was so great at being an advertising executive that he took on a mysterious, almost mythical status to those that worked under him. The problems of his personal life were always covered up by his powerful voice in the advertising community and his uncanny ability to creatively mitigate problems for his firm. But maybe his success at work and lack of success with marriage aren't separate—maybe he needed the affairs, rye whiskey benders and debauchery to propel him forward in his career?

which he said—*5 years down the line, if that urge comes back, if the Bulls will have me, if David Stern lets me back in the league, that's an option that I'll never close on*—I don't think the Stern comment is nearly as damning as many online conspiracy theorists do, but he did follow the statement with the exact same cring-ey face you make when you remember that awkward comment you made two years ago.

It's unclear when MJ's gambling reached an obsessive level, but as early as the summer of 1986, he was beginning to associate with shadowy North Carolina-based characters in pursuit of his gambling fix. MJ met James 'Slim' Bouler that summer and according to Slim, they golfed together in the ballpark of 50 times between 1986 and 1991. Their meetups would typically involve golfing during the day and high-stakes card games at night where it was common for each guy to cover one another depending on who had more cash. Allegedly, Bouler failed to mention that he was a convicted cocaine dealer, and when he was apprehended in October 1991 on 12 counts of drug conspiracy, firearms possession and money laundering charges, among his assets that were seized was a $57,000 cashier's check signed by Michael Jordan. MJ originally claimed the money was a loan for Bouler to build a driving range, but when Jordan was forced to testify, under oath, in October 1992, he admitted that it was to cover a gambling debt.

Jordan's involvement with another questionable-at-best metro-Charlotte character came to light a few months after Jordan's cashier's check to Bouler was discovered. In February 1992, a bail bondsman named Eddie Dow was gunned down in the carport of his home near Charlotte. The four assailants, including one young man who had previously worked for Dow, took $20,000 from his briefcase. Also in his briefcase were three cashier's checks, totaling $108,000, that were signed by Michael Jordan, and payable to Dow and two other Charlotte-area characters for gambling debts. Dow was known in the area as a gambler, hustler, and to have arranged many high-stakes card games. MJ's John Hancock on those checks prompted the NBA to investigate Jordan's gambling activity—both in regard to the overall breadth of his gambling, but also to ensure he wasn't gambling on NBA games. On March 31st, 1992, after bringing Michael in and providing his assurance that he would be more selective with whom he shared his company, the NBA concluded the investigation and absolved Jordan of any wrongdoing.

One year later, in May of 1993, Jordan's Bulls were matched up against the New York Knicks in the 1993 Eastern Conference Finals. Jordan left his team between game one and game two to go to Atlantic City for the night, where he was seen gambling until 3:00am, making it back to New York sometime the next day before game two tipped off.[299] There were a handful of reports like this, to which Jordan frequently justified by saying some version of him being 'too wound up to sleep'.

Shortly after the Bulls beat the Knicks, and throughout June of 1993, Jordan was plagued by more allegations related to gambling. A 38-year-old San Diego sports executive named Richard

---

[299] Jordan was 12 for 32 from the field in a game two loss. Down 0-2, Jordan went 3 for 18 from the field in game three, but the Bulls won the game in large part to 29 from Scottie Pippen on 10 of 12 from the field.

Esquinas published a book that month entitled *Michael & Me: Our Gambling Addiction...My Cry For Help!* The book detailed a gambling-driven lifestyle that included private jets, cards, girls, late nights and early mornings dedicated to golfing. Their shared gambling habit led them to do so in San Diego, around Jordan's Hilton Head condo, around the Charlotte area in North Carolina and even around metro-Chicago. The most damning allegation, and ostensibly Esquinas' purpose in publishing the book was the claim that MJ refused to pay the $1.2 million-dollar debt that he owed the San Diego resident. He elaborated by saying that he'd negotiated the debt down to $300k with MJ, in an attempt to recoup some of the winnings. Jordan, when pressed publicly, admitted to the $300k claim, but scoffed that the debt was ever close to the alleged $1.2M. The NBA responded by bringing back Frederick Lacey, a former federal judge and also the individual tasked to conduct the investigation in March of 1992, to open up another investigation into Jordan's gambling activity.

The cast of shadowy characters in Jordan's gambling life, that we know about, to say nothing of the one's we don't know about, were never going to drag down his reputation. He was Michael Jordan, and all he had to do was remind people that he was Michael Jordan, that they were shadowy characters, and they would ultimately get brushed aside. Later that summer, across 23 days, a very strange saga played out around the death of James Jordan—Michael Jordan's father:

- July 22nd, 1993—The last time Michael Jordan's father was seen alive, as he drove away from a co-worker's funeral in Wilmington, North Carolina. [300] James Jordan left around midnight to start the 3 ½ hour drive back to Charlotte.
- July 23rd—Around 2am, he pulled off the road to take a nap in Robeson County.
  - At some point that night, James Jordan is shot once through his chest and killed.
  - Teenage friends Daniel Green and Larry Demery heist Jordan's red Lexus, and later dispose of his body in a swamp, 30 miles away in McColl, South Carolina.
  - Among 36 phone calls made from Jordan's car phone, which ultimately led to Green and Demery's capture, a call is made to Hubert Larry Deese, the son of then Robeson County Sheriff, Hubert Stone—whose office conducted the investigation of Jordan's murder.
- July 26th—Jordan's car is stripped and dumped near Fayetteville, North Carolina.
- August 3rd—Jordan's body is found, but unidentified and listed as a John Doe.
- August 5th—Police are notified of the stripped-down Lexus in Fayetteville.
- August 7th—Jordan's body is cremated by a South Carolina coroner as a John Doe.
- August 12th—Jordan's family files a missing-persons report.
- August 13th—Jordan's body is identified using dental records.

---

[300] Wilmington is where the Jordan family grew up. If James Jordan were apprehended the night he disappeared, it's conceivable that contacts in Wilmington knew of his whereabouts and plans.

On October 6ᵗʰ, 1993, after a few days of swirling rumors, Michael Jordan publicly retired from the NBA. He didn't bring up baseball once during the press conference, and he claimed that his father's death had nothing to do with his decision.

On October 9ᵗʰ, 1993, the NBA announces that the probe into Jordan's gambling had completed with the determination that no wrong-doing had occurred.

Okay. I'm not a detective, and I need to start by saying that the unusual circumstances of Jordan's father's death don't have to be related to Jordan's penchant for consorting with sketchy figures across North Carolina and South Carolina. They could be related, but you might have to squint to get there.

The circumstances of what happened the night of the murder are only truly known by the two who were charged with the murder—whose stories naturally don't line up, and it's clear one or both tried to flip on the other—so, I don't think it's worthwhile to pry at the hearsay details of how Jordan wound up dead. The phone call to the Robeson County Sheriff's son, however, was clearly linked to some level of funny business that was never further investigated. The Sheriff's son, Hubert Larry Deese, was a known drug trafficker in the area. 7 months after James Jordan's murder, he was put away for 10 years on drug trafficking charges that linked him directly to Colombia. But somehow, Deese was never questioned during the investigation. Even after receiving a call on a dead man's phone from the two people who were convicted of the murder. Even more, in the early 2000s, the Robeson County Sheriff's office was the subject of a federal corruption probe entitled 'Operation Tarnished Badge'. The probe led to 22 officers being charged with varying combinations of money laundering, perjury and drug trafficking.

The other part that's rather sticky is how there wasn't a missing-persons report filed for James Jordan until 21 days after he actually went missing—how the hell does *that* happen? It took some very clever internet research to determine that, while James was still legally married to Michael's mother, Deloris, reportedly, they were living in different locations in the Charlotte area at the time of Jordan's death. That was an important discovery, and definitely made it feasible for Jordan to be uncontacted for 21 days before he was reported missing. Although, July 31ˢᵗ, 1993 would have been Jordan's 57ᵗʰ birthday, but he wasn't reported missing for another 12 days?

So, if you were writing the 8-episode Netflix series around the conspiracy behind Michael Jordan's 1993 retirement—which, I think we can agree would be incredible—what is the underlying theory you'd attempt to lay out? The showrunners would have to create a link between the shady Robeson County Sheriff's office and not only someone Jordan had gambled with, but someone Jordan had lost to, and someone who Jordan was refusing to pay—someone who wanted to hurt MJ, and was connected enough to make it happen. I suppose the showrunners would also have to make the nature of James Jordan's actual murder premeditated, which seems difficult given the circumstances—the crime is hard to spin as anything other than an armed robbery gone wrong, or maybe a kidnapping gone wrong if you stretch some of the crime scene inconsistencies. Perhaps though, once James Jordan (or his unique car with the vanity plate, UNC0023) was identified, it's conceivable that a ransom plot unfolded (that would play with why his disappearance wasn't reported for three weeks). Or maybe intercepting James Jordan on his way back from that funeral was the plan the whole time by some backwoods crooked Sheriff's office and a few teenage knuckleheads that carried it out and ultimately took the wrap.

We'll never know for sure because those two kids were the only (known) witnesses to the murder, but there's a chance one of those knuckleheads will walk free at some point in the future. Daniel Green, who has always maintained that while he assisted in disposing of the body, wasn't present when Jordan was murdered, has a good chance at getting a re-trial because of how horribly the investigation was conducted by the Robeson County Sheriff's office. Those sound like semantics to me and he's still guilty as fuck, but he does keep the door cracked open on the conspiracy by repeating for the last 30 years that he and his accomplice were 'just pawns in a game'.

I have to let it go at this point, because I'm two degrees of separation from launching a true-crime podcast because of this shit, and if I continue to follow the open threads I still have, my wife might actually kill *me* for workshopping all the various angles of the crime to her. Pulling up these harsh realities might be hurtful to anyone that was close to the heinous crime, regardless of what actually happened that night. If you find any of this to be disrespectful, I'm sorry, but I felt that getting into the granular details of the case was better than slopping together some favorable narrative that subjectively favored the conspiracy.

Was MJ's father killed because of an unpaid debt to someone who was connected with a sketchy backwoods cop shop in rural North Carolina? I have my doubts, but it's certainly possible. Both sketchy characters that were found with gambling debt checks signed by MJ were North Carolina guys, meaning that Mike was, at minimum, visible in some shady circles around Charlotte and maybe beyond. One thing I do know is that things were just easier to get away with before the internet-era, and I'm not talking about the circumstances of James Jordan's death. I'm talking about his son galivanting around the country for gambling binges with all manner of shady characters—that shit isn't possible for C-List celebrities today, much less the 6'6" *most famous person in the world*. Michael Jordan's pathological competitiveness was much darker than I thought, even if his gambling and extracurriculars had nothing to do with his old man's death. His greatness on the court insulated him from the perils that come with surrounding yourself with criminals. But winning is the magic pill in our culture. There's no end to the nice things people will say about you if you continue to win. Everything else gets pushed aside. Everything.

19.

Per the NBA rulebook—a steal is credited to a player that legally takes the ball away from an opponent, intercepts a pass, or otherwise obtains possession of the ball following an opponent's turnover (provided the ball has remained in bounds and the clock has not stopped). If a player deflects a pass or dribble and controls his deflection either away from an opponent or towards a teammate resulting in eventual possession for the defense, the player causing the deflection is credited with the steal.

Steals are kind of a weird stat. The multi-term incumbent marker of a quality perimeter defender ran unopposed for decades, but tracking data, on-off figures, hustle stats and the requirement in the pace-and-space era for more nuanced observational techniques have challenged exactly what a steal says about a player's defensive ability. The stat that I predict to emerge most prominently will be deflections. Beginning with 2016-17', the stat has been tracked as part of NBA.com's Hustle Stats dashboard, and because steals are only credited to a player if the deflection results in his team's possession, it may be a more complete defensive activity metric. But while deflections are a good marker for how active a player's arms are, James Harden finishing second in deflections during the 2018-19' season demonstrates how fraught a measurement it is for how active a player's legs are.

The most fraught way to apply steal figures to a player's defensive profile is to elevate their defensive reputation if they lead the league in steals once, or have a few seasons where they rank toward the top of the league. For instance, Steph led the league in steals during his virtuoso 2015-16' season, but reasonably speaking, of the 5 teammates he played with the most—Klay Thompson, Harrison Barnes, Draymond Green, Andrew Bogut and Andre Iguodala— Steph is the least dynamic defender overall (considering Klay, Draymond, Bogut and Iggy have all made All-Defensive teams). Steph's steal numbers are steady and reliable over the years, but they peaked in 2014-15' and 2015-16', perhaps when those Warriors were flying around the court it created more live ball turnovers. And again, he certainly benefited from playing with a supporting cast of high-level, multi-talented defenders. Steal numbers are more indicative of quality defenders when they routinely finish toward the top of the league. Chris Paul, insane defender, led the league in steals 6 out of 7 seasons between 2007-08' and 2013-14'. John Stockton, maniacally consistent guard defender, finished top ten in steals 15 of his 19 seasons in the league, and holds the all-time record for steals. Michael Jordan was an unbelievable defender—both on-ball, and a doctorate-level, ball-denial maestro off-ball. With the exception of his final two seasons in Chicago, MJ finished top five in steals for each full season he played with the Bulls (landing him third on the all-time steals list):

- 1984-85' [4th]
- 1986-87' [2nd]
- 1987-88' [1st]
- 1988-89' [2nd]
- 1989-90' [1st]
- 1990-91' [3rd]
- 1991-92' [4th]
- 1992-93' [1st]
- 1995-96' [3rd]

18.

To say nothing of how bad Charlotte has been under his leadership, Jordan's entry into NBA ownership was a brilliant and prudent move. BET founder and the first African American billionaire, Robert L. Johnson, also became the first majority African American owner in U.S. major professional sports when his ownership group paid a $300 million expansion fee to see the Charlotte Bobcats enter the NBA for the 2004-05' season. After the 2005-06' season, a deal was struck for Michael Jordan to not only become a minority owner, but for him to also head up basketball operations. Under Johnson's ownership, it's said that the team was losing around $20 million per season. In 2010, Johnson decided to sell the team to MJ, as so much of Johnson's wealth was tied up in non-liquid assets and he'd burned through too much of his cash through ownership of a flailing NBA franchise. Jordan only had to put up $25 million in the transaction that landed him as the franchise's majority owner because the remainder of the team's $275 million valuation was the assumption of debt from Johnson's ownership. The NBA board of governors had no problem with the unusual circumstances of the sale because Michael Jordan owning a team was always going to be positive for the league.

Coup is probably a more appropriate term than sale for how MJ ended up the primary owner of an NBA franchise. But whether it was a calculated business move or just being in the right place at the right time, the investment clearly paid off as the Charlotte Hornets were valued at $1.5 billion in February 2020 by Forbes.

17.

When you win, you don't have to answer questions.. but ..there's a dirty little secret about Jordan's success in the 1990s. To even speak of it could be heresy, because winning is winning, and I subscribe to that too. However, it's undeniable that the league's talent cupboard was desperately empty toward the end of the 1990s. On top of that, between the 1985-86' and 1995-96' seasons, the league expanded from 23 to 29 teams, so whatever talent was coming into the league was being further spread out across several new franchises. Using career Win Shares, let's look at the top 20 players to come out of the NBA drafts between 1986 and 1994, and the top 20 players to come out of the NBA drafts between 1995 and 2003:

Drafted 1986-1994	Career Win Shares	Drafted 1995-2003	Career Win Shares
Shaquille O'Neal (1992)	181.7	LeBron James (2003)	236.4
David Robinson (1987)	178.7	Tim Duncan (1997)	206.4
Reggie Miller (1987)	174.4	Dirk Nowitzki (1998)	206.3
Gary Payton (1990)	145.5	Kevin Garnett (1995)	191.4
Jason Kidd (1994)	138.6	Kobe Bryant (1996)	172.7
Scottie Pippen (1987)	125.1	Paul Pierce (1998)	150.0
Horace Grant (1987)	118.2	Ray Allen (1996)	145.1
Dikembe Mutombo (1991)	117.0	Pau Gasol (2001)	144.1
Jeff Hornacek (1986)	108.9	Steve Nash (1996)	129.7

Eddie Jones (1994)	100.6	Vince Carter (1998)	125.3
Grant Hill (1994)	99.9	Shawn Marion (1999)	124.9
Vlade Divac (1989)	96.4	Chauncey Billups (1997)	120.8
Kevin Johnson (1987)	92.8	Dwayne Wade (2003)	120.7
Mark Jackson (1987)	91.8	Tony Parker (2001)	111.3
Hersey Hawkins (1988)	90.6	Elton Brand (1999)	109.6
Dennis Rodman (1986)	89.8	Manu Ginóbili (1999)	106.4
P.J. Brown (1992)	89.8	Chris Bosh (2003)	106.0
Alonzo Mourning (1992)	89.7	Rasheed Wallace (1995)	105.1
Glen Rice (1989)	88.7	Tyson Chandler (2001)	102.1
Sam Cassell (1993)	87.5	Jason Terry (1999)	102.0
	2,305.7		**2,816.0**

No doubt the 1995 through 2003 drafts ushered in a golden generation for the NBA—shit, Allen Iverson and Carmelo Anthony didn't even qualify here. Comparatively, let's focus on the top of both of these lists for a minute. After Magic and Kareem's Lakers, Bird's Celtics and the *Bad Boy* Pistons had all petered out, there simply weren't any players left that were great enough to be the best player on a championship team. It wasn't Drexler, it wasn't Barkley, it wasn't Malone, and it might have been Olajuwon, but he peaked and won his titles in the two seasons that Jordan was playing baseball. In my estimation, and you'll probably agree with me, that of the players drafted between 1986 and 1994, only Shaq would prove capable of being the best player on a championship team. Conversely, the first five players listed in the 1995-2003 group *all proved* that they were capable of being the best player on a championship team. Even more, 3 of the 20 best players drafted between 1986 and 1994 were enormous contributors to Chicago championships—Horace Grant was a key player for the 1991, 1992 and 1993 titles, Rodman was instrumental to the 1996, 1997 and 1998 titles, and Scottie Pippen was the second best player for all six championships.

Players Drafted 1986-1994		Players Drafted 1995-2003
27	Championships	39
15	Championships (without MJ)	39
2	League MVPs	12

Without question, it was a weak generation of players who were uniquely spread out across a rapidly expanding league, and some of the best players from that group were fighting with Jordan instead of preventing him from winning more championships. This chasm in NBA talent and the overall lack of dominant teams helped Jordan succeed during the first Chicago three-peat, but it really manifested during the second three-peat. Give the late 90s Jazz teams credit—they outlasted Barkley's Suns, Hakeem's Rockets, Payton's Sonics and Robinson's Spurs with their core intact and a model for winning that worked against everyone in the league .. except for Jordan's Bulls. But if Stockton and Malone in the middle of their 30's were MJ's greatest adversary—doesn't that say as much about the state of the NBA as it does about Mike's dominance?

The subtext here is how many more all-time great players LeBron James had to mitigate on his path toward championships than Michael Jordan did—in that context we're not done with this conversation. But for now—you may just attribute Mike's own greatness to there not being teams great enough to challenge his own, but I think we may want to re-think that to a certain degree, and acknowledge that he benefited from a noticeable lack of competition.

16.

I grew up in the late 1990s and believe me when I say that it was harder then to familiarize yourself with NBA rosters outside of your home team's. I was introduced to a broader NBA universe through the same medium as many kids my age—video games. Dating back to 1973, there had been roughly 45 basketball-themed video games released prior to *NBA Jam* changing the game in 1993. Shortly after that, games that had full NBA rosters starting coming out like *NBA Live 95'*. For me, *NBA In The Zone 2,* which came out in November 1996 on my beloved original PlayStation, introduced me fully to the world of the NBA.

Well, not fully. Because as much as I loved playing with prime Penny Hardaway, or rocking the Jazz because Jeff Hornacek's three-ball was totally unfair, I wanted to play as MJ, duh! It kind of made sense to me when I was a kid because he towered over the basketball world in every way and maybe he was just too good to be in the game (?). Turns out that his exclusive rights deal with Nike caused him to opt-out of the NBA Players Association group license that allowed NBA players likenesses to be used for endeavors such as video games.

NBA Live 96' embedded a cheat code that would allow you to play as MJ, but the NBAPA got wise to it and shut it down. From then on you would get the generic players in place of stars whose likenesses weren't allowed to be in the game—i.e. 'shooting guard #23 for the Chicago Bulls'. Into the 2000s, playable Jordan characters became more available after he retired. In *NBA Live 2000,* MJ appeared as the final boss in the 'one-on-one' mode, and you were able to play as him after beating him. *NBA Street* (2001) also implemented Jordan as a boss character (alongside Steph Marbury and Rafer Alston—yikes—2001 NBA, ladies and gentlemen). *NBA Street Vol. 2* (2003) offered three different Jordan versions—1986 Bulls, 1996 Bulls and the topical 2003 Wizards versions. Finally, *NBA 2K11* broke it wide open by allowing you to play as the super realistic version of Jordan—the tongue, the hands on the hips, the shorts, the ferocity—and he's been available in every version of the franchise since.

By far the best story regarding MJ and video games surrounded *NBA Jam* in the mid-90s. In an August 2019 interview, Tim Kitzrow, the iconic voice of the *NBA Jam* games, said that Michael Jordan, Gary Payton and Ken Griffey Jr. all wanted to be in the game very badly but MJ was held back for the reasons I mentioned, Payton hadn't yet been developed into the game and Griffey .. uh .. wasn't in the NBA. However, in response to their desire to be in the game, *NBA Jam's* developers created a version that included all three athletes and sent copies to each of them. Legend has it only 4 or 5 copies of that custom version of *NBA Jam* exist in the world.

15.

We can all agree that there have been a lot of contemporary discussions about rest and load management. I'm not sure where I land, but I do lean toward the opinion that the way the game is played now with all the cutting, running and closeouts, players are at a much higher risk of injury than when the game was slower and less sophisticated schematically. Sometimes when someone is engaged in this ongoing debate, they'll reference the fact that Mike Jordan was able to play virtually every game without rest, so 'why shouldn't everyone else be able to?' Well, simply put, there was only one MJ, and his extraterrestrial physical durability should never be the model for other mere mortals.

Jordan only missed seven regular season games, and never missed a playoff game.[301] He played all 82 games eight times out of twelve full seasons with the Bulls, including starting every single game of the Bulls 1996-1998 three-peat. It's hard to fathom how many hangovers and downright buzzes he played through. There was something that drove him that no one can really understand, and it helped that he was also a thermo-nuclear physical specimen, bio-engineered to play shooting guard.

14.

For all the things Mike was great at, it's easy, at least for me, to sometimes forget what a raw athlete he was. When you watch him on tape there are two dimensions to his athleticism that leap off the screen (pun intended).

1) [The First Step] It's genuinely a thing of beauty. Even the best defenders of their respective time—Joe Dumars, Sidney Moncrief, Dennis Johnson, Michael Cooper, Alvin Robertson—they were all powerless to stay in front of 1987-1993 Michael Jordan. He weaponized his first step to get himself countless jumpers, clear lanes to the rim and continual mismatches for an unprepared defense.

2) [The Hangtime] Another thing of beauty. His ability to hang in the air on approach to the rim allowed him to shift according to his defender's position. As impressive as the dunks are, the rim attacks where he shifts, then re-shifts, his weight to position himself for a lay-in might be even more impressive. On jumpers, his ability to hang in the air allowed him to make last-minute passes to an open teammate, and also made his shot virtually impossible to adequately defend.

This got me thinking about the most purely athletic players in the history of the NBA. Using very anecdotal markers for speed, dexterity, leaping ability and strength, I decided to put together my first, second and third 'All-Athlete' teams across the history of the NBA.

First-Team

---

[301] Excluding the season he broke his foot, the vastly shortened season during which he returned from baseball, and the Wizard years.

(PG) Russ Westbrook [2015]
(SG) Michael Jordan [1988]
(SF) LeBron James [2009]
(PF) Giannis Antetokounmpo [2020]
(C) Kareem Abdul-Jabbar [1972]

Second-Team
(PG) Derrick Rose [2011]
(SG) Kobe Bryant [2002]
(SF) Julius Erving [1977]
(PF) Kevin Garnett [2002]
(C) Wilt Chamberlain [1962]

Third-Team
(PG) Luka Dončić [2020][302]
(SG) Dwayne Wade [2006]
(SF) David Thompson [1978]
(PF) Dennis Rodman [1990]
(C) Shaquille O'Neal [2000]

13.

We all miss Kobe in one way or another. Personally, I'd been so hunkered down in the trench warfare of convincing people that LeBron was a greater player that it blinded me to what an incredible human we had in Kobe. All the people I look up to embody so many of the traits that constituted Kobe's personality, especially the version we got to see of Kobe after his playing career—less competitive psychopath and more relatable visionary. Kobe's death impacted me way more than I could have expected, and most of me refuses to believe he's gone because his legacy lives on in my mind, in this book and in the memories of anyone that gave half a shit about sports over the past two and half decades.

For Michael Jordan, losing Kobe had to of felt like losing a child. Kobe was Mike's most devout disciple. Kobe's career was virtually an homage to MJ.

[Record Scratch] Color me a cynic, but Jordan gave Kobe his blessing because he knew that Kobe wasn't going to surpass his legacy through a karaoke-ed version of himself. With all due respect to their relationship, which ostensibly was close, it's obvious to me that Jordan saw Kobe's career as a stylistic tribute to himself. I know it sounds unsavory and I don't doubt that losing Kobe was difficult for MJ, but can we be honest with ourselves here? Jordan is still the guy that doesn't give anyone credit in the NBA world because he refuses to dilute his own accomplishments in any kind of meaningful way. He's never given LeBron the time of day

---

[302] Laugh if you must, but athleticism isn't just 'going', 'jumping' and 'sprinting'. Being able to decelerate and/or stop is a marker for athleticism too. No one does it better than Luka.

because he's known all along that Bron posed a genuine threat to his legacy. But because Kobe's approach and methodology so resembled Michael's, yet was always bound to fall short—because no one 'out MJ's MJ'—Jordan chose to support Kobe, because it ultimately supported his own legacy.

12.

There are so many juicy Michael Jordan stories. We already hit on perhaps my favorite—when he paid off a baggage handler to ensure his bag would come out first at baggage claim, allowing him to wager against his teammates, while they waited for their bags to come, on whose bag would come out first. That's some cold shit.

Instead of force-feeding you a list of MJ stories that you've probably already heard, I have one story that you may not have heard that seems to best illuminate the maniacal competitive spirit of Mike Jordan. In November of 2019, NHL great, Jeremy Roenick, went on the *McNeil & Parkins Show*—a Chicago-based sports talk radio show. Roenick, who was a mega-famous super athlete in his own right in the early 1990s, recalled a time that Jordan and he golfed, gambled and drank the morning of a Bulls' home game:

> *Meet me at Sunset Ridge, early. We're gonna go play 18 holes.*
>
> *We played a round, I beat him for a couple thousand and got ready to leave. Now, the Bulls are playing that night. They played Cleveland that night. I'm thinking he's leaving, it's 10 o'clock. He goes, 'No, let's go play again'.*
>
> *So, we go and fill up a bag full of ice and Coors Light and walk again. We roll around another 18 and I take him for another couple. Now we've been drinking all afternoon and he's going from Sunset Ridge to the stadium to play a game. I'm messing around, I'm like, 'I'm gonna call my bookie. All the money you just lost to me, I'm putting on Cleveland'. He goes 'I'll tell you what. I'll bet you that we'll win by 20 points and I have more than 40'. I'm like 'done'. Son of a gun goes out and scores 52 and they win by 26 points or something.*
>
> *He had maybe 10 beers. The man, Michael Jordan to me, is probably the best athlete I've ever seen.*

The story didn't *fully* check out, as he must have been referring to the March 28th, 1992 Chicago home game in which MJ got *44* points on 21 of 32 from the field, and the Bulls beat the Cavs by *24* points. Crazy mother fucker still won the bet.

11.

Similar to the volume of Jordan stories out there, trying to compile a list of Jordan's finest moments is a pretty challenging exercise. I'd made a note to do so for LeBron's profile, but it would have been more self-serving than anything else. I profiled his finest moment at the beginning of the book—the moment Bron took charge of his legacy, the moment he said 'enough is enough' against Boston in game six of the 2012 Eastern Conference Finals. For Jordan, take your pick:

- *The Ehlo Shot*—1989 Eastern Conference 1st round—when he basically hit two consecutive series-winning shots, the last at the buzzer to eliminate the Cavs. If you Google 'The Shot', the moment is properly immortalized and recognized by the internet as that singular moment.
- *The 1998 Walk-off*—1998 NBA Finals'—when he steals the ball from Karl Malone on the defensive end, and struts into retirement on the crest of an NBA championship-winning shot over Bryon Russell.
- *'God disguised as Michael Jordan' game*—1986 Eastern Conference first-round—MJ gives the 86' Celtics 63 points in a 135-131 double overtime loss.[303] Bird said after the game he was the best player he'd ever seen, and that 'it's just God disguised as Michael Jordan'.

There are a dozen moments you could cherry pick from Jordan's career that could rightfully serve as his finest moment. For me there is one that stands above the rest. One that tests and proves the theory of Mike's drive that constituted his immaculate invulnerability. You may remember it as game five of the 1997 NBA Finals', but you definitely remember it as 'The Flu Game'. Let's set the stage.

John Stockton and Karl Malone's first NBA Finals' berth in 1997 was the result of their steady consistency throughout the 1990s. They routinely found themselves in the mix but after reaching the Western Conference Finals in 1992, 1994, and the year before in 1996, they fell short of the NBA Finals' to Drexler's Blazers, Hakeem's Rockets and Payton's Sonics in respective order. Leading into game one, Utah swept the Clippers in the first round, beat the baby Shaq & Kobe Lakers in the second round, and took down the Hakeem-Barkley-Drexler fake super team in six games during the Western Conference Finals. When the NBA Finals' tipped off on June 1st, 1997, Stockton (35) and Malone (33) were entering their respective final chapters. Having already established distinguished statistical careers, they were seeking the ultimate and final validation.

MJ, Pippen, Rodman and crew were all more than validated, but their 72-win championship-winning 1995-96' masterpiece season didn't stop them from following it up with 69 wins in 1996-97'. They entered the 1997 postseason as heavy championship favorites, and they made

---

[303] This was the year Jordan broke his foot, but was able to come back for the playoffs, and despite a 0-3 series loss to Boston, he certainly foreshadowed what was on the horizon for the NBA.

pretty quick work of the Eastern Conference—they swept the Washington Bullets in the first round, then spotted Atlanta and Miami each a game in consecutive five-game series' wins before reaching the NBA Finals' once again. It was Chicago's fifth NBA Finals' in seven seasons, and with MJ at the tip of the spear, they were looking to extend their perfect record. For Mike specifically, the Jazz were a new group of players for him to dominate on the highest stage— Utah was the fifth Finals' opponent in Mike's five Finals' appearances up to that point. Jordan was eager to slam the door shut on whatever hope Stockton and Malone were holding onto that it was *their* time.

Game one was a bloodbath. The score was tied 10 different times and there were 23 lead changes over the course of the game. In the final moments of an 82-82 tie, a missed Stockton three resulted in a loose ball foul on Rodman—putting Karl Malone on the line for a pair of free throws with 9 seconds left in the game. Malone misses both—a tough look for my guy—until MJ walked up the final possession and drained a buzzer beater to take game one for the Bulls— it then turned into a miserably bad look for the ole' Mailman.

Game two was going to Chicago from the opening tip. There were zero lead changes and zero ties in the 97-85 victory for the Bulls. Utah seemed content leaving Jeff Hornacek on an island against MJ during game one, and he'd done a decent job—MJ had a modest 31 on 27 shots in game one. After game two, that strategy might have needed some re-tooling—MJ had 38 on just 20 shots in game two. Malone continued to struggle and was 16 of 42 through the first two games.

Game three swung back in Utah's direction, as the venue of the 1997 Finals' also switched back to Salt Lake City for games three, four and five.[304] The Jazz gave MJ more to think about in game three by giving more minutes to Howard Eisley, Bryon Russell and found particular success in matching up the 6'8" Chris Morris on Mike. The result was a stunted Chicago offense and MJ getting just 26 on 22 shots. On the other end, refusing to lie down (yet), Karl Malone fueled the crucial Utah victory with a pretty efficient 37 points.

Game four was another bloodbath—the 78-73 rock fight Utah victory had 10 ties and 17 lead changes. The Jazz upped Bryon Russell's minutes from 33:33 in game three to 43:09 in game four. He became Jordan's primary defender throughout the game and Mike's defender for the duration of game four's crunch time—Utah seemingly had found the right matchup for MJ. Despite a rough shooting game for Chicago, the Bulls were up 5 points with 2:42 left, and MJ was seemingly zoning in on a victory, after finding a rhythm in the fourth quarter that had eluded him all game. However, Chicago failed to score in the game's final two minutes, and John Stockton refused to go silently into the night. Stockton was superb in the clutch and Karl Malone didn't pee his pants, so the Jazz evened up the series. The stage was set for a crucial game five in Salt Lake City, where the Jazz were now 10-0 in the 1997 postseason.

---

[304] R.I.P. 2-3-2 format (1985-2013)

Game five was set to take place on Wednesday June 11th, 1997 at 7:00pm local time in Salt Lake City. Early Wednesday morning, around 2:00am, Jordan called his personal trainer to his room where he found MJ curled up in the fetal position, barely able to move. Per Tim Grover—Mike's trainer—he had ordered and retrieved a pizza for Jordan before they'd gone to sleep earlier that night, and MJ was the only one that had eaten any of it. Grover is 100% sure that Jordan was in the full throws of food poisoning because of that late-night pizza. Jordan spent the next day in bed, unable to eat and only got out of bed to get to the arena less than two hours before tipoff. Marv Albert, Matt Goukas and Bill Walton were on the call for the NBC broadcast, and Marv barely introduced his broadcast partners before providing the latest on Jordan's status, which leading right up to game time was uncertain. Jordan did start for the Bulls, but he was visibly struggling.

Out of the gate, the Delta Arena, which was packed to the stations with screaming Mormons, helped fuel an early lead, and Chicago only managed 2 points in the first 5 minutes of play. Jordan hit a few jumpers, confirming that he would at least be able to contribute in some way. Scottie Pippen, visibly determined to make up for whatever percentage of Michael Jordan that was absent, was pressing hard in the first quarter. He was overly eager in trying to get to the rim early on, which resulted in a handful of poor Chicago possessions. He was also reaching on defense and picked up a quick second foul before the start of the second quarter. The Jazz sprinted to a 29-16 lead by the end of the first quarter.

Jordan was laboring with every movement, but he started ramping up in the second quarter. He led the Bulls back from a 16-point deficit and helped get their offense going by getting a few fast break buckets and generating better offense out of the post. Still, Chicago only managed a 1-point lead after the surge by MJ and the energy in the arena clarified the uphill battle required if the Bulls were going to squeak out a win. Karl Malone was engaged and effective in the first half, but a third foul in the second quarter kept him on the bench for several minutes before halftime, which likely disrupted his rhythm. Utah carried a 53-49 lead into halftime.

The game really settled into a brawl by the third quarter. Chicago called fewer plays for MJ in the 3rd quarter, ostensibly to save his efforts for the fourth. Karl Malone was just 1 of 4 in the third quarter and he was settling for jumpers because Chicago had deliberately pushed him away from his spots. Despite his struggles, strong efforts from Stockton, Greg Ostertag and Bryon Russell kept the Jazz on course toward a victory. The Jazz led 72-67 heading into the fourth quarter.

Per Chicago's game plan, Jordan, who was now completely exasperated, came out gunning in the fourth. A three-pointer from MJ evened the score 77-77 with 9:07 left in the game. From that point on, the game resembled the trench-warfare Finals' game sevens of 2010 and 2016—each team was afraid to blink. Neither team led by more than two points until the game's critical sequence that occurred with less than a minute left. Down 1 point, Jordan gets fouled by Stockton with 46 seconds left, and earns two free throws—he makes the first, misses the second, Malone blows the box out and Chicago gets another possession with the game tied. After trying to get Pippen a post touch, the Jazz decided to double so he kicked out to Jordan for a go ahead three-pointer attempt. Jordan's focus tapped into a reservoir that no other human has ever been born with, and he splashed a monumental three-ball to take a three-point lead with 25 seconds left. For all of Chicago's efforts in this game, it still felt like Utah would manage to win throughout the entire game .. until that moment. The Bulls won 90-88.

Jordan finished with 38 points on 13 of 27. Including 17 points in the second quarter when the Bulls needed to rally, and 18 points in the fourth quarter when the game was in the balance. By the time he was being interviewed by Ahmad Rashad at the game's conclusion he was barely able to stand up on his own.

There is rear-view conjecture that perhaps Jordan was hungover or maybe not as sick as he was portending to be during this game. As you know, I know full well that Jordan had 'habits' off the court, but I don't think there's any reason to believe that he wasn't sick for this game.[305] Even if he was hungover .. even if he was 100% healthy and faking every single mannerism that suggested he was legitimately ill .. he still hung a pretty efficient 38 points, on the road, in a pivotal NBA Finals' game. When you accept the probable likelihood that he managed to accomplish that in a physical state that would relegate you or I to the fetal position next to a toilet, you arrive at just why Jordan was the all-time apex predator. On paper, the Chicago Bulls had no business winning that game—the Jazz were dominant at home, they'd seized momentum of the series, and the Bulls' best player had just been poisoned by the late-night shift manager at the Park City *Pizza Hut*. But MJ refused to see that game as a schedule loss. Karl Malone's second half floundering (1 for 6 from the field) kept the door open, and if we've learned anything about Mike, a small opening is all he needs.

10.

To win on the scale that Michael Jordan did, you can't do it on sheer greatness alone. We talked about how the league's talent was relatively down during the late 1990s, and how expansion had spread that talent out across a wider NBA landscape. The finest talent was also concentrated in the Western Conference, especially after Shaq decided to play in Los Angeles after the 1995-96' season. MJ also needed elite teammates to be able to win that many championships. The 'underrated' trope attached to Pippen has gotten enough tread at this point, but I'm not sure it's been fully established how truly instrumental both his talents and his massively under-market-value contract were to the creation of Jordan's unassailable legacy.

After Chicago's first championship in 1990-91', Pippen locked himself into a seven-year deal that paid him between $2.2 and $3.4 million per season. It was several times what his rookie deal had been paying him and the years brought a semblance of security to him and his family.

---

[305] I really doubt it had something to do with drinking—the game was at 7:00pm the next day, so that would have had to be some kind of hangover. On top of that, this was the Salt Lake City area in 1997. I don't know how much you know about the LDS church, but drinking is forbidden, and even in 2020 it's difficult to get alcohol in SLC. If he'd been out drinking, there would have only been so many places to do it—he was staying in Park City which was nowhere near the tourist spot that it is today, and everyone knew which hotel he was staying at. The better conspiracy is obviously who poisoned that pizza...

For Chicago's front office, the contract made the agonizing exercise of constantly re-tooling a perennial championship contender much easier. When your second-best player is locked in for that long and being paid like your sixth-best player, you have a meaningful advantage in financial flexibility. It was a huge win for Chicago as a franchise, but for Scottie, the moment he signed that deal, it was a massively below-value contract for one of the league's best players.

Scottie Pippen was First-Team All-Defense for each season of that seven-year contract. He also made an All-NBA team each of those seven seasons—3x First-Team, 2x Second-Team, 2x Third-Team. Here's a riddle—how many players have ever made seven consecutive First-Team All-Defense teams while also making an All-NBA team in each of those seasons? Time's up .. there's only one player to have ever done that, and his name is Scottie Pippen.

Pippen was vital in all six of the Chicago championships. Like I said in his profile, there's not a precedent for a player being the second-best player on six different championship-winning teams. He's historically, criminally under-praised for his singular two-way skill profile. In this context, Jordan was fortunate to have been paired with such a multi-talented player, who was also, until the very end of the Chicago run, willing to play for a fraction of his value.

9.

Sometime in 2018, I jumped in an elevator and noticed a girl wearing the LeBron XII's—the 12's are my favorite because that was the shoe Bron wore during the 2014-15' season.[306] I'm not a sneaker guy, but I am a LeBron nerd and can point out all of his shoes by the season he wore them. I found it curious that this girl was wearing a rather clean pair of LeBron's that were from years prior, so I asked her, despite definitely knowing the answer:

> *Me:* Are those the 12's?

> *Her:* Oh, no, these are *LeBrons*

> *Me:* Yeah, I'm just trying to place which season they're from (lie)

> *Her:* Oh, I don't know

That was the moment I knew that LeBron had no chance of capturing a fraction of the commercial or cultural acceptance that Jordan's shoes have. See, as plenty of you already realized, she was sure that I was asking which model of *Jordans* she was wearing. Jordan's shoes are so incredibly popular that they've transcended commercial success. The shoe line is so culturally resonant and well-known that espousing that a certain model is your favorite genuinely reveals something about the type of person you are. In social currency, wearing a certain model in a certain colorway is an expression all its own. The best part is that people

---

[306] There's a special place in my heart for LeBron's performance in the 2015' Finals'. Despite the loss, that MF went down fighting.

seek them out not to be worn on a basketball court, but to be worn as fashion statements (or to sit in a closet in their original box). Jordan's line of shoes were the first to be treated this way, and their demand drives the multi-billion dollar men's collector shoe industry.

How the hell do you build a brand that powerful? I think it starts with an on-court brand that is virtually untarnished, and the shoes' popularity have simply stood the test of time. Shit, I found a pair of 5's in my dad's closet when I was a kid, and let's just say my dad was not a basketball fan. But, apparently, Jordan's allure and greatness has been a selling point for decades, even among people that don't follow the NBA.

In 2020, almost 20 years since Jordan's final retirement, he still owns the shoe game. Of the $3.14 billion in revenue that Jordan brand made in 2019, Jordan's cut was a whopping $130 million. Basketball's second-highest earner in the sneaker game was LeBron James, who earned around $32 million. The money Jordan earns off his shoes alone is more than the total earnings of the world's highest paid athlete—Lionel Messi—who took in $127 million in 2019.[307] Jordan brand continues to print money, and lucrative deals with mega brands like soccer club Paris Saint-Germain and The University of Michigan indicate that the future is also very bright for 'the brand'.

Professional athletes had been used to peddle products long before Jordan, but no athlete before Jordan had ever been as pristinely marketable. Phil Knight, Nike's co-founder, has cited several times that signing Michael Jordan to that first five-year contract in 1984 was a turning point for the company. Over the term of that first contract, Nike got a taste for the explosive commercial and cultural potential that comes with selling the signature shoes of the world's most exciting athlete. During Mike's second Nike contract, when he started collecting Larry O'Brien trophies, his marketability went nuclear and the basketball shoe revolution was fully realized.

Jordan was such a firestorm of popularity during his ascent in the late 80s and 90s, that it was no surprise companies were tripping over themselves to pay him to represent their brands. I guess that's why it makes sense why the Jordan brand is still so viable—if you're wearing articles with that symbol, or you're sporting sneakers that MJ actually wore, you're attaching yourself to all the superlatives attached to Mike. As Don Draper says:

You are the product. You feeling something—that's what sells.

8.

Speaking of cultural influence, has any man in history done more for the single hoop earring or beret? It took a confident man to rock that combo, but Jordan was never lacking in that category. MJ gets beat up for a lot of his style choices and the criticism is mostly fair—the dad

---

[307] Jordan also owns a car dealership, three restaurants and still has endorsement deals with Gatorade, Hanes and Upper Deck—combined those net him around another $15 million per year.

jeans, the overall 'bougie yet frumpy uncle' aesthetic that we've grown accustomed to in Jordan's post-retirement years. But let's give credit where credit is due. Having the stones to rock the hoop and beret meant that he didn't give any fucks, and when you're in the unique influential position that Mike was during the 1990s, those stylistic choices reverberate a resounding declaration about his status in that moment—*I'm on top, fuck off if you're not down with it.* Draymond Green was on the inaugural episode of *The Shop*, when it aired on HBO in August 2018. Draymond similarly emblemizes the hoop earring[308] during a monologue about LeBron realizing he was in that same airspace:

> *I think Bron over the last four years became LeBron James. And it wasn't nothing to do with winning and it wasn't nothing to do with stats. He found himself. People didn't start to view him as they view him now, until he became that force, that man to say, 'I'm here'. I feel like for years, he shied away from saying 'I'm here'. And when he started to say, 'Fuck y'all, I'm here', that's when he became who he is, and no one would have ever said that until he did it himself. Motherfuckers fucked with Mike because Mike was like, 'I'm Mike with my hoop earring. Fuck all y'all, I'm here'. And until he did that, that's when he became the figurehead that he is. So many people shy away from that and that's why they never reach their full potential.*

7.

In case there were any question about it, Michael Jordan was the greatest pure scorer in the history of the NBA, and it's not especially close. He won all of his championships, and enjoyed all of his postseason success, during the lowest scoring decade in the NBA since the 1950s. For his postseason career, he averaged a ridiculous 33.4 points per game. That figure's insanity is intensified given the decade he played in, and that he got to that number despite defenses throwing out their game plans to key on trying to slow him down. That postseason scoring average stands almost 4 full points per game better than the player with the second-highest mark (29.7—Allen Iverson). He also boasts the highest regular season scoring average at a little over 30 points per game.

MJ basically led the league in scoring ten consecutive seasons. In the 12 seasons between 1986-87' and 1997-98', Jordan led the league in scoring each season (less the two seasons he was primarily playing baseball). For historical context, no one has ever come close to leading the league in scoring for ten total seasons, and to do it in sequential seasons is totally unthinkable. In the history of the league, the players with the most scoring titles are as follows:

	Scoring Titles
Michael Jordan	10
Wilt Chamberlain	7

---

[308] LeBron's equivalent to the hoop and beret? Popularizing the dad hat—a gigantic feat unto itself.

Allen Iverson	4
Kevin Durant	4
George Gervin	4

When you consider what a statistical aberration Wilt Chamberlain was, it's not hard to realize that MJ stands in his own tier as a scorer.

I'll spare you a diatribe about efficiency and advanced stats (for now), but it's worth mentioning how efficiently Jordan arrived at his gaudy scoring numbers. For his career, he shot just a hair under 50% from the field—very impressive for someone that led the league in field goal attempts nine different times. That freakshow athleticism allowed him to get off clean jumpers and open driving lanes for dunks or trademark mid-air-shifting layups.

His three-point numbers won't blow anyone away, but if his scoring was that inelastic to the scoring trends of the era he played in, he would have figured out a reliable three-ball if the league trend suggested he do so. His jumper was silky smooth—what's a few feet further back?

6.

IN FACT—Jordan's jumper was at the heart of his stone cold most savage flex over an opponent. Leading up to the 1992 NBA Finals', support for Clyde Drexler was swelling in the NBA community. As we know, Drexler was drafted a year before Jordan, and Portland passed on Jordan because they felt their need for a shooting guard was already fulfilled based on Clyde's projected ability. Both Drexler's Blazers and Jordan's Bulls were actually on similar arcs for the handful of years after they were drafted—making the playoffs, but only becoming legitimate contenders toward the end of the 1980s.

As the new decade began, Drexler became the first of he and Mike to reach the NBA Finals', when the Blazers earned the right to get smoked by the Pistons in June of 1990. Jordan finally outlasted those same Pistons and broke through himself to play against the Lakers in the 1991 Finals'. Scottie Pippen forced Magic to seriously consider retirement in those Finals', and the Bulls rolled to their first championship. Any doubt that Drexler was on Jordan's level should have been extinguished. But when Drexler's Blazers and Jordan's Bulls each found their way to the 1992 NBA Finals', many media members had talked themselves into there being a genuine debate to be resolved at the conclusion of the series. David Halberstam wrote in *Playing for Keeps: Michael Jordan and the World He Made*:

> But of course, it was intensely personal for him, the perfect challenge for
> a man who always wanted and always need challenges, and he used all
> the comparisons with Drexler, all those nonbelievers who thought
> Drexler as good as he was, to motivate himself. He set out to do nothing
> less than destroy, not just Portland, but Drexler as well.

In the first half of game one, it was clear that Portland made the deliberate choice to allow MJ to shoot from the outside—there had been thinking in that moment that it was the way to beat Jordan. Naturally, this came as a personal afront to Mike. Jordan proceeded to bang down five threes in the first half. On the sixth attempt, Danny Ainge stopped short of fully closing out on Jordan's shot (proving the Portland strategy of letting him shoot), Jordan banged home another three-ball, turned to walk back down the court and shrugged as if to say 'I don't know, I guess you're right, I can't shoot'. The Bulls won game one in a route, and despite a legitimate challenge from the Blazers, Chicago won the 1992 NBA Championship in six games. Per Halberstam:

> Later, Danny Ainge, who was Drexler's Portland teammate that year, said that there was a certain inhumanity to what took place on the court in that series. Drexler chose to give Jordan the outside shot in the beginning and Jordan hit six threes in a row ... When the Trail Blazers had the ball, Ainge thought, it was as if Jordan had a terrible personal vendetta against Drexler. If it was not personal, it most certainly looked that way. Jordan barely let Drexler touch the ball on offense. Ainge sensed that it was as if Jordan had taken all those newspaper articles and television stories about Drexler as nothing less than a personal insult.

That same summer was the 1992 Barcelona Summer Olympics, and Jordan and Drexler were *Dream Team* teammates. MJ relentlessly attacked Drexler in practice, and this excerpt from Halberstam's book really drives home how lethal Jordan's psychological arsenal was:

> Jordan did not pass up the opportunity to talk some trash as he brought the ball up court. "Didn't I just kick your ass? ... Anything here look just a little familiar? ... Think you can stop me this time, Clyde? ... Better watch out for the threes, Clyde." Eventually some of his Dream Team colleagues suggested that Jordan cut back on the trash talk with Drexler because they were all teammates now and there was no need to reopen wounds still so fresh. Back off he did, but the coaches noted that every time Jordan guarded Drexler in scrimmages, he took the defensive level up more than anyone else...

> Michael reported gleefully to the Bulls' coaches that one day Clyde Drexler showed up at practice with two left sneakers. Unwilling to admit his mistake and borrow a shoe from someone else or go back and get another one, he went out and played with a sneaker on the wrong foot. To Michael Jordan, who always looked for psychological weaknesses in his opponents, that was a sure sign of Drexler's insecurity. He carefully filed it away, to be used some other day if necessary.

There's a lot of speculation, as well there should be, about what would have happened if Jordan hadn't retired, and how the Bulls would have matched up against Olajuwon's Rockets in the 1994 and 1995 Finals'. Historically, I've been of the belief that 'championship fatigue' would have caught up to Chicago eventually, and the two-year hiatus was the perfect prescription to allow the Bulls to extend their dynasty. However, while I can't speak to the hypothetical outcome of the 1993-94' season, had Jordan participated, I can speak definitively to how a Houston-Chicago 1995 Finals' would have played out. Drexler was traded during the 1994-95' season from Portland to Houston and was instrumental to the Rocket's 1995 championship. If Jordan hadn't spent most of that season playing baseball and the Bulls managed to make the 1995 NBA Finals', there's no fucking way in hell that Jordan let's Clyde get the best of him in those Finals'. Hell, for all we know, Jordan stopped playing baseball to do his part in preventing Drexler from ever winning a ring. It's true that Jordan never had a career-long rival to keep pushing him. Instead there were characters that came and went, but Jordan was always the victor. Drexler was as close as it came to being that arch-nemesis, but it's possible Jordan didn't have lasting rivals because no one could endure the wrath of a motivated MJ.

5.

Jordan's Hall of Fame acceptance speech wasn't that bad.

The sharpest dig is toward Jerry Krause—the primary front office architect of the Chicago dynasty—but we've all seen *The Last Dance,* and this surprises no one. Jordan spends a lot of time thanking his family for sparking his competitive fire, but also singles out the following NBA personalities for varying reasons:

- o   Scottie Pippen—in the first minute of the speech he acknowledges Scottie for being beside him for all of Chicago's championships.
- o   LeRoy Smith—who famously made MJ's high school team when Jordan was cut. He doesn't undercut him, but states that he was emblematic of what Jordan aspired to be.
- o   Buzz Peterson—Jordan's first roommate at UNC, who was also North Carolina's reigning high school player of the year. Mike talks about how that honor also drove him to be better.
- o   Dean Smith—Michael's legendary college coach who Mike brings up because Smith did not select Jordan to be on the *Sports Illustrated* cover with him because Jordan was a freshman at the time. Another motivating factor for MJ.
- o   Isiah Thomas, George Gervin and Magic Johnson—Jordan isolates them for the theory that those three froze him out at his first All-Star game in 1985 by not passing him the ball.
- o   Pat Riley—This is probably my favorite moment of the speech. Riley, a notoriously competitive person in his own right, battled with MJ throughout the 1990s, and Jordan recognized Riley as a kindred personality because of their shared competitive nature. Jordan reminisces how Riley wouldn't allow his players that were friends with MJ—Patty Ewing, Charles Oakley—to fraternize or even go out to lunch with him because they

were rivals. He does go on to call Jeff Van Gundy the 'little guy' that took over as the Knick's coach after Riley left—an unsubtle jab.
- ○ Bryon Russell—Jordan tells a story of how Russell ran into Jordan while Jordan was playing baseball and Russell said to MJ: *Why'd you quit man? You know I could guard you. If I ever see you in a pair of shorts.. If I ever see you in a pair of shorts..* Jordan made sure everyone in the audience knew how much that motivated him, and he's definitely calling Russell out, but it wasn't over the top.

Jordan speaks warmly of plenty of characters from his epic story—Phil Jackson, Jerry Reinsdorf, everyone in his family, his Chicago teammates—but did we really expect the most competitive person of all-time to not attribute most of his accomplishments to those that doubted him? For the most part he does so in a good-natured way. I think it's time we revise the notion that MJ's Hall of Fame speech was 23 minutes of self-deluded, self-congratulatory hubris.

4.

Jordan was the highest usage player of all-time. Per *Basketball Reference*, whose servers have been under unprecedented strain since I began writing this book, define Usage Percentage as an estimate of the number of team plays used by a player while he was on the floor. Basically, you're calculating what percentage of a team's possessions are taken by a certain player's field goal attempts, drawn fouls, or turnovers. By this metric, Jordan was the most ball-dominant player of all-time:

	Usg%
1) Michael Jordan	33.26
2) Russell Westbrook	32.69
3) Kobe Bryant	31.85
4) Allen Iverson	31.83
5) DeMarcus Cousins	31.82

What's wild about Jordan's usage is both how efficient he was and similarly, how few turnovers he committed. This top five is rounded out by prolific volume scorers, but players who have often been criticized for arriving at gaudy scoring numbers on below average efficiency. MJ's historic usage didn't just allow him to hang huge volume scoring figures, but he's also the most efficient scorer ever. That insanity is, again, compounded by his playing in a slow era of the NBA where defenses were always keying on him. As you could expect, the highest-usage players tend to have the highest turnover rates, but Jordan eludes that trend as well. On my list, only Duncan, KG, David Robinson, Draymond, Rodman, Dirk and Chris Paul have averaged fewer turnovers per game. With the exception of Chris Paul,[309] these are players that mainly play out of the post. So, Jordan had the ball in his hands more than any player in modern history, still managed to be the most efficient scorer ever, and turned the ball over significantly less than all of his historical contemporaries. Yikes.

---

[309] Behold, the Point God.

3.

Six Finals' MVPs, bro? *Six??* There's nothing that makes Mike's legacy feel more invincible than his clean sweep of the Bill Russell NBA Finals' Most Valuable Player Award. Jordan made six NBA Finals' appearances, his team won all six times, and the motherfucker won all six Finals' MVPs. The lack of a historical precedent,[310] or anything even close, speaks loudly to Jordan's granite-solid case for being the best player of all-time.

2.

Jordan's flawless NBA Finals' record speaks for itself on the stone-cold trophy count alone. But the fact that none of his Chicago teammates snagged even one of those Finals' MVP trophies says something more about Jordan's refusal to allow any force greater than his own dictate the environment he dominated. From a young age he always had a problem with anyone that was perceived to have been better than him, and that only escalated as he rose to the platform of being the greatest player on earth. His refusal to allow anyone to enter that airspace, teammate or opponent, led to his stature of invulnerability—the most powerful weapon in his legacy's arsenal.

1.

(a) Advanced stats don't matter. Evaluation of NBA player performance is shifting into a world of advanced data that is dismissed by fans at large. Fundamentally, I understand the pushback, and to some degree basketball will always be about toughness, imposing your will and winning the ongoing psychological battle versus your opponent.

(b) Michael Jordan is the greatest NBA player of all-time. The lack of precedent for his accomplishments, the adoration of his competitive spirit, the way he's bridged his basketball greatness into lucrative off-court endeavors—he definitely makes the best case for claiming the mantle.

What if I told you agreeing with (b) means you disagree with (a)? Michael Jordan probably boasts the most impressive advanced stat profile of all-time, and the way that aligns with where many people believe he belongs in the anecdotal greatest-ever conversation, it serves as one of the strongest arguments for why advanced stats work.

Jordan has the best PER (regular season and postseason), the best Win Shares Per 48 (regular season and postseason), and the best Box Plus-Minus (regular season and postseason). Compared to LeBron and Kareem, Jordan had a significantly shorter career and wasn't able to

---

[310] The award started being handed out with the 1969 NBA Finals'. The players closest to Jordan in number of Finals' MVP trophies are LeBron (4) and then Shaq, Magic and Duncan (3).

compile the numbers they've been able to. But when it comes to sheer efficiency of play, there's no one on his level.

If you watched Jordan play in the 90s, you didn't need advanced stats to tell you he was the greatest player you'd ever seen—he just was. Advanced stats shouldn't be the foundation of your opinion for a player, but reinforce what you believe you're already seeing. Jordan's unmatched advanced profile offers the intersection of old world and new world basketball thinking, and drives home (even further) the notion that we'll never see a player cast a larger shadow across the entire league.

Why Is Jordan The Greatest Player Ever? Because he has the most compelling case. There isn't a chink in any of his profiles—statistically, anecdotally, volume of trophies etc. I have doubts about the quality of the competition during his most celebrated triumphs, but Mike is the greatest because, well, simply, he just is. I think all four players in this tier have their own case for being the best ever, but the other three are handicapped not only against Michael's accomplishments, but against the universal determination of his status in popular culture. When someone wants to metaphorically compare someone as the greatest at what they do, they proclaim them 'The Michael Jordan of _____', because even non-basketball-going folks will understand the reference. That's a powerful challenge to LeBron.

Tier I Recap.

As the great British philosopher Mick Jagger once said—*You are left out, out of there without a doubt 'cause baby, baby, baby, you're out of time.*

We're almost out of time, but there are a few important conversations we've yet to have.

Of the 30 great players profiled here, four of them truly stand apart. It's also no accident that the careers of the four greatest players in NBA history have unfolded in succession, with very little overlap. Russell's career ended in the summer of 1969—the same summer Kareem began his NBA career. It wasn't until the sixteenth of Kareem's twenty seasons that Jordan joined the NBA. When Jordan retired in the summer of 2003, LeBron officially began his NBA career a few weeks later.

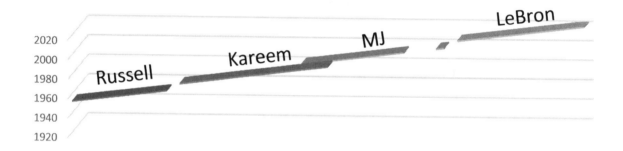

When I was trying to think about what the appropriate Tiers would be, all of my plans were based around my initial confidence that these four players *had to* comprise Tier I. I've made a few adjustments to Tier II and Tier III selections through the course of writing this book, but have adjusted Tier I exactly zero times. These players truly define their respective eras, and while I've had to make plenty of adjustments during this project, there's nothing I'm more sure of than these players being, in some order, the four greatest players of all-time.

On February 27th, 2020, Ryen Russillo had broadcasting legend Craig Kilborn on his podcast. Among various topics covered, they talked about the NBA in a big picture sense and Kilborn joked that after a few drinks, he could occasionally talk himself into Tim Duncan being the greatest player ever. That struck a chord with me because that was roughly my appraisal with Duncan during this project—he was the only player on the outside of Tier I that I genuinely considered.

Most Screwed Over	Considered.. Kind of	No Chance
Tim Duncan	Kevin Garnett	Steph Curry
	Hakeem Olajuwon	Wilt Chamberlain
	Shaquille O'Neal	Oscar Robertson
		Kobe Bryant
		Larry Bird
		Magic Johnson

Ultimately, the environmental circumstances of Duncan's career seem so uniquely favorable that his championship output would need to be a little higher and/or the peak of his efficiency would need to be higher for consideration. When I was considering him for a spot, it was definitely the sheer prolific-ness of his career that kept enticing me toward his inclusion. Garnett and Olajuwon were glancingly considered, but never seriously. Watching those two players on tape is truly a delightful experience, and I have a soft spot for hyper-switchable big men with accomplished (albeit varied) offensive profiles. Starting with Russell, that prototype proves to be a winning player in any era. As for Shaq, it was pretty striking looking at how consistently great, offensively, his teams were throughout his prime, regardless of the jersey he was wearing. I could never realistically make a case given the lack of reliability in his defense, and while it's controversial, I also think his skills were maximally realized during a super slow stretch of NBA basketball. Would he be effective in a faster, more stretched-out NBA? Absolutely. However, he struggled to step out on the perimeter during a super-iso heavy era of the NBA, and I think he would get cooked on defense in stretches of the NBA that required him to be in constant motion defensively.

The four players that do comprise Tier I are etched in stone. Unlike the Tier II and Tier III spots that fill out the magic number of 30, a Tier I membership is for life and not vulnerable to relegation—the reward for being the player of your generation. However, Tier I is open for expansion. As LeBron's window begins to close, there are a couple players in the mix for the next spot.

Etched in Stone	In Play..
Bill Russell	Steph Curry
Kareem Abdul-Jabbar	Giannis Antetokounmpo
Michael Jordan	Kawhi Leonard
LeBron James	Luka Dončić

My book was authored at the conclusion of a Golden State Warrior season that has them poised to win at least one championship in the next three seasons. If they do, Steph will begin submitting his paperwork for a Tier I spot. I think it would take two more Golden State championships to stem the tide of anti-Steph sentiment, forcing everyone to begin considering him a mountaintop-level player. It's totally conceivable given Golden State's current assets and championship-caliber players who have meaningful tread left on their tires. In my assessment, just one more championship and a few more All-NBA-caliber seasons will be enough for me to consider Steph. I do think Steph is a favorable symbolic choice for Tier I. Irrefutably, Steph Curry has been the emblem of the pace-and-space era, and that cohesively goes along with the stylistic impact that existing Tier I players had across their respective careers. Ultimately, I think Steph will remain a Tier II player, as I've fast-tracked his candidacy for that tier to some degree. Possessing a larger body of work isn't necessarily important when you're the most important player on a team that made five straight Finals'—a mantle you and Russell share with no one else. However, this incoming twilight of his career will have to be really magical for him to force his way into Tier I.

We're watching Giannis' Tier I campaign begin to blossom. He has a lot of ground to make up, but he's well positioned from a team perspective, and he probably has to be the odds-on favorite for the next Tier I spot. Milwaukee bringing in Mike Budenholzer quickly ignited a system capable of obliterating their competition during the regular season (while compiling freakish stat profiles for the player at the center of the system). But questions rightfully remain about the system's postseason viability. Giannis is still in 'darling' status around the league, but if a championship isn't in his immediate future, he'll start to endure the pessimism and scrutiny that accompany MVP-level players without championships. There's no question about his ability—he's the contemporary Wilt Chamberlain—but there are questions about his current team's championship potential, and, of course, the question hanging over the city of Milwaukee like a thick fog—will he be there much longer?[311]

Kawhi Leonard has a puncher's chance of retiring the next Tier I player, but I'm pessimistic about both how much longer his prime will last, and his case being a little harder to make given the limited, intermittent top-of-the-food-chain impact he's had on the NBA. Kawhi has a chronic, degenerative issue with his thigh and every day that passes, the ceiling of his athleticism decreases. He's an incredible player who possesses a great deal of physical strength that will help to compensate for this over the coming seasons, but I'm confident the injury will start to cost him playing time that won't be attributed to load management. The bigger challenge in Kawhi's Tier I pursuit will be overcoming the limited amount of time Kawhi's spent as one of the league's best players. He'll be hard-pressed to legitimately contend for another league MVP, and 2017 was the only campaign during which he was a true candidate. Even if he does secure another Finals' MVP, joining LeBron as the only player to have done so with three different franchises, it's hard to argue that he hasn't had immaculate fortune in terms of where he's played in his career. He was drafted by a franchise uniquely positioned to sculpt his raw talents, and San Antonio was playing in the NBA Finals' during his second and third NBA seasons. After the injury debacle with the Spurs, his subsequent trade was to a turn-key championship contender. Another championship or two would make it very hard to keep him out of Tier II, but it's hard to envision Kawhi landing in Tier I.

He's not without question marks himself, but I think Luka Dončić will be the next member of Tier I. Luka's been playing professional basketball for a handful of seasons, and was conditioned for the on-court and off-court aspects of NBA stardom in a way that no other player has been in the history of the game. Off the court, at just 21, he already grasps exactly what it means to be a celebrity. Luka's social media footprint and aesthetic demonstrates a person who already knows how to portray the simple, sanitized, corporate, team-centric messaging of a veteran NBA star. He's not privy to controversial statements regarding other players, nor is he prone to the voicing of opinions or grievances that draw negative press to

---

[311] You're going to love Toronto, big fella. Trust me.

himself. While other 21-year old NBA players are just immersing themselves in the mitigation of stardom, Luka already possesses a master's-level understanding of how to protect his brand and how to avoid the perils of being a celebrity.

On the court, the command and confidence with which Dončić orchestrates the Dallas offense is way beyond his years. He was a fringe MVP candidate in 2019-20', just his second season, and unlike so many young stars over the course of league history, he doesn't rely on raw athleticism to play at an MVP-level. Luka is also in great hands with the Dallas Mavericks— Rick Carlisle will get the most out of his talent, Mark Cuban will make sure there is premier talent around him, and Dirk Nowitzki is whispering in his ear about how best to sculpt his talent going forward. Luka landing in Dallas—an established, championship caliber organization—also lowers the likelihood he'll have to force his way out or want to leave in free agency.

On the skeptical side, I'm concerned about Kristaps Porzingis' reliability as Luka's counterpart-star. Kristaps is ultra-skilled for his frame, but when players with his frame have lower-body injuries early in their career, as Porzingis has had, they tend to always have lower-body injuries. Starting with 2020-21', Dallas has Porzingis on the books for $29, $31, $33 and a player option at $36 million in 2023-24'—I'm fearful that there will be a lot of dead money across those years if Dallas doesn't decide to move Kristaps' contract (which I suggest ASAP). How Dallas fills out the roster around Luka, and perhaps in place of Porzingis, will serve as the uncertainty in Luka's chase of Tier I status. But there are a few things that are certain going forward—Luka Dončić was probably the best 20-year old player in the history of the NBA, he's playing for a very institutionally-sound NBA franchise, and he's been groomed for NBA superstardom unlike any professional athlete in history.

The great British philosopher Mick Jagger is the front man for a little band called The Rolling Stones who, as of 2020, have pressed exactly 30 studio albums since their debut record in 1964. Across their sprawling catalog, the Stones capture the urgency, messiness and gritty essence of rock music. For all the important moments in the Rolling Stones' musical index, that essence is most purely refined across exactly 4 albums, which were pressed in succession as the turbulent 60s became the uncertain 70s:

Beggars Banquet (1968)
Let it Bleed (1969)
Sticky Fingers (1971)
Exile on Main St. (1972)

The first track on *Beggars Banquet*—*Sympathy For the Devil*[312]—marked the beginning of a new era for the Stones. It was the most powerful track they'd released up to that point, and it made clear that the band had leveled up from Britpop blues covers and Beatles' karaoke. *Let it Bleed's* first track—*Gimme Shelter*[313]—captures the angst, uncertainty and downright

---

[312] #32 on *Rolling Stone's 500 Greatest Songs of All Time.*
[313] #38 on *Rolling Stone's 500 Greatest Songs of All Time.*

apocalyptic tenor of late 1969 in The United States of America.[314] It's also an absolute motherfucker of a rock song. The Rolling Stones began the next decade with two more top-to-bottom classic rock albums. *Sticky Fingers* is a 10-track masterpiece of production that traverses the genres of country, blues and soul to form their cleanest and most peerless record on file. *Exile on Main St.* was released just a year later, but is practically the creative inverse of the polish, precision and pursuit of sonic clarity that *Sticky Fingers* strived for and accomplished. *Exile* is an 18-track masterpiece of a more raw and unbridled sort—stitched together with the blues and country present in all their prior music—but tinged with gospel and swing, the record sounds like an impromptu club gig (and you're the only one in the audience).

These four records crystalized the cultural upheaval the 60s had excavated from post-WWII life in western society. The Stones emerged from the emotional rubble of the 1960s and continued to level up their cultural and sonic importance on *Sticky Fingers* and *Exile on Main St.* The Rolling Stones made a few more great albums in the 70s—*Goat's Head Soup* (1973), *Black and Blue* (1976) and *Some Girls* (1978)—and while they've kept the pedal down ever since, they would only provide albums that mattered in the rock canon intermittently through the 80s, 90s, 2000s and 2010s. Nothing like that historic run that began in the late 60s, when they gave us four consecutive albums that continue to stand apart from their other twenty-six records.

.. Except ..

If we're really being honest with ourselves .. *Sticky Fingers* and *Exile on Main St.* create a binary argument over which is truly the greatest Stones' record.

Sticky Fingers is basically perfect. It's just ten songs, but each track is its own dynamic composition, and the album doesn't really have a low point. The record has the perfect rock song—*Sway*—the perfect blues cover—*You Gotta Move*—the perfect country song—*Wild Horses*—and as much as Jagger detested them, the perfect ballad—*Moonlight Mile*.

Exile on Main St. is perfectly imperfect. It's a whopping eighteen songs, and while its peak is higher (*Sweet Virginia*[315]), its valleys are lower (*Happy, All Down the Line*). You're not wrong to believe either album is the Stones' best, but one thing is for certain—a thorough examination of each album's candidacy is a worthwhile exercise.

Michael Jordan's legacy is virtually perfect, unassailable in the context of all the criteria by which we generally appraise all-time NBA players.

---

[314] Tension over US involvement in Vietnam. Racist pushback to the Civil Rights movement, leading up to Martin Luther King Jr.'s assassination. Violent mass murders were on the rise, from Richard Speck, to the Texas Tower Sniper, to the Manson murders. Bobby Kennedy's assassination—who was a viable presidential candidate running on a platform of unity and the advancement of Civil Rights—yielded a Nixon presidency, that all but burst the counter-cultural bubble.

[315] For my money, a finer distillation of all the elements that constitute rock n' roll music does not exist. You won't convince me otherwise

LeBron James' legacy isn't perfect using that same criteria, but his prolific stature and accomplishments across a golden generation of NBA talent speaks loudly on its own merits toward greatest-ever[316] status.

The argument between these two players is largely a generational one, with the two camps hunkered down behind their battle lines. Irrefutably, Jordan has more troops on the ground. His base, those born before 1982 and who watched at least some of Jordan's triumphs in the 90s, are largely resolute in the belief that it's not even worth having a conversation over who is the greatest-ever. The LeBron camp is more of an insurgent movement, that's steadily been accepting enlistees since 2016. This punchy group of rebels are definitely out-numbered, but their cause does have a few opportunities that their majority adversary does not have.

First, LeBron is still playing at an MVP-level, and if his dynamism is able to decline on the Kareem Abdul-Jabbar diet, Bron has the chance to add meaningful layers to his legacy over the next three to four seasons. Second, the LeBron camp's intelligence officers have acquired credible intel that has become a popular recruiting tool in growing their army—the evidence that LeBron has navigated an appreciably more competitive league in pursuit of NBA championships.

What else can I say about Jordan that I didn't drool over in his profile? What other positive aspects of Jordan's legacy are there that *The Last Dance* didn't exaggerate one hundred times over? Examining the resistance LeBron faced over the course of his career has to be the entry point to this conversation. It represents the only chance for malleability in a dialogue that is otherwise destined to be cast in iron.

The great basketball philosopher Amin El-Hassan once said that the NBA has a low barrier for fanhood but a high barrier for mastery. In no other aspect of NBA discourse is this more true than in appropriately ranking all-time players. This discourse is usually strained by reductive ring-counting suggestions and dismissive blanket statements about whether or not a player 'was a winner' or not.

That baggage need not enter the courtroom in the high-profile litigation of James v. Jordan (2020). While the trial will be ongoing, correlative with the unknown duration of LeBron James' career, Jordan's prosecution team has now given their final remarks via a 10-hour propaganda film. The defense will continue to monitor the investigation unfolding in Los Angeles, but it's their prerogative now to begin discrediting the quality of competition that Michael Jordan encountered en route to his success. This is the defense's only course of action in the interim, given it's not their mission to prove LeBron has been an equally dynamic basketball player—that much is clear to those with a mastery of the historical NBA landscape— the real objective is proving that LeBron is a superior player in a vacuum of equal competitive circumstance.[317]

---

[316] Everyone needs to stop saying goat or GOAT or G.O.A.T. or using the goat emoji. It's diluted the value of actually being the greatest ever, but more importantly, it's annoying the motherfuck out of me.

[317] Yes, I have sympathies to the LeBron cause and perhaps that means I should recuse myself from a trial of such magnitude. I admit fully to an unhealthy LeBron complex, but remember, that goes both ways—I'm fully aware of the moments for which LeBron should be deified, but also those that he rightly should be crucified. Maybe it's a sign that I should be recused as I continue to use biblical allusions to LeBron's legacy. Alas! You're stuck with me as the presiding judge, even though I might be a Manchurian plant for the LeBron camp.

Exhibit A—NBA Finals' Opponents

Of Michael Jordan's six trips to the NBA Finals', only once were his Bulls not favored to win the championship. Of LeBron's ten trips to the NBA Finals', only three times have his teams been favored to win the championship. To quantify the impact of each player's Finals' opponents, I'm going to start by using SRS—Simple Rating System—which we've gone over previously, but I suspect we're due for a refresher on.

SRS is a team rating that takes into account average point differential and strength of schedule. While the statistic's makeup has been adjusted to create postseason ratings, it was designed as a measure of a regular season team's impact versus the rest of the league. It's been the prevailing statistic used in attempts to determine the greatest *teams* of all-time because it adjusts for generational nuances that raw numbers like wins and raw margin of victory are unable to capture. You'd probably agree that the top five teams in history, by way of SRS, are fairly in line with the way that conversation goes in the barbershop:

(1) 1970-71' Milwaukee [+11.92][318]
(2) 1995-96' Chicago [+11.80]
(3) 1971-72' Los Angeles [+11.65]
(4) 2016-17' Golden State [+11.35]
(5) 1996-97' Chicago [+10.70]

All of these teams won championships. All of them were also unique composites of all-time talent. Topically, two of them were also led by Michael Jordan—let's take a look at who his teams played in the Finals', and the rest of LeBron and MJ's Finals' opponents:

Jordan Finals' Opponent	SRS	LeBron Finals' Opponent	SRS
1990-91' Lakers	+6.73	**2006-07' Spurs**	**+8.35**
1991-92' Blazers	+6.94	2010-11' Mavs	+4.41
1992-93' Suns	+6.27	2011-12' Thunder	+6.44
1995-96' Sonics	+7.40	2012-13' Spurs	+6.67
1996-97' Jazz	+7.97	**2013-14' Spurs**	**+8.00**
1997-98' Jazz	+5.73	**2014-15' Warriors**	**+10.01**
		2015-16' Warriors	**+10.38**
		2016-17' Warriors	**+11.35**
		2017-18' Warriors	+5.79
		2019-20' Heat	+2.59

Five of LeBron's Finals' opponents had a higher rating than the highest-rated of Jordan's opponents—those five are in bold type. Numerically, this pseudo-justifies LeBron's 1-4 record

---

[318] Behold, Oscar Robertson, the original *Point God.*

against those teams (LeBron's team was the underdog all five times). Generally speaking, this also tells us that Jordan didn't have to go through Duncan's Spurs or Steph's Warriors (two of those teams were Duncan's Spurs and three were Steph's Warriors).

The 2019-20' season was an outlier in myriad ways, and the Miami Heat's good but 'far-from-historic' +2.59 SRS from the regular season certainly doesn't tell us much about the very different team that met LeBron in the Finals'. SRS is a good measure of a team's overall quality, but as the Miami Heat showed us during the 2020 Bubble Playoff, a team with a great SRS score—the +9.41 Milwaukee Bucks—are still vulnerable to the challenges that postseason basketball present.

Let's also measure these opponents not by their regular season performance which preceded their Finals' matchup with either LeBron or MJ, but by their postseason Net Rating for the playoff run that included that Finals' matchup:[319]

Jordan Finals' Opponent	Playoff Net Rating	LeBron Finals' Opponent	Playoff Net Rating
1990-91' Lakers	+1.1	2006-07' Spurs	+4.5
1991-92' Blazers	+3.5	2010-11' Mavs	+6.6
1992-93' Suns	+0.8	2011-12' Thunder	+4.4
1995-96' Sonics	+1.6	2012-13' Spurs	+7.6
1996-97' Jazz	+3.8	2013-14' Spurs	+10.0
1997-98' Jazz	+2.4	2014-15' Warriors	+8.2
		2015-16' Warriors	+4.4
Average	+2.2	2016-17' Warriors	+13.5
		2017-18' Warriors	+10.3
		2019-20' Heat	+2.0
		Average	+7.2

The Miami Heat not only claim the lowest regular season SRS in the canon of LeBron Finals' opponents (+2.59), but also have by far the lowest Playoff Net Rating as well (+2.0). Turns out the SRS was a pretty accurate indicator of Miami's effectiveness, but I do think this weaker LeBron opponent sheds some light on the average Michael Jordan Finals' opponent. The Heat may have been LeBron's weakest opponent statistically, but they appear to be equal in quality to Jordan's average Finals' opponent. Furthermore, with the exception of the Heat, all nine of LeBron's other Finals' opponents had a higher Playoff Net Rating than the highest of any MJ Finals' opponent.

---

[319] Net Rating is an estimate of point differential per 100 possessions—the differential between a team's offensive rating and their defensive rating. It's an awfully trendy measure of modern team performance in the NBA writer circles. It was also the best measure of performance for a team's postseason that works across multiple eras. Naturally, Jordan's opponents will have diminished ratings because their postseason Net Rating includes the Finals' loss to a Michael Jordan team. However, all three of the teams LeBron beat in the Finals' still have better ratings than all six of the teams Jordan beat.

I initially attributed this massive gulf in the cumulative averages to the increase in league scoring during the 2010s, but it turns out that postseason scoring is fairly static across the LeBron and Jordan eras. In the six postseasons which Jordan reached the NBA Finals', playoff teams averaged 97.7 points per game. In the ten postseasons which LeBron reached the NBA Finals', playoff teams averaged 98.9 points per game.

LeBron faced tougher Finals' opponents because those teams were constructed with greater players. This opens up the broader conversation about the amount of overall talent in the league while Jordan played versus while LeBron's played—something we touched on—but now is time for a deeper examination, mainly because there wasn't anything in Jordan's universe close to LeBron James.

Exhibit B—Overall NBA Talent Pool

Remember this chart?

Drafted 1986-1994	Career Win Shares	Drafted 1995-2003	Career Win Shares
Shaquille O'Neal (1992)	181.7	LeBron James (2003)	236.4
David Robinson (1987)	178.7	Tim Duncan (1997)	206.4
Reggie Miller (1987)	174.4	Dirk Nowitzki (1998)	206.3
Gary Payton (1990)	145.5	Kevin Garnett (1995)	191.4
Jason Kidd (1994)	138.6	Kobe Bryant (1996)	172.7
Scottie Pippen (1987)	125.1	Paul Pierce (1998)	150.0
Horace Grant (1987)	118.2	Ray Allen (1996)	145.1
Dikembe Mutombo (1991)	117.0	Pau Gasol (2001)	144.1
Jeff Hornacek (1986)	108.9	Steve Nash (1996)	129.7
Eddie Jones (1994)	100.6	Vince Carter (1998)	125.3
Grant Hill (1994)	99.9	Shawn Marion (1999)	124.9
Vlade Divac (1989)	96.4	Chauncey Billups (1997)	120.8
Kevin Johnson (1987)	92.8	Dwayne Wade (2003)	120.7
Mark Jackson (1987)	91.8	Tony Parker (2001)	111.3
Hersey Hawkins (1988)	90.6	Elton Brand (1999)	109.6
Dennis Rodman (1986)	89.8	Manu Ginóbili (1999)	106.4
P.J. Brown (1992)	89.8	Chris Bosh (2003)	106.0
Alonzo Mourning (1992)	89.7	Rasheed Wallace (1995)	105.1
Glen Rice (1989)	88.7	Tyson Chandler (2001)	102.1
Sam Cassell	87.5	Jason Terry (1999)	102.0
	2,305.7		**2,816.0**

I was trying to show how weak the generation of players was, relatively speaking, that should have been pushing Jordan late in his career. The right column showed how brilliant the generation of players was that immediately preceded LeBron's entry to the league. This didn't show the players that were drafted before Jordan, so to fully demonstrate the universe of players that Jordan contended with throughout his career, I looked at the top 20 players by Career Win Shares, that were drafted between 1977 and 1991 (seven drafts before Jordan, Jordan's draft, and seven drafts after Jordan). Shockingly, the total Career Win Shares from the top 20 players across those 15 NBA drafts barely eclipsed the 9 drafts preceding and including LeBron's draft.

Drafted 1977-1991	Career Win Shares	Drafted 1995-2003	Career Win Shares
Karl Malone (1985)	234.6	LeBron James (2003)	236.4
Michael Jordan (1984)	214.0	Tim Duncan (1997)	206.4
John Stockton (1984)	207.7	Dirk Nowitzki (1998)	206.3
David Robinson (1987)	178.7	Kevin Garnett (1995)	191.4
Charles Barkley (1984)	177.2	Kobe Bryant (1996)	172.7
Reggie Miller (1987)	174.4	Paul Pierce (1998)	150.0
Hakeem Olajuwon (1984)	162.8	Ray Allen (1996)	145.1
Magic Johnson (1979)	155.8	Pau Gasol (2001)	144.1
Larry Bird (1978)	145.8	Steve Nash (1996)	129.7
Gary Payton (1990)	145.5	Vince Carter (1998)	125.3
Clyde Drexler (1983)	135.6	Shawn Marion (1999)	124.9
Patrick Ewing (1985)	126.4	Chauncey Billups (1997)	120.8
Scottie Pippen (1987)	125.1	Dwayne Wade (2003)	120.7
Buck Williams (1981)	120.1	Tony Parker (2001)	111.3
Horace Grant (1987)	118.2	Elton Brand (1999)	109.6
Dominique Wilkins (1982)	117.5	Manu Ginóbili (1999)	106.4
Dikembe Mutombo (1991)	117.0	Chris Bosh (2003)	106.0
Kevin McHale (1980)	113.0	Rasheed Wallace (1995)	105.1
Jack Sickma (1977)	112.5	Tyson Chandler (2001)	102.1
Terry Porter (1985)	110.4	Jason Terry (1999)	102.0
	2,992.3		2,816.0

- o **5)** Career Win Shares is a cumulative stat, and if nothing else, this chart shows how much longer players are playing in the modern game. The players on Jordan's side of the chart averaged 16.3 seasons in their career, while the players from LeBron's draft class and the eight preceding drafts played 18.7 seasons on average.

- o **4)** Important to note that this is an incomplete list because the meter is still running on all-time great players that came after LeBron—Giannis, Steph, Harden, Durant, Lillard, CP3—many of whom have stood directly in the way of LeBron's pursuit of championships. When LeBron retires, and because LeBron's career will be appreciably longer than Jordan's, running the experiment for 9 seasons before LeBron's draft, LeBron's draft, then 9 seasons after LeBron's draft would be more appropriate given how long his peak will have been (but many of the players having come after LeBron are still playing at a high level).

○ **3)** Players from Jordan's universe tended to not play on the same team because the league expanded from 23 to 30 teams over the course of Jordan's career, which generally spread out the talent further (especially into the 90s). LeBron has always played in a league with 30 teams. Players from Jordan's era also had less maneuverability via free agency, and it was more frowned upon to team up with other great players in an attempt to skip steps toward a championship.

○ **2a)** Because team's during LeBron's era were more prone to create clusters of talent, it's kind of wild to look at how many times LeBron had to face composite clusters from players on his side of the chart (in high profile situations, no less):

Garnett/Pierce/Allen [Celtics]—2008 EC Semis, 2010 ECF, 2011 EC Semis, 2012 ECF.[320]
Terry/Chandler/Marion/Nowitzki [Mavs]—2011 NBA Finals'.
Wallace/Billups [Pistons]—2006 EC Semis, 2007 ECF.
Duncan/Parker/Ginóbili [Spurs]—2007, 2013, 2014 NBA Finals'.

If you fold in players that entered the league seven seasons after LeBron did:

Durant/Harden/Russ [Thunder]—2012 NBA Finals'
Steph/Durant [Warriors]—2017, 2018 NBA Finals'

○ **2b)** Jordan also played combinations of the great players from his universe:

McHale/Bird [Celtics]—1986 1st round, 1987 1st round.
Williams/Drexler/Porter [Blazers]—1992 NBA Finals'
Malone/Stockton [Jazz]—1997, 1998 NBA Finals'

But .. obviously less frequently, and Jordan's Bulls were swept both times they played Bird's Celtics. This is probably because Jordan was at the center of, arguably, the best cluster of talent from his generation of players—himself, Scottie Pippen and Horace Grant—who played together for six seasons from 1987-88' through 1992-93'.[321] Now obviously Jordan was the centerpiece of every team he's ever been on, but maybe MJ should be a little less salty toward the late Jerry Krause, given how important it was that Krause drafted two of the best players from Jordan's era on the same night, and those two became irrefutably instrumental to Jordan's legacy.[322]

---

[320] Technically, Rasheed Wallace was on that 2010 Celtics team too, but he was cooked by that point.
[321] *The Last Dance* sure went out of its way to villainize Jerry Krause. But the guy pulled Scottie Pippen and Horace Grant in the same draft. Maybe Jordan gets reinforcements to Chicago by some other means if Krause doesn't pull off that heist at the 1987 draft, or maybe Jordan has to leverage his way to another franchise to try and win his rings, like say, LeBron James did.
[322] Fundamentally, I think this is the exact difference between LeBron and MJ's legacy—Jordan received legitimate reinforcements after his third NBA season in the form of Grant and Pippen, and LeBron never did. Or we can say

- 1) Ultimately, I'm at the same conclusion as when we first went through this chart during Jordan's Tier I profile. Stockton and Malone, in their mid-30's, were Jordan's toughest adversary as his legacy came to a close. Those two were great players in their own right, but it speaks clearly to the lack of real competition, especially late in Jordan's career, that Mike had to contend with. If Jordan's 1997 and 1998 Bulls reached the Finals' and were staring down the 2017 and 2018 Warriors, how sure are you that the Bulls win either of those matchups?[323]

Exhibit C—The Ghost of Jordan's Era

The 1985-86' Celtics are on the short-list within the debate for greatest team of all-time. Shortly after they put the finishing touches on their championship campaign, improbably, they held the second-overall pick in the 1986 NBA draft.

Red Auerbach, a draft-pick swindler of the highest order, had traded Gerald Henderson to Seattle prior to the 1984-85' season, and received Seattle's 1986 first-round pick in return. The 1986 Draft Lottery furthered the Celtics' good fortune when that pick became the second overall pick. When asked if it was fair that Boston, already rich with assets, became even richer, Red responded:

> I think it's very fair .. After all, we had to give up a player to get that
> pick, and so did Philly [who held the first pick]. Gerald Henderson is a
> fine player. But there a lot of fine 6'2" players.

Classic. With that pick, Boston claimed the rights to a fireball of a skilled power forward out of Maryland. His name was Len Bias. With their Bird/McHale/Parish/Johnson[324] core intact, the addition of Lenny Bias made it very easy to see the Celtics competing for championships into the 1990s. Maybe even beyond that if Bias were able to become an All-NBA or MVP-level contributor. Initially, Boston intended to play Bias off the bench—a luxury they could afford—or at least that's what they told Bias immediately following the draft:

> They've told me I'll be the sixth man. They said I'd get plenty of playing
> time. I'm not worried about that.

---

that he did receive reinforcements in the form of Mo Williams, J.J Hickson, over-the-hill Antawn Jamison, way-over-the-hill Shaq, but we'd be lying to ourselves, right? LeBron did manage to become the centerpiece of a dynamic cluster of talent when he leveraged his way to Miami with Chris Bosh and Dwayne Wade. They enjoyed a lot of success as a team, but in the context of this experiment, what if they were able to join together earlier than each player's 8th season in the league? Jordan entered his 4th NBA season with Grant and Pippen flanking him—what if LeBron entered his 4th season flanked with dynamic young talent? LeBron still managed to make the NBA Finals' in his 4th season, but it was with very little talent around him.

[323] Scottie Pippen was a savage for gutting out game six of the 1998 NBA Finals' with that back injury. But beyond a shadow of a doubt, if the Warriors are the opponent, they hunt Scottie down like a wounded gazelle and force him off the court by constantly putting him into actions that require him to move on defense.

[324] Dennis Johnson or DJ. 5x All-Star. 9x All-Defense. 1979 Finals' MVP for Seattle.

As a prospect, Len Bias looked unusually polished. He was definitely a freakazoid 6'8" power forward in terms of his athleticism, but the totality of his offensive game suggested he was going to be a dominant NBA player. He had a structurally beautiful jump shot, not just from the catch-and-shoot, but it was also reliable fading toward either baseline and spotting up off-the-dribble. He had great footwork that you could see in how well he used the up-fake and up-and-under moves. On top of being a skilled, athletic precursor of the stretch-four, Lenny Bias played with an undeniable dose of 'fuck-you' in his game. There was a swagger in his approach to the game, and he often finished his dunks with a 'fuck-you/KG-esque' ferocity. Ed Badger, Boston's director of scouting in 1986, had this to say in his appraisal of Len Bias:

> He's maybe the closest thing to Michael Jordan to come out in a long time [even though Jordan came out just two years prior (?)]. I'm not saying he's as good as Michael Jordan, but he's an explosive and exciting kind of player like that.

The comp wasn't ridiculous then, and it's not ridiculous now when you look at tape of Jordan's final season at North Carolina and Bias' final season at Maryland. Jordan's athleticism and propensity to create fast-break dunks separate him on tape, but it's impossible not to be equally impressed by Bias' skillset, especially considering his position. Bias and Jordan both played in the ACC, and they actually played against each other in Jordan's final two collegiate seasons, and Bias' first two collegiate seasons. Take college stats for what they are, but remember that in the mid-80s, all of the amateur basketball talent was consolidated in the NCAA instead of sitting on the bench in the NBA. These are Jordan and Bias' stats from their final collegiate seasons:

		PPG	FG%	FTr	FT%	TS%
Michael Jordan	Junior (UNC) 1983-84'	19.6	55.1%	.324	77.9%	.587
Len Bias	Senior (Maryland) 1985-86'	23.2	54.4%	.493	86.4%	.613

What's incredible to me is how accomplished Bias was, as a 6'8" power forward who would also play center, at getting to the free throw line and capitalizing once he got there. During that senior season he averaged 7.6 FTA per game and made 86% of them. FTr—or Free Throw Rate—is the number of free throw attempts per field goal attempt. .493 is an utterly ridiculous figure for a power forward who so frequently played on the perimeter offensively. For example, James Harden, the master of swindling defenders into cheap fouls, put up a .502 FTr during his 2017-18' league MVP season. I assure you that Lenny Bias wasn't tricking ACC defenders into cheap fouls with exaggerated head-jerks and deliberate iso-ball, he just had a really refined offensive game and knew how to get where he wanted to.[325]

---

[325] You may dismiss the impact a rookie, even one of Len Bias' quality, may have had on the Celtics. But you can't overstate how impactful rookies could be during that era. Magic won a title in his first season. Bird won a title in his second. Hakeem made the Finals' as his team's best player in his second season.

This doesn't mean that Len Bias was going to step in and be a superior player to Michael Jordan at some point, especially given Jordan had a two-year head start in terms of NBA experience. But Lenny Bias was going to the team that just swept Jordan's Bulls in the 1986 postseason. A team that went 40-1 at home the previous season, won 67 regular season games, and a team that only lost 3 games in their romp of the 1986 postseason. A team that now had the Eastern Conference by the balls for the foreseeable future, and were also prohibitive favorites for the NBA championship. A team that was also now graciously positioned to force fewer minutes on players like Larry Bird, Kevin McHale and Robert Parish. A much-needed reprieve for Boston's nucleus who had then played in three consecutive NBA Finals'.

That reprieve never came, because Len Bias died two days after he was drafted by the Celtics.

It just doesn't matter ultimately. But, the ripples of Len Bias' death are so far-reaching, and undeniably relevant in the context of Michael Jordan's legacy. Bias and Jordan were separated by just 9 months in age, and had Bias played, even conservative extrapolation of his career meant he and Jordan would have tangled on several high-profile occasions. Aggressive extrapolation of Lenny Bias' career could see him carrying the Boston torch well into the 90s, and maybe becoming the legitimate nemesis that MJ never had.

Instead, Boston played on, swept Jordan's Bulls again, and still managed to make the 1987 NBA Finals'. However, the Finals' berth (and subsequent defeat to the Lakers) came at a tremendous tangible cost to their viability as a championship contender going forward. Bird was forced to play 40+ minutes per game on a back that was already bothering him. McHale, who was enjoying his best NBA season to-date during the 1986-87' season,[326] broke his foot shortly before the playoffs began. Knowing that the team didn't have much behind him in the way of a backup, he decided to play through the injury, dramatically shortening his career and the injury still bothers him to this day. Boston gave way to Detroit in the 1988 playoffs, and the franchise failed to compete for a championship for two decades after that. For Jordan's Bulls, shortly after their second-consecutive sweep to the Celtics, they snagged Horace Grant and Scottie Pippen in the 1987 NBA Draft. That initiated their ascent in the Eastern Conference, which now had one fewer contender to deal with.[327]

You don't even need to squint to see how impactful Lenny Bias would have been if he'd played. Boston extending their dynasty is so believable that you can almost wrap your arms around it.

---

[326] He was First-Team All-NBA, and became the first player ever to average 60% from the field and 80% from the free throw line.

[327] There's definitely nothing like this that happened during LeBron's era. The closest hypothetical would have to involve Chris Paul, who was the premier player drafted from the 2005 draft, two drafts after LeBron entered the league. Instead of CP3 going to New Orleans, he somehow gets drafted by Detroit (<3 <3 <3), who were already in position to control the Eastern Conference and prevent LeBron's Cavs from advancing *before* acquiring a generational talent. But then CP3 tragically passes away right after the draft. Behold, the hypothetically deceased *Point God*.

Almost. Alas, all we can do is ask questions that won't ever have answers. If Lenny Bias had played, he'd certainly be one of those 20 players charted by Career Win Shares in Jordan's universe, and Jordan is unquestionably fortunate to have not had to play against a Boston team that included Len Bias.

Closing Argument

Ladies and gentlemen of the jury, we can all agree that for extraordinary events to happen, extraordinary circumstances must present themselves. A player, even one as great as Michael Jordan, doesn't win six championships in six NBA Finals' appearances on the heels of their sheer greatness alone. Jordan needed elite supporting talent to be consolidated in Chicago, which it was. Jordan needed the Boston dynasty to crumble earlier than expected, which it did thanks in large part to the death of Len Bias. Into the 90s, Jordan needed the overall NBA talent pool to be spread thin, which it was, thanks to aggressive league expansion between 1985 and 1995. None of this is to say that Michael Jordan was not the greatest player we've ever seen, because he likely was. But even if that is your determination in the case versus LeBron James, be careful in attributing Chicago's success exclusively to the individual greatness of Michael Jordan. There was a confluence of circumstantial undercurrents that allowed a player to succeed as frequently as Michael Jordan did during the 90s.

Deliberation & Verdict

While I do believe all of that information is important, I'm also not blind to the fact that it falls on deaf ears. Winning is winning is winning is winning is winning, and when the foundation of the argument between LeBron and Jordan looks like this, the details that arrive at these figures don't seem to matter as much to most people:

	Jordan	LeBron
NBA Championships	6	4
Finals' MVPs	6	4
League MVPs	5	4
Greatness Index	**447.28 (1ˢᵗ All-Time)**	441.81 (2ⁿᵈ All-Time)
All-NBA First-Team	10x	**13x**

Jordan claims the highest ever averages for WS/48, playoff WS/48, PER, playoff PER, BPM, and playoff BPM—he's truly the greatest-ever from an advanced perspective, and you know how much I value advanced stuff. LeBron has the second highest average ever in 5 of those 6 categories, an impressive standing compared to, well, any other player in history not named Michael Jordan. LeBron's freakshow 2008-09' season overshadows many of the peak comparisons, but that season failed to yield a championship, unlike Jordan's freakshow 1990-91' season where he did break through for his first championship. We're going to bring this conversation home by splicing the question—*who is the greatest ever?*—into more specific questions about each player's legacy and/or career. The first one gets at the heart of why Jordan was able to break through in 1990-91' and why LeBron was not in 2008-09'.

WHO HAD BETTER TEAMMATES?

Beginning with a broad snapshot of All-League selections, this chart shows how many times each player had a teammate selected to the teams listed:

	LeBron	Jordan
First-Team All-NBA	1x	2x
Second-Team All-NBA	1x	2x
Third-Team All-NBA	3x	2x
First-Team All-Defense	1x	7x
Second-Team All-Defense	-	2x
	6x	**15x**

Stunningly, prior to 2019-20' and the LeBron-AD pairing, LeBron had never played with a player who was selected to First-Team All-NBA *or any* All-Defensive team (AD was selected to both). There's something to be said about LeBron's style of play, and how it can choke off the ability for teammates to rise toward All-Star or All-NBA levels. However, I'm sure you'll remember a segment in Jordan's profile where we illuminated Mike's status as the highest usage player in history—but that didn't stop Scottie Pippen from continually being selected for All-NBA teams. This chart is basically a banner for Pippen's importance to Chicago's success and the construction of Jordan's legacy. 13 of the 15 selections belong to Pippen, with a Second-Team All-Defense selection for Horace Grant in 93' and a First-Team All-Defense selection for Rodman in 96' being the other two. Broadly speaking, because of Scottie Pippen, the answer to this question is Michael Jordan by a decent margin.

However, It would be unfair to suggest that teambuilding was the same in the 1990s as it was in the 2010s. LeBron was a pioneer, a homesteader if you will, on the forefront of player self-determination and player empowerment. Whether you think that distinction should come with praise or criticism, you can't deny that LeBron had more agency than Jordan in selecting his teammates. The Miami Heat triumvirate of Dwayne Wade, Chris Bosh and LeBron was a success—four Finals' trips and two championships in four seasons. The Cleveland Cavaliers reboot in 2015 with Kevin Love, Kyrie Irving and LeBron was also a success—four more Finals' trips and the 2016 NBA Championship across four seasons. The Los Angeles Lakers slap together a championship contender in 2019-20' after acquiring Anthony Davis, and it quickly became a success—hanging a banner for the Lakers in the first season of what will, presumably, be several seasons of this roster dynamic.

LeBron, the homesteader, travelled away from his home in search of better teammates that could improve his odds at winning championships. Broadly speaking, he succeeded in doing so, but left a lot of franchise debris in his wake. Bron definitely screwed over Pat Riley when he left Miami,[328] and by the end of the second Cleveland term, the Cavs were Kyrie-less, and way over the salary cap[329] with a roster destined for the lottery. Again, broadly speaking, he left Cleveland the first time to win a few rings, and he's done that. But when you're forced to live the transient championship-contender lifestyle, things get a little messier as you switch from team to team.

Jordan didn't have to leave the franchise that drafted him, because Chicago built the walls of a championship contender around his other-worldly talents. Jordan is a fairly petty guy, I don't think I'm stepping on any toes by saying that. His disdain for Jerry Krause—the Chicago Bulls' General Manager from 1985 to 2004—was not hidden and it was sourced from Jordan's perception that Krause believed that front offices built championships (not players). Krause seemed like a prick (may he rest in peace), but he wasn't wrong to stand up for the importance of a competent front office when it comes to championship building.

For everything Michael Jordan has, and he has a lot, there are few people he should be thanking more than Jerry Krause. I know, shit, we all know that Michael thinks he could have done it alone. But we all know he's wrong. These crucial front office moves insulated Jordan's abilities in an environment where he was free to play his style of basketball, and there were certain to be quality supporting players around him—a luxury that Jordan still takes for granted to this very day.

- o   1987 NBA Draft—After being swept in the first round of two consecutive postseasons to the Boston Celtics, the Bulls trade the eighth-overall pick, Olden Polynice, and future draft considerations to the Sonics for their fifth-overall choice, Scottie Pippen.[330] The Bulls also draft Horace Grant with the tenth-overall pick. I know I keep banging the drum of how important this draft was, but invariably, these were the second and third best players on the 91', 92' and 93' championship teams for Chicago.

- o   1988—Krause traded Charles Oakley, Chicago's enforcer and Jordan's best friend on the team, for Bill Cartwright. This angered Jordan at first, but Cartwright was a key rotational piece during the Chicago's first three-peat, as he was especially proficient at guarding big men, namely Patrick Ewing, in the post.

- o   1989 NBA Draft—The Bulls draft B.J. Armstrong (eighteenth-overall) who appears in 81 games as a rookie and played in every single playoff game of the Bulls' 91', 92' and 93' championship seasons.

---

[328] Can it finally be funny that LeBron encouraged the team he'd just spent four years playing for to draft a certain player, then ended up leaving that team anyway? Can LeBron shadow drafting Shabazz Napier finally be funny? Please?

[329] Thanks to LeBron's insistence that players like J.R. Smith and Tristan Thompson get paid way more than they were worth.

[330] If just this trade isn't made .. where would Jordan's legacy have fallen?

- 1990 NBA Draft—Chicago drafts Toni Kukoč (twenty-ninth-overall) and while he did not debut in the United States until just after Jordan's first retirement, he was integral to the success of the second Chicago three-peat, and won NBA Sixth Man of the Year in 1995-96'.

- 1994—Chicago signs Ron Harper as a free agent and he played in every playoff game of the Bulls' second three-peat.

- 1994—Krause trades Stacey King for Luc Longley. Luc and Jordan never got along, but he was an important player in Chicago's rotation for their 96', 97' and 98' championships.

- 1995—Krause controversially trades Will Perdue for Dennis Rodman. The Bulls had been dominated down low by the Magic in the 1995 playoffs, and Krause pulled the trigger on acquiring the immensely talented (and colorful) Rodman. Rodman was instrumental to the success of the second Chicago three-peat.

Jordan can hate Jerry Krause all he wants, but Krause's front office consistently constructed championship-level supporting casts for MJ throughout his career. He wasn't afraid to make aggressive trades and he nailed no fewer than a handful of draft picks. That cannot be said for how Cleveland's front office constructed a team around LeBron James.

(Takes deep breath)

LeBron was drafted by Cleveland in 2003 and left for Miami in 2010. The failure to build a true contender around him during the seven seasons of his first Cleveland stretch has to be one of the great front office failures in the history of North American professional sports. Cleveland was gift-wrapped a player with greatest-ever upside and through abortion after abortion of intense front-office malpractice, they forced that player's hand in necessitating a move to play for another franchise. Cleveland's failure to find a running mate (or two) for LeBron during this stretch, in the context of the MJ and LeBron conversation, put LeBron behind schedule for years in climbing up toward Jordan's legacy. Fair warning—the festering anger I have over Cleveland's failure will not be camouflaged while we revisit who LeBron's teammates were during the first seven seasons of his career. You were warned.

The Cleveland Cavaliers were fucking it up well before LeBron's arrival. Before drafting LeBron in 2003, the Cavs held top-ten picks in the 2000, 2001 and 2002 NBA Drafts. This is who they took:

Draft	Pick	Player	Result
2000	8th	Jamal Crawford	Traded Draft night for Chris Mihm who didn't do shit in the NBA (13.3 Career Win Shares).
2001	8th	DeSagna Diop	Didn't do shit in the NBA (12.8 Career Win Shares). Missed on Joe Johnson (10th) and Richard Jefferson (13th).

2002	6th	Dajuan Wagner	Literally didn't do shit in the NBA (0.0 Career Win Shares). In succession, the players drafted after him—Nenê (7th), Chris Wilcox (8th), Amar'e-fucking-Stoudemire (9th), Caron Butler (10th).

This front office buffoonery was orchestrated by Jim Paxson—brother of MJ's Chicago teammate, John Paxson—who was promoted to General Manager of the Cleveland Cavaliers in 1999. I don't love cherry-picking draft mistakes, but these three colossal misses became retroactively important when LeBron James fell into their lap in 2003 (especially that 2002 nightmare). Because in short order, LeBron would raise the floor of the team and top ten draft picks would quickly be a thing of the past. In the 2004-05' season, Paxson's buffoonery climaxed in a deal he made for a completely forgotten NBA player named Jiri Welsch. At the 2005 trade deadline, Paxson sent the Cavaliers unprotected 2005 first round pick for Jiri Welsch, a player who'd already been traded twice in his 18 months since joining the NBA. The Cavaliers, who were 31-21 at the time of the trade, went 11-19 down the stretch. Paxson was fired two months after the trade, and Welsch was dealt again 4 months after the trade to acquire him at the deadline. Good job everyone. Enter Danny Ferry as the Cavaliers General Manager and Dan Gilbert as the franchise's majority owner—what could go wrong?

The Cavaliers notched 50 wins for the first time in the LeBron era during the 2005-06' season, their first season under coach Mike Brown. Behind LeBron's rapid ascent, the Cavaliers managed to push a really good Pistons team to seven games in the second round of the postseason. They lost, and it's probably because their second-leading scorer was averaging 11 PPG in the postseason:

Cleveland Starters 2006 Postseason	PPG	TS%	PER
LeBron James	30.8	.557	23.2
Larry Hughes	11.1	.395	9.2
Zydrunas Ilgauskas	10.4	.501	15.2
Eric Snow	6.6	.484	8.2
Drew Gooden	8.2	.576	16.4

Not Great. Big changes were needed .. and none occurred! Great job, Danny Ferry! Signing Larry Hughes and Donyell Marshall in the summer of 2005 is all you'll ever need to do! The 2006-07' regular season reflected the same number of wins and relative efficiency as the previous season, but LeBron leveled up massively in the playoffs and Cleveland's improbable Eastern Conference Finals win over Detroit somehow landed them in the NBA Finals'. They were innumerably outmatched against the 2007 Spurs, and their starting five—by a wide margin, the worst starting five to ever take the floor in an NBA Finals'—put up these numbers for the postseason, which exposed the same problem they had in the previous postseason:

Cleveland Starters 2007 Postseason	PPG	TS%	PER
LeBron James	25.1	.516	23.9
Larry Hughes	11.3	.450	9.5
Zydrunas Ilgauskas	12.6	.553	18.0
Sasha Pavlović	9.2	.447	6.7
Drew Gooden	11.4	.523	15.7

The Cavs clearly needed a second star, and it wasn't going to fall out of thin air. But apparently Danny Ferry thought that it would, as he made no changes to the roster until the 2008 trade deadline! Nice work, pal! Maybe don't fall asleep when Kevin *fucking* Garnett is on the table in the summer of 2007, and Minnesota took a poo-poo platter centered around Al Jefferson and draft picks to move Garnett to a city he didn't even want to play in! But it's okay, because Danny Ferry saved the day at the 2008 trade deadline by acquiring .. wait for it .. nearly washed Wally Szczerbiak, fully washed Ben Wallace, fully washed Joe Smith and Delonte motha-fucking West! Full steam ahead, destination championship!

In the second round of the 2008 playoffs, the Cavaliers lost in seven games to the eventual champions—Kevin *fucking* Garnett's Boston Celtics. Good job everyone. The stats for Cleveland's starters in the 2008 postseason demonstrate a few new faces with a similar problem:

Cleveland Starters 2008 Postseason	PPG	TS%	PER
LeBron James	28.2	.525	24.3
Delonte West	10.8	.551	11.5
Zydrunas Ilgauskas	13.1	.533	17.2
Wally Szczerbiak	10.8	.510	9.2
Ben Wallace	3.2	.490	12.5

LeBron went to the Olympics that summer, won a Gold Medal, and with the help of an impromptu mentorship from Kobe Bryant, became the best player in basketball during the 2008-09' season. In Danny Ferry's God's honest best move during his illustrious Cleveland tenure, he traded Damon Jones and Joe Smith[331] for Mo Williams before the season. The Cavs won 66 games in 2008-09' and Mo Williams was moonlighting as the second scorer that might finally get the Cavaliers over the top. But he wasn't. After sweeping the first two rounds of the 2009 postseason, Cleveland found themselves in a dogfight against a Magic team with an ingeniously simple strategy—*let LeBron do whatever he wants, because these other fucking bums will not beat us.* LeBron went nuts, Mo Williams and Delonte West struggled to shoulder the bigger loud, and the Cavs got absolutely nothing out of their bench. They lost in six games to the Magic and their 2009 postseason starting five looked like this:

---

[331] But mercifully Joe Smith signed back with the Cavaliers after clearing waivers because where would the Cavs be without 33-year-old Joe Smith as the first guy off the bench? Stab me, just fucking stab me.

Cleveland Starters 2009 Postseason	PPG	TS%	PER
LeBron James	35.3	.618	37.4[332]
Mo Williams	16.3	.530	13.0
Zydrunas Ilgauskas	10.5	.482	14.5
Delonte West	13.8	.550	12.6
Anderson Varejão	8.2	.576	13.0

A much better starting five boasting much better stats, but a championship starting five this was not. The Cavs set out on their 2009-10' suicide mission with LeBron, Delonte and Mo Williams as their three most important players. Danny Ferry, in full-on-panic-mode, acquires worthless Jamario Moon, worthless Leon Powe, a washed Anthony Parker, and a super-washed Shaquille O'Neal prior to the season. Then, reaches for the fences at the 2010 trade deadline and lands his big fish—the also-washed Antawn Jamison. A couple months later, The Cavs met the Celtics again in the second round of the playoffs. They lost in six, because they had no answer, whatsoever, for Kevin .. fucking .. Garnett. Mike Brown gets fired. Danny Ferry resigns (good job, big guy, BRAVO!). LeBron splits for Miami.

What the fuck were we talking about? Oh, who had better teammates between LeBron and MJ? Yeah, it's MJ. It was crucially important to Jordan's legacy that he was partnered, relatively early on, with another premier player. It was substantially detrimental to LeBron's legacy, reputation and confidence, that he was not.

WHO WOULD WIN ONE-ON-ONE?

Completely, utterly, hypothetical. I mean, one-on-one technically isn't even basketball, even though it's played *with* a basketball. I guess we'd have to start by picking which version of each player would be best suited to win versus the other.

For LeBron, it would need to be a version that is still athletically competent enough to stay with Jordan on defense, but equally important, a version of LeBron that would be psychologically impervious to the inevitable trash-talk and mind games that Jordan would wade into. Pre-championships LeBron would be out, because those versions just wouldn't be confident enough. I think somewhere between 2013 and 2016 LeBron would be the sweet spot. I'm going to go with 2013 Miami LeBron—still hyper athletic, has recently added the post game, and has a championship but is still hungry.

For Jordan, I'm tempted to take a later 90s, savvier version who could out-smart LeBron. I just think that he'll need every ounce of athleticism, so I won't overthink it and I'll go with 1992 Jordan—championship hardened and confident, but still a freakshow athletically.

---

[332] lolololololol

LeBron is smart enough to know that he has an advantage in the post, and in a normal basketball game, with referees, he could properly exploit that. But there's no way Jordan lets him do that. Jordan would just foul, or at least force LeBron to call fouls when LeBron settled into his spots on the block. Jordan had an incredible mid-range shot, and because of its ability to demoralize an opponent, I think he would try to get to his spots in the midrange. Even at Mike's peak athleticism, LeBron wouldn't get lost staying with him on the way to the rack, and could recover any lost ground with his much longer frame, so I wouldn't see Mike basing his strategy on attacking the rim.

I think LeBron wins. He has at least 40 pounds on Mike, but he also doesn't give up any agility or speed to him. LeBron could definitely bully him in the post if Jordan doesn't give him the flagrant treatment every time. If LeBron could get even a micro-step on Jordan in his first step, he could euro-step or give Mike the spin-cycle treatment before a dunk. I think Jordan needs to be absolutely draining the jumper to win. He had an incredible jumper, and that's absolutely possible. I just think LeBron has the path to higher-percentage shots that Jordan would not in a one-on-one matchup.

WHO WOULD WIN IF FIVE LEBRONS PLAYED AGAINST FIVE JORDANS?

Even *more* fun hypothetical! I've almost forgotten that we were just talking about the eternal sting that the 2010 Cavaliers put on my psyche. Let's say you have to pick different versions of each player to fill out the starting five, but can't repeat any of them.

For LeBron, as much as I'd like to lean in on athleticism, I think I'll just go in order from 2013 and draft the 2013, 2014, 2015, 2016 and 2017 versions. Actually, let's sub in 2009 for 2017 just for shits and gigs.

For Jordan, he'll be physically overwhelmed at every spot, so I think it's important to take all three of the first three-peat versions—the post Detroit Jordan—so, 1991, 1992, 1993 Jordan for sure, and round it out with the savvy 1996 and 1997 versions.

It's a fascinating prospect. Jordan was a great off-ball player with his cutting and edging, but LeBron was also an excellent off-ball defender. Both teams would absolutely sizzle in transition. Ultimately, if Jordan's team could find a way to consistently get buckets at the rim, it would be a close matchup. Otherwise, I think the physical advantage LeBron has plays out even more strongly in an exhibition like this.

I think LeBron wins. Offensively, the five LeBrons would be like a goddam hive mind, anticipating the perfect cut or the outlet pass that hasn't even opened up yet. Again, I think LeBron's team would have a path to easier buckets. 2009 LeBron could be vulnerable to trash-talk, as I would imagine he would take primary on-ball responsibilities instead of the older, wiser versions. But I think the veteran teammates shepherd young LeBron through any adversity, and it becomes another outcome determined by whether or not Jordan's(ssss) jumper is locked in or not.[333]

WHO HAS THE MORE SIGNIFICANT NON-BASKETBALL LEGACY?

This is a tough one, and I think you have to qualify what the question is really asking. Aside from Michael Jordan *playing basketball*, the legacy that his merchandise and brand have established are nothing short of legendary and culturally revolutionary. However, we're still talking about *basketball* shoes, and largely speaking, Jordan's legacy is always intertwined with something to do with basketball. Jordan and LeBron are very different people, and Jordan clearly draws most of, if not all of, his self-worth from his basketball accomplishments, and the opportunities yielded from those accomplishments. Because, frankly, he doesn't want people to know about his non-basketball life and maybe we shouldn't blame him.

There's a story to be told here about identity and what being better than everyone else can do to a person and their priorities. We all probably know a person with a winning complex, or an obsession with being better than others at something, and it could be anything—fantasy football, rec bowling league, consistently having the best sales at the office, pick-up hoops, golfing circles, etc. If that person is telling themselves a story about how much better they are than other people at something, it starts becoming their identity, and that dominance over others or mental reward you get from winning becomes addictive. Jordan just continued to win, and continued to receive more adoration from fans, sponsors, peers, fucking every person in the world. That compounded and compounded over the course of his career, and he got addicted to being told that he was better than everyone else at something. In a way, we created the ego that Jordan has, and it's not really his fault that he's become so prickly.

We shouldn't be surprised that Jordan is notoriously prickly toward anyone that slights him. Even micro-slights. Like Chuck Barkley jabbing him for the ineptitude of the NBA team that Jordan owns, and Jordan subsequently shutting out their decades-long friendship. Or, I don't know, making a TEN-HOUR documentary about your career. Because, obviously, a 1, 2 or 3-hour documentary detailing all of your accomplishments just wasn't enough. Not even a 4, 5, or 6-hour documentary would be long enough to interweave every positive clip ever captured of you on film. *Not even a 7, 8 or 9-hour documentary is long enough to capture the true story that just needed to be told!* Yes .. it had to be ten hours .. no shorter. That's just who he is—he

---

[333] And let's be clear about something here—one of the Jordan's, after not getting the ball enough, is absolutely starting a fight with another of the Jordan's, right?

never wants to let go of the thing that made him so happy with himself—basketball—and we can't really blame him.

LeBron has eyes for plenty of things beyond basketball. I don't think it's controversial to say that his non-basketball legacy is already more significant than Jordan's, and will continue to surge in the coming years. Jordan made the calculated decision to stay away from political issues for the entirety of his playing career—commercially, probably a good move and you can't really knock him for it.

Conversely, LeBron's willingness to interject his opinions about social and racial inequality allow citizens of the world, particularly those of color, to connect with him in a way that people weren't able to with MJ. LeBron is this generation's Muhammad Ali, and I mean that.[334] People now anticipate and expect LeBron to give his input on matters of inequality in America. Because of his willingness to voice these opinions from his huge media platform, he's drawn criticism from high-profile conservative voices. It's not especially flattering for LeBron James to have his name slandered frequently on Fox News, until you broaden the context to include LeBron as just the most recent example of how this pattern works.

It's the same thing they did to Owens, to Robinson, to Gibson, to Russell, to Baylor, to Brown, to Robertson, to Clay (but especially Ali), to Rudolph, to Alcindor (but especially Abdul-Jabbar), to Smith & Carlos, to Ashe, to Abdul-Rauf, to Williams, and to Kaepernick.

When high-profile African American athletes speak out against injustice they perceive in America, defamatory assaults on their credibility are sure to follow. LeBron's money and fame don't shield him from the same brand of attacks that befell those brave men and women who were also instructed to 'shut up and dribble' when they protested racial inequality. Honestly, being singled out by right-wing voices is about the greatest recognition a speaker in their position can achieve.

While the stakes aren't as high for LeBron, and he's been able to prosper in large part to the volume of efforts that came before him, we still need to acknowledge his acceptance of the same burden that was embraced by his cultural predecessors. LeBron James earned our respect because he chose to carry the torch, absorb the inevitable daggers, and not sit on the sidelines by saying shit like 'republicans buy sneakers too'.

While we shouldn't blame Michael Jordan for his non-basketball stances, or criticize him for having fewer of them in total, we need to reward LeBron for choosing to stand up, and for maintaining a level of humanity that often eludes athletes chasing down 'greatest-ever' status.

---

[334] But let's be clear about what I mean—he's this generation's most famous athlete who also frequently speaks out on inequalities for African Americans. The difference between Bron and Ali is the stakes. When Ali made his stand against the Vietnam War, he was risking everything—his livelihood, his name, his reputation (amongst whites and blacks) .. and shit, his life. LeBron might be risking a few extra dollars from 'whiter' sponsors and a lower overall approval rating when he speaks out on racial injustices, but what he's putting on the line is nothing close to what Ali was.

For as much media scrutiny as has been shoveled on him, somehow there are no skeletons or scandals in LeBron's closet. He doesn't appear to have any vices, and his dedication to being a great Dad in his kids' lives creates another opportunity for everyday people to connect with him, where they might have felt shut off when it came to MJ. Maybe it was just the era I was growing up in where athletes were more frequently engaged in after-hours knuckleheadery, but I seem to remember the constant call for athletes to serve as better role models. As this generation's most-recognized and famous athlete, could LeBron have answered the call any better?[335]

WHO HAD THE BETTER CAREER?

Now this, my friends, is a juicy question. I'm going to start with a stat called MVP Award Shares—which demonstrates the percentage of voting points that a player received out of the total possible votes in a given season (for league MVP). It slides well across eras because it's a percentage of the vote, and I think you'll see some familiar faces in the top-ten:

	All-Time MVP Award Shares
LeBron James	8.813
Michael Jordan	8.115
Kareem Abdul-Jabbar	6.105
Larry Bird	5.612
Magic Johnson	5.104
Bill Russell	4.748
Shaquille O'Neal	4.380
Karl Malone	4.296
Tim Duncan	4.278
Kobe Bryant	4.202

Another stat that ranks LeBron and Jordan in the top two, but this one really drills home the division from the other all-time greats. It's a cumulative stat and it's really a reflection of how present a player was at the very top of the league (and for how long). But as we focus back in on LeBron and MJ, it opens up a question about how you value LeBron's impact beyond the number of years that Jordan played.

When you see this question, it looks interchangeable with 'who is the greatest player ever?'. But what I'm really asking is how we should view LeBron having a substantially longer career

---

[335] I mean, Jordan *is a dad*, technically. But how many times were his kids even mentioned in the 10-HOUR DOCUMENTARY about him. Little known fact, because *The Last Dance* surely wasn't going to tell you, MJ was married across the vast majority of the time documented in the films, and I'm pretty sure his wife is mentioned .. once. Cool .. ?

than Jordan, while maintaining an All-NBA level of play across substantially more seasons. I think the quick answer, and it might just be the correct answer is simply—Jordan—he won a lot more championships, had fewer blunders and typically completed his accomplishments in more convincing fashion.

If your answer is—LeBron—it's because he built more cumulative championship equity over the course of his career, and even if this is the wrong answer, it's worth taking a deeper look at. All-NBA teams are not easy to make, and chances are your favorite player made fewer in his career than you think. If your favorite player is LeBron, like me, then you know that he's been selected to more All-NBA teams overall, and more First-Team All-NBA teams, than any other player in history:

	LeBron James	Michael Jordan
All-NBA Selections	**16x**	11x
First-Team All-NBA Selections	**13x**	10x

We know that Jordan's career was relatively short compared to many other all-time greats, and this isn't an attack on his career. But the sheer volume of elite, elite, elite, level contribution to winning basketball in the margin between each player's selections here is fascinating to me.

Think about it this way, LeBron has 5 more All-NBA selections than Jordan, and 3 of them to the First-Team. Kawhi Leonard has 3 First-Team selections over his entire career. Allen Iverson made 3 First-Team All-NBA squads in his whole career. *Steph freaking Curry* has only 3 appearances on the All-NBA First-Team. Isiah Thomas, for the length of his career, made exactly 5 All-NBA teams, and 3 of them were to the First-Team—the exact difference between MJ and Bron's total selections.

Whether this matters to you or not, it's important to remember that additional peak LeBron seasons are not equal in value to, say, Karl Malone eating up seasons on an All-NBA team.[336] If LeBron made the First-Team, that meant he was in the MVP hunt—which is why he's accumulated so much tread in MVP Award Shares. Plus, an elite LeBron season also meant that his team was, at minimum, obliquely in the championship conversation. Maybe it only matters if he won the championship, and I won't blame you if that's your line of thinking. But if the difference between LeBron and MJs career, in terms of how many great seasons they had, is a wide enough margin to encompass entire careers of dynamic, historic NBA players, that has to be worth something.

Michael Jordan's career was like an hour-long workout where you burned 1,000 calories and maintained an average heart rate of 170. A fucking massacre of a workout. LeBron's career will have been like an hour-and-a-half workout where you burned 1,250 calories, but your average

---

[336] That is to say, LeBron is not a rich man's Karl Malone. LeBron being prolific and Malone being prolific are different animals.

heart rate was 164. A fucking brutal workout in its own right, but not quite as intense throughout.

Ultimately, I think this is incredibly close, and it's probably the portion of the—*who is the greatest ever?*—question that will continue to unravel in LeBron's favor over the coming years. I would have deferred to Jordan for a long time, in respect of his championship success, but I think LeBron has had enough championship success now to validate the Pacific Ocean of accumulated greatness that he's shown us. I'll take *The King* in the question of who had the better career.

WHO IS BETTER AT BASKETBALL?

Framing it as each player at their peak—2013 or 2014 LeBron, 1991 or 1992 MJ—I just think the apex version of LeBron has more tools in his bag. He's more impressive physically, and possesses an ability to distribute that Jordan didn't have. They're both incredible two-way players at their apex, and I'll hear the argument that Jordan won a Defensive Player of the Year award, whereas LeBron did not. But, LeBron finished second on two different occasions, and without any legitimate argument to be made on the side of Jordan, the best version of LeBron is an appreciably more versatile defender.

In a vacuum of equal competitive circumstance and era-specific nuances, I think apex LeBron— 2013 through 2016 LeBron—is the most competent overall basketball player we've ever seen.

SO, WHO IS THE GREATEST-EVER?

It's LeBron James.

I haven't thought this way for long, and in fact, I was a holdout on LeBron's status until the Los Angeles championship. As I eluded to during LeBron's profile, I believe LeBron's position as the best player on four championship teams for three different franchises is as good a claim to the throne as exists in the NBA universe .. and that includes Jordan's once unassailable trophy count from his trips to the NBA Finals'.

If you can follow me to a place where LeBron's four championships for three different franchises is an equal accomplishment to Jordan's six championships for the same franchise, then we can suspend the 'count the rings' methodology and begin contextualizing each player's career and what the NBA looked like while they were playing.

I think it's clear that LeBron has played in a more competitive NBA, a more stylistically diverse NBA, and an NBA that was clustering talent more often in pursuit of championships. Simply put, I think teams in LeBron's era have just been smarter about positioning themselves to win championships. But Jordan could say the same thing about Kareem's era, and Kareem could definitely say the same thing about Russell's era—when Red Auerbach's foresight was enough to embargo the rest of the NBA from winning for more than a decade. Basketball advances, therefore, basketball's generational players advance correlatively.

The construction of this book was based on the premise that Tier I could only, truly, be made up of the four players that I selected for it. It's up to you to decide if *Beggars Banquet*, *Let it Bleed*, *Sticky Fingers* or *Exile on Main St.* was the greatest Rolling Stones record. I'll respect your choice, regardless.

You're far from wrong for thinking it's *Sticky Fingers*. It showcases an immaculate and tidy collection of Rolling Stones' songs that construct a seemingly perfect record. The brilliance of *Exile on Main St.* is more subtle, and certainly less tidy, but if you listen to both records enough, you'll see the inevitable advancement of the Stones' sound that occurs across their four album peak, which crests with the final album of that run, *Exile on Main St.*

Thanks for going on this journey with me. My updated ranking of the 30 greatest players ever by Tier I, Tier II and Tier III distinction can be found, in perpetuity, at strainofdiscourse.com.

Acknowledgements.

- Rebecca—thanks for believing in me, supporting me, encouraging me, and most of all, pretending like you didn't want to punch me while I was writing this thing. You're the best person I've ever met and it's my great fortune to be your husband.

- Mom and Mike—thanks for always encouraging me to chase down shit I care about.

- James—thanks for showing me what courage and perseverance look like.

- Lauren—thanks for showing me what it looks like to be an adult (maybe one day).

- Mike—thanks for accepting me and going out of your way to create our friendship.

- Dad and Tree—thanks for your ever-present support.

- Kenny—thanks for letting me workshop insane ideas with you.

- Roger—thanks for reading through some tough anti-Kobe versions of this book, happily clenching your teeth the whole time. (Champs, son!!!!!)

- Zach—thanks you son of a bitch, for staying in my ear about a certain player who you strongly believed needed to be on this list. You were right.

- Greg—thanks for always supporting me and being a great friend.

- Brian—thanks for nothing you ding dong! JK, thanks for encouraging me and being an awesome friend.

Quentin Tarantino—thanks for not going to film school and film-nerding your way into a massively prolific career.

Matthew Weiner—thanks for paying the Beatles estate, by way of AMC, $250,000 for using *Tomorrow Never Knows* in S5:E8 of *Mad Men*. Because, let's be honest, it had to be that song.

Kanye West—thanks for always going the other way.

- Thanks to Jacob Goldstein for all your help with integrating PIPM.

- Thanks to Coach David Thorpe for letting me bounce ideas off of you.

- Thanks to Rob Parker for encouraging me to *keep dreamin' and keep workin'*.

Attribution.

Foreward

"Basketball Statistics and History." *Basketball*, 13 Apr. 2018, www.basketball-reference.com/.

"Middle Ground." *The Wire.* HBO. Dec 12. 2004. Television.

Sports Illustrated. 18 Feb. 2002, https://vault.si.com/vault/2002/02/18/ahead-of-his-class-ohio-high-school-junior-lebron-james-is-so-good-that-hes-already-being-mentioned-as-the-heir-to-air-jordan.

St. Vincent-St.Mary's vs. Oak Hill Academy. ESPN 2. Dec 12 2002. Television.

Beck, Howard. "James Takes Game 6 Personally." *The New York Times*, The New York Times, 8 June 2012, www.nytimes.com/2012/06/08/sports/basketball/james-leads-heat-to-game-7-against-celtics.html.

"Who Goes There." *True Detective.* HBO. Feb 9. 2014. Television.

"The Godfather: Part One." Paramount/Alfran, 1971. Film.

"Training Day." Warner Bros, 2001. Film.

"Basketball." *The Office.* NBC. Apr 19. 2005. Television.

Mad Men. AMC. 2007-2015. Television.

"Episode 2." *The Shop.* HBO. Oct 12. 2018. Television.

"Transformed at Last." *Dragonball Z-Frieza Saga.* Fuji TV. Oct 18. 1999. Television.

"No Country For Old Men." Miramax Films/Paramount Vantage. 2007. Film.

Manfred, Tony. "Here's Proof That Lebron James Played One Of The Best Playoff Games Ever Last Night" *Business Insider*, Business Insider, 8 June 2012, www.businessinsider.com/lebron-james-celtics-game-6-2012-6.

Boston Celtics vs. Miami Heat. ESPN. Jun 7. 2012. Television.

"Space Jam." Warner Bros. 1996. Film.

Introduction

"Basketball Statistics and History." *Basketball*, 13 Apr. 2018, www.basketball-reference.com/.

"Season 2 Episode 6: The Internet & Moment in the Life of Lil Jon." *Chappelle's Show*. Comedy Central. Feb 25. 2004. Television.

Rolling Stone. "500 Greatest Albums of All Time." Rolling Stone, Rolling Stone, 29 July 2019, www.rollingstone.com/music/music-lists/500-greatest-albums-of-all-time-156826/.

Simmons, Bill. Gladwell, Malcolm. *The Book of Basketball: The NBA According to The Sports Guy*. Ballantine Books Trade, 2011.

Taylor, Ben. "The Backpicks GOAT: The 40 Best Careers in NBA History." *Back Picks*, 25 June 2019, backpicks.com/2017/12/11/the-backpicks-goat-the-40-best-careers-in-nba-history/.

Duncan, Nate, host. *Dunc'd On Basketball NBA Podcast*. Spotify. Jun 7. 2020.

Simmons, Bill, host. *The Bill Simmons Podcast*. The Ringer. Spotify. Jun 7. 2020.

Lowe, Zach, host. *The Lowe Post Podcast*. ESPN. Spotify. Jun 7. 2020.

Goldstein, Jacob. "Player Impact Plus-Minus." *Basketball Index*, 29 Mar. 2019, www.bball-index.com/player-impact-plus-minus/.

Silver, Nate. "Introducing RAPTOR, Our New Metric For The Modern NBA." *FiveThirtyEight*, FiveThirtyEight, 10 Oct. 2019, fivethirtyeight.com/features/introducing-raptor-our-new-metric-for-the-modern-nba/.

Ilardi, Steve. "The next Big Thing: Real plus-Minus." *ESPN*, ESPN Internet Ventures, 7 Apr. 2014, www.espn.com/nba/story/_/id/10740818/introducing-real-plus-minus.

dantheman9758. "r/Nba - Here's 135 NBA Games Where Blocked Shot Data Exists for Bill Russell (and Compared with Wilt Chamberlain's 112):" *Reddit*, 10 Nov. 2015, www.reddit.com/r/nba/comments/3s9669/heres_135_nba_games_where_blocked_shot_data/.

Sepinwall, Alan, and Matt Zoller Seitz. *TV (the Book) Two Experts Pick the Greatest American Shows of All Time*. Grand Central Publishing, 2016.

Rolling Stone. "500 Greatest Albums of All Time." Rolling Stone, Rolling Stone, 29 July 2019, www.rollingstone.com/music/music-lists/500-greatest-albums-of-all-time-156826/.

Julius Erving:

Sports Reference LLC "Julius Erving Stats." Basketball-Reference.com - Basketball Statistics and History. https://www.basketball-reference.com/. Sept 9. 2018.

Taylor, Ben January. "Backpicks GOAT: #16 Julius Erving." *Back Picks*, 1 Jan. 2018, backpicks.com/2018/01/01/backpicks-goat-16-julius-erving/.

Goldstein, Jacob. Walker, Nathan. "Player Impact Plus-Minus." *Basketball Index*, 29 Mar. 2019, www.bball-index.com/player-impact-plus-minus/.

"Semi-Pro." New Line Cinema. 2008. Film.

"NBA-ABA: Erving, Other Stars, Recall Days in ABA." *UPI*, UPI, 7 Mar. 1987, www.upi.com/Archives/1987/03/07/NBA-ABA-Erving-Other-Stars-Recall-Days-in-ABA/1906542091600/.

"Michael Scott Paper Company." *The Office*. NBC. Apr 9. 2009. Television.

(Hubie Brown excerpt). MacMullan, Jackie. Bartholome, Rafe. Klores, Dan. *Basketball: A Love Story*. Broadway Books, 2019.

Lowe, Zach, host. Buss, Jeanie, guest. *The Lowe Post Podcast.* ESPN. Spotify. Jan 22. 2019.

Goodman, Elizabeth. *Meet Me in the Bathroom: Rebirth and Rock and Roll in New York City 2001-2011*. Faber & Faber, 2019.

(Mike Vaccaro excerpt). MacMullan, Jackie. Bartholome, Rafe. Klores, Dan. *Basketball: A Love Story*. Broadway Books, 2019.

Scottie Pippen:

Sports Reference LLC "Scottie Pippen Stats." Basketball-Reference.com - Basketball Statistics and History. https://www.basketball-reference.com/. Oct 2. 2018.

Taylor, Ben. "Backpicks GOAT #23 Scottie Pippen." *Back Picks*, 13 Feb. 2018, backpicks.com/2018/01/29/backpicks-goat-23-scottie-pippen/.

Goldstein, Jacob. Walker, Nathan. "Player Impact Plus-Minus." *Basketball Index*, 29 Mar. 2019, www.bball-index.com/player-impact-plus-minus/.

"Without Bias." ESPN Films. Nov 3. 2009. Television.

Manfred, Tony. "27 Examples of Michael Jordan's Extreme Competitiveness." *Business Insider*, Business Insider, 5 May 2020, www.businessinsider.com/michael-jordans-insane-competitiveness-2014-7.

Smith, Sam. "Scottie Pippen Still Battling a Curse - a Migraine Headache - That Has Haunted Him." *Chicagotribune.com*, Chicago Tribune, 27 Apr. 2020, www.chicagotribune.com/news/ct-xpm-1991-05-24-9102160600-story.html.

Simmons, Bill. Gladwell, Malcolm. *The Book of Basketball: The NBA According to The Sports Guy*. Ballantine Books Trade, 2011.

Elgin Baylor:

Sports Reference LLC "Elgin Baylor Stats." Basketball-Reference.com - Basketball Statistics and History. https://www.basketball-reference.com/. Oct 10. 2018.

Taylor, Ben. "Backpicks GOAT: #36-40." *Back Picks*, 3 Mar. 2018, backpicks.com/2018/03/08/goat-36-40/#Baylor.

Goldstein, Jacob. Walker, Nathan. "Player Impact Plus-Minus." *Basketball Index*, 29 Mar. 2019, www.bball-index.com/player-impact-plus-minus/.

Rolling Stone. "500 Greatest Albums of All Time." Rolling Stone, Rolling Stone, 29 July 2019, www.rollingstone.com/music/music-lists/500-greatest-albums-of-all-time-156826/.

Spitz, Bob. *The Beatles: The Biography*. Aurum, 2007.

McKenna, Dave. "Elgin Baylor Is Finally Ready To Tell People He Was Great." *Deadspin*, 16 Apr. 2018, deadspin.com/elgin-baylor-is-finally-ready-to-tell-people-he-was-gre-1825284896.

Schwartz, Larry. "Before Michael, There Was Elgin." *ESPN*, ESPN Internet Ventures, www.espn.com/sportscentury/features/00014086.html.

Reid, Jason. "Dr. J on Elgin Baylor: 'He Was Just Ballet in Basketball'." *The Undefeated*, The Undefeated, 18 Apr. 2018, theundefeated.com/features/dr-j-on-elgin-baylor-he-was-just-ballet-in-basketball/.

Easton, Ed. "Celebrating the Basketball Life of Lakers Legend Elgin Baylor." *Hoops Habit*, FanSided, 10 Apr. 2018, hoopshabit.com/2018/04/10/celebrating-basketball-life-lakers-legend-elgin-baylor/.

Ganguli, Tania. "Elgin Baylor, in Bronze, Gets Place of Honor." *Los Angeles Times*, Los Angeles Times, 7 Apr. 2018, www.latimes.com/sports/lakers/la-sp-lakers-report-20180406-story.html#.

Simmons, Bill. "Ewing Theory 101." *ESPN*, ESPN Internet Ventures, 9 May 2001, www.espn.com/espn/page2/story?page=simmons/010509a.

Chris Paul/Isiah Thomas:

Sports Reference LLC "Chris Paul Stats." Basketball-Reference.com - Basketball Statistics and History. https://www.basketball-reference.com/. Oct 15. 2018.

Sports Reference LLC "Isiah Thomas Stats." Basketball-Reference.com - Basketball Statistics and History. https://www.basketball-reference.com/. May 24. 2020.

Taylor, Ben. "Backpicks GOAT #21: Chris Paul." *Back Picks*, 17 Feb. 2018, backpicks.com/2018/02/19/backpicks-goat-21-chris-paul/.

Goldstein, Jacob. Walker, Nathan. "Player Impact Plus-Minus." *Basketball Index*, 29 Mar. 2019, www.bball-index.com/player-impact-plus-minus/.

Young, Shane. "A Case For Chris Paul, Second-Best Point Guard Of All Time." *Medium*, The Cauldron, 26 July 2016, the-cauldron.com/a-case-for-chris-paul-second-best-point-guard-of-all-time-a64f168054a6.

Redick, JJ, host. Paul, Chris, guest. *The JJ Redick Podcast.* The Ringer. Spotify. Mar 8. 2019.

"Players Clutch Traditional." *NBA Stats*, stats.nba.com/players/clutch-traditional/?sort=GP&dir=-1.

Karl Malone:

Sports Reference LLC "Karl Malone Stats." Basketball-Reference.com - Basketball Statistics and History. https://www.basketball-reference.com/. Oct 26. 2018.

Taylor, Ben. "Backpicks GOAT: #13 Karl Malone." *Back Picks*, 7 Apr. 2018, backpicks.com/2018/02/08/backpicks-goat-13-karl-malone/.

Goldstein, Jacob. Walker, Nathan. "Player Impact Plus-Minus." *Basketball Index*, 29 Mar. 2019, www.bball-index.com/player-impact-plus-minus/.

Dirk Nowitzki:

Sports Reference LLC "Dirk Nowitzki Stats." Basketball-Reference.com - Basketball Statistics and History. https://www.basketball-reference.com/. Nov 1. 2018.

Taylor, Ben. "Backpicks GOAT: #18 Dirk Nowitzki." *Back Picks*, 25 Feb. 2018, backpicks.com/2018/02/26/backpicks-goat-18-dirk-nowitzki/.

Goldstein, Jacob. Walker, Nathan. "Player Impact Plus-Minus." *Basketball Index*, 29 Mar. 2019, www.bball-index.com/player-impact-plus-minus/.

"The Lion King." Buena Vista Pictures/Walt Disney Pictures. 1994. Film.

"Star Wars: Episode IV—A New Hope." 20th Century Fox/Lucasfilm Ltd. 1977. Film.

Campbell, Joseph. *The Hero with a Thousand Faces: a Brilliant Examination, through Ancient Hero Myths, of Mans Eternal Struggle for Identity.* Fontana Press, 1949.

Vogler, Christopher. *The Writers Journey: Mythic Structure for Writers.* Michael Wiese Productions, 1998.

Preston, Richard E. "The Hero's Journey in Game of Thrones: Daenerys Targaryen." *Winter Is Coming*, FanSided, 19 Mar. 2016, winteriscoming.net/2016/03/19/the-heros-journey-in-game-of-thrones-daenerys-targaryen/.

"The Story Structure of True Detective." *Articles - Narrative First*, narrativefirst.com/articles/the-story-structure-of-true-detective.

SportsDayDFW.com. "Sefko: Dad Teased Dirk about Playing 'Woman's Sport' but Is Proud Mav Remained Well-Grounded." *Dallas News*, The Dallas Morning News, 27 Aug. 2019, sportsday.dallasnews.com/dallas-mavericks/sportsdaydfw/2012/10/03/sefko-dad-teased-dirk-about-playing-woman-s-sport-but-is-proud-mav-remained-well-grounded.

MacMullan, Jackie. "Inside The NBA - Sports Illustrated Vault." *Sports Illustrated Vault | SI.com*, 15 June 1998, www.si.com/vault/1998/06/15/244497/inside-the-nba.

Wise, Mike. "The Americanization of Dirk Nowitzki." *The New York Times*, The New York Times, 7 Feb. 2001, www.nytimes.com/2001/02/07/sports/pro-basketball-the-americanization-of-dirk-nowitzki.html.

Mad Men. AMC. 2007-2015. Television.

Lowe, Zach, host. Beck, Howard, guest. *The Lowe Post Podcast.* ESPN. Spotify. Mar 27. 2019.

Lowe, Zach, host. Nowitzki, Dirk, guest. *The Lowe Post Podcast.* ESPN. Spotify. Feb 1. 2019.

Stein, Marc. "Sources: Dirk Sends Opt-out Letter." *ESPN*, ESPN Internet Ventures, 29 June 2010, www.espn.com/dallas/nba/news/story?id=5339661.

Stein, Marc. "Sources: Dirk, Mavs Have $80M Deal." *ESPN*, ESPN Internet Ventures, 4 July 2010, www.espn.com/dallas/nba/news/story?id=5352960.

Jerry West:

Sports Reference LLC "Jerry West Stats." Basketball-Reference.com - Basketball Statistics and History. https://www.basketball-reference.com/. Nov 11. 2018.

Taylor, Ben. "Backpicks GOAT: #17 Jerry West." *Back Picks*, 17 Dec. 2017, backpicks.com/2017/12/18/backpicks-goat-17-jerry-west/.

Goldstein, Jacob. Walker, Nathan. "Player Impact Plus-Minus." *Basketball Index*, 29 Mar. 2019, www.bball-index.com/player-impact-plus-minus/.

Thomas, Greg. "Constructing a Winner: The Genius of Jerry West." *Golden State Of Mind*, 31 Dec. 2016, www.goldenstateofmind.com/2016/12/30/14122696/constructing-a-winner-the-genius-of-jerry-west.

Dwayne Wade:

Sports Reference LLC "Dwayne Wade Stats." Basketball-Reference.com - Basketball Statistics and History. https://www.basketball-reference.com/. Nov 15. 2018.

Taylor, Ben. "Backpicks GOAT: #22 Dwyane Wade." *Back Picks*, 12 Feb. 2018, backpicks.com/2018/02/15/backpicks-goat-22-dwyane-wade/.

Goldstein, Jacob. Walker, Nathan. "Player Impact Plus-Minus." *Basketball Index*, 29 Mar. 2019, www.bball-index.com/player-impact-plus-minus/.

Steve Nash:

Sports Reference LLC "Steve Nash Stats." Basketball-Reference.com - Basketball Statistics and History. https://www.basketball-reference.com/. Nov 19. 2018.

Taylor, Ben. "Backpicks GOAT: #19 Steve Nash." *Back Picks*, 20 Feb. 2018, backpicks.com/2018/02/22/backpicks-goat-19-steve-nash/.

Goldstein, Jacob. Walker, Nathan. "Player Impact Plus-Minus." *Basketball Index*, 29 Mar. 2019, www.bball-index.com/player-impact-plus-minus/.

"The Godfather: Part Two." Paramount/The Coppola Company, 1974. Film.

Merron, Jeff. "The Suns Rise in Phoenix." *ESPN*, ESPN Internet Ventures, www.espn.com/espn/page2/story?page=list/050110/nbaturnarounds.

Heifetz, Danny. "Tyrion Used to Drink and Know Things. Now He Just Drinks." *The Ringer*, The Ringer, 17 Apr. 2019, www.theringer.com/game-of-thrones/2019/4/17/18412187/tyrion-used-to-drink-and-know-things-now-he-just-drinks.

Leibowitz, Ben. "Phoenix Suns: Worst Trades of the Last Decade." *Bleacher Report*, Bleacher Report, 3 Oct. 2017, bleacherreport.com/articles/1015694-the-worst-phoenix-suns-trades-of-the-last-decade#slide9.

McPeek, Jeramie. "Surprised But Happy, Nash Is a Sun Again." *Phoenix Suns*, NBA.com/Suns, 5 Oct. 2004, www.nba.com/suns/news/tribune_041005.html#gref.

Cuban, Mark. "Steve Nash, Part 1." *Blog Maverick*, 3 July 2004, blogmaverick.com/2004/07/03/steve-nash-part-1/.

Moses Malone:

Sports Reference LLC "Moses Malone Stats." Basketball-Reference.com - Basketball Statistics and History. https://www.basketball-reference.com/. Nov 26. 2018.

Taylor, Ben. "Backpicks GOAT: #24 Moses Malone." *Back Picks*, 6 Jan. 2018, backpicks.com/2018/01/08/backpicks-goat-24-moses-malone/.

Goldstein, Jacob. Walker, Nathan. "Player Impact Plus-Minus." *Basketball Index*, 29 Mar. 2019, www.bball-index.com/player-impact-plus-minus/.

Papanek, John. "THERE'S AN ILL WIND BLOWING FOR THE NBA - Sports Illustrated Vault." *Sports Illustrated Vault | SI.com*, 26 Feb. 1979, www.si.com/vault/1979/02/26/823411/theres-an-ill-wind-blowing-for-the-nba-attendance-is-slipping-and-the-leagues-tv-ratings-have-plummeted-leading-to-a-lot-of-cries-and-whispers-about-the-real-problems.

Dennis Rodman:

Sports Reference LLC "Dennis Rodman Stats." Basketball-Reference.com - Basketball Statistics and History. https://www.basketball-reference.com/. Dec 2. 2018.

Goldstein, Jacob. Walker, Nathan. "Player Impact Plus-Minus." *Basketball Index*, 29 Mar. 2019, www.bball-index.com/player-impact-plus-minus/.

User: Kendrick. "Why Dennis Rodman, Not Jordan Should Have Been '96 Finals MVP." *HBCU Sports Forums*, HBCU Sports Forums, 14 Dec. 2018, www.hbcusports.com/forums/threads/why-dennis-rodman-not-jordan-should-have-been-'96-finals-mvp.136320/.

Draymond Green:

Sports Reference LLC "Draymond Green Stats." Basketball-Reference.com - Basketball Statistics and History. https://www.basketball-reference.com/. Feb 3. 2019.

Goldstein, Jacob. Walker, Nathan. "Player Impact Plus-Minus." *Basketball Index*, 29 Mar. 2019, www.bball-index.com/player-impact-plus-minus/.

Mahoney, Rob. "Through Small Ball, Warriors Amp up Their Stylistic Advantage." *Sports Illustrated*, 21 May 2015, www.si.com/nba/2015/05/21/draymond-green-warriors-rockets-nba-playoffs-small-ball-stephen-curry.

Hughes, Grant. "Andrew Bogut's Value to Golden State Warriors Has Never Been Higher." *Bleacher Report*, Bleacher Report, 17 Aug. 2017, bleacherreport.com/articles/2532139-andrew-boguts-value-to-golden-state-warriors-has-never-been-higher.

Jenkins, Lee. "How a 3 A.m. Text and a Team Staffer Helped the Warriors Win Game 4." *Sports Illustrated*, 12 June 2015, www.si.com/nba/2015/06/12/warriors-steve-kerr-nick-uren-andre-iguodala-andrew-bogut-nba-finals-cavaliers.

David Robinson:

Sports Reference LLC "David Robinson Stats." Basketball-Reference.com - Basketball Statistics and History. https://www.basketball-reference.com/. May 6. 2019.

Taylor, Ben. "Backpicks GOAT: #15 David Robinson." *Back Picks*, 2 Feb. 2018, backpicks.com/2018/02/05/backpicks-goat-15-david-robinson/.

Goldstein, Jacob. Walker, Nathan. "Player Impact Plus-Minus." *Basketball Index*, 29 Mar. 2019, www.bball-index.com/player-impact-plus-minus/.

"Scott's Tots." *The Office*. NBC. Dec 3. 2009. Television.

Upscale. "CHARITY ADMIRAL DAVID ROBINSON." *Upscale Magazine*, 2 Feb. 2016, upscalemagazine.com/charity-admiral-david-robinson/.

"The Buys." *The Wire.* HBO. Jun 16. 2002. Television.

John Havlicek:

Sports Reference LLC "John Havlicek Stats." Basketball-Reference.com - Basketball Statistics and History. https://www.basketball-reference.com/. Jul 18. 2018.

Taylor, Ben. "Backpicks GOAT: #32 John Havlicek." *Back Picks*, 6 Jul. 2018, backpicks.com/2018/03/12/backpicks-goat-31-40/#Havlicek

Goldstein, Jacob. Walker, Nathan. "Player Impact Plus-Minus." *Basketball Index*, 29 Mar. 2019, www.bball-index.com/player-impact-plus-minus/.

Araton, Harvey. "John Havlicek, a Dynamo in Two Eras of Celtics Glory, Dies at 79 (Published 2019)." *TheNewYorkTimes*,25Apr.2019,www.nytimes.com/2019/04/25/sports/basketball/john-havlicek-dead-boston-celtics-hall-of-famer.html. Accessed 16 Oct. 2018.

"Havlicek Wearing 17 Last Time (Published 1978)." *The New York Times*, 9 Apr. 1978, www.nytimes.com/1978/04/09/archives/havlicek-wearing-17-last-time-what-might-have-been.html. Accessed 22 Jul. 2018.

Herald, Tom Keegan | Boston. "Boston's Top 10 Athletes, No. 6: No. 17 John Havlicek." *Boston Herald*, 27 Mar. 2020, www.bostonherald.com/2020/03/27/bostons-top-10-athletes-no-6-no-17-john-havlicek/. Accessed 16 Oct. 2018.

"'Hands off Havlicek' | Pro Football Hall of Fame Official Site." *Www.Profootballhof.Com*, www.profootballhof.com/blogs/stories-from-the-pro-football-hall-of-fame-archives/hands-off-havlicek/. Accessed 16 Oct. 2020.

Kevin Durant:

Sports Reference LLC "Kevin Durant Stats." Basketball-Reference.com - Basketball Statistics and History. https://www.basketball-reference.com/. Jul 18. 2019.

Taylor, Ben. "Backpicks GOAT: #26 Kevin Durant." *Back Picks*, 6 Mar. 2018, backpicks.com/2018/03/05/backpicks-goat-26-kevin-durant/.

Goldstein, Jacob. Walker, Nathan. "Player Impact Plus-Minus." *Basketball Index*, 29 Mar. 2019, www.bball-index.com/player-impact-plus-minus/.

"The Night Lands." *Game of Thrones.* HBO. Apr 8. 2012.

"Walk of Punishment." *Game of Thrones.* HBO. Apr 14. 2013.

"D2: The Mighty Ducks." Buena Vista Pictures/Walt Disney Pictures. 1994. Film.

Cotton, Anthony. "NBA's New Collective Bargaining Pact Raises Interesting Questions." *Los Angeles Times*, Los Angeles Times, 5 June 1988, www.latimes.com/archives/la-xpm-1988-06-05-sp-6494-story.html.

Whitehead, Todd. "How Free Agency Changed NBA Team Building." *FanSided*, FanSided, 7 Sept. 2016, fansided.com/2016/09/07/free-agency-changed-nba-team-building/.

Alvarez, Edgar. "How Kevin Durant's Attempt to Clap Back at Trolls Backfired." *Engadget*, 6 Mar. 2020, www.engadget.com/2017/09/22/kevin-durant-twitter/.

(Bill Simmons excerpt). MacMullan, Jackie. Bartholome, Rafe. Klores, Dan. *Basketball: A Love Story*. Broadway Books, 2019.

"Baelor." *Game of Thrones*. HBO. Jun 12. 2011.

Tier III RECAP

"Basketball Statistics and History." *Basketball*, 13 Apr. 2018, www.basketball-reference.com/.

"Paint it Black." *Aftermath*. The Rolling Stones. Decca Records, 1966.

"No Country For Old Men." Miramax Films/Paramount Vantage. 2007. Film.

Rolling Stone. "500 Greatest Albums of All Time." Rolling Stone, Rolling Stone, 29 July 2019, www.rollingstone.com/music/music-lists/500-greatest-albums-of-all-time-156826/.

Beck, Howard. "A Coach With a 'Situation' for Almost Any Occasion." *The New York Times*, The New York Times, 14 May 2011, www.nytimes.com/2011/05/15/sports/basketball/for-lakers-phil-jackson-situations-could-turn-on-a-trifle.html.

Oscar Robertson:

Sports Reference LLC "Oscar Robertson Stats." Basketball-Reference.com - Basketball Statistics and History. https://www.basketball-reference.com/. Dec 13. 2018.

Taylor, Ben. "Backpicks GOAT: #12 Oscar Robertson." *Back Picks*, 20 Dec. 2017, backpicks.com/2017/12/21/backpicks-goat-12-oscar-robertson/.

Goldstein, Jacob. Walker, Nathan. "Player Impact Plus-Minus." *Basketball Index*, 29 Mar. 2019, www.bball-index.com/player-impact-plus-minus/.

"Cincinnati Royals." *Sports Ecyclopedia*, 19 Apr. 2020, www.sportsecyclopedia.com/nba/cincy/cincyroyals.html.

"Royals Trade Robertson to Bucks for Robinson and Paulk, Rookie in Army." *The New York Times*, The New York Times, 22 Apr. 1970, www.nytimes.com/1970/04/22/archives/royals-trade-robertson-to-bucks-for-robinson-and-paulk-rookie-in.html.

Pelton, Kevin. "Where the Warriors Rank among the NBA's 50 Greatest Teams of All Time." *ESPN*, ESPN Internet Ventures, 2 June 2015, www.espn.com/nba/story/_/id/13000418/where-golden-state-warriors-rank-50-greatest-nba-teams.

"Oscar Robertson Biography." *HOME*, 8 June 2020, www.oscarrobertson.com/about.

Kevin Garnett:

Sports Reference LLC "Kevin Garnett Stats." Basketball-Reference.com - Basketball Statistics and History. https://www.basketball-reference.com/. Aug 9. 2019.

Taylor, Ben March. "Backpicks GOAT: #8 Kevin Garnett." *Back Picks*, 17 May 2018, backpicks.com/2018/03/19/backpicks-goat-8-kevin-garnett/.

Goldstein, Jacob. Walker, Nathan. "Player Impact Plus-Minus." *Basketball Index*, 29 Mar. 2019, www.bball-index.com/player-impact-plus-minus/.

Reusse, Patrick. "Tom Gugliotta Visits, Brings to Mind the Wolves' Chaos Years." *Star Tribune*, Star Tribune, 3 Sept. 2018, www.startribune.com/tom-gugliotta-visits-brings-to-mind-the-wolves-chaos-years/492269871/.

Wilt Chamberlain:

Sports Reference LLC "Wilt Chamberlain Stats." Basketball-Reference.com - Basketball Statistics and History. https://www.basketball-reference.com/. Aug 21. 2019.

Taylor, Ben. "Backpicks GOAT: #9 Wilt Chamberlain." *Back Picks*, 6 Jan. 2018, backpicks.com/2017/12/04/backpicks-goat-9-wilt-chamberlain/.

Goldstein, Jacob. Walker, Nathan. "Player Impact Plus-Minus." *Basketball Index*, 29 Mar. 2019, www.bball-index.com/player-impact-plus-minus/.

Seitz, Matt Zoller, et al. *Mad Men Carousel: The Complete Critical Companion*. Abrams Press, 2017.

"Signal 30." *Mad Men*. AMC. Apr. 15. 2012. Television.

"Collaborators." *Mad Men*. AMC. Apr 14. 2013. Television.

"A Day's Work." *Mad Men*. AMC. Apr 20. 2014. Television.

Mikaelian, Zarouhi. "How an NCAA Superstar Quit Basketball After Playing a High Schooler Who Would Become a Legend." *Obsev*, 1 Aug. 2018, www.obsev.com/sports/bh-born-wilt-chamberlain/.

Cherry, Robert Allen. *Wilt: Larger Than Life*. Triumph Books, 2006.

S, Will. "Wilt Chamberlain vs Muhammad Ali: A Fight That Never Happened." *Basketball Network*, 17 July 2019, www.basketballnetwork.net/wilt-chamberlain-vs-muhammad-ali-a-fight-that-never-happened/.

Kobe Bryant:

Sports Reference LLC "Kobe Bryant Stats." Basketball-Reference.com - Basketball Statistics and History. https://www.basketball-reference.com/. Sep 1. 2019.

Taylor, Ben. "Backpicks GOAT: #14 Kobe Bryant." *Back Picks*, 7 Apr. 2018, backpicks.com/2018/03/01/backpicks-goat-14-kobe-bryant/.

Goldstein, Jacob. Walker, Nathan. "Player Impact Plus-Minus." *Basketball Index*, 29 Mar. 2019, www.bball-index.com/player-impact-plus-minus/.

Davis, Scott. "Kobe Bryant Was Known for His Intense Work Ethic, Here Are 24 Examples." *Business Insider*, Business Insider, 26 Jan. 2020, www.businessinsider.com/kobe-bryant-insane-work-ethic-2013-8#he-texts-business-leaders-at-all-hours-of-the-day-including-3-am-to-pick-their-brains-24.

Staff, Viral Hoops. "18 Motivational Kobe Bryant Work Ethic Stories from Other NBA Players & Coaches." *Viral Hoops*, 15 Oct. 2014, www.viralhoops.com/kobe-bryant-motivational-stories/.

Olympics:

Leopold, Bill, and Ben Teitelbaum. "Red, White and Bronze: The Death and Rebirth of USA Basketball." *NBC Olympics*, 2 Aug. 2016, archiverio.nbcolympics.com/news/red-white-and-bronze-2004-death-and-rebirth-usa-basketball.

Orange County Register. "Kobe Bryant Credited with Reshaping Culture of USA Basketball, Helping Lead Team to 2008, 2012 Gold Medals." *Orange County Register*, Orange County Register, 12 Aug. 2016, www.ocregister.com/2016/08/12/kobe-bryant-credited-with-reshaping-culture-of-usa-basketball-helping-lead-team-to-2008-2012-gold-medals/.

Abrams, Jonathan. "How Kobe Bryant Led the Rebirth of USA Basketball." *Bleacher Report*, Bleacher Report, 12 Sept. 2018, bleacherreport.com/articles/2795121-how-kobe-bryant-led-the-rebirth-of-usa-basketball.

Sheridan, Chris. "Despite Gaffe, Kobe the Star at the End." *ESPN*, ESPN Internet Ventures, 22 July 2007, www.espn.com/nba/columns/story?columnist=sheridan_chris&id=2945741.

"USA Basketball Announces 12-Member 2008 Men-s Senior National Team." *Team USA*, 23 June 2008, www.teamusa.org/News/2008/June/23/USA-Basketball-Announces-12-Member-2008-Men-s-Senior-National-Team.

Himmer, Alastair. "King Kobe Rules 'Bling Dynasty' in China." *Reuters*, Thomson Reuters, 20 Aug. 2008, www.reuters.com/article/us-olympics-basketball-men-bryant/king-kobe-rules-bling-dynasty-in-china-idUST28948520080820.

Staff, Viral Hoops. "A Team of NBA Superstars Were Put to Shame by Kobe Bryant's Work Ethic." *Viral Hoops*, 6 Feb. 2016, www.viralhoops.com/kobe-work-ethic-team-usa/.

Hakeem Olajuwon:

Sports Reference LLC "Hakeem Olajuwon Stats." Basketball-Reference.com - Basketball Statistics and History. https://www.basketball-reference.com/. Sep 12. 2019.

Taylor, Ben March. "Backpicks GOAT: #6 Hakeem Olajuwon." *Back Picks*, 22 Mar. 2018, backpicks.com/2018/03/25/backpicks-goat-hakeem-olajuwon/.

Goldstein, Jacob. Walker, Nathan. "Player Impact Plus-Minus." *Basketball Index*, 29 Mar. 2019, www.bball-index.com/player-impact-plus-minus/.

"Phi Slama Jama." ESPN Films. ESPN. Oct 18. 2016. Television.

Ebert, Roger. "Pulp Fiction Movie Review & Film Summary (1994): Roger Ebert." *Movie Review & Film Summary (1994) | Roger Ebert*, 14 Oct. 1994, www.rogerebert.com/reviews/pulp-fiction-1994.

Galloway, Stephen, and Matthew Belloni. "Director Roundtable: 6 Auteurs on Tantrums, Crazy Actors and Quitting While They're Ahead." *The Hollywood Reporter*, 4 June 2014, www.hollywoodreporter.com/news/ben-affleck-quentin-tarantino-4-394576.

Lee, Nathaniel. "How Golden Globes Winner Quentin Tarantino Steals from Other Movies." *Business Insider*, Business Insider, 6 Jan. 2020, www.businessinsider.com/quentin-tarantino-movies-steals-cinema-homage-reference-2019-7.

"Death Proof." Troublemaker Studios/Dimension Films. 2007. Film.

"The Hateful Eight." The Weinstein Company. 2015. Film.

"Django Unchained." Columbia Pictures/The Weinstein Company. 2012. Film.

Bembry, Jerry. "A Golden Opportunity for Olajuwon U.S. Citizen Finally Gets -- Shot at Olympics." *Baltimoresun.com*, 23 Oct. 2018, www.baltimoresun.com/news/bs-xpm-1996-07-06-1996188003-story.html.

"Kill Bill Vol. 2." Miramax Films. 2004. Film.

"Kill Bill Vol. 1." Miramax Films. 2003. Film.

Lucier, Maddy. "Dominate the Post With the Hakeem Olajuwon." *STACK*, 9 Aug. 2011, www.stack.com/a/dominate-the-post-with-hakeem-olajuwons-dream-shake-code.

"Jackie Brown." Miramax Films. 1997. Film.

"Reservoir Dogs." Miramax Films. 1992. Film.

"Pulp Fiction." Miramax Films. 1994. Film.

"Once Upon a Time… in Hollywood." Columbia Pictures/Sony Pictures Releasing. 2019. Film.

Ryan, Chris, host. Fennessey, Sean, host. Simmon, Bill, host. *Once Upon a Time… in Hollywood.* The Rewatchables Podcast. The Ringer. Spotify. Feb 5. 2020.

"Inglorious Basterds." Universal Pictures/The Weinstein Company. 2009. Film.

Ryan, Chris, host. Fennessey, Sean, host. Rubin, Mallory, host. *Inglorious Basterds.* The Rewatchables Podcast. The Ringer. Spotify. Jul 16. 2019.

Steph Curry:

Sports Reference LLC "Steph Curry Stats." Basketball-Reference.com - Basketball Statistics and History. https://www.basketball-reference.com/. Sep 22. 2019.

Taylor, Ben. "Backpicks GOAT: #31-35." *Back Picks*, 14 Mar. 2018, backpicks.com/2018/03/12/backpicks-goat-31-40/#Curry.

Goldstein, Jacob. Walker, Nathan. "Player Impact Plus-Minus." *Basketball Index*, 29 Mar. 2019, www.bball-index.com/player-impact-plus-minus/.

Thompson II, Marcus. "Thompson: Five Years Ago, Steph Curry Signed the Contract…" *The Athletic*, The Athletic, 4 Nov. 2017, theathletic.com/142451/2017/10/31/thompson-five-years-ago-steph-curry-signed-the-contract-that-set-up-a-dynasty/.

Torre, Pablo S. "How Stephen Curry Got the Best Worst Ankles in Sports." *ESPN*, ESPN Internet Ventures, 10 Feb. 2016, www.espn.com/nba/story/_/id/14750602/how-golden-state-warriors-stephen-curry-got-best-worst-ankles-sports.

Spitz, Bob. *The Beatles: the Biography*. Aurum, 2007.

Shiller, Drew, et al. "Curry Has Chance to Make Free-Throw History in NBA Finals." *NBCS Bay Area*, 30 May 2019, www.nbcsports.com/bayarea/warriors/steph-curry-has-opportunity-make-free-throw-history-nba-finals.

"Players Clutch Traditional." *NBA Stats*, stats.nba.com/players/clutch-traditional/?sort=GP&dir=-1.

Silver, Nate. "Introducing RAPTOR, Our New Metric For The Modern NBA." *FiveThirtyEight*, FiveThirtyEight, 10 Oct. 2019, fivethirtyeight.com/features/introducing-raptor-our-new-metric-for-the-modern-nba/.

Shaquille O'Neal:

Sports Reference LLC "Shaquille O'Neal Stats." Basketball-Reference.com - Basketball Statistics and History. https://www.basketball-reference.com/. Oct 20. 2019.

Taylor, Ben March. "Backpicks GOAT: #5 Shaquille O'Neal." *Back Picks*, 28 Mar. 2018, backpicks.com/2018/03/29/backpicks-goat-5-shaquille-oneal/.

Goldstein, Jacob. Walker, Nathan. "Player Impact Plus-Minus." *Basketball Index*, 29 Mar. 2019, www.bball-index.com/player-impact-plus-minus/.

"Report: Kobe Said Shaq Paid Women Hush Money." *ESPN*, ESPN Internet Ventures, 29 Sept. 2004, www.espn.com/nba/news/story?id=1891629.

Larry Bird/Magic Johnson:

Sports Reference LLC "Larry Bird Stats." Basketball-Reference.com - Basketball Statistics and History. https://www.basketball-reference.com/. Oct 27. 2019.

Sports Reference LLC "Magic Johnson Stats." Basketball-Reference.com - Basketball Statistics and History. https://www.basketball-reference.com/. Oct 29. 2019.

Taylor, Ben February. "Backpicks GOAT: #11 Larry Bird." *Back Picks*, 10 Jan. 2018, backpicks.com/2018/01/11/backpicks-goat-11-larry-bird/.

Taylor, Ben. "Backpicks GOAT: #10 Magic Johnson." *Back Picks*, 11 Jan. 2018, backpicks.com/2018/01/15/backpicks-goat-10-magic-johnson/.

Goldstein, Jacob. Walker, Nathan. "Player Impact Plus-Minus." *Basketball Index*, 29 Mar. 2019, www.bball-index.com/player-impact-plus-minus/.

"The Dark Knight." Warner Bros. Pictures/DC Comics. 2008. Film.

"Land Of Basketball.com." *Larry Bird vs. Magic Johnson Comparison*, www.landofbasketball.com/player_comparison/larry_bird_vs_magic_johnson.htm.

Guralnick, Peter. "Elvis Presley: How Sam Phillips Discovered a Star." *The Independent*, Independent Digital News and Media, 30 Oct. 2015, www.independent.co.uk/arts-entertainment/music/features/elvis-presley-how-sun-records-boss-sam-phillips-discovered-a-star-in-1954-a6713891.html.

Rubino, Michael. "Larry Bird's Greatest Shot Was the One He Didn't Take." *Indianapolis Monthly*, 22 Oct. 2019, www.indianapolismonthly.com/longform/larry-birds-greatest-shot-one-didnt-take.

Tim Duncan:

Sports Reference LLC "Tim Duncan Stats." Basketball-Reference.com - Basketball Statistics and History. https://www.basketball-reference.com/. Nov 24. 2019.

Taylor, Ben March. "Backpicks GOAT: #7 Tim Duncan." *Back Picks*, 21 Mar. 2018, backpicks.com/2018/03/22/backpicks-goat-7-tim-duncan/.

Goldstein, Jacob. Walker, Nathan. "Player Impact Plus-Minus." *Basketball Index*, 29 Mar. 2019, www.bball-index.com/player-impact-plus-minus/.

Taylor, Ben, host. Snellings, Andre, guest. *#41: Duncan vs. Garnett | Andre Snellings, Great Debates.* Thinking Basketball Podcast. Jan 10. 2020.

Lombardi, Esther. "Every Nobel Prize Winner in Literature." *ThoughtCo*, 28 Sept. 2019, www.thoughtco.com/nobel-prize-in-literature-winners-4084778.

Beviglia, Jim, et al. "Bob Dylan & The Band: The Basement Tapes Complete " American Songwriter." *American Songwriter*, 14 Sept. 2018, americansongwriter.com/bob-dylan-band-basement-tapes-complete/.

"Bob Dylan." *Spotify*, open.spotify.com/artist/74ASZWbe4lXaubB36ztrGX.

TIER II RECAP

"Basketball Statistics and History." *Basketball*, 13 Apr. 2018, www.basketball-reference.com/.

"Think." *Aftermath.* The Rolling Stones. Decca Records, 1966.

"Blood Money." *Breaking Bad.* AMC. Aug 11. 2013. Television.

Lowe, Zach, host. Beck, Howard, guest. *Howard Beck.* The Lowe Post. ESPN. Spotify. Jun 15. 2018.

Beck, Howard. "Kobe Bryant, NBA Greats Get Lathered About LeBron's Legacy." *Bleacher Report*, Bleacher Report, 11 June 2018, bleacherreport.com/articles/2780523-kobe-bryant-nba-greats-get-lathered-about-lebrons-legacy.

Ginsburg, Steve. "LeBron Surpasses Kobe as the Top Player: Jerry West." *Reuters*, Thomson Reuters, 18 May 2009, www.reuters.com/article/us-nba-west/lebron-surpasses-kobe-as-the-top-player-jerry-west-idUSTRE54H5PF20090518.

Fischer, Jake. "Front Office Hopefuls Gather for an NBA Bootcamp." *Sports Illustrated*, 22 Sept. 2017, www.si.com/nba/2017/09/22/nba-hackathon-warriors-clippers-kings-adam-silver-chris-pickard.

"Hackathon." *NBA Basketball Analytics Hackathon*, hackathon.nba.com/2016-basketball-analytics-hackathon-recap/hackathon/.

Rooney, Kyle. "ESPN Sports Science Breaks Down LeBron James' Epic Block On Andre Iguodala." *HotNewHipHop*, HotNewHipHop, 21 June 2016, www.hotnewhiphop.com/espn-sports-science-breaks-down-lebron-james-epic-block-on-andre-iguodala-news.22398.html.

"Players Clutch Traditional." *NBA Stats*, stats.nba.com/players/clutch-traditional/?sort=GP&dir=-1.

"Hamsterdam." *The Wire.* HBO. Oct 10. 2004. Television.

"Threat Level Midnight." *The Office.* NBC. Feb 17. 2011. Television.

Abbott, Henry. "The Truth about Kobe Bryant in Crunch Time." *ESPN*, ESPN Internet Ventures, 28 Jan. 2011, www.espn.com/blog/truehoop/post/_/id/24200/the-truth-about-kobe-bryant-in-crunch-time.

Kareem Abdul-Jabbar:

Sports Reference LLC "Kareem Abdul-Jabbar Stats." Basketball-Reference.com - Basketball Statistics and History. https://www.basketball-reference.com/. Feb 2. 2020.

Taylor, Ben. "Backpicks GOAT: #1 Kareem Abdul-Jabbar." *Back Picks*, 11 Apr. 2018, backpicks.com/2018/04/12/backpicks-goat-1-kareem-abdul-jabbar/.

Goldstein, Jacob. Walker, Nathan. "Player Impact Plus-Minus." *Basketball Index*, 29 Mar. 2019, www.bball-index.com/player-impact-plus-minus/.

Abdul-Jabbar, Kareem, and Raymond Obstfeld. *Becoming Kareem: Growing up on and off the Court*. Little, Brown and Company, 2018.

Schwartz, Larry. "Kareem Just Kept on Winning." *ESPN*, ESPN Internet Ventures, www.espn.com/classic/biography/s/abdul-jabbar_kareem.html.

Zillgitt, Jeff. "LeBron James Opens up and Reflects on Kobe Bryant after Passing Him on NBA Scoring List." *USA Today*, Gannett Satellite Information Network, 26 Jan. 2020, www.usatoday.com/story/sports/nba/lakers/2020/01/26/lebron-james-reflects-on-kobe-bryant-nba-scoring-list/4579971002/.

Eig, Jonathan. "The Cleveland Summit and Muhammad Ali: The True Story." *The Undefeated*, The Undefeated, 2 June 2017, theundefeated.com/features/the-cleveland-summit-muhammad-ali/.

"Muhammad Ali Refuses Army Induction." *History.com*, A&E Television Networks, 16 Nov. 2009, www.history.com/this-day-in-history/muhammad-ali-refuses-army-induction.

Staff, SI. "January 29, 1968 - Sports Illustrated Vault." *SI.com*, 29 Jan. 1968, vault.si.com/vault/42398.

Abdul-Jabbar, Kareem. "Colin Kaepernick Is the Black Grinch for Those Who Dream of a White America." *The Guardian*, Guardian News and Media, 5 Dec. 2019, www.theguardian.com/sport/2019/dec/05/colin-kaepernick-kareem-abdul-jabbar.

Bonk, Thomas. "JUNE 16, 1975: A BANNER DAY FOR LAKERS : KAREEM TAKES HIS POST : 4 Players Bucks Got in Trade Gone, but He's Still on Job." *Los Angeles Times*, Los Angeles Times, 25 Dec. 1987, articles.latimes.com/1987-12-25/sports/sp-21142_1_national-basketball-assn.

Ramirez, Joey. "Kareem Abdul-Jabbar Awarded Presidential Medal of Freedom." *Los Angeles Lakers*, NBA.com/Lakers, 5 Dec. 2016, www.nba.com/lakers/news/161122-kareem-abdul-jabbar-presidential-medal-freedom.

Bill Russell:

Sports Reference LLC "Bill Russell Stats." Basketball-Reference.com - Basketball Statistics and History. https://www.basketball-reference.com/. Feb 19. 2020.

Taylor, Ben. "Backpicks GOAT: #4 Bill Russell." *Back Picks*, 2 Apr. 2018, backpicks.com/2018/04/02/backpicks-goat-3-bill-russell/.

Goldstein, Jacob. Walker, Nathan. "Player Impact Plus-Minus." *Basketball Index*, 29 Mar. 2019, www.bball-index.com/player-impact-plus-minus/.

Russell, Bill, and Alan Steinberg. *Red and Me: My Coach, My Lifelong Friend.* Harper, 2010.

Brooks, Bucky, host. Jeremiah, Daniel, host. Meyer, Urban, guest. *Urban Meyer discusses building a winning culture & shares stories from his coaching days.* Move The Sticks Podcast with Daniel Jeremiah & Bucky Brooks. NFL.com. Spotify. Nov 6. 2019.

Bird, Hayden. "How Red Auerbach Used the Ice Capades to Add Bill Russell to the Celtics' Best Draft Class." *Boston.com*, The Boston Globe, 22 June 2016, www.boston.com/sports/boston-celtics/2016/06/22/bill-russell.

"Territorial Pick." *Basketball Wiki*, basketball.fandom.com/wiki/Territorial_pick.

Swain, Christian, host. *Episode 4: The Change of the Guard.* Rock N Roll Archeology Podcast. Pantheon Media. Spotify. Dec 22. 2015.

"Boston Bruins Yearly Attendance Graph." Hockeydb.com, https://www.hockeydb.com/nhl-attendance/att_graph.php?tmi=4919

"Boston Celtics Attendance by Season." *Boston Celtics Attendance by Season - CelticStats.com*, www.celticstats.com/misc/attendance.php.

LeBron James:

Sports Reference LLC "LeBron James Stats." Basketball-Reference.com - Basketball Statistics and History. https://www.basketball-reference.com/. Feb 27. 2020.

Taylor, Ben. "Backpicks GOAT: #3 LeBron James." *Back Picks*, 3 Apr. 2018, backpicks.com/2018/04/05/backpicks-goat-3-lebron-james/.

Goldstein, Jacob. Walker, Nathan. "Player Impact Plus-Minus." *Basketball Index*, 29 Mar. 2019, www.bball-index.com/player-impact-plus-minus/.

"Devil In a New Dress (featuring Rick Ross)." *My Beautiful Dark Twisted Fantasy.* Kanye West. Def Jam/Roc-A-Fella. 2010.

McCarthy, Erin. "Roosevelt's 'The Man in the Arena.'" *Mental Floss*, 23 Apr. 2015, www.mentalfloss.com/article/63389/roosevelts-man-arena.

"Episode 6." *The Shop.* HBO. Sep 3. 2019. Television.

"Background: Life Cycles of Stars." *NASA*, NASA, imagine.gsfc.nasa.gov/educators/lessons/xray_spectra/background-lifecycles.html.

"Chapter 2." *House of Cards.* Netflix. Feb 1. 2013. Television.

@kirkgoldsberry. "Most Effective Post-up Players, 2019-20*." *Instagram.* Feb 13. 2020. https://www.instagram.com/p/B8gmiEGlJde/?utm_source=ig_web_copy_link

@kirkgoldsberry. "Most Corner 3s Assists Last 5+ Seasons*." *Instagram.* Jan 22. 2020. https://www.instagram.com/p/B7oKBdMlA01/?utm_source=ig_web_copy_link

@kirkgoldsberry. "Top Scorers By Zone, 2010s." *Instagram.* Feb 21. 2020. https://www.instagram.com/p/B81s7n2FB31/?utm_source=ig_web_copy_link

"The D.E.N.N.I.S. System." *It's Always Sunny in Philadelphia.* FX. Dec 10. 2009. Television.

Taylor, Ben, host. *#50: Top scorers in NBA history revisited.* Thinking Basketball Podcast. Spotify. Mar 24. 2020.

Axson, Scooby. "How Many Consecutive NBA Finals Has LeBron James Made?" *Sports Illustrated*, 3 May 2018, www.si.com/nba/2018/05/03/lebron-james-consecutive-nba-finals-streak.

Vergara, Andre. "The Top 10 Players with the Most Consecutive NBA Finals Appearances." *FOX Sports*, 31 May 2017, www.foxsports.com/nba/gallery/top-10-players-with-most-consecutive-nba-finals-appearances-lebron-james-bill-russell-james-jones-053017.

Katz, Sharon B. "LeBron's Finals Record Isn't Really A Disappointment." *FiveThirtyEight*, FiveThirtyEight, 2 June 2016, fivethirtyeight.com/features/lebrons-finals-record-isnt-really-a-disappointment/.

Taylor, Ben, host. *#48: Tatum vs. Giannis & BPM 2.0! Inside Basketball-Reference's new metric.* Thinking Basketball Podcast. Spotify. Feb 29. 2020.

Steinbeck, John. *East of Eden.* Penguin Books, 2017.

THE HOLY BIBLE: NEW STANDARD VERSION. *Bible.* Oxf. U.P.

King James Bible. Holman Bible Publishers, 1973.
"New God Flow." Kanye West & Pusha T. GOOD/Def Jam. 2012.

Michael Jordan:

Sports Reference LLC "Michael Jordan Stats." Basketball-Reference.com - Basketball Statistics and History. https://www.basketball-reference.com/. Mar 26. 2020.

Taylor, Ben. "Backpicks GOAT: #2 Michael Jordan." *Back Picks*, 8 Apr. 2018, backpicks.com/2018/04/08/backpicks-goat-2-michael-jordan/.

Goldstein, Jacob. Walker, Nathan. "Player Impact Plus-Minus." *Basketball Index*, 29 Mar. 2019, www.bball-index.com/player-impact-plus-minus/.

Lifton, Dave. "Why the Beatles Failed an Audition for Decca Records." *Ultimate Classic Rock*, 1 Jan. 2016, ultimateclassicrock.com/the-beatles-decca-records-audition/.

Spitz, Bob. *The Beatles: The Biography*. Aurum, 2007.

Astramskas, David. "Remembering When The Chicago Bulls Drafted (but Didn't Want to Draft) Michael Jordan with the 3rd Pick." *Ballislifecom*, 19 June 2015, ballislife.com/bull-draft-jordan/.

Lauria, Peter. "Michael Jordan Bails Out a Billionaire." *The Daily Beast*, The Daily Beast Company, 31 Mar. 2010, www.thedailybeast.com/michael-jordan-bails-out-a-billionaire.

Walton, Michael, et al. "The Legend of the 'Michael Jordan Edition' of NBA Jam." *NBC Sports Chicago*, 21 Aug. 2019, www.nbcsports.com/chicago/bulls/legend-michael-jordan-edition-nba-jam.

Clark, Emma. "A History of Michael Jordan in Video Games." *Independent*, Independent.ie, 24 Feb. 2016, www.independent.ie/business/technology/tech-gaming/a-history-of-michael-jordan-in-video-games-34462060.html.

Fischer, Mark. "Michael Jordan Destroyed Cavaliers Hours after Beer-Filled Golf Gambling: Jeremy Roenick." *New York Post*, New York Post, 9 Nov. 2019, nypost.com/2019/11/09/michael-jordan-destroyed-cavaliers-hours-after-beer-filled-golf-gambling-jeremy-roenick/.

ESPNChicago.com. "Trainer: MJ Had Food Poisoning." *ESPN*, ESPN Internet Ventures, 17 Apr. 2013, www.espn.com/chicago/nba/story/_/id/9183990/michael-jordan-flu-game-was-really-food-poisoning-trainer-says.

Badenhausen, Kurt. "How Michael Jordan Will Make $145 Million In 2019." *Forbes*, Forbes Magazine, 3 Sept. 2019, www.forbes.com/sites/kurtbadenhausen/2019/08/28/how-michael-jordan-will-make-145-million-in-2019/#2ca047d81064.

"Episode 1." *The Shop.* HBO. Aug 28. 2018. Television.

Ruiz, Steven. "Michael Jordan's Famous 'Shrug Game' Had a Pretty Dark Story behind It." *USA Today*, Gannett Satellite Information Network, 4 June 2018, ftw.usatoday.com/2018/06/nba-michael-jordan-shrug-game-trail-blazers-clyde-drexler-story.

Halberstam, David. *Playing for Keeps: Michael Jordan and the World He Made*. Random House, 2013.

Conspiracy:

Jackson, David. "Michael Jordan's Acquaintances in a Shadowy World." *Chicagotribune.com*, 29 Mar. 1992, www.chicagotribune.com/news/ct-xpm-1992-03-29-9201280815-story.html.

Isaacson, Melissa. "JORDAN LEAVES GAMBLING STORY UP IN AIR." *Chicagotribune.com*, 17 Oct. 1992, https://www.chicagotribune.com/news/ct-xpm-1992-10-17-9204040081-story.html

Roth, David. "That Time Michael Jordan Allegedly Ran Up a Million-Dollar Golf Debt." *Vice*, 15 June 2017, www.vice.com/en_us/article/43y5x9/that-time-michael-jordan-allegedly-ran-up-a-million-dollar-golf-debt.

Wiederer, Dan. "Absence of Answers: The James Jordan Murder." *The James Jordan Murder -- Chicago Tribune*, 9 Aug. 2018, graphics.chicagotribune.com/james-jordan-murder/index.html.

Swenson, Kyle. "He's in Prison for Murdering Michael Jordan's Father. New Evidence Could Change Everything." *The Washington Post*, WP Company, 6 Dec. 2018, www.washingtonpost.com/nation/2018/12/06/hes-prison-murdering-michael-jordans-father-new-evidence-could-change-everything/.

Starr, Mark. "The Mysterious Death Of 'Pops'." Newsweek. 22 Aug. 1993, https://www.newsweek.com/mysterious-death-pops-192652

Roberts, Mark, et al. "Man Convicted of Killing Jordan's Father Breaks His Silence." *WRAL.com*, WRAL, 4 Aug. 1998, www.wral.com/news/local/story/130818/.

Tier I RECAP

"Basketball Statistics and History." *Basketball*, 13 Apr. 2018, www.basketball-reference.com/.

Goldstein, Jacob. Walker, Nathan. "Player Impact Plus-Minus." *Basketball Index*, 29 Mar. 2019, www.bball-index.com/player-impact-plus-minus/.

"Out of Time." *Aftermath*. The Rolling Stones. Decca Records, 1966.

Russillo, Ryen, host. Kilborn, Craig, guest. *Craig Kilborn | The Ryen Russillo Podcast.* The Ryen Russillo Podcast. The Ringer. Spotify. Feb 27. 2020.

Beggars Banquet. The Rolling Stones. Decca Records, 1968.

Let It Bleed. The Rolling Stones. Decca Records. 1969.

Sticky Fingers. The Rolling Stones. Rolling Stones records. 1971.

Exile on Main St. The Rolling Stones. Rolling Stones records. 1972.

Rolling Stone. "500 Greatest Songs of All Time." *Rolling Stone*, Rolling Stone, 29 July 2019, www.rollingstone.com/music/music-lists/500-greatest-songs-of-all-time-151127/.

Partnow, Seth, host. DuFour, Dave, host. Arnovitz, Kevin, guest. Elhassen, Amin, guest. Abbott, Henry, guest. *Sloan Conference Meeting of the Minds with Amin Elhassen, Kevin Arnovitz & Henry Abbott.* Back To Back: A Show About the NBA. The Athletic. Spotify. Mar 8. 2020.

McManis, Sam. "Rich 76ers and Celtics Get Richer in Lottery." *Los Angeles Times*, Los Angeles Times, 12 May 1986, www.latimes.com/archives/la-xpm-1986-05-12-sp-3324-story.html.

Jenkins, Sally. *The Washington Post*, WP Company, 18 June 1986, www.washingtonpost.com/wp-srv/sports/longterm/memories/bias/launch/bias2.htm.

staff, Plain Dealer. "Danny Ferry Timeline as General Manager of the Cavaliers." *Cleveland*, 5 June 2010, www.cleveland.com/cavs/2010/06/danny_ferry_timeline_as_genera.html.

"Gimme Shelter." *Let it Bleed.* The Rolling Stones. Decca Records, 1969.

Profile Index.